THE MAKERS OF CIVILIZATION IN RACE & HISTORY

THE MAKERS OF CIVILIZATION IN RACE & HISTORY

AUSTINE L. WADDELL

GYAN

Published by

GYAN

Gyan Publishing House
5, Ansari Road
Daryaganj, New Delhi-110002
Phone: 011-47034999, 9811692060
E-mail: books@gyanbooks.com

Distribution Network
gyanbooks.com
India, USA, Canada, UK, Australia

ISBN: 978-93-7225-144-9 (PB)

First Published, 1929

2nd Impression 2025

Printed at: Gyan Press, Delhi.

THE MAKERS OF CIVILIZATION IN RACE & HISTORY
Author: AUSTINE L. WADDELL

THE MAKERS OF CIVILIZATION IN RACE & HISTORY

THE MAKERS OF CIVILIZATION IN RACE & HISTORY

SHOWING
THE RISE OF THE ARYANS OR SUMERIANS
THEIR ORIGINATION & PROPAGATION OF CIVILIZATION
THEIR EXTENSION OF IT TO EGYPT & CRETE
PERSONALITIES & ACHIEVEMENTS OF THEIR KINGS
HISTORICAL ORIGINALS OF MYTHIC GODS & HEROES WITH DATES
FROM
THE RISE OF CIVILIZATION ABOUT 3380 B.C.
RECONSTRUCTED FROM BABYLONIAN, EGYPTIAN, HITTITE
INDIAN & GOTHIC SOURCES

BY

L. A. WADDELL

LL.D., C.B., C.I.E.

Fellow of the Royal Anthropological Institute
and Linnean Society, Honorary Correspondent of
Indian Archæological Survey, Ex-Professor
of Tibetan, London University.

WITH 25 PLATES, 168 *TEXT ILLUSTRATIONS & 5 MAPS*

LONDON
LUZAC & CO.
46 GREAT RUSSELL STREET, W.C.
1929

PLATE I (*Frontispiece*).

PORTRAIT (? CONTEMPORARY) OF FIRST ARYAN OR SUMERIAN KING DUR OR THOR, *c.* 3380 B.C.

On carved ivory handle of stone-knife from (?) Cappadocia, found in Egypt, of predynastic age, now in Louvre 2/1. (After M. Bénédite, *Mons. Académie des Inscripts.*, xii, 1.) Note the King, in Gothic dress and horned hat, with his Goats (Goths), is taming (civilizing) the Phrygians (of Asia Minor) and Urs (of Chaldea), represented by their totem animals (lion and wolf), and on reverse in human form (Pl. V). The shaggy-maned lions are of palæarctic type and the prick-eared wolves are collared. For same scene on Sumerian and Ancient Briton monuments, see Figs., pp. 195, 607, 608; and for details, see Fig., p. xlvi.

PREFACE

"The Message for the Future
Is the Message of the Past."

It is a commonplace that, in order to achieve real Progress in the Present, it is necessary to know what has been accomplished in the Past. Thus, if we are to apply usefully to the Present the accumulated knowledge we possess of the Origin and Growth of the Sciences, of Art, of Literature, of the Free Institutions of Society, the forms of Religious Belief and of Government; and more particularly of these as forming the basis for further Progress in the Present and the Future, it is first of all necessary, in order to avoid useless waste of effort in directions already exploited, to know exactly what has been achieved in these directions in the Past, and the manner and circumstances in which it was achieved and by whom.

Yet, in respect to our Civilization, the supreme movement of existence towards a higher and fuller state of being, which embraces all these departments of knowledge and institutions, which enriches our lives and has effected the phenomenal Rise of Man from savagery and barbarism to sunlit heights, and on which the Present as well as the Future Progress of the World mainly depends, it is notorious how little definitely has been known of its origin, early growth and development and its authors. Nothing whatever has been known of the personalities of its gifted authors who originated and established Civilization for us in very much the same form in which it still exists, nor of their names, home, race, the manner and circumstances and form in which they invented it, developed it and began its dissemination over the world, nor even their approximate date.

At the present time, especially is this information desirable and necessary in view of the unrest which is threatening the Progress, if not the very existence of Civilization, and the menacing revolt by masses of the people, and even otherwise educated people, against its obligatory burdens, obviously in ignorance of how the priceless boon of civilization was achieved and of the superior race quality and higher intellects which made it possible, and which are still necessary for the continued efficient existence and Progress of that elaborate complex of social and political organization called "Civilization." For biologists have conclusively shown that civilization is fundamentally conditioned by a superior quality of race, and that in the classic Greek period civilization reached its zenith under the Aryan or Nordic Race (which still forms a leading element in the foremost European nations to-day); and that it waned and became practically extinct in later Greece with the weakening and practical extinction there of that racial element.

That hitherto missing elementary knowledge as to the origin, names and personalities, home, race and date of those originators of creative genius who invented, established and first developed and propagated civilization over the world, is now offered in these pages from arresting new discoveries of concrete contemporary history from documents revealed by the spade on the horizon of written history.

This work now recovers for us those epoch-making culture heroes who originated civilization, with their long-lost real names, personalities and authentic records of achievements and exploits, *as truly historical kings of fixed dates*, who have left us many of their actual contemporary inscribed monuments, along with full lists of their early kings and dynasties with their regnal years, extending continuously back to the rise of civilization; for they are disclosed as being already at that epoch a scientific people, accustomed to writing and calculation by calendar years and possessed of a keen historical sense. It also recovers for us a mass of new concrete inscriptional and other authentic history regarding the personalities of the early propagators of civilization by land and sea over Asia Minor, Mesopotamia, Egypt, Indo-Persia, the Mediterranean, Crete and Ancient Europe, including Britain, with their dates in times hitherto considered "Prehistoric," along with some light upon the lowly aboriginal races of the Old World and their debasing cults, who were reclaimed by civilization from savagery. It moreover discloses the hitherto unknown and unsuspected manner in which Civilization was mainly propagated abroad from one common centre from the earliest times down to the opening of the classic period in Europe. And most startling of all, perhaps, it establishes the fact that the Aryan Race—now chiefly represented in purest form in North-western Europe, including the British Isles as the "Nordic" Race—which has hitherto been generally regarded by historians, philologists and anthropologists as the Cinderella of the civilized races, as having been the youngest and latest of all, and as having borrowed its civilization and monotheistic religion all ready-made from Semites and others, is now on the contrary disclosed to be the oldest of all the civilized races and the parent of all the other civilizations.

This book is also offered as a pioneer contribution towards a *true* Universal History of Man from the earliest civilized period founded on concrete Facts, as contrasted with current dogmatic Theories appealing to tradition and prejudice, and often it is to be feared designed in the interest of those who profit by the maintenance of Error—theories which by mere mechanical repetition have come to be believed, but have befogged and blotted out like a smoke-screen the vista of the originators of civilization, their race and date and the essential Unity of the World's Civilization. The practical importance of the recovery of this lost history is obvious, for a knowledge of the manner in which these ancestral people evolved and developed civilization and overcame its blights in the Past, is essential to us at the present day for assistance in solving the vital problem of the factors which make for real and solid Progress in the World's Civilization and National Life in the Present and in the Future. And a noted writer has recently declared that "there can be no common peace or progress without common historical ideas"; and that these historical ideas must be founded upon *true* History; and that a true Universal History of Man should "*form the backbone of a general education.*" These discoveries of authentic new basic history, therefore, should awaken and engage the interest of the general educated reader, as well as the historian, seeking for the Truth on those subjects of such vital importance.

The new keys, which have unlocked for us the hitherto sealed doors of the inscriptions that enshrine this lost history of the Past, are chiefly those that I found embedded in the official King-Lists and Chronicles of the early Aryans —that is the tall, fair and long-headed race of people, the "Aryan Race" of Huxley, now usually called "Nordic," through its purer elements now being located mostly in North-western Europe, including especially the British Isles and Scandinavia, and to which belonged the classic Greeks, patrician Romans, Medo-Persians, Hittites, early Phœnicians, the ancient Hindus, the Goths and old Rhine and Danube tribes, Ancient Britons, Normans and Anglo-Saxons.

These old official Aryan King-Lists and Chronicles, which have been uniquely and faithfully preserved down through the centuries by the eastern or Indian branch of the Aryans, are now seen to be a complete authentic official record of the names and achievements of the Aryan kings continuously back to the epoch of the Rise of Civilization. It now transpires that on the final break-up of the old Aryan headquarters in Asia Minor, by the savage exterminating wars of the Assyrian King, Sargon II, the ruling caste of the eastern or Indian branch of the Aryans carried off with them from their central archives, in their migration eastwards to the new colonial land of their adoption in Gangetic India, those cherished ancestral chronicles as their most precious heirlooms, like Æneas carrying with him in his exile into Italy his cherished household gods, and they embedded them bodily with scrupulous care in India into their great "Epic of the Ancient (Aryan) Heroes"—the *Purānas*—at the beginning of the seventh century B.C. There these uniquely precious historical documents, extending to many hundreds of pages of manuscripts, have lain down through the centuries neglected, and wholly unappreciated as to their historical significance; and have even been contemptuously rejected as fabulous by our European Sanskrit Vedic scholars, merely because the latter could find no traces of those early Aryan kings in India, for the very good reason, as now seen, that very few of these kings had ever been in India at all, and those few only temporarily resident as local governors of their rich Indus Valley colony on the north-west frontier of India before their accession to the imperial Mesopotamian throne ; as they all belong to the pre-Indo-Aryan period, the so-called " Vedic period," now disclosed to have been non-Indian, except for the Indus Valley, and before the great migration of the Eastern Aryans from Asia Minor into Gangetic India in the 7th century B.C., with which Indian post-Vedic history and the history of the heart of " India," as now generally understood, first begins.

On being led, however, by the various clues, described in my former works, to observe that the Indo-Aryans had obviously come from Asia Minor and Mesopotamia, I picked up these despised and rejected ancient chronicles. I then found that many of the leading kings of the Early Aryans in these ancient records bore substantially the same names with the same achievements and occupied the same relative chronological position as leading kings of the ancient Sumerians in Mesopotamia—the Sumerians being the oldest known of all civilized peoples of the Ancient World and the founders of Civilization in Mesopotamia ; and the marvellous remains there of their vast cities, with public buildings, palaces and temples, rich in art treasures, archives and libraries, and inscribed monuments adorned with sculptures, that have been unearthed by the spade during the past few decades, form one of the modern " Wonders of the World." And further comparative scrutiny disclosed that all the kings' names and their exact chronological order were identical in both lists, Indo-Aryan and Sumerian.

In former works, I have demonstrated with full scientific proofs the hitherto wholly unsuspected radical identity of the Sumerians with the Aryans, ancient and modern—in Europe, Asia Minor, Syrio-Phœnicia, Indo-Persia and also as regards the ruling race in Ancient Egypt—in physical type, language and writing, free institutions, art and science, traditions, religion, mythology and symbolism, thus proving them to be one and the same people. And Menes, the founder of the First Dynasty of Egypt, whose origin and antecedents were wholly unknown and his date the subject of widely conflicting conjecture, was now discovered by my new keys to be a famous Aryan king and " world-emperor " of known ancestry and fixed date. He was disclosed to be at one and the same time the Sumerian emperor of Mesopotamia and Pharaoh of Egypt, a land which his grandfather and father the Sumerian emperors before him had annexed (as "pre-dynastic Pharaohs") and introduced into it the Sumerian civilization, which on latterly acquiring in the Nile Valley a local complexion is nowadays called " Ancient Egyptian " Civilization, and supposed to have been of wholly independent and local origin. The Egyptian hieroglyphic writing also, I demonstrated was all unsuspectedly derived from the Sumerian picture-writing and possessed essentially the same forms, phonetic values and meanings as the parent Sumerian word-signs, and the radical elements in the Ancient Egyptian language were demonstrated to be Sumerian and Aryan. This disclosed the Unity of these three oldest civilizations and their authors, the Mesopotamian, Ancient Egyptian and Indian, each of which had hitherto been supposed to have originated wholly independently, in separate water-tight isolated centres.

A dramatic sequel to the publication of my first work on this subject, *which announced and established the discovery of the Sumerian Origin of the Indo-Aryans and their civilization and of the Indian language and writing*, was the unearthing *some four months later* of the ruins of two Sumerian cities in the Indus Valley in North-western India. Amongst other objects unearthed there were several sacred seals and burial amulets, inscribed with the old Sumerian cursive writing. And my pioneer decipherment of these inscriptions published a few months later in my *Indo-Sumerian Seals Deciphered* disclosed that these seals and amulets were chiefly those of ancient Sumerian government officials and priests of this Sumerian colony of about 3100 B.C. to 2300 B.C., the name of which was specified; and some of them were celebrated in the ancient Vedic Psalms of the Hindus as patronizing the Indus Valley. Two of the seals were the official imperial state signets of two of the contemporary suzerain Sumerian emperors in Mesopotamia, including the great world-emperor Sargon-the-Great himself, whose conquests in the Indus Valley I cited from the ancient Indian Chronicles; and in the pages of the present work they are cited in detail with their Indian names deciphered for the first time from his own inscriptions in Mesopotamia.

The present volume forms really the foundation-stone on which all my former works have been built, for its main material was amassed by me before the issue of those works, although its own publication has been unavoidably delayed for the reasons explained in the text. It establishes in detail the personal identities of the originators of the World's Civilization and of its early developers and their Aryan or Nordic Race continuously back to the Rise of Civilization with concrete dates. This it does by demonstrating the absolute identity of the Sumerian kings by their still existing contemporary monuments and official dynastic lists with regnal years from the first king of the First Sumerian Dynasty at the Rise of Civilization above the twilight of its Dawn at Ukhu (Pteria in Cappadocia), who was the traditional founder of Civilization, continuously downwards in a long unbroken line to the later Babylonian period within the classic historical era, with the traditional kings of the Early Aryans as faithfully preserved in the official king-lists in the Ancient Indian Chronicles from the first King of the First Aryan Dynasty at the same epoch, who was also the traditional founder of Civilization, continuously downwards to the classic period.

This identity of these kings, Sumerian and Aryan, is complete, not only in respect of their names and titles, but also as regards their exact chronological position and order of succession and in the achievements of the leading kings throughout this very long period of over two millenniums of years—an overwhelming proof of identity unparalleled perhaps elsewhere in the annals of History. This identity extends into such minute details as the names of queen-consorts, and of sons. Thus for example, in regard to an early Sumerian sea-emperor who had five famous colonizing sons, whose inscribed contemporary portraits are preserved in a family group (figured in these pages) it is found that the names and achievements of the sons as well as of their father are absolutely identical in the Sumerian and in the Early Aryan records preserved in the Indian Chronicles for the same chronological period. And the identity of names, periods and exploits is further confirmed by identities in the two records in physical type and culture, language and writing, traditions, symbolism and religion. With reference to the last, several of the hymns of Sumerian priest-kings that have been unearthed are shown to be substantially the same hymns as those of the corresponding Early Aryan priest-kings of the same name and period which have been preserved in the Indian Vedas.

The epoch-making first king himself, the traditional builder of the first city and the founder of Civilization, which changed the whole history of mankind, has his personality and achievements preserved in considerable circumstantial detail in the numerous early representations of him (see Frontispiece, etc.), and in the celebrations of his fame and his benefactions to humanity in Sumerian literature, and in the Indian Chronicles and Vedas and in the great Gothic epics of the Nordics, the Eddas, and for those benefactions he was latterly canonized and deified. These records disclose him as a supremely gifted, tall and fair and bearded heroic chief of Nordic or Gothic racial type, a superman and Sun-worshipper, the foremost leader of the most advanced race in the opening of the Metal Age, a practical scientific discoverer and especially the inventor of an improved method of Fire-production, an invincible warrior and wise statesman and administrator, who with rare creative genius arose to fashion the higher destinies of men, and by great practical improvements in the culture of his time, within one generation he raised it up with the aid of his hardy sons and men of the same Gothic breed and established it firmly on a higher plane as "Civilization," which the tides of Time can never wash away.

He and his early descendants are represented in the earliest carvings, sculptures and sacred seals as clad in Gothic dress. And we shall find that they were, in fact, the Early Goths, the most typical of the Nordic race. Most of the leading kings of the Early Sumerian dynasties, including

"Sargon-the-Great" and Menes the first Pharaoh of the First Dynasty of Egypt repeatedly call themselves in their official documents and seals *Gut* (pronounced *Goot*) or *Got*. And one of the more progressive Early Sumerian Dynasties in Mesopotamia called themselves *Guti* or *Goti*; and "Goti" was the regular title of the Goths in Europe—the aspirated form "Goth" having been coined merely by the Romans and never used by these people themselves. And significantly the princes of this Gothic Dynasty over forty-three centuries ago already use, as we shall see, the especially Gothic titles of "Duke" and "Earl."

His personal name in Sumerian is *Dar, Dur*, or *Tur*, which latterly aspirated as *Thur* or *Thor* has given us our modern weekday name of "Thursday," the "Thor's day" of the Anglo-Saxons and "Jupiter's day" of the Romans and Latin nations. He also bears amongst his Sumerian titles that of *Ia*, disclosed as the Sumerian source of *Iu-piter* or "Father Iu" or Ju-piter of whom he is seen to be the human original. And of his titles of *Pur* or *Bur* and *Mit*, the former is now disclosed as the Sumerian source of his Indian title of "Purū of the Sun," for the first Aryan King, the bringer of Fire to the home-hearths of men; and along with the latter title the source of Thor's Gothic title of *Bur Mioth* as I show in my new literal translation of the Nordic Eddas. This latter title also, with his identical achievements, identifies him as the historical human original of the greatest of all Greek culture heroes, the Fire-hero Pro-metheus, with whose real history, however, great liberties seem to have been taken by the later myth-mongering Hellenic bards; just as our later English and Welsh bards in the medieval period when tournaments were in vogue have taken free license with the real, original, and very long pre-Christian hero King Arthur or Ar-Thur or Her-Thor of the Nordic Eddas, who we shall find is made a somewhat quixotic reflection of his real self—this same invincible beneficent culture hero, the first "universal king" and institutor of town or city life and monogamous marriage, the Sumerian King Dur or Tur, the first Aryan king and founder of Civilization, and now made historical and of fixed date.

As this long line of recovered historical Aryan kings and dynasties from the first king onwards, with their achievements adown the ages, now passes like a pageant before our eyes, we see for the first time the true perspective of Ancient History from its beginning, with the names and titles, personalities, Aryan race and relative fixed dates for the authors and the early developers and propagators of Civilization. The hitherto "Pre-historic" Period back to the Rise of Civilization now becomes Historic. And so far from having been a period as supposed of dead stagnation, it is one of ceaseless movement and progress. Civilization from its start is seen to have been fashioned essentially on the same fundamental lines as at the present day; and the astonishing "modernness" of its scientific authors and their outlook on life makes them feel quite near to us, though separated by thousands of years; as they are found to be our own kith and kin. And through their inscriptions in primitive Aryan or Sumerian speech, still uttering their messages, they seem to stretch out their hands and speak to us in fellowship and understanding with trumpet-tongues down the long corridor of Time.

We see them as a vigorous, thriving, industrial people living in cities, and spreading their civilization and ordered government with free institutions amongst the wild aboriginal races, whom they welded into civilized nations. We seem to hear the tramp of their well-disciplined legions and see the glitter of the sun on their spears as they repel the attacks of the would-be destroyers of their civilization, as is recorded in their inscriptions and represented on their monuments. We see the just laws they enacted for championing the cause of the weak and poor and needy, their great public works, and temples and libraries and palaces adorned with sculptures and other works of high and naturalistic art. And we see them engaged in industries and as daring pioneer mariner merchantmen, in their small winged galleys, scouring and exploring the wide seas and confines of the unknown Ancient World.

The point when Civilization emerges on the horizon of written History, hitherto the subject of vague and vastly conflicting conjecture, is now fairly fixed. And it is all unsuspectedly located in Cappadocia in Asia Minor—the land of St George of England, and a land which scientists have shown is really a part of Europe geographically, geologically, zoologically and botanically and climatically, so that *Civilization and its authors were European.* Here in Cappadocia we find the first civilized king established himself and built the first town or city and formed the first civilized state according to the Sumerian accounts; and the Indian Chronicles also locate him and his capital in Asia Minor. There is some evidence indicating that this first king with his adventurous band of fellow-tribesmen came from the old Gothic land of the Euxine and Danube Valley of S.W. Europe. Then forty-three years later, we find his son and successor descending from the uplands of Asia Minor with his army of civilized Aryan tribesmen as an armed peasantry into the rich alluvial plains of Mesopotamia to form there a great empire, building there the first cities in "The Land of Shinar" and civilizing "the black-headed people," the Semitic Chaldean aborigines. It is this advent into Mesopotamia of this immigrant ruling and civilizing Aryan or Nordic race that is now disclosed to be what nowadays is called by Assyriologists "The Coming of the Sumerians."

From this epoch of the advent of the Aryans into Mesopotamia as "Sumerians"—the historical "Sumerians" of this epoch having been hitherto unrecognized by Assyriologists—we can now trace in continuous dated detail Civilization developing and advancing down the ages in the hands of the descendants of its Aryan originators, who are seen to have formed the exclusive imperial ruling caste in the civilized states of the Ancient World. We thus gain a new aid of immense importance towards historic reconstruction and the factors making for Progress in Civilization and towards a new synthesis of the mental and physical sciences.

Thus, the reason for the remarkable Unity in the elements of the various ancient local civilizations hitherto inexplicable—a Unity hitherto logically recognized as implying Unity in Civilization only by Professor Elliot Smith and his school, who, however, ascribe its originating and propagating centre to Egypt—is now seen to be found in the newly-elicited fact that the authors of the supposedly independent ancient civilizations were one and the same ruling race, the Aryans, who spread their civilization over the ancient world by their world-wide imperial sway and colonial rule. Thus Egyptian Civilization is disclosed by the new evidence, which includes actual surviving inscriptions in Egypt of the "world-monarch" Sargon-the-Great and his father and grandfather before him as "Pre-dynastic" Pharaohs, to be of Sumerian or Aryan origin; and introduced fully-fledged into Egypt from Mesopotamia by those Aryan emperors from Mesopotamia. And the First Dynasty of Egypt or Menes' dynasty is demonstrated to be identical with that of Sargon's son Manis-the-warrior or "Menes" in Mesopotamia, of which empire Ancient Egypt is disclosed to have been a colony or dependency. And Menes' Dynasty in Egypt are shown to use generally the same names and territorial titles in their Egyptian inscriptions—hitherto undeciphered by Egyptologists, as they are written in Sumerian script and in the Sumerian language—as they used in their inscriptions in Mesopotamia.

Menes, moreover, is demonstrated to be identical with King Minos, the traditional founder of civilization in Crete. And the other ancient civilizations of Asia Minor, Elam, Persia, the Indus Valley and Mediterranean are shown likewise to be of Sumerian or Aryan origin—the remaining ancient civilization also, namely that of China, which dates traditionally only to about 2200 B.C., has previously been shown with considerable probability by Professors De Lacouperie and Ball to be, along with its hieroglyph system, derived from the Sumerian. The history of Civilization and its propagation is thus disclosed to be a unity to a much greater extent than has hitherto been supposed.

Amongst the important new historical information elicited in regard to these Early Aryan emperors who developed and propagated civilization is that which discloses the hitherto unknown identity and Aryan royal ancestry of the father of Sargon-the-Great; and the pre-history of Sargon himself and his son Menes. Thus it is found that Menes, whose origin and antecedents have been wholly unknown, early revolted against his father and seized Egypt and established there the first local dynasty, detaching it from his father's empire, when he was still crown-prince and governor of the Indus Valley colony of his father's empire. In his official seals which I have found amongst those unearthed in the prolific second batch of seals in the latter colony —and deciphered for the first time in this work along with several scores of others of these Indus seals of the second batch, hitherto wholly undeciphered, and proving to be of immense historical importance for the recovery of the History of the World's Civilization—he also styles himself *Paru* or " Pharaoh." And along with these are other official signet seals of his father Sargon, in addition to those I have previously deciphered and published of the first batch of those Indus Valley seals; and in these Sargon also calls himself " Pharaoh." Moreover, Menes' route for his conquest of Egypt is indicated *via* the Persian Gulf, Indian Ocean or Arabian Sea and the Red Sea.

Most pathetically tragic of all perhaps is the discovery that the hitherto unread long record inscribed on the great Ebony Label found in the " tomb " of Menes at Abydos in Upper Egypt, and written in the Sumerian script and language of his time, and now deciphered and translated for the first time, narrates in graphic and circumstantial detail how this great admiral and " world emperor " in his old age on " a voyage of exploration with his fleet " made the complete course to " The Furthest West Sunset-Land in the Western Ocean " and there met his tragic death; and it states that his " tomb " in Egypt remained empty, and was merely a cenotaph and " place of the hanging wood-label." And the place-name of the island in the Far Western Ocean, which appears to read " Urani," suggests the place of his death and real tomb as " Erin " or Ireland.

Apart from the flood of new light thus gained on the personality, achievements, methods and race of the hitherto unknown, but now historical, individuals who originated and early developed civilization, and of the relatively little known early propagators of civilization over the Ancient World, and the manner in which they did it, the new method of research is of great service to scientific History by the more accurate Chronology which it introduces. Through the recovery by our new keys of the complete list of the Sumerian or Aryan kings continuously back to the first king of the First Sumerian Dynasty and bridging over the gaps which have hitherto existed, we are enabled for the first time to recover the exact dates to within a few years for the entire main line of Sumerian or Aryan kings back to the first king at the Rise of Civilization. Thus the real date for the first Aryan or Sumerian king becomes about 3378 B.C.; and the real date of Menes, the founder of the First Dynasty of Egypt becomes about 2703 B.C. And the great confusion that arises from the enormous discrepancies in the extravagantly conjectural and calculated dates for these epochs by the rival schools amongst Assyriologists and Egyptologists, none of which are anywhere near the mark, will soon it may be hoped disappear from our research records and text-books. The determination of the real date of Menes will not only bring due order into Egyptian Chronology, but must react beneficially on inquiries into the history of the countries with which Egypt was connected during the period covered by its earlier dynasties, including Ancient Britain.

In speaking of the Sumerians or Early Aryans of the fourth millennium B.C. as the Founders of Civilization, and of the Rise of Civilization as a now relatively fixed and dated historical epoch, one has to be on one's guard against misconception. Civilization was not the sudden affair we sometimes imagine it. The progress which the Sumerians brought to fruition was a slow growth from remote beginnings. It was the outcome of a long, slow process of evolution from the primitive culture with fire-production, cookery and beginnings of art of the tall, long-headed, big-brained, Crô-Magnon race of men of the last stage of the Old Stone Age about 20,000 B.C. onwards to the later New Stone Age men on the threshold of "The Dawn of Civilization" with domestication of animals, sporadic agriculture and social organization with fixity of customs. It was not until the relatively recent period of the Metal Age that the most highly-developed race of men (presumably the descendants of the cultured Cro-Magnon race) invented Writing and built the first cities, thus putting the coping stone, so to speak, on the edifice that had been so long building, and giving us at last "Civilization" in its dictionary sense.

The first builder of a city or town was, according to the old Sumerian records, the first king of the First Sumerian Dynasty, who was the traditional founder of Civilization, and he was we find familiar with Writing and lived at the opening of the Metal Age. His date by our new chronological evidence of about 3378 B.C. thus becomes technically the date for "The Rise of Civilization" with which began the glorious new era of human progress.

Of other far-reaching historical effects of the new evidence several are indicated in the concluding chapter. Here may be mentioned the new light which is shed on evolution of heroic mythology, on the very early Aryan institution of monotheism some two thousand years before Abraham; on the evolution of the anthropomorphic idea of God and its date, on the Aryan-Sumerian basis of the Mosaic, Roman and other law-codes, on the inspiration drawn by Greek art from the naturalistic art of the Sumerians, Hittites and Aryan Babylonians, the derivation of the applied and industrial arts and sciences including astronomy, the arch in building, measures of weight, surface, capacity, time, etc., hydraulic and sanitary engineering and deep-sea navigation.

Heroic Mythology has its historical human basis now disclosed for the first time, showing the identity between the civilized traditions of the East and West, and the connection of both with the primitive Aryan or Nordic race and language. We get behind the beginnings of heroic mythology. A vast deal of what has hitherto been looked upon as "prehistoric" and mythical becomes historic and real. Heroes who have been raised into gods again take form as men, and as historic early Aryan kings of relatively fixed dates. Gods and demi-gods of the ancient Greeks and Romans, Egyptians and Hittites, Persians and Indo-Aryans, as well as of the Goths, Scandinavians and Germans, Ancient Britons, Irish and Anglo-Saxons, such as Zeus, Jove or Ju-piter, Indra, Prometheus, Atmu, Addamu, Adam, Ad or Odin, Thor or Her-Thor or Ar-Thur of the Round Table with his Sumerian "Holy Grail" (now discovered as still existing and identical with the magical stone-bowl or cauldron captured from the weirds at the Well-of-Urd by Her-Thor), Sir Gawain, Conn-the-hundred-Fighter, Cain, Enoch, Noah and Japhet, Nimrod the mighty hunter and city-builder, Dardanos, Erich-thonias, Hercules, Bacchus, Osiris with Isis and Horus, Barat or Brihat the eponymous ancestor of Brutus-the-Trojan and the British, St George of Cappadocia and of "Merrie England" with his Red Cross, St Andrew, St Michael the Archangel and Tascio of the Ancient Briton pre-Roman coins and prehistoric monuments in Britain, are found before their deification or canonization to have been famous Sumerian or Early Aryan kings and emperors of relatively fixed dates, most of them with still existing contemporary monuments, whose histories can be reconstructed by the Sumerian monumental inscriptions and records, supplemented with the accounts of them preserved in the Indian Chronicles and the Gothic or Nordic Eddas.

Thus we find that, after all, the god Zeus, Jove or Ju-piter or Thor-Odin in historical fact was before his deification the actual human ancestor in lineal ascent of many of the famous kings and heroes of antiquity. This justifies the proud boast of many of the early Sumerian kings that they were "The son of God Zax (Zeus)," who was also called Ia (Jah or Jove); and that they "suckled at the breast" of his queen "The Lady of the Mountain or Innini (= Juno)," that is to say they were vicariously so nourished as the lineal descendants of his son the second Aryan king, as shown in the dynastic genealogies in the Appendix. This was just as in later times the Anglo-Saxon and other Nordic kings claimed to be descended from Odin; and in classic Greek and Roman myth, many of the leading heroes are made to be the sons of Zeus or Jupiter, that is to say they traced back their descent to him in human form; though the later mythmongering bards, in ignorance of the real history and reflecting the lax morality of their time, ascribed the descent to direct illicit amours on the part of Zeus or Jupiter and so grossly traduced his noble character. Even the old traditions of the later Chaldean and Egyptian priests, reflected by Berosos and Manetho, that the first earthly kings were "gods" is now seen to be based on historical fact. And the leading Heraldic Animals and associated Crosses on modern national and family escutcheons are seen to have been used in similar fashion by our Sumerian or Early Nordic forbears, the animals being usually rebuses for their clan names.

The innate relationships of Civilization to the Aryan Race from the earliest period disclosed by this new evidence are, it is interesting to note, fully in agreement with the recent researches of Professors W. M'Dougall and Hans Günther in their classic analyses of the racial elements in European Civilization from the Greek period downwards to the modern, in which they reach the same conclusion as to the leading part played by the Nordic Race, that is the Aryans, and that racial impoverishment in that element tends to the weakening of Civilization.

In this regard, the staggering fact now emerges from the united testimony of the entire body of Sumerian and Babylonian monumental and literary history, as interpreted by the new official Indian keys to the Aryan ancestry and the traditional forms of the names of the kings, that *no Semitic dynasty whatsoever is to be found in Mesopotamia throughout the whole period of recorded history from the Rise of Civilization downwards until the Semitic Assyrian period of about* 1200 B.C. All the dynasties before this period which are alleged by Assyriologist Semitic scholars to be "Semitic" are now disclosed to be purely and unequivocally "Sumerian" or Aryan and Non-Semitic. It now transpires that Assyriologists, possessed of no key whatever to the traditional forms of any of these kings' names to guide them in "restoring" the names from the ambiguous "polyphonous" Sumerian syllabic signs, have under the spell of their Semitic theories forcibly Semitized the names of those Sumerian kings by arbitrarily substituting often Semitic values for the normal Sumerian or Aryan values of the syllabic signs by which the kings' names are written, in order to give the names a Semitic semblance and thus support their inveterate theory that the Semites were the originators of Mesopotamian civilization. This falsification of the History of Mesopotamia and of Civilization has hitherto grossly misled historians in general. But all of these so-called " Semitic " dynasties, as well as their individual kings, including, for example, " Sargon-the-Great " (who, however, never called himself " Sargon," nor was so called even in late Babylonia), and King Khammu-Rabi of Law-code fame, are now conclusively proved in this work from their own contemporary records to be Sumerians or Aryans in race ; and each and all of them are recognized Early Aryan kings and dynasties of the Indo-Aryans, several of them being famous Early Aryans mentioned in the Vedic psalm literature of the orthodox Hindus, and one of them is the famous epical Aryan king Rāma Chandra, the hero of the *Rāmāyana* romance and the most popular ancient heroic Aryan king in India to-day. And it is difficult to acquit altogether from blame those distinguished Assyriologist scholars who mechanically following each other, have allowed the spell cast by their Semitic prejudice to blind them for so long to the real facts.

Geographically, considerable insight is gained incidentally through these earliest inscriptions regarding leading place-names of the Ancient World, and the unsuspected wide prevalence of deep-sea Navigation by the Early Aryans and their Phœnician branch in times hitherto deemed " prehistoric." In Menes' day, over forty-five centuries ago, we find large three-decked ships scouring the seas " in fleets," and which " made the full course," implying that the courses were already mapped out. The remarkable persistence of place-names is also demonstrated, Whilst some of the ancient names, such as " Kham " or " Ham " for Egypt, have long become obsolete, though now found in the newly deciphered inscriptions many centuries earlier than previously known, others like *Parahsi* or " Persia " and *Mushsir* or Egypt—the modern vernacular name of which is still " Misr "—disclose the currency of the modern names a millennium or more before that hitherto recorded. And besides locating definitely the lost pre-Indian homeland of the Indo-Aryans, the historical original of the real " Garden of Eden " paradise is found in a location far from that hitherto imagined for it.

Zoologically, also we recover admirable naturalistic contemporary portraits of animals, wild and domesticated, at early periods which can now be definitely dated, and in habitats where they have long been extinct, such as, the woolly-maned lion, rhinoceros and tiger, and amongst the domesticated animals we find at these early dates the prick-eared wolf, Brahminy bull, buffalo, elephant, and goats of different species.

On the origin of civilized writing from Sumerian pictographs—selected signs of which I have shown were the parents of our modern alphabetic letters with their phonetic values—considerable light is thrown by the early Indus colony writers having preserved fuller pictographic forms of many of the signs than in the Mesopotamian script. Thus many of the hieroglyph signs in the latter which are drawn so abbreviated and diagrammatically that the original object which they pictured is doubtful or unknown, that object now becomes recognizable.

Such are a few of the many outstanding results which so far have followed from comparison of the monumental inscriptions with the literary remains of our Aryan ancestors. Important in themselves, by placing universal history on a firmer foundation than before, they are still more so by the promise they afford of the harvest of new knowledge that awaits us when the methods of research, of which this comparison is the key, have been more fully exploited.

The enforced delay of nearly a quarter of a century between the making and publishing of most of these discoveries, however regrettable, has not been without its compensations. The interval has witnessed the remarkable confirmation of my observations as to the Sumerian origin of the language and civilization of India that is supplied by the unearthing of two dead Sumerian cities in the Indus Valley, with numerous monuments and inscribed seals, the first batch of which in my pioneer readings of the inscriptions disclosed the name of that Sumerian colony and of several of its chief governors and high priests, the Sumerian emperor who founded the colony, and the date; and also furnished the key to that early form of cursive Sumerian script, for writing with pen and ink on parchment. It has afforded, by the unearthing of fresh inscriptions, further and more complete old Sumerian king-lists, and also titles of many of the kings, which confirm the unique historicity of the official Indian king-lists and chronicles as an independent source of Sumerian history, and also confirm my readings of the Indo-Sumerian seals and my revised readings of the personal names of " Sargon " and others. It has seen my opinions on the drift of Civilization from the Near East to the West, as to the part played in its dissemination by the Phœnicians as a sea-going branch of the Aryans, as to the unique cultural value of the Aryan tradition and physique, as to the decadence produced by some and the improvement resulting from other mixtures of the Aryans with foreign race strains, and as to the comparatively small account of Semitism as an original creative force, supported independently by antiquaries who have approached these problems from the Western side, so that it has become a commonplace of anthropologists that " all over North-western Europe the descendants of the men who built the palace of Minos plied their industries and buried their dead."

As this volume, like its predecessors in the series, is primarily intended for the educated general reader as well as the historian, I have placed as far as possible the more technical details and the attestation of proofs in foot-notes and appendices. And I have arranged the chapters generally in the order in which the discoveries were achieved. Thus the reader may take part, as it were, step by step in the adventurous exploration into the Unknown and gain acquaintance across " The Gulf of Time " with our noble Aryan ancestors in their moulding the destinies of the world, in their struggles with the hordes of primitive men in establishing Civilization, not only for themselves but for the welfare of mankind, and the manner in which they developed and propagated and controlled it by world-wide empire, ensuring widespread peace (like an embryo League of Nations), and welded the heterogeneous primitive tribes into nations, and the apparent causes leading to the decline of civilized nations. The exploration is thus perhaps not one of the least attractive of the " romances of Science," in which " Truth is stranger than Fiction."

The not infrequent references to my former works have been found necessary in order to avoid needless repetition of the proofs which are already detailed there, especially as this work forms part of the same series, and most of these references are to new research and new discoveries not to be found elsewhere. A few of these references are to the proofs in refutation of some of the more common, false and misleading statements which are mechanically repeated through ignorance by writers, such as that "Aryan" is not a racial but a linguistic term; that the Khatti or "Hittites," an early stock of the Aryans, were "Armenoids," or low-browed Semites; that "Caucasian" is a synonym for Aryan and Nordic, despite its unscientific inclusion of Semites and other round-headed people; that the "Phœnicians" properly so-called were Semites, and so on. The somewhat positive style of expression adopted in many instances will, I believe, be found justified by the fully attested facts on which they are based.

In the Appendices will be found details of the official signets of the Egyptian Pharaohs and of the Gothic dynasty of Mesopotamia recently unearthed in the Indus Valley and now deciphered for the first time, as well as of the Sumerian writing on prehistoric pottery from the Danube Valley attesting the early presence of the Sumerians or primitive Goths in Middle Europe. An unusually full Index is supplied in order to facilitate reference to the vast number of new historical facts elicited. And a perusal of the Contents Table will help the reader to keep a clear view of the immense extent of time and territory over which the work travels.

No pains have been spared to make this pioneer work as free as possible from errors of commission. Covering such a vast and as yet largely unexplored field with so many aspects of history, prehistory, civilization, religion and historical geography, with the ransacking of ancient sites and museums and specialist works and periodicals scattered over the world, and "fishing up Truth from the bottom of her well," it is too much to hope that no mistakes may have crept in. Yet were these far greater and more numerous than is at all likely, they are, I believe, relatively insignificant and cannot affect the force of the main facts and the cumulative effect of the great mass of concrete historical proofs.

My cordial thanks are due to the authors, Sir Flinders Petrie and others, and the publishers mentioned in the text for their courtesy in permitting the reproduction from their books and journals of plates of inscriptions and contemporary portraits of some of the leading Ancient Aryan or Sumerian and Egyptian kings from their own monuments. To Mr David Couper Thomson of Dundee I owe most grateful thanks for supplying many references to recent excavations in different parts of the world; and to the Venerable Archdeacon G. H. Cameron, Westminster; Rev. L. G. Hunts, Munsley Rectory, Ledbury, Herefordshire; H. C. Lawlor, M.A., Esq., and A. Pringle, Esq., Belfast, and others, for photographs and notes on the markings on prehistoric monuments in Britain and Ireland; and to Sir Gerald Strickland, G.C.M.G., Dr A. K. Chalmers, LL.D., and other friends for various useful suggestions. I am deeply indebted in an especial degree to my old friend, Dr Islay Burns Muirhead, M.A., for perennial encouragement in the research, helpful criticism and painstaking revision of the proof-sheets. And I have pleasure in acknowledging the exceptional care bestowed by The Edinburgh Press on their setting up and printing of the book with its many tables of technical difficulty and numerous plates and text illustrations.

L. A. WADDELL.

April 23, 1929.

CONTENTS

CHAP. PAGE

APPENDICES.

FIG. A. Portrait (? contemporary) of First Aryan or Sumerian King Dar (Thor or St George of Cappadocia) taming (or civilizing) the Lion totem tribes, from ivory handle of stone-dagger, *c.* 3380 B.C. See Frontispiece for photograph.

Note his Gothic horned hat and dress, and compare with his later representation as the Sun-god by King Khamu-Rabi, *c.* 2000 B.C., see Fig. B below.

FIG. B. First Aryan-Sumerian King deified as the Sun-god, on King Khamu-Rabi's Law-code stele, *c.* 2000 B.C. And see photograph and note in Pl. XXIV.

Drawn from original monument and several photographs in different lightings. Note the four horns (set in sockets) on his conical hat in series with the representation in above Fig. A, and innumerable Sumerian and Hittite Seals., *e.g.* Figs. pp. 64, 149, 406, 608; and on Ancient Briton monuments, Figs. 195, 607.

LIST OF ILLUSTRATIONS

PLATES

ILLUSTRATIONS IN TEXT

MAPS.

ABBREVIATIONS

AE.	Ancient Egypt ed. Sir F. Petrie. London.
AIC.	Académie des Inscript. et Belles Lettres, Comptes Rendus. Paris.
AJ	The Antiquaries Journal. London.
B.	Origin and Development of Babylonian Writing, 2 vols. G. A. Barton, Leipzig, 1913.
B.	Bismya. E. J. Banks, New York, 1912.
BD.	Egyptian Hieroglyphic Dictionary. E. W. Budge, 1920.
BHE.	History of the Egyptian People. E. W. Budge, 1914.
Br.	Classified List of Sumerian Ideographs. R. Brünnow, Leyden, 1889.
BSK.	Sea-Kings of Crete. J. Baikie, 1920.
CAH.	Cambridge Ancient History, I. 2nd Ed., 1924.
CD.	Pali Dictionary. R. Childers, 1875.
CIWA.	Cuneiform Inscriptions of W. Asia. H. Rawlinson and T. G. Pinches.
CMC.	Mission en Cappadocia. E. Chantre, Paris, 1898.
CPN.	Personal Names of Cassite Period. A. T. Clay, 1912.
CSH.	La Glyptique Syro-Hittite. G. Contenau, Paris, 1922.
CT.	Cuneiform Texts in the British Museum.
DCO.	Cylindres Orient. du Mus. du Louvre. L. Delaporte, Paris, 1923.
Déc.	Découvertes en Chaldée. E. de Sarzec et L. Heuzey, Paris.
DP.	Délégation en Perse Mémoires.
DS.	Die Entstelung das altesten Schriftsystems. F. Delitzsch.
EB.	Encyclopædia Biblica. T. K. Cheyne.
EM.	The Palace of Minos. A. Evans, 1921.
ERE.	Encyclopædia of Religion and Ethics. J. Hastings.
FB.	Die Boghaz Koi Texte-Umschrift II. 1. Leipzig, 1922.
FD.	Documentes Pre-Sargoniques. A. de la Fuye.
GH.	Hieroglyphs. F. L. Griffith, 1898.
GLH.	Land of the Hittites. J. Garstang, 1910.
HA.	Hilprecht Anniversary Volume. 1909.
HASK.	Akkadischo und Sumerische Keilschrift-texte. P. Haupt.
HCC.	Clavis Cuneorum. Howardy, Lipsia, 1904 f.
HG.	Geographie und Geschichte d. Alten Orients. F. Hommel.
HI.	Hittite Index. Mayer and Garstang.
HL.	Sumerische Lesestücke. F. Hommel.
HNE.	Ancient History of Near East. H. R. Hall, 1918.
HOB.	Old Babylonian Inscriptions. H. V. Hilprecht, 1896.
HWU.	Ur Excavations, I. H. R. Hall and C. L. Woolley, 1927.
IA.	Indian Antiquary, Bombay.
JAOS.	Journal of American Oriental Society. Newhaven, U.S.A.
JEA.	Journal of Egyptian Archæology.
JRAI.	Journal Royal Anthropological Institute.

JRAS.	Journal Royal Asiatic Society.
JRB.	Religious Belief in Babylonia. M. Jastrow, 1911.
KCB.	Chronology of Early Babylonian Kings. L. W. King, 1907.
KHS.	History of Sumer and Akkad. L. W. King, 1916.
KIB.	Inscription of Darius the Great at Behistun. L. W. King, 1907
KTA.	Keilschrift texte aus Assur. Inhalts, 1920.
LHF.	Historical Fragments. Univ. Pennsylvania. L. Legrain, 1922.
LMJ.	Museum Journal. Univ. Pennsylvania 1920 art. L. Legrain.
M.	Seltene Assyrische Ideogramme. B. Meissner, 1910.
MBt.	Mahā-Bhārata.
MD.	Dictionary of Assyrian Language. W. Muss-Arnolt, Berlin, 1905
MDC.	Dawn of Civilization. G. Maspere, 1922.
MDOG.	Mitteilung d. Deutschen Orient-Gesellschaft.
MKI.	Vedic Index. Macdonell and Keith, 1912.
MVM.	Vedic Mythology. A. Macdonell.
MS.	Sumerian Administrative Documents. D. W. Myrrnan.
MWD.	Sanskrit-English Dictionary. M. Monier-Williams, 1899.
PB.	Babylonian Tablets, Berens Collect. T. G. Pinches, 1915.
PGG.	Galatie et Bithynie. Perrot and Guillaume.
PHE.	History of Egypt. Sir F. Petrie, 1923.
PḤT.	Historical Texts, Univ. Pennsylvania. A. Poebel, 1914 f.
PIT.	Ancient Indian Historical Tradition. F. E. Pargiter, 1922.
PRT.	Royal Tombs, I and II. W. M. Flinders Petrie, 1901.
PSL.	Sumerian Lexicon. J. D. Prince, 1908.
PZ.	Præhistorische Zeitschrift. Berlin.
RA.	Revue d'Assyriologie.
RB.	Early Babylonian History. H. Radau, New York, 1900.
RHP.	History of Phœnicia. G. Rawlinson, 1889.
RSH.	Sumerisch-Babylonisch Hymen. G. A. Reisner.
RV.	Rig Veda.
Sb.	Syllabar of the Second Class, C.T. xi.
SI.	Ilios. H. Schliemann, 1880.
SS.	Syllabar Verzeich der Akkad. u. Assyr. Wörtes. Strassmaier.
SSS.	Sculptured Stones of Scotland. J. Stuart, 1856.
STE.	Textes élamites-sémitiques. V. Scheil.
TDC.	Les Chronologie des Dynasties de Sumer et d'Accad. F. Thureau-Dangin, 1918.
TDI.	Les Inscript. Sumer et d'Akkad. F. Thureau-Dangin, 1905.
UE.	Ur Excavations, I. H. R. Hall and Woolley, 1927.
VD.	Icelandic Dictionary. G. Vigfusson, 1874.
WAOA.	Aryan Origin of the Alphabet. L. A. Waddell, 1927.
WBC.	Weld-Blundell Collection of Cuneiform Texts. Oxford, 1923.
WBT.	The Buddhism of Tibet. L. A. Waddell, 1895.
WISD.	Indo-Sumerian Seals Deciphered. L. A. Waddell, 1925.
WPOB.	Phœnician Origin of the Britons, Scots and Anglo-Saxons. 1924.
WSAD.	Sumer-Aryan Dictionary, A-F. L. A. Waddell, 1927.
WSC,	Seal Cylinders of W. Asia. W. H. Ward, Washington, 1900.
WVP.	Vishnu Purana trans. H. H. Wilson, ed. F. Hall, 1864.
ZA.	Zeitschrift für Assyriologie.

THE MAKERS OF CIVILIZATION IN RACE & HISTORY

I

INTRODUCTORY—MY PREVIOUS HISTORICAL DISCOVERIES LEADING UP TO THE PRESENT ONES

> "*There was and is an Aryan Race, that is to say the characteristic modes of speech termed Aryan were developed among the Blond Longheads alone, however much some of these may have been modified by the importation of Non-Aryan elements.*"—HUXLEY.[1]

ALTHOUGH there is nowadays a considerable consensus of opinion in favour of attributing to the Aryan race—the race now generally called Nordic or North European—a special share in the invention and diffusion of our Civilization which is the prime factor for the Progress of Mankind, and more especially in the invention and diffusion of European and Indian Civilization, as the languages of Europe and India are of the Aryan family, there has so far been little or nothing known as to the origin and early history of that race, or even its early homeland. Arguing from the location of its chief modern representatives, historians have variously placed our primitive Aryan stock in Central Asia, in N.W., Central and S.E. Europe; and have been hoping that archæological research in one or other of those regions may unearth the lost history of the Early Aryans.

Hitherto that hope has not been realized, and authorities, whilst adhering to their opinion as to the special Aryan race-strain in Civilization, and its vital importance for the Progress of Civilization, are inclining to look upon the problem of its beginnings and the personalities of its authors as insoluble from the point of view of existing scientific data.

1 "The Aryan Question," *Nineteenth Century*, November 1890, 766.

In former works, I have suggested that a chief cause of the failure to solve these problems was the non-recognition by scholars of the essentially Aryan character of the earliest extant written records, those namely on the Mesopotamian and Egyptian monuments. And I have given many illustrations of the way in which my discovery of the predominantly Aryan character of the language of these inscriptions, and the Aryan personalities and histories of their authors assist us in identifying the Civilization from which our own has descended, and in recovering the lost history of the Aryan Race continuously back to the Rise of Civilization.

A brief reference to some of the main results of these earlier researches will prepare the way for a right understanding of the present work.

Nothing had been known of the racial and linguistic affinities of the "Sumerians," the oldest of all civilized peoples, whose vast city ruins in Mesopotamia with magnificent inscribed and sculptured monuments and other works of art, with libraries and hundreds of thousands of official and private documents, etc., began to be unearthed some fifty years ago and whose treasures now enrich and adorn the galleries of the national museums in Europe and America; but who seemed themselves, after suddenly appearing there with a fully-fledged higher civilization, to have as suddenly disappeared after a comparatively brief existence as a nation, leaving no descendants to continue their culture and language.

Study by leading Assyriologists of their language and writing tended rather to deepen than dispel the mystery surrounding them, for it led to the conclusion, crystallized by continual repetition into a dogma, that these people while certainly not Semites, or "Children of Shem" like the Jews, bore no affinity to the Aryan or Nordic race nor other well-known type, and that their language had no affinity with any recognized linguistic group, and that in particular it had no affinity whatever with the Aryan languages—the English and the continental languages of Europe and India.

Thus the Sumerians with their marvellously high civilization, art, culture and language have hitherto been universally

SUMERIAN HEADS OF ARYAN OR NORDIC TYPE.

From ancient statues, *c.* 3050 B.C. *A-B* (top), shaven prelate in profile and semi-full face, in Berlin Museum. *C* (lower), shaven priest, and *D*, long-haired layman, in Imperial Ottoman Museum, Constantinople. (After Banks, B.B. 253-4).

regarded as a sort of fossil curiosity, a remote and totally extinct alien race in no way related to any modern people nor to their civilization or language; though from the monosyllabic and "agglutinative" forms of their early language they are supposed by many to have been physically related to the Chinese and Finno-Tartars.

Aryan Race of the Sumerians discovered

The direct reverse of these current views on the Sumerians was I observed the fact, and I established it in my previous works, by a mass of fully-attested concrete scientific proofs. This new evidence proved conclusively that the Sumerians were Aryans in physical type, culture, religion, language and writing; and that they were our own kith and kin, living under our Aryan civilization and laws and speaking radically the same tongue.

Their Aryan racial physical type I showed was clearly seen in their portraits on their own contemporary sculptures (see Plate II.) [1] and seals from the earliest period downwards, and it was especially evident in the engraved portraits on their seals.[2] This disclosed them to be preponderatingly of the longish-headed, broad-browed and large-brained Nordic type; and they were obviously fair in complexion as attested by the blue eyes of white shell inlaid with lapis lazuli stone inset in some of their statues, as also by the darkish colour of much of their jewellery; and of fair hair, as their general term for their subject people was "the black-headed (haired) people." And the kings and officials on state occasions usually wore the Gothic horned head-dress of the Ancient Britons and Anglo-Saxons. This Aryan

[1] Both marble heads in Plate II.B. from Bismya, the ancient Adab, were found without the bodies of their statues by Mr Banks, who believed them to be of the same "age," as they were of the same type, as the statues of the ancient Sumerian king excavated by him from the same mound, and itself the oldest Sumerian statue, carved in the round, as yet known, and bearing his name in pre-Sargonic Sumerian writing as King Bidsar (cp. BB. 190 f. 196), and now disclosed as probably the pre-Sargonic Sumerian king Bidash of about 2950 B.C., see No. 17 in King-list, p. 104. The long hair of the layman is in series with that found on the earliest Sumerian seals and bas-reliefs.

[2] See the very numerous illustrations of their seals in WSC. *passim*; DCO.; and in WPOB and in the present work.

physical type of the Sumerians has significantly just been confirmed (1927) by Sir Arthur Keith's examination of several skulls unearthed from Sumerian cemeteries at Ur.[1]

Linguistically also, I proved that the Sumerian Language was radically Aryan in its words and structure, and that it was the parent of all the Aryan family of languages, ancient and modern, as demonstrated in my *Sumer-Aryan Dictionary*. And in particular it was the parent of the English Language, over seventy-five per cent. of the English words being shown to be derived from Sumerian roots with identical forms, sounds and meanings. The Aryan Alphabets, including the European or "Roman" writing, I demonstrated in my *Aryan Origin of the Alphabet* to be derived from Sumerian picture-writing with the same phonetics.

The Culture and Religion also of the Sumerians, I showed were identical with the Aryan, and the Sumerians worshipped the same god or gods under the same names and under the same representations with the same attributes and symbols as the Aryans, ancient and modern, including the Britons, Anglo-Saxons, Irish Scots, Scandinavians, classic Greeks and Romans in pre-Christian Europe, and in present-day India. And they possessed the same heroes and saints.

The name "Sumerian"

The name "Sumerian," which has been arbitrarily applied by Assyriologists to this ancient imperial people now disclosed to be the Early Aryans, was never used by these people themselves. That name is merely coined by Assyriologists from a Semitic territorial title "Shumer" for the name spelt by these people *Ki-en-gin*, and supposed to designate Lower Mesopotamia, to which these people have hitherto, but as now seen erroneously, been believed to have been restricted.[2] That name "Sumer" or "Shumer"

[1] He concludes: "They (the Sumerians) certainly belong to the same racial division of mankind as the nations of Europe, they are scions of the Caucasian stock." (HWU. 215). The earlier skulls exhibited greater width while being also long-heads. "There is no evidence of the presence of any people of Mongol affinities, nor of any showing the characteristic Armenoid form of head." (HWU. 226).

[2] The name "Shumer" is first found in a bilingual inscription of King Khammu Rabi about 1980 B.C., as the Semitic term for the Sumerian territorial name of "Kiengin"; and it is once applied to the language of

indeed, well illustrates the unscientific methods of leading Assyriologists in the fantastic liberties they take with these old names. Thus they dogmatically declare that "*the ideogram Ki-en-gin according to phonetic laws became Shumer.*"[1] (!) As also showing its ambiguous character and usage, this "Sumer" title was for long applied by Assyriologists in the diametrically opposite sense, namely to the supposed Semitic people of Mesopotamia and their language now called by them "Akkad," and who were then called by them "Sumerian"; but latterly by a complete somersault they arbitrarily interchanged these titles. As, however, the name "Sumerian" has obtained currency for several decades as the title for these earliest civilized imperial people in Mesopotamia, we are now forced to continue its use as a general designation for them.

The name "Aryan"

The title *Ārya*, Englished into "Aryan," is the usual term employed for the white race, now called from its western stock "Nordic," from the very earliest Vedic period by the eastern or Indian branch of that race who have uniquely preserved its early traditional history and records; and the same race is similarly so termed by the Ancient Persians who also belonged to its eastern branch. And the title was and *is solely used by them in a racial and in no other sense;* and especially it is never used by them in a linguistic sense as is popularly supposed—a usage which was only introduced by European philologists a few generations ago. That title Ārya literally means in both the Indian Sanskrit, the old classic language of India, and in the Ancient Persian language "the exalted or noble one"; and it is derived as I have shown from the Sumerian *Ar*, *Ara* "exalt, lofty, shining, glory";[2] which is also disclosed as the remote Sumerian root of our modern word "Aristocrat" or "noblest or most excellent governor," derived through the Greek, a word which well defines the older ethnic meaning of the word "Aryan." For the civilizers of

that land (cp. MD. 1062), and to the contemporary people of that land in Babylonia, but merely in the form "of Shumer" (MD. 737); and at a period after the Sumerians had become extinct according to Assyriologists.

[1] S. Langdon, *Sumerian Grammar* I.

[2] WSAD. 15.

the old world are now disclosed to have been more or less exclusively of this Aryan stock, which was essentially an aristocracy of master-men, the ruling race who established Civilization and who civilized the aborigines by their enlightened rule and science; just as in the Greek classic period of Europe, Greek Civilization reached its zenith under a military aristocracy of this same Aryan race, and weakened and became practically extinct with the weakening and practical extinction of this Aryan racial element from the population there. Indeed the later Sumerians do appear also to have used this title in a racial sense in the aspirated form of *Ha-ra*, which is defined in the bilingual Assyrian glossaries as "The host of the nation or people."[1]

This title *Ara*, *Ārya* or "Aryan" is found as a designation of rulers or masters to run throughout the whole family of the Aryan languages, including the Egyptian, presumably because the early rulers and masters were of this race. Thus it is in aspirated form the *Her*, *Hera*, *Hearra* or *Herr*, "lord or master" of the Goths, Scandinavians, Germans and Anglo-Saxons, the *Aire* "chieftain" of the Irish Scots and Gaels and so on.[2] It is the *Arios*, *Harios* or *Harri* of the Medes, and *Arya* and *Airya* of the Ancient Persians in a similar exalted and racial sense; and it is thus proudly used by Darius-the-Great on his tomb where he calls himself "An Arya of Arya(n) descent," and Xerxes called himself a "Harri." The early sea-going branch of the Sumerians, the Morites or Amorites who have left many "prehistoric" inscriptions in the British Isles, whilst calling themselves *Mur*, *Gut* or "Goth" and *Kad* (forms of *Khatti*, *Catti* or "Hitt-ite"), also called themselves *Ari*,[3] which now appears to be a dialectic form of this title "Aryan."[4]

SUMERIAN ORIGIN OF THE BRITONS, ANGLO-SAXONS, CYMRI, IRISH SCOTS, SCANDINAVIANS, EARLY GERMANS & GOTHS & THEIR CIVILIZATION, LANGUAGE & WRITING

Detailed proofs are given in my former works for the "Sumerian" origin of the Britons, Anglo-Saxons, Cymri, the fair Scots and Irish, Scandinavians, Early Germans and

[1] Br. 5915, 8206, 6352. [2] WSAD. 15. [3] M. 5328.
[4] WPOB. 257 f.; WISD. 51 f. 100; WSAD. 18.

Goths, with approximate dates for the Sumerian mining and colonizing occupations of parts of the British Isles by several immigrations from the Sargonic period of about 2700 B.C. onwards. The evidence included a few linear Sumerian inscriptions, the first decipherment of the Sumerian sacred "cup-mark" inscriptions on the prehistoric monuments in the British Isles with their Sumerian symbolism, including votive inscriptions to the Sumerian Sun-angel

FIG. 1.—Ancient Briton Coins of pre-Roman "Catti" kings of about second century B.C., inscribed *Tascio* and *Tascif*, with portraits of that Sun-archangel of the Hitto-Sumerians. (Coins after Evans.)

Note head and beard as in archaic Hittite or "Catti" sculpture of him as Tash in Fig. 6 (p. 14); and corn crosses of Indara or Andrew ✕ type.

Tasia, who I showed was identical in name, representation and functions with *the well-known "Tascio" figured and inscribed on the pre-Roman coins of the "Catti" kings of Ancient Britain*,[1] and the decipherment of a bi-lingual inscription of a Brito-Phœnician king of the fourth century B.C.

The identity also of the religion and leading folk-lore of the Ancient Britons and Goths with that of the Sumerians was demonstrated. In particular it was shown that the patron saints St George, St Andrew and the tutelary Britannia, as well as St Michael, King Arthur and his Grail legend and the Thor-Odin legend of the Britons and Scandinavians were of Sumerian origin, all of which is now

[1] For numerous representations see WPOB.

confirmed in the present work, which discloses the human originals of these saints and heroes as historical Sumerian kings of fixed dates with an existing contemporary inscribed monument.

FIG. 2.—Ancient Briton Coins of the pre-Roman "Catti" kings of about the second century B.C., with symbols of the Sumerian Sun-archangel Tasia. (After Poste.)

Note the crosses around sun-horse, ears of corn on reverse, and in second coin the contraction of *Catti* into *Att*. The "EL" between the face and back of coin = "Electrum" alloy of gold, of which coin consists; and *AV* = Aurum or "gold." And compare with Fig. 1 (p. 7) for the name and representations of *Tascio*.

THE ANCIENT GREEKS, ETRUSCANS & PATRICIAN ROMANS & THEIR CIVILIZATION, LANGUAGE, WRITING & RELIGION OF SUMERIAN ORIGIN

The Sumerian origin of the Ancient Greeks, Etruscans and patrician Romans and their civilization, with its language, writing and religion was also evidenced. On the Sumerian origin of Greek art see the instances incidentally demonstrated in Figures 6 and 7 and Plate III, on the Hitto-Sumerian origin of the crested helmet of the Greeks and of the Grecian representation of the god Bacchus or Dionysos. And the shorter form *Att* for *Khatti*, as in Briton coins, was seen to be probably the source of the Greek *'Atti-kē*, *'Atti-gē* or "Attica," wherein the affix represents the Sumerian *Ki* or *Gi* "Land."

TROJANS, IONIANS & CRETANS, AND THEIR CIVILIZATION, LANGUAGE, WRITING & RELIGION OF SUMERIAN ORIGIN.

The Trojans and Ionians and their civilization were demonstrated to be of Sumerian origin in considerable detail. The Sumerian linear and "cup-mark" inscriptions on the Trojan amulets[1] were deciphered for the first time, and disclosed the same religion with the same invocations and symbols of the same deities as on the grave-amulets of the Sumerian and on the Indo-Sumerian seals, and as on

[1] WPOB. 238, 254

HITTITE SOLDIERS OF ARYAN OR NORDIC TYPE.

On bas-relief at Carchemish, *c.* (?) 2500 B.C., in British Museum. (After Hogarth, *Carchemish*, Pl. B. 2). Note their crested helmet as obvious source of the crested Greek helmet.

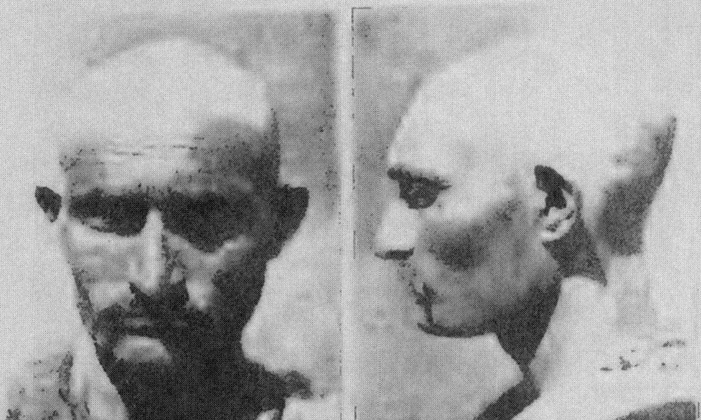

MODERN KURD PEASANT OF ARYAN AND HITTITE TYPE.

From Mt. Nimrud district in E. Asia Minor. (After Prof. von Luschan, JRAI. 1911.)

the prehistoric monuments in Ancient Britain. The Ancient Trojans physically were of the Aryan or Nordic or Sumerian type as evidenced by their skulls and skeletons. And historical and other evidence was cited confirming the authenticity of the Ancient Briton traditional chronicles of Geoffrey that Britain was first systematically colonized by King Brutus the Trojan and his tribe about 1103 B.C. The Ionians of the same area in Western Asia Minor, who had previously been identified by Indianists with the *Yavan* branch of the Aryans in the Indian epics and chronicles had that identity further confirmed. And evidence was adduced for the Sumerian origin of Minos the Cretan and his civilization, and real date, which is now fully confirmed and established in the present work.

"Hittites" & Amorites & their Civilization, Language, Writing & Religion of "Sumerian" or Aryan Origin

The so-called "Heth," "Hitt" or "Hitt-ites" of the Hebrew Old Testament, the great civilized pre-Israelite people of Jerusalem and Palestine, who called themselves and were called by the Babylonians *Khatti* or *Hatti*, and by the Ancient Egyptians "The Great *Khata*" or "*Kheta*," who were "The White Syrians" of Strabo, and of whom the "Catti" kings and their ruling tribe of Britons in Ancient Britain I showed were a branch, were the immemorial civilized rulers of Palestine (with their sacred city at Jerusalem, a Sumerian and non-Semitic name), Syria-Phœnicia and Asia Minor, and were fully identified by me as a residual stock of the Early Aryans or Sumerians.

Their old imperial "Hittite" capital at Pteria in the heart of Cappadocia (see map) is now disclosed in the present work as a pre-Mesopotamian capital of the "Sumerians." Their monuments and numerous artistic and delicately engraved seals disclose them as of a fine Aryan type (see Plate III,[1] and Fig. 3), and they usually wore the Gothic dress with the conical "Phrygian" (red) cap, which was

[1] This slab owes its well-preserved condition to its being sculptured in basalt and early covered up by the debris from above.

often adorned with horns like that worn by the Ancient Britons, European Goths and Anglo-Saxons.

The current statement by anthropologists, the one

FIG. 3.—Early Khatti or "Catti" or "Hitt-ites" in their bas-relief rock-sculptures at Iasili-Kaia of about ? 3000 B.C.[1]
(After Perrot & Guillaume.)[2]

Note the Aryan or Nordic types, Gothic dress, "Phrygian" cap of men and snow-boots. The scene is part of a religious procession, fully detailed in the Nordic Eddas.[3] And note the double axe of man on the right.

mechanically repeating the other, that the Hittites were "Armenoids," that is a Semitic people of the Armenian type with round heads and low receding brows, was shown

[1] The rock-galleries where these sculptures are carved are near Boghaz Koi, the ancient Hittite capital. This date seems indicated by the symbolic spread-eagle, which in Mesopotamia was current in and restricted to the Sumerian dynasty of King Uruash of this period. The name Iasili Kaia is Turkish for "written stones."

[2] PGG. pb. 47. From rock bas-relief in Iasili rock-chambers below Boghaz Koi or Pteria in Cappadocia.

[3] See my new literal translation of The Eddas.

to be purely fictitious and grossly misleading, and merely based on a false impression gained from a few rude Hittite rock-carvings and from some of the conventional drawings by the Egyptian artists of the rather vain-glorious Ramses II depicting disparagingly his conquests of the Hittites, wherein

FIG. 4.—Hittite priest-king conducting a priest (?). From Iasili rock-chambers at Boghaz Koi of about ? 3000 B.C. (After Perrot and Guillaume, pl. L.)

Note the intertwined serpent Caduceus rod on his hat and compare with Fig. 15; and the Sun-Hawk above.

Ramses himself significantly is also sometimes figured with receding brow. These writers entirely disregard the much more important and patent facts that in the numerous fine Hittite sculptures, as well as in the finer rock-carvings, this feature is wholly absent, and that even in the Egyptian drawings on the same monument the Hittites are also represented without receding brows and of fine Aryan type, see, for example, Fig. 5.

The monuments of the Hittites themselves naturally furnish much more authentic evidence of the Hittite physical type than those of their rivals and enemies, the later Egyptians. The numerous fine Hittite sculptures uniformly represent these people of good Nordic or Aryan type, as for example in Plate III, picturing their soldiers of

FIG. 5.—Hittites of Aryan type in their War-chariots as pictured by Egyptians in thirteenth century B.C. (Bas-reliefs of Ramses II at Abydos after Roselini 103.)

Note.—Hittites or Khatti used war-chariots like the Ancient Briton "Catti"; but are here pictured of slender build as in the usual conventional style of Egyptian drawing.

about 2000 B.C. and in much more realistic and artistic style than the Egyptian. Below this Hittite sculpture, I have placed for comparison a photograph of a modern Kurd from the eastern Hittite area in Asia Minor, as the Kurds are disclosed in these pages to be remnants of the old imperial Hittite ruling race; and they still speak an Aryan language, and are of good Aryan physical type, fair in complexion and mostly with blue eyes and "yellow" hair (xanthochroic Aryans of Huxley).[1] And the numerous

[1] F. v. Luschan JRAI, 1911, 229f.

Hittite sacred seals[1] uniformly picture the Hittites of good Aryan type and wearing Aryan dress, and often with horns on their caps like the Anglo-Saxons and Ancient Britons. Incidentally, those portraits of Hittite warriors in Plate III disclose *the Hittite or northern "Sumerian" origin of the crested war-helmets of the Ancient Greeks.*

The Hittite language also, as written in their cuneiform tablets (their old hieroglyphic writing not having yet been deciphered by Assyriologists) is found by Prof. Hrozny to be radically Aryan, though incorporating many alien words, as indeed was to be expected in the language of a great imperial people, whose archives in their old capital cities contain also many official documents written in the foreign languages of their tributaries. And their Law Codes, earlier than the Babylonian, from which latter the Mosaic code was derived, are substantially identical with the Sumerian, which are essentially Aryan.

In Religion also, it was demonstrated that the Hittites were Sun-worshippers and of the Sumerian or Aryan type and terminology and symbolism of that cult. Even in their later period when they formed a pantheon of the local patron saints or godlings of their provincial states, the Sun continued to be the first invoked, as in their treaty with Ramses II of Egypt, who is usually regarded as "the pharoah of the oppression" of the Israelites in Egypt. And significantly their next highest divinity Tash-of-the-Plough (*Tash-up*), see Fig. 7, was demonstrated to be the Solar archangel tutelary and Corn-Spirit, *Tasia* or *Tashia* of the Sumerians, so freely represented as I showed on Early Sumerian seals and monuments, and proved to be *identical with the "Tascio" of the Ancient Briton monuments and of the Catti* (i.e., *Khatti*) *pre-Roman Briton coins*, on which latter he is represented in practically the same form and with the same ears of corn as in the Hittite sculptures (see Figs. 1, 2, 6), and seals, and in the Sumerian seals and in Phœnician coins.[2] It was also shown that he was the deified

[1] See the numerous representations on Hittite seals in WSC. 284 f., and CSH., and in WPOB.; and for sculptures see British Museum *Carchemish*, Garstang's *Land of the Hittites*, Ed. Meyer *Reich und Kultur der Chetiter*.

[2] See WPOB. 339 f. for numerous representations.

second Aryan or Sumerian King who developed Agriculture and invented the Plough and bore in Sumerian the title of *Bakus* with the epithets "The Lord of Plants" and "Libator of the Wine of Life," and he was disclosed as the human historical original of the later Aryan god Bacchus of the Greeks and Romans in name, representation and function.

Hitto-Sumerian Origin of Greek Art with reference to Bacchus & his Representation

This early Hittite representation of the second Aryan or Sumerian king, Bakus, the *Bauge* lord of agriculture and

Fig. 6.—Hittite or Catti portrait of Bacchus, the deified second Sumerian or Aryan King, surnamed "Tash-of-the-Plough" (Tash-up), the Corn-Lord "Tascio" of the coins of the Catti in Ancient Britain. From archaic rock-sculpture, with hieroglyphs at Ivriz in Cappadocia. (After von Luschan and see Pl. VI.) *B*. Hittite piper, from a fragment in Berlin Museum, after Puchstein.)

Note.—He is dressed as a Goth, with snow-boots, and goat horns on his conical "Phrygian" cap, and he carries stalks of barley corn with bunches of grapes; and behind him is a plough, of which he was the traditional inventor. The adoring priest-king has Swastika Sun-crosses in key-pattern embroidered on his dress. Comparison of this drawing with the photograph in Plate VI shows that the nose is straighter in the original than in this sketch.

mead of the Nordic Eddas, and the *Basu* lord of grain and wealth of the Hindoos, the traditional Sumerian extender of agriculture and wine-lord, was shown to be of immense historical importance in disclosing the Hitto-Sumerian source of the Greek tradition regarding Bakchos (or Dionysos), not

FIG. 7.—The Greek Bacchus or Dionysos and Satyr (Seilenos). From Hieron cylix of about fifth century B.C.

Note its derivation from the Hittite in Fig. 6.

only of his name and functions, but also of his representation in early Greek art; and of the identity of the Greek tradition and mythology with the Hitto-Sumerian. This Hittite source of Greek art and mythology is strikingly shown by the comparison of Figs. 6 and 7, representing alongside respectively the forms of this god in the early Hittite rock-sculpture and in one of the earliest Greek drawings of him. It is seen that the Greek artists over two thousand years later bodily took as the model for their selfsame "Greek" god the old conventionalized and ready-made Hittite picture of him, and reproduced it in all its essential details. They merely modernized his old "uncouth" Gothic dress of the mountains to adapt it to the fashion in vogue in their warmer clime of Hellenic Greece. In both he is bearded and has long curly hair. In both the grapes are disposed fore and aft on a vine passing over his left shoulder. In both, the corn stalk reaches the ground below, with its ears on a level with his face. The pointed ornaments on his chaplet in the Greek version are presumably modelled on the pointed horns decorating his cap in the Hittite original. And even the satyr, which is added by the Greek artist, is taken from the old stereotyped Hittite piper with double pipes, of which a representation from a fragment of Hittite sculpture is placed in Fig. 6 for comparison. Here again we thus have another instance of the Hittite source of Greek art, as well as of mythology, and the Hittites I showed were Nordic and an early stock of the "Sumerians," just as the Greeks themselves were a later branch of the same stock.

The sacred symbols of the Hittites also, including the True Cross or the Sun-Cross, or the Red Cross of St George of Cappadocia and England and the St Andrew's Cross, are identical with those Sun crosses of the Sumerians, Trojans and Ancient Britons as displayed in my comparative plates of these crosses;[1] and St George and the Dragon and St Michael are represented on their early seals.[2] And their grave-amulets bear the sacred cup-mark script with invocations to the same divinities as the Sumerians, Trojans, and Ancient Britons.

The Morites or "Amorites," the Muru or Maruta of the Sumerian, were shown to be the early sea-going branch of the Sumerians and identical with the early "Phœnician" mariner and merchant colonist branch of the latter.

"Phœnicians" & their Civilization, Language, Writing & Religion of Sumerian or Aryan Origin

With the "Phœnicians" we reach a paradox. According to current modern opinion the "Phœnicians" are universally

[1] WPOB. 294 f. [2] *Ib.* 319, 334 f.

believed to be Semites, that is "Children of Shem," Shem being the traditional ancestor of the Hebrews, though incongruously made by them the uterine brother of Japhet the Aryan, in their impossible scheme of the origin of the different races of mankind from one immediate common father, entailed by their having killed off all other human beings by their Flood Myth. And this supposed Shemite racial origin of the Phœnician is nevertheless believed, notwithstanding the stultifying fact that the real Semites, the Hebrews, who ought to know best who were Semites and who were not, definitely state in their Old Testament that the Phœnicians, therein called "Canaan-Sidon," were *not* "The Children of Shem" at all, but were "The Children of Ham,"[1] that is of Egypt, the old name for which was Ham or Kham; and which land we shall see in the present work was the chief settlement of the Early Phœnicians on their advent to the Mediterranean from the Persian Gulf.

Despite this positive testimony of the Semites themselves against the Phœnicians being Semites, modern writers nevertheless arbitrarily call them such, and point to the inscriptions of the later Phœnicians of Phœnicia and Carthage from about the ninth century B.C. onwards as being written in a Semitic dialect, and inscribed in the reversed or retrograde direction, from right to left, with reversed letters, as adopted by Semitic scribes.

But mere retrograde writing with reversal of letters does not imply that it was written by Semites. The Early Sumerians regularly wrote in the reversed direction in their sealings. Some of the Greek writing in the sixth century B.C. and earlier is in the retrograde direction with reversed letters, and sometimes the lines run alternately left and right in the "ox-plough-furrow" fashion as with the Hittite hieroglyphic writing. And the great Indo-Aryan emperor Asoka in the third century B.C. wrote his edicts in the reversed direction with reversed letters in those provinces of his mighty empire where the majority of the population were Semites and accustomed to retrograde reversed writing. Yet no one has ever on this account called the Greeks and Asoka "Semites." And we shall

[1] Gen. x. 6 f.

find in the present work that Sargon-the-Great and his dynasty, whose Aryan race is completely established herein, whilst writing their official documents in Mesopotamia in the non-retrograde direction and with non-reversed signs, write most of their documents in Egypt, where the bulk of their subjects were Semites, in the retrograde direction with reversed signs. Similarly the Greco-Roman overlords of Egypt wrote their edicts there in Egyptian in reversed writing. And as to the so-called "Semitic" Phœnician alphabet of these later Mediterranean Phœnicians, I have demonstrated that this alphabet was derived from the non-Semitic Sumerian signs for those alphabetic letters.[1]

Moreover, I showed that the relatively few words of these later "Semitic Phœnicians" of the Mediterranean basin which are known to us are radically Sumerian, that is Aryan,[2] though written generally in a Semitized idiom; that some of these Mediterranean Phœnicians wrote in Aryan non-reversed style and in the Aryan language;[3] and that the Phœnician religion and civilization were essentially Sumerian or Aryan and *non*-Semitic. And it is a matter of common observation that no Semitic nation, ancient or modern, has ever been known as a great sea-faring people.[4] Besides, Herodotus specially records that while the residents in Phœnicia, that is the Semites who formed the bulk of the population there, practised circumcision; on the contrary the Phœnician mariners, that is the real Phœnicians, who traded with Greece, the chief mart for the Phœnicians of Tyre and Sidon, were uncircumcised.[5] And the monuments and coins of these Mediterranean Phœnicians show them to be of fine Aryan physical type, and *non*-Semitic, as seen in the accompanying illustrations.

It is thus evidenced that even the later "Phœnicians" of the Mediterranean basin, who are regarded by modern European writers as the typical "Phœnicians," were not

[1] WAOA. [2] WSAD *passim*. [3] WPOB 33, 43, 55 f.

[4] The Moors of Mauretania and Morocco, I have shown were leavened by the civilization and settlers of the Sumerian sea-going colonizers, the Muru or Maruts, a title of the Early Aryan Phœnicians, see WPOB., 216 f.

[5] H. ii. 104.

traditionally " Semites " at all, but were classed by the real Semites as *non*-Semites ; that their civilization and religion was Aryan and *non*-Semitic ; that the so-called " Semitic " Phœnician letters were derived from the Sumerian or Early Aryan writing ; that some of these Mediterranean later Phœnicians wrote in the Aryan language and in non-reversed

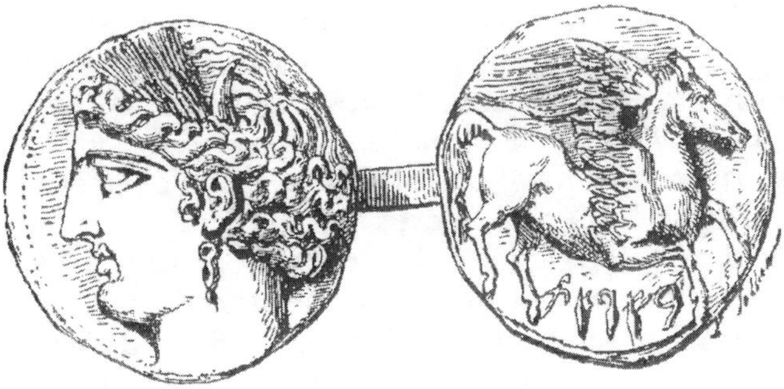

FIG. 8.—Aryan or Nordic racial type of Phœnicians in their coins, from Carthage, about 300 B.C. (After Druruy, *Hist. romaine*, reproduced by photography.

Note on obverse the Aryan facial type, broad-browed, with straight nose and long head of their sea-tutelary *Bārāt*, whose name is engraved on the reverse below the winged Horse of the Sun, a purely Aryan and non-Semitic symbol, but which is extremely common on the pre-Roman coins of the Ancient Britons.

writing ; that their seafaring instincts and achievements were non-Semitic ; that they were uncircumcised ; and that they were of fine Aryan or Nordic racial physical type, see Figs. 8 to 11.

FIRST " PHŒNICIAN " DYNASTY IN PERSIAN GULF, ABOUT 3100 B.C., OF ARYAN ORIGIN

The Aryan racial origin of the ancient Phœnicians was demonstrated in my former works, and is fully confirmed and established by a mass of new historical proofs in the present volume. These daring pioneer mariners of the Ancient World were disclosed to have originated within the clan of the first great Sumerian colonizing sea-emperor, King Uruash, of about 3100 B.C. (see his contemporary archaic portrait in Plate VII). He had his capital at the seaport city of "Lagash"[1] at the head of the Persian Gulf, where the Fish-men legends of the later Chaldeans are probably based to some extent on the memory of the early conquests of the sea there by this famous sea-emperor and his dynasty, most of the emperors of which bore the title of "Sea-king." Like the later Phœnicians in the West, whilst *worshipping his deified ancestor, the first Sumerian or Aryan King, who we found bore the surname of Gūur, the historical original of St George of the Red Cross*,[2] *his especial patron saint was St Michael, the canonized second Aryan King* (see below), *who was the patron saint of his city-port*. He was also discovered to have established a great overseas colony in the Indus Valley in North-West India, which is now confirmed in these pages by further concrete historical evidence including seals of his dynasty there.

He was also shown to be identical with the great sea-going Early Aryan emperor Haryashwa (the Indian writing for the Sumerian "Uruash") of the Indian Chronicles and King-Lists of the Early Aryans, and who was also a sea-farer. And the dynasty he established is significantly called in the Indian Chronicles "The excellent or able *Panch* (*Panch-āla*).[3] Now this title *Panch* appears, as I showed, to be the equivalent of the popular title by which his descendants and their tribe were latterly known as the sea-farers of the Mediterranean to the Ancient Egyptians as *Fankhu* and *Panag*, and to the Greeks and Romans as *Phoinix;* from which latter name the Greeks coined the name of *Phoinikē* for their land of Tyre and Sidon,[4] which the Romans later called *Phœnicia*, whence obviously was derived our modern word "Phœnician."

[1] "Lagash" is a conjectural reading by Assyriologists of the Sumerian signs for this city name which is written *Shir-la-pur* or *Shir-pur-la* on the monuments, and the first sign has also the value of *'A* or *'I*.

[2] For this King's archaic representation with his Red Cross standard, see Fig. 16.

[3] Āla = "excellent" in Sanskrit, WSD. 153, and cognate with *Al* "able"; both with similar meanings in Sumerian: WSAD. 10 f. *Panch* is interpreted by the Brahmans (who we shall find give patently false etymologies to the proper names in the Indian Epics) as *Panchan* "five," as this emperor in question chanced to have five sons.

[4] No such territorial name was used by the "Phœnicians" themselves, who merely called their land after their city ports.

This Persian Gulf location for this First *Panch* or "Phœnician" dynasty about 3100 B.C. is significant; for it is strikingly confirmed by the Syrio-Phœnician tradition recorded by Herodotus. That great historian was informed by the Phœnicians on his visit to Tyre that that city was founded by the Phœnicians "two thousand three hundred years" before his day,[1] that is to say *about* 2750 B.C. And he further records that these Phœnicians who founded Tyre, Sidon, etc., "anciently dwelt on the Persian Gulf and having crossed over from there had settled on the seacoast of Syria."[2] All this traditional history preserved by Herodotus is seen to be in exact agreement with the mass of new history we elicited from the contemporary monumental and other inscriptions, and which is still further confirmed in these pages by fresh material.

The world-wide conquests of far-flung empire by this Panch (or Phœnician) dynasty are thus summarized in the Indian epics:—

> "The excellent Panch setting out to invade the Earth
> Brought the whole World under their sway."[3]

THE "PHŒNICIANS" AS BARATS OR "BRIT-ONS" & THEIR SEA-TUTELARY AS "BRITANNIA"

It is significant also of the Aryan origin of the Phœnicians, that they called themselves in Europe sometimes *Parat*, *Prut*, *Prydi*, and *Barata*,[4] just as the Aryan Panch ruling and colonizing people called themselves *Bárata*, after the patronym of their famous earlier emperor Bárata, Brihat or Prithu (the famous historical Sumerian emperor Bartu, Barti or Pirtu of about 3180 B.C., whose inscriptions are given later on in these pages); and from whom I showed, and further show in this work, the Brit-ons ultimately derived that patronymic name—the name "Britain" being spelt dialectically with a *P* initial as *Pretan* by the great Ionian navigator Pytheas, who circumnavigated the British Isles in the fourth century B.C.,[5] and it is still spelt by Welsh bards as "Prydain."

[1] H. 2, 44.
[2] H. 7, 89.
[3] MBt. 1, 91, sloka 3738.
[4] WPOB. 53, 55 f.
[5] WPOB. 146 f.

Similarly also, like the Early Aryan Barats of the Panch dynasties, the European Phœnicians also named their sea-

FIG. 9.—Brit-annia tutelary of Phœnicians in Ancient Egypt as *Bāīrthy*, "The Mother of the Waters" (*Nut* or "Naiad"). (After Budge.) Compare the horns on her head with those of Bārāt on her coin from Carthage, Fig. 5 p. 12.

tutelary *Barati*, after their own tribal title. And this Aryan tutelary I showed was also the source of the *Bāīrthy* water-

FIG. 10.—Phœnician Sea-tutelary Bārāt as "Britannia." From coins of the Barats of Lyconia in Asia Minor of third century A.D. *a.* from Barata City. *b.* from Iconium.[1] (After Ramsay.)

Note in *a* she is seated beside a rudder amidst the waves symbolized by a swimming water-sprite, wears a city-turret for a helmet, and bears in left hand the horn of Plenty. In *b* she holds the rudder and beside her throne is her shield emblazoned with the Red Cross of St George.

[1] From W. Ramsay, *Cities of St Paul*, 368 and 415. And cp. photographs in G. F. Hill, *Coins of Cilicia*, pl. 1, figs. 3 and 9.

tutelary of the Ancient Egyptians[1] (see Fig. 9), and of the British sea-tutelary Britannia, not only in name and function, but also in her representations (see Fig. 10).

St Michael the Patron Saint of the Sumerian First "Phœnician" Dynasty in Mesopotamia also the Patron Saint of the European Phœnicians.

In religion also, it was shown that the Phœnicians, even in their late period in the Mediterranean were essentially Sun-worshippers (a wholly non-Semitic cult), like the

Fig. 11.—Phœnician worship of the Sun-god. From a Phœnician stele (or altar) of about fourth century B.C. (After Renan, Mission de Phénicie, pl. 32.)

Note the rayed halo of the Sun-god.

Sumerians or Early Aryans. Thus see Fig. 11 for a Phœnician stele or altar to the Sun-god—the Sun-god being latterly represented by the Sumerians in human form as a reflex of their deified first king Dar or Tur (Thor of the Eddas) who

[1] *Ib.* 60 f.

established Sun-worship as part of his system of Civilization. I also demonstrated that these Western Phœnicians also worshipped the almost equally distinguished sire of the first Sumerian king, the second Sumerian king, whom the Sumerians deified as the Archangel of the Sun-god under the title of *Muku* or *Mukhla*, the invincible warrior, and surnamed Tasia, and who I showed was the historical human Sumerian original of our St Michael the Archangel, and was identical with *Miok*, the son of King Thor in the Nordic Eddas, which ancient Gothic epics are seen in my new literal translation to be essentially historical and not mythological as hitherto supposed.

FIG. 12.—St Michael, the Archangel, or "Lord *Mukhla*" of the Sumerians, on Phœnician coins of Cilicia of the fifth century B.C. (After Hill, see WPOB. 349 for details.) Compare with Ancient Briton forms in Fig. 13.

Now the European Phœnicians in Cilicia in the fifth century B.C., I showed, represented Michael the Archangel as their patron saint with wings (see Fig. 12), under the name of *MKLU* (short vowels not being expressed in their writing of that period), thus giving him the name of *Mikalu*. And it is noteworthy that they represented him there as associated with the rayed disc of the Sun and Corn and the Sun-bird, the latter being in the form of the Phœnix or Goose, and disclosed as apparently the source of the "Michaelmas Goose" associated with the festival day of that Saint in modern times. And I also showed that *St Michael is similarly represented as in these Phœnician coins on the coins of the pre-Roman and so-called "pagan" Early Britons* (see Fig. 13), and significantly therein identified with Tascia or Tcvi of the Early Britons, which was shown to be the *Tasia* title of Michael the Sun-angel amongst the Sumerians.

This now explained why the western Phœnicians named their chief seaport in Ancient Britain, like the First Dynasty of Phœnicians their patron saint of their seaport in Mesopotamia, after St Michael, namely their tin-port of St Michael's Mount in Cornwall; and it also explained why it was called by the Cornish folk, "The Fort of the Sun" (Din-Sol).[1] It also explained why so many of the old St Michael foundations throughout Britain are in the neighbour-

FIG. 13.—St Michael the Archangel, on the pre-Roman coins of the Ancient Britons, identifying him with *Tcvi* or Tascia. Compare with Phœnician representations in Fig. 12. (See WPOB. 349 f. for details.)

hood of prehistoric mine-workings and prehistoric monuments of the Ancient Britons inscribed with the Sumerian cup-marked writing. For it was shown that these western Phœnicians exploiting the British Isles for its minerals, eventually settled there and colonizing it became the ancestors of the Early Britons properly so-called, that is the civilized white elements of Aryan racial stock in Britain, as opposed to the dark Pictish descendants of the un-civilized aborigines of non-Aryan race. It was also seen that those earlier waves of these tin-exploiting Phœnicians

[1] WPOB. 281

of the Morite or Amorite period probably introduced the Bronze Age into Britain about 2700 B.C. or earlier.[1]

And it was seen that this western branch of these Aryan Barat Phœnicians as merchant princes and adventurous sea-traders, from the beginning of the 3rd millennium B.C. onwards, scoured the wide seas and uncharted oceans of the old Western World seeking for new sources of tin, copper, lead, gold, amber, etc., bartering their wares with the various lowly aboriginal tribes, and establishing posts at their chief trade ports and mining stations, most of which gradually developed into colonies, and later into separate civilized nations, through these ruling Aryans welding together the varied aboriginal tribes into free states with their Aryan Civilization. In this way Civilization, originated by the Aryans, was evidently spread over the Western World by Aryan agency and thus accounted for the unity in the essentials of the Ancient Civilizations.

The title "Phœnician" seldom used by the Phœnician themselves

But the title "Phœnician," or its dialectic equivalent, was scarcely ever used by themselves. Thus although *Panch* is a title for them preserved in the Indian epics, that title has not hitherto been found in Mesopotamian records. Nor amongst the very many hundreds of "Phœnician" inscriptions unearthed in Phœnicia, Carthage and the Mediterranean generally has even one been found so far as I have scrutinized them, containing the name "Phœnician" or "Punic." This discloses the futility of trying to trace the settlements of these famous colonizers and civilizers through that title, except in the several old seaport or islet stations, which retain their name in the form of Phœnice, Venice, etc. The Phœnicians, whilst occasionally calling themselves Ari, Muru (or Amorite), Gut or Goth, Kad, Khad, Barat, Part or Prat, the equivalent as we have seen of Brit-on, usually called themselves and were called after their city-ports or city-states, such as "Tyrian" after Tyre (or Zur), Sidonian after Sidon, and similarly after their colonies in Karia, Lydia, Phocia, Cilicia, Thebes, Carthage, Mauretania, Gades,

[1] On Phœnicians in Norway see S. Nilsson, *Prim. Inhabs. Scandinavia.*

etc., etc. That is in agreement with the practice of our British colonists at the present day, who call themselves Canadian, Australian, New Zealander, Newfoundlander, etc.

And even the sneer of their political rivals, when the great services of the earlier Phœnicians to their own civilization were forgotten, that the later Phœnicians were unscrupulous and faithless, expressed in the derogatory *Punica fides*, is seen to be in a way perhaps another evidence of their Aryan origin, by having presumably as little justification as the analogous modern cry of *Perfide Albion*, applied also to a seafaring trading people, who from the new evidence are seen to be largely the descendants of the old Aryan Phœnicians.

Indo-Aryans & Ancient Medes & Persians & their Civilization of Sumerian Origin.

The Indo-Aryans and Ancient Medes and Persians with their Civilizations were shown to belong to the Eastern branch of the Sumerians. The Sumerian origin of the Indo-Aryans, with their leading kings, and of their civilization, including traditions, language, religion, and symbols, I demonstrated in considerable detail. This discovery significantly *was published before the discovery of the great ruins of Ancient Sumerian cities in the Indus Valley.* And my pioneer decipherment of the Sumerian seals then unearthed in the Indus Valley disclosed for the first time the Sumerian race and historical identity of the founders of that great colony about 3100 B.C.; and also the fact that it continued to be held as a colony of Mesopotamia down through the Sargonic period to at least the Ur Dynasty of about 2260 B.C., to which the latest seal in that first unearthed batch belonged.

The identity of the Sumerians with the Early Aryans was now made positive and absolute by the discovery of the identity of these historical Sumerian kings who held the Indus colony with the Early Aryan kings of the same name and same chronological period, and whose activities in the same region are preserved in the Indian Epic Chronicles and the Vedas. This identity was shown in detail in regard to the Sumerian Dynasty which established that colony, namely the dynasty of the famous sea-king Uruash and his five famous sons, which was demonstrated to be identical with that of the Aryan sea-emperor Haryashwa and his five famous sons of the Indian lists. This identity extended not only to the names of that king and his five sons but also to their achievements and to the names of their successors in the dynasty, which were in the same chronological order in both lists, Sumerian and Indo-Aryan.

This absolute proof of the identity of the Sumerians and Early Aryans is now further confirmed in these pages by proofs which for documentary force are unparalleled in the annals of history. These show that *the long list of Early Aryan kings and dynasties from the First Aryan Dynasty down through the long period of over two thousand years are in absolute agreement with the king-lists of the Sumerians from the First Sumerian Dynasty down throughout this period, not only in names and achievements, but also in the precise chronological order of their succession.*

This new evidence, moreover, besides yielding further confirmation of the Sumerian colonization of the Indus Valley confirms my pioneer decipherment and readings of the Indo-Sumerian seals.

Egyptian Civilization, Predynastic & Dynastic, & its Authors of Aryan or Sumerian Origin

The supposed "indigenous" Civilization of Ancient Egypt was likewise shown to be of Aryan Origin, and introduced fully fledged by Aryan or "Sumerian" world-emperors as the earliest Pharaohs of the Nile Valley. Its ancient solar religion also and its chief deities and sacred symbols were shown to be of Aryan or "Sumerian" origin, with the same names, functions, representations, and symbols; and now more fully confirmed in the present work. The Egyptian Language and its Hieroglyphic Writing and its ancient use of Alphabetic Letters were likewise demonstrated in my *Sumer-Aryan Dictionary* and *Aryan Origin of the Alphabet* to be radically of Aryan or "Sumerian" origin. And the discovery was announced that the "oldest" of the Predynastic Pharaohs, that is the Pharaohs before the First Dynasty which was established by Menes, who have left records, was none other than the great Aryan world-monarch "Sargon of Agade" himself; and that his son Manis-the-Warrior, the famous emperor and Sun-worshipper of Mesopotamia, was identical with Menes, the founder of the First Dynasty of Egypt.

In the present work are given the full contemporary documentary proofs for the latter discoveries from the actual inscriptions of Sargon and his son Manis as Pharaohs respectively of Predynastic and First Dynastic Egypt and from the inscriptions of their successors in that dynasty. Menes, the founder of the First Dynasty of Egypt and his successors in that dynasty are discovered to bear the same names and with the same achievements in Egypt as the emperor Manis and his successors in his dynasty in their own inscriptions in Mesopotamia; and they are all in the same identical order of succession in Mesopotamia and in Egypt; and several of the kings of Menes' dynasty in their Egyptian inscriptions call themselves King of Kish (in Mesopotamia) and King of the Lands of the Lower Sea (Persian Gulf and Indian Ocean) as they did in their inscriptions in Mesopotamia.

That these discoveries were not made before is seen to be largely because the records of the Predynastic and First Dynasty Pharaohs are written, not in the later conventional form of Egyptian hieroglyphs to which Egyptologists are accustomed, but in Sumerian script and in the Sumerian language, and have in consequence not been deciphered or translated before. A great deal of important new information is recovered from these inscriptions supplemented by the Indian Chronicles in regard to these earliest of the Pharaohs. And the fact emerges that the great Aryan-Sumerian world-monarch Sargon and his dynasty selected for their mausoleums and their new homeland that more favoured and relatively temperate part of their vast empire which lay on the banks of the fruitful Nile, that poured its waters northwards into the cool basin of the Mediterranean, which was a more natural homeland for that Nordic ruling race than the sun-baked mud plains of Mesopotamia.

The Predynastic higher culture and art in Egypt, which has been assumed to be indigenously developed, is also seen to be of Sumerian or Early Aryan origin. Thus, for example, the Predynastic flint-knife with sheet-gold handle decorated with designs in *repoussé* work (Fig. 14) is seen to bear on the latter as a chief design the Lion attacking Goats, a

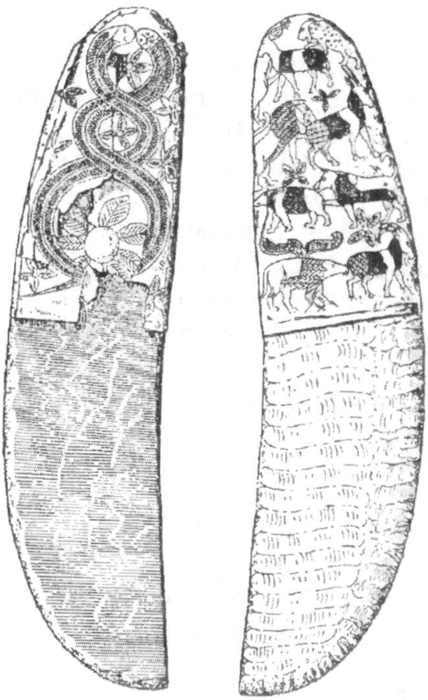

FIG. 14.—Flint Knife of "Predynastic" Egypt, with gold handle decorated with designs of Sumerian type found also on the monuments of Ancient Britain. (After de Morgan.) ½

Note Lion attacking Goats, as in Sumerian and Phœnician seals, and coins of latter, and in Ancient Briton monuments, compare figures in p. 607 and WPOB. 334 f.; and for the intertwined Serpents and leaf-crosses.

familiar motive of the early archaic and pre-Sargonic Sumerian sacred seals, on Hittite and Phœnician seals and on coins of the latter, and found also on Ancient Briton monuments.[1] The intertwined serpents on the reverse occur in an archaic pre-Sargonic Sumerian seal,[2] and later it is found

[1] See Figs. in WPOB. 334 f., where the historial meaning of this symbolism is explained. And for Sumerian cp. WSC. 69, Fig. 179; KHS. 175.

[2] WSC. 95. And see Early Hittite Sculpture, Fig. 4.

in the more developed form seen in Fig. 15 on the votive Serpent-Dragon vase which King Gudia (see his photograph in Plate XVI) about 2370 B.C. dedicated to his patron saint Mukhla [1] or St Michael, the canonized second king of the Sumerians or Early Aryans, as we have seen, and who as I found captured for his father the central fetish Stone-Bowl of the Serpent-Dragon-worshipping Chaldea aborigines

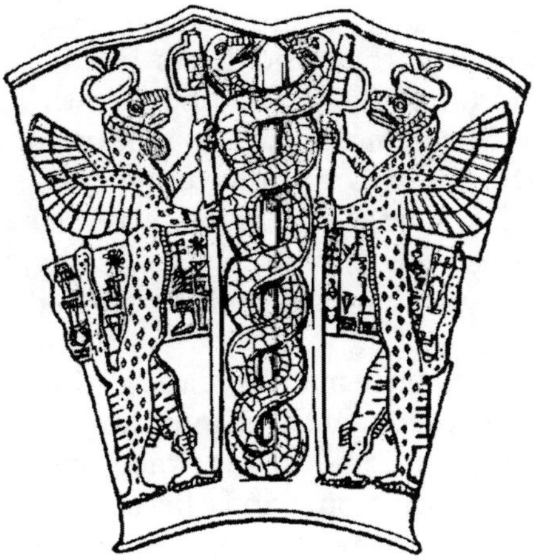

FIG. 15.—The intertwined Serpents on a Sumerian votive stone-bowl or vase dedicated to Lord Mukhla or "St Michael," 'the canonized second Sumerian King, by King Gudia about 2370 B.C. (From *Déc.*, pl. 44, 2.) Note the Dragons on either side protecting the double Serpent.

who, with their degrading sanguinary sacrifices of Hell, opposed the innocuous and exalting Sun-cult of Heaven introduced by his father, King Dur or Tur, the leader of the Sumerians or Early Aryans in their regeneration and civilization of the Old World. And further I showed that on account of this capturing achievement with the slaying of the Serpent-Dragon priest, which dealt a death-blow to the degrading Serpent-Dragon cult of the Ancient World, Mukhla became afterwards canonized as "St Michael the Archangel of Heaven and Vanquisher of the Dragon"; and that this

[1] Under his title of *Ni-mish-zi-da* ("Nin-gish-zidā"), and see later under second king.

Serpent-Dragon fetish Stone-Bowl was afterwards consecrated to the Sun-cult by his father King Tur, the Her-Thor of the Nordic Eddas, and became the original of the famous "Holy Grail" of King Arthur.[1] All this is now fully confirmed and established in the present work by a mass of concrete documentary proof from contemporary and other early Sumerian inscriptions and hymns celebrating the event, and from the Eddas. And as this new evidence discloses that the Holy Grail of King Tur, like that of King Ar-Thur, had for long mysteriously disappeared (having been buried about a thousand years before Gudia's day by the great grandson of King Tur underneath the foundations of the oldest Sun-temple in Mesopotamia, where it was unearthed with his inscription some years ago), it now seems that King Gudia had evidently piously made and offered this magnificent new Serpent-Dragon Stone-Bowl to its deified capturer as a substitute for the lost Holy Grail.

The intertwined serpents decorating this bowl, and embossed on the predynastic Egyptian knife-handle, are moreover found on prehistoric monuments of Ancient Britain and Scandinavia, and became latterly conventionalized into the "rope-pattern decoration" so common on the ancient pre-Christian Sun-crosses, monoliths and funereal monuments in the British Isles.[2] And the "leaf-rayed" or properly Corn-rayed Crosses, also symbolic of St Michael or Tascio, which are figured on both sides of this predynastic Egyptian stoneknife-handle, were also shown by me to occur on the amulet whorls of Ancient Troy and on the prehistoric monuments and coins of Ancient Britain, as part of their solar symbolism.[3]

All this strikingly disclosed *the essential identity in the traditions, legends, symbols and mythology of the Ancient Aryan Britons, Scandinavians and Trojans with the Sumerians, as it does also of the predynastic Egyptian civilization with the Sumerian.*

[1] WSAD, 42, 64 f. [2] WPOB, 94 f.

[3] SI. Figs. 1903-1910. This symbolism is explained in WPOB. 238 f., 316 f.

A Synchronism between Ancient Egypt & Mesopotamia discovered fixing the Date of Menes & the First Dynasty of Egypt.

A synchronism was also found for the first time between Ancient Egypt and Mesopotamia which fixed for the first time the critical date of Menes, a date which has hitherto been the most disputed of all dates in ancient history and variously estimated discrepantly from 5546 B.C. to 3300 B.C., according to different schools of Egyptologists, with correspondingly wide divergence in the chronology of the theoretical dates for the European and other Civilizations associated with the Egyptian. The real date of Menes was disclosed to be many centuries later than even the lowest date of the "short" school of Egyptologists; and this is now fully confirmed and established in the present work by a mass of concrete historical proofs which fix the date of Menes' accession at no earlier than about 2704 B.C.

As these discoveries were achieved mainly through the official King-Lists and Chronicles of the Early Aryans lying embedded and hitherto wholly unappreciated by Vedic scholars in the Indian Epic of Ancient Heroes (the *Purānas*); but which have preserved the complete lists of the Sumerian kings of which only fragmentary lists have been recovered in the Babylonian dynastic lists, and have also preserved uniquely the traditional forms of the names of the Sumerian kings which have hitherto been wholly unknown to Assyriologists in their conjectural "restorations" of the kings' names from the ambiguous polyphonous Sumerian and cuneiform writing, it is desirable now for us to examine the authenticity and date of these Ancient Aryan King-Lists and Chronicles which have proved to be such unique and fundamentally important keys to the recovery of Sumerian and Early Aryan History and the dated Early History of the World's Civilization.

II

Indian Official King-Lists & Chronicles of the Early Aryans discovered as Unique Historical Keys to Names of the Sumerian Kings continuously back to the Rise of Civilization.

Discovering Sumerian Origin of Lists & their Date, the Unknown Pre-Indian Homeland of the Indo-Aryans, their Migration to India, & its Causation & Date, *and Date of the Great War of the Bhārats for the Partition of India.*

> "*Hear now, as I recite the recorded Genealogy that is sacred!*"—Herald's prelude to the Indian Epic King-Lists.[1]

The manner in which I was led to find that the traditional King-Lists and Chronicles of the Early Aryan kings, which are embedded in the ancient epics of the Hindus and esteemed sacred, were the genuine official lists and chronicles of the historical kings of the Early Aryans *of the pre-Indian period which had been brought to India by the Eastern branch of the Aryans from their hitherto unknown pre-Indian homeland at the time of their "Great Migration" thence into the Ganges Valley or "Hindustan,"* is detailed in my former works. And this discovery was led up to by my previously finding the hitherto unknown pre-Indian homeland of the Aryans whence the Great Migration obviously came, with its apparent causes, route and date.

Unique Historical Importance of Indian Official Lists of the Early Aryan Kings, for recovery of Lost Sumerian History & Names of Kings

The altogether unique and fundamental historical importance of these ancient King-Lists and Chronicles of the

[1] *Mahā-Bhārata* epic, 1, 75. Similar declarations of their sacred character are prefixed to the *Purāna* epic lists, see *e.g.*, WVP. 3, 230.

Early Aryans, not only for recovering the lost history of the Early Sumerians, but also the lost Early History of the World's Civilization, is that these lists uniquely preserve the complete line of Sumerian kings and dynasties extending in unbroken line continuously back to the first Sumerian king of the First Sumerian Dynasty at the Rise of Civilization (whereas no complete lists have hitherto been known from Mesopotamian or Babylonian sources); and that these lists also uniquely preserve the traditional forms of the names and titles of the Sumerian kings which have hitherto been unknown to Assyriologists, whose conjectural "restorations" of these names from the ambiguous polyphonous Sumerian writing, without any keys whatever to the traditional forms of these names and by mere guesswork, are more often than not totally different from the real form of these names, and have thus been grossly misleading historians.

The Date of the Indian Lists *re* Date of the Great Indo-Aryan Migration

In order to fix the Date when these old King-Lists and Chronicles of the Early Aryan kings brought by the Indo-Aryans from their old homeland in their migration to Gangetic India were closed, as well as to establish their official and authentic character, it is necessary here to describe briefly how I was led to discover the hitherto long lost and unknown pre-Indian homeland of the Indo-Aryans—one of the great unsolved problems in Ancient History—and the historical evidence for their Great Migration and its Cause and its Date.

The Great Migration of the Eastern Branch of the Aryans into the Ganges Valley of India & its Date

It is with the arrival of this "Great Migration" of Aryans into the Ganges Valley of Mid-India, or the so-called "Great Aryan Invasion of India," according to the universal opinion of European (and American) Indianist scholars, that "the Indian Civilization" first begins, the Ganges Valley having hitherto been regarded by them as the centre of that civilization from the earliest historical and prehistoric periods; and it is that central Ganges Valley also which is believed by the

Brahman priests to have been not only the centre of origin of Indian Civilization and Religion, but also the original homeland of the Aryan Race itself. The fact of the immigration there of the Aryans was solely discovered by European archæologists and historians, just as was Alexander's invasion of the Indus Valley which was quite unknown to the later Brahmans and to indigenous vernacular Indian history. The Indus Valley on the north-west frontier of India, in which a very much more ancient Sumerian Civilization has recently been discovered, was never thought of either by these European scholars or by the Brahmans as the ancient centre of Indian Civilization, though it is occasionally mentioned in the Vedas or ancient psalms of the Hindus as a settlement of some early Aryan merchants, princes and sages. And it even now appears probable that the Sumerian colonization of the Indus Valley was not extended, at least in a like systematic manner with city settlements, to the Ganges Valley, the heart and centre of what has hitherto been called " The Indian Civilization," which is seen to have begun suddenly there with its fully-fledged Civilization with the arrival of a great body of Aryans with their families in what is termed " The Great Aryan Migration " or " The Great Aryan Invasion of India," and which is now found to be of very much later date.

The great migration eastwards into the Gangetic Valley of India of the race of people afterwards known as the " Indo-Aryans," and the traditional founders of " The Indian Civilization," as a branch of the Aryan stock, was inferred by European scholars mainly from the following facts. Firstly, when local Indian literary history first suddenly opens about the sixth century B.C., in the post-Vedic period, Gangetic India is the centre of an already fully-fledged Indian Civilization, with social institutions, religion *with the completed Vedas* and the Hindu language substantially the same as it has continued down to modern times. Secondly, no evidence of any ancient civilization before that epoch was or has been found in Gangetic India, such as is found in the seats of the older civilizations of Ancient Egypt and Babylonia. Thirdly, no traces whatever of any of the Vedic kings have ever been found in Gangetic

India, and to this may be added the fact that much of the climatology and topography of the old homeland of the Early Aryans contained in the Vedas differs markedly from that of Gangetic India.

It thus became evident that the *Aryas* (or " Aryans "), as this race called themselves and were so called in their Vedas, and who are therein described as tall and strong, of fair complexion, and the hair sometimes specified as tawny or ruddy, and in their sculptures from the earliest period downwards are figured of Aryan or " Nordic " racial type, and whose civilization, religion and language were of Aryan type, had entered Gangetic India in a great immigration, accompanied by their wives and families and priests from an older homeland, bringing with them their fully-fledged civilization, and their Veda Bible already closed.[1]

Location of the Pre-Indian Homeland of the Indo-Aryans and Theories Thereon

The question then arose: Whence and by what route and at what date did these Aryans come into the Ganges Valley with their ready-made Civilization?

As the Central Asian theory of the " Home of the Aryans " was at that time, and still largely is, in vogue, locating that homeland in the high steppes and tablelands of Turkestan and its Oxus Valley to the east of the Caspian Sea and north of Afghanistan, which was separated from India on the south-east by the vast towering Hindu Kush range or the Indian Caucasus on " The Roof of the World," the majority of European Sanskrit scholars fixed on that region as the immediate home of the Early Aryans before the migration of their eastern branch to Gangetic India, and made the Indo-Aryan branch penetrate the Hindu Kush in order to

[1] Most Sanskrit scholars conjecture that the Indo-Aryans entered the North Punjab and Gangetic India from the Hindu Kush about 1000 B.C. to 1500 B.C., with their Vedic period not yet closed, though they are totally ignorant of the relative chronology of all the kings mentioned in the Vadic psalms. But there is no evidence of any such early settlement there, not until Gangetic India is reached at a somewhat later period, apart from the recently discovered Indo-Sumerian city at Harappa on the Ravi, an outpost of the Sumerian colonial seaport city at Mohenjo Dara at the old mouth of the Indus on the south.

reach Gangetic India by way of the Upper Punjab. And such is still the view generally held at the present time by Sanskrit scholars, the so-called Hindu Kushites. A small minority of these scholars, recognizing that the Ancient Persians were manifestly of the same stock as the Indo-Aryans in civilization, language, religion and physical type, made the latter separate from the former in Persia and brought them to India *via* Persia and Kandahar.

This Central Asian location for the original homeland of the Early Aryans as well as of the Sumerians, on the grass-lands between the Caspian and the sandy deserts of Eastern Turkestan, was supposed to be confirmed by the excavations made by the Carnegie expedition under Mr R. Pumpelly in 1903–4 at the Anau oasis, near Askabad, in the province of Russian Turkestan. He found on excavating the older mound there, in the stratum immediately above the Stone-Age culture, a more advanced culture with remains of houses built of sun-dried bricks and containing fragments of delicate *hand*-made polished and painted pottery decorated with geometric designs, including the chevron zigzag, and generally resembling some of the old earthenware found at old Sumerian sites in Mesopotamia and Elam. And in the somewhat later mound site to the south, with a culture of the Copper Age, he found rude clay figurines (children's toys ?) generally resembling those found in Sumerian sites in Mesopotamia and Elam, and also lately in the Indus Valley Sumerian city sites. He thus assumed that the grassy plain of Turkestan, previous to its undergoing the climatic change of desiccation with encroachment of the sandy desert, had been the home of the Aryans in their pastoral stage as well as that of the Sumerians, before the appearance of the latter in Mesopotamia. This view was supposed to be further confirmed by the finding of somewhat similar painted pottery in the Danube Valley of Europe, the immemorial home of the Goths, who were a leading branch of the Nordic Race ; and one of these find-sites was at Hallstatt in Austria, where the Iron Age of mankind is supposed to have been originated by the Nordic Race, on the evidence of the abundance of that metal in a large prehistoric burial-ground there, and the long period of development that is seen to have elapsed in attaining the conventional forms of iron tools and weapons, which elsewhere suddenly appear in those conventional shapes.

Against this Turkestan location for the original homeland of the Aryans and of the Sumerians—which incidentally is nevertheless significant in linking together unconsciously the Aryans with the Sumerians—it has with justice been pointed out as regards the latter [1] that the Anau pottery, which is solely hand-made, is decidedly different in many ways from the Sumerian, which was largely made by a potter's wheel; and that the designs found on the Anau pottery are of the late highly conventionalized kind towards the decadence of that style of pottery amongst the Sumerians, and exhibit none of the earlier and intermediate stages, and thus indicating that the Anau people had borrowed that art from elsewhere. In addition, *the total absence of any form of writing* tells forcibly against any close or even a necessary racial relationship with the Sumerians, or with the Goths, amongst whom the chevron zigzag was a favourite decorative design as it was with the Nordic Race throughout Europe. The evidence rather points to mere contact between Anau and the Sumerians of Mesopotamia and Elam in Persia; and that the Sumerians were in commercial relations with Turkestan is evidenced by the large employment by them in Mesopotamia of lapis-lazuli stone, which does not occur in Mesopotamia but which had to be obtained from Turkestan.

The Hindu Kush itself opposes an almost unsurmountable barrier to this theory of the Hindu Kushites. It is clear that the advocates of this theory have not realized the practical impossibility of a host of civilized people, with their wives and families, cattle and goods and chattels penetrating through the vast snowfields and long rugged solitudes and defiles of this most inhospitable of lofty mountain ranges; and this, even although the indomitable Alexander-the-Great managed, with extreme privations, to bring his army from Bactria through one of its lower passes near Kabul into the Upper Indus Valley. The practical impossibility, however, for a great body of emigrants with their wives and families and chattels crossing this range was forcibly brought home to me on traversing part of the modern improved caravan

[1] See, for example, KHS. 357 f.

route to Chinese Turkestan flanking that mighty range, in the Chitral direction in 1896.

Besides, such a Central Asian location for the immediate pre-Indian homeland of the Indo-Aryans of Gangetic India is altogether put out of account by the fact that these people suddenly appear in the Ganges Valley with their fully advanced civilization of the Iron Age and with their vast literature of the Vedas and their bulky official king-lists and chronicles of their ancient Early Aryan kings extending back for some thousands of years previously, with mighty kingdoms and innumerable populous cities with fertile cultivated plains watered by great rivers flowing into the ocean.

Discovery of the Pre-Indian Homeland of the "Indo-Aryans"

On the other hand, I observed, by personally visiting most of the oldest reputed city sites in Gangetic India and studying all the archæological reports of the excavations made of all such sites, and most of them went through all the strata down to the virgin soil, that *no trace whatever of any ancient Civilization in Gangetic India has been found which can be dated earlier than about the seventh century* B.C., *and no inscription before the fourth century* B.C. And this still remains the case at the present day. It thus became evident that the Indo-Aryans with their ready-made Civilization and Vedas and their long lines of kings and dynasties of their pre-Indian period, had entered Gangetic India about the beginning of the seventh century B.C., that is shortly before the Great War of the Bhārat Aryans (as the ruling Indo-Aryan princes called themselves as we shall see) [1] for the partition of Gangetic and Southern India and Rajputana, as described in their great Indian epic, the Mahā-Bhārata. And this epoch was also shortly before the epoch of Gautama Buddha, the founder of Buddhism, whose birth in India is placed

[1] The *Bharats* were the descendants of the famous king and emperor Bharata, the tenth Aryan king, who is now disclosed in these pages as a historical Sumerian emperor of Mesopotamia, with existing contemporary inscriptions and fixed date. Most of the later Aryankings, princes and nobles claimed descent from him, so that most of the leading Aryan clans claimed to be Bharats, and especially those forming this great immigration, which warred amongst themselves for the partition of Gangetic India.

about 557 B.C.,[1] when Indian Civilization burst suddenly into view with its fully-fledged Civilization and Brahmanism and bulky Indian literature and writing, with continuous Indian history down to the present day. Moreover, the Kurus who formed the leading Aryan tribe in the great war of partition of Gangetic India, preserved the tradition that they were driven forth from their old homeland in *Kuru* by a "curse."

Then, the clues to the pre-Indian homeland of these Aryan immigrants into Gangetic India obtained by my critical comparative study of their ready-made civilization with its social and political constitutions, laws, religion, and its Vedic literature, led me to Mesopotamia and Asia Minor of the Hittites (the ancient name of which, including Syria, was *Kur*), with their correspondingly advanced Civilization of the same type.

I then picked up the traditional King-Lists of the Early Aryan kings which are embedded in the Indian epic of "The Ancient Heroes," the *Purānas*—epics which have hitherto been scornfully rejected by all Vedic scholars as fabulous, merely because they could find no traces of those Early Aryan kings in India, for the good reason as now transpires that most of those kings had never been in India at all. Comparison of these Pauranic King-Lists with those of the Sumerians, Babylonians and Hittites disclosed that several of the names of the Early Aryan kings were substantially identical with those of the Sumerian and Babylonian king-lists *and occupied the same chronological position, and were substantially identical also in the exploits of those kings*. And further scrutiny disclosed, as shown below, that *all the names and titles of those early kings were identical in both lists, Sumero-Babylonian and Indo-Aryan, from the first king of the First Sumerian Dynasty continuously downwards to the end of the Kassi Dynasty in the later Babylonian period, not only in the names and titles, but also in their exact chronological order and in the achievements of the leading kings*.

This central discovery, therefore, established absolutely

[1] His birthplace at Kapilavastu in the Indian terai of Nepal was first located by me and subsequently confirmed by the discovery there of the great pillar of the Emperor Asoka of the third century B.C., recording that event at the spot of his birth, see JRAS. 1897, 644 f.; 1898, 201 f.

the identity of the Sumerians with the Early Aryans. And it was also found that most of the leading historical Sumerian kings and priest-kings were celebrated in the Vedic psalms of the Hindus as famous kings and priest-kings of the Aryan race, and some of them as authors of Vedic psalms. It was thus disclosed that Mesopotamia of the Sumerian period had been for long a homeland of the Early Aryan ruling race, whose later eastern branch had migrated to Gangetic India as the Indo-Aryans about the beginning of the seventh century B.C.

Further comparison with the king-lists of the *Khatti*, Hatti or "Hitt-ites" of Asia Minor and Upper Mesopotamia accounted for the Indo-Aryan branch of the Aryans in the interval between the twelfth and seventh centuries B.C. I observed that the names of many of the "Hittite" kings, and more especially those subsequent to the fall and expulsion of the Kassi Dynasty of Babylon, with the end of the Sumerian rule in Babylonia, bore names substantially identical with, and in the same chronological order as, the later pre-Indian kings of the Indo-Aryan lists in the *Kuru* Dynasty. Now *Kur*, literally meaning "Mountain-land," was an old Sumerian name for Asia Minor,[1] and especially its eastern portion, and I have shown that this *Kur* was also obviously the source of *Suria* of the Greeks, the "Syria" of the Romans, and that Suria was a name for Cappadocia in the time of Herodotus,[2] and was also used for Central and Eastern Asia Minor by the Seleucid Greeks.[3] The leading clans also of the Indo-Aryans who formed "The Great Migration" to Gangetic India are often bracketed together in the Vedas as the *Kuru-Panch(-āla)*, which corresponds as I observed to the *Surio-Phoiniki* of the Greco-Romans,[4] that is the "Syrio-Phœnicians"; and in the Vedas the "Panch (āla)," that is the Aryan Phœnicians, bear also the title of *Krivi*, which is obviously dialectically derived from this

[1] WPOB. 12 f. The name appears to survive in Kurdistan, for S.E. Asia Minor, and in the Giaour title for Mt. Amanus and numerous old Hittite sites in Asia Minor.

[2] *Ib.*, 12. And see also its use by Alexander's historians, who included in Syria all Upper Mesopotamia west of the Tigris. Arrian, *Anabasis*, 5, 25; 7, 9, etc.

[3] *Ib.*, 12. [4] *Ib.*, 13.

Kur or "Syria."[1] Besides this, as associating the Indo-Aryan remnant of the Sumerians with the Khatti or "Hitt-ites," it was significant that all the Indo-Aryan princes of the Great Migration and who were of the Bharat line, who shortly after their arrival in Gangetic India fought amongst themselves for the partition of India in the Great War of the Bhārats, called themselves and were called *Khattiyo,* which in the old Indian Pali and in its later Sanskrit form possesses the identical literal meaning of "ruler" or "ruling caste" as the *Khatti* title of the "Hitt-ites" has in both the Hittite and Sumerian languages.[2]

This Kur Land, or Eastern Asia Minor with Syria, was also significantly in its south-eastern province of Comagene in "Upper Syria," bordering Cappadocia, as shown in these pages, the old homeland of the Aryan Kassi or *Kashi* or *Kashshi* Dynasty who ruled Babylonia for over six centuries till about 1200 B.C. Their old Syrian capital there was presumably at their eponymous city latterly called Gashshia or Kishshia above Carchemish, the Samosta capital of Comagene of the Greeks, with old Hittite remains, at the first bridge over the Euphrates, where Strabo records began the overland caravan road to India. It was natural that the remnant of the Kassi or Kashi Dynasty with their clansmen should return to their old home on expulsion from Babylonia by the Semites; and we find members of this Kāshi clan amongst the emigrants to India, the road to which from Asia Minor and Syria ran from their old capital on the Upper Euphrates.

Still further, I observed that the *last historical king of the Khatti or Hittites, namely, WI-SI-TI-the-Hero*[3] *with his capital at Carchemish in Upper Syria, was identical with VICITRA (or Wicitra)-the-Hero,*[4] *of the Kuru Line, the father of the First traditional King of Gangetic India (Dhrita-Rāshtra) who was*

[1] *Ib.*, 13. [2] WPOB. 8 f.

[3] *Wi-si-ti-Ish* (or *-Bir*). On *ti*, cp. Br. 2550 and 9518. And on *Ish*= "hero," Br. 5707; PSL. 134; MD. 19. And it has the alternative value of *Bir* or *Bar* (MD. 281, Br. 1724), which discloses the Sumerian origin of the Latin *Vir*, the Sanskrit *Virya*, "hero."

[4] *Vicitra* (or *Wicitra*) *Virya*. On Virya, "hero," see previous note. The *r* in Wicitra is presumably the *r* which the Sanskrit frequently intrudes Cockneywise into the old Pali and Sumerian names.

the first semi-historical king of Gangetic India and who in his old age was the contemporary of The Great War of the Bharats (*or Khattiyo*) for the partition of Gangetic India, at the dawn of the historical period in Gangetic India.

These significant new historical facts, the details of which are fully given in my forthcoming "Origin of Indian Civilization," conclusively fixed not only the fact of that Great Migration of Aryans of the Kuru line to Gangetic India as the Indo-Aryans, but also showed that *it came mainly from Eastern Kur or Asia Minor and Syria of the Hittites*, and consisted of the remnants of the Sumerian or Aryan stock left there with accretions from Persia; and there was also disclosed the Cause of that Great Migration to Gangetic India, which brought there the official King-Lists and Chronicles of the Early Aryans, and its exact Date.

Cause of "The Great Migration" of Aryan Remnants from Eastern Kur or Asia Minor (and Syria) to Gangetic India, and its Date

The immediate cause which led to this Great Migration of the Kurus, as the remnants of the "Sumerians" or Early Aryan stock left in Kur or Eastern Asia Minor, including Syria-Phœnicia and Kurdistan, was obviously the devastating and annihilating war of extermination waged by the notorious Semitic Assyrian king Sargon II against the cluster of old mountain states of Eastern Asia Minor to the north and west of Assyria and Babylonia, from Lake Van in Armenia to Cilicia and Syria-Phœnicia in the west. It was the last straw after the series of similar ruthless conquests by his predecessors, who brutally butchered their victims, crucifying and flaying them alive and transporting many of the remainder wholesale into captivity, as they did likewise to the Jews. Sargon II captured the southern Hittite capital Carchemish in 717 B.C. and killed[1] its king Wisiti-the-Hero, the last of the once mighty Hittite kings, and reduced Carchemish to a province of his empire under an Assyrian governor. And concurrently the Cimmerians had occupied the greater part of Cappadocia in the north. Thus, caught between the two jaws of a vice, the Great Migration of the Kurus, with

[1] According to one account "carried off."

their princes and priests and their families and army of retainers to Gangetic India is disclosed as a great flight of refugees fleeing from Carchemish and Syria-Phœnicia, Kurdistan and Armenia, to escape from the atrocities of the barbarous Assyrian victors, and the probable attack by the Cimmerians on the north. This now explains for the first time the cryptic reference in the early post-Vedic literature that the Kurus were driven out of their old home of Kuru-Land by a curse;[1] and it also explains why the "*Asuras*" are called "devils" in Indian literature. But Asia Minor's loss was India's gain; and amongst other things it preserved for us from destruction the uniquely complete official King-Lists and Chronicles of the Early Aryan kings.

The apparent line of this great flight of the Kuru-Panch (-āla) Khattiyo or "Hittites" through Persia and Seistan-Gandhara across the Indus Valley and border of Rajputana to Gangetic India is traced in my "Origin of Indian Civilization."

The Date of the King-Lists & Chronicles of the Early Aryans of the Indo-Aryans

We now gain through the above historical criterions, which fix the date of the Great Migration that brought to India the official King-Lists and Chronicles of the pre-Indian period of the Indo-Aryans, the necessary chronological material for fixing also the date when these King-Lists of the Early Aryans now embedded in the Epic of the Ancient Heroes—the *Purānas*—were closed.

That date according to the most recent estimates by European Sanskrit scholars, although made in ignorance of the locality of the pre-Indian homeland of the Indo-Aryans and of the date of the migration and of the date of the Great Bharat Wars, is nevertheless remarkably in general agreement with our newly found facts. By finding references to the *Purānas* as being already in existence and esteemed sacred in the very earliest post-Vedic literature,[2] and by the internal evidence of the *Purānas* themselves, which divided their king-lists into those of "The Past" (that is the pre-

[1] MKI. I, 166.

[2] The Atharva Veda and Shatapatha Brahmana, cp. PIT. 54 f.

Indian lists with which the old lists closed), and those of "The Future" (that is in the Indian period, beginning with kings immediately after the Great War of the Bharats for the partition of India), they place the "probable" date for the closing of the old list variously at 600 B.C. to 950 B.C.[1] The latter earlier date is got by including a considerable number of the kings of the Vedic period, which period, however, we shall find ended before this Great Migration.

Now, however, we find by our more precise historical data that these old King-Lists were closed on or about 717 B.C., when the great flight from Kur Land in Eastern Asia Minor with Upper Syria took place eastwards to India through Persia on the tragic death of the ill-fated king Vicitra. And allowing sixteen years or so for a temporary sojourn in Persia, of which I have found evidence, the date of arrival in Gangetic India would be about 700 B.C.

The leader of that migration into Gangetic India was clearly the son and successor of King Vicitra in the lists, namely "Dhrita-of-the-Empire" (Dhrita-Rāshtra),[2] who is now disclosed as the first historical Aryan king of Gangetic India, and significantly he was made in the later Indian mythology the white guardian emperor of the Eastern quarter of the world.[3] By the time of the outbreak of the Great Bhārat War amongst his sons and other followers for the partition of India, he was "very old and blind." Thus by allowing him forty-six years' reign after the death of his father in 717 B.C. (and his father was an elderly man, as he paid tribute to the Assyrian king Tiglath-Pileser III in 738 B.C.) until the epoch of the Great War, this would make *the date of that Great Bhārat War about* 670 B.C., and this date is in general agreement with its estimates from the calculated dates for the semi-historical Indian kings who now begin to appear for the first time in Gangetic India, though the

[1] PIT. 54, 182.

[2] In Pali *Dhata-Rattho.* In early post-Vedic literature he is the son of Vicitra (cp. MKI. 1, 403), but the later Brahman editors of the *Purānas* make him the son of the widow of Vicitra by a Brahman priest, which is clearly fictitious.

[3] WBT. 84. He is white in complexion and king of the Gandharvas, who seem to be a mythic memory of the Gandharas or natives of old Candahar.

first fixed date in Indian history is not until Candra-Gupta in 321 B.C., who was a contemporary of Alexander the Great.

Moreover, it is clear that the King-Lists of "The Past" Early Aryan kings *were already closed before the Great War of the Bhārats* from the fact that these lists are stated in the Epic of that war (the Mahā-Bhārata) to have been recited to King Dhrita (or Dhata) on his arrival in Gangetic India along with the enumeration of all the provinces and tribes in (this new land of) India, of which he claimed to be the emperor, which is also confirmed by his title of Rāshtra.

Thus the King-Lists and Chronicles of the Early Aryans of "The Past" or pre-Indian period embedded in the *Purānas* were evidently closed about 717 B.C. So we now can pass on to the examination of these King-Lists themselves.

The Official Character of the Indian King-Lists & Chronicles

No more eloquent testimony to the sincerity of the Indian belief in the historic genuineness of this genealogical tradition of the ancient kings and heroes of the Aryans could perhaps be desired than the simple opening sentence above quoted in the heading of this chapter, by which the heraldic bard in the Epic introduced his official proclamation of these lists, of which he was presumably the official custodian. The material had already, in Ancient India, become so venerable as to have acquired a sacred character.

The ancient Indo-Aryans treasured as sacred those memories of the beginnings of their Aryan nation, the names of the famous heroes, from their first Aryan king onwards, who had led the tribes to victory, or who had welded together the divers tribes into a nation and enlarged their liberties. Ages had not dimmed the shining glory of these names, which were handed down with scrupulous care in writing, with all the sanctity of a popular cult. This explains why they have been so carefully preserved and why they have so manifestly escaped the Brahman censor, when the Epics were Sanskritized about the beginning of the Christian era and enlarged by the Brahman priests by the introduction of religious dogmatics.

General Form of the Indian King-Lists of the Early Aryans

These Early Aryan King-Lists are for the most part bald strings of names and relationships of the kings and of the rise of new dynasties, interspersed with occasional episodes in regard to leading kings, as with modern writers' and speech-makers' use of episodes to break the monotony, though the story at times is eked out with details sometimes rather puerile and obviously expanded by later Brahmans through false etymology of some of the names, analogous to "the confusion of tongues" fable manufactured by the Hebrews from a false etymology of "Babel." They possess no positively expressed chronology of regnal years, though contemporaries are sometimes mentioned.

Their unique merit is that they are arranged in a strict chronological sequence upon a complete scheme of succession from the first king of the First Aryan Dynasty on the horizon of history continuously onwards down to the later historical period. They thus supply the material framework from which a dated history can be constructed. They are unique also in preserving the full list of the Sumerian kings of the Great Gap of lost kings in the Sumerian and Babylonian lists, for 420 years in the "Second Dynasty," as well as bridging the gap between the Isin and Babylonian First Dynasty.

The actual dates can now be obtained through the Sumerian and Babylonian king-lists of the same kings which preserve the traditional number of years' reign for each king; and then calculation by the process of dead-reckoning backwards from a fixed date yields us the actual dates approximately to a few years, as detailed in the chapter on Chronology. Thus the Indian and Sumerian king-lists supplement and complement each other.

Different Versions of the Indian Epic King-Lists

These official Indian King-Lists of the Early Aryans purporting and found in fact to extend continuously down without a break from the first king of the First Aryan Dynasty to the beginning of the later historical period in

India, fortunately exist in several distinct and independent versions, as preserved independently by the different clans of the eastern branch of the Aryans on their great migration to Gangetic India, when they were afterwards gathered together in their present form, reduced to alphabetic writing, and embedded in their great national Epics.

The Epics which contain the full official king-lists are called *Purānas* or "The Ancients (Heroes)." And as becoming their sacred character, they have latterly had prefixed to their king-lists a late post-Vedic mythical account of the creation of the universe and the genealogy of the later gods with dogmatic theology, the whole forming a bulky set of Hindu Scriptures. These *Purānas* exist in over a dozen different and independent clan or sectarial versions or recensions. Of these versions the *Vishnu*, *Vāyu* and *Bhagavata* are regarded as the oldest and most authentic, the *Vāyu* being regarded as the oldest; and they are generally in agreement and complement each other, some of them giving occasionally titles, solar or lunar, in place of the personal names given by the others.

The phonetic and other variations in the spelling of the same name or title in these separate and independent clan versions in transliterating the old Sumerian syllabic writing into the latter alphabetic Indian writing, as well as the scrupulous care with which the Indian copyists of the manuscripts have endeavoured to retain the original spelling in the different versions, further attest their independence and authenticity.

Solar & Lunar Versions of Aryan King-Lists

Each of the *Purāna* Epic versions of the King-Lists contains nine or more main lines of kings, and these lines are broadly divided into "Solar" and "Lunar." This presumably denotes that these different lines were originally compiled respectively and independently by Sun-worshipping and Moon-worshipping Aryan clans before the advent of the members of these clans to India, when they were amalgamated independently in one common text.

The *Solar* lines are two in number, and are now called by the Brahmans the *Ayodhyā* and *Videha* or *Mithila* lines respectively, after the old capitals of two chief dynasties in the Solar line; and thus presumably designating the two cities where these two lists were compiled or preserved. The Ayodhyā city we shall find is "Agade" or properly *Agudu*[1] city of the Mesopotamian records; and the Ayodhyā list is the most complete of all.

The two chief *Lunar* lines are named *Yadu* and *Puru* respectively after the names or titles of their ancestral king in the fourth generation of descent from their common parent the first Aryan king. The Puru line version is admittedly the youngest, and as we shall find is the most tampered with by the Indian Brahmans, who have through ignorance dislocated the succession from King Puru by interposing a dynasty of a later king of the same name which comes as shown by its synchronisms about thirty generations later (see Appendix I, col. 4).

The *Mahā-Bhārata*, or Epic of "The Great War of the Bharats" over the partition of Gangetic India, also contains embedded in it two abbreviated versions of the lunar Puru traditional king-lists with the same displacement in the beginning of the lists, and exhibiting several discrepancies, like the two different accounts of the succession of the patriarchs from Adam in the Hebrew Genesis. Yet these preserve some traditional details regarding several of the kings, which prove from the Mesopotamian and Egyptian contemporary inscriptions to be genuine tradition. The *Rāmā-yana* Epic tradition of the king-lists on the other hand is much later and almost wholly corrupt and historically worthless.

The Main Lines of the different Versions of Indian King-Lists contain the Same Kings under different Titles, Solar, Lunar, Regnal, etc.

Hitherto each of the Main Line King-Lists, solar and lunar in the *Purānas* has been believed by modern Brahmans and by all Sanskrit scholars to catalogue totally different lines of totally different kings and dynasties, although each,

[1] On the *gu* and *du* values of the signs in this name *A-gu-du*, usually restored as *A-ga-de*, see SS. 244 and M. 3099.

solar and lunar, begins with and continues for some distance with the same ancestral kings.

On placing, however, these main line lists as represented by the four chief lines above specified alongside each other in parallel columns (see Appendix I), I observed that the names of leading kings come out in the corresponding place in each of the tabulated lists. Thus, for example, the tenth king Barata, with his dialectic variants of Brihad, Brihat, Prithu and Pārtha; the fifteenth king Haryashwa with his five sons, the thirty-seventh king Śakuni or Sagara (who we had found was "Sargon" of Agade with his identical history and achievements), occupy the same relative chronological position in all these main-line lists. And a great number came out substantially identical with merely variant phonetic spellings in two or more of the columns.

This clearly showed that the various main line lists, solar and lunar, were merely variant versions of the same main line or imperial line, in which the kings were called respectively by their solar or lunar religious title, or by their personal name, or by their regnal or other title. And this was fully confirmed by further comparative scrutiny, as shown in Appendix I.

Plurality of Titles of Early Aryan or Sumerian Kings

The Solar Title, we find, was presumably the chief regnal title of the Early Aryan kings, who in the early period we have seen were purely Sun-worshippers, whilst the Lunar Title was apparently adopted to conciliate their Moon-worshipping Chaldee or Semitic subjects. This is borne out, as we shall see, by the multiple Sumerian titles of these self-same Aryan kings in the Sumerian records, the first king of the First Sumerian Dynasty for example bearing no less than seven different Sumerian names or titles in the Sumerian records.

This plurality of names and titles for Sumerian kings and princes is also well illustrated in the famous inscribed plaque of King Uruash (see Fig. 20), in which that emperor portrays himself with his five sons in two scenes, and gives each of them different names or titles in the upper scene from the lower; and significantly both of these different forms of name and title for each of his sons are duly given as in the different versions of the Indian King-Lists, as detailed in Chapter VI. And their father, King Uruash, bears in the victory seal of his crown-prince A-Madgal the same title of "Barama'hasha," which as King Haryashwa, the father of the crown-prince Mudgal, bears in the Indian King-Lists.[1]

This plurality of the names and titles of the Early Aryan or Sumerian kings thus discloses the Aryan origin of the multiple names and titles borne by the Egyptian kings from Menes downwards—all of the Pharaohs bearing at least five different names or titles, solar and other, down to the latest period.[2] Plurality of names or titles of Aryan kings and heroes was still in vogue in Homer's day. And the present-day multiple names of kings is perhaps founded on this ancient Aryan custom.

Comparison of the Early Aryan King-Lists with the Sumerian King-Lists

Having thus established a standard list or codex of the Ancient Aryan kings in the main or imperial line from the first king of the First Aryan Dynasty, with their various specific titles, solar and lunar, as recorded in the four columns of the table in Appendix I, I then turned to the Sumerian King-Lists to compare their names in detail with those of the Early Aryan kings of the Indian lists, being led to institute this comparison by the affinities and agreements discovered in my early researches and described in previous works.

Wide Disagreements in the "Restorations" of Sumerian Kings' Names by Assyriologists

In essaying a detailed comparison between the Indo-Aryan King-Lists and the Sumerian, I was met at the outset by the staggering and seemingly insuperable obstacle that Assyriologists were not agreed in their reading of the names of Sumerian kings, so that there was no one standard list of Sumerian kings to refer to. These scholars, I observed, differed enormously amongst themselves in their readings

[1] See App. I, No. 15, and cp. WISD. 35 f.; 131 f.
[2] BKE. 1, xii. f.

or "restorations" of the names of the Sumerian and Babylonian kings. Scarcely any two of these scholars read the names of the majority of these kings and heroes in the same form, and not infrequently they produced totally different forms for the name of the self-same king in the self-same Sumerian or Babylonian writing in the self-same text.

Thus the personal name which one scholar read *Izdubar*, another read *Gishtobar* and a third *Gilgamesh*. What one read as *Ālūsharshīd* another read *Urumūsh*. What one read as *Eriaku* another read *Rimsin* or *Bur-Sin*; and *Uru-Enzū* of one was *Aradi Nannar* of another. What one read as *Ugur* others read as *Urid, Urlammu* or *Urnammu*. What one read as *Dingirān* another read as *Ilūma*, and so on. And similarly was it with city names: what one read as *Umma*, another *Gishkhu*; and *Shirpurla* of one is *Lagash* of another, and so on.

Cause of Disagreements in "Restoring" Sumerian & Babylonian Kings' Names is the want hitherto of any Key to the Form of Names in the ambiguous Sumerian & Babylonian Writing

I then observed that this wide dissimilarity in reading or "restoring" the same name from the same text by Assyriologists was owing to their *total want of any key whatever to the traditional forms of the names* of the Sumerian and Early Babylonian kings and their cities in "restoring" the names from the ambiguous Sumerian and Babylonian syllabic writing, in which nearly every syllable possesses two or many more, usually half a dozen or more, totally different syllabic phonetic values or spellings. This is owing to the syllabic signs by which names are spelled out, being polyphonous, each sign possessing not only the name of the object which it pictures but also the various synonyms for that name.[1] Thus the Sumerian and Babylonian syllabic sign *Sar* in "Sargon," which is the pictograph of a garden, possesses also the other phonetic values of *Kesh, Khir, Ma, Mu, Nisigū, Sakar, Shar, Sher, Sir* and *Xir*, any one of which may be the form intended in writing that syllable in a particular name.

[1] WSAD. xxxii. f.

As a consequence of this want of any key to the traditional form of the kings' names each Assyriologist in reading a proper name is in the habit of arbitrarily selecting one or other of these polyphonous forms by mere guesswork, each according to his own individual fancy, and thus they fabricate more or less totally dissimilar forms of name, as often as not fictitious, for the same king; and being all Semitic scholars they tend to give many of the Sumerian names Semitic, and therefore false, forms.

It thus became clear that no positive reliance whatever could be placed on the forms of Sumerian and Early Babylonian kings' names thus arbitrarily "restored" by Assyriologists, except in the relatively few cases where the syllabic sign possessed only one phonetic value, which thus could not distort the true form of the name beyond recognition.

In this dilemma, I approached one of our foremost English Assyriologists for assistance in ascertaining whether the Sumerian kings' names that intervened between the few outstanding ones which I found manifestly agreed in form and in chronological position with those of Early Aryan kings in the Indian lists, might also on revision by their other polyphonous values agree with the names in the latter lists. But, while admitting the conjectural manner in which they "restored" the names, and the neglect to warn readers that the names so restored were largely conjectural in the absence of any keys to the forms of the names, he shared the universal prejudice that the Sumerians were not related to any other civilization and language, and in particular the Aryan, and on the plea that such a comparison would be a sheer waste of time, he refused assistance.

It now became a question of only two alternatives. Either I must give up all hope of comparing in detail the Indian king-lists with the Sumerian, and abandon my long search for the lost Aryan Origins, despite the innumerable clues I had elicited; or, I must begin late in life the acquisition of another and extremely difficult new language, with a new and formidable hieroglyphic and cuneiform writing, in order personally to compare at first hand the Indian king-lists of the Early Aryan kings with the Sumerian. I chose the latter alternative, and leave the results to speak for themselves.

Indian King-Lists of the Early Aryans supply the Unique Key to the Traditional Forms of the Sumerian Kings' Names

Forced in this way over twenty years ago to take up seriously the study of the Sumerian language and its linear, pictographic and cuneiform writing in order to compare in detail the names of the Sumerian and Early Babylonian kings with those of the Early Aryan kings preserved in the Indian lists, I soon began to find that the names of the Sumerian kings from the First Sumerian Dynasty onwards were all in substantial agreement with the names in the Indian king-lists, and the leading kings had the same achievements attached to them in both Sumerian and Indian records.

Further comparison showed that this agreement and identity extended throughout both lists from the First Dynasty continuously down to the later historical period both in names, achievements, and precise chronological sequence.

Thus the Indian king-lists of the Early Aryan kings proved to be official and authentic and independent historical records of the Sumerians, and they provide an unique key to the restoration of the traditional forms of the names of the Sumerian and Early Babylonian kings, for which hitherto there has been no key whatever. More than this, they preserve the full list of the lost names and succession order of the Sumerian kings of the great gap in the Babylonian lists of Sumerian kings. And they complete the positive identification of the Sumerians with the Early Aryans in personalities, race, civilization and language.

We now proceed to examine the Sumerian King-Lists and compare them in detail with the Early Aryan versions preserved in the official Indian Lists.

III

Sumerian Dynastic Lists in Kish Chronicle of about 2650 B.C. from First Sumerian Dynasty to the Guti or Gothic Invasion

Disclosing Date of First Sumerian Dynasty at about 3378 B.C., *and the Great Gap in the Kish Chronicle*

On the Sumerian side, no official systematic traditional king-list of the Sumerians was found until 1911, when The Kish Chronicle, named after the very ancient Sumerian capital city where its tablet was unearthed, and containing the first five Sumerian dynasties, was published by Prof. V. Scheil.[1] The recent excavations at this ancient city site by the joint Oxford and Chicago expedition of Weld and Field are yielding a rich harvest of remains of the earliest Sumerian period; for the view that whilst the culture is Sumerian and decidedly non-Semitic, the people are possibly pre-Sumerian, is not at all supported by the objects themselves, nor by their inscriptions and form of writing, which latter is similar to the cursive Sumerian of the Indo-Sumerian seals and the Sumerian writing in the Predynastic and First Dynasty inscriptions in Egypt.

The Kish Chronicle

Characteristically, although this Kish Chronicle was published by the veteran Assyriologist Prof. Scheil as "The most Ancient Dynasties known of Sumer-Accad"; and his colleague found that the capital of the first of these dynasties was "very probably a Sumerian city,"[2] and the Sumerians are admittedly far older than the supposedly Semitic "Akkads," modern Assyriologists, nevertheless, with their

[1] AIC. Octr. 1911, 606 f., and amended in plates in RA. 1912, 69. The Fourth or Sargon's Dynasty is now conclusively proved in these pages to be also Sumerian.

[2] TDC. 61.

PLATE IV

KISH CHRONICLE TABLET OF SUMERIAN KINGS.

From First Sumerian Dynasty to Gothic Invasion of *c.* 2650 B.C., obverse and reverse, 1/2, now in British Museum, No. 108857. (After Prof. V. Scheil RA. 1912.)

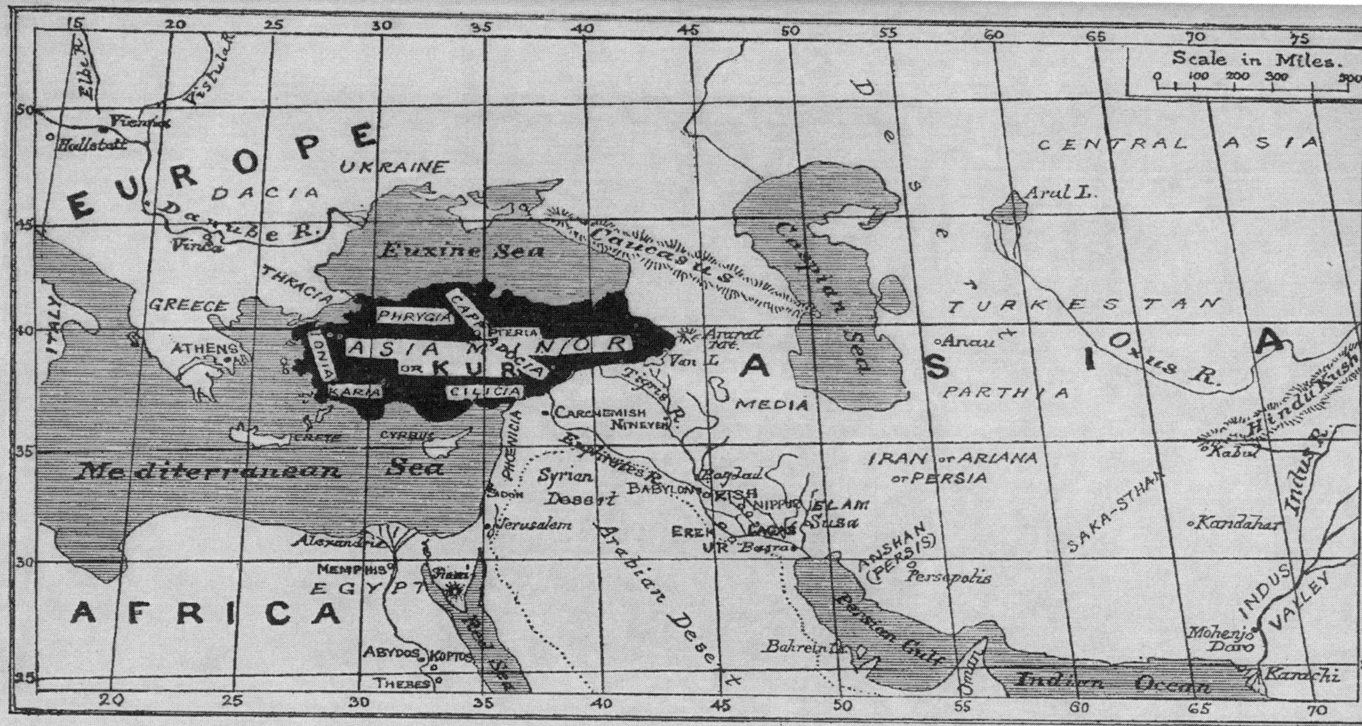

MAP I ASIA MINOR AS LAND-BRIDGE BETWEEN EUROPE, MESOPOTAMIA (IN ASIA) AND EGYPT (IN AFRICA)

inveterate Semitic theories, have arbitrarily seized on these first two dynasties as "Semitic" (!); and this notwithstanding also that they have been unable to find any contemporary inscriptions of those very ancient kings, and that the names of those kings, as well as their personalities, are Sumerian.

This Kish Chronicle is an official Babylonian clay-tablet copy made about the epoch of King Khammu Rabi (c. 2000 B.C.) from an original, dating presumably to about five centuries earlier, as its record ends there. And we shall find that it is the most authentic of all Babylonian records extant of the Sumerian dynasties from the First Sumerian Dynasty continuously down through the Sargonic period to the Guti or Gothic invasion about 2495 B.C. The other later unearthed and published Babylonian king-lists by the myth-mongering priests of Isin are all betrayed by their own records, as we shall find, to be wholly fictitious in prefixing dynasties and chronology before the First Sumerian Dynasty of this Kish Chronicle. This Chronicle is fully confirmed with its first dynasty as the First Sumerian Dynasty by the Indian lists, and by the contemporary Sumerian monuments and archaic king-lists embedded in the prefixed Isin lists, and especially by the contemporary genealogy of the first Sumerian king inscribed on the votive stone-bowl of his great-grandson King Udu (see Chap. V), and the earliest of all known historical Sumerian inscriptions.

Early Provisional King-Lists of the Sumerians

Previous to the finding of this Kish Chronicle, the only lists of the Sumerian kings available were the fragmentary provisional ones compiled by Assyriologists from the stray inscribed monuments and tablets of isolated kings, in several of which their paternity for one or two generations was sometimes recorded. These were then arranged in approximate chronological order by the palæographic forms of their writing, which was gradually changing from the simple linear form of the earliest pictographs and hieroglyphs into a cuneiform or "wedge-form" style for writing on clay-tablets; and this supplied an approximate clue to the relative antiquity and chronology of the kings who inscribed them. But as with mere archæological inferences for chronology several of them proved to be wrongly placed chronologically, when fuller historical inscriptions and the traditional king-lists were latterly forthcoming.

The Kish Chronicle Text

This Chronicle, written on a clay-tablet (see Plate IV), is of fundamental importance for all Ancient History and for the History of the World's Civilization. It was found by Prof. Scheil in a private collection with the report of having been unearthed from the ruins of Kish, the old imperial Sumerian capital at the site of the modern Arab village of El Ohmeir on the old channel of the Euphrates, about twelve miles east of Babylon (see Map). It was latterly acquired by the British Museum,[1] where it is now preserved.

Its Official Character & Date

It is a simple tablet inscribed on both sides and is complete in itself. It is written in Babylonian cuneiform script of about the period of King Khammu Rabi, of the famous law-code, about 2000 B.C. It is a certified copy by a scribe of an older record, which closing with the Guti or Gothic Invasion of about 2495 B.C. presumably dated from that epoch.

It commences without any reference to any previous dynasty, and gives systematically the names of the kings, in successive order from its first dynasty onwards, with the lengths of the reign of each king separately and their relationships to their successors, and the city which was their capital; with, in addition, the total number of kings and regnal years collectively for each dynasty. It records five successive "dynasties" according to their respective capital cities. The penultimate or Fourth Dynasty is that of "Sargon-the-Great of Agade," and hitherto conjectured to be "Semitic" by Assyriologists, with their inveterate Semitic prejudice, just as they have arbitrarily dubbed the first two of these dynasties "Semitic." But their "Sargon-the-Great," who is called in this Kish Chronicle and in many of his own inscriptions "King Kīn" in series with the usual form of his

[1] BM. No. 108857.

name in the Indian Lists and Chronicles, where he is one of the most famous Aryan emperors, is conclusively proved in these pages to be along with his entire dynasty of the Aryan race.

Decipherment & Translation of The Kish Chronicle

The pioneer decipherment and translation of this Chronicle by Prof. Scheil has been amended or altered in a few of the names by later scholars.[1]

My revised decipherment and reading of the names in the light, for the first time, of the traditional forms of the kings' names furnished by the new Indian keys is given below, and the Babylonian text in App. II. All my readings of the names when they differ from those phonetic values hitherto conjecturally selected from the ambiguous polyphonous values of the Sumerian writing without any key whatever to the forms of the names, are fully attested in the list in Appendix II from the latest standard Sumerian lexicons, as in all my former works, and cannot be gainsaid.

The " dynasties " are not so termed in the text nor are they there numbered, but I have for facility of reference inserted numbers within square brackets. And the contents of the broken lower edge of the obverse of the Kish tablet containing part of the continuation of Sargon's dynasty is restored within square brackets from the Nippur and Isin versions of this same dynastic list.. The proper names which agree with those in the Indian Lists are printed in capitals.

Kish Chronicle Text

(Revised reading of names ; for text see App. II.)

Obverse.

[1st Dynasty at Ukhu, Uxu or Akshak.]

Line.

1. " At UKHU City UKUSI became king and — reigned 30 years
2. AZAG, the (mighty) handed AMA (or BĀ'KUS or BĀ'SAM) — reigned 12 years
3. TAN-TAN — " 6 "

[1] TDC. 58 f., and Gadd, *Early Dynasties of Sumer and Akkad*, 1921, 1 f.

Line		
4.	NAKSHA-ANSIR	reigned 20 years
5.	Ishuil	„ 24 „
6.	Shuanenzu, son of Ishuil	„ 7 „
7.	6 kings	„ 99 „
8.	At Ukhu the rule was changed: its royalty passed to KISH City.	
	[2nd Dynasty at Kish.]	
9.	At KISH City AZAG, Lord BAKUS (or BASAM), Libator of Ale (*Ul*) of Life, founded Kish City,	
10.	becoming king, he	reigned 64 years [1]
11.	NAKSHA-ANENUZU, son of Azag Lord Bakus	„ 25 „
12.	The Devotee of Lord Sagaga, s. of Naksha Anenuzu	„ 6 „
13.	ZIMUGUN (or GINMUGUN)	„ 30 „
14.	UZIWITAR s. of Zimugun	„ 6 „
15.	UGUN-MUTIN	„ 11 „
16.	IMUASHU	„ 11 „
17.	NAILĪANA	„ 3 „
18.	8 [2] [+] Kings	„ 586 „
19.	At Kish the rule was changed: its royalty passed to Unug (Enoch) City.	
	[3rd Dynasty at Unug or Enoch.]	
20.	At Unug City King ZAGGISI became king, he	reigned 25 years
21.	1 king	„ 25 „
22.	At Unug the rule was changed, its royalty passed to AGUDU (“ Agade ”) [3] City.	

[1] On this figure see text in App. II, and discussion in next Chapter.

[2] See note on this number in App. II, and next Chapter.

[3] This capital city name is usually transcribed *A-ga-de* to equate it with *Akkadu*; but the Indian Chronicles preserve the traditional name as *Ayodhya*, which indicates that the Second and Third Sumerian signs should read by their other phonetic values of *gu* (SS. 244; Br. 6103, which is the sign-name), and *du* (M. 3099), thus giving the form *Agudu*.

[4th Dynasty at Agudu (or " Agade ").[1]]

Line

23. At AGUDU City SHARRU-KĪN . . .
a gardener (acolyte) cup-bearer
24-25. devotee of Lord Sagaga and King
of Agudu City who . . . built
26. Agudu being king reigned [55] years [2]
[a.b. The hero MŪSH, son of Sharru-Kīn „ 9 (15)[3] „
[c.d. MANIS-TĪSSHU, elder brother of
the hero Musūsh
[e.f. Son of Sharru-Kīn reigned 15 (7)[3] years
[g.i NARĀM, Lord ENZU, s. of Manis-
Tisshu „ 56 (38) [3] years]

Reverse.

1. SHAR-[GANI King ERI reigned 24 years]
2. Who was king ? Who was not king ?
3. IGIGI [4] king IMI king
4. NANUM king IAMA king
5. These 4 „ 3 „
6. DUDU „ 21 „
7 SHUDUR-KIP son of Dudu „ 15 „
8. 12 (?11) kings „ 197 „
9. At Agudu City its rule was changed
10. Its royalty passed to UNUG (Enoch) City

[5th Dynasty at Unug (Enoch).]

11. At UNUG City Uru-NIGIN being king reigned 3 years
12. URISGINAR, son of Uru-Nigin „ 6 „
13. KUDDA „ 6 „
14. NAGSHALILI „ 5 „
15. URASHUTU „ 6 „
16. 5 kings „ 26 „

[1] The defaced lines after the 26 are replaced, within square brackets, from the other perfect later copies from Nippur and Isin.

[2] The years' sign, defaced in the tablet, is restored, within curved brackets, from other and generally accepted inscriptions.

[3] These variant totals in different MSS. are discussed in Chapter on Chronology.

[4] Or *Ni-gi-gi.*

Line
17. At Unug (Enoch) its rule was changed:
18. Its royalty passed unto the Troops of GUTI Land

. . . .

Written in the month of In (May-June) 30th day."

DATED CHRONOLOGY OF KISH CHRONICLE DISCLOSES DATE OF FIRST KING OF FIRST SUMERIAN DYNASTY AT ABOUT 3378 B.C.

The full traditional regnal years for each king separately and the total years collectively for each dynasty from the first Sumerian king of the First Sumerian Dynasty continuously onwards preserved by the Kish Chronicle, giving a continuous chronology from the earliest historic period down to and beyond Sargon's dynasty, is universally admitted by Assyriologists (though ignorant of the fact that the first dynasty therein is the First Sumerian Dynasty) to be historically authentic. For, where they can be tested, as in the case of the long reigns of Sargon and his grandson "Naram Sin" these regnal years are in general agreement with the facts of contemporary history.

This traditional chronology, therefore, enables us by a process of dead-reckoning back from the relatively fixed date of about 2725 B.C. for "Sargon," or properly *Sharru Kīn* or "King Kīn," as he is called in the Kish Chronicle by one of his later and well recognized dialectic variants in spelling—to fix the initial date of the first king of the First Sumerian Dynasty. This latter date, we shall find, in the following chapters and in detail in the chapter on Chronology, gives the accession of King *Ukusi* of *Ukhu* City, the first king of the First Sumerian Dynasty, and now disclosed as identical with King *Ikśh-Vāku* the first Aryan solar king of the First Aryaṇ Dynasty of the Indian lists at about 3378 B.C.

Such a date for the first king of the Sumerians or Early Aryans, at about 650 years before King Sargon, is in general agreement with the palæography and archæology of the period of the First Sumerian Dynasty—the difference in writing, art and civilization being practically no greater than between those of King Alfred and Queen Elizabeth.

The Great Gap in the "Second" Sumerian Dynasty of Kish Chronicle of 430 years is filled by the Indo-Aryan King-Lists and Chronicles.

The most outstanding feature in this Babylonian chronology of the Early Sumerian kings in the Kish Chronicle is the Great Gap of 430 years in the Second Dynasty of that chronicle, in which the names of all the kings beyond the eighth were lost to the Babylonian scribes of that chronicle and of the one of which it is a copy.

Whilst the total duration of the Second Dynasty is given as 586 years, only the names of the first eight kings reigning for a period of 156 years are preserved, thus leaving the kings for the long period of 430 years a total blank.

Here the unique and full historical record preserved by the Indian King-Lists of the Early Aryans now comes to our aid and completely fills up this Great Gap of names in the Kish Chronicle. The Indian lists, whilst giving us the names of the Early Aryan kings from the first king of the First Aryan Dynasty down to the end of Sargon's Dynasty and far beyond, which names are in dialectic agreement with all the corresponding kings' names in the Kish Chronicle and also significantly in the same identical order of succession, also *preserve between the 8th king of the Second Dynasty of the Kish Chronicle and the first king of the Third Dynasty of that chronicle the lost names of the* 27 (*or* 28) *kings of the Great Gap of* 430 *years in that chronicle.*

These 27 (or 28) kings reigning for 430 years give an average reign for each of 16 years, which is a fair average regnal length. But we shall find that the actual traditional reign for several of the leading kings of this gap are preserved in other later found Sumerian and Babylonian king-lists.

This total loss by the Babylonian scribes of the names of these 27 (or 28) ancient Sumerian kings of the Great Gap, now explains for the first time, the hitherto inexplicable absence of all mention of the great pre-Sargonic Sumerian dynasties of Uruash or "Ur-Nina" and of "Urukagina" in both the Kish Chronicle and in its later Nippur and Isin versions of this "Second Dynasty." But these missing Sumerian kings with their dynasties are now disclosed by the Indian lists all in their true chronological sequence and fill up this Great Gap in the Second Dynasty of the Kish Chronicle, as we shall see later on in Chapters VI f.

We are now in a position to compare the Sumerian King-Lists from the First Sumerian Dynasty preserved in the Kish Chronicle with the Early Aryan King-Lists from the First Aryan Dynasty preserved in the Indian Lists down to the Great Gap in the former chronicle.

FIG. 15A.—Deified First Aryan-Sumerian King, Dur or In-Dur or Ia (Jah), as Lord of the Deep Waters, and bestower of the Waters of Life. From a Sumerial seal of the Gothic King Gudia (c. 2370 B.C.). After Delaporte D.C.O. I, enlarged 1½ diameters.

Note the horned head-dress and the flounced and other costumes; and the shaved upper lip of the god and his attendant.

IV

Comparison of Kish Chronicle & Indian Lists of the Early Aryan Kings discloses their Identity and Site of their First Sumerian and Aryan Capital in Asia Minor

Discovering also The Advent of the Sumerians into Mesopotamia & its Date as *c.* 3335 B.C., *Overlapping of 1st and 2nd Dynasties of Kish Chronicle, Identity of 1st Sumerian King with Indra, Thor or King Ar-Thur or St George with Date, and Location of First Capital in Cappadocia.*

THE comparison of the Sumerian King-Lists of the Kish Chronicle from the First Sumerian Dynasty onwards with the Indo-Aryan King-Lists of the Early Aryans from the First Aryan Dynasty onwards discloses the complete identity of the Sumerian with the Aryan kings. This identity is evidenced not only by the equation in the form of their names and titles, but also by the same identical order in their succession or chronological position. Moreover the achievements of the leading kings are identical in both the Sumerian and Aryan records, as far as the latter go in regard to the achievements.

Variant Phonetic Spellings of Proper Names in Sumerian & Indian Records

As in modern European languages before the invention of the printing-press, which has tended to fix rigidly the spelling of words and names—though even long after that invention Shakespeare, for instance, we are told, continued to spell his own name in over half-a-dozen different ways—the Sumerian kings are found to spell their own names in their own inscriptions sometimes in different phonetic ways. Moreover the later Babylonian scribes of the period to which the Kish Chronicle belongs, in repeating the names of the early kings, spell their names in still other different phonetic ways, according presumably to their pronunciation of that period; analogous to our modern use of the name "English" for the word variously spelt by the Anglo-Saxons *Angel, Angle, Engel, Engle, Engla, Ingle,* and "Britain," which the Anglo-Saxons variously spelt *Bryten, Breten, Breoten, Brittan, Broten,* or *Brytten.*

Thus we find King Barat in his own inscriptions spells his name so as to read variously *Bardi, Bardu, Pardi, Pardu* or *Pirdu;* whilst later Sumerian and Babylonian scribes spelt it variously as *Baratutu, Bardudu, Burudu, Bardu* or *Badu.* And the Indian lists in different independent versions, solar and lunar, obviously owing to these differences in the Sumerian and cuneiform documents which they copied, spell this name variously as *Barata, Brihat, Brihad, Partha* and *Prithu* (see App. I, No. 10). Again "Sargon-the-Great," as his name is written by Semitic scholars, spells his own name in different ways, though never as "Sargon"; but usually as *Gani, Sar-Gani* or *Sir-Gani*, or "King Gani," and later Sumerian and Babylonian scribes spell it in a very great variety of different ways, as we shall see later on.

Comparison of the Kish Chronicle Names with their Indian equivalents

In comparing the orthography of the Sumerian Kings' names of the Kish Chronicle with that of the Early Aryan kings' names preserved in the Indian lists, it is necessary to remember that besides these different phonetic spellings by individual scribes there are also the following important factors which produce different phonetic spellings of the same name:

(*a*) The Kish Chronicle forms of the personal names are written by scribes of a later period who do not always spell the name or title precisely as spelt by the early Sumerians themselves, but according to their own phonetics;

(*b*) the Indian List forms of the names of the Sumerian kings are manifestly taken independently from quite other documentary sources than the Kish Chronicle source, and, as we shall see, form much more complete sources without any gap, such as exists in the Kish Chronicle, and different Sumerian records often exhibit phonetic differences in the spelling of the same names;

(*c*) whilst the Kish Chronicle is written in *syllabic* spelling, the Indian Lists are written in *alphabetic* letters. Thus in the process of reducing the old Sumerian or cuneiform script into alphabetic spelling by single letters—a system invented only about 1200 B.C.[1]—slight variations in the original spelling are inevitable;

(*d*) the Indian Alphabet omits the letter *Z*, a phonetic which is frequently used in Sumerian inscriptions, and in its place uses *J*, a letter which often lapses into *Y* and sometimes exchanges with *S* and *Sh*;[2]

(*e*) and the Indian Lists sometimes *translate* the ancient Sumerian name or title into the Indian Sanskrit or Pali vernacular, for the information of Indians unacquainted with the old Sumerian, giving it the same or similar meaning as it has in the Sumerian —a practice which alters the equation in form sometimes, but not altering the recognizable identity. Thus see for example under the grandson of "Sargon" named *Naram-Enzu* rendered in the Indian Lists as *Karam-Ba*, and the Indian translation of Khammu Rabi's name.

The Indian Forms of the Kings' Names & Titles

Still with all these factors tending to differences in the phonetic spelling and form of proper names in the Sumerian, Babylonian and Indian writing, it is remarkable how well the Indian scribes, with their scrupulous and meticulous care in copying these ancient sacred names in their manuscripts continuously down through the centuries, have preserved the general phonetic forms of the original Sumerian names.

And it is especially noteworthy that the Indian King-Lists of the Aryans preserve substantially the original Sumerian names and titles of the Sumerian kings *much more*

[1] WAOA. 68 f. [2] WAOA. 54 f.

faithfully and more in agreement with the original Sumerian monuments than do the analogous Egyptian papyri and Manetho's versions in regard to the Early Kings of Egypt in comparison with the Egyptian monuments:[1] which versions nevertheless are accepted by Egyptologists and historians as authentic and historical.

The Indian forms of the names and titles of the Early Aryan kings used in this comparison with the Kish Chronicles are taken from the standardized list of their names and titles compiled from the Indian Epic King-Lists in Appendix I.

Kish Chronicle Forms of the Kings' Names and Titles.

This comparison of the Kish Chronicle names of the Sumerian Kings with their independent Indian King-Lists of these same kings discloses the significant fact that the Kish Chronicle uses largely the *titles*, solar or lunar of the Sumerian kings instead of their proper *personal* names—the use of a plurality of titles by the Early Sumerian Kings being common, as we shall see later on, just as the Indian lists also disclose these titles for the Aryan Kings. Thus the Kish Chronicle calls the first king of the First Sumerian Dynasty not by his personal name of Dur, Tur, Daru or In-Dara,[2] but by his solar title of "*Ukusi* of *Ukhu* City" or of "The Sun-Hawk City"—that is *Iksh-Vāku* or "*Iksh*-the-Hawk," the solar title of the first Aryan Kings of the First Aryan Dynasty in the Indian lists. Similarly with the second and fourth kings, the Kish Chronicle does not call them by their personal names but by their lunar titles respectively of *Azag*, with variants *Ama* or *Basam* and *Naksha-Anenuzu*, corresponding to the Indian-list lunar titles for these kings of *Ayus* with variants *Ama Basu* and *Nahusha* and *Anenas*. And we shall find later that the *Nahusha* of the Indian lists is justified by the earlier Sumerian spelling of that name as *Unnusha*, showing that the Indian lists are more authentic in some respects than the Kish Chronicle.

[1] Cp. lists in PHE. 1, 7 f.

[2] See later, and WSAD. 51, 63 f.

Comparison of Kish Chronicle First and Second Dynasties with Indian Lists of Earliest Aryan Kings.

	Kish Chronicle of Sumerian Kings.			*Indian Lists of Earliest Aryan Kings.*	
1st Dyn.	1. UKUSI of UKHU City, 1st king	r. 30 yrs.	=	IKSH-VĀKU, 1st solar king of Aryans.	1.
1st Dyn. and 2nd Dyn.	2. AZAG, AMA, BAKUS or BASAM	r. 12 yrs. at Ukhu	=	AYUS, AMA-BASU or BIKUKSHI, s. of 1.	2.
	1. AZAG, BAKUS or BASAM	r. 64 yrs. at Kish			
2nd Dyn.	2. NAKSHA AN-ENUZU, s. of 1.	r. 25 ,,	=	NAHUSHA, ANENAS, Pur-ANJAYA, s. of 2.	3.
,,	3. The devotee (*Uru*) of Lord Sagaga, s. of 2.	r. 6 ,,	=	UDĀ-VASU, YODHANA, YADU, YAYATI, s. of 3.	4.
,,	4. ZIMUGUN or GINMUGUN,	r. 30 ,,	=	JANAMEJAYA or JINA, or PURU, s. of 4.	5.
,,	5. UZIWITAR, s. of 4,	r. 6 ,,	=	WISHTARA or VISHTARA, s. of 5.	6.
,,	6. MUTIN (Ugun-),	r. 11 ,,	=	MATINĀRA	7.
,,	7. IMUASHSHU,	r. 11 ,,	=	VISHAMSU or TAMSU, s. of 7.	8.
,,	8. NAILĪANA	r. 3 ,,	=	ILINA, ANILA or (?) DUSHYANTA, s. of 8.	9.

Equation of Indian King-Lists of the First Aryan Dynasty with Kish Chronicle First and Second Sumerian Dynasties

In comparing in above table the Sumerian King-Lists of the First and Second Sumerian Dynasties of the Kish Chronicle down to the Great Gap of that chronicle alongside the Aryan First and succeeding Dynasties of the Early Aryan kings from the Indian lists, I have adopted the Indian King-List on the right-hand side of the table as the standard for the main-line succession. For we shall find that the "Second Dynasty" of the Kish Chronicle *overlapped and was contemporary with the First Dynasty* of that chronicle, after the first king of the latter, as disclosed by the Indian lists; and this is fully confirmed by the mass of Sumerian evidence cited presently.

The first king of the "Second Dynasty" of the Kish Chronicle is seen to be identical in name with the second king of the First Dynasty of that chronicle.

The numbers placed on the Indian side of the table are the actual succession numbers in the Indian lists from the first Aryan king downwards. Whilst the numbers placed on the Kish Chronicle side are the succession numbers for the First and Second Dynasties of that chronicle. In the table *s.* = "son."

Identity of Sumerian 1st & 2nd Dynasty Kings with Aryan 1st Dynasty Kings demonstrated

This striking equation in the names of the Sumerian kings of the First and Second Sumerian Dynasties of the Kish Chronicle down to its Great Gap with those of the Aryan kings of the First Aryan Dynasty of the Indian lists, with merely slight dialectic phonetic variations in spelling, coupled with the strict agreement in their relative order or chronological succession, and also with agreement in the achievements of the leading kings, as we shall find later on, proves the absolute identity of these earliest Sumerian kings with the earliest kings of the Aryans.

This comparison, moreover, proves the identity of the Sumerians with the Aryans in race and language and tradition.

LOCATION & NAME OF THE FIRST CAPITAL OF THE SUMERIANS AT UKHU CITY

The name and location of the capital of the First King of the Sumerians are of great historical importance, as disclosing the centre from which civilization was spread over the world in "prehistoric" times which now become historical.

The name of the capital of the first king of the First Sumerian Dynasty in the Kish Chronicle is *Ukhu* City, or literally "The Hawk or Eagle City,"[1] wherein the name Ukhu is written by a pictogram of the flying disc or winged Sun above an arm, suggesting a falconer and the Sun-Hawk or Sun-Eagle, which latter is figured on Sumerian seals as the heraldic symbol of this first king after his deification, as it latterly was also with his Greek form as Zeus or Jove, and as it is with his Indian form as Indra. But that city is also called by other names or titles in other Sumerian lists and in Sumerian literature, as we shall see.

That name "Ukhu City" is given in bilingual glossaries the synonyms of *Kieshi* and *Kiissa*,[2] with the Semitic values of *Kēshu, Akshak* and *Upē*. In the latter form it was obviously the Babylonian name for the city of Opis on the Tigris to the north of Babylon, celebrated by Xenophon in the March of the Ten Thousand, hence the capital of this dynasty now disclosed as the First Sumerian Dynasty, has hitherto been placed in Southern Assyria.[3] There is no doubt that a city in this neighbourhood bearing a name written with this Ukhu or Akshak or Upē sign was already in existence in the time of the Sumerian king Bidashnadi ("Eannatum") the seventeenth Sumerian emperor in the main line about 3050 B.C. (see list, p. 104), as he refers to having defeated its king to the north of Kish along with the local king of Maer or Marri far up the Euphrates towards Carchemish. But this is now seen to be obviously a namesake

[1] *Ukhu*, B. 346, Br. 8125, 8130, defined with prefix *Ish* or "Great or Ruling" as "The Wind-Bird," which fittingly described the Eagle or Hawk. Cp. WSAD. 9.

[2] TDC. 61.

[3] It has been conjecturally located by Winckler near Seleucia, below Bagdad, and by Lt.-Col. W. H. Lane (*Babylonian Problems*) much farther north at the junction of the Adhem with the Tigris, about fifty miles above Bagdad.

of the older Ukhu (if indeed it were ever so called, and not merely Upē), just as we shall find there were earlier cities called Ur and Eridu or Urudu in Upper Mesopotamia before the later ones were founded in Lower Mesopotamia.

Location of First Capital of Sumerians, Ukhu City, at Pteria in Cappadocia of Asia Minor

Our new evidence shows that this capital city *Ukhu*, or "Eagle or Hawk City," of the First King of the Sumerian lists stood to the north of Mesopotamia and Carchemish in Asia Minor, which we have seen is physically and naturally a part of Europe, with its people, flora and fauna, and that it was probably at Pteria City of Herodotus, the capital of the White Syrians of Strabo, which is generally identified with the ancient capital of the imperial Hittites at the ruins near the modern Turkish village of Boghaz Koi in the Halys valley in the heart of Cappadocia, on the old trade-route leading from the Mediterranean at Tarsus in Cilicia, and from Mesopotamia, northwards to Sinope port on the Euxine or Black Sea (see Maps I and IV), and the Eagle is frequently found in prehistoric bronzes in Cappadocia (see Pl. IVA).

The name itself for this capital city, "The Eagle or Hawk City," places it outside both Mesopotamia and Southern Assyria, where these sky-soarers are naturally absent. On the other hand, the Indian epic King-Lists in their lunar version of this first Aryan king, who in the solar version bears the name of Iksh-Vāku (that is Ukusi of Ukhu City of this Kish Chronicle), give the name of the land in which his children were born to him by his queen Urv-Ashī as "*Kuru Land*,"[1] which land we have seen was Asia Minor and especially Central and Eastern Asia Minor, including Cappadocia, the home of St George; and it is the natural habitat of the Eagle and Hawk.

An interesting reference to the Eagle as a badge of royalty on the eastern border of this Asia Minor region is

[1] WVP. 4, 8 f. The Indian Chronicle here is expanded by later Brahmans with silly tales transparently founded on false etymologies of the proper names. But the name of his capital as Alakā is significant, as it was the capital of that king under his deified title of Kubera (Sumerian Kubabbar, a title of the solar god), the God of Wealth and Produce, and placed on Mt. Meru or Su-Meru, the Olympus of the Hindus.

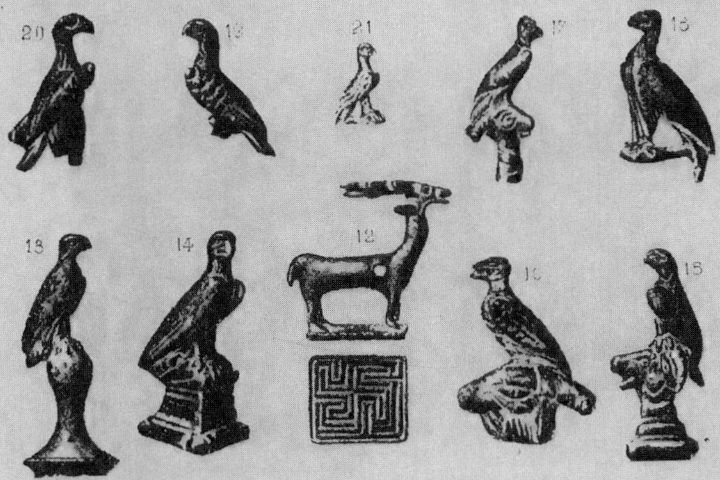

HAWKS & EAGLES, IN BRONZE, OF PREHISTORIC AGE, FROM CAPPADOCIA.

From Boghaz Koi and Cæsarea (after Chantre, CMC. Pl. XXVI). Note also the Goat symbol and the Swastika Sun-Cross in bronze.

LION-GATE OF HITTITE CAPITAL AT BOGHAZ KOI (PTERIA).

(After O. Puchstein, *Boghaz Koi Bauwerk*, Taf. 23.) Note lions of the type in Pl. I, and for inner view, see Pl. IVB.

LIONS ON PREHISTORIC ROCK-CUT TOMB IN PHRYGIA.

Near Ayazin, S.W. of Midas' Tomb (after Hogarth) as at Lion-gate in Mycenæ. Note the shaggy lions, about 40 ft. high, of same type as in Pl. I.

PLATE IVB.

LION-GATE OF OLD HITTITE CAPITAL AT BOGHAZ KOI (PTERIA).
Inner view showing Gothoid arch. (After Puchstein, *op. cit.*)

made by the famous Venetian traveller and geographer Ser Marco Polo, the genuineness of whose records has been established by scientists in most of their details. In his travels through the old province or state of Georgia on the western flank of the Caucasus he says as follows: "In Georgiana there is a king called David Melic, which is as much as to say 'David King.' He is subject to the Tartar. In old times all the kings were born with *the figure of an Eagle upon the right shoulder*."[1] He goes on to say, "The people are very handsome, capital archers and most valiant soldiers." And as regards the Hawk, which we have seen is also a meaning of Ukhu, he adds, "This country produces the best goshawks in the world, which are called Avigi. It has indeed no lack of anything, and the people live by trade and handicrafts." And the editor notes that the goshawks which are much used in Persia still come largely from this region of the Caucasus.[2]

The Eagle significantly is figured in the ancient Hittite sculptures at Boghaz Koi (see Fig. 3), and also at the neighbouring ancient Hittite city at Eyuk to the north on the old trade-road in spread-eagle form with two heads. But it is figured in single-headed and lion-headed form at the sea-port city of Lagash on the Persian Gulf by the Sumerian emperor Uruash about 3100 B.C.[3]; and as an attendant on their deified first king on Sumerian seals, and on sculptures by the grandson of Uruash, see Fig. p. 122.

"Pteria" Name for First Sumerian Capital

The "Pteria" name and location for this Ukhu City is supported by the Indian Chronicles, which give the name for the city occupied by the first Aryan king under his lunar title as *Prati*-shthana or "*Prati*-place,"[5] wherein *Prati* seems the equivalent of "Pteria," and we have seen that the land in which his children were born was Kuru Land or Asia Minor.

This "Pteria" name and location for him is also supported

[1] YMP. 1.50 f. [2] *Ib.*, 57. [3] *Déc.*, pl.31, *bis*, No. 1. [4] WISD. 41.
[5] WVP. 3, 237. The affix *Sthāna* in Sanskrit = "place," "abode," MWD. 1263; and is a country appellation still in Asia Minor, etc., as "Kurdi-stan," or Land of the Kurds, Albistan, Hindu-stan, etc.

by the Nordic Edda name for the land on which King Thor's capital was built, which is called "*Vidar* Land" (*V*, *B* and *P* being freely interchangeable dialectically and *V* being a late letter.[1] And it was from this territorial title that Thor's son and crown-prince Vidar-the-Asa (or "lord Vidar") took that title. Now this identity is supported by the Sumerian, wherein *Bidarra* was evidently the name of a land also rich in gardens,[2] and it was situated in the mountains, from the references to several valuable mountain-plants growing there and to "Bidarra, the garden on the mountain of cultivation (or abundance or plenty)."[3] Bidarra likewise, as with Vidar in the Eddas, was in Sumerian evidently the name of a lord or king, as a plant is called "The plant of the lord Bidarra the king,"[4] and significantly the word here for "lord" is *Ash*, which I have shown was obviously the Sumerian source of the Eddic title of Asa or "lord" applied to Thor and to his son Vidar. This essential similarity thus equates:

Greek and Phrygian.	Indian.	Sumerian.	Eddic.
Pteria =	*Prati* =	*Bidarra* =	*Vidar*.

The prominent reference to the plant and garden under this Bidarra name, seems significant, especially as in the Sumerian the son of this first Sumerian king is repeatedly called "Lord of Plants"[6] and "The Lord Digger of the Earth"[7] and in the Eddas Vidar is the leader of the husbandmen of his father King Thor. And a Sumerian synonym for Bidarra is *Ukush*, in series with Ukhu.

Another Sumerian title for the capital city of the first Sumerian king is given in an old Sumerian king-list, cited hereafter, as *In-an-na Inn-ash-na*,[8] which literally means "The divine Stone House (or *Inn*)"; and in a bilingual glossary where it bears the prefix of "Mountain" and the affix of "City," it is translated in the Semitic as "The Mountain abode of Plenty"[9] Here the "Mountain" prefix is significant as well as its description of "Plenty" from its gardens, etc., and its Sumerian affix of "Stone." For

[1] WAOA. 49 f. [2] M. 8371.
[3] M. 8362 and B. 58; and cp. Br. 10893-4.
[4] M. 8370. [5] WSAD. 19. [6] *Ib.*, 22. [7] *Ib.*, 62.
[8] The double *n* is given by the affix *ni* in Br. 6237.
[9] M. 4441, Shad-Bi-ta-lal.

in the Eddas a frequent title for King Thor's capital is *Inn-Stane* or "The Stone (built) House or *Inn*," which is in agreement again with this Sumerian title for his capital.

Further Evidence locating Site of First Capital at Pteria in Cappadocia

Further striking confirmation for the location of this mountain capital of the first king of the First Sumerian Dynasty in Cappadocia in the direction of Pteria is found in the Eddas—those Nordic epics which prove to be, not as hitherto imagined mere fantastic bardic tales of gods and goblins, but reflections of genuine historical tradition on the family of the First Aryan Dynasty by King Thor, as is fully demonstrated in my forthcoming literal translation and reconstruction of these ancient Nordic epics.

In the Eddas Thor's capital is described as located above the hot plains of *Ginung Gap* or "The Gape or Gulf of *Ginung*," which name is now seen to preserve the old Sumerian name of *Gi-in-gin* or *Kan-in-gi* [1] for the plains of Mesopotamia, which viewed from the hills, especially in the flood season must have seemed to the hillmen as a wide gulf or "Gap." Thor's mountain kingdom was separated from the torrid plains—which were peopled by a dark race that raided his land—by a great river which bounded his eastern frontier called the *Vimur* which was fordable at certain seasons. This river is now disclosed to be the Euphrates, which in the Greco-Roman period still bore in its main upper course the name of *Omiras*, of which Vimur or Wimur is seen to be evidently a variant; and the present-day Turkish name for the Euphrates as *Murad* is possibly a variant of the same ancient name.

The chief fort of these enemy plains people of Ginung was situated lower down that river where the latter formed the great "pool" and became thenceforth unfordable. It was called *Gymis garda* or "Gymis garden" and also *Jœro-velli*, which identify it with *Gar-Gamish* or "Fort Gamish," the "Carchemish" of the Hebrews, the *Iero-polis* of the Greco-

[1] On *Gi* or *Kan*, see Br. 9617, 9623; on *in* Br. 2808; and the third syllable has the phonetic values of both *gi* and *gin*. This name has also been read *Ki-en-gin*.

Romans and the *Jerablus* of the modern Arabs. Besides the equation of the names and its geographical position, the topography of Carchemish is also in agreement with the Eddic descriptions, and it is situated on the deep water channel of the Euphrates below the last ford, in what is now called the plains of Upper Syria but which are really within Mesopotamia. And King Thor, in his expeditions against this fort of those hostile Ginung people, from his mountain capital at Vidar had to descend through wooded ravines,

FIG. 16.—First Sumerian King Dar (or Thor or St George) as First Crusader. (From a seal-cylinder, probably about 2000 B.C., after Ward, No. 1071.

Note the king bearded and in Scythic or Gothic dress is taking up Sun-Cross standard of "Celtic" type with Eagle in front, and his eponymous He-Goat antelope (Dar) prancing before him.[1]

according to the remarkably detailed traditional and circumstantial accounts preserved in the Nordic Eddas of the Goths, for several days and cross mountain torrents, and at one season on those expeditions he crossed one of them by "a snowbridge," such as might be met with in crossing the Taurus. And significantly *he carried as his banner the Sun-Cross surmounted or attended by an Eagle,* as seen in the early seal-cylinder in Fig. 16, in which the remarkably artistic and naturalistic drawing and technical skill in engraving will be appreciated when it is remembered that the picture is cut on the hardest stone and within a space of little more than a square inch.

Altogether the mass of cumulative evidence locates this

[1] The details of this crusading scene from Sumerian sources are given in my new translation of the Eddas.

PHRYGIAN & UR ABORIGINES IN INTERNECINE COMBAT BEFORE TAMED (CIVILIZED) BY KING DUR.

Reverse of ivory handle in Pl. I (after M. Bénédite), 3/4. Note the men are naked, save a loin girdle; the armed men are mostly crop-haired, and the unarmed long-haired. The upper boats are straight-bodied, high-prowed and sterned like Mediterranean ships, whilst the lower have curved bodies like river-boats. Both have a goat's head on their prow, or inside it, suggesting that they are Gothic.

Ukhu City or " Eagle City," the capital of the first king of the First Dynasty of the Sumerians in the Kish Chronicle in the heart of Cappadocia in Kur Land and presumably at Pteria, the old capital of the later Hittites or White Syrians. That no inscriptions in Sumerian writing have yet been found there is probably because the excavations there hitherto have been mainly confined to the relatively later fort and two palaces, the oldest of which dates only from King Khantilis about 2000 B.C., who built about that period the existing fortifications of cyclopean stone walls adorned in places with many fine sculptures: and it is noteworthy that the " King's Gate " there has a massive arch of Gothoid type. The ancient Hittite sculptures in the vicinity of Boghaz Koi, however, at the Iasili rock chambers (see Fig. 3 for part of one panel) are very much older, and represent in that scene as I find from their Hittite hieroglyphs (which Assyriologists have failed to decipher) this first King Thor in a religious procession which is literally described in the Nordic Eddas. But the publication of the details of the decipherment of these and the other Hittite hieroglyph inscriptions requires a volume to themselves.

The site of Pteria, as located at Boghaz Koi in a ravine of great natural strength on the eastern side of the valley of the Halys River, occupied the unique strategical imperial position of standing on the great land-bridge connecting and commanding the convergent ancient overland trade-routes between the three continents of Europe, Asia and Africa (through Syrio-Palestine and Egypt). And it is highly significant that the New Turkish Empire, the modern successors to the imperial Hittites in this area, and whose language exhibits several affinities with the Sumerian, has selected as its imperial capital Angora, which similarly stands in a corresponding position on the other or western side of the Halys Valley and on the same ancient Hittite trade-road and in the same latitude as Boghaz Koi; thus attesting its natural suitability for administration and commercial purposes, and it was similarly selected by the Romans for their provincial government. And to the south-west of Angora also are archaic rock-sculptures of the Hittites.

The selection, therefore, of this Cappadocian site for his capital by the first Sumerian king, Ukusi of the Kish Chronicle, otherwise surnamed in other following Sumerian lists *Dur* or *Tur*, *i.e.* the first Gothic king *Thor*, attests his wise statesmanship and generalship. For it afforded him a unique centre for dominating and controlling the primitive aboriginal tribes throughout Asia Minor in his struggle for the establishment there of the Aryan Civilization with its agriculture, industries, and well-ordered government, and for hammering the wild tribes into shape by "the hammer of Thor," and welding the regenerates into a civilized nation. The land from whence he and his civilized Sumerians came is indicated as the Old Gothic land of south-west Europe.

We are now in a position to begin the detailed comparison of the names of the individual kings of the First Dynasty of the Kish Chronicle and their achievements with those of the kings of the First Dynasty of the Early Aryans in the Indian lists and chronicles.

First Sumerian King "Ukusi of Ukhu" as First Aryan King Iksh-Vāku of about 3378 to 3350 B.C.

The earliest and presumably contemporary representation of the portrait of this first Sumerian king in Gothic dress is seen in a scene in Frontispiece, described in the Eddas.

Our comparative table on p. 69 demonstrates that the first Sumerian king of the First Sumerian Dynasty in the Kish Chronicle under his solar title, namely, "*Ukusi of Ukhu City*" (or of "The Eagle or Sun-Hawk City"), is identical with the first Aryan king of the First Dynasty of the Early Aryans in the Indian Lists and Chronicles under his solar title of *Iksh-Vāku*.

Interesting confirmation of his identity under this title of Ukusi associated with the Sun Hawk is found in the bilingual Sumerian and Babylonian glossary tablets. In these under his later deified form as the Father god, Bel of the Babylonians, he is called in Sumerian "The Hawk Lord *Ukuzu'i*," and is defined as "The Lord (or god) *Sakh* (or *Zax*), called the Judge of the Mass of the People."[1] And we shall see in next chapter that *Sakh* or *Zax* is one of his most common

[1] Br. 2051.

titles in the Sumerian and in the Aryan languages generally and has the variant synonyms of *Dur* or *Tur*, and *Bur* or *Pur*. This Ukusi title is also variantly spelt in Sumerian literature as *Ugu*.[1] We thus get the equation for this solar hawk title for him as:

Kish Chronicle	Sumerian Literature	Indian Solar Lists
Ukusi or *Ukuzi* =	*Ukuzu'i*[2] or *Ugu* = or *Sakh* or *Dur* or *Dar*[3] or *Pur*[4]	*Iksh-Vāku* (*Purū*-of-the-Sun in Lunar lists with variant *Indra* [Sakko])

First King's Personal Name & his "Indar" Title

His personal name in Sumerian, as differentiated from his titles, as I have shown in the former volumes and as we shall further find in these pages, was *Dar*, *Dur* or *Tur*; or with the prefix of "King" or "Lord" (*In* or *Ash* or *An*), it was *In-Dar*, *In-Duru* or *In-Dur*, *i.e.* "King Dar, King Dur or Tur." And it was also shown that he was the historical human original not only of the later Sumerian god bearing those names, but also of the god *Indra* of the Indo-Aryans, *Indara* of the Hittites and Mitani or Early Medes, and of *Thor* or *Her-Thor* the first traditional king of the Goths in the Nordic epics, the Eddas (wherein he is also called *Eindri* and *Andvara*, now seen to be dialectic spelling of *Indara*); and that he was the original King *Ar-Thur* of the Grail Legend, of which latter we find further and concrete contemporary proof in the next chapter.

"Indra" is not a name directly applied to this first human king in the Indian King-Lists and Chronicles nor in the Vedas, as both of these classes of literature were compiled in their present form long after the deification of this king under the name of Indra with the reservation of that name solely for that father-god. But a confused memory of the original identity of Indra with the first human Aryan king survives in Vedic literature under his lunar title of *Purū*-of-the-Sun (Purū-Ravas), and we have seen above that *Pur* was a Sumerian synonym for his king *Dur* title. This very early Vedic commentary, which is nearly as old as the present

[1] Br. 2870. [2] Br. 2051. [3] Br. 2948 and 11319.
[4] Br. 11318, synonym of *Dur*.

Vedic text itself, makes the god Indra to be "jealous of his (the first Aryan king's) cohabitation in wedlock with her (the queen of this first Aryan king) *as if he* (*the first Aryan king*) *were* INDRA."[1]

HIS HISTORY UNDER HIS SOLAR TITLE IN INDIAN CHRONICLES & THE VEDAS

His fuller history as regards his introduction and establishment of civilization, and his welding of the primitive tribes into civilized nations, are elicited under his personal name and lunar titles in the Sumerian, Babylonian, and Indian texts in the following chapters. But here it is desirable to cite some of the brief references to him under his solar title of Iksh-Vāku preserved in the Indian chronicles and Vedic hymns.

The Indian Chronicles record respecting him under his solar title that:

> "Iksh-Vāku was born from . . . Manu, the Sun-born[2] . . . He had a hundred sons (or descendants), of whom the eldest were Bikukshi-Nimi and Danda. Fifty of these, Sākuni [" Sargon "][3] and others were the protectors of the northern countries. Forty-eight were the princes of the south."[4]

The special record here that "Sargon-the-Great," the famous world-monarch was a direct descendant of the first Aryan (or Sumerian) king is of immense historical significance as we will see later on, he records it himself.

In the Indian Vedic hymns this first king is several times referred to under his solar title as the founder of a family of illustrious kings; and in the following hymn he is made not only a votary of Indra (that is his later deified self), but appears to be made after his death a ministering angel of Indra *in Heaven* "dazzling bright," that is in a solar celestial paradise, in company with other members of the blessed dead of the Five Tribes of the Aryans. This reference to the paradise of the blessed dead of the Aryans being in

[1] *Brihad-devata*, ed. A. Macdonell, 2, 290.

[2] *Manu Vaivasvati*, WVP. 3, 15, 231 f. It is significant that *Man* in Sumerian = "The Sun," cp. WPOB. 342.

[3] On the identity of Sākuni with "Sargon," see Chap. XIII.

[4] WVP. 3, 259.

Heaven and in the Light is noteworthy as it is diametrically opposed to the devil-infested underground afterworld of the Greeks and Romans (through their having adopted largely the mythology of the aboriginal Earth Mother-Goddess with its subterranean cult) and the paradise of the Osirian Egyptians and of the Jews, which was not celestial at all, but was in the dark subterranean world of Hades or Hell.[1] That Vedic hymn to Indra sings:

"Him (Indra) in whose service flourishes Iksh-Vāku, rich and dazzling bright,
As [others of ?] the Five (Aryan) Tribes that are in Heaven!
Indra! Support the princely power of Ratha-Proshthas, match'd by none,
Even as the Sun for all to see."[2]

In the Atharva Veda this king is represented as a sage of remote antiquity who knew the virtues of the "all healing" Costus shrub, the medicinal species of which was obtained significantly from "the snowy mountains." In celebrating this famous Costus drug that Veda sings:—

"Thou (Costus)[3] whom Iksh-Vāku of old knew . . . thou all-healing."[4]

Second Sumerian King Azag or Bakus as Second Aryan King Āyus-Bikuksi. *Disclosing the human historical original of Bacchus & his Date, about* 3348 B.C.

Similarly regarding the second king, from our comparative table on p. 69 it is seen that the second king of the First Dynasty of the Kish Chronicle *Azag* is identical with *Ayus* the second king of the First Dynasty of the Early Aryans —the Indian alphabet having no *z* spells this sound by *y* and the soft *g* by *s*. And this identity is not confined to that solar title of this king, but also extends to all the other three variant titles of this king in the Kish Chronicle, all

1 The name "Hell" is obviously from the Sumer *Hal*="imprisonment, lamentation, distress," Br. 10978, MD. 383; and as "Serpent, evil demon spirit," Br 10979, MD. 1078. The Chaldeans called it *Aralu*, with seven evil spirits M.D. 101.

2 RV. 10, 60, 4-5.

3 *Costus speciosus*, in Skt. *Kūshtha*.

4 *Atharva Veda*, 19, 39, 9.

of which are reproduced in the Indian version of that second king's titles, as seen in the following equation:

Kish Chronicle.		*Indian Lists.*
Azag or	=	Ayus or
Ama Basam or	=	Ama Basu (or Vasu) or
Bakus	=	Bikukshi

He is recorded in the Indian lists to be the son as well as the successor of the first king, and in Sumerian and Babylonian literature as well as in the contemporary inscription in next chapter he is similarly cited under one of his other titles. And his achievements are celebrated in considerable detail in both Sumerian and Indian epic literature, as we shall see later on.

This second Sumerian king (whose archaic portrait we have seen in Fig. 6, p. 14 and Pl. VI) proves to have been nearly as famous an historical figure as his transcendent father. He was a great warrior and formed a great empire, and extended the establishment of the Aryan civilization over a wider area; and especially he systematically developed and extended Agriculture and was the traditional inventor of the Plough, for which services to mankind he was afterwards deified by the grateful ancients under his Sumerian title of *Bakus* or "Bacchus," whose *Iakchos* Greek title is in series with his Sumerian Azag and Aka titles and his Indian Ayus title.[1] He was also frequently styled by the Sumerians as already seen *Tasia*,[2] and is *Tash*-of-the-Plough (*Tash-ub*) of the Hittites[3] *Resef* the Corn-god and warrior of the Egyptians[4], and *Tascio* the Corn-Spirit of the Ancient Britons, and his name with fine representations adorn thousands of the Early Briton coins of pre-Roman Britain as we have seen;[5] and his name I have also demonstrated is widely invoked for Resurrection from the Dead on the prehistoric tomb monuments of Ancient Britain,[6] as it was also so invoked as I showed amongst the Sumerians and Babylonians[7] and Trojans.[8] His function of solar Arch-

[1] See WSAD. 7.
[2] WPOB. 243 f., and many details in present work.
[3] *Ib.*, 261, 338 f. [4] *Ib.*, 339 f.; 350 f.
[5] WPOB. 335 f., with very numerous illustrations.
[6] *Ib.*, 243 f. [7] *Ib.*, 255 f. [8] *Ib.*, 254 f.

SECOND ARYAN KING BAKUS (BACCHUS), MUKHLA (MICHAEL), TASIA (TASCIA), OR GIN (CAIN), FOUNDER OF ENOCH CITY.

From gigantic rock-sculpture at Ivriz in Cappadocia, of about 2700 B.C. (after von Luschan, *loc. cit.*). See Fig. 6 and description, pp. 14 f.

angel of Resurrection arose presumably from his association with the renewal of vegetation life in the Agricultural Era which he so widely established for increased food supply.

His early evolution as the god Bacchus we have already seen in his representation on the archaic gigantic rock-cut sculpture at Ivriz in the Taurus, on the old road leading to Pteria from the Mediterranean seaport of Tarsus in Cilicia, with inscriptions in Hittite hieroglyphics. Carrying heads of corn and bunches of grapes, this archaic sculpture of the second Sumerian king strikingly discloses the early Hittite sources from which the Greek artists and mythmongers derived their ready-made ideas and models for their representations and functions of Dionysos or Bacchus. This sculpture is also notable as picturing a ploughshare presumably of bolted metal behind him, of which agricultural implement he was the traditional inventor. He was also the first traditional builder of cities in Mesopotamia including Kish and Erech or *Enoch*; and he is in these pages proved to be the historical original of Nimrod of city-building fame, which name is now disclosed to be derived from his Sumerian title of *Nimirrud*—and his *Nimi* title in the solar versions of the Indian king-lists and chronicles.

"Second" Dynasty of Kish Chronicle is a Continuation of & partly Contemporary with the First Dynasty of that Chronicle

It now transpired from our further comparison of the First and Second Dynasties of the Kish Chronicle (see p. 69) with the aid of our Indian key lists, that this King Azag Bakus, the second king of the First Sumerian Dynasty of the Kish Chronicle, *was identical with the first king of the Second Dynasty of that Chronicle*; and also that the fourth king of the First Dynasty (Naksha Ansir) *was identical with the Second king of the Second Dynasty of that chronicle,* who was the son and successor of King Azag Bakus; whilst the third king of the First Dynasty, namely, *Tantan* was *Danda* of the Indian lists, the younger brother of the second king.[1]

This clearly showed that the so-called "Second" Dynasty of the Kish Chronicle was a continuation of and partly

[1] Cp. *Danda*, WVP. 3, 259.

contemporary with the First Dynasty of that chronicle; and that the "Second" Dynasty was merely a change of capital by the second king of the First Dynasty in the thirteenth year of his reign, by which he transferred his capital from Ukhu City in Cappadocia (see map) to Kish City which he built in the plains of Mesopotamia which he had conquered and annexed to his empire; and that he was succeeded at Ukhu by his younger brother Tantan, who after a short reign of six years (the Indian Chronicles record that he was killed by a hostile chief [1]) was succeeded by his nephew, the son of Azag who afterwards succeeded the latter on the imperial throne at Kish as second emperor of the so-called "Second" Dynasty. This discovery was then fully confirmed by the official Indian king-lists of the imperial line, which omit altogether from their main line-lists the local kings of the First Dynasty of the Kish Chronicle after the second king Azag Bakus (though recording that Danda was early slain by a hostile chief), and go on with the second king of the Second Dynasty of the Kish Chronicle followed by the others of that "Second" Dynasty in strict agreement in name and chronological order in both lists, Sumerian and Indian, see Table, p. 69. And this continuity of the First Dynasty of the Kish Chronicle with the "Second" Dynasty of that chronicle was fully confirmed by the later discovery of older Sumerian king-lists than the Kish Chronicle, in which the kings of the First Dynasty of that chronicle after the second king are entirely omitted, and their king-lists are identical with the Indian key lists (see Chap. VIII.).

Conquest & Annexation of Mesopotamia by Azag Bakus second King of First Sumerian Dynasty about 3335 B.C.

It is thus disclosed that the second king of the First Sumerian Dynasty, the mighty civilizing, agricultural and

[1] The younger son of the First King Ikshvāku, named Danda, was killed by Sudyumna, otherwise called Idā or Ilā, who was a hermaphrodite, WVO. 3, 234 f. This double sex appears to be a confused memory of his being the devotee of the hostile cult of the Mother-goddess, Idā or Ilā. And he appears to be the aboriginal *Śutu* enemy of King Dur or Adar of the Babylonian legend of *Adamu* and *Shutu*, see later.

warrior king Azag Bakus[1] in the thirteenth year of his reign at Ukhu in Cappadocia, conquered and annexed Mesopotamia, and transferred his imperial capital in his thirteenth year to Kish on the Euphrates, which city we are told in the Kish Chronicle he founded and built, which is confirmed by other Sumerian records. There at Kish City, according to that chronicle, he reigned sixty-four years, making a total reign with his twelve years at Ukhu of seventy-six years ; and such a long reign is in keeping with the tradition of his manifold achievements, great empire and the number of cities which he founded, as seen later on. And it is also in agreement with his title of Ayus in the Indian records, which means " The aged," to which word the later Indian scribes obviously equated his name from the universal traditions of his exceptionally long life. This would also explain at last circumstantially the tradition cited by Strabo that the god Bacchus built a bridge over the Euphrates.

This discovery now led to our even more fundamentally important historical discovery of the epoch-making Advent of the " Sumerians " into Mesopotamia and its Date.

The Advent of the " Sumerians " into Mesopotamia & its Date about 3335 B.C.

There now emerged the great fundamental historical discovery that this invasion and annexation of Mesopotamia by the second Aryan king of the First Aryan Dynasty, from his capital at Ukhu or Pteria in Cappadocia, was the epoch-making " Advent of the Sumerians " into Mesopotamia, and there was also disclosed its hitherto wholly unknown date. That date is now exactly fixed by our new evidence at about 3335 B.C., with only a very few years possible variation one way or other.

This discovery of the fixed datum point for the advent of the " Sumerians " into Mesopotamia, it will be seen, revolutionizes all the extravagantly conjectural chronology hitherto

[1] Assyriologists universally, the one mechanically repeating the other, read the name of this mighty Sumerian warrior king as *Bau*, a Semitic Chaldee title of the Mother-goddess, and *make him to be a woman and " a emale wine-seller !* " from his title as " Libator of Ale."

current amongst Assyriologists in regard to ancient Mesopotamia and its civilization, and its repercussions revolutionize all the early chronologies of the other later civilizations of Ancient Egypt, Crete, Ancient Europe and Indo-Persia.

First to Eighth Sumerian Kings of Second Dynasty of Kish Chronicle identical in Sumerian & Indian Lists

Continuing our comparison of the Kish Chronicle lists of the Second Dynasty kings with our Indian lists of the Early Aryan kings, we find that all the kings from the second king of that Dynasty onwards to and inclusive of the eighth king of that dynasty *are identical in name and in exact chronological order* with those of the official Indian king-lists of the Early Aryans (see table p. 69). This again further establishes the identity in race and tradition of the Sumerians and Early Aryans.

But with the eighth king of this Second Dynasty of the Kish Chronicle the list of the kings of that dynasty suddenly ends in that chronicle leaving a great gap of 430 years, for which the names of the kings were obviously lost to the compilers of that Kish Chronicle.

The Great Gap of 430 Years with 27 Kings in the Second Dynasty of Kish Chronicle is completely Filled up by the Official Indian Lists of the Early Aryan Kings

Scrutiny of the Kish Chronicle king and dynastic lists disclosed the hitherto unnoticed fact that the Second or so-called Kish Dynasty (so named because its imperial capital was mainly at Kish City) contained a Great Gap of 430 years. This was evidenced by the total reign of that dynasty being recorded therein as 586 years, whereas the reigns of its first eight kings who are alone cited total only 156 years, thus leaving 430 years wholly unaccounted for; and the Kish Chronicle then passes on without any explanation to the very much later king who immediately preceded Sargon-the-Great. This shows that the list of the kings of the Great Gap had been lost to the compilers of the Kish Chronicle.

Comparison then with our official Indian king-lists of the Early Aryans (App. I.) disclosed that the latter contained no fewer than 27 kings intervening between the last of the 8 kings of the Kish Chronicle above cited (who is No. 9 on the list of Aryan kings of the main line) and the name of Sargon-the-Great (who is No. 37 on the main line Aryan list). This indicated that *the lost kings of the Great Gap of the Kish Chronicle were preserved in the Indian lists*, and that they numbered 27 (or 28); and these reigning for the total period of 430 years of the gap gave an average reign for each king of about 16 years, which was quite a fair average reign when compared with the other dynasties of that chronicle. And the fact of the existence of this Great Gap in the Kish Chronicle, along with the absolute authenticity of the Indian lists in their preservation of the missing kings of that gap and in their exact chronological order, was subsequently confirmed and established by the discovery announced in these pages of other Sumerian king-lists older than the Kish Chronicle which gave the full lists of the kings of this Great Gap which had been lost to the compilers of the Kish Chronicle but which were preserved in full detail and in their exact chronological order in the Indian lists of the kings of the Early Aryans.

Before proceeding to compare in detail the Sumerian accounts of the personalities and achievements of the kings anterior to the Great Gap of the Kish Chronicle with the accounts of the same kings preserved in the Indian chronicles and to some extent in the Vedas, it is desirable now for us to examine the positive and contemporary proof for the identity of the first four Sumerian kings with the first four Aryan kings, which I have discovered in the genealogy recorded by the fourth king himself, King Udu, upon the votive Stone-Bowl of his great-grandfather, the first king of the Aryans or Sumerians, which Bowl is disclosed to be the historical original of the long-lost " Holy Grail " of King Arthur (or Ar-Thur, Her-Thor or King Thor), and its inscription is the oldest known historical Sumerian inscription, and the oldest known historical inscription in the world.

V

Udu's Stone-Bowl ("Holy Grail") Contemporary Genealogy of First Sumerian Dynasty in Agreement with Indian Lists, Kish Chronicle & Nordic Eddas

Disclosing Original "Holy Grail" of King Ar-Thur, the Magic "Cauldron" of Thor, and the oldest known Historical Inscription in the World.

THE identity of the first four Aryan kings of the Indian lists with the first four Sumerian kings of the main line in the Kish Chronicle is now strikingly confirmed by *the actual contemporary record of the genealogy of those kings*, which I find is inscribed on the war-trophy sacred Stone-Bowl of the first Aryan or "Sumerian" king by the fourth king of that main line who was the great-grandson of the first king himself. The genealogy here recorded is not only in agreement with the Kish Chronicle, but is confirmed by the older Sumerian King-Lists (see table opposite p. 140) and by the Indian lists and the Nordic Eddas.

King Udu's Stone-Bowl as "The Stone Cauldron of Thor" & "The Holy Grail" of the historical King Ar-Thur

This sacred trophy Stone-Bowl of the first Sumerian king Ukusi or Dur (or Tur) is inscribed and dedicated to the latter by his great-grandson King Udu of Kish City, the fourth imperial king of the First Aryan Dynasty. And it is now disclosed as the actual material original of the famous vanished "Holy Grail" of King Ar-Thur, and the famous war trophy magical stone-bowl or "cauldron" captured from the weirds at the Well of Urd (Urudu) by Her-Thor as detailed in the Nordic Eddas. It was unearthed in a fragmentary condition, but with its inscription practically intact, by the Pennsylvanian University expedition from deep down below the foundations of the central tower of the oldest Sun-temple in Mesopotamia at Nippur, on the old channel of the Euphrates south-west of Babylon (see map), where it had been deposited by this fourth king and great-grandson of King Dur, Thor, or Ar-Thur about 3245 B.C., at a spot which has been personally inspected by me. And this fragment of this famous magic bowl bearing that inscription is now in my possession.

Pre-history of the Magic Stone-Bowl of King Dar, Dur or Sagg, King Her-Thor or Ar-Thur with King Udu's Inscription

This famous magical Stone-Bowl of King Dar or Dur or Sagg or Sakh, the large fragment of which was inscribed by his great-grandson King Udu of Kish with the genealogy of the latter back to that first king and deposited by him beneath the central tower of the oldest Sun-temple in Mesopotamia at Nippur, is frequently referred to in early Sumerian sacred literature as one of the most celebrated war-trophies captured by that first king. And significantly it is specially associated therein with the first Sumerian king under his *Sakh* title (earlier *Sagg*) as written on this Bowl, that is the *Sig* title of Thor in the Nordic Eddas. Thus the first Sumerian king under his Sakh title in the bilingual Sumerian and Babylonian glossaries (wherein *Sakh* is shown to be an equivalent of Sagg or Sa-ga-ga and of *Adar* of the later Babylonians [1]) is called "The Lord (or King) Sakh, Ugu the king of the Precious Stone, the Hidden Vessel of Kish Land, the King of that Hidden (or Disappeared) Vessel." [2] And it is also called "The Serpent-Stone-vessel" see below.

This Bowl is disclosed by our new evidence to have been the central fetish magical stone-bowl of the aboriginal Chaldean Serpent-worshippers. They violently opposed the establishment of King Dur or Sagg's Civilization with its

[1] *Adar* we shall find is a Babylonian form of In-dar; but it is also found as a form of one of Thor's titles in the Nordic Eddas.

[2] Br. 2870. *U-gu shar-ri u-shu u-shu-u Kish-mad sharru shu.* On the *gu* value in U-gu, see SS. 244 and Br. 6103. The last *shu* sign means "hidden (Br. 10831) also "broken" (Br. 10838).

bland Sun-worship which destroyed the immemorial debasing superstitions of those Serpent and Lion worshippers, with their animal and human sacrifices of devil-worship and their swarms of wizards and weirds of that Mother-Son cult who battened on and terrorized the people, yet the latter nevertheless implicitly believed their sorceries as the Serpent and Lion were the totems of their tribes.

The capture of this central fetish bowl of that Serpent-Lion cult is thus celebrated in a Babylonian copy of a fine old Sumerian hymn; wherein the later Babylonians have made *Adar* the son of King Sakh instead of himself.[1]

> "The tooth of the Lion, and the mighty Serpent of Ilu, thou (Adar) removest, making (them) to turn away from the land.
> Adar, the king, the son of the god King Sakh, has caused (? them) to turn unto (? themselves).
> He is the warrior whose lasso overthrows the foe.
> O Adar! the fear of thy shadow inclines towards the world.
> He assembles his people in strength to invade the hostile land.
> Adar the Warrior who knows not fear (has driven away) the pest.
> The strong *Darru* before whom the foe exists not,
> Adar, manly exalter, who makes joyful his side,
> Has driven the chariot over the mountain, has scattered wide the seed.
> (Men) altogether have proclaimed his name for sovereignty over them.
> In their midst like a great wild bull has he lifted up his horns.
> The *Shū* (Vessel) Stone, the precious [stone of the Chaldees], the strong stone, the Serpent-Stone (of) the mountain-stone,
> That Warrior—the Fire-Stone [Cauldron] too—the Hero has carried (off) to the city."[2]

[1] *Ibid.*

[2] SHL. 479 f. In l. 1 *Labi*="Lion." In l. 2 for *Mul-lil*, a "reading long given up" is given its literal reading of In-Sakh or "King Sakh."

The Nordic Eddas also celebrate repeatedly the capture of this Stone-Bowl by King Thor, who also bears therein the title of *Adar* and *Sig* "The Victorious" (*i.e.* a dialectic form of the Sumerian *Sagg* or *Sakh* as seen below); and significantly he also bears therein the prefixed title of *Asa* "Lord or king," just as Sagg in this Bowl bears the prefix of *Ash* "lord or king." The Eddas relate that Thor, in a punitive expedition against the raiding *Gald* (=Kaldu or "Chaldee") people of the plains of Ginung (Mesopotamia), carried off from the weirds at the Well of Urd at Jöro-velli (which we have seen was Carchemish on the Upper Euphrates), their most treasured magical Stone-Bowl or "Cauldron," which was the central fetish of their Serpent cult.

The Eddas further relate how after its capture King Thor[1] or Sig consecrated this "Life-giving" Stone-Bowl as a sacred vessel in his own Sun-cult.[2] The disappearance of this "Holy Grail" of Her-Thor and the futility of its quest, except in visions, is now accounted for by its having been so deeply buried by his great-grandson Udu or Utu (? Otto) over fifty-one centuries ago down beneath the foundations of the oldest Sun-temple in Mesopotamia, until it was unearthed a few decades ago.

This identity in the Nordic or Gothic tradition with the Sumerian, forms still another of the many striking proofs of the identity of the Early Sumerians with the Early Goths or Nordics, who were the ancestors of the Anglo-Saxons, Norse, Swedes and Britons. And it is significant that amongst the modern descendants of the latter Nordics, the traditional memory of this famous historical incident of about fifty-three centuries ago has still survived; though the Ar-Thur versions of this "pagan" event have been modernized by later bards embellishing them as well as King Ar-Thur himself with Christian embroidery.

1 "Thor" is a late spelling for *Dūr* or *Dur*, which latter occurs as another spelling for "Thor" in the Eddas, and see on *Th*, and *o* for *u* in WAOA. 28 f., 48 f.

2 For full details, see my new literal translation of The Eddas.

Inscription on the Stone-Bowl by King Udu

The inscription on this Stone-Bowl of King Dar or Dur is the earliest of all known historical Sumerian inscriptions, and thus the earliest known historical inscription in the world. But its unique historical importance consists in its inscription being written by the great-grandson of the first "Sumerian" king, the founder of Civilization, and in its recording at first hand his own genealogy in full, back to that first Sumerian Aryan king.

The inscriber and dedicator calls himself in his inscription by his personal name *Udu* (or *Utu* or *Uduk*), and he uses the title of "The Priest-King of Kish City." But he is shown in the old Sumerian king-lists (see Table opposite, p. 140) to be the fourth Sumerian king in the imperial line, all of which kings as we shall see were *ex-officio* "priest-kings." In the solar version of the Indian Lists of the main line he, as the fourth imperial king, is called *Udā-Vasu* or "*Udā* of the Vase," a title which is now seen to have designated him as the custodian of this sacred Stone-Bowl. In the lunar version of the Indian lists he is called *Yayāti*, *Yati* or *Yadu* (see Appendix I). In the Kish Chronicle as the fourth king in the imperial line (*i.e.* the third king in the so-called "Second" or Kish Dynasty there), he is not called by his personal name, but is styled "The Devotee of Lord Sagg (Uru Ash-Sa-ga-ga)," wherein as we have seen *Sagg* is one of the favourite old Sumerian titles of King Ukusi or Dur, and is the *Sig* title of Thor in the Eddas, and the *Sakko* title of Indra in the old Indian Pali. And it is significant that that *Sagg* is also the title actually used by King Udu for his great-grandfather in his inscription on this Bowl, thus confirming his identity with "The Devotee of Lord Sagg" in the Kish Chronicle. And it now appears probable that it was this King Udu, the expressed devotee or worshipper of his radiantly illustrious great-grandfather, who first deified the latter as "The god Sagg (Sakh or In-Dur, whose name also reads IA, the source of JAH, or "Father Ju" or Ju-piter or Jove, borrowed by the Hebrews as *Yahve* or "Jehovah"). For the prefixed title *Ash* (or *An*) for "Lord" or "King" tends in this Bowl inscription and hereafter in Sumerian and

Babylonian inscriptions and literature to have the sense of "God" as well as of "Lord." And this now seems to explain for the first time why the later descendants of this deified first Aryan king called themselves "the sons of God," for they were the lineal descendants of that man who was made by the later people the type of the Father God.

Decipherment & Translation of the Bowl-Inscription

This critically important inscription, written in the most archaic linear form of Sumerian script, was first published by Prof. Hilprecht,[1] and has been translated by him and several other Assyriologists,[2] without any knowledge of the significance or identification of its names or of the royal identity of its author or his date. But from the palæography of his writing he is placed by Assyriologists as the earliest known historical high-priest of Kish; and his inscription is generally regarded as the earliest known Sumerian historical inscription. And this is now confirmed by our new evidence.

I here give my revised reading and translation of this inscription, in the light of our Indian and Eddic keys to the personal names and titles, which we shall find are fully confirmed by the old Sumerian king-lists and Sumerian literature. The authority for all my readings, when they differ in any way from the previous ones which were made without any keys, are fully cited from the standard Sumerian lexicons and cannot be gainsaid. The several Sumerian synonym titles given for the name of the first king as Sagg (or Sa-ga-ga), as written on this bowl, while illustrating the plurality of titles borne by the Early Aryan kings, and by the first king in particular, are of immense importance in his establishing his identity in the different king-lists, where he often appears under one or other of these different titles cited in the table over the page, and all of which are given in the bilingual Sumerian and Babylonian glossaries as synonyms of this name as written on this Bowl of Udu.

The inscription written in eight lines, separated by horizontal strokes forming separate compartments, reads as follows: —

1 OBI. pl. 46. Nos. 108-9, and p. 263. 2 Thus TDI. 229.

DECIPHERMENT AND TRANSLATION OF UDU'S BOWL INSCRIPTION

Translation.	Sumerian Text.
l. 1. To King (or Lord) SAGG (or ZAGG)	Ash Sa-[ga-ga][1] (or Za-ga-ga)
(or ,, ,, ,, SAKH	(or In-Sakh.[2]
DAR, DUR or IN-DARA	,, In-Dara (or Dar or Dur).[3]
UDU-DUR or-BUR-PUR	,, -Udu-Dur (or -Bur or -Pur).[4]
GURUSHA-A-DUR or -PUR	,, U-Gurush-a (or -Dur or Bur or -Pur).[5]
GAR	,, Gar.[6]
UKUZU'I	,, Uku-zu-'i.[7]
MID, MIT	,, Mid or Mit.[8]
IDIM	,, Idim.[9]
ETIL	,, Etil.[10]
PIR or BAR	,, Pir or Bar.[11]
ADAR)	,, Adar.[12])
2. UDU (or UTU or UTUK)	U-du (or U-tu or U-tuk-).
3. priest-king or Khatti ruler	Khat (or -Khut-) ti- [sig] (or pa-te-si).[13]
4. of Kish City	Ki[sh-ki].
5. (son of) ENUZUZU (or INZUZU)	Enu-zu-zu (or In-zu-zu).[14]
6. (son of) GIN the established (son),	Gin-zi.[15]
7. (the) KHAMAZI City	Kha-ma-zi-ki.
8. choice broken (Bowl) has deposited.	sag-gaba-du.

[1] All Assyriologists agree that the name here, of which the last two signs are broken off, is the well-known early god-name which reads *Sa-ga-ga* or *Za-ga-ga*, no other early god-name having this initial sign. And as the *ga* sign latterly became the alphabetic *g*, the name was probably pronounced *Sagg* (see WAOA 62). It tended early to become obsolete and was replaced by *Sakh*. The prefixed title *Ash*, literally meaning " King " or " Lord " (Br. 428, 439) was latterly used for " god."

[2] *In-Sakh* or " King *Sakh* " and all its other synonym titles which follow here are given in the bilingual glossaries through the synonym for Sagaga, with *Nin-Dar* or *Nin-Dara*, Br. 11761—the later Babylonians, who wrote these glossaries, having dialectically used *Nin* for the old *In* prefix by the dialectic alteration of " Nunnation " ; just as in modern times Edward becomes *Ned* and Ann becomes *Nan*. On Sagaga=Sakh, Br. 11761, 11096, 2870. *In*=" King or Lord," Br. 2813-16, 10985.

[3] In-Dara, *Dar* or *Dara*, see previous note. On *Dur*, cp. Br. 10475 and 6644, 6661 and 3331.

[4] Br. 11761, 11096, 8820, see note 2. *U*=" King or Lord," especially religious, Br. 8659, 8754. *Udu*, 10673.

[5] Br. 11761, see note 2. *Gurush*, Br. 11096, 6197, meaning " Lord or Supreme Ruler." The affix *A*=*Dur*, Br. 11319 ; also *Bur* and *Pur*, Br. 11818.

[6] *Gar*, Br. 11761, cp. Br. 6236 and 11189.

[7] Br. 2051 and see note 2.

[8] *Mid* or *Mit*, see Br. 2870, 1481, and note 2. [9] *Idim*, *ib.*, Br. 1480.

[10] *Etil*=" Lord," Br. 2870, 1506. Is Thor's clan name in Ædl in Eddas.

This Bowl inscription thus reads:

"To King (or Lord) Sagg (or Zagg, Sakh, Dar, In-Dara or Dur, Udu, Gurusha or Adar), Udu, the priest-king of Kish City, the son of[1] Enuzuzu (or Inzuzu), the son of Gin the established son (of King Sagg), the Khamazi City choice broken (Bowl) has deposited."

Location of Khamazi City where the Bowl was Captured as "Car-chemish"

It has been generally considered by Assyriologists that this broken Stone-Bowl which had been esteemed of such importance as to have this ancient genealogy inscribed on it and termed "precious or choice" and given the chief place of honour in the Sun-cult by being deposited under the foundations of the tower in the oldest Sun-temple in Mesopotamia, must have been a famous war-trophy captured at the city of Khamazi. But where the latter place was situated has hitherto been quite unknown. It is, I now find, undoubtedly "Car-chemish" of the Hebrew Old Testament,

---

11 *Pir* or *Bar*, Br. 11096 and 1722-24.

12 *Adar* is Semitic title for this king in all the foregoing notes Nos. 1-5, see Br. 11096 and 10492. It is presumably founded on his *Udu* title, which may also read *Odo* (see WAOA. 48 f.), which as well as *Adar* and *Adr* occur in the Eddas. And all these are probably related to Sumerian *Ad, Adda,* "Father."

13 *Khat*, Br. 5573. *ti*, Br. 7685; and see footnote p. 154.

14 The first sign here is clearly the Throne sign *En, Ene*, or *In*, B. 112. Br. 2806-8.

15 Br. 11900, B. 530. The second sign B. 481 has clearly the phonetic value of *Zi* (Br. 10519), with the meaning of "stable, established" (Br. 10528). For the same personal name is written in the glossaries (Br. 11921), with the Reed sign *Zi* (B. 91), which has also the same meaning (Br. 2313), and it is called "a lofty name." This sign is also given the Semitic value of *Dāmu* (M. 7978), which = "son" (MD. 252). And significantly that sign has the Sumerian value there of *Tuku,* which sign in the glossaries with the affix of *a* is defined as "The god Mar-tuk," *i.e.*, Mar-duk, or "The Son *Tuk* or *Duk*," of whom I have shown this second Sumerian king (Gin) was the human historical prototype. It thus appears that whilst the identity of King Gin as the human original of "Marduk" is thus confirmed, the affix here meaning literally "the established" was intended to read "the established son," that is the crown prince son of King Sagg who heads the inscription.

---

1 In ancient Sumerian genealogies the sonship is not always expressed, but is indicated merely by the order of succession of the personal names.

which we have seen was the last stronghold of the Hittites on the Upper Euphrates, where the river debouches on to the Mesopotamian plains; and it was called by the Babylonians *Kar-Kamish* or *Gar-Gamish*, that is "The Fort of Kamish or Gamish." And it is at this site also that the Nordic Eddas locate the capture of the Stone-Bowl, namely, at "The Fort of Gymi or Gymis" at Urd, the headquarters of the weirds of the Mother-Son and Serpent cult or Jöro-velli, now identified with Hieropolis Jerablus or Carchemish.

It is significant also that the Bowl is described in the inscription as "broken"; for the Eddas specially detail the circumstances as to how the bowl became broken during its capture by Thor and his son.

The title "city" (a Sumerian word also meaning "town") which is applied to Khamazi does not necessarily imply that that place was a "city" at the time of the capture of the Bowl. On the contrary, the Sumerian literature credits King Sakh (or Sagg) with founding the first city in the world, and his son with founding the first city in Mesopotamia. And the Eddas have preserved us the tradition that this "Fort of Gymis" consisted of a collection of underground burrows and "cellars," and its fort was presumably a stockade. But the Eddas add that after its capture it was made into a city by Thor and his descendants. The reference to it as a "city" by King Udu, thus doubtless refer to its condition at the period when he wrote.

Title of 1st King on the Bowl & his Identity with 1st King in Kish Chronicle and as Historical Human Original of Indra, Thor & Zeus

The identity of the king [1] to whom this Bowl is dedicated, namely, King Sagg or Zagg (Sa-ga-ga or Za-ga-ga), with the first king of the First Dynasty of the Kish Chronicle is evidenced at the outset by *both of these kings being respectively the traditional father of the same famous son Bakus*,[2] who was

[1] We have seen that his title *Ash* or *An*="King," also "Lord." Only the first bears this king title and the dedicator calling himself only "priest-king." "Lugal," the later title for "King," is of much later origin.

[2] See Br. 122, where, however, with the usual Assyriologists' confusion of Bakus with the Semitic woman's name of Bau, Bakus is made to be the "wife" of Lord Sagaga! This title of "Protector of Plants" (Gu-la) is also confused with that of *Gulu* for "woman."

afterwards deified as Bacchus for his vast developments in Agriculture and his invention of the Plough. And King Udu, who dedicates this Bowl, and who is shown in the Kish Chronicle and the other lists to be the grandson of King Bakus, is significantly called in the Kish Chronicle "The devotee of King Sagg (or Sa-ga-ga)," that is, this very king his great-grandfather) to whom he dedicates this Bowl, and whom he appears to have been the first to deify.

This title of Sagg or Zag (Sa-ga-ga or Za-ga-ga) is seen to have been a very early regnal title for this first "Sumerian" or Aryan king. It was also retained for long as an early title for him after he was deified as the Father-god, and it survived with the Indian branch as the *Sakko* name for the god Indra in the old Indian vernacular in Pali dialect; and it was Sanskritized later by the Indian Brahmans by introducing an *r* into it Cockney-wise and aspirating its *S* into *Shakra*, as a title of the god Indra.

The name Sa-ga-ga or Zagaga, which was presumably pronounced Sagg or Zagg, means in Sumerian "The established Lord or Leader."[1] It is obviously a syllabic spelling of the regular Sumerian word *Sag* or *Zag* for "Lord or Leader" which is written with the pictograph of a capped man's head and neck,[2] for which the sign-name is *Saggu* or *Zaggu*;[3] and this sign besides its primary meaning of "Head" also means "The First,"[4] and thus for the leader is analogous to the Teutonic *Fürst* title for "Sovereign or Prince." And the affix *ga* means "established."[5]

After his deification, this title of Sagg is found remodelled on the same general form as *In-Sakh* (or *In-Zakh*) or King *Sakh* or *Zakh*, meaning literally "King of the Winds,"[6] and thus making his title truly mythological, and obviously connecting it to his Sun-Eagle or Sun-Hawk emblem of his Sun-worship. This *Zakh* name has also the phonetic Sumerian value of *Zax*, and it was through this value, as well as the *Zagg* form with the soft *g*, that I have shown the Greeks obviously derived their name for him of "Zeus."

On the same phonetic model was latterly coined his

[1] Br. 6477, 6468.
[2] Br. 3509.
[3] Br. 3501 and 6459.
[4] Br. 3523.
[5] Br. 5417.
[6] Br. 5933. On *In* or *En*="King," see before.

Sumerian variant title of *Sig*,[1] which is written with the picture of a Horn, and defined as " Horn, exalted, Prince as Decider," and also " overthrow " in sense of " Victorious." It is this *Sig* form of his title which persists in the Nordic Eddas as a common title of Thor.

The other title for this first king which are given in the glossaries as synonyms for him, as noted in column I of the above decipherment Table, will be referred to when they occur later on in other Sumerian king-lists or inscriptions.

" Gin " Name of Second King on the Bowl & in Agreement with the other Lists

The name *Gin* for the second king in this Bowl inscription is seen to be a dialectic form of his *Gan* or *Kan* agricultural title in other Sumerian lists and a synonym of his Bakus or Bacchus title. *Gin* means " The Increaser " ;[2] and *Gan* or *Kan* means " Cultivate, beget of Plants, make abundant," also " Field and Produce " ;[3] and thus this *Gin* title confirms his identity with Bakus the second king in the Kish Chronicles, and the son of the first king.

His identity as son of the first king of the First Sumerian Dynasty Sagg or Ukusi is further confirmed by his being designated in the inscription as " the established (son ?) " by the same word-sign which is applied later to the almighty Babylonian Mar-Duk, the deified son of the Father-god Bel, and of whom we have seen that this second king was the human original and prototype, just as his father had been deified as Bel. This is still further confirmed under his title Bakus (who was traditionally the son of King Sagg or Sa-ga-ga) whereunder he is called " the son of Udu "[4] Udu being as we have seen a synonym of the first king of the First Dynasty of the Kish Chronicle and the *Odo* title of Thor in the Eddas. And he is also called " The Great Storehouse, called *Ama* of the Jar " (Br. 4078), wherein Ama we have seen on p. 82, is his title in the Indian lists, and also in Sumerian (p. 59.)

[1] Br. 3378, 3410 f. [2] M. 9168. [3] M. 2690 f. Br. 3177-80.
[4] Br. 4078, 9867. Bakus is here also called " The Great Digger."

Comparison of Bowl Genealogy with Kish Chronicle & other Sumerian & Indian Lists & Nordic Eddas showing Identity

The identity of the Bowl genealogy is established by comparison with the Kish Chronicle and other Sumerian[1] and Indian Lists of these first kings and with the Nordic Eddas. In this comparison it is to be remembered: (*a*) that the Chronicle inscription uses the solar title of Ukusi for the first king, which is found also as a title for him in another Sumerian list and is his Iksh-Vāku solar title in the Indian lists; and (*b*) that the Eddas, dealing solely with the rise of the Goths under their first king Thor, do not extend beyond the third king, and thus contain no mention of the fourth king Udu or Utu (? Otto) who wrote this inscription.

The equations of the names and synonymous titles of these earliest Sumerian or Aryan kings are here tabulated for reference (see Table, p. 100):

It is thus seen from this comparative table that the four kings in the genealogy inscribed on this Stone Bowl by King Udu are identical with the first four kings of the First Dynasty of the Sumerians as recorded in the Kish Chronicle, with its imperial extension to Kish in Mesopotamia; and they are identical with the first four kings of the First Dynasty of the Early Aryans; and they are identical, as regards the first three, with the first traditional kings in the Nordic Eddas. Their chronological order also, as well as their achievements, are identical, and thus collectively they establish the identity of the Sumerians and Early Aryans or Nordics.

The dedicator of this Bowl to King Sagg, who is disclosed as the great-grandson of the latter, is called in the Kish Chronicle not by his personal name, but by his title of "The devotee of King (or Lord) Sagg."[2] And it is seen that he had elevated the great and brilliant personality of his matchless great-grandfather as the originator of Civilization into a religious cult within his Sun-worship.

[1] For the old Sumerian King-List in column 3 of Table, see Table opposite p. 101 and App. III.

[2] With this compare the title "The Devotee of Nimirrud" *i.e.* the "Nimrod" title of the second king, namely Bakus. See later and compare Br. 11267

Bowl Genealogy compared with First Four Kings of Sumerians and Early Aryans.

Sumerian Lists.			Indian Lists.	Nordic Eddas.
Udu's Bowl.	Kish Chronicle.	Old Sumerian List. (See Table opp. p. 140.)		
SAGG or Sa-ga-ga (or SAKH) (or INDARA)	UKUSI of Uku	AGUSHE-ir or SAGKI	IKSH-VĀKU, SAKKO or INDRA	OKU or SIG or ANDVARA, EIN-DRI
GIN the established (son ?)	AZAG, BAKUS or BASAM	GAN, GUN or KAN s. of 1	ĀYUS or BASU or BIKUKSHI, s. of 1	ÆGIS or BAUGE, GUNN or KON, s. of 1
ENUZUZU or IN-ZUZU, s. of 2	NAKSHA, ANENUZU, s. of 2	IN, ENU, UNNUSHA	NAHUSHA, ANENAS or JANAK, s. of 2	HŒNI
UDU or UTU, UDUK, s. of 3.	Devotee of King SAGG or Sa-ga-ga.	(U)-DUKU	UDĀ of the Vase, s. of 3, or YADU or YA-YATI.	

And in the Indian King-Lists of the solar version this fourth king Udu is called " Udā of the Vase (Udā-vasu)," wherein the vase in question is disclosed as being this famous trophy magic Stone-Bowl captured by his great-grandfather King Ikshvāku Indara, Dar or Dur.

This Stone Bowl on which this record is engraved is thus disclosed as the actual material original of the central fetish-magic Stone-Bowl or " Cauldron " of the Serpent cult of the precivilized period of the ancient world, and captured from the weirds of Urd by King Thor and his son, and afterwards consecrated by the former, as is circumstantially described in the Nordic Eddas. And King Thor's or Her-Thor's son, who bears the title of Gun and Kon in the Eddas, and was the champion knight-errant of his father, Thor, and has the Sun-falcon as his special emblem, and who is Gan, Gun or Kan in the Sumerian amongst his other titles, is now disclosed with his fixed date as the historical original of Sir Gawain, the chief champion knight-errant of King Ar-Thur in the Arthurian Legends.

We now proceed to the recovery of the lost kings of the Great Gap of 430 years in the Kish Chronicle, existing between the eighth king of its " Second " Dynasty and its pre-Sargonic king of its " Third " Dynasty. These kings who had all been lost to the Babylonian scribes are now discovered to be all duly preserved in the Indo-Aryan King-Lists and Chronicles, and all in their due chronological order with the achievements of the leading kings.

FIG. 16A.—Sun-Hawk or Eagle triumphs over the Serpent of the Mother Cow-cult. From a pre-Christian Cross at Mortlach, Banff. (After SSS. T. pl. 44.)
Note the Serpent is given the form of the British adder.

VI

The Great Gap in 2nd Dynasty of Kish Chronicle of 430 Years with 27 Kings is filled by Indian King-Lists

Disclosing King Barat, Uruash's *Dynasty with his Five Sons, and* "Meshannipadda" *and other pre-Sargonic kings, including Sargon's Father, in their due Chronology for the first time, and the "Garden of Edin" paradise in the Indus Valley founded by King Uruash, and Sargon I discovered as first historical Predynastic Pharaoh of Egypt and his son as Menes, the founder of the First Dynasty of Egypt.*

We have found in Chapter III that the Kish Chronicle after enumerating eight kings of its Second Dynasty who reigned for a period of only 156 years, gives the total reign for that dynasty at 586 years, thus leaving the kings for a period of 430 years a complete blank. It then passes on to the relatively late king immediately preceding Sargon-the-Great, as its "Third" Dynasty, a king or "Dynasty" whose period is admitted by Assyriologists, for palæographic reasons, to be about eight centuries later than King Udu of the Stone-Bowl inscription,[1] who we have found was the third king of that "Second" Dynasty of the Kish Chronicle. And this Great Gap in that chronicle, of which the kings had been lost to its scribe and in the original form which he copied, is also mechanically repeated in all the later found Babylonian lists of the ancient Sumerian kings.

The Indian King-Lists fill up the Great Gap of the Kish Chronicle & other Babylonian King-Lists

Fortunately for history, the uniquely complete official Indian King-Lists of the Early Aryan kings now come to our aid in preserving the full list of all the missing kings of

[1] For example, CAH. 1, 667 and 669.

this Great Gap, and in their due chronological order of succession. These missing kings of the Kish Chronicle gap of 430 years are disclosed by the Indian Lists to number twenty-seven,.that is with an average reign of about fifteen years each, and they continue the main or imperial line of the Early Aryan kings from No. 10 down to No. 37 in the main-line list of the Aryan kings (see annexed Table and Appendix I). Most of the kings are famous emperors, whose inscribed monuments exist, but could not be definitely placed chronologically. But the recovery of the official Indian King-Lists of their succession now enables us to place them in their due chronological positions.

Besides this recovery of the full list of missing kings and the fixing of the chronological position of the stray kings of monuments in the gap period, the Indian Chronicle also preserves important records of the achievements of the leading kings which are unknown in the fragmentary Babylonian records, yet which are of great historical importance, and in keeping with the wide location of their monuments, as showing that they were great emperors, and not the petty kinglets of single cities or single city-states as hitherto erroneously supposed. And amongst the critically important information thus recovered is a full account of the hitherto unknown personality and history of the father of Sargon-the-Great as a hereditary Aryan emperor in the main-line succession from the first Aryan king, which effectually destroys the universal theory of Assyriologists that Sargon was a low-born Semitic adventurer.

The Sumerian Kings & Emperors of the Great Gap Recovered by the Official Indian King-Lists

The Sumerian kings and emperors of the Great Gap of the Kish Chronicle who are now fully recovered in their chronological order by the official Indo-Aryan king-lists, are detailed in the following list extracted from Appendix I. :—

(*See the Table over the page.*)

SUMERIAN OR ARYAN KINGS OF THE GREAT GAP OF 430 YEARS DISCLOSED BY THE INDIAN LISTS

Nos. in Main Line.	Indian List Names.	Sumerian Inscription Names.
10.	B'ARATA, BRIHAD-Uktha or PRITHU, s. of Dushyanta or Dushmanta.	BARTI, BARDI or BARDU, s. of Duimushsu-Dussh.
11.	GOTAMA, TAMAS or DHUNDHU-*mara*.	
12.	DWAT, DHRITI or CANDRA-*ashwa*.	
13.	AJA-*mīdha* or SITESHU.	
14.	CHAXUS, CAKSHUS, RIKSHA, RUCAKA or RUK-MESHU.	GISHSAX or ISZAX ("Gilgamesh").
15.	HARYASHWA or B'ARMYASHWA.	URUASH KHĀD, URUSAG KHADDU or BARAMA'HA-SHA.[1]
16.	MUDGALA or MOGALLO (*P.*) or *Akrish, Samkatāshwa*.	A-MADGAL or A-KURGAL.
17.	BADRY-ashwa, BHUJYU or PASENADI (*P.*) (with collateral line)	BIDASHNADI, BI(D)SAR, or BIUGUN[2] of Kish (with collateral line).
18.	YUWAN-ASHWA II, brother.	INASH-*nadi*, brother.
19.	DĀSA (*Divo-*, or "divine"), MANDHĀTRI or TRASA-DASYU I, s. of 17.	TARSI (*Ene-* or "divine") priest-king of Lagash.
20.	METTIYO (*P.*) or MITRAYU.	MEDI or METI, k. of Kish.
21.	CYAVANA, MUCCH-KUNDA or CIDI (Break of Dynasty).	[KI]-AGA (or (?) MŪKUDA),[3] k. of Kish. (Break of Dynasty).
22.	*Su*-DĀSA I or DUSSAHA or TRASA-DASYU II.	TARSI, k. of Kish.
23.	SOMAKA or SAHA-*deva* or SAUDASA.	
23A.	JANTU I. or *Anaranya*, slain by Ravana.	ANTA k. of Lagash.
24.	PRISHADA or *Suvarna*-ROMAN.	PĀSHI-PADDA (so-called "*Meshanni-padda*").
25.	DRUPADA I, HRASHWA-ROMAN or ROHIDA-ashwa.	DURUASHI-PADDA (so-called "*Anni-padda*").
26.	VASUMANAS, VYOMAN.	PĀSHUNU-tu (so-called "Meskalam-dug").
27.	JĪMŪTA.	
28.	BHANU or BAN-*kirti*.	
29.	SATYA-BRATA (or *Tri-shanku*).	
30.	HARISH CANDRA.	
31.	HARITA or *Rohita-ashwa*.	
32.	CUNCU or DHUNDU.	(?) KINGUBI-DUDU, k. of Erech.[4]
33.	VIJAYA.	
34.	B'ARUKA or RURUKI.	
35.	*Wri*-TAKA.	
36.	PRA-CIN-wat, BĀHU, B'ARADWAJA or BAHU, f. of S'akuni or "Sargon," dethroned by Haibaya chief, and defeated by Sakuni.	BAR-GIN, BUU, URUDUGINA dethroned by Zaggisi, 3rd Dyn. Kish Chronicle who was defeated by Sargon.

[1] WISD. 35 f.

[2] Hitherto read *Enbi Ishtar*, by Semitic values; but last sign is *ugun* in Sumerian (M. 6636).

[3] King of Adab, and his name hitherto read *Anna Mundu*.

[4] Hitherto read *Kigubni-dudu*.

Alongside the Indian forms of their names are placed for comparison the Sumerian forms of the names from the stray inscriptions of those kings amongst them whose inscriptions have hitherto been unearthed[1]—excluding their Indo-Sumerian seals, wherein several others of them are recorded, as seen later on.

The numbers given on the left-hand margin, beginning with No. 10, are the serial numbers of those kings in the main or imperial line from the first Aryan (or Sumerian) king of the First Aryan Dynasty onwards. The preceding kings, Nos. 1 to 9, are cited in Chap. IV, p. 69. The relationship of the succeeding kings is usually stated to be "son" of the preceding king, unless where otherwise specified. The letter *P* designates the old Indian Pali form of the name.

Identities in the Names of the Kings of the Great Gap in Sumerian Contemporary Inscriptions & in the Indian Lists

Here again, the substantial equations in the further strings of names of Sumerian kings in their own inscriptions with those preserved in the official King-Lists of the Early Aryans in the Indian Lists establishes still more solidly the identity of the Sumerians with the Early Aryans. And the unique historical importance of the Indian Lists in recovering the traditional forms of the names of the kings from the polyphonous Sumerian writing, and in fixing the unknown chronological position of those stray kings of this Great Gap period of the Kish Chronicle, whose monuments exist, is evident.

It is now desirable to glance briefly at some of the outstanding new evidence in regard to the leading Aryan or Sumerian emperors of this period of the Great Gap who played an important part in the development and propagation of the Aryan Civilization as elicited by the Indian Chronicles, supplemented by the evidence from their own Sumerian inscriptions.

[1] On these Sumerian names and the inscriptions whence they are derived for Nos. 14-21, see WISD. 32 f., and my article in *Asiatic Review*, October 1925, 676 f.

KING BARAT OR BRIHAT, THE EPONYMOUS ANCESTOR OF THE BRITONS & EASTERN BARATS *c.* 3180 B.C.

The first of the Sumerian kings and emperors of the Great Gap of the Kish Chronicle is seen to be Barata or Brihat. He is the famous great Aryan emperor from whom, as I have shown,[1] the Britons and the Eastern and Indian and Parthian Barats—the leading branch of the Indo-Aryans in the Vedas and Indian epics—derived their patronym. I have shown that his actual inscribed monuments exist in Mesopotamia at Adab as King of Kish, with his name splet *Bardi*, *Barti* or *Bardu* " son of *Duimushsu-Duash* "—corresponding to his father's name of " Dushyanta, son of Tamsu " in Indian lists—and disclosing him as an historical Sumerian king of relatively fixed date about 3180 B.C.[2]

In the Indian epics he is called " emperor " (*cakra-vartin*[3]) and in the Vedic literature his birth-place was Nādāpit.[4]

King Barat greatly enlarged the prosperity of the Arayns (or Sumerians), and developed the Fire-cult ritual,[5] so that his descendants proudly called themselves after his name. Thus most of the Aryan kings in the Indian Vedic psalms style themselves " Barats," and the leading stock of the later Indo-Aryan race habitually uses this title which is thus referred to in the Indian epics : " And King Barat gave his name to the Dynastic Race of which he was the founder ; and so it is from him that the fame of that dynastic people hath spread so wide." [6]

The leading clans of the Barats forming the leading section of the Aryan race were the *Kurus* (or Syrio-Asia Minor) and the " able *Panch*—whom I have shown to be the Early " Phœnicians." And still to the present day the eastern branch of the Aryans, the Indo-Aryans proudly call their

[1] WPOB. 1 f., 52 f., 188 f. ; WSAD. 35 f.

[2] Two inscriptions of Barat were unearthed at Adab by Mr Banks (BB. 201, 266), who read the name as *Bar-ki*. But the 2nd signs are respectively *du* (B. 417) and *di* or *ti* (B. 415) ; and the full inscription reads *Bar-ti* (or *-di*) *lugal-Kish ban Du-im-u-uś-su-Du-ash*, as above translated, cf. on father's name Br. 9577, 4736, 10509, 515. This seems to identify him with Tamsu, but the expanded Ind. lists make Barat a grandson of Tamsu.

[3] MBt. 1, 2983, 3120.

[4] MKI. 1, 440.

[5] WPOB. 292.

[6] MBt. 1, 94, sloka 3704.

country "B'arat country" (B'arat-varsha) and themselves B'arats, just as the leading western branch of the Aryans call themselves "Brit-ons."

GISHSAX OR ISSAX (OR GILGAMESH) OF ERECH OR CHAXUS OF INDIAN LISTS, THE SUMERIAN HISTORICAL ORIGINAL OF HERCULES OF THE PHŒNICIANS *c.* 3120 B.C.

The fifth king of the Great Gap is the famous Sumerian Hercules named *Gishsax* or *Issax*, with the title of *Gamesh*, or "Lord of Oxen," the *Caxus Chaxus, Cakshus* of the Indian lists; and whom I have shown to be the historical original

FIG. 17.—King Gishsax or Issax of Erech, the historical original of Hercules, slaying the Lion. From a Sumerian seal of about 2500 B.C., now in British Museum.

Note the trees or reeds of the (Nemean ?) grove. On the right the hero is crushing the lion, and on the left is lifting the dead beast.

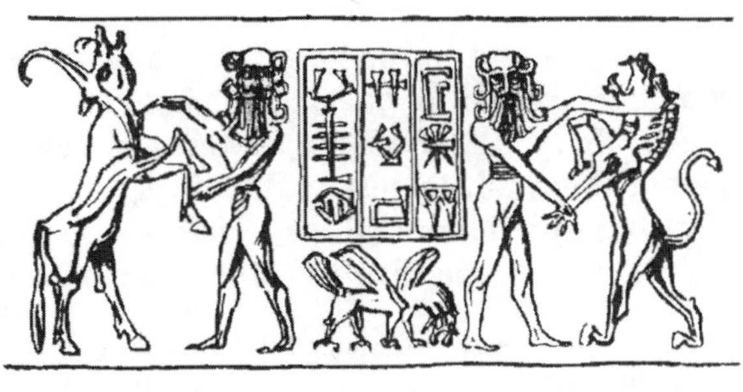

FIG. 18.—King Gishsax or Chaxus of Erech, the Sumerian original of Hercules wrestling with a wild Bull and Lion. From a Sumerian seal of Uruash, son of "The Priest-king of Adab." c. 2500 B.C. (After Banks, BB. 303.)

of Hercules or Herakles of the Phœnicians and Greeks,[1] who also was a " Lord of Oxen." He is now recorded in his due chronological position for the first time by the Indian lists. He is usually represented wrestling with lions and wild oxen in Sumerian, Hittite, Babylonian and Phœnician seals, as in Figs. 17 and 18.[2]

He is recorded in the Indian lists, under the name of Chaxus or Caxus (see Table, p.) as father of the emperor Haryashwa, the founder of the First *Panch* or " Phœnician " Dynasty, that is the Sumerian sea-emperor Uruash (" Ur Nina "), which accounts for the Phœnician worship of Hercules. This paternity is confirmed from Sumerian sources, as we shall find later on.[3]

THE SEA-EMPEROR URUASH (" UR-NINA ") OR HARYASHWA & HIS FIRST PHŒNICIAN " DYNASTY OF ARYANS *c.* 3100 B.C.

The sixth king of the Great Gap is the famous Sumerian emperor Uruash (hitherto conjecturally read " Ur Nina "), the Aryan emperor Haryashwa of the Indian lists, and one of the best known of the Early Sumerian kings from his prolific monuments and portraits (see Plate VII A). He is called in the Indian epic " The Restorer (of the Empire)." [4]

He was the founder of the great dynasty of sea-kings with their seaport at Lagash on the Persian Gulf (see map) ; and a great builder of temples, granaries as insurance against famine, embankments, canals for irrigation, etc. And his dynasty's numerous inscribed monuments, sculptures, cultural objects and records still form the greater bulk of the Early Sumerian remains hitherto unearthed, and now mostly in the Louvre Museum. Yet, despite all this concrete evidence in which all of them call themselves " Kings," Assyriologists have hitherto regarded him and his dynasty as being merely petty kinglets of a single city or city state, obsessed with

[1] WISD. 134 f., for complete details of his identity with Hercules.

[2] See WISD. for many representations from Sumerian seals.

[3] And see WISD. 129 f. Uruash usually calls himself in his inscriptions " son of Gunidu, son of Gur-sar." This may be a contracted genealogy claiming descent from more remote ancestors.

[4] *Parā-vrit.* See App. I., No. 15.

A

A. KING URUASH, FOUNDER OF Ist PHŒNICIAN (PANCH) DYNASTY, *c.* 3100 B.C., WITH HIS 5 SONS.

From contemporary votive plaque (after Heuzey, *Déc.*, Pl. II, *bis*). In upper register as priest-king building temple. In lower, in hermitage performing a ritual. For details, see pp. 111 f.

PLATE VII.

B

B. KING BIASNADI, 3RD KING OF PHŒNICIAN DYNASTY, LEADING HIS TROOPS IN BATTLE.

From his victory stele, *c.* 3050 B.C. (after Heuzey, *Déc.*, Pl. III *bis*). Note soldiers led by king, instinct with movement, advancing in solid phalanx. In upper scene, front rank, shielded by 4 bucklers, between which protrude their spears, marches over enemy dead. In lower, the king, protected by shield, is throwing a spear with left hand, and darts in pocket of shield.

their theory that no real kingship arose in Mesopotamia till many centuries later.

His Foundation of Overseas Colony in the Indus Valley

On the other hand, I have shown that Uruash and his descendants in this dynasty were emperors not only of the whole of Mesopotamia, but of colonies beyond, and that both he himself and most of his descendants call themselves in their inscriptions besides their local title of King of

Fig. 19.—Madgal, Crown-prince of Emperor Uruash, as "Lord and Capturer of the Edin" colony in Indus Valley, c. 3070 B.C. From his victory-seal. (After Delaporte.) For detailed decipherment and identification of the symbols, see WISD. 35 f.

Lagash, also "King of Kish," that is the recognized title in the Sumerian period for "Emperor of Mesopotamia." I have also shown that he founded the great overseas Sumerian colony of Edin in the Indus Valley, as attested by the contemporary victory-seal of his crown-prince Mudgal—Mudgala of Indian lists and Vedas, the first governor of that colony (see Fig. 19), and by the other official Sumerian seals found there. And the kings of his dynasty are the chief Aryan kings mentioned in the Indian Vedic hymns as seafarers and the subjects of shipwreck, one in "a ship of a hundred oars" and associated with the Maruts or Amorites.[1]

1 WISD. 30 f.; 129 f.; and my article in *Asiatic Review*, 1925, 676 f.

The great seafaring dynasty founded by King Uruash is called in the Indian epics and Vedas "The able *Panch*" (Panch-āla), which I have shown was the First *Phœnician* Dynasty, and the obvious source of the name "Phœnician."[1] The descendants of this dynasty using the title of *Panch* for themselves and their Aryan officials and people, became the chief clan of the ruling and seagoing Aryans. And I demonstrated that the later Phœnicians also occasionally called themselves *Barat* or *Parat* or *Part*, the patronym of their famous ancestor King Barat, and also called their patron sea-tutelary and goddess *Bārāt*, who I have shown was the Sumerian origin of our "Britannia."[2] This now explains for the first time the tradition of the Phœnicians of Tyre as recorded by Herodotus that the Phœnicians came from the Persian Gulf to Tyre 2300 years before his period, that is about 2750 B.C.

The absolute identity of this Sumerian king Uruash and his dynasty with the Aryan emperor Haryashwa and his dynasty of the Indian lists and chronicles is now evidenced by positive forceful proof seldom equalled in ancient History. This identity in Sumerian and Aryan is proved (*a*) by the identity of his own name and titles, (*b*) by identity of the names of his five famous sons and in the same relative order, (*c*) by the identity in the names of his descendants in the dynasty and in their precise chronological order of succession and (*d*) by identity in achievements.

These identities thus establish still more firmly the identity of the Sumerians with the Early Aryans in personalities and race; and they demonstrate the Aryan racial character of the Early "Phœnicians."

THE FIVE FAMOUS SONS OF THE EMPEROR URUASH IDENTICAL IN SUMERIAN RECORDS & INDIAN LISTS IN NAMES, TITLES & ACHIEVEMENTS

No more striking and absolute proof of the identity of the Sumerian emperor Uruash with the Aryan emperor Haryashwa is possible than that now demonstrated not only of the identity of himself and his dynasty, but also of his

[1] See p. 19, Chap. I.

[2] WPOB. 8 f., 53 f.

five famous sons in their names, titles, relative order and achievements in Sumerian and Aryan.

The names and representations of King Uruash himself along with his five famous sons are preserved in his well

FIG. 20.—King Uruash (Haryashwa of Indian Lists), Sumerian Emperor of Mesopotamia and priest-king with his five famous sons. From contemporary votive plaque of limestone at Lagash City, and see photograph in Pl. VII A. (After Heuzey *Déc*, pl. 2 bis.)

Note in upper register the king as priest-king with shaven head and face, as a workman carrying a basket of bricks to build his temple to Nimirrud (or St Michael), the patron saint of the city, with his family whose names are written across their woollen skirts. His daughter Lidda stands in front. Next is the crown-prince Madgal, holding a jar in his right hand, and his third son (Baridishshu) is behind his father holding up some object; and his other three sons stand in order behind the crown-prince. In lower register the king is seated holding a sacrificial cup (of fire or oblation) with four sons taking part in the rite, the foremost holding out his right hand for the cup, and behind the king, the same son as in top-register bearing a mace or other object.

known inscribed votive plaques (see Plate VII A and Fig. 20).

These plaques carved somewhat roughly in limestone and pierced by a hole, presumably for attachment to the wall or pillar of a temple, represent him with his five sons in two different scenes, and each individual bears his or her own name written across their body or skirt. In the upper scene he is depicted as a priest-king with shaven head and face, garbed in the woollen embroidered flounced kilt of royalty of that period in the sun-baked tropical plains of Mesopotamia, and building or rebuilding a temple to the Sumerian patron saint of his sea-port capital of Lagash, namely the canonized second Sumerian King *Nimirrud*,[1] who we shall find is the Sumerian historical original of "Nimrod" of city building fame in Chaldea, Shinar or Mesopotamia. And in the lower register he as priest-king is celebrating with his sons a Fire-cult ritual in a hermitage on Mount Māl. This latter scene illustrates the extreme antiquity of the practice, so often referred to in the Indian epics, of ancient Aryan kings retiring for ascetic contemplation into hermitages. And in many of the sculptures of this and the later Sumerian period the priest-king or priest is figured shaven and with the right shoulder bare as in the well known representatives of the India Buddha.

The special importance of these inscribed double scenes on the same monument, for our present purpose, is that the top scene gives the ordinary *personal name* of each of his sons, whilst the lower scene gives their *titles*. And significantly *in the upper scene the sons of the king are enumerated by name in the identical order in which they are enumerated in the Indian Chronicles*, with the exception that the third son who was presumably an adept priest by profession is placed behind him holding up some object.

The identity in the names and order of the sons in the upper scenes from left to right of the king with those preserved in the Indian Chronicles [2] is displayed in the following table. The eldest son A-Madgal holding the vase occupies the position nearest the king and behind his sister and his brother behind him with folded hands in adoration. Their names are written across their skirts, whilst their father's, the king's, name is written in front of his mouth; and the authorities for my readings of the signs of the words when differing from previous readings are cited from the standard Sumerian lexicons under each name.

[1] See App. V. for the first decipherment of this name.
[2] WVP. 4, 144.

IDENTITY OF NAMES OF URUASH'S FIVE SONS ON UPPER REGISTER IN SUMERIAN & INDO-ARYAN

Order in plaque.	Sumerian Name.	Indian Chronicle Name.	Order in Indian Lists.
1.	(A-)MADGAL,[1] son (holding Jar)	=MUDGALA, son, " Leader of Jar."[2]	1.
2.	SIRIM [3](King-), son	=SRIN-Jaya, son	2.
5.	(left). BARID-ISHSHU[4]	=BRIHAD-ISHU, son	3.
3.	ANIARRA,[5] son	=YAVINARA, son	4.
4.	(*Mu*-) GAMIMLA,[6] son	=KĀMPILYA, son	5.

It is thus seen that the names of King Uruash's five sons are identical in Sumerian and Indo-Aryan; and similarly their order is identical, the third son being placed alongside his father owing to his position presumably of domestic priest—his smaller size is owing to the exigencies of space under the inscriptions. Moreover it is specially noteworthy that the crown-prince Madgal (or "*The* son Madgal" i.e. *A-Madgal*) [1] the Mudgala of the Sanskrit, who in the Sumerian picture holds the Jar, *actually bears in the solar version of the Indian King-Lists the title of "Leader of the Jar"* (*Ni-kumbha*), see Appendix I. No. 16.

THE FIVE SONS' TITLES IN LOWER REGISTER

In the lower scene in the hermitage on Mount Māl, as it is called in the inscription, his five sons are mostly labelled with their *titles* instead of their personal names. All five are his sons although only the first three on the left-hand side are actually called there " son," a word which is omitted in the other two presumably from want of space.

1 The prefixed *A*=" *The* son" or " The," title of the Crown-prince, see WISD. 32; and WSAD. 1.

2 Ni-Kumbha.

3 Br. 4300.

4 The initial *Bar* is clearly written by the ᒋ sign, as in the Indus Valley seals of this period, see WISD. 31, 40. The second sign, the hand-sign with the value ID is also clear, The next sign has the value I (Br. 5307), and the following signs *ish* and *shu* (B. 311 and 7065) are distinct.

5 The third sign is not *kur*, but the plough sign *ar* (B. 261, Br. 5776).

6 The first sign *Mu*=" named." The second to fourth signs are *Ga* (B. 275), *mim* (B. 116), and *la* (B. 440, Br. 10082, with a blemish stroke).

Their Sumerian titles are compared in the table below with their lunar titles in the Indian lists [1] shown on the right hand side of the table. Some of these titles agree substantially in form in the Sumerian and Indian, as for example the last two; whilst the others generally agree in their *meaning*, the Indian scribes having translated the names into the Indo-Aryan vernacular of their period.

IDENTITY OF TITLES OF THE FIVE SONS OF LOWER REGISTER IN SUMERIAN & ARYAN

Order in Plaque.	Sumerian Title.	Indian Chronicle Title.	Order in Indian Lists.
1.	*Lakh*[2]-MAD-GAL[3]-*Gut* (or Goth) [4] or "The Shepherd Madgal, the Warrior."	= RUK-MESHU or "Shining Arrow."	1.
2.	A-NUN-PAD or "Sea-lord Commander," son	= JYĀ-MAGHA or "Overpowerer of Magha Island.	3.
5. (right).	SAG-ASH-DUK or "Duke of Troops" [5]	= PRITHU-RUKMA or "P. of Shining Disc."	2.
3.	*Uru*-PAL[6] or "Pal the Protector," son	= PALITA or "The Protector."	4.
4.	AD-TUR-TA, "The child of his Father," son.	= HARITA.	5.

The first son, next the king's front, is clearly again the crown-prince Madgal, for he bears therein the latter name, with in addition the prefixed title of *Lakh* or "Shepherd" and the affixed title of *Gut* or "Goth" or "Warrior"—the last sign being pictured by the head of an ox as described later on. And significantly his Indian equivalent title of *Rukmeshu* means "The Shining Arrow," [1] and we shall find that in a later Sumerian text he bears also the title of "Shepherd," and so also in his Indus seals (Pl. IX.).

Similarly with the other sons, the second bearing the title of "sea-lord" is seen to be the second son of the upper scene,

[1] WVP. 4, 64. [2] *Lakh*="shepherd," Br. 4940.

[3] The first sign is *Mad*, B 9264, and second seems to be *Gal*, Br. 2254.

[4] On *Gut* sign and values, see later.

[5] On Sumerian *Duk*=Duke, see WSAD. 61.

[6] *Uru*, "protect" (B. 238), and not *Men* (B. 240). Second sign is clearly *Pal* (B. 9, Br. 262).

and the third and fourth are in the same order as in the upper scene. The fifth son, behind his father, is clearly as in the upper scene, the third born son of the Indian lists of names, as his priest-name *Prithu* is dialectic for the *Brihad* in the upper list, and his title *Rukma* or " The Shining Disc," is in keeping with the mace-like object which he holds in the lower Sumerian picture, and in agreement with his Sumerian title of " Duke of the Troops."

The achievements of the sons also, as well as their relative positions and titles, are in agreement with the Indian Chronicles. These state that the eldest son Ruk-Meshu (*i.e.* Madgal) succeeded his father in the sovereignty. His brother Prithu, " the Duke of the Troops " in Sumerian, who is figured behind the king, remained in the service of his elder brother on his becoming king. The youngest brother Palita and Harita were set over the Videha Lands. And the third brother Jyā-Magha or " Overpowerer of the Island of Magha," and " The Sea-lord Commander " in the Sumerian, went forth to conquer new lands, including " Madhya-Land, Mekala and the Shuktimat Mountains," and established a Cidi or Cedi or " Phœnician dynasty," [1] presumably in Phœnicia.

Thus the identities of the Five Sons of King Uruash are found to be alike in names, titles and order of birth and position, in agreement in the Sumerian records and in the Indian Chronicles. This striking agreement again proves the identity of the Sumerians with the Aryans in personality and in race. It also again illustrates the scrupulous care taken by the Indian scribes in copying the official lists of the names of the historical ancient Aryan kings down through the ages to the present day. And it again attests the authenticity and historicity of the Indian King-Lists and Chronicles as an independent source of Sumerian or Early Aryan history.

" Edin " or " Garden of Edin " Name for the Indus Valley Colony of King Uruash confirmed by Sargon's Chronicle.

In my former work on *Indo-Sumerian Seals Deciphered* I have given detailed proofs for my reading of the name of

[1] WVP. 4, 64.

the Indus Valley city-state founded by King Uruash through its signs engraved on several of the seals recently unearthed there, as *Edin* or *Etin*,[1] after the name of its great city-fort on the Indus; and have shown that while in later

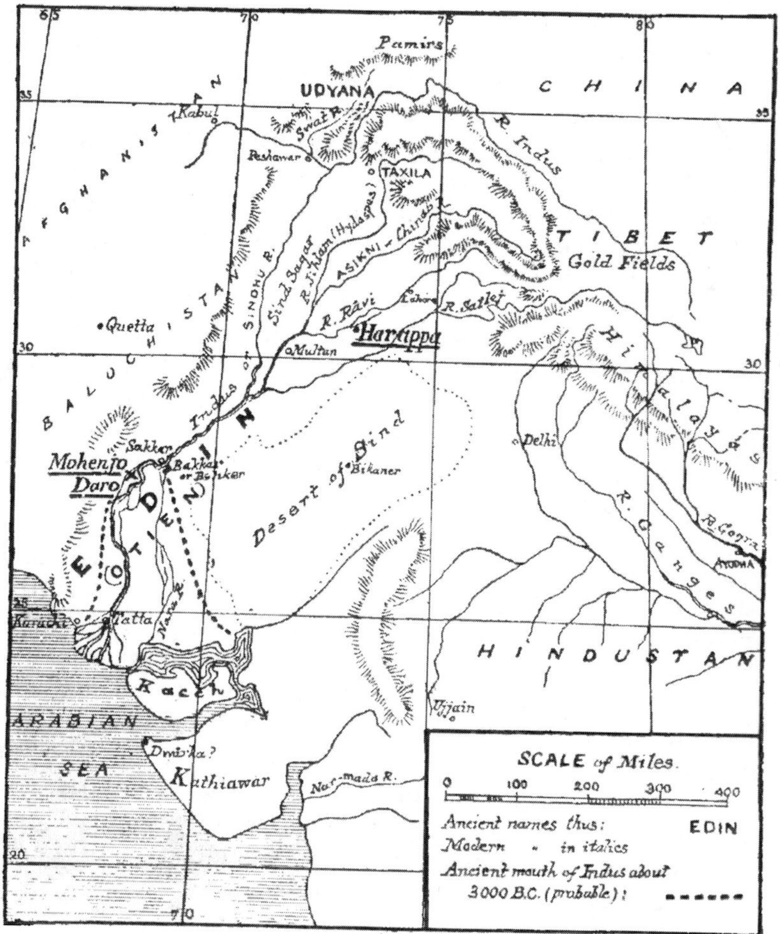

L.A.W. del.

Map of the Sumerian Colony of Edin in the Indus Valley.

Sanskrit it was called *Udyana*, it was still locally known as *Otien* at the visit of the famous Chinese Buddhist pilgrim and geographer, Huien Tsang, in the seventh century A.D. (see accompanying map).

[1] WISD. 7, 29-33, 49, 57, 102 f.

Striking additional confirmation of my reading of the name *Edin* or *Etin* now comes from the Chronicles of Sargon-the-Great—the seals of which emperor from the Indus I had deciphered, along with details of his recapture of that revolted province as preserved in the Indian Epics. In the Chronicles of Sargon I find is described his conquest or reconquest of this Indus Valley, under the circumstances detailed in the later chapter devoted to the new evidence now elicited regarding him and his world-empire.

In Sargon's Chronicle, as extracted in the Omen literature of the later Babylonians, he calls this distant land far to the east of Mesopotamia " The Good Edin (or Etin) Land " (*Su-Edin-ki*)—a name which has hitherto been arbitrarily disguised by modern translators as " Subartu " ![1] And it is called by Sargon's son King Manis-Tusu " The Garden of EDIN, the Fruitful "[2]—a name also hitherto disguised by all previous translators and writers on Babylonian history as " Sirihum " ![3] And this " Garden of Edin " is definitely placed by Manis-Tusu's own inscriptions to the east of Anshan (Persis) of Persia and bordering the Arabian Ocean or " Lower Sea " of the Sumerians, as we shall see later on from the many seals of Manis-Tusu and his dynasty actually found there, and now deciphered for the first time.

So rich was this flourishing arcadian Indus Valley colony of Edin in cultivation, fruits, orchards, flocks and herds of cattle and horses, in gold and other metals and produce, that it was given by the Sumerians the title of " The Good Abode " (*Su-bati*)[4] *a term which significantly exists literally and in the self-same sense, in the India Pali as Su-vatthi " happiness, blessing, welfare,"*[5] *and in the Sanskrit* as *Su-vati* (" *Heaven of the Indian Buddhists,*")[6] *and as Su-vata* (" *Full of Joy or Pleasure* ").[7] This affords another striking example

[1] See, for example, KCB. 2, 36, and all subsequent writers.

[2] *Shu-Edin-hum.* See later on Manis-Tusu's reconquest of it. On *Shu*=" Garden," Br. 10509 and 10539, and MD. 568; and on *hum*=" Fruitful," Br. 11183.

[3] See references later under Manis-Tusu's conquests.

[4] Br. 1723 and 1696. [5] CD. 483.

[6] MWD. 1221. The paradise of Amitābha Buddha, see WBT. 127, 217. It was in the West, and this Old Indus Valley seaport is west of India proper. [7] MWD. 1221.

of the radical origin of the Aryan languages in the Sumerian language, of which I give thousands of other instances in my *Sumer-Aryan Dictionary*.

From the glowing references to this "Garden of Edin" colony in Sumerian and Indian Vedic and Buddhist literature as a terrestrial paradise and the actual material evidence in the profusion and magnificence and luxuries of the Sumerian palaces and other buildings and the wealth of artistic objects recently unearthed at this Edin on the Indus, its memory would seem to have eclipsed the other and older "Eden" which I have shown was situated at Carchemish on the Upper Euphrates, as the lost earthly paradise of the Semitic legend.

Uruash's Successors in Dynasty from Madgal to Tarsi or Trasa-Dasyu in full Agreement in Sumerian & Indo-Aryan

The successors also of the emperor Uruash in his *Panch* or "Phœnician" Dynasty from his son King Madgal or Mudgala (see his portrait on p. 109) down to Tarsi king of Kish, the Trasa-Dasyu II of the Indian Lists were, I found, in strict agreement in name and chronological order in both their own Sumerian inscriptions and in the Indian King-Lists of the Early Aryans, as shown in Table facing p. 140. And I demonstrated the agreement in considerable detail as regards their achievements in my *Indo-Sumerian Seals Deciphered* with reference to their great imperial colony of Edin in the Indus Valley, which I showed was established by the crown-prince Madgal "The Shepherd (of the people)" as its first Sumerian governor,[1] and see further details in later chapters.

The imperial character also of King Madgal's son and successor, King Bi(d)asnadi, the Pasenadi of the Indian records, was also demonstrated, as king of Kish, carrying the imperial suzerain title, as well as king of various other Mesopotamian cities, in his own inscriptions. And his portrait as a warrior-king was reproduced. He has also left his fine statue as a priest-king with shaven head and face at Adab, see Plate VIII. This fine statue, the earliest known

[1] WISD. 35 f.

PLATE VIII.

KING BI(D)SAR (BI[D]ASNADI OR B'UJYU) AS PRIEST-KING, *c.* 3050 B.C.

From Adab (after Banks, BB. 191). And see Pl. VIIB.

statue of an early king cut in the round, was unearthed by Mr Banks of the Chicago Expedition at Adab. It represents him of fine Aryan type, with straight nose, and attired as a priest in the flounced embroidered woollen petticoat, with arms and shoulders bare in the tropical Mesopotamian climate; and significantly this petticoat or kilt is similar to that which he wears as warrior in his victory stele in Plate VII. B. The eye-sockets, which are now empty, had been filled with eyeballs of ivory and stone or enamel, as in later statues of this kind with hollowed eye-sockets, giving a vividly life-like aspect. His name and title engraved on the right upper arm read "*Bid-sar* King of the City, King of 'Adab' City" in which "Bidsar" is seen to be a dialectic form of his name.

The so-called "Mesannipadda" and "Annipadda" Kings are long subsequent to Uruashi's Dynasty, and of relatively Fixed Date

Amongst the Sumerian kings of this Great Gap thus disclosed as *subsequent* to Uruash's (or Ur Nina's) Dynasty, it is especially to be noted, is the king whose name from his inscription has been conjecturally read as "Annipadda," and that of his father referred to in that inscription which has been conjecturally read as "Mesannipadda," and both of them have been arbitrarily placed about one and a half thousand years before King Uruash (or "Ur Nina")! But our Indian Key-Lists of the Sumerian kings duly record them by the traditional forms of their names and in their real chronological position, which is respectively 11 *and* 12 *generations* AFTER *King Uruash* (*or* "*Ur Nina*"), and their names are disclosed to read in Sumerian properly *Pāshi-padda* and *Duruashi*-padda, as we shall find later on.

Sargon's Father & his Royal Aryan Origin discovered by the Indian Lists in the Great Gap of the Kish Chronicle

The remaining kings of the Great Gap of the Kish Chronicle, but preserved in the Indian lists, who have left some of the monuments hitherto found, are shown in their due chronological position by the Indian lists in the Table facing p. 140.

The last of the kings of the Great Gap is now disclosed to be the father of Sargon-the Great, and he is discovered by the Indian lists as the hereditary Sumerian king of Kish, and identified with "Uruka-Gina" of the monuments—one of the great developers of Sumerian laws and civilization, as we shall see along with several of his seals from the Indus Valley. These discoveries of the royal Aryan ancestry of Sargon's father with fresh historical light on the birth and upbringing of Prince "Sargon," detailed in the subsequent chapters, effectually dispose of the theory universally held by Assyriologists that Sargon-the-Great was a low-born adventurer who seized the Mesopotamian throne, and that he was a Semite.

Sargon I discovered as First Historical Predynastic Pharaoh of Egypt and his Son as Menes, the Founder of First Dynasty of Egypt

Most startling of all these discoveries made through the Indian Lists and Chronicles is perhaps the discovery that Sargon was the first of the historical Predynastic Pharaohs of Egypt, and that his son Manis-Tusu or "Manis the Warrior" is identical with Menes, the founder of the First Dynasty of Egypt and that all the succeeding Pharaohs of that dynasty bear in their own Egyptian inscriptions the same names and titles as they possess as emperors in Sargon's dynasty in Mesopotamia, and that Egyptian civilization was derived from the Sumerian or Aryan as detailed in the later chapters.

These discoveries made by our Indian Chronicle of the Early Aryan kings now explain for the first time why Assyriologists have never been able to find any reference whatever to the famous emperor Uruash and his dynasty and the other isolated pre-Sargonic kings in the Kish Chronicle, or in any other of the subsequently found king-lists of the early kings of Mesopotamia. The reason is now disclosed to be because these kings belonged to the period of the Great Gap, whose kings were lost to the Kish Chroniclers and other Babylonian scribes, but preserved in the Indian Chronicles of the Early Aryan kings.

How Publication of these Discoveries was Delayed

Just as I was about to publish in 1914 the fuller details of these discoveries above summarized, disclosing the historicity of *the Kish Chronicle as an authentic record of the Early Sumerian kings from the First Sumerian Dynasty* down to the period of the Guti or Gothic Invasion of Mesopotamia by a fresh tribe of Goths from Asia Minor about 2600 B.C., and filling up its Great Gap of lost kings of its "Second" Dynasty from the Indian King-Lists, which disclosed for the first time the chronological position of Uruash's Dynasty and the other stray pre-Sargonic kings of the monuments, there was found a series of other cuneiform clay-tablet lists of the early kings of Mesopotamia compiled by the priests at Isin about 2200 B.C., which differed widely in their chronology from the Kish Chronicle.

These new Isin king-lists or chronicles, whilst repeating the First and following four dynasties of the Kish Chronicle almost verbatim, *placed before them long strings of other dynasties with vastly fabulous supernatural ages and purporting to extend back to "The Flood,"* the aboriginal Chaldean or Semitic myth of which had about this period come into vogue amongst the Semites. These lists were very fragmentary, being fragments of five copies of the same list.

On examining these fragmentary Isin lists, I observed that the prefixed strings of dynasties placed in front of the First Dynasty of the Kish Chronicle began and continued on with variant titles of the kings of the Second Dynasty of that chronicle and of its Great Gap, and in their same relative order of succession, although all were prefixed to the First Dynasty of that chronicle, and to all of them vastly superhuman ages and lengths of reign were attached by the Isin priests. It thus appeared that these Isin dynastic lists with their fabulous ages prefixed to the First Dynasty of the Kish Chronicle were presumably old Sumerian lists of the kings of the Great Gap which the Isin priests failing to recognise had fictitiously placed in front of the Kish Chronicle.

As, however, these prefixed Isin lists were so fragmentary, I was forced to delay the publication of my discoveries through the Indian Key-Lists and confirmed by the Kish

Chronicle, in the hope that a more complete version of the Isin lists might turn up. This hope was eventually realized in 1924, when a practically complete copy of the Isin lists was found and published. This version of the Isin lists went to further excesses even than the previous ones, and carried the prefixed dynasties back to 241,200 *years before the Flood!* Yet strange to say, these Isin lists of the credulous Isin priests, with their fictitious and vastly fabulous chronology prefixed to the First Dynasty of the Kish Chronicle, are nevertheless now accepted by all the leading Assyriologists and text-books as the basis of their early Mesopotamian history![1] This is another striking illustration of the sort of foundation upon which the latest "authorities" have fabricated their "History" of Mesopotamia and of the world's earliest Civilization, to the gross misleading of students of true History and the public at large.

But the utter falsity of these dynasties and their chronology prefixed to the First Sumerian Dynasty of the Kish Chronicle is betrayed by the Isin prefixed lists themselves, as disclosed in the next and following chapters.

[1] See, for example, CAH. 1 ed., 1924, *passim.*

FIG. 20A.—Canonized 2nd Sumerian King, Gin, Nimrod or Michael, with Chaldee infidels in net of the Sun-god. From victory Stele of King Bidasnadi, c. 3050 B.C. After Huezey *Déc.*
Note Sun-Hawk in his hand, and another in fragment of same monument on left.

VII

The Isin Chronicles of about 2050 B.C. & the Falsity of their "Dynasties" & Chronology prefixed to the First Dynasty of the Kish Chronicle

Disclosing Falsity of all the current Assyriologists' "History" and Chronology of the Sumerians of Mesopotamia based upon the Prefixed Dynasties of the Isin Chronicles

As related in the previous chapter, when I was about to publish the full corroboration of the historicity of the Kish Chronicle, as an authentic record of the earliest Sumerian kings *from the First Sumerian Dynasty* onwards, by means of the official king-lists of the Early Aryan kings from the First Aryan Dynasty onwards preserved in the Indian Epics, and proving that the First Sumerian Dynasty dated no earlier than about 3380 B.C., there was found another purported king-list or chronicle of the earliest kings of Mesopotamia compiled by the myth-mongering priests of Isin near Babylon about 2050 B.C., in which strings of alleged earlier dynasties with vastly fabulous ages were prefixed to the First Sumerian Dynasty of the Kish Chronicle.

The Isin King-Lists or Chronicle and their Fantastically Fabulous Chronology

These Isin king-lists or chronicles were discovered in fragmentary condition by Prof. Poebel in 1914 [1] amongst the thousands of cuneiform clay-tablets unearthed by the Pennsylvania Museum Expedition from 1893 onwards at the old Sun-temple at Nippur (where Udu's Bowl was found). The five fragments found were portions of five different copies of a large tablet-chronicle in twelve columns, containing lists of names of ancient kings and "eight or ten" dynasties of Mesopotamia, mostly with vastly superhuman

[1] PHT. iv. 1914, 73 f.; and Texts v. 1914.

ages, purporting to go back some tens of thousands of years before the 1st Dynasty of the Kish Chronicle to "The Flood!" These Isin lists, moreover, as evidencing their late origin, continued the line of dynasties downwards from the end of the Kish Chronicle through the Guti or late Gothic dynasty to the end of the Isin Dynasty contemporary with King Khamu Rabi's Dynasty of Babylon about 2000 B.C. And one fragment, No. 5, is still later, as it contained some names in the second half of Khamu Rabi's dynasty.

These fragments of the Isin Chronicle showed that they were compiled on the model of the Kish Chronicle, giving the name of each king, with his capital city, length of reign, relationship sometimes to his predecessor and total number of kings and years' reign for each dynasty. And a further fragment from the same collection, published by Dr L. Legrain,[1] contained three additional prefixed dynasties.

The Prefixed Isin Chronicle Dynasties with their Fabulous Chronology accepted by Assyriologists as Basis of their Sumerian and Babylonian History and Chronology!

Despite the preposterous and vastly fabulous ages in the string of ten or more "dynasties" prefixed by the Isin priests to the First Dynasty of the Kish Chronicle, ranging from 241,200 years for their "Antediluvian Dynasty" with individual kings reigning on an average about 30,150 years, and for their so-called "First Postdiluvian Dynasty" with individual kings reigning from 1200 years down to still vastly superhuman ages in the other prefixed "dynasties," and the fact that not one single one of those prefixed kings could be found by Poebel and others on any monument in Mesopotamia,[2] these prefixed lists of the Isin Chronicle, with their Semitic "Flood" myth, were nevertheless at once accepted by all Assyriologists, who regard them as genuinely historical! And this fabulous chronology is actually made the basis of the Early History of Mesopotamia and of the World's

[1] *Museum Journal*, Pennsylv. Univ., Dec. 1920, 175 f.

[2] The "Mesannipadda" king-name of Ur unearthed three years ago refers to a king who was long subsequent to the Second Dynasty kings cited in the Kish Chronicle, as we shall see.

Civilization as written by Assyriologists in our latest "authoritative" text-books on History ! [1]

On the other hand, I had already established, as we have seen, the authenticity of the First Dynasty of the Kish Chronicle as the first of all historical Sumerian dynasties, and was long accustomed to the Semitic vagaries and prejudices of Assyriologist "authorities" [2]—thus one of them in dogmatically dismissing a fundamental Sumerian problem declares "I am convinced . . . [although] the problem has not occupied my attention." (!) [3]

On scrutinizing the kings' names in these prefixed fragmentary Isin lists by my Indian keys, I observed that the earliest of these names were obviously variant dialectic spellings of the names or titles of the kings of the First and Second Dynasties of the Kish Chronicle and its Great Gap, that they followed one another in the same relative order of succession, and that several of these same names or titles were repeated lower down as fresh dynasties. It was thus evident that these so-called "dynasties" prefixed by the Isin priests to the First Dynasty of the Kish Chronicle if not fabricated had been obtained from various old fragmentary Sumerian lists of the names and titles of kings of the Great Gap, and had been strung together and then fictitiously placed in front of the Kish Chronicle First Dynasty.

Owing to the fragmentary character of these prefixed Isin lists, preventing my dealing with them satisfactorily, I waited in the hope that a more complete version might be found. This hope was eventually realized in 1924.

Isin Prefixed "Antediluvian" & "Early Post-diluvian" Dynasties showing growth of the Perversion of Sumerian Chronology & Arbitrary Prefixion of Dynasties to the Kish Chronicle

A practically complete version of the Isin Chronicle with its prefixed dynasties was found and published in 1923,

[1] For example, *Cambridge Ancient History* I., 1924, *passim*.

[2] On the persistent obstruction by Assyriologists to progress in our knowledge of the Sumerians, see WSAD. xxi f.

[3] S. Langdon, *Sumerian Grammar* II.

from the Weld-Blundell Collection at Oxford.[1] It is inscribed on a large clay " prism " with two columns of closely written text on each of its four faces.

This version of the Isin Chronicle, written by the Isin priests about 42 years later than those fragmentary ones published by Poebel & Legrain[2], shows how rapidly the legend of prefixed kings had grown in the hands of the Isin priests, obsessed with the Semitic " Flood " myth, in these few decades. It prefixes to the earliest " Postdiluvian " dynasty in Poebel's version a new *Antediluvian* dynasty of eight kings, reigning for a period of 241,200 years with an average reign for each of 30,150 years ! This is even more than in the mythical list of antediluvian kings of the late Chaldean priest Berosus. And it gives generally the same fabulous ages as the previous Isin Chronicle to the eleven dynasties which it prefixes to the First Dynasty of the Kish Chronicle, which latter moreover it characteristically mutilates.

Falsity of all the current Assyriologists' " History " & Chronology of the Sumerians & of Mesopotamia based upon the Prefixed " Dynasties " of the Isin Chronicles

To the ordinary matter-of-fact and scientific student of history, such vastly absurd and fabulous superhuman ages and chronologies are merely preposterous and foolish. Not so are they however, to that Assyriologist scholar who publishes this latest Isin Chronicle. He thinks that " it (this Isin Chronicle) constitutes the most important historical document of its kind ever recovered among cuneiform records." [3] He makes it the framework of his chronology and history of Ancient Mesopotamia and Babylonia ; and even goes the length of saying dogmatically—in defiance of the historical axiom that contemporary records are more trustworthy than later ones—that " in the inscriptions before the time of Sargon no confidence can be placed in records of local scribes unless they are confirmed by the

[1] WBC. 1923. Clay prism, No. WB. 444, 1923.

[2] The later date is evidenced by later Isin kings being mentioned in the Isin dynasty.

[3] WBC. II., 1. 1913.

dynastic (Isin) lists."[1] (!) And merely because he cannot find the great Sumerian emperor Uruash (" Ur Nina ") and his dynasty (so prolific in inscribed monuments) in this Isin Chronicle, or any other of the early Sumerian kings who have left their inscribed monuments, he declares that Uruash and these other emperors, whose monuments form the bulk of the early Sumerian remains, were but impostors in calling themselves " kings " at all ![2]

But the facts, as we shall now find, prove quite the contrary. These dynasties prefixed to the Kish Chronicle by the credulous myth-mongering priests of Isin are betrayed by their own records to be merely duplications of the First and Second Dynasties of the Kish Chronicle which have been arbitrarily misplaced in front of the latter. And the whole fantastic scheme of fictitious and extravagant Mesopotamian chronology and history founded on them in the latest text-books of ancient history and complacently adopted by the archæological excavators, crumbles ingloriously to the ground. On the other hand the First Dynasty of the Kish Chronicle emerges still more strongly established as the First Sumerian Dynasty, with its first king Ukusi (Dur, In-Dara, Gaur or George, Thor-Eindri or Andrew) and identical with the First Dynasty of the Early Aryans and Goths, and at a date no earlier than about 653 years before the reign of Sargon-the-Great, that is about 3380 B.C.[3]

[1] *Ib.*, 7. [2] Cp. *ib.*, 7. [3] See Chapter on Chronology.

FIG. 20A.—First Sumer King, In-Daru (Ukusi, Gaur or St George) slaying the human sacrificing Dragon of the Semitic Chaldees. From Cappadocian Hittite seal of about 2000 B.C. (After Ward 584, enlarged 2 diameters.)

Note the Andrew's X in his hat. Full description in WPOB. 319.

VIII

ARCHAIC SUMERIAN KING-LIST OF ABOUT 3150 B.C. DISCOVERED MISPLACED IN ISIN CHRONICLE, CONFIRMING KISH CHRONICLE, INDIAN & EDDIC KING-LISTS

Disclosing ODIN-THOR *of the Nordic Eddas as First Sumerian King, King* BARAT *amongst the "Antediluvians" and the Sumerian or Aryan Origin of the "Antediluvian" Kings of Berosos.*

ON scrutinizing the names in the so-called "Antediluvian" dynasties prefixed by Isin priests to the Kish Chronicle, and revising the reading of the polyphonous Sumerian written signs by the standard Sumerian lexicons in the light of our Indian and Nordic Edda keys, I made a discovery of fundamental importance for Ancient World History.

THE SO-CALLED "ANTEDILUVIAN" KINGS ARE MERELY MISPLACED OLD SUMERIAN VERSIONS OF 1ST & 2ND DYNASTY KINGS OF KISH CHRONICLE WITH FABULOUS AGES ADDED

I observed that this list of so-called "Antediluvian" kings, although used to fabricate a false chronology, was really a genuine old Sumerian version of the King-List of the Early Sumerian kings of the First and Second Dynasties of the Kish Chronicle down to and including King Barat, the first king of the Great Gap of that chronicle; and that as the list ended with that king it was presumably originally compiled in the reign of King Barat, that is about 3150 B.C. Its list of eight kings, or in the second version ten kings, was, I observed, substantially identical in names and titles and in chronological order of succession with the first ten Sumerian kings in the Kish Chronicle (including the first king of the gap, Barat), and in the Indian Aryan lists; and as regards the first three kings it was identical with the first three kings in Udu's Bowl and in the Nordic Eddas. And it contained besides this several other, but well recognizable, titles for certain of these kings additional to those in the Kish Chronicle and Udu's Bowl and in agreement with the Indian lists.

THE "ANTEDILUVIAN" KINGS OF THE ISIN CHRONICLE

The Isin list of these "Antediluvian" kings occurs in column I of the Weld-Blundell prism (WB. 444) and gives eight kings. But it is supplemented by a later and fuller list in the same collection (WB. 62) giving ten kings.[1] My revised readings of these two documents are given in detail in Apps. III and IV, with full proofs from the Sumerian lexicons for the readings when they differ from those hitherto conjecturally read.

IDENTITY OF "ANTEDILUVIAN" KINGS WITH EARLIEST SUMERIAN KISH CHRONICLE & UDU'S BOWL KINGS, & EARLIEST INDO-ARYAN & EDDIC KINGS

In the annexed Table is exhibited the identity of these "Antediluvian" kings of the Isin and Babylonian lists with the First and Second Dynasty main-line kings of the Kish Chronicle, with the first ten Aryan kings in the Indian lists (see Table, p. 130), with the first four Sumerian kings on Udu's Bowl, and with the first three Gothic kings in the Nordic Eddas as far as their king-list goes. It will be noticed that the Isin list, WB. 444 version, omits the sixth and ninth king, whilst WB. 62 version gives the full ten, and in their precise order as in the Indian lists. The serial numbers on left hand give the order of the names in the Isin list, and on right hand the order of the names in the Indo-Aryan lists. The syllables placed within square brackets are introduced as possible restorations of the text where it is destroyed or illegible.

[1] Another copy of this tenfold series was found by Weidner.

[*For Table see over page.*]

TABLE SHOWING ISIN "ANTEDILUVIAN" KINGS AS MISPLACED 1ST & 2ND DYNASTY KINGS OF KISH CHRONICLE, INDIAN LISTS, UDU'S BOWL & EDDAS.

"Antediluvian" Kings in Isin List.		Sumerian 1st & 2nd Dynasty.		Nordic Eddas.	Indian Lists.	
WB. 444	WB. 62.	Udu's Bowl.	Kish Chronicle 1st & 2nd Dynasty.			
1. UDUIN (or ODOIN) from Heaven made kingship at *Urdu*.	UDUIN (or ODOIN).	SAGG or SAGA-GA, or UDU-DUR or SAKH or DAR, DUR. GIN.	UKUSI	ODO, ODIN, SIG, YGG, or THOR or DUR from Heaven made kingship at *Urd*	SAKKO title of Indra or PURŪ-rawas, or IKSH-*Vāku*.	1.
2. ĀMA-Lord (or AKU) of the Jar.	. . . -AMA of the Jar.		AZAG, AMA (or AKA)[1].	ÆGIS, AMA, GUN.	ĀYUS, AYU, AMA of Jar.	2.
3. ENU, Priest-king, Lord of men.	[ENU]-KIDU, UNNUSHA.	ENUZUZU.	NAKSHA, EN-UZU, s.	HŒNI.	NAHUSHA, AN-ENAS	3.
4. Lord Enchanter, Great Lord.	[U]-DU-KU.	UDU, priest-king.	UDU or UDUK of Lord Sagg, s.		UDĀ	4.
5. DUMUZI or DUMU-GIN the Shepherd.	[DUMU]-ZI or -GIN.		ZIMUGUN.		JANAMEJAYA.	5.
6.	. . . EN, Lord of men		*Uziwitar*.		*Vishtara*.	6.
7. SHIBAZI.	. . . SHIBAZI, Lord.		*Mutin* (Ugan-)		*Matindra*	7.
8. UMUSH.	PISH [-MA-MA]		IMUASHSHU.		VISHĀMSUTAMSU or DUSHYANTA.	8.
9.	SUMADDI, s. of *Pishmama*		NAILINA.		ANILA, or ILINA or ? SUMANTA.[2]	9.
10. BARDUDU or BAR-ATUTU, at Sum-adru City. The Flood.	BAR-RA-DU (GIN-) or ZIU-SUDU. The Flood.		[BARDU, BAR-TU of inscrip.]		B'ARATA, BRI-HAT, PRITHU or YĀSHAS, s.	10.

[1] *Aka* is Sumerian synonym for *Azag*, WSAD, 7.
[2] *Sumanta* is called "brother" in late MSS., but may be a surname of Dushyanta.

Historical Importance of Isin "Antediluvian" King-Lists as Genuine Old Sumerian King-Lists Misplaced

It is thus demonstrated by the table that these so-called "Antediluvian" kings of the Isin Chronicle, although falsely called "Antediluvian," and merely a variant version of the Kish Chronicle kings of the First and Second Dynasties of the latter, are nevertheless *genuine independent old Sumerian lists of the earliest known Sumerian kings, and thus of immense historical importance.*

Their historical importance is all the greater as they continue the list from the first Sumerian king down to and inclusive of the first king of the Great Gap, Barat; and they preserve for the first king his ancient Sumerian titles of Udu or Odo and *Uduin* or *Odoin*, which along with his position and successors identifies him unequivocally with the first Nordic Edda king, Odin, Odinn or Odo.

It thus transpires that this list of kings existed in the Isin period as a floating traditional list of the very earliest known Sumerian kings, and presumably compiled in the age of the last or the tenth king; and that the Isin priests, not being able to equate their names with those in the First and Second Dynasties of the Kish Chronicle, in despair pitch-forked them in front, and in the remotest age they could think of, namely, before "The Flood," the Semitic myth of which had just come into vogue in Babylonian literature.

Odin, Thor or Sig, the First King of the Goths, is the First King of the Sumerians

The most outstanding fact that emerges from this ancient Sumerian list of the earliest Sumerian kings, thus fortunately preserved to us by these Isin scribes in their "Ante-diluvian" Dynasty (see Appendix III and Table), is that the first Sumerian king bears the name of *Uduin*; and we have seen that his title of Sagg (or Sagaga) on Udu's Bowl inscription had the synonym in the bilingual glossaries of *Udu-Dur* as a recognized variant title for this king.

Now it is admitted by Sumerologists that some of the six Sumerian signs at present transliterated as U had an O phonetic value; and I have shown that one at least of those "U" signs written by the O sign of the solar disc had clearly this O value and was the parent of the letter O in all the alphabets.[1] But be this as it may, these *Uduin* and *Udu* names for the first Sumer king clearly equate with those for the first Gothic king in the Eddas, as *Odin* or *Odinn* and *Odo*.

Striking confirmation of this identity of the first Sumerian king Uduin with Odin of the Eddas is found in the bilingual Sumerian glossaries which define King Uduin as "King UDU, the *Etil* (Lord), the First Leader of Men."[2] And here the title *Etil* or "Lord" is the same title which is a synonym for the first king as Sagg on his Stone-Bowl (p. 94), and is as we shall see the Sumer source of Thor's royal clan-title of ŒDL or ÆDL in the Eddas.

Moreover, the Star named after King Uduin is called "The Star of The Lord King ME-TI-RA,"[3] which discloses the Sumerian origin of the Sanskrit title of *Mitra* and the Persian *Mithra* for the Sun, which luminary was the sole "star" worshipped by the first king and his Goths in the Eddas. Still further the Planet *Jupiter*, named as we have seen after the first Sumer king's title of *Ia* or *Ja*, was called by the later Sumers "The planet UDU, the *Etil* (Lord), the GŪT,"[4] wherein *Gūt*, here spelt with signs meaning "The Bull of the Sun," is as we shall see later the ordinary Sumerian form of the word *Goti* or "GOTH."

This identity is further confirmed by this Sumerian record stating (see Appendix III) that "Kingship from Heaven was made arise. At Urdu City kingship was. . . . At Urdu City Udu-in the king reigned." This is in strict agreement with the Nordic Eddas which state that Thor, also called in different stanzas of that episode *Odo*, descended from his Himin, *i.e.* "Heaven" and enthroned himself as king at Urd.[5]

"ODO" & "ODIN" IN THE NORDIC EDDAS ARE TITLES SOLELY OF THOR, THE FIRST KING OF THE GOTHS & NOT OF WODAN

"Odo," "Odin" and "Odinn," as is clearly shown in my new literal translation of the Gothic Eddas, are solely the

[1] WAOA. 38 f., 48 f., and pl. II.
[2] Br. 10723 and cp. 1506.
[3] Br. 10724 and cp. 8201.
[4] Br. 51.
[5] See my new translation of The Eddas.

names or titles of Thor, Andvara or Eindri, the first king of the Goths in the older Edda texts; and they are never applied therein to Wodan, with whom Odin was confused by the later Norse and Teutonic Wodan-worshipping bards, who arbitrarily transferred the Odin stanzas of the Edda epic poems to Wodan in order to exalt the latter after that Chaldean chieftain was deified by his descendants and votaries.[1]

Wodan always appears in the older Eddas as a non-Goth, non-Aryan and non-Asa, and as an aboriginal Galdr or Chaldean sorcerer who was the arch-enemy of Thor or Odin in the latter's establishment of Civilization in Cappadocia and elsewhere in Asia Minor and in Carchemish. Wodan is usually called in the older Edda texts by the name of *Bodo* or *Bauta*, a shortened form of his full name of *Budhnya*, which is preserved in the Sanskrit Vedic hymns, in his later demonified form of "The Serpent of the Deep," who significantly is also made in the Vedas to be the arch-enemy of Indra, that is In-Dara, In-Dur, Dur or Thor. In the Eddas, Wodan is regularly represented as an aboriginal serpent-worshipping Chaldee priest and latterly sometimes mythically as a serpent; and hence his inveterate antipathy to Thor and his Aryan Sun-cult. Wodan's name is also preserved in its more proper form in our modern week-day name of "Wednes-day" or "Woden's-day" of the Anglo-Saxons, a people who latterly adopted the Teutonic Wodan or Woden or "The Fury" as their god of War instead of Mars and the serpent-rod bearer Mercury of the Romans. Whilst Thor's name survives in our "Thurs-day" or "Thor's-day" —preserving the older form of *Thur* for *Thor*—the Jupiter's day (*i.e.* Indra's day) of the Romans, when the Roman (and also Aryan-Sanskrit) notation of planets and god-names for the week-days was adopted by the Anglo-Saxons and Britons in Britain.

IDENTITY OF ODO OR ODOIN, 1ST SUMERIAN KING WITH ODO, ODIN OR THOR, 1ST KING OF THE GOTHS

The identity of this Odo or Odoin title and personality of this first Sumerian King, with the Gothic *Odo* or *Odin*,

[1] See details in my new literal translation of The Eddas.

a title of the first Gothic King, is evidenced not only by identity in that name and in the other titles of that personage as *Sakh* and *Dur*—the Eddic *Sig* and *Thor* or *Dur*—but also by his identity in the premier position and in the names and order of his successors, as seen in the comparative Table on p. 140.

In achievements also the identity is evident. In both Sumerian and Gothic records Odo, Odoin or Odin " descended from heaven " to make kingship at *Urdu* or *Urd*, which city I show was Carchemish on the Upper Euphrates, and the headquarters of Wodan, who with his son was vanquished and their Chaldean capital annexed and civilized by Thor, Sig, Odo or Odin, as detailed in my new literal translation of the Eddas.

We thus gain further striking Sumerian confirmation for the racial identity of the Sumerians with the Early Goths as Nordic Aryans.

King Barat, the Eponymous Ancestor of the Britons as an " Antediluvian " King of the Isin Chronicle

It is especially noteworthy that the last of these so-called " Antediluvian " Sumerian kings in both versions is the famous Aryan emperor Barat or *Brihat* of the Indian lists, the eponymous ancestor, as we have seen of the Britons and British (see p. 106). It is now historically important to find this independent Sumerian testimony to his existence and to his occupying therein the tenth place in the list of the earliest Sumerian kings, just as he also does in the list of the earliest Aryan kings in the Indian lists (see p. 130).

The new information we now gain regarding King Barat, who greatly extended the Aryan empire, from this Old Sumerian misplaced king-list is that it records his capital as being called Sumadru. This city has been supposed to be identical with " Shuruppak " on the site of the modern Arab village of Fara on the old Euphrates channel, not far to the south of Bismya or Adab (see map), where the contemporary inscriptions of this king were found. The name of this city may possibly be called after King Barat's uncle's title of *Sumanta* in the Indian epics,[1] which is presumably intended for the Sumerian *Sumadi* title of Barat's predecessor in the second version of this "Antediluvian" list.[2] In this latter also Barat bears the prefixed title of *Gin* (or *Zi*), meaning "ruler," and also "move, rise, extend, fill, full.[3] This *Gin* seems to be the title of Barat which the Indian scribes have translated into Sanskrit as *Shravas*, meaning "flow, gush, swift,"[4] and in a later Sumerian list we shall find that Barat bears the title of *Gani* or *Guni*, which may be a variant of the same.

Berosos' legendary "Antediluvian" Kings of Chaldeans are Misplaced Aryan Kings of 1st & 2nd Dynasties of Kish Chronicle with fabulous ages attached

This Isin list of "Antediluvian" Sumerian kings in Mesopotamia or Chaldea, naturally suggested comparison with the late Chaldean priest Berosos' list of "Antediluvian" kings in the same region, compiled about the third century B.C.[5] Such a comparison, hinted at by Poebel from his fragmentary Isin lists, has been attempted by the publisher of this fuller version of these lists, and shows a considerable amount of similarity in several names and in relative sequence; but the first name in the Isin list is read therein as "Alulim" (wherein the *A* belongs to the previous word, see App. III) in order to equate somewhat with the *Alorus* of Berosos; and the second name is read Ālalgar to resemble somewhat his *Alaparos*, but this name clearly reads in the second version *Āma*-gar, that is "*Āma* of the Jar," that is of Udu's Bowl, in the capture of which the second Sumerian king assisted his father Thor.

[1] In modern MSS. of the Indian epics Sumanta is made a "brother" of Barat's father, but this word seems to have been a title of the latter; for the later Indian scribes, in expanding the text, have clearly made separate personages out of adjoining aliases and surnames, as shown by the evidence of the Sumerian monuments with regard to the second main-line king and others.

[2] *Sumati* is given in some MSS. as a title of the preceding or eighth main-line king Tamsu. WVP. 4, 129 f.

[3] Br. 2038, 2396; M. 1342.

[4] MWD. 1097.

[5] Cory's *Ancient Fragments*, 51 f.

TABLE SHOWING ISIN "FIRST POSTDILUVIAN" &
1ST & 2ND DYNASTIES O

1st &c. "Postdiluvian" Prefixed Dynasties in Isin Lists.		Isin "Antediluvian" Dynasty.	
Kish Dynasty.	Unuk or Erech Dynasty.		
1. GAUR from Heaven, made kingship at Kish City.	SAGGI, AGUSHE-*ir*, s. of UDUIN at Inanna or Biddingir-City.	UDUIN from Heaven, made kingship at Urdu City.	UKUS
2. MUKHLA, TASIĀ or AZAG, Lord of Grain.	MŪKU of Plants, GĀN, GUN or KAN, s. of 1, K. and builder of Unuk City.	ĀMA, AKU of Jar.	AZAG (AK Kish
3. (Illegible).	IN, Shepherd of Vessel.	ENU, INU, UNNUSHA.	NAKS Devot
4. ,,	—	[U]-DUKU.	
5. ,,	DUMUZI or DUMUGIN, Prince PUR.	DUMUZI or DUMUGIN.	ZIMU
6. ,,			
7. MA (or BA(?)) . . .	—	. . . EN.	UZIWI
8. PIASH-ENZU.	—	SHIBAZI.	MUTIK
9. [. . . tab-ba].	—	PISH-[MAMA].	IMUA
	—	SUMADDI, s. of Pishmama.	NAILI
10. BŪRUDU (Gani or Guni).	—	BARDUDU, BARATUTU, BARRADU (GIN-) or ZIUSUDU ["The Deluge came up"].	
11. GAUDUMUMU or DŪDU-MUMU.	—	—	
12. DUTU-GINDARA.	—	—	
13. AZAG(?), or ASHITA-AB(?).	—	—	
14. AZAGBA(?) or ASHITABBĀ(?).	IZZAX GAMESH, s. of Zax.	—	
15. ARWASAG, s. of Mesh-RASAX.	URUASH, Great Sea-lord, s.	—	
16. GAL, Lord MA-RUD, ETANA, shepherd (colonizer), who made foreign lands faithful.	MUKH of the Sea-lands, s.	—	
17. BAGU(B)U, s. of 16.	BAUSSA, the swift.	—	
18. ENISHIB, Sea-lord.	ENNUN-NAD, Lord.	—	
19. —	DIXXI, The Divine (*Di*).	—	
20. MEDE of Kish, s. of 18.	MEDE, the Lord.	—	
21. GAAG or MUG (priest), Sea-lord, s. of 18.	KIAGA, King.	—	
22. DIXSAAX.	—	—	
23. TĪZAMA.	—	—	
24. RUMAU.	PĀSHIPADDA at Uri City.	—	
25. RUTASA-RĀUMAU.	URUDUKI-RAMAN.	—	
26. —	[EAMA . . .).	—	
27. —	[. . . (?)Biama].	—	
28. —	(Illegible), at Awau.	—	
29. —	,,	—	
30. —	,,	—	
31. —	,, at Kish.	—	
32. —	DUDU GUN-GUN	—	
33. —	MAMA-GAL ("Great in ships").	—	
34. —	KĀLBU . . ., s. of 33.	—	
35. —	TUKE.	—	
36. (En-mēn) BARA-GIN, Lord.	BURU-GIN, PURU-GIN, Sea-lord.	—	(ZAG "S
37. SHA-GIN, SHA-KIN, SHAGUR, s. of 36.	GANNI (or GUNNI) -PUR or -BUR, the Horizon-quartering.	—	SHA
37A. —	MU, k. in whose reign Kish smitten.	—	
38. —	KHA-(?)DANIS or KHA-(?)MANIS. of Khamazi.	—	MUS MAN
39. —	ENUGGE-ANNA	—	NAR BA

…VING PREFIXED DYNASTIES AS MISPLACED
…CHRONICLE & ITS GAP

THE GREAT GAP OF 430 YEARS.

…Chronicle. …d Dynasties.	Sumer Inscriptions. (*U.*) = Udu's Bowl.	Aryan Kings in Indian Lists. (*P.*) = Pali.	
. City.	SAGG, SAGAGA (*U.*), or INDARA, GAR, UDU-DUR, SAKH, DAR, DUR, PUR.	IKSH-VĀKU, SAKKO (*P.*), title of INDRA or PURŪ-*ravas.*	1.
…r BASAM, BAKUS …ator of Wines, built	GIN (or BĀS'UA) (*U.*).	ĀYUS, AYU, AMA-BASU, BIKUKSI, s. of 1.	2.
…ZU, s.	ENUZUZU, INUZUZU, s. (*U.*).	NAHUSHA, ANENAS, JANAK, s. of 2.	3.
. SAGG.	UDU, UTU, UDUK (*U.*).	UDĀ-*Vasu*, YADU, YAYATI, s. of 3.	4.
	—	JANAME JAYA or JINA or PURU.	5.
	—	WISHTARA or VISHTARA, s. of 5.	6.
	—	MATINĀRA.	7.
	DUIMUSHSU-DUASH.	VISHAMSU or TAMSU DUSHYANTA.	8.
	—	ILINA ANILA, or (?) SUMANTA.	9.
	BARDU, BARTU, BARTI, PIRTU, s. of *Duag.*	B'ARATA, BRIHAD, PRITHU, s. of *Dushyanta.*	10.
	—	GAUTAMA, TAMAS, DHUNDHU-*maru.*	11.
	—	DWAT, DHRITI, CANDRA-*aśwa.*	12.
	—	AJA-*Midha* or SITESHU.	13.
	IZZAX, GISHSAX.	CHAXUS, RIKSHA, RUCAKA or *Ruk-Meshu.*	14.
	URUASH-*Khūd*, URUSAG-*Khaddu*, or BHRAMA'HASHA.	HARYASHVA or BARMYASHYA, s. of Rucaka, Riksha, or Ruk-Meshu.	15.
	MADGAL, A-(A-MADGAL).	MUDGALA or MOGGALLO (*P.*) MARU.	16.
	BI(D)ASHNADI, BI(D)SAR, BIUGUN.	B'ADRY-ashwa, B'UJYU or PASENADI (*P.*).	17.
	ENASH-NADI, brother.	YUVAN-ASHVA, b. of 17.	18.
	TARSI (*Ene-* or "Divine").	DĀSA (*Divo-*, or "Divine"), or TRASA-DASYU I.	19.
	MEDI or METI.	METTIYO (*P.*), MITRAYU.	20.
	[KI]-AGA or MŪKUDA.	CYAVANA, MUCU-KUNDA.	21.
	TARSI, K. of Kish, or (?)SHU-DIG ("Shubad"), K. of Ur.	*Su*-DĀSA I, DUSSAHA, TRASA-DASVU II.	22.
	—	SOMAKA, SAM-*bhuta*, s. of 22.	23.
	ANTA (*Lugal-*).	JANTU.	23A.
	PĀSHI-PADDA ("*Mesanni-padda*").	PRISHADA or Suvarna-ROMAN.	24.
	DURUASHI-PADDA ("Ānni-padda").	DRUPADA I, HRASHWA-ROMAN, or ROHITA-ASHWA.	25.
	—	VASUMANAS, VYOMAN.	26.
	—	*Jimūta.*	27.
	[(?)PA-UNU-KHA ("Meskalamdug")].	*Bhanu* or *Ban-Kirti.*	28.
		Satya brata.	29.
	—	*Harish-candra I.*	30.
	—	*Harita* or *Rohita-ashwa* (?) *II.*	31.
	KINGUBI-DUDU, K. of Erech.	DHUNDU or CUNCU.	32.
		Vijaya ("The Conqueror").	33.
	—	B'ARUKA or RURUKI.	34.
	—	*Vri*-TAKA or Dhri-TAKA, or *Urja-vaha.*	35.
…rech), dethroned by	(URUDU-GINA, dethroned by Zaggisi),	PRA-CIN-wat, B'ARADVAJA, BĀHU or BAHUKA or PURU II.	36.
	BAR-GIN (BURU-), PARDUIBUZ-um.	SHA-KUNI, KUNI, SAGARA or PRA-VĪRA SU-VIRA.	37.
at Agade.	SHAR-GANI, GIN.	—	37A.
of 37.	MŪSH (Uru-).	MANASYU, PRAB'U of Gopta (Egypt), or Asa-MANJA, s. of 37.	38.
…U, s. of 37.	MANIS-TUSU (or -TUŚŚU).		
ENZU or NARĀM-	NARĀM, Lord ENZU or BA.	ANJANA, ANSU-mat or KARAM-B'A.	39.

On revising the readings of the Isin-list names, I observed further agreements in other names, as shown in the accompanying table, in which my revised readings duly attested are shown in col. 2.

BEROSOS' "ANTEDILUVIAN" KINGS COMPARED WITH SUMERIAN IN ISIN LISTS

Berosos.	Isin "Antediluvians."	
1. *Alōr-os*, appointed by God as Shepherd of Men.	(*A*)-*lu-in*.[1]	1.
2. *Alapar-os*.	*A-(?)lal-gar*[2] or *A-ama-gar*.	2.
3. *Amel-ōn* with OANNES, *Annedotus*.	*Enu, Unnusha Enmen-lu-anna*.[3]	3.
4. *Ammen-ōn*.	*En-men-gal-as-na* [*Udu* or *Uduk*].	4.
5. *Megalar-os*.	*Dumuzi*.	5.
6. *Daōn-os* or *Daōs*, the Shepherd.	. . . *en*.	6.
7. *Euedorach-os* with *Odakon*.	*Shibuzi*, the Shepherd.	7.
8. *Amempoin-os*.	*Pishmama*.	8.
9. *Ōpart-ēs*.	*Sumaddi*.	9.
10. *Xisouthr-os*, son of 9, the *Xasiwadra* of later Babylonian myth.	*Baratutu*. or *Ziusudu*.[4]	10.
— The Flood —	— The Flood —	

With reference to the name of *Alorus* given by Berosos to the first "Antediluvian" king, it is noteworthy that the first Gothic king Odo, Odin or Thor, bears in the Eddas the title of *Hloridi*, while in the Indian Epics and Vedas the first Aryan king bears also the title of *Aila*.[5] The name of

[1] The second or properly first sign here *lu* has also value of *udu*.

[2] This sign is transcribed *lal* in eye-copy in WB. 444; but it is clearly *ama* in second version WB. 62.

[3] *An-na* or "lord" also reads *ash-na*.

[4] This is an alternative of the tenth king's name in second version, where the same signs also read, *Zi-Barrachi*, see App. IV.

[5] WVP. 3, 168. This *Aila* title is interpreted by Sanskritists as a patronym or metronym of the first Aryan king, as "the son of *Ila* or *Ilā*," his reputed father or mother, the latter a title of Mother-goddess. It seems to be possibly derived from the Chaldean *Ilu*, "god," designating him as "The Son of God," a title used for him in later Sumerian literature, where he, besides being called *Adar*, is also called *Adamu*, "the Son of God" (WPOB. 239, 253) in series with the description of Adam in the New Testament, "Adam which was the son of God" (Luke iii. 38).

this first king in the Isin "Antediluvian" list may read *A-lu-in* by including the *a* from the previous word. The fourth name of Berosos, *Ammenon*, seems to be the synonym title *Enmen* of the third king which has got out of place. *Odakon*, a contemporary of the seventh king, is presumably *Uduk* of the Vase, the fourth king of the Aryan and Sumerian main line, who has also got out of place in Berosos' list. The ninth king is clearly intended for Barat or Baratutu, the tenth king in the Aryan and Sumerian main line. And the tenth king *Xisouthros*, the Flood-hero of the late Chaldean and Babylonian legends, is obviously intended for *Ziusudu*, the synonym or surname of Barat in the second "Antediluvian" version, and the equivalent of the *Uchathya* title of the latter in the Indian epic-lists (see App. I. No. 10).

Historical Results of these Discoveries that the "Antediluvian" Kings are Aryan

Altogether, it is thus evident that the "Antediluvian" kings of the Isin priests and of Berosos in his Chaldean corrupt version of the same are now disclosed to be merely the Sumerian kings of the First and Second Dynasties of the Kish Chronicle *with the inclusion of the first king of the Great Gap of that chronicle* (*Barat*) *and identical with the first ten Aryan kings in the main line in the Indian lists*, who have been thus far misplaced before "The Flood" and assigned fabulous ages by the myth-mongering Isin and Chaldean priests.

The date on which the original lists thus preserved were compiled was presumably in the reign of the last king in the list, namely the tenth king Barat about 3150 B.C.; and the archaic spelling is in keeping with such an early date.

These results therefore establish still more fully the fact that the Kish Chronicle First and Second Dynasties are the First and Second Dynasties of the Early Sumerians, and the identity of the Sumerians with the Early Aryans.

IX

TWO FURTHER OLD SUMERIAN KING-LISTS DISCOVERED OF ABOUT 2700 B.C. & 2600 B.C., MISPLACED IN ISIN CHRONICLE, CONTAINING MISSING KINGS OF THE GREAT GAP & CONFIRMING KISH CHRONICLE & INDIAN KING-LISTS OF THE EARLY ARYANS.

Disclosing the GAUR *or* " ST GEORGE " *title of 1st Sumerian King Odin or Thor, the* MUKHLA *or* " ST MICHAEL," TASIA, KAN, GAN *or* " GAWAIN " *titles of his son & Historical Originals of* ADAM, CAIN, ENOCH, NOAH & JAPHETH AS ARYAN KINGS, WITH FIXED DATES AND CONTEMPORARY MONUMENTS.

TURNING now to the so-called " First Postdiluvian " and other Dynasties prefixed by the Isin priests to the First Dynasty of the Kish Chronicle, we find that *these prefixed dynasties are merely a repetition of the self-same Sumerian or Aryan kings of the First and Second Dynasties of the Kish Chronicle, in the same order of succession and expanded beyond the eighth king of the Second Dynasty of that Chronicle with the lost twenty-six kings of the Great Gap in that chronicle, from King Barat onwards, and extended down to Sargon-the-Great and part of his dynasty under the old forms of their names and titles preserved in the Indo-Aryan Lists and in their Indus Valley Seals.*

Indeed, the fact that this so-called " First Postdiluvian " Dynasty was merely another version of the self-same kings who were arbitrarily projected before it by the Isin priests as " Antediluvian," should have been apparent to any critical Assyriologist from the circumstance that the self-same preface in identical words is prefixed to both of them, namely: " Kingship from Heaven Udu, Sakha (or Sakh, Dur or Pur) made." This implies that each of these two lists had evidently been separate independent traditional lists of the Sumerian kings from the first king of the First Sumerian

Dynasty. But the credulous Isin priests, failing to recognize either this or their relationship to the Kish Chronicle lists, arbitrarily termed the older of the two lists " Antediluvian " and the later " First Postdiluvian " and then attached fabulous ages to the kings and their reigns.

Immense Historical Value of the Misplaced Isin Lists as authentic Old Sumerian Versions of the Missing Kings of the Great Gap.

Here again, as with the prefixed " Antediluvian " kings, the prefixed " Postdiluvian " kings, these prefixed dynasties whilst entirely fictitious as regards their chronological position anterior to the Kish Chronicle, prove nevertheless in themselves to be of immense historical importance in preserving old independent traditional lists of the earliest Sumerian kings, which extend in two different and independent versions from the first king of the First Sumerian Dynasty more or less continuously down to Sargon and his dynasty, and include between them all the kings of the Great Gap, whose names are lost in the Kish and other Babylonian chronicles.

We thus recover, in addition to a duplicate copy of the first ten kings, two independent old Sumerian lists of kings of the Great Gap to supplement and confirm those preserved in the Indo-Aryan Lists, which led to these discoveries. And they preserve amongst other critical details the name and titles of Sargon's father as king of Kish, in agreement with those preserved in the Indian lists and on his Indus Valley seals.

Date of Compilation of the Two Old Sumerian King-Lists misplaced by the Isin Priests at about 2710 B.C. and 2600 B.C.

The respective dates of compilation of these two independent sets of Old Sumerian King-lists which the Isin priests thus misplaced is presumably indicated by the last king's name recorded in each list respectively. This postulates a date for the " First Postdiluvian " or " First Kish Dynasty " list in Sargon's reign that is about 2720 B.C.; and a date for the second list in the reign of Sargon's grandson, Naram-Enzu or Naram-Ba (the so-called "Naram-Sin") about a century later. And this is in keeping with the Indian Epic tradition regarding Sargon, where he is we shall see repeatedly referred to as a leading descendant of the *first* Aryan king, implying that he had on record a continuous genealogy back to that first Aryan or Sumerian king.

"First Postdiluvian" Prefixed Dynasty of Isin Chronicle as Misplaced Kings of 1st to 4th Dynasties of Kish Chronicle

This so-called "First Postdiluvian" Dynasty which the Isin priests have prefixed with its fellows to the Kish Chronicle is made by them to reign at Kish City at a vastly remote period immediately after "The Flood." It consists of 23 kings who are made by the Isin priests to reign 31,762 years before the First Dynasty of the Kish Chronicle and to reign for a period of 24,510 years!

On making a revised decipherment of the names in the prefixed list (see App. III) [1] and on placing their names as revised by the Indian Key-Lists alongside those of the previous "Antediluvian" Dynasty and those of the Kish Chronicle and Indo-Aryan King-Lists I observed that they were the self-same kings in the self-same order in all these lists, merely differing somewhat in phonetic spelling and in the occasional use of a different but recognizable title, solar or lunar; and extending more or less continuously down through the Great Gap to Sargon's Dynasty.

Comparative Table showing all Isin Prefixed "Postdiluvian Dynasties" are Misplaced Kings of 1st to 4th Dynasties of Kish Chronicle

This identity is exhibited in the accompanying table, in which I also place the strings of names of the next following "Early Postdiluvian" and other prefixed dynasties, all of which we shall find are similarly a further repetition of the

[1] My revised readings of the names in this text by the Indian Keys are given in App. III, where every reading of the ambiguous polyphonous Sumerian signs which differ from those hitherto conjecturally read without any keys to the form of the name are each and all duly attested by the standard Sumerian lexicons. See pp. 530 f.

kings of the Kish Chronicle First and Second Dynasties, but including the kings of its Great Gap down to Sargon's Dynasty.

In this table it will be seen that the chief difference between the "First Postdiluvian" Dynasty with its capital at Kish (col. 1) and the "Second Postdiluvian" Dynasty at Erech (col. 2) with its following prefixed dynasties, is that besides the occasional use of other titles, solar or lunar for certain of the kings, the latter (or Erech Dynasty) list gives a contracted early genealogy after the third king down to the fourteenth king. Beyond this it continues on with its successive prefixed dynasties giving the full list of the kings of the Great Gap down to Sargon's dynasty. Both these lists begin with the same king, the first Sumerian king of the First Dynasty of the Kish Chronicle, and give him several of his titles as in the "Antediluvian." His *Sagg* or *Sakh* title is spelt by the first list as *Sakh* or *Sakha* and by the second as *Saggi*, whilst his *Ukusi* title of the Kish Chronicle is spelt in the second list as *Akgushe*. The "First Postdiluvian" list of the "Kish Dynasty" ends with "Sargon" whose name is here spelt *Shāgin*, *Shākin* or *Shāgur*, in series with the Indian forms of his name, whilst the second string of prefixed dynasties (col. 2 of Table) carry the list down to Sargon's grandson Naram Enzu, here spelt *Enuggeana*, in series with the Indian list form of his name *Ansu* or *Anjana*.

Results of this Tabular Comparison prove First Dynasty of Kish Chronicle about 3380 B.C. to be the First of all Sumerian Dynasties, Recovering Old Sumerian King-Lists of Great Gap & Absolute Identity of Sumerians with Early Aryans

This comparative table demonstrates in the most conclusive manner possible by its positive and cumulative proofs in the extremely long string of mainline Sumerian or Aryan Kings, 39 in number, from the First Sumerian Dynasty continuously down to Sargon's Dynasty: (*a*) the fictitiousness of the Isin chronology in placing those strings of dynasties, so-called "Antediluvian" and "Early Postdiluvian" before the First Dynasty of the Kish Chronicle;

(*b*) the identity of the prefixed Isin "First" and other "Postdiluvian" and "Antediluvian" dynasties with the First and Second Dynasties of the Kish Chronicle; (*c*) the Recovery by these prefixed Isin dynasties of two genuine independent Old Sumerian King-Lists preserving the names of the last kings of the Great Gap of 430 years in the Second Dynasty of the Kish Chronicle; (*d*) *the unique historical authenticity of the Indian King-Lists of the Aryans in preserving the full list of the Sumerian Kings and in their due chronological order and in their traditional forms of names and titles;* (*e*) the uniqueness of the Indian Lists as a Key to the forms and restorations of the names and titles of Sumerian kings from the First Dynasty onwards; and (*f*) the absolute identity in tradition, language and race of the Sumerians with the Early Aryans.

ADDITIONAL SUMERIAN TITLES OF KINGS RECOVERED BY THE OLD SUMERIAN KING-LISTS

This tabular comparison of these different Old Sumerian versions of the main line Sumerians king and dynasties with the Aryan also discloses several additional titles of leading kings which are of immense historical importance in confirming the identifications, and all of which are in series with Aryan or Gothic multiple titles of those kings—and see on the use of plural titles by the Early Sumerian and Aryan kings, chap. II, p. 51. Amongst these multiple titles of these Sumerian kings thus preserved, the following are of especial historical importance and significance.

GAUR OR GAOR OR "ST GEORGE" TITLE OF 1ST SUMERIAN OR GOTHIC KING OF CAPPADOCIA & THE "GŒR" TITLE OF THOR IN THE NORDIC EDDAS

Amongst the other historically important Sumerian titles of the earliest kings in these old Sumerian King-Lists, thus fortunately preserved in the Isin Chronicles, is the significant one of *Gaur* or *Gaor* for the first Sumerian King, Udu, Odo, Indar or Dur, who had, as we have seen, his early capital at Ukhu, the immemorial capital of Cappadocia, the traditional home of "St George of merrie England," of whose name the Sumerian *Gaur* or *Gaor* is now seen to be an early form, in series with its dialectic variant of *Gar* on Udu's Bowl. This personal name for him is also written in Sumerian as *Guer*, *Goer* or *Gur*.[1]

In the Indian Sanskrit also *Gaura* or *Guru* are names for the planet Jupiter *i.e. Indra;*[2] and in the old Indian Pali Thursday *i.e. Thor's*-day is called *Guru*-day.[3]

This further confirms the identity of the Sumerians with the Goths, which latter people in their great national epics, the Eddas, give Thor the title of "*Geor*" or *Geir*, especially when he carries his standard of *The Red Cross* and in his slaying of the Dragon-worshipping aboriginal Chaldean chief who oppressed the people and opposed King Thor in his establishment of the Higher Civilization in Cappadocia and Mesopotamia.[4]

These new historical facts now fully identify the first Sumerian king with the historical original of St George of Cappadocia, the patron saint of England, who is still the patron saint of Asia Minor and the adjoining lands. The identity is still further confirmed by the title of his Cappadocian capital preserved in this Isin Chronicle, and in the phrase that King Odo, Dur descended "from Heaven" to establish kingship in Mesopotamia. For the Gothic Eddas relate that King Odo Thor's capital at Oku in Cappadocia, the Sumerian *Ukhu* capital of the first Sumerian king in the Kish Chronicle and the Pteria capital of the later Hittites (see map), was also called "Heaven" (*Himin*, the *Imin* or "Heaven" of the Sumerians[5]; and it is related that he "descended from his Heaven" to conquer and civilize Urd at Carchemish in Mesopotamia; and in the "Antediluvian" Isin list his Mesopotamian capital is called *Urdu* (see accompanying Table, col. 3). Similarly in the second Isin list version, his original city is called *Inan-na* (see Table, col. 2) wherein the affix *na* in Sumerian = "Stone"; just as in the Eddas the old Cappadocian capital of Odo Thor is often called "Inn-Stane," that is "Inn-Stone." Moreover, I have shown

1 WPOB. 319 f.

2 MWD. 359, 369. The later Brahmans, of course, try, as with other old titles, to translate this title to find a meaning and render it "teacher."

3 CD. 151.

4 WPOB. 304 f., 318 f., 320 f. And see my new translation of the Eddas.

5 WPOB. 241, 251; WISD. 94, 97.

in former works that this first Sumerian or Aryan king, who was afterwards deified for his benefactions to humanity by the grateful later Sumerians, Babylonians, Hittites, Indo-Aryans, Greeks and Goths is represented in the literature and mythology and art of all these several people as slaying the destructive world-menacing Dragon, and usually in association with his demon-dispelling solar Red Cross of St George.

"MUKHLA" OR "ST MICHAEL" AND "TASIA" TITLES OF 2ND SUMERIAN OR GOTHIC KING *re* "TASCIO" OF THE ANCIENT MONUMENTS & COINS OF THE ANCIENT BRITONS

Equally important historically are the *Mukhla*, *Mūku* and *Tasia* titles for Azag or Bakus, the human original of Bacchus or Dionysos, the son and successor of the First Sumerian king, preserved in these prefixed Sumerian King-Lists in the Isin Chronicle and referred to generally in a previous chapter. They confirm from independent old Sumerian sources the historical human original of St Michael the Archangel, the vanquisher of the great Dragon, with *Tasia* the solar Archangel of the later Sumerians, Babylonians, Hittites, Phœnicians and Ancient Britons as I had already demonstrated from quite different sources.[1]

The historical human original of St Michael the Archangel, I have shown was the son and successor of the first Sumerian, Aryan or Gothic king, Indara, Dur or Thor, and was identical with the Gothic *Miok*, a name equating with the Sumerian *Muku* of the second version of this Isin Chronicle and with the modern "Mike" contraction for "Michael." *Miok* is the Eddic title for Thor's son and chief-champion—otherwise called *Aegis* or *Bauge*, *i.e.* this Sumerian Azag or Bakuus who assisted his father in slaying the Dragon-chief and who himself also slew the almost equally malignant Dragon in the person of the son of the old Dragon-chief. He is *Miklu* the Archangel of the Aryans, Phœnicians and Greeks on the ancient coins of Cilicia and Phœnicia; (see Figs. 12, 13)[2] and the patron saint of the western Phœnicians

[1] WPOB. xv. 243 f., 338, 354 f., with many illustrations from Sumerian, Babylonian, Hittite and Phœnician seals and monuments, and Ancient Briton monuments and coins and from Phœnican coins.

[2] WPOB. 249 f., 319 f., 334 f., 349 f., 357 f.

who named after him their chief tin-port in Ancient Britain "St Michael's Mount."

Tasia, as his other title is preserved in this Isin Chronicle in keeping with its usual form in Sumerian and Babylonian literature, is of immense historical importance in confirming his identity as the historical human origin of this solar archangel *Tasia* of the later Sumerians, Babylonians (who also called him *Duk* and *Mar Duk*) [1] Hittites, Phœnicians, Trojans and Greco-Romans, the *Daxa* of the Indo-Aryans, and the *Tascia* solar archangel of the Ancient Britons so freely invoked on the prehistoric monuments and figured on the pre-Roman coins of Ancient Britain,[2] as we have seen in Figs. 1, etc.

Kan, Gan, Gin or Gun, title of 2nd Sumerian King Discloses the historical human origin of "Sir Gawain" of the Arthur legend & of "Cain"

The *Kan*, *Gan*, or *Gun* title of the second Sumerian king preserved in the Old Sumerian King-List in the Isin Chronicle (see col. 2 in Table), wherein he is also recorded as the builder of the city of Unuk, that is "Enoch," identifies him on the one hand as the historical original of "Sir Gawain" of the King Arthur legend, and on the other hand with Cain, the builder of Enoch city of the biblical legend, in which however his noble character and birth are mutilated and spitefully perverted.

The King Arthur (or properly Ar-Thur) legend, as we have already found, is a medieval romantic version of King Thor or Her-Thor, the first king of the Goths, in the Nordic Eddas, who we have found is identical with the first king of the Sumerians, Dur, In-Dur, or In-Duru, wherein the prefix *In*="king"; and *D* freely interchanges with *T*, and latterly *T* with *Th*. King Thor's son and chief knightly champion warrior in the Eddas bears amongst his other titles that of *Gun*, *Gunn* or *Kon*, and is the traditional "Conn the Hundred Fighter" of the Irish-Scots legends. He is also now discovered to be the historical original of "Sir Gawain" the young knightly champion of King Arthur in

[1] WPOB. 259 f., 343 f.

[2] WSAD. 53; WISD. 37, 79; and see foregoing notes 1-3.

the modern bardic versions of that legend. In the Eddas prince Gunn or Kon performs the same feats of knight-errantry in single combat as does Sir Gawain and he also vanquishes "The Green Man" who was the champion as now disclosed of the aboriginal Chaldees and son of the mother-weird.[1] In the later versions of the Arthurian legend Sir Gawain is arbitrarily made by later bards the "nephew" of King Arthur, but he was really as now seen his son.

"Adam" of "The Garden of Eden" Legend as a Travesty of the First Historical Aryan King with his History & Character perverted

It now transpired from our discovery of this *Kan* or *Gan* title for the second Aryan or Sumerian king, in view of his being recorded as the builder of the City of Enoch (Unug or Erech), and as the son of *Adar, Adda* or *Addamu* and as the father of Enu, Enuzu, Naksha or Nahusha the father of "Ia-patesi," that *Kan or Gan was obviously the historical original of the "Cain" of the Hebrew Genesis* with the genealogy of "Adam, Cain, Enoch or Enos, Noah and Japhet"; and that his father, King Adar or Adda or Addamu, was the historical original of "Adam" of "The Garden of Eden" legend of the Hebrew Genesis, with his history and character perverted by the Semites.

Further examination fully confirmed this chain of identities. And it showed that the Hebrew rabbis who composed Genesis with its Garden of Eden and Creation of Man story had manifestly helped themselves to the floating traditional history in late Babylonia in respect to the oldest kings known to the ancient world, namely the kings of the First Aryan Dynasty. But not understanding it, they had travestied the historical facts and the noble character of the great King "Adam," by making "Adam" to be the first lowly "created" man, instead of the first man and superman, several geological periods subsequent to the advent of man in the world, who first made men of the Pre-Adamite men. His date also they did not get quite correctly, but evidently took the late Babylonian estimate which placed

[1] See my new translation of the Eddas.

him several centuries before his true date. Thus they made their date for the "creation" of Adam and the "Creation of the World" to be 3761 B.C.; whereas the year on which King "Adam" ascended his throne, as we now find by the new historical evidence, was about the year 3378 B.C.

THE NAME "ADAM" IN RELATION TO TITLES OF THE FIRST ARYAN OR SUMERIAN KING DUR, BUR OR THOR

We already observed in the Bowl genealogy of Udu that he calls himself therein by the title *Patesi* or "Priest-king," and in the Kish Chronicle he is called "The devotee of Lord Sagg, whose later reflex was called *Ia* (or "Jah"), whence as *Ia-patesi* or "Priest-king of Ia" seems to have been coined his title of "Iapetos" or "Japhet." The First King, in addition to his personal name of *Dar, Dur* or *In-Dar*, bore also the titles of *Sagg* or *Sakh, Udu* and *Adar—Odo* and *Adar* being also names of Thor in the Eddas. Now the Semitic synonym for this Sumerian king (or god) *Dar* is ADDA;[1] and *Adda* was made by the priests "The God of the Thunder Storms," just as King (or Lord) Sakh was latterly made so by the Sumerians, and just as he was as Indra made by the Indian Brahmans "The God of Thunder and Rain," and as *Zeus* (the Sumerian *Sakh, Zakh* or *Zax*) he was made by the Greeks "The God of the Thunder-bolt." And *Idim* we found was a synonym for King Sakh's title as *Sagg* on Udu's Bowl, and the vowels are freely interchangeable in Sumerian.

Later, we find that in the polytheistic stage the priests, in extending their mythology, made a human reflex of this deified Adda (*i.e.*, the deified King Dar or In-Dur himself) to bear the name of "The Man *Ad-mu* (or *Adda-mu*),"[2] who retained a memory of the original human character and exploits of King Dar or Sakh of the Sun-Hawk cult. They gave this "Man Addamu" the characteristic title in Sumerian of "The Man *Sig*, the Hawk-Man (or Sakh)"[3]—wherein *Sig* we have seen was a Sumerian variant of Sakh and is a common title for Thor in the Nordic Eddas. But

[1] M. 1868; B. 113. Also spelt by Semites *Adad*.

[2] Br. 3426. On *Adda*, Br. 4165.

[3] Br. 3426 and 2051.

here now comes the significantly historical fact that they define this Sumerian title for this Admu or Addamu "the Hawk-Man" in Semitic as "the Man ADMU, *The Revolutionist, The Caster down*, the Bird (Hawk)-Man."[1]

Here then we have Babylonian references not only to the Semitic application of the name Admu or Addamu to the human form of the first Aryan or Sumerian king, but also *the memory of King Dur's or Sakh's great Revolution, by which he rebelled against the Pre-Adamite Semites' "god" and cast down their Serpent-Lion and Mother-Son demonistic cult by his establishment of Civilization and civilized rule;* and thus evoked upon his head and name the spiteful vilification of the Semites down the centuries—a vilification which was continued even after the Semites adopted "Adam's" idea of God in Heaven in place of their own old demonist totems the Serpent and Lion of the underworld that demanded sanguinary sacrifices.

KING ADAM'S OR ADDAMU'S REVOLT AGAINST THE PRE-ADAMITE DEMONISTIC SERPENT CULT IN BABYLONIAN ART AND LITERATURE

Apart from the systematic references to Lord Sakh, Dar or Adar's overthrow of the Serpent-Dragon cult of the Chaldeans in Sumerian and Babylonian sacred literature (as instanced in the old hymn cited at p. 150, and in the many seals I have figured in previous works), a Semitic reflection of the human King "Adam's" epoch-making revolt against, and overthrow of, that Semitic demonolatry is, I find, preserved in the well-known later Babylonian legendary poem on "How Adamu broke the Wing of Shūtu, the South Wind," in which Adamu is in human form though semi-mythical. The tablet on which it is written dates to about the fourteenth century B.C., that is to a period when the Semitic Babylonians had largely given up their Serpent and demonist worship, and had borrowed King "Adam's" or Dar's idea of Heaven and God, and also the later Sumerian idea of an anthropomorphic god, and had personified Heaven as an anthropo-

[1] *Ib.*, and 2050-3. On *Te-esh lu-uku*, cp. *Teshu*, "revolution," "rebellion," and *lakū*, "to cast down," M.D. 1199 and 479.

morphic Father-god, " Anu," forming with two other gods, namely, the Moon and In-Dur himself, a trinity god-head.

In this poem, with a vague memory apparently that Adamu was related to In-Dur or Ia, " The Lord god Dur " (that is to his deified self), he is made " the son " of that divinity, who had become in their polytheism " The god of the Deep Waters or Flood " ; and his epithet here as " The son of the god Ia," is in series with Adam's title in the New Testament as " Adam, the son of God (Iah or Jah).

FIG. 21.—Trial of " Adamu, the son of God Ia," for casting down the Semitic " god " Shûtu. From a seal of about 2500 B.C. After WSC. 300 b.

(For explanation of the Bird-form of the lower half of his body, see text.)

But the story was current much earlier, as it was a favourite subject on seals of about 3000 B.C. or earlier (see Fig. 21), which represents Adamu as being tried before a god for the heinous offence and " sin " of a mere man casting down and maiming a " divinity." And the god before whom he is brought as a prisoner is seen on the earliest seals to be, not the Semitic Anu, but In-Dur or Ia,[1] that is his own deified reflex. This is exactly paralleled in the later Indian Vedas, as we have seen, where the *man* Indra was made by the Brahmans, who had forgotten the origin of their god, to be the object of jealous malevolence by their *god* Indra who was developed from him. In these seals, Adamu is pictured conventionally as a Bird-Man, his upper body

[1] Cp. WSC. Figs. 291-8, where the water streams and fishes are diagnostic.

being human and his lower with the body, feet and tail of a bird—this, however, appears to be merely a graphic device to represent him by the hieroglyphs of his title of "Bird-Man" or devotee of the Sun-Hawk, for distinguishing purposes.

The name of Adamu's enemy is given in the poem as *Shūtu*, and he was latterly identified mythologically with the destructive and dreaded scorching South Wind. But it seems to me that he was Shūtu "the Slinger of the (Chaldean) Mother-goddess."[1] For this same outrage inflicted by him on Adamu with the same retaliation by the latter is related of Thor in the Nordic Eddas as inflicted by his arch-enemy *Surt*, who was the fiery stone-slinger of the Mother weird of Urd and the prototype of Satan.[2]

In the following translation of this poem, however, I retain the later mythological reading of "South Wind," and for "hand" read accordingly "wing."

"How Adamu broke the Wing of the South Wind (Shūtu)

In this legendary form the tablet literally records:[3]

"Shūtu in angry scorching [raged] and ducked him (Adamu) under:
Unto the dwelling of . . . [the fishes] he made him (Adamu) sink.
[Quoth Adamu] 'O Shūtu . . . [thou hast played] me bitterness,
For that I will bind you! Thy wing will I break!'
As with his mouth he had said, [so] of the South Wind the wing was broken.
For seven days the South Wind over the land did not rage.
God Anu to his minister Lord Ila-abrat spake:
'Why has the South Wind for seven days over the land not raged?'

[1] Cp. MD. 1131, No. 4; and *gishparru*, 233.
[2] See my new translation of the Eddas.
[3] The text was published by H. Winckler in *Der Thontafelfund von El Amarna*, 166; and reproduced KFS. 215 f. And several translations practically identical are extant.

His minister Ila-abrat answered him : ' My Lord !
Adamu the son of god Ia, of the South Wind the wing has broken.'
When Adamu before the god Anu, the king, drew near,
The god Anu saw him and said : ' Come, Adamu !
Why of the South Wind, the wing didst thou break ? '
Adamu to the god Anu made answer : ' Lord, for the house of Lord Ia
In the midst of the sea, fish I was catching,
[When] the South Wind blew and me did he duck under,
To the dwelling of the fishes he made me sink ! ' "

From this trial scene, it seems clear that the later Semitic story of the " Sin " of Adam for his " disobedience " of the Semitic " God " was already beginning to be concocted by the Chaldean priests in Babylonia.

But it is characteristic of the truer tradition of the Nordics, that there is no such " trial " scene in the Eddic version, for the reason that Thor Adar was supreme and those Semitic gods had not yet been invented. And a memory of the truer history of King Adamu was still evidently retained by the British bard Caedmon in the seventh century A.D. through his Nordic runic literature, as in his famous poem on the Hebrew Genesis he makes *Adam to be an enthroned king living in joy* while the vanquished Serpent, Satan of Eden, laments, saying :

" That is my greatest grief that Adam, wrought of earth
Should hold my firm-set throne and live in joy,
While we endure this bitter woe in Hell." [1]

Cain, Enoch, Noah and Japheth as Early Aryan or Sumerian historical Kings of fixed Dates and Contemporary monuments

Similarly the identity of King " Adam's " descendants and successors as historical Aryan kings who were bodily borrowed by the Hebrew scribes for their Genesis legend became more evident on further examination.

" Cain " in the Biblical legend is the son of Adam and is made the first man to be born in the world, yet building

[1] Caedmon's Poems, 383-7. Transl. by C. W. Kennedy, 19.

the city of Enoch—a city of which the now historical King Kan or Gan, the second Aryan or Sumerian king and son of King Udu or Adar, was the traditional builder. His name is spelt in the Hebrew *Qin*, and is thus in series with the *Gin* title for the second Sumerian king in Udu's Bowl—the hard *G* and *Q* being interchangeable in Babylonian and other languages. Moreover, this Sumerian *Gin* sign has the Semitic value of *Qanu*,[1] which is in series with the later Hebrew spelling of *Qain* for the name rendered "Cain" in our English version.

Significantly also Cain, the son of Adam, is called in Genesis[2] by the title of *Aysh or Aish*, which appears to be a memory of the Sumerian royal title of Gin as *Azag*, the *Ayus* of the Indian epic versions, and his *Ægis* title in the Eddas.

Cain, moreover, so far from being an outcast, accursed, and a fugitive, is admitted to have been the greatest man of his time and "the first" builder of cities in the ancient world, according to the Semitic compilers of Genesis. Thus we are told: "Cain . . . builded a city and called the name of the city after the name of his son Enoch" (Genesis iv. 17), wherein the name "Enoch" of the English version is written in Hebrew as "*Hanuk*." This city in question built by Cain is admitted by all Biblical authorities to be identical with the old Sumerian seaport city of *Unuk*,[3] in Lower Mesopotamia, on the Persian Gulf to the west of Lagash city (see map). It was latterly called "Erek" by the Chaldeans and is the modern Warka, now left far inland by the downward silting-up of the Euphrates delta. Now this city of Unuk or "Enoch" is recorded in this second version of the Old Sumerian king-list in the Isin Chronicle to have been built by Gan, Gun or Kan, the second Sumerian king and son of King Odo, Dur or Adar. And this is confirmed by many references in Babylonian literature. Moreover, that city of Unuk or Enoch is specially recorded in the Creation myths of the later Babylonians as having been built by Mar-Duk (a title which is defined as "The Son

[1] Br. 2384 and 11900.

[2] Gen. iv. 1, where the word is translated in our English version as "a man."

[3] EB. 623 f.

of the Sun"), who as we have seen was this deified second Sumerian king Gina, and son of the deified Dar or In-Dara or Bil. Thus one of these texts says:

> "Lord Mar-Duk . . . he built the city,
> [He built the city of Nippur], he built the temple,
> He built the city of Unuk (Enoch), he built the temple of Anna."[1]

The identity of Prince Gunn or Kon or Miok (St Michael) of the Eddas, the son and successor of the first Gothic King Odo, Thor or Adar with the Cain of Genesis is confirmed by the Eddic poems which record his slaying under his title of *Miok* of the Chaldean *Epli* (*i.e.* "Abel") of *Iotun-gardi* ("Garden of Eden"), who was an elderly aboriginal Dragon-chief and the arch-enemy of Prince Gunn's or Miok's father, opposing the latter in his establishment of civilization. This incident evidently discloses the historical human originals and personalities of St Michael slaying the Dragon Apollyon. And we shall find that "Nimrod," the name of a great traditional builder of cities in Early Mesopotamia in the Old Testament was a title of "Cain" (see Appendix IV).

Enoch or *Hanuk*, the son of Cain—a spelling which equates with its *Janak* form in the Indian Epic—is regarded by Biblical authorities as being identical with Noah of the Flood myth, who is also called "Hanuk" in the Bible—the list of nine or in second version ten antediluvian patriarchs therein having been formed by repetition of titles.[2] This identity of Enoch and Noah is now confirmed by the Sumerian variants in spelling the third Sumerian king's name as Enu, Enuzu, Unnusha and Naksha. The uncertainty also of the Hebrew compilers of that genealogy in regard to Enoch seems evident from their statement that Enoch did not die, and that he lived for 365 years—a statement which is regarded by Biblical authorities as indicating his *solar* character through the number of days in a solar year,[3] and we have seen that his ancestors and descendants were Aryan Sun-worshippers. And the statement that "Enoch

[1] Zimmern, EB. 623. The temple of Anna was at Unuk.
[2] On the identity of Enoch or Enos with Noah see EB. 623.
[3] EB. 624.

walked with God," is obviously a confused memory of the fact that Enoch was contemporary with " and walked with " his grandfather King Odo or " Adam," who was afterwards deified under the title of IA (*Jah*) as the ideal Father-God.

" Japhet," the son of Noah, has his name spelt in Hebrew as I-P-T or Y-P-T that is *Iapat* or *Yapat*. This *Iapat* suggests that this name was borrowed from the title of the fourth king, Udu son of Enu or Enuzu as " priest-king," namely *Patesi*.[1] King Udu inscribes himself as " *Patesi* of the Lord Sagga." In later times Sagga became the Father-god, and in still later times this Father-god was called *Ia* or " In-Duru." [2] Thus the title *Ia-patesi* or " priest-king of God Ia " could easily be corrupted into *Iapat* the Hebrew for " Japhet." And one of the Indian variants of this king's name as *Yati* or *Yayati* approximates somewhat *Iapat* or *Yapat*.

Adam, Cain, Enoch, Noah & Japhet, Names & Genealogy borrowed by Semites from those of the First Sumerian or Aryan Kings & Culture Heroes

Genealogically, therefore, as well as in the form of the names, the identity of the names of the Biblical patriarchs Adam, Cain, Enoch, Noah and Japhet, with the names of the first Sumerian kings and culture heroes, is indicated, as here tabulated in their genealogical order:

Sumerian.	Eddic Gothic.	Hebrew Genesis.
1. *Udu* (or Odo) or *Adar* (*Adamu*).	*Odo, Adar* or *Adr.*	*Adam.*
2. *Gin, Gun, Kan-*, or *Azag*, s. of 1.	*Gunn, Kon* or *Ægis*, s. of 1.	*Qin* or " Cain " or *Aysh*, s. of 1.
3. *Enu, Enuzu, Unnusha*, s. of 2.	*Hoeni*, s. of 2.	*Enoch* or *Hanuk* or *Enos* or Noah, s. of 2.
4. *Udu-Patesi*, s. of 3.	—	*Iapat* or " Japhet," s. of Noah.

The borrowing of these famous names of the earliest Sumerian or Aryan kings and culture heroes—the most

[1] *Pa-ti-si* is a variant Sumerian value for this *Khat-ti-si* title, see p. 94 *ti* has also the value *te*, Br. 7685; and I have shown that *Khatti-sig* was probably a title of Sumerian rulers as " Rulers of the Khatti or Hittites."

[2] WPOB. 244 f., 259 f., 323 f.; WISD. 70, 127.

famous of all names in the Old World—by the Hebrew compilers of Genesis for their version of the origin of civilization, seems to be sufficiently explained by the fact that according to the best modern Biblical authorities those compilers based their version of the Creation myth upon borrowings from the later Babylonian and Chaldean Creation myths which included these heroes and made these First and Second Sumerian Dynasty Kings " Antediluvian "—the " Flood " myth having come into currency about the period of the Isin Dynasty. And the " Sons of God " who married " the daughters of men " in the Hebrew legend are seen to have been obviously the Aryan " sons " or descendants of the Aryan King " Adam " who introduced Civilization with the idea of a God of Light in Heaven into the Old World of lowly pre-Adamite men, Chaldean and Semitic worshippers of the Old Serpent and malignant demons of Darkness and the underworld demanding sanguinary sacrifices. But presumably owing to imperfect knowledge of the historical facts they mutilated the tradition and degraded these illustrious kings into their own primitive pre-Adamite ancestors, notwithstanding that these famous kings were not Semitic in race at all, but Sumerians, Early Aryans, or " Nordics " or Goths.

Fundamental Importance for Ancient History of the Discovery of Two additional independent Old Official Sumerian King-Lists of First & Second Dynasties of Kish Chronicle, & Disclosing further Sumerian Titles of First historical Sumerian Kings

Thus our comparative table of the so-called " Early Postdiluvian " Dynasties prefixed in the Isin List to the First Dynasty of the Kish Chronicle, discovers that these prefixed king-lists are in fact two additional independent genuine Old Sumerian King-Lists of the First to Fourth Dynasties of the Kish Chronicle, which the Isin priests being unable to identify had bodily prefixed them, end to end, before the First Dynasty of the Kish Chronicle—*the only genuine continuous* chronicle of the Sumerians from the First Dynasty down to the later historical period.

The first ten kings of these so-called " Early Postdiluvian "

Dynasties are disclosed by our Comparative Table to be merely a repetition of the ten "Antediluvian" kings of the still earlier prefixed list with the addition in some cases of other titles; and they correspond to the first nine kings of the First and Second Dynasties of the Kish Chronicle main line with the addition of the first king of the Great Gap in that chronicle; and they are in strict agreement with our Indian King-Lists of the Early Aryans, and with Udu's Bowl contemporary genealogy of the kings of the First Sumerian Dynasty, and with the first Gothic Dynasty as far as the Edda Epics of the Goths go.

The further Sumerian Titles borne by these kings in these two Old Sumerian King-Lists are of immense critical historical importance as they preserve amongst others the Early Sumerian forms of the titles of *St George* of Cappadocia and England, *St Michael*, or *Tasia*—the "Tascio" of the pre-Roman coins and monuments of the Ancient Britons, and the *Gan* or "*Sir Gawain*" title of the son of King Her-Thor or Ar-Thur, who we have found to be the first Sumerian, Aryan or Gothic king and of fixed date. And all these title identifications are confirmed by the independent Indian King-Lists and Chronicles, Udu's contemporary Bowl inscription of the First Sumerian Dynasty and by the Gothic Eddas and the Arthurian tradition.

The further analysis and comparison of these two additional Old Sumerian King-Lists now requires a separate chapter.

FIG. 21A.—St Michael or Tasia (Tashub) the Sun-archangel in Hittite seal of about 2000 B.C. After Ward 873. Note winged type of saint, Sun-Cross emblems, and dress of votaries with amulet-seal tied to wrist.

X

THE TWO OLD SUMERIAN KING-LISTS MISPLACED IN ISIN CHRONICLE PRESERVE THE MISSING 27 KINGS OF THE GREAT GAP OF 430 YEARS IN KISH CHRONICLE IN COMPLETE AGREEMENT WITH INDIAN OFFICIAL LISTS:

Disclosing further information regarding King BARAT *and his son* GAUTAMA; URUASH'S *Dynasty of Sea-empire and Colonization of Indus Valley by his son Madgal; and King Tarsi of Kish or Su-Dāsa and his Battle against the* 10 *confederate Kings.*

OF equal fundamental and extreme historical importance is the discovery—resulting from the comparison of these two independent Old Sumerian King-Lists misplaced in the Isin Chronicle with the Kish Chronicle and the official Indian King-Lists of the Early Aryans, see Comparative Table, p. 140—that these two independent Old Sumerian King-Lists thus misplaced by the Isinites preserve the missing names of the Sumerian kings of the Great Gap of 430 years in the 2nd Dynasty of the Kish Chronicle, which have otherwise been completely lost in the Babylonian lists, but which are fully preserved in our official Indo-Aryan King-Lists.

Between them, these old Sumerian King-Lists are seen to fortunately preserve the complete list of the Sumerian kings of this Gap, except four whose names are illegible. And significantly they are seen in the table to agree both in general form and in strict chronological sequence with the names of these kings as preserved in our official Indian lists of the kings of the Early Aryans.

These Old Sumerian King-Lists of the Great Gap supply, besides the names, some additional information regarding certain of the leading kings which is of much historical importance or significance in supplementing our knowledge regarding them. Some of this additional information now calls for notice.

KING BARAT & HIS SON GAUTAMA OR GOTAMA

We gain from the first of these Old Sumerian lists further confirmation of the identity of Barat the first king in the Gap and tenth in the main-line list in both versions, Sumerian and Aryan, and further light regarding him in addition to that on p. 106. His name is not only substantially identical in both, but so also are the names of his successors. His name here as King of Kish is dialectically spelt in the Sumerian *Būrudu* or *Piurudu*, in series with the *Bardu* or *Pirtu* in his inscriptions and the *Prithu* dialectic variant in the Indian lists. He bears also the prefixed title of *Gani* or *Guni*,[1] which seems a variant of his *Gin* title in the "Antediluvian" list, see table opposite p. 140.

His identity with the famous Indian emperor Barat or Barata is further strikingly confirmed by the names and order of his successors. His immediate successor is *Gaudumu* which equates so literally with *Gautama*, the son of King Barata by Queen Mamatā in the Indian Epics.[2] King Gautama's Indian variant of "Dhundhumara" in some MSS. is also interesting as being explicable by a variant reading of the polyphonous Sumerian signs for this name *Ga-udu-mu*. The first sign has the polyphonous values of both *Ga* and *Du*, and with the latter the name can be read as *Du-udu-mu*, which seems the source of the "Dhundhumara" of those Indian versions. It thus appears that the latter was a reading of this name by Indian scribes who knew the polyphonous Sumerian values of the signs in transliterating the Sumerian syllabic script into the later alphabetic writing; and that the *mu* affix was later converted by Brahmans into the Sanskrit *mara*, in order to extract some meaning from the name and to fabricate a legend therewith.

Gautama, the son of King Barat, also called dialectically Gotama, is still in modern India one of the most revered of royal sages. He is in the Vedas frequently mentioned as a special worshipper of the Sun and Fire in association with Indra, and bears the title of Rahugana, and in the

[1] On *Gu* value, cp. Br. 6103, which is the name for this sign and SS. 244.

[2] WVP. 3, 16. On *Uthathya* or *Ucatha*, title for Barata, cp. PIT. 157 f.

Epics is called "The good Worshipper" (*Su-yaj-na*). He is also associated with the sea-god Varuna. In the Epics also he is called Dīrgha Tamas, who lived at Saradwant, and was a great sailor and delivered from dangers of rivers;[1] and under this title he is traditionally the father of Prince Kakshivan, "the far-famed merchant prince," whose official seal, or that of a descendant bearing his patronym, was found, as I have shown, in the Indus Valley.[2]

This old Sumerian list, moreover, helps us to disentangle the great confusion in the Indian list genealogy of this period in the Brahmanist Puru versions of these King-Lists, which obscure the direct succession and introduce many branch dynasties here claiming immediate descent from this famous emperor Barat. Thus the third in succession from the latter is called in the Sumerian *Azag* (?) or *Ashita-ab*, who is seen to be substantially identical with *Aja-midha* of the Puru lists and *Shiteshu* of the Yadu lists (see Appendix I, No. 13), and thus disclosing the real main-line succession.

King Uruash's Parentage, Sea-Emperorship and Colonization of the Indus Valley by his son Madgal

Important additional information to that previously elicited (on p. 108) is also supplied by these two Old Sumerian King-Lists in regard to King Uruash, his parentage, and to other members of his dynasty and their seafaring achievements—this dynasty being the *Panch* Dynasty of the Indian Epics, which we have found was "The First Dynasty of the Phœnicians," and of Aryan race. And we shall find that *in their Indus Valley seals this dynasty used retrograde writing like the later Phœnicians* (see Plate VIII).

Uruash, the Emperor *Haryashwa* of the Indian chronicles (see Fig. 20), bears in the first of these two old Sumerian King-Lists the phonetic form of name of *Arwasag*, which is in series with the form in one of his own inscriptions as King of Kish, namely *Urusag*, inscribed on the votive alabaster vase which was unearthed from the foundations of the tower of the old Sun-temple at Nippur, close to the site where were unearthed the inscribed fragments of Udu's Bowl. In this Sumerian King-List as "*Arwasag* king of

[1] RV. I, 158, 3 f.

[2] WISD., 42 f.

Kish" he is called "son of the priest (or *Mash*) *Rasax*"; whilst in the second old Sumerian King-List his father is called "*Iszax* prince of Oxen (or *Gamesh*)," a name and title which has hitherto been read as "Gilgamesh," the famous Sumerian Hercules, who also was a "prince of Oxen," and who I have demonstrated was the historical original of that hero of the Phœnicians and Greeks.[1]

Now this old Sumerian form of Uruash's father's name as *Rasax* equates with the Indian variant forms of his name as *Rucaka* and *Riksha*; and with its prefix *Mash* it equates with the Indian variant of his name as *Ruk Meshu* (see Appendix I, No. 14).

We further learn from the second Sumerian version that Uruash's father was "son of *Gela* or *Zaxla* and Lord of Zirabba, Sirabba or Kulabba; and that Uruash himself bore the title of "Great Sea-lord."

King Uruash as Sea-Emperor

Besides bearing personally in this list the title of "Great Sea-lord," most of his descendants in the dynasty also bear the title of "Sea-lord" in both lists; and his usual title in his inscriptions at Lagash city seaport admittedly designates him as "of the House of the Fishes," that is "of The Sea," giving the title of "Ruler of the Waves."

That King Uruash and his *Panch* or "Phœnician" Dynasty were seafaring people is abundantly evidenced by the numerous finds in the stratum of their period at their seaport city of Lagash of fish-hooks, fishing-tackle, harpoons, the Net as a figure of the king's power in sculptures,[2] sea-shell ornaments finely carved and used also for inlaid work, the offering of oars to the patron saint of

[1] See WISD. 134 f., with many illustrations for Sumerian and Phœnician seals. Uruash calls himself usually in his inscriptions at Lagash, "son of *Guni-du*, son of *Gar-sar*"—neither of which names have been identified in inscriptions. It is thus possible that *Guni-du* may be a title of Uruash's immediate father, Iszax; but it seems more probable, I think, a contracted genealogy claiming descent from the second Sumerian king, *Gun* or *Gunu*, and his father, *Gaur* or *Gur*, the first Sumerian king. This latter is in strict series with the practice of the later Sumerian kings Gudia and Dunji, who claimed to be the sons of these two first Sumerian kings under their other titles of *Nimirrud* ("Ningirsu") and Sakh ("En-Lil").

[2] See WISD. 41, 128 f., and Fig. 32.

the city of Lagash (see Fig. 22) and the pictographic use of a sail with the meaning of "winds, watery space and sea," with the phonetic value of *Mar* or *Muru*, which I have shown is the Sumerian or Early Aryan origin of our modern Aryan words for "sea," in French *Mer*, Latin *Mare*, Eddic Gothic *Marr*, Irish and Gaelic *Muir*, English *Mere*, Mar-ine, Mar-iner, Mar-itime, Marsh, etc.; and also the Sumerian origin of the title of the early sea-going branch of the Sumerians, the *Muru* or *Marut* and the Sanskrit *Marutas* or "Morites" or "Amorites" who have left their name in Mauretania or Morocco to the west of Carthage.[1]

FIG. 22.—Offering of Oars to temple of Nimirrud (Nimrod), patron-saint of Lagash, about period of Uruash, 3100 B.C. (After Heuzey, *Déc*, pl. I *bis*, Fig. 1.)

Positive evidence of the seafaring activities of this dynasty is also found in the fact that King Uruash or Haryashwa and his dynasty are almost the sole Early Aryan kings who are celebrated in the Vedic psalms as sea-goers and the subjects of shipwreck in mid-ocean; and a "ship of a hundred oars" is mentioned therewith.[2]

URUASH'S TITLE OF KHĂD OR KHADDI AS "SEA-EMPEROR" OR "RULER OF THE WAVES"

The title which King Uruash habitually uses immediately after his personal name in his Lagash inscriptions reads by

[1] WPOD. 216 f., 243, 260, 343.
[2] WPOB. 13 f., and see previous note.

its ideographic Sumerian values, as I have shown *Kha-ad* or *Khăd*[1]—a title which has hitherto been read through a very late Semitic Assyrian gloss as "*Ninā*"; and by dropping out the second syllable of his name *ash*, his name has been transformed into "*Ur-Ninā*"! That title *Kha-ad* is pictured (see Fig. 20)[2] by the sign of a Fish inside the sign for "House-Father" (*Ad*), and thus designates him literally as "House-Father of the Fishes," and "House of the Fishes" is poetic for "The Sea."

Significantly also in his Kish inscription as *Uru-sag*, wherein *sag* has the meaning of "Lord," just as the last syllable *ash* in *Uruash* also has in his Lagash inscriptions,[3] that king uses the title of *Khad-di*. This title is written by the signs of the Sun (*Khad*)[4] + a Foot (*di*),[5] meaning primarily "the going forth of the Sun," and secondarily "The East or Orient."[6] It thus appears to have designated King Uruash as "King of the Orient," and the orient from the locality of Lagash on the Persian Gulf was the Persian Gulf and Indian Ocean, the so-called "Lower Sea" of the later Sumerians, in contradistinction to the Upper Sea or Mediterranean.

His "Khâd" or "Khaddi" Title as Title of "Phœnicians" & *re* "Catti" & "Goth"

This title of *Khăd* or *Khaddi* used by King Uruash, the founder of the *Panch* or "Phœnician" Dynasty, suggests that it is the origin of the title *Kad* or *Qad*, which I have shown was apparently used by the Phœnicians in their place-names, Kadesh, Qadesh and Gades, with the meaning of "House of the Kads or Qads or Gads,"[7] and as *Qadi* or *Qeti* by the Ancient Egyptians for the sea-land of Phœnicia and the Levant. It was presumably coined on the model of

[1] WISD. 30 f., 123 f. As *Khab* it may be source of the Phœnician *Kabiri*.

[2] The sign is above the nose of the King in upper register of the plaque. An account presumably of the number of fin strokes of the Fish, the X element in the sign is often omitted.

[3] Br. 6477. [4] M. 5741 f. [5] Br. 4859.

[6] A later value given to this compound sign, according to the bilingual Assyrian glossaries was *E*, with the same meaning of "going forth" and "East," see WSAD. 68 f.; but its ideographic reading is *Khad-di*.

[7] WPOB. 74, 78, 159 f., 173 f., 180 f.

the *Khat* or *Khatti* "ruler" title, which we have seen was apparently used by the Early Sumerians as a clan title for that ruling race;[1] and which was the obvious source of the *Catti* title of the Ancient Briton ruling kings and their Aryan clans. And this title of *Khad* or *Khat* we have seen is in series with *Gut* or "Goth"—a title which was applied to Madgal in his father Uruash's plaque, and is now discovered to be used by him and by others of his dynasty and by succeeding Sumerian dynasties including the Great Sargon's in their Indus Valley seals (see Plates VIII-XII and Appendix VI). It thus appears that the adoption of the *Khad* or *Kad* title by the "Phœnicians" was in series with the adoption of the "Barat" patronym by the chief ruling clans of the Aryans, including the Indo-Aryan Panch or Phœnicians themselves.

The form *Cedi, Chedi, Caidya* or *Cidi* used in the Indian Epics for a branch dynasty of the Panch Dynasty of this period, which had its capital at Tripuri,[2] is clearly a phonetic variant derived from this *Khād* or *Khaddi* title of Uruash.

In series also with this title is the *Qadu* or *Qetu* title applied by the Ancient Egyptians to the sea of the Levant along with the Eastern Mediterranean, which they called "Sea of the *Qadu* or *Qetu*[3]—this being the especial sea of the Phœnicians as the chief mariners in Europe: and the Phœnicians were also called by the Ancient Egyptians by the name of *Fankhu*, as early as the Sixth Dynasty of Egypt,[4] and latterly *Panag* and *Panasa*, that is "Phœnician."[5] And the whole tract of land between the Levantine coast of the Mediterranean and the Euphrates was known to the Egyptians as *Qadi, Qet* or *Qeti*,[6] and included also the Asia Minor coast of the Mediterranean.[7]

THE "NUN" OR "NUNNA" TITLE OF URUASH & HIS DYNASTY AS "SEA-LORD"

In this Phœnician dynasty of Uruash there first appears the title of *Nun* or *Nunna*, which is applied to most of its

[1] See p.211, re *Khatti-sig* or "Ruler of the Khatti."
[2] WVP. 4, 67 f.; 5, 118.
[3] BD. 780.
[4] Sethe, *Zeitschrift f. Ægypt. Sprache*, 1908, 7 f.
[5] WPOB. 39 f.
[6] BD. 1045.
[7] BD. 142.

kings in one or other of both versions of these Old Sumerian prefixed King-Lists of the Isin scribes. It seems to be the equivalent of the Fish symbolism of the Khād title of Uruash with the same meaning of "Sea-Lord." This sign *Nun* is written by a pictogram supposed to be diagrammatic of a Fish; but which may be a Serpent—a Sea-serpent—in which the cross-bars represent the coils.[1] It is defined in the bilingual glossaries as "fish" also "great, majestic, and lord,"[2] and is a title of Lord Dara or In-Duru as "Lord of the Abyss (or Sea)"[3] For Uruash in the second list it has the affix "great," thus designating him as "Great Lord of the Sea."

We now gain further confirmation through these lists of King Uruash's annexation of the Indus Valley to his sea-empire, which is still further strikingly confirmed by my discovery of signet seals of this dynasty in the second batch of seals unearthed at the old capital there and now deciphered for the first time (Plate IX and App. VI).

King Madgal's Annexation of the Indus Valley as the Colony of Edin or Etin

We have already found from the victory-seal of King Uruash's son and successor, the crown-prince Madgal, containing the fine contemporary portrait of the latter (Fig. 19, p. 109), that King Uruash or Haryashwa annexed permanently the Indus Valley province called Edin or Etin, through his son the crown-prince Madgal, who calls himself in his victory-seal "Lord of Edin, the Capturer (of Edin)." And this Edin or Etin, I proved from the seals locally found there, was the name of the great city-state in the Indus Valley where the rich remains of two or more palatial Sumerian cities have recently been unearthed, and their first batch of official seals deciphered by me, with identifica-

[1] In Babylonian myth the Spirit of the Sea is often represented as a Serpent with the head of a human king. And in Indian myth the old legendary human kings are represented as Sea-serpents or *Nāga,* and one of these is called *Panch-ālo,* (see my article on *Nāga Rājas* in *Jour. R. Asiatic Soc.*, 1894, 91 f.). And it is significant that this Sumerian sign Nun also reads *Nūk* (cp. Br. 3622 and 5912), and thus equates with Sanskrit *Nāga*, a Serpent of the Waters, and the *Nāg* of modern Indians.

[2] Br. 2627-9. M. 1726.

[3] Br. 2625.

PLATE IX.

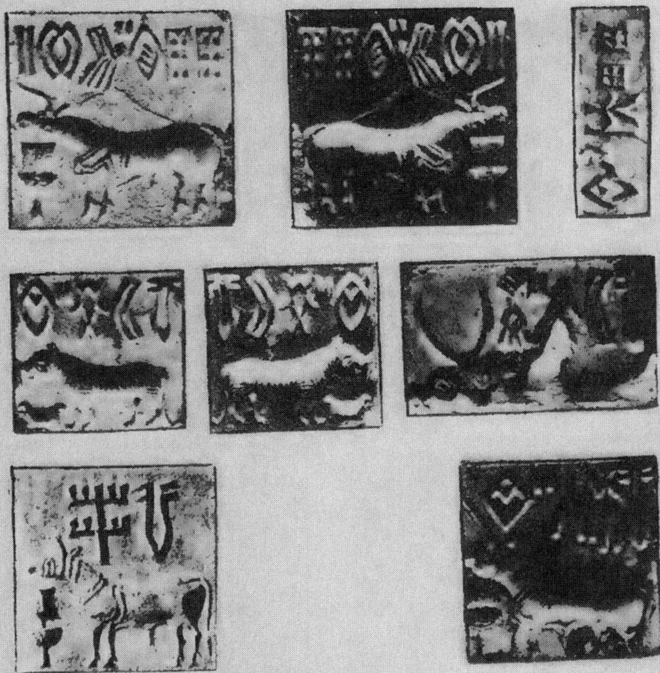

INDUS VALLEY SEALS OF KING MADGAL OR AKUR (MUD-GALA) & HIS GRANDSON KING TARSI (TRAŚA-DASYU), *c.* 3070 & 3030 B.C.

(Photographs after Sir J. Marshall.) For decipherments and translations see pp. 168 f., 545 f.

tions of their owners as historical Sumerian kings, princes, or famous Vedic Aryan princes and priests, some of whom were actually located in the Indus Valley by the ancient Indian Vedic psalms, and represented as merchants, rich in cattle and horses, trading in gold and other metals and protected by the Maruts, who were shown to be the Morite or Amorite or Early Phœnician branch of the Early Aryan mariners.

This achievement of Prince Madgal is reflected in the Indian Vedic hymn, cited in my previous work, which relates that Mudgala "recovered" vast herds of stolen cattle, implying that he and his Aryan people had been settled there for some time and had been raided by the aborigines or neighbouring tribes. Or it may imply that the Sumerians had already established a tributary colony on the Indus, which had revolted and was recovered. In any case it showed that this Indus colony was consolidated and extended and formed into a great civilized Sumerian province by Prince Madgal, who remained there for a time as governor and "Lord of Edin or Etin." All this is now strikingly confirmed by my discovery of five actual official signets of Madgal and of his great-grandson Tarsi amongst the seals latterly unearthed at the old Sumerian seaport city there (see Plate IX and App. VI). In one of these, Madgal or A-Kur-gal calls himself "The Minister of Edin" by the self-same signs as in his Victory plaque, and in two of them he also calls himself "The Shepherd of Shepherds of Edin Land" in agreement with his title of "The Shepherd" in his father's plaque (see p. 111).

The imperial policy of this First *Panch* or "Phœnician" Dynasty we have seen indicated by the title given to its founder as "The Restorer (of the Empire)"; and in his famous Sumerian plaque the crown-prince is called "The Shepherd Madgal, the Warrior,"—the name Madgal or A-Kur-gal being an honorific title—meaning "The Prince or Great One (*Gal*) of the Land (*Mad* or *Kur*)."

Striking confirmation of all this is now supplied by these two old Sumerian King-Lists. In the first of these the successor to King Arwasag (*i.e.* Uruash or Haryashwa), and who we find was his son Mad-Gal, was evidently called in the old Sumerian text copied by the Isin priests "*The Shepherd of Etin(a), Gal of Ansha(n), the One who made the Foreign Lands faithful*" (see App. III for text).

MADGAL AS "LORD ETANA" & HERO OF THE ROMANCE OF "ETANA & THE EAGLE"

But these myth-mongering Isin priests obsessed by their Flood and later Babylonian legends are now seen to have identified this "Shepherd" or "Lord of Edin or Etin," with the hero of the late Babylonian legend of "Etana and the Eagle" (or properly the Sun-Hawk which is called *Aukh* in the texts of that story. In that legend the hero is named Lord *Etana* or *Etina*,[1] that is precisely as in Madgal's own seal, where he calls himself "Lord Etin,"[2] the possessive suffix being as very usual not expressed in Early Sumerian. The Isin scribes have thus assumed "Etana" or "Etina" to be the personal name of the hero instead of his mere territorial title.[3] That legend goes on to relate that Lord Etana was invited by his "friend" the Sun-Hawk (*Aukh*)[4] to cling to it and be carried up to Heaven—and we have seen that Madgal and his dynasty were famous Sun-worshippers. Consenting, he is carried up by the Hawk, and on the way is shown the vast dwindling panorama of earth and sea, and eventually reaches Heaven; which significantly is the heaven of the late Babylonian trinity of Father Anu, Lord Sakh or Bel and In-duru, a Chaldean trinity fabricated out of titles of the deified Gothic king In-dara, and showing the late date of this legend.

Under the influence of this legend and obviously unaware that the hero of Etin was Mad-Gal the son and successor of King Uruash, the Isin priests in keeping with the mess they made of Mesopotamian early history through ignorance of the historic names of Uruash and his dynasty, have read the *Gal* and *Ansha(n)* of this text as grammatical terms and made the record to read: "Etana, the Shepherd who to

[1] A *ti* value is suggested for the *ta* syllable by PSL. 395.

[2] WISD. 35.

[3] Somewhat similarly the name "Jupiter" was sometimes used by the Romans for "Heaven, Sky and Air."

[4] On *Akh* or *Uka* as "Eagle" or "Sun-Hawk," see WSAD. 9.

heaven ascended, who made the foreign lands faithful became king and reigned 1500 years"!

"Etana" or "Etina" in this old Sumerian record, thus slightly mutilated by the Isin scribes, is clearly the *Etin* name of the Indus Valley city-state of which Prince Madgal claims in his victory-seal to be "The Lord (of) Edin, the Capturer," and of which city-state in the same record his father Uruash is called "The King of Etin." And *An-sha(n)* is obviously *Anshan*, the ancient Sumerian name for Persis on the Persian Gulf in Southern Persia to the east of Elam, which latterly had its capital inland at Persepolis, which was still called "Anshan" by Cyrus who had his imperial capital there.[1] This would presume that Madgal held the Persis province of Persia midway down the Persian Gulf, as a halfway station between Lagash port in Mesopotamia and the Indus Valley, just as we shall find Sargon and his son Manis-Tusu did some centuries later.

The identity of King Madgal as "Lord of Etin" with Lord Etana or Etina of this old Sumerian King-List is further confirmed by his title of "The Shepherd who made the Foreign Lands faithful." This identifies him with King Uruash's eldest son on the plaque, who as we have seen bore therein the title of "The Shepherd Madgal, the Warrior" or *Gut*; and significantly he bears both of these titles of "Shepherd" and of "Warrior" or *Gut* (or "Goth") in his seals from Edin as now deciphered for the first time (Pl. IX, Nos. 1-6 and App. VI).

Further confirmation of this identity is afforded by the second version of these old Sumerian King-Lists (see Table, p. 140). This gives his name as "son of King Uruash" as "*Mukh* of the Lands." Here the term "Lands" is evidently correlated to *Mad*, "Land," in his usual name of Madgal. And *Mukh* equates with the dialectic form of his name in the old Indian Pali as *Moggalla*[2] instead of the Sanskrit form *Mudgala* or *Mugala*[3]; and in one of his Edin seals his initial title also reads *Makkas* (Pl. IX, 3).

Still further confirmation of Madgal's activities in the Indus Valley seems indicated by his *Maru* title in the many

[1] Cp. PHT. 4, 234. [2] CD. 248.
[3] On *Mugal* and *Mohugal*, see WBT. 98. f.

MSS. of one of the solar versions of the Indian Lists (see App. I, No. 16). This appears to associate him with the Sindh Desert of the Indus Valley in which the old Sumerian cities are located there as oases. *Maru* in Sanskrit means " Sandy Desert," and curiously that is a meaning of *Etin* or *Edin* in Sumerian,[1] so that Maru might be a translation of *Etin* or *Etina*. The name *Maru* or " The Desert " still survives in the name of Marwar for the Rajputana section of the great Sindh Desert of the Indus Valley. But significantly Madgal is actually called *Mar* and *Marru* in his seals (Pl. IX 3–4).

Uruash's Imperial Dynasty in Old Sumerian King-Lists in Agreement with Inscriptions & Indian Lists

The members of Uruash's (*Panch* or Phœnician) Imperial Dynasty in these two recovered Old Sumerian King-Lists of the Great Gap are found to be in strict agreement with both the contemporary inscriptions of these Sumerian kings themselves, and with *the official king-lists of the Early Aryan kings preserved in the Indian Lists, which have proved to be the sole and unique key which has recovered not only the traditional forms of the names of these Sumerian kings, but also the real chronological position and date of Uruash's great Dynasty hitherto unknown, and the full list of the lost Sumerian Kings of the Great Gap.*

This agreement is displayed in the accompanying table, which also illustrates the *variant phonetic spelling* both in those several king-lists and in the actual inscriptions of the kings themselves. The order of the kings is that preserved in the Indian Lists which is seen to be precisely that of the Old Sumerian King-Lists as now recovered from the misplaced prefixed dynasties in Isin Chronicles. The rule of his descendants in the Indus Valley as a Sumerian colony of Mesopotamia is attested by their seals. And the 3rd king, Bidasnadi (see for his contemporary portraits Plate VII B, and Fig. 20, p. 111), extended the Indus Valley colony by conquests in the Upper Indus.[2]

[1] Br. 4526-9.

[2] WISD. 108.

URUASH'S OR HARYASHWA'S "PANCH" OR FIRST "PHŒNICIAN" DYNASTY OF SEA-EMPERORS, C. 3100 B.C. TO 2950 B.C.

Old Sumerian King-Lists.		Sumerian Inscriptions in Mesop.	Indian Lists (P.=Pali).	
1st (Kish City).	2nd (Erech City).			
1. *Arwasag*, s. of *Rasax*.	*Uruash*, s. of *Isshax Gamesh*, k. of Erech.	*Uruash* Khād, *Urusag* Khaddi.	*Haryashwa*, s. of *Rucaka*, *Riksha* or *Ruk-Meshu*.	1.
2. *Gal* of Ansha(n), Etana, Shepherd, s. of 1.	*Mukh* of Lands, s. of 1.	*Madgal*, *A-Madgal*, Shepherd, s. of 1.	*Mudgala*, Moggalla (P.), s. of 1.	2.
3. *Bigu(b)axu*, s. of 2.	*Bishīr*, the protector.	*Bi(d)ashnadi*, *Bi(d)sar*, *Biugun*, s. of 2.	*Badhry-ashwa*, *B'ujyu*, Pasenadi (P.), s. of 2.	3.
4. *Enme-nunna*, sea-lord.	*Ennun*-nad, lord.	*Enash*-nadi.	*Yuvan*-ashwa, s. of 2.	4.
5. —	*Dixxi* (*Di-*, Divine).	*Tarsi* (*Ene-*, or Divine, s. of 3.	*Dāsa* (*Divo-*, or Divine), *Trasa-Dasyu*, s. of 3.	5.
6. *Mede*, k. of Kish, s. of 4.	*Mede*, the lord.	*Medi* or *Meti*.	*Mettiyo* (P.), *Mitrayu*, s. of 5.	6.
7. Bar-*Mug*-nunna, sea-lord, s. of 4.	*Kiaga*, king.	[*Ki*]-*aga*, *Mūkuda*, k. of Kish and Adab.	*Cyavana*, *Mūcchkanda* or *Pijavana*, s. of 6.	7.
8. *Dix-saax*, s. of 7.	—	*Tarsi*, k. of Kish.	*Su-Dāsa*, *Dus-siha*, (?) *Trasa-Dasyu* II, s. of 7.	8.
9. *Tīz-ama*, s. of 8.	—	—	*Somaka*, *Sambhuta*, s. of 8.	9.

The end of Uruash's Dynasty with the seventh king, Kiaga, in the second version of those Old Sumerian Lists misplaced by the Isin priests is in agreement with the Indian Lists in several of the lunar versions which end the Panch Dynasty there.[1] Similarly the continuation of the dynasty in the first Isin version with two more kings (see col. 1) is also paralleled in other lunar versions of the Indian Lists which carry it on for two generations further and add a tenth (Jantu), and continue it on to include the next four kings of the solar list as being of the Panch Dynasty as well.[2]

The reason for these varying lengths of this Panch Dynasty

[1] WVP. 4, 147. [2] *Ib.*, 4, 148.

is presumably due to revolts with loss of several of the chief cities of the empire. Thus it appears Erech was lost in the reign of the seventh king; whilst Kish appears to have been held and continued as the imperial capital. And the omission in the Isin list of the tenth king of the Indian List is presumably owing to his short reign, as he is stated in the latter to have been slain by one Ravana and succeeded by his " brother " *Prishada*, with whom the Isin lists, as we shall see, start a new " dynasty " at Ur, which we compare in the next chapter.

Indeed, we have striking traditional evidence of these revolts and confederated attacks in the latter part of this dynasty preserved in the Indian Vedic Hymns with regard to the eighth king of the dynasty, Su-Dāsa or Trasa-Dasyu, now disclosed as the historical Sumerian King Tarsi of Kish of the inscriptions.

King Tarsi of Kish or Trasa-Dasyu or Su-Dâsa & his famous Victory over Ten Confederate Kings

Celebrated in his Battle-Hymn in the Vedas

The chief battle-hymns in the Indian Vedic psalms of the Early Aryans are those celebrating the victories of King Su-Dāsa now disclosed as King Tarsi of Kish. There are many references to his victories throughout the Vedas. The chief of these are in the special hymn which is generally known as " Su-Dāsa's Battle-Hymn of Victory over the Ten confederated Kings." As he is now identified with King Tarsi, the numerous details in its names of the chief kings and tribes or nations in the hostile confederacy of this period are of much historical importance, so that I cite here the hymn for reference.

This hymn was compiled and sung, as stated in its first four stanzas by King Su-Dāsa's chief priest named Vasishta—a title used for a class of sacrificing priests in the Vedas and derived as I have formerly suggested from the Akkadian *Pashishutu*, " a class of anointing priests " in Mesopotamia.[1] The King's own warrior-people are called *Tritsus*.

Significantly the name of the chief river in the hymn at

[1] MD. 847.

the seat of the first battle is called in Sanskrit *Parushni*, which is clearly intended for the Sumerian name of the Euphrates as *Puranunu*[1] or *Puratti*. The other river is called *Yamunā*; and mention is made of his victories on "seven rivers." In another Vedic hymn he celebrates victories on the Vipās and Sutudri, which are usually identified by Sankritists with the Bias and Sutlej tributaries of the Indus,[2] and thus may relate to his recovery of the Indus Valley colony. And with characteristic piety the victories are ascribed by Su-Dāsa and his priest to Indra, that is the In-Dara or In-Duru or Lord Sakh of the Sumerians, of which deity they were the votaries.

This hymn,[3] which is full of the stirring movement of battle, opens with Su-Dāsa's, somewhat miraculous crossing of the flooded Parushni river (Euphrates), by the aid of his patron god Indra, while the returning waters drowned most of the enemy host—just as such a miraculous passage story was later attached by the Hebrews to the crossing of the Red Sea by Moses and the Israelites. The simile in verse 17 of the Goat through Indra's aid doing the Lion to death, is significantly a favourite scene on Sumerian, Hittite and Phœnician sacred seals, and on Phœnician coins,[4] and on ancient Briton monuments; and the Lion attacking the Goats is seen on the Predynastic Egyptian knife handle (Fig. 14, p. 30), and in the Frontispiece, where the champion of the Goats (or Goths) Thor, Adam or In-Dur defeats the enemy Lions. And the striking synchronism is noteworthy in verse 10, where *Prishni* the Maruta or Morite is named as aiding King Su-Dāsa with horsemen whom he "sent down," and who is clearly *Vrishni*, a cousin of Su-Dāsa's father in the collateral dynasty of the Cedi or Cidi branch of the Panch or "Phœnicians." (see App. I, No. 21, col. 3).

The first four verses celebrate the almightiness of Indra and cite the bard's name as Vasishtha.

[1] Cp. PSL. 7. [2] RV. 3, 53, 9 f. [3] RV. 7, 18.
[4] See for representations WPOB. 334.

Battle-Hymn of Victory of King Su-Dāsa or Trasa-Dasyu or King Tarsi from Vedas

5. "Though the floods spread widely, Indra made them shallow and easy for Su-Dās to cross;
He (Indra) worthy of our praise, caused the *Simyu* foe of our hymn, to curse the rivers' fury.

6. Eager for spoil was (the enemy leader) Turvasa Puro-Dās, fain to win wealth, like *Matsya* (fishes) urged by hunger;
The *Bhrigus* and the *Druhyus* quickly listened to him: friend joined friend amid the two distant peoples.

7. Together came the *Pakthas*, the *Bhalānas*, the *Alinas*, the *Sivas*, the *Vishānins*;
But to (Su Dās') *Tritsus* came the Aryans' Comrade (Indra) to lead these heroes on in war and spoil.

8. The (enemy) fools in their folly, fain to waste her waters they parted inexhaustible Parushni (Puratti or Euphrates);[1]
But the Lord of the Earth (Indra) with his might repressed them: still lay the herd and their affrighted herdsman.

9. As to their goal they sped to their destruction: they sought Parushnī; but even their swift men returned not;
Indra to Su Dās, the manly, abandoned the swiftly flying foes, unmanly babblers.

10. The fleers rushed like kine unherded from the pasture, each clinging to a friend as chance happened;
But the Maruts driving dappled steeds sent down by *Prishni*[2] gave ear, these warriors and their harnessed horses.

[1] This is interpreted by Sanskrit scholars as an attempt by the enemy confederates to make the flooded river fordable by digging canals to divert the stream, but the river rushing back to its natural bed drowned the men when crossing the stream.

[2] This *Prishni* is evidently King *Vrishni* of the collateral *Panch* Dynasty in Maghya Land, being the clan title of *Cedi* or *Cidi*, which branched off with the third brother of King Madgal (see col. 3 in Table, App. I). He was contemporary with Su-Dāsa's father, and also as now seen with Su-Dāsa himself, and was therefore a "cousin" of the latter.

11. The King who (singly) scattered one-and-twenty houses of both *Vaikarna* tribes with glory—
As the skilled priest clips grass within the shrine, so hath the hero Indra wrought their downfall.

12. Thou thunder-armed Indra overwhelmest in the waters the famous old Kavasha, and then the Druhyu ;
Whilst thy votaries, O Indra! with thy friendship were made joyful.

13. Indra in conquering might demolished all their strongholds and their seven castles ;
The goods of *Anu's* son he gave to (Su Dās') Tritsus. May we by our sacrifices conquer scornful *Pūru !*

14. The Anus and Druhyus seeking spoil have slept, the sixty hundred, yea the six thousand,
And six and sixty of their heroes. For his votaries were all these mighty deeds done by Indra.

15. The Tritsus under Indra's careful guidance sped on like loosened waters rushing downwards,
The foemen with reluctance abandoned to Su Dās all their treasured stores.

16. The vaunted heroes who drank (Indra's) dressed oblations, Indra's deniers, far o'er the earth he scattered them :
Indra laid low the fierce destroyers' fury, He set them different roads (in flight), did he the paths Controller.

17. E'en with the weaker he worked this matchless triumph : E'en with a Goat he did to death a Lion.[1]
He pared the pillar's angles with a needle. Thus to Su Dās Indra gave all their treasured stores.

18. To thee (Su Dās) have all thine enemies submitted ; e'en the fierce *Bheda*, hast thou made thy subject.
Cast down thy sharpened thunder-bolt, O Indra, on him who harms the men who sing thy praise !

19. Yamunā (River) and the Tritsus aided Indra. There he stripped Bheda bare of all his treasures.
The *Ajas* and the *Sigrus* and the *Yakshus*, brought in to him as tribute heads of horses.

[1] Indra, with his attendant sacred Goat, vanquishing the Lion is a frequent scene on Sumerian, Hittite and Phœnician sacred seals, and on Phœnician coins. See for representations WPOB. 334.

20. Not to be scorned but like recurring dawns, O Indra, are thy favours and thy riches.
Devaka, Manyamāna's son thou slewest, and smotest *Sambara* from the lofty mountain.

21. We (priests) who from home, have gladdened thee,
Thy servants Parāshara, Vasishtha, Satayatu
Will not forget thy friendship, bountiful Giver ;
So shall the days dawn prosperous for the princes.

24. Him (Su Dās) whose fame spreads 'tween wide earth and heaven, who as dispenser gives each chief his portion :
Seven flowing Rivers glorify him like Indra. He slew *Yudhyāmadhi* in close encounter.

25. Attend on Su Dās ye Marut heroes as on his (fore-) father Divo-Dāsa !
Further Pijavan's son's desire with favour. Guard faithfully his lasting firm dominion ! "[1]

Historical Results of this Discovery of Two Old Sumerian King-Lists of the Great Gap in Second Dynasty of the Kish Chronicle

Thus our comparison between these two old Sumerian King-Lists, prefixed to the Kish Chronicle by the Isin priests, and our Indian Lists and Chronicles of the Early Aryan kings which have provided the key to the discovery and identification of these lists, supplemented by comparison with the existing inscriptions of the leading kings themselves in these lists, discloses that these two Old Sumerian King-Lists prove to be two independent versions of the lost king-list of the Great Gap in the second Dynasty of the Kish Chronicle, which was lost to the Kish Chronicle, Isin and other Babylonian scribes.

The immense and fundamental importance of this discovery for Ancient History is that it recovers from old Sumerian sources two independent old official lists of the lost kings of the Great Gap for a period of 430 years with 27 kings, including the great Aryan Emperor Barat and Uruash's First *Panch* or " Phœnician " Aryan Dynasty and

[1] This translation is based on R. Griffith's *Hymns of the Rig-Veda*, 2, 17.

others, and gives us the true chronological positions of these famous kings and dynasties which were hitherto unknown.

At the same time, this discovery further conclusively exposes the entire falsity of the chronology prefixed by the Isin priests to the first Dynasty of the Kish Chronicle—a wholly false chronology which nevertheless is universally accepted by Assyriologists for their "reconstruction" of the Early History of Babylonia and of the Rise of Civilization, and thus has been misleading students of history.

Moreover, it strikingly confirms the authenticity of the official Indian King-Lists and Chronicles as a unique key to the King-Lists of the Sumerians and to the traditional forms of the kings' names, and as an independent and fertile source of authentic traditional information on lost Sumerian history.

And it again affords still further conclusive proof of the identity in race, language and tradition of the Sumerians with the Early Aryans.

XI

Remaining Kings of the Great Gap from Ur Dynasty, including Drupada & Sargon's Father as King of Kish in Old Sumerian King-Lists in complete Agreement with Indian Official Aryan Lists

Disclosing the real Date of " Mesannipadda " *of Ur and his Dynasty at about* 2900 B.C.

The remaining kings of the Great Gap of the Second Dynasty of the Kish Chronicle, subsequent to Uruash's Dynasty, from the Kings of Ur—whose marvellously rich tomb remains and massive buildings have recently been unearthed by the British and Pennsylvania Museums Joint Expedition under Mr Woolley [1]—down to Zaggisi of the " Third " Dynasty of that chronicle (see p. 60) and the immediate predecessor of Sargon-the-Great beginning the Fourth Dynasty of that chronicle, are now disclosed in the present chapter by means of the Indian King-Lists and confirmed by the two Old Sumerian King-Lists recovered and identified, as described in the preceding chapter.

Recovery of Old Sumerian Lists of Kings of Great Gap from King Pashipadda (" Mesannipadda ") of Ur Dynasty

These two Old Sumerian King-Lists, as seen in the Table at p. 140 (cols. 1 and 2), preserve also the names—the first version in summary and the second version in full detail—of the remaining 13 kings of the Great Gap of the Kish Chronicle subsequent to Uruash's Dynasty; and are in complete agreement with the Indian King-Lists (see App. I, Nos. 24-36).

[1] UE. 1, 1927.

REMAINING KINGS OF GREAT GAP FROM URUASH'S DYNASTY TO SARGON'S FATHER.

	Old Sumerian King-Lists.		Sumerian. Inscriptions in Mesop.	Indian Lists.	
	1st (Kish City).	2nd, &c. (Uri, &c., Cities).			
24.	*Rumau.*	*Pāshipadda* at Uri City.	*Pāshipadda* of Ur ("Mes-annipadda").	*Prishada* or *Roman* (Suv-arna-).	24.
25.	*Rutasa-Rāma.*	*Uruduki-*RAMAN.[1]	*Duruashipadda* ("Annipadda").	*Drupada, Rohi-dashwa* or *Hrash-wa Roman.*	25.
26.	—	[*Eamu* . . .].	—	*Vasumanas,* Vyoman.	26.
27.	—	[*Biama* . . .].	(?) *Paunutu* ("Mes-kalam-dug").	*Jīmūta.*	27.
28.	—	(Illegible) at Awan.	—	Bhanu or Ban-kirti.	28.
29.	—	,,	—	Satya-brata (or Trisanku).	29.
30.	—	,,	—	Harish-candra.	30.
31.	—	,, at Kish.	—	Harita or Rohit-ashwa II.	31.
32.	—	*Dadasig* or *Gun-gun.*	Kingubi-Dudu, k. of Erech.	*Dhundu* or *Cuncu.*	32.
33.	—	*Mamma-gal* ("Great in ships").	—	Vijaya ("The Conqueror").	33.
34.	—	*Kālbu-* (?) *ru,* s. of 33.	—	B'aruka or Rur-uki.	34.
35.	—	*Tuke.*	—	Wri-*Taka,* Dhri *Taka* or Urja-vaha.	35.
36.	En-men *Bara-Gin-ma,* father of S'agin or S'agur (or "Sargon").	*Buru-Gina* at Kish or *Puru-Gin,* sea-lord.	*Urudu Gina,* de-throned by Zaggisi.	*Pra-Cin*-wat, *B'aradhwaja,* or *Bahu,* de-throned by Haihayas.	36.

This agreement is displayed in the above Comparative Table, which is an abstract of the second group of the Great Gap kings on p. 140. It similarly shows in the first two columns the names and their chronological order as found in the two Old Sumerian lists misplaced by the Isin priests; in the third column are given the names of those of the kings as found written in their own or in contemporary inscriptions, and in the fourth column are their

[1] On this reading with Akkad value of *Raman,* see App. III.

names as preserved in the Indian King-Lists of the Aryans and in their chronological order of succession in the latter, which is seen to be identical with that in these two Old Sumerian lists. The detailed translations of these Sumerian texts are given in App. III, where the authority for my revised readings of the names is duly cited wherever it differs from the previous conjectural readings made without any key to the forms of the names. Nos. 26 and 27 illegible in this text are restored from Poebel's Nippur versions.

This Comparative Table now calls for our scrutiny and detailed analysis. For the evidence fixing No. 36 in that position in the contracted list of the first of the Old Sumerian lists, see Table, p. 140.

KING PASHIPADDA (SO-CALLED "MESANNIPADDA") OF UR & HIS DYNASTY ABOUT 2900 B.C.

The most outstanding fact of critical historical importance discovered by this Comparative Table is that the first of these kings of Ur, whose name has hitherto been conjecturally read as "Mesannipadda," reigned subsequent to the dynasty of King Uruash, and his date is thus definitely fixed for this first time.

Hitherto his date has been placed by the Isin priests in their misplaced prefixed king-lists at 4942 years before the First Dynasty of the Kish Chronicle, or about 7000 B.C.(!) according to the Isin list chronology, which despite its obvious fabulousness is nevertheless now universally accepted by Assyriologists as the basis of their "history," though with characteristic liberty they arbitrarily reduce the date to "about 4216 B.C." ![1]

But this king is now disclosed by our Table and Indian key-lists to be the historical Sumerian king whose name reads in Sumerian *Pāshipadda*, and whose traditional form of name preserved in the Indian King-Lists reads *Prishada* or *Prishata* in two absolutely independent versions solar, and lunar respectively.[2] And his real date, so far from being

[1] *Cambridge Anc. Hist.*, I, 666. And note the ingenious exactitude!

[2] This agreement in the form of his name in both solar and lunar lists is all the more remarkable as no Brahman or Sanskrit scholar ever suspected any connexion between these solar and lunar lists which were supposed to be of totally different lines of kings, until I placed them alongside and identified them as representing the same Kings.

4942 years *before* the First Dynasty of the Kish Chronicle, is now disclosed to be *about* 500 *years* AFTER *the first king of the First Dynasty of the Kish Chronicle, and no earlier than about* 2900 B.C.

The historicity of this king is attested by an inscription of his son and successor at Ur city recently unearthed there by the joint Museum Expedition. In this inscription[1] his son calls his father by the identical name of *Pāshipadda* (hitherto misread "Mesannipadda") as in these two Old Sumerian King-Lists. And significantly the profuse cultural remains of this period unearthed from the tombs of his dynasty at Ur are all of a relatively late type and clearly of the post-Uruash period, in keeping with his real date as now elicited of about 2900 B.C.

The remarkable authenticity of the Indian lists in the preservation of his name and titles is also seen in the fact that he is given therein the title of "The Golden *Roman* (*Suvarna Roman*)—a title meaning in Sanskrit "The Golden Haired"—which may possibly refer to the golden locks of fair hair of this king, or to his institution of a period of lavish use of gold for decoration, as in the massive golden crowns unearthed from the royal tombs of his period and probably including his own tomb, the profusion of golden articles in florid style unearthed recalling those of the type of Tutankhamen's tomb in Egypt. Now, in agreement with this title of *Roman* for him in the Indian lists, we find that he is also called in the second of the Old Sumerian lists by the title of *Rumau*, thus equating substantially with his title in the Indian lists, and suggesting that the Indian scribes altered this title to *Roman* so as to extract a Sanskrit meaning from it.

King Duruashipadda (so-called "Ānnipadda") or Drupada, the Panch or "Phœnician" of Indian Chronicles

The son of the former king is now a well-known historical personage from the inscriptions and numerous cultural remains unearthed from his buildings and possibly also from his royal tomb at Ur, above referred to. His name, without

[1] UE. II, 126.

any clue to its traditional form in the polyphonous Sumerian writing in which his name is inscribed, has hitherto been conjecturally "restored" as "Ānnipada." But the Indian lists preserve his name as *Drupada*, thus disclosing that his name was read in full as *Duruashipadda* or *Duruashipada*, and the fact that the mid-portion of his full name was pronounced *ash* is evidenced by one of the independent solar versions of the Indian lists giving his name as *Haryashwa II* (see App. I, No. 25).

The identity of this Indian king Drupada with this Sumerian king Duruashipadda, quite apart from the proofs by the identity of his name, genealogy and location in the Indian and Sumerian lists, is again confirmed by identity in his *titles* in the Indian and Sumerian. In the two Old Sumerian lists of the Great Gap kings he is given the titles of *Rutasa-Rāma*, and *Uruduki-Raman*. Now the Indian lists in the solar and lunar versions give him also the titles respectively of *Rohidashwa* and *Hrashwa-Roman*, thus yielding the equation :

Sumer Lists.		Own Inscript.		Indian Lists.
Rutasa-Rāma	=		=	*Rohidashwa.*
Uruduki Raman	=		=	Hrashwa-Roman.
		Duru(ashi)padda	=	Drupada.

This comparison of his titles in the Sumerian and Indian lists seems further to confirm his identity by his Sumerian title of *Uruduki*. We have seen that the early Indian scribes in transcribing the names and titles from the Sumerian not infrequently translated the latter into the Indian Sanskrit or Pali vernacular. Now *Urudu* in Sumerian means "bronze," and is cognate with Old English *Āre*, "bronze," and Anglo-Saxon *Ār* "brass"; [1] and we find it stated in the Indian chronicles that this king was "The Destroyer of the Brazen (or Copper) faced Foes." [2] This appears to be a legend founded on the Sumerian element in his name meaning "Bronze;" from which the later Indian scribes coined the legend that he destroyed "Aryan faced foes."

And it is significant that this famous heroic Aryan king

[1] WSAD. 16.

[2] WVP. 4, 68. This occurs under his lunar title of Dashārha, and see App. I, No. 25.

SUMERIAN HARPIST WITH WORSHIPPERS.

From bas-relief, *c.* 2500 B.C., at Lagash. (After Heuzey, *Déc.*, Pl. XXIII). Note the harp has twelve strings as in the old Irish harp of A.D. 800; and it has carved on its stem the Bull symbol of God Ia or Dur. The player and worshippers are bearded and long-haired, while a shaven priest stands in front of harpist.

Draupada is described in the Indian Chronicles, like Uruash and his dynasty, as a *Panch-āla, i.e.* as we have seen, "Phœnician." Thus his dynasty was evidently "The Second Phœnician" Dynasty of the Sumerians.

King Drupada as "Leader of Praise or Worship" (? Harpist)

Another title borne by King Drupada in the Indian epics is "Leader of the Praise, Prayer, or Worship" (*Yajna-sena*). This suggests that he may be the unknown king of this period, whose name has not yet been found in an inscription, whose royal tomb at Ur contained amongst its magnificent equipment of objects interred for his use and enjoyment in the underground world of the after-life, a splendidly decorated harp of twelve strings, suggesting that he was a harpist and musician. The harp occurs in Sumer sculptures (Pl. IXA); and "a harp of a 100 strings" is cited in the Vedas and the Indian harp is of the same form as the Babylonian.[1]

Romance of King Drupada in the Indian Epics

In the Mahā-Bhārata epic[2] this King Drupada is the hero of a lengthy romance which now acquires general interest in view of so many of the splendid personal belongings and works of art of his dynasty, if not of himself, having been unearthed at the royal tombs at Ur. Briefly that romance tells us that Drupada was a school-fellow and friend of the Brahman priest Drona, son of Bharadwaja, who became the religious tutor of the Kuru and Pāndu princes —which seems an anachronism, as these princes are made later to take part in the great intertribal war of the Barats over the partition of Gangetic India; though it is possible that the old tale of Drupada and the Pandus had been transplanted into the Mahā-Bhārata epic, which contains many anachronisms, as we shall see. Drupada mortally offended his friend Drona, when on succeeding to the throne he repudiated his acquaintance with the latter, who in revenge instigated his pupils the Kuru and the five Pāndu princes to capture Drupada and his kingdom. This the five

[1] G. Birdwood, *Indian Arts*, II., 67.

[2] MBt. I. Slokas, 5511 f.

brother Pāndu princes accomplished, but Drona spared Drupada's life and restored to him the southern part of his kingdom.

Drupada's daughter Krishnā, otherwise called Draupadī, was a princess of rare beauty. Many princes sought her hand, but her father decided to hold a tournament to enable her to choose a heroic husband. The successful suitor in the tournament was the third of the five Pāndu prince brothers named Arjuna, who was the fairest and handsomest of them all and an invincible bowman. The story goes on to relate that by the princess marrying one of the brothers she became the joint-wife of all the five, and on this episode it has been supposed that polyandry was prevalent at that time.

The rest of the tale relates that the elder brother of the five, Bhīma, was an inveterate gambler—*and significantly a finely inlaid gaming-table, with men and dice, was unearthed in one of these royal tombs at Ur.* And in playing against his cousins the Kuru (or Syrian) princes, he staked and lost his kingdom, and thereafter staked and also lost his wife, the princess Draupadī, the joint-wife of all the five brothers and of his pre-eminently as the eldest brother. After this the princess Draupadī, who becomes a slave, suffers innumerable vicissitudes and gross insults ; but is eventually restored to her fivefold husbands.

As for King Drupada himself, he is said to have been killed and beheaded by his arch-enemy Drona, who in turn was killed by Drupada's son and successor Dhrista-Dyumna ; but this may refer to a second Drupada or Drupada II at the later epoch of the Great War of the Barats.

Funerary Murders or Immolations *re* "Satti" in this Ur Dynasty

The startling discovery disclosed by the Ur excavations of the prevalence in the period of this Ur Dynasty of the barbarous burial practice of immolating the wives, concubines and personal servants of the dead king in the royal tomb shows how degraded this particular "Phœnician" dynasty had become by the adoption of this revolting aboriginal Chaldean Semitic custom, analogous to the adoption of human sacrifice by some of the later Phœnicians of Carthage.

No reference to, or suggestion of, such a repulsive practice of human sacrifice has ever been found in Sumerian literature. On the other hand the Semites are well-known to have been addicted to human sacrifice from time immemorial.

These funerary murders as disclosed in this Ur tomb are obviously related to the Hindu custom of *Satti* or self-immolation of widows on the pyre of their deceased husbands —a long-established custom in India, which has only been stopped by stringent British legislation since a few generations ago, though isolated cases still occur. In this *Satti*, which was actively supported and urged by the Brahman priests as orthodox, the victim was usually a consenting party. And these discoveries at the Ur cemetery appear to disclose the period and circumstances in which this inhuman degraded practice crept in to the rites of the Indo-Aryans.

And it is of historical interest to find that in the Indian epic romance of King Drupada there is an actual reference to the practice of funereal immolation. This states that Drupada's daughter, the princess of Draupadī, whilst a slave-girl, was beloved by Prince Kīchaka, the leading man in the kingdom of Wirāta (? Ur), who was at the instigation of Draupadī slain by the senior husband of the latter, Bhīma, the same who had sent her into slavery. Whereupon she was ordained to be burnt alive on the funeral pyre of the dead prince, but was rescued.

Sumerian Royal Tombs at Ur as Source of Egyptian Type of Tombs

The great discovery of the royal cemeteries at Ur by Mr Woolley, and subsequently at Kish by the Weld-Field Expedition, has disclosed that these Sumerians of this period buried their royal dead in very much the same fashion as the Egyptians of the Old Kingdom buried theirs. The resemblance is so close that it cannot be explained as of separate or independent origin; but suggests that the Egyptian fashion was borrowed from the Sumerian. And I have already shown, and we shall further see, that Egyptian civilization was derived from the Sumerian subsequent to the period of this dynasty at Ur.

Both in Sumerian and in Egypt the tomb seems to have been a shaft with the chamber at the bottom; and in both the body was accompanied by an equipment for the use and enjoyment of the deceased in the underworld, in the same belief in the immortality of the soul. In the Sumerian tomb of Ur the funerary equipment is more extensive than in Egypt. Amongst other things, besides changes of apparel, there was found the king's chariot along with the bodies of the pair of favourite chariot asses.[1]

In the Sumerian colony in the Indus Valley, which was contemporary with and dated from the previous dynasty, as we have seen, the dead were buried in bricked shallow shafts, often near houses, but the details have not yet been published.

Embalming of the corpse is also referred to in the solar version of the ancient Indo-Aryan chronicles. This states that the body of the second king of the First Dynasty (under his title of *Nimi*, which I have shown is the equivalent of his Sumerian title of *Nimirrud* or "Nimrod") was so preserved. The record says: "The corpse of *Nimi* was preserved from decay by being embalmed with fragrant oils and resins; and it remained as entire as if it were immortal."[2]

Successors of Duruashipadda or Drupada (including "Meskalamdug") in the Great Gap

The equations between the names of the successors of King Duruashipadda or Drupada of the Great Gap in the Sumerian and Indian Lists are seen in the Table. This exhibits substantial equation in the forms of the names, where these are legible in the Sumerian text, and absolute relative identity in the chronological order and number of the kings in the Sumerian and Indian. Thus again is attested the remarkable historical authenticity of the Indian Lists, and the fact that the First Dynasty of the Kish Chronicle is the first dynasty of the Sumerians.

The name of an apparently royal personage whose tomb,

[1] A chariot was found in Tutankhamen's tomb. [2] WVP. 3, 328.

that of the immolated victims, was unearthed at Ur—who seems to have been royal, judging from the pomp and magnificence of the objects buried with him, but whose inscription does not call him "king"—has been read "Mes-kalam-dug." This name, however, reads also *Pa-unu-du* or *Pa-unu-khi*.[1] He may therefore possibly be one of the *Pāndu* princes of the Drupada legend; or might possibly be *Bhānu* or *Ban-kirti*, the third king in succession to Drupada and twenty-eighth in the list. Significantly, whilst his body was not found in the tomb, there was found there a massive life-sized golden mask, modelled as a prince's head wearing a fillet, with embossed features and with the hair engraved, and it was pierced at the lower border to carry a sewed-on cloth. This suggests to me that this personage had possibly been beheaded in battle or in a duel, as we have seen Drupada is reputed to have been in the feuds then rampant.

The last Sumerian or Aryan King of the Great Gap of the Kish Chronicle is disclosed by our Comparative Table, and confirmed by a mass of concrete historical and other evidence to be the father of Sargon-the-Great as hereditary king of Kish—a position for him hitherto altogether unknown and unsuspected, as Sargon is universally believed by Assyriologists to have been merely a Semitic adventurer and of low birth. As this king now proves to be an imperial personage of great critical importance in Ancient History, he requires a special chapter to himself.

[1] Br. 8647, 8204, 8207.

XII

Sargon's Father discovered as Hereditary Sumerian or Aryan King of Kish and his Dethronement by Zaggisi—Completing the Recovery of all the Kings of the Great Gap, Establishing Authenticity of First Dynasty of Kish Chronicle as First Dynasty of the Sumerians & the Identity of the Sumerians with the Early Aryans:

Disclosing Unknown Name, Personality and History of Sargon's Father, his Identity with King "Uruka-Gina" and his seal in the Indus Valley colony.

Another of the outstanding discoveries of universal importance which is now made by our Indo-Aryan keys is that the last king in the Great Gap of the "Kish Dynasty" in the Kish Chronicle is the hitherto unknown father of Sargon-the-Great, with his unknown name and titles and ancestry. And along with this is the discovery of his official seals in the Indus Valley and now deciphered for the first time.

"Sargon's" Aryan or Sumerian Race & Paternity.

Hitherto "Sargon"-the-Great has been dogmatically stated by all Assyriologists, followed mechanically by all modern writers, to have been a lowly-born adventurer and a Semite in race,[1] notwithstanding that there is nothing whatever to support such conjectures. On the contrary, neither in his own records nor in those of his dynasty nor elsewhere is there any reference whatever to his being a Semite or non-Sumerian. All his inscriptions that have hitherto been found in Mesopotamia are written in the standard Sumerian script of his time, in the Sumerian or Aryan sun-wise direction of left to right, and usually if not

[1] *E.g., Camb. Anc. Hist.*, I, 403 f. and *passim.*

altogether in the Sumerian language—the very occasional introduction of a Semitic word or idiom (which is doubtful in regard to Sargon's own inscriptions),[1] was obviously, as I have shown, because by far the great majority of his subjects in his vast empire were Chaldeans or Semites who spoke a Semitic language, and Sargon himself doubtfully but certainly his successors in the dynasty, tended to embody a few Semitic words in their official inscriptions for imperial purposes, just as other Aryan Emperors did in later times. His religion also was purely Sumerian and Aryan; he worshipped and invoked solely the Sun (a non-Semitic cult) with its associated later Sumerian or Aryan deity Sagg or Sakh, and neither he nor his dynasty ever once mentions a Semitic deity.

And now we have discovered positive contemporary documentary proof that his father was not only an Aryan or Sumerian in race but the lineal descendant of the first Sumerian or Aryan king, of whom he was the 36th in descent in direct succession in both the Indo-Aryan and the Old Sumerian King-Lists of the Isin Chronicles (see p. 140); and he was the hereditary Sumerian King of Kish which carried with it the imperial Sumerian title.

"Sargon's" Father's Unknown Name Disclosed

"Sargon" never mentions his father's name in any of his own extant contemporary inscriptions, nor is it mentioned in any of those of his descendants.

"Sargon's" own proper personal name we shall find in the next chapter was not "Sargon"; but it was variously phonetically spelt in Sumerian by himself and others "*Gin* or *Gani*, *Guni*, or *Shar-* or *Sha-Guni*" (*i.e.*, "Lord Guni"), with the title of *Shagur;* and thus equating with his name in the Indian King-Lists and Chronicles as *Kuni* or *ShaKuni* with the title of *Sagara*—the current modern name "Sargon" being merely a Semitic corruption arbitrarily adopted by Assyriologists to make the name of this great Sumerian and Aryan Emperor equate with the Hebrew Old Testament name for the notorious Semitic Assyrian king who sent

[1] Thus his mace-head inscription can be read as purely Sumerian. CT. BM. xxi. pl. I.

the Jews into captivity; and thus introducing another of their many confusions into Sumerian and Mesopotamian or Babylonian history. As this fictitious name "Sargon," however, has thus been forced into currency, we are now compelled to use it; but the reader must bear in mind that it does not express the real form of that great emperor's name, but rather disguises it.

The only instance hitherto known in which Sargon's father's name is mentioned in Babylonian records is in a cuneiform tablet copy of about 2200 B.C. of an old Sumerian record found at Warka, the site of Old Erech, narrating Sargon's negotiations with the usurper King Zaggisi of Erech, who had dethroned Sargon's father. In that cuneiform tablet the name of Sargon's father is given, and it has hitherto been conjecturally read as "Laipūm." But, as shown in detail in next chapter, it reads in the polyphonous Sumerian writing, as deciphered by our Indian keys to the traditional forms of the ancient names, *Bar-gin-i-buz* or *Barduibuz-um*.

That name thus equates substantially with the forms of Sargon's father's name in the Old Sumerian lists misplaced in the Isin Chronicle (p. 140), and with those preserved in the Indian Lists. And it is confirmed by the shorter forms of his name on his official seals found in the Indus Valley colony as *Bargin* and *Buruubuz*.[1] Thus we get the equations for these variant phonetic spellings of Sargon's father's names by different scribes as follows:—

In Erech Tablet.	Old Sumerian.	Indus Valley Seals.	Indian King-Lists.
Bar-gin-i-bu-um =	*Baragin-ma* =	*Bargin* or *Pargin* =	*Pracin-wat* or *Puru*.
Barduibuz-um =	*Buru* or *Puru* =	*Buruubuz* =	*B'aradwaja*.
f. of King *Kin*, K. of Kish or "Sargon."	f. of K. Ganni, *Sha-Gin* or *Sha-gur*, K. of Kish or "Sargon."	(*Urudu-Gina*).[2]	*Bāhu* or *Bāhuka*, f. of K. *Kuni*, *Shakuni* or *Sagar* or "Sargon."

[1] See Plate X and Appendix VI for details.

[2] He is seen to be identical with King Urudu-Gina or "Uruka-Gina" of the Lagash inscriptions. The second syllable of that name reads *du* (Br. 506) as well as *ka*; and *du* seems to be the correct form, in view of one of the Indus versions giving his name as *Baradwaja*. And the first syllable *Uru*, the sign for "city," presumably had also a *Buru* or *Puru* value in view of the usual Sanskrit name for "city" being *Pura*, and the Anglo-Saxon being *Burh*, the source of our English word "Borough."

The equations of the Sumerian *Baragin, Bargin* and *Barduibuz* with the Indian *Pracin* and *B'aradwaja* are noteworthy.

His Empire, including the Indus Valley.

King Buru Gina or Bara Gin(ma) is described as King of Kish in the imperial main-line in the Old Sumerian King-Lists, just as he as Pracin-wat or B'aradwaja, the father of Sakuni or "Sargon" is described as an emperor in the corresponding position in the main line in the Indian lists. And he bears in the Old Sumerian lists the title of "Sea-lord" like the members of Uruash's Dynasty, who held the Indus Valley.

In keeping with this Sumerian account of his empire, the Indian Epics record that "*Pracinwat conquered all the eastern countries to the very confines where the Sun rises.*"[1] This seems to be a genuine tradition of his imperial colony in the Indus Valley, as attested by his inscribed official seals there as now discovered and deciphered here for the first time.

His Indus Valley official seals (Plate X, Nos. 3-4), are inscribed in the old cursive Sumerian pictographic writing to which I have already furnished the keys to its sign-lists in my pioneer decipherments of the Indo-Sumerian seals. And significantly, like all the other Indus Valley seals, the direction of their writing in the seal-impressions is *in the retrograde direction.*[2] Of these seals, it will be seen that one (Plate X, No. 4), reads and translates from the detailed decipherment tables in Appendix VI as follows :—

Reads : *Buru umun-buz bar-gin gu uri-du-ash.*
Transl. : Buru (or Puru), Lord Buz Bar-Gin of Uridu Land.

[1] MBt. I, ch. 95, sl. 3696 ; and WVP. 4, 127.

[2] The supposition that the photographs of the first published batch of Indus Valley seals were of *impressions* of the seals, and not the seals themselves, is now seen to have been a mistake. Those photographs were of the seals themselves, which latter are graved in the non-retrograde direction, but give the writing in the reversed or retrograde direction in their impressions or sealings. Thus the inference in my *Indo-Sumerian Seals Deciphered,* that the writing was non-retrograde, applies only to the graving on the seals themselves and not to their sealings. This, however, in nowise alters the decipherments and readings of those seals in that book.

Here his *Buru* title, with the personal name *Bargin*, equates with his name and title in the Old Sumerian lists of Buru-Gin, and Priest-Lord Bara-Gin(ma) and with the Indian form Pracin-wat. His title of Lord or King of Uridu is also implied in his imperial title of "King of Kish" in the Old Sumerian king lists of the Isin Chronicle, a title as we have seen which carried kingship of the individual cities. His *Buru* title, moreover, which has the variant of *Puru*, clearly identifies him with the Indian "Puru" name for the father of "Sargon" under the latter's lunar title in the Puru version as Puru II and Pra-Vira,[1] wherein the latter part of that name equates with Sargon's *Pir* title in the Old Sumerian Lists (see table opposite p. 140). His variant title of Bāhu or Bāhuka in one of the solar versions of the Indian Lists is obviously derived from the common contracted Sumerian variant of *Bu-u* or *Bū* for the *Buz* sign of his name. In his own Mesopotamian inscriptions at Lagash, he usually spells his name Uru-du Gina, a name hitherto conjecturally read as "Urukagina," wherein the first syllable *Uru* had presumably a fuller value of *Buru* or *Puru*.[2]

His Great Reforms & Free Institutions

Sargon's father, under his name of King Urudu Gina (or Uruka Gina)—a name obviously dialectic with his name and title Buru-Gina in the Old Sumerian lists and cognate with Barduibuz, equating with the Indian form of his name as "B'aradwaja"—of the most famous reforming kings of the Sumerians. Indeed, so great and enlightened a statesman was he and reformer of abuses in the public service, in priestcraft, in the administration of justice and in championing the welfare and freedom of the poor, and so very "modern" his ideals and methods that they bear favourable comparison with those of present-day Europe in the twentieth century of the Christian era, and show *how very little real progress has been made in civic government legislation for justice and free institutions since the days of those Aryan Sun-worshippers about five thousand years ago.* They also show all unsuspectedly that a great deal of the administrative talent

[1] WVP. 4, 127. [2] See footnote on p. 188 and table, p. 140.

of Sargon, by which he held and extended his patrimonial empire, was obviously inherited from his father.

Fortunately, several detailed copies of King Urudu Gina's edicts and law-codes have been unearthed from the ruins of the old Sumerian seaport city of Lagash, in which he styles himself "King of Lagash," just as his predecessors of Uruash's Dynasty were Kings of Lagash as well as of Kish. He appears to have resided a great deal, latterly, at Lagash in purging its administration from the gross abuses which had crept into the local government there.

In one of his edicts[1] he describes the rampant oppression and corruption by a great army of officials, lay and priestly, which had prevailed in the Lagash city-state "since distant days"; and he then goes on to enumerate the reforms which he introduced by which he claimed to have ameliorated the people's lot. These contemporary records give a vivid glimpse of the economic and social conditions of his time and of the daily life and occupations of the people. He especially lightened the grievous burden of taxes and of forced feudal labour which oppressed the people. There were, he says, armies of corrupt tax-inspectors and priests who plundered the populace wholesale and grew rich themselves at the expense of the state and their temples, and deprived the impoverished people of the fruits of their own labour in trade and in produce of their fields.

Urudu Gina in attacking the abuses abolished the greater number of the tax-inspectors and cut down the fees of the extortionate priests and lay officials. There were inspectors of granaries, fisheries, boats, cattle and herds, and others who farmed out the revenues, all over the state and "down to" the sea. All officials who had taken money (shekels) in place of tribute, and who had given bribes to the priests and higher officials were dismissed. The fees of the priests were reduced by more than half. Thus the burial fees of the priests for an ordinary burial which had been to the chief priest, 7 urns of wine, 420 loaves of bread, 120 measures of corn, a garment, a kid, a bed and a seat, were reduced by King Urudu Gina to 3 urns of wine, 80 loaves of bread, a bed and a kid; and

[1] For texts, see TDI. 68 f.; and English translations of several portions in KHS. 178 f., from which several of these extracts are cited.

likewise the fee of the priest's assistant was reduced from 60 to 30 measures of corn. And similarly the other fees of the priests and of the lay officials were revised, reduced, and regulated. The laws regarding murder or theft of goods and cattle were enforced with drastic penalties.

He especially sought to protect the poorer classes of his subjects against the oppression of their richer and more powerful neighbours. Thus he enacted that if a good ass were foaled in the stable of any subject of the king, and his superior or richer neighbour wished it, he must buy it at a fair price, and that if the owner refused to part with it his superior must not molest him. And so with other properties. And he alleviated some of the grievances of the feudal forced labourers. He also abolished the practice of superstitious divination by oil, by which the priests extracted huge sums of money from the people. In divorce cases, the governing officials charged 5 shekels of silver and the Grand Vizier an extra one, and they justified these high charges on the plea of deterring divorce. But as divorce and infidelity were rife the king abolished the divorce fees, but inflicted severe penalties for infidelity on the part of the wife.

Altogether the king claims that " he is the champion of the weak against the strong; in place of servitude, he established liberty; he delivered the children of Lagash from want, theft, murder and other ills. In his reign, to the widow and the orphan the strong man did no harm."

Significantly, his Sumerian law-codes are generally similar in character to those latterly codified by Hammurabi which were obviously derived from the same Aryan or Sumerian source, and we shall see in next chapter the traditional version of the Aryan commandments in which the prince Sargon was instructed, as preserved in the Indian Epics. It is also noteworthy that King Urudu Gina piously ascribed his codes to Lord Nimirrud (Nimrod) the patron-saint of Lagash, who, we have seen, was King Cain the canonized second king of the Sumerians and son of the first king Ukusi or "Adam," the Sun-worshipper; just as later the Babylonian Aryan king Khammurabi ascribes his famous law-codes on "a table of stone" to the Sun-god, whose representation he models on that of the bearded and Gothic horned-capped, deified first Aryan or Sumerian king, Sakh or Induru or Thor. And still much later the Hebrews, in extracting from the Aryan law-codes the leading ethical commands for their Mosaic code, also borrowed this legend of their divine origin and of their being graven on "tables of stone."

His Dethronement by the Usurper Zaggisi

This last king of the Great Gap of the Kish Dynasty of the Kish Chronicle was dethroned as detailed in the next chapter by the usurper Zaggisi, who had been local governor and priest-king at Umma City to the north of Lagash, and was the son of the former governor there who bore the solar name of Ukush.

Zaggisi, who was evidently considered a usurper by the Indian annalists, as they do not give him a place in the Indian main-line lists, became emperor and transferred his capital to Erech. From his votive inscriptions at Nippur we learn that he claimed to have "conquered the land from the Rising of the Sun to its Setting, and made straight the path from the Lower Sea (Persian Gulf and Indian Ocean) over the Euphrates and Tigris unto the Upper Sea (Mediterranean)." This was presumably the same extent of empire over which Sargon's father ruled. Like the latter also he claimed to be "King of Uri," which he spells as *Ki-uri*.[1] Significantly he was a devotee of the Chaldean or Semitic Moon-cult of Ur and claimed the Moon-god and several goddesses as patrons; although he also invokes the Sun and Lord Sakh, to which latter he ascribes his victories. He also claims to have rebuilt during his 25 years of reign the chief temples in the land and to have dug canals; and that "he caused the lands to dwell in security, he watered the lands with the waters of joy."

Zaggisi's harrowing sack of the Sumerian seaport of Lagash is described in an unofficial tablet by an eyewitness, wherein the dethroned king is called *Urudu-* (or Uruka-) *Gina*. Zaggisi forms by himself the so-called "Third

1 PHT. iv. 183. But *Ki-uri* may also mean "Syria" in its broader sense of Asia Minor—the *Kuru* of the Indian Epics and Vedas.

Dynasty " of the Kish Chronicle immediately after the last king of the Great Gap in that chronicle, in regard to which the term " dynasty " is used by modern writers for a change of capital. Zaggisi was dethroned by " Sargon " and the " Fourth Dynasty " then follows as " Sargon's " dynasty, which now requires separate chapters, on account of the vast amount of new historical discoveries now elicited regarding him by our new keys and new inscriptions.

Complete Recovery of All the Kings of the Great Gap Establishing the Authenticity of the First Dynasty of Kish Chronicle as the First Dynasty of the Sumerians

Thus, we have now in the foregoing seven chapters identified all the Sumerian Kings of the First and Second Dynasties of the Kish Chronicle, as well as those of its Great Gap disclosed by our official Indian King-Lists of the Aryans, with historical kings, most of the leading ones of whom have left inscriptions, notwithstanding that no trace whatever of any of the kings of the First and Second Dynasties of the Kish Chronicle had hitherto been found by Assyriologists. The historicity and chronology of the Kish Chronicle First and Second Dynasties is confirmed by the testimony of three independent Old Sumerian King-Lists discovered misplaced in the king-lists prefixed by the Isin priests to the Kish Chronicle. And the names, order and achievements of these Early Sumerian kings equate strictly with those of the Early Aryan kings preserved in the Indian King-Lists and Chronicles of the Early Aryans, which have formed our chief key to these discoveries, and which are now established as historical and unique independent sources of Early Sumerian History.

As a result, we have established the historicity and genuine chronology of *the Kish Chronicle with its First King and First Dynasty as the first of all Sumerian kings and the First Dynasty of the Sumerians, and at a date no earlier than about* 3378 B.C. as detailed in the Chapter on Chronology.

Recovery of True Chronology of Sumerian Period & Identity of Sumerians with Early Aryans.

We also have established the identity of the First and

following Sumerian dynasties with the First and following dynasties of the Early Aryans and, therefore, *the identity of the Sumerians with the Early Aryans in race, tradition and achievements.* And thus we recover for the first time the fundamental basis of Early Sumerian or Early Aryan History, the oldest concrete history in the world, with its real Chronology.

At the same time the falsity of the chronology of the Isin Chronicle with its dynasties of fabulous ages prefixed to the First Dynasty of the Kish Chronicle is fully exposed, and the hopeless current confusion introduced into Mesopotamian and World History by the too credulous acceptance of this fabulous Isin chronology is now effectually got rid of by the recovery of the genuine History and true Chronology by means of our Indian keys.

FIG. 22A.—First Aryan King In-Dara taming the Lions (tribal Chaldee totems) from pre-Christian Crosses in Britain (*l* and *m*), for comparison with Sumerian in Frontispiece. Tasia-Michael on Catti coins of Anc. Britain of 2nd cent. B.C. (*h.* and *i*). Andrew's (Indara's) Cross on Anc. Briton coins c. 2nd cent. B.C. (*k*); and see Figs. 141, 142, pp. 607, 608.
(For detailed descriptions see WPOB. 335-337.)

XIII

" SARGON "-THE-GREAT DISCOVERED AS HEREDITARY ARYAN KING OF KISH WITH HIS LOST PRE-HISTORY & " WORLD MONARCHY "

Disclosing his Aryan Race, unknown Royal Ancestry, Posthumous Birth, Training by Priest Aurva, Recovery of Father's Kingdom and attainment of World-Empire, including Britain, Mediterranean, Asia Minor, Syria, Mesopotamia, Persia, Indus Valley and Egypt.

> " **Ikshvāku (First Aryan King) had a hundred sons (or descendants) of whom the eldest were Bikukshi-Nimi (Bacchus-Nimrod) and Danda. Fifty: SHAKUNI (" Sargon ") and others, were the protectors of the northern countries,"** ***Vishnu Purāna*** **Epic.**[1]

HAVING established through our Indian key-lists, confirmed by the Old Sumerian King-Lists misplaced by the Isin priests, and by a mass of concrete inscriptional evidence including Udu's Bowl record (*a*) that the Kish Chronicle is the sole authentic Babylonian chronological record of the Sumerians from their First Dynasty continuously down to the later historic period, (*b*) that the First Dynasty of the Kish Chronicle is the First Dynasty of the Sumerians, and (*c*) that the last king of the Great Gap in the Second Dynasty of that chronicle is the father of " Sargon "-the-Great as king of Kish, we now come to the glorious King " Sargon " himself—an epoch-making hero who never calls himself by that name, which is merely a Semitic corruption of his name adopted by Assyriologists and adding to the confusion they have introduced into History.

" Sargon," whose proper name is disclosed below, with his dynasty forms the " Fourth " Dynasty in the Kish Chronicle

[1] WVP. 3, 259.

(see p. 61), in which the "Third" Dynasty consists merely, as we have seen, of King Zaggisi of Erech, who dethroned "Sargon's" father and who was in turn dethroned by "Sargon."

By the Indo-Aryan Chronicles, which are especially rich in records regarding his birth, Aryan genealogy, upbringing, and exploits, we recover a great deal of "Sargon's" lost history for the first time, which revolutionizes the hitherto current conjectures in regard to his origin, birth, and race, and make him now one of the best-known great emperors of the ancient world, of which he held the vastest empire.

"Sargon's" Aryan Race, Royal Birth & World Empire

This famous "world-monarch," who has hitherto been universally regarded by Assyriologists, and through them by all writers on Ancient History, as a low-born adventurer of a "lowly mother" and a Semite in race, is now discovered on the contrary to have been the son of a mighty emperor and his queen and the hereditary King of Kish, and a Sumerian and Aryan in race.

By his great world-conquests he was esteemed by the Babylonians and Assyrians as the most mighty and famous of all kings; and in the Indian Epics and Chronicles also he is an Aryan "world-monarch" under his solar title of "Sagara"; and as "Shakuni" he is, as cited in the heading, the especial lineal descendant and chief representative of the first Aryan king Ikshwāku, the first Sumerian king Ukusi of the Kish Chronicle. And "Sargon" himself in his own inscriptions repeatedly states, as we shall see, that his patron-lord or "god" is Sagga, the name of the Bowl hero, and equating with the "Sakko" title of the first Aryan king, the deified Indra, and the "Sig" title of Thor, the first king of the Goths in the Eddas.

The extent of his empire has hitherto been only vaguely inferred and greatly underestimated from his title in his inscriptions as "King of the lands of the Lower Sea and the Upper or Western Sea"—terms in which "Lower Sea" has been supposed to be restricted to the Persian Gulf, and in which "Upper Sea" or "Sea of the West or of the Setting Sun" though rightly recognized as meaning the Mediterranean, has been interpreted by Assyriologists as meaning no more than the Syrian coast. Now, however, he is seen to have ruled an empire in the Ancient World so vast that it has perhaps never been equalled in the Old World. It is seen to have included, besides Mesopotamia and the greater part of Asia Minor and Syrio-Phœnicia, also Egypt and the Mediterranean basin, Persia and the Indus Valley with the Arabian Sea, and extending beyond the Pillars of Hercules to Britain.

"Sargon's" Name & Titles in Sumerian & Babylonian Inscriptions & in Indian Chronicles, not "Sargon"

The current name "Sargon" for this great Sumerian-Aryan emperor, is merely a Semitized corruption adopted by Assyriologists who have supposed him to be a Semite, in order to assimilate his name to the Hebrew name for the relatively late notorious Semitic Assyrian king who sent the Jews into captivity. And to distinguish him from this late Semitic Assyrian they call him "Sargon I" or "Sargon of Agade," after his capital city on the Euphrates above Babylon, the site of which has not yet been found, but the name of which appears to be more properly spelt *Agudu* [1] as it is preserved in the Indian Chronicles as *Ayodhya.*

Neither "Sargon" himself nor Babylonian scribes are ever found to have spelt his name so. That emperor himself usually spells his own name in his very few inscriptions as yet unearthed in Mesopotamia as *Shar Ga-ni, Sir Ga-ni* or *Shar-Gu-ni.*[2] It has hitherto been usual to regard the whole of these three latter syllables as forming the king's personal name. But our new evidence obtained from the old Sumerian forms preserved in the prefixed Isin Lists, where he is called *Ganni* or *Gunni* and *Sha-Gin* or *Sha-Kin ;* and in the Indian Lists where his personal name is *Kuni* with variant *Sha-kuni,* indicates that his personal name was intended to be

[1] On *gu*, Br. 6103 and SS. 244, and on *du* M. 3099.

[2] The second syllabic sign here (B. 275) which I have shown in its earliest Sumerian form pictures a buffalo's head (WSID. 57 f.), has the sign-name of *Gu* (Br. 6103), which is its basal value ; and is a value given by SS. No. 244 ; and it is the same sign as in the name of his capital in foregoing note, *A-gu-du.*

read "Lord *Gani* or *Guni*"—the prefix *Shar* or *Sir*[1] or *Sha* (surviving in the Persian *Shah*) meaning in Sumerian "Lord,"[2] And this is confirmed by his own inscription in Egypt, as we shall see.

This form for his personal name of "Lord (or Sir) *Gani, Ganni, Guni* or *Gunni*," in series with the Indian *Kuni*, is supported by the usual style of writing his name in Babylonian and Assyrian, in which the Sumerian sign for "king," has the Semitic value of *Sharru*, which is substituted for the *Shar* or *Sir* sign of the original writing of his name, and thus gives the reading, "King *Gani, Gina* or *Gin*." This is also supported by the form of his name in old Sumerian inscriptions at Nippur and elsewhere in which he is called "*Shar* (or *Sir*)-*um* GIN,"[3] which appears to designate him as "Lord of Lords" (or Master-Lord) GIN,"[4] a fitting title for him as the greatest of emperors.

VARIATIONS IN THE SPELLING OF "SARGON'S," OR PROPERLY KING GUNI'S OR GANI'S NAME

The great variations in the spelling of "Sargon's" name in his inscriptions and in the copies of his inscriptions made by Babylonian and Assyrian scribes are here tabulated for reference in their *Gin, Kin, Gani, Guni* and *Sagara* series, and with the prefixed *Shar* and *Sha* or *Sa*,[5] all of which latter merely mean "King" or "Lord." As the form with prefixed *Sharru* only occurs in copies made by late Semites it is placed within brackets.

GIN.	KIN.	GANI or GUNI.	SAGARA.[8]
Shar-GIN.	Shar-um KÎN.	Shar-GUNI.	SHAGUR.[7]
Shar-um-GIN.	She-KIN.[7]	Shar-GANI.	
Shar-GENA.[6]	(Sharru-KIN).	Sir-GANA.[8]	
(Sharru-GIN).	(Sharru-KÎN).	Sha-GUNI.	
(Sharru-GINA).			
(Sharru-GIUNA).			

[1] This Sumerian *Sir*, "Lord" (Br. 4306) is disclosed as presumably the Sumerian source of our English *Sire* for "King" or "Majesty" and of "Sir."

[2] This *Sha* sign in Sumerian = "Lord," Br. 2776.

[3] PHT. iv. 173, 176, and elsewhere.

[4] *Um* is obviously *Umu, Umun* "Lord, Master." This *um* sign literally means "Mother" in Sumerian; and if used in this sense would be analogous to the Oriental title for a patron of "Father and Mother."

[5] Cp. PHT. iv. 130.

[6] King Nabonidus (555-538 B.C.).

[7] Isin Lists, see table opposite p. 140.

[8] On seals, WISD. 63, 65, 68.

This analysis of these variants shows that "Sargon's" proper personal name was "King *Gani*, *Guni*, *Gin* or *Kin*, which is in agreement with his usual name in the Indian Lists as "King *Kuni*"; and that the prefixed *Shar*, *Sharru* and *Sha* corresponding to the Indian *Sha-Kuni* [1] merely meant "Lord" or "King." Whilst *Sagara* was his solar title, and exists both in his Sumerian inscriptions and in the Indian Epics.

"Sargon's" Dynasty in Kish Chronicle & Prefixed Isin Lists in Agreement with Indian Lists of Early Aryan Kings

The agreement between "Sargon's" Dynasty in the Kish Chronicle and in the prefixed Old Sumerian king-lists in the Isin Chronicle, and in the Indian Lists of the Early Aryan kings is displayed in the accompanying table—for Kish Chronicle list see p. 62; for Old Sumerian king-lists see Table p. 140; and Appendix III; and for the Indian Lists see Appendix I, Nos. 36 to 42.

The Indian Lists exhibit considerable variation in the names of the successors after No. 39 Karam B'a or Narām-Ba ("Narām Sin") of the Sumerian, and especially in the lunar Puru version. But this period, we learn from the Kish Chronicle and the Babylonian records, was a period more or less of anarchy, with different claimants to the imperial throne. The use in the Puru version (which we have seen was misplaced by the later Puru priests) of the title for "Sargon" of *Pra-Vira* or "Foremost Hero" or *Su-Vira* or "Good Hero" is noteworthy, as it seems to have been coined by the later Indian priests on his Sumerian title of *Pir* or *Pur* (see col. 2 of Table). It is also noteworthy that all the Indian Lists omit Sargon's younger son Mūsh or Uri-Mūsh and make the eldest son Manasyu or Asa Manja, *i.e.* Manis-Tusu the immediate successor of "Sargon," which is in keeping with the later Babylonian history which makes no mention of that younger son, who obtained the throne

[1] *Sha* in Sanskrit = "auspicious, the best, teacher," MWD. 1074, 1107; and thus agrees somewhat with the Sumerian. It is obviously a shortened form of *Shar* "Lord or King," and is presumably the source of the Persian *Shah* title for "King."

of his father as we shall see during the absence of his elder brother Manis-Tusu.

This agreement between the Indian and Sumerian King-Lists affords still further confirmation of the remarkable historicity of the Indian Lists of the Early Aryan Kings as an independent record of Sumerian history; and of the Aryan or Nordic racial and traditional identity of the Sumerians and Aryans.

"Sargon's" unknown Royal Aryan Ancestry & Posthumous Birth Disclosed by the Indian Chronicles

Nothing has hitherto been known of the antecedents and parentage of "Sargon" beyond the so-called legend of his birth in the late Babylonian version of his autobiography which gives no names for his parents and is supposed to represent him of "lowly" birth and illegitimate. Nor has any reference to "Sargon's" parentage been found in any inscription of himself or descendants, or in any of the Babylonian records, except one fragment in which the name of his father has been read "Luipum"; [1] but no royal position is accorded to him in the existing portion of that fragment.

Fortunately, however, for history a fairly full account of this great world-emperor is now found to be preserved in the Indian Chronicles of the Early Aryan Kings, which we shall find is supported in most of its critical details where these can be verified by the actual Babylonian inscriptions and records.

It is under his imperial solar title of *Sagara*—a title used by himself in one of his Indus Valley seals [2]—that the fullest account of his biography is preserved in the Indian Epics. In Sumerian *Sa-gar* is the title for "Lord of Lords" [3] that is "emperor." Under this title of Sagara he is significantly the father of *Asa-Manja* or "*Manja* the Shooter," who we shall find is identical in both name and achievements with "*Manis* the Warrior" or Manis-Tusu, the famous son and successor of Sargon. And under this title his royal Aryan ancestry is carried continuously back through the self-same

[1] See later on. [2] WISD. 64, 66, 68.
[3] *Sa-gar* as "Lord of Lords," Br. 447 and cp. Br. 6532.

ancestors as under his personal name of Kuni or Sha-Kuni, to the first king of the First Aryan Dynasty, Ikshvāku, who we have found is identical with King Ukusi, the first Sumerian king of the First Sumerian Dynasty of the Kish Chronicle, and with King Agushe, the first Sumerian king of the First Sumerian Dynasty in the second version of the Old Sumerian King-Lists in Table opposite p. 140. And this is the identical ancestry recorded for him as King Sha-Kuni or Kuni in the epic extract cited in the heading of this chapter, and claimed by himself in his own inscriptions.

This Indian Chronicle of the solar version relates that Sagara's (*i.e.* "Sargon's") father, under his title of Bāhu (a title obviously coined from his Sumerian name of *Bu-u* for *Buz* as above seen), was the hereditary king in the Aryan main-line with his capital at Ayodhya (Agudu or Agade), and was dethroned by his distant kinsman the chief of the Haihaya tribe, who we have seen in the previous chapter was King Zaggisi of Erech. We are informed that as the fugitive ex-king he died later in exile at the hermitage of the Fire-Priest Aurva, and that his posthumous son and heir was born at that hermitage, where tutored by the priest Aurva in the Vedic religion and in science and the art of war, he on reaching manhood wrested back his patrimonial kingdom and became a "world-monarch."

Here let the Indian Chronicle text speak for itself:

"Sargon's" Posthumous Birth & Upbringing by the Fire-priest Aurva, Regaining his Patrimonial Throne & Achievement of World-Empire in Indian Chronicles

This Indian Chronicle records: [1]

"The son of Uri-Taka was Bāhu (of Ayodhya). This king was vanquished by the tribes of the Haihayas and Tālajanghas,[2] and his country overrun by them, in consequence of which he fled into the forests with his wives. One of these was pregnant. . . . Bāhu died in the neighbourhood of the hermitage of the sage Aurva or Ūrva—the Fire-priest. His queen having constructed his funeral pyre, ascended it

[1] WVP. 3, 289 f.

[2] On these tribes see later in the narrative.

a

b

LADIES' (SUMERIAN) DRESS COIFFURE AND JEWELLERY.

a. Sumerian lady spinning, from bas-relief *c*. (?) 2500 B.C. (after DP. 1, Pl. XI). Note her elaborate coiffure and dress; her attendant with fan; and legs of table and stool ending artistically in claws.

b. Bracelets of gold and blue enamel of Queen of Sargon's great-grandson (Gin-Eri), on her mummy in Egyptian tomb, *c*. 2570 B.C. (after Sir F. Petrie, PHE. 1, 16).

c. Sumerian lady's coiffure carved in diorite, offered to the goddess Innina on behalf of King Dungi, *c*. 2330 B.C., in British Museum (No. 91075).

with the determination of accompanying him in death. But the sage, the Aurva, who knew all things, past, present and to come, issued forth from his hermitage and forbade her, saying: 'Hold! Hold! This is unrighteous! A valiant prince, the monarch of many realms, the offerer of many sacrifices, the destroyer of his foes, a universal emperor is in thy womb. Think not of committing so desperate an act!'

"Accordingly, in obedience to his injunctions, she relinguished her intentions. The sage then conducted her to his abode, and after some time a very splendid boy was there born. Aurva, after performing the ceremonies required at birth, gave him the name of *Sagara*. The same holy sage celebrated his investiture with the cord of his class, instructed him fully in the Vedas and all sciences, and taught him the use of arms, especially those of Fire, called after the Bhrigu or Fire-priest.

"When the boy had grown up and was capable of reflection, he said to his mother (one day): 'Why are we dwelling in this hermitage? Where is my father?' His mother, in reply, related to him all that had happened. Upon hearing this he was highly incensed, and vowed to recover his patrimonial kingdom, and exterminate the Haihayas and Tālajanghas and others by whom it had been overrun.

"Accordingly, when he became a man, he put nearly the whole of the Haihayas to death, and would also have exterminated the Shakas, the Yavanas, Kāmbojas, Pāradas and Pahlavas, Mahishikas, Dārvas, Daradas and Khashas, but they applied to Vasishtha, the family priest (of Sagara) for protection. Vasishtha, regarding them as deprived of power, though alive, thus spoke to Sagara: 'Enough, enough, my son! Pursue no further these objects of your wrath, whom you may look upon as no more (dangerous?)' Sagara in compliance with the advice of his priest contented himself therefore with imposing upon the vanquished nations peculiar distinguishing marks (as punishment). He made the Yavanas (Ionians) shave their heads entirely;[1] the

[1] Prof. F. Hall notes on this: "Amongst the Greeks it was common to shave the forepart of the head, a custom introduced according to Plutarch by the Abantes, whom Homer calls *Opiden xomoōntes* (Iliad 2, 542)." WVP. 3, 294.

Shakas (Scyths of Indus Valley, etc.)[1] he compelled to shave the (upper) half of their heads; the Pāradas to wear their hair long, the Pahlavas to let their beards grow, in obedience to his commands. . . .

"Sagara, after the recovery of his kingdom, reigned over the seven-zoned earth with undisputed dominion."

Confirmation of Indian Chronicle Record of "Sargon's" Birth & Upbringing by the Fire-Priest Ūrva in the Babylonian Autobiography of "Sargon"

Remarkable, and in essential respects almost literal, confirmation of the foregoing Indian Chronicle record of "Sargon's" birth and upbringing by the Fire-priest Ūrva is found in the famous Babylonian autobiography of "Sargon." This latter document, now found to be of the greatest historical importance, occurs in a late Assyrian cuneiform tablet copy of about 700 B.C., and has hitherto been supposed to be merely a mythical romance in regard to the circumstances of Sargon's birth and upbringing; but that opinion is now seen to be mainly owing to mistranslation of several critical words by our English translators, the one mechanically following the other.

The narrative is in the form of an autobiographical poem, the words being put into the mouth of Sargon himself. It relates how "King Ginna" (arbitrarily translated hitherto as "Sargon) "knew not" his father, that on his birth he was set adrift on the Euphrates River by his mother in a basket of rushes (a legend later attached by the Hebrews to Moses), that his mother according to our previous English translators was "a lowly woman,"[2] that the babe was picked up and adopted by an "irrigator" say these translators, and made by him a gardener, and that he was beloved by the goddess Ishtar and became a great king.

On revising, however, the reading of this cuneiform text[3] I was surprised to find that so far from his mother being described therein as "lowly," she is stated therein, on the

[1] See WISD. 59, 63, 101, 103, 108.

[2] *Camb. Anc. Hist.*, I, 403. KFS. 222 and others.

[3] Tablet in CIWA, 3, pl. 4, No. 7, and reproduced in part with a translation in L. King's *First Steps in Assyrian*, 222.

contrary, to be "a princess," and there was nothing about "an irrigator," *but, on the contrary, his tutor is named* "URU" *the Shepherd (priest) and* "*the Man of Fire,*" *as in the Indian Chronicle.*

AUTOBIOGRAPHY OF KING GINNA OR "SARGON" FROM ITS BABYLONIAN VERSION

My revised reading of this important historical text, and in which the critical words are duly attested from the standard lexicons, is as follows:

"King GINNA, the mighty king, King of *Agudu*[1] (am) I.
My mother was a princess.[2] My father I knew not.
The brother of my father dwells in the mountain.
Where the city of *Azutu*,[3] my (paternal) remainder,[4] on the bank of the Euphrates stands,
There she conceived me, (my) mother the princess. In concealment she bear me.
She set me in a basket of rushes, with bitumen my door she closed.
She gave me to the river which (rose) not over me.
It bore me, the river, to ANAKKI,[5] to the Man of Fire[6] it carried me,
Anakki, the Man of Fire into his dwelling[7] (he) URU . . . (like) a shepherd[8] lifted me up.
Anakki, the Man of Fire, as the Man of the Garden (? Oracle)[9] he instructed me.[10]

[1] On *Agudu*, see previous notes.

[2] *enitum*="princess," MD. 73.

[3] *tu*, Br. 7967.

[4] *raxāni*="remainder," cp. MD. 959.

[5] The initial vertical wedge, which is not prefixed to any other proper name in this text, forms obviously part of this personal name and has the value of *An*.

[6] *Awelu Nāq-me*=*Awelu*," man," and *Naqmū*, "fire," cp. MD. 719.

[7] *ina du*, cp. MD. 235.

[8] Several words are illegible after *Uru*, but *udu* or *re'a*, "shepherd" (M. 8181) is distinct.

[9] In this phrase reading *Nu-gish-shir-ti* or *Nu-iz-shir-ti*, the *shirti* appears to me to mean "Oracle," cp. MD. 1123 and 1156. Whilst *Nizirti* ="curse" also "blessing" of an oracle. The word *Nu-iz* (or *gish*) is usually supposed to mean "garden."

[10] *Kunani*="instruct, teach," B. 82; MD. 405.

As the Man of the Garden (? Oracle) the Lord Sakhar-Tar[1] loved me.
For . . . (? fifty) and four years the kingdom I ruled.
The men of the blackheaded race (Chaldees) I ruled, I . . .
Over rugged mountains in bronze chariots I rode.
I (ruled) the upper mountains.
I (ruled) the rulers of the lower mountains.
To the (Upper ?) Sea-coast, I thrice advanced: *Iatu* (or *Pu*) Land (Egypt)[2] submitted;
The fortress of *Durash* (? *Dur-Ilu*),[3] the great city, bended . . .
I destroyed . . . (illegible) . . ."

The specific agreement in so many details between this Babylonian autobiography of "Sargon" and the tradition preserved in the Indian epics regarding him is of great historical importance, in that while it confirms the authenticity of the latter it also discloses again the historical value of the Indian records as an independent source for explaining and complementing Babylonian history in regard to the Sumerians.

Thus the expression that Sargon "knew not his father," from which it was inferred that he was illegitimate, is now disclosed by our Indian evidence to be because he was born posthumously; and the statement that his mother was "lowly" is seen to rest merely on a mistranslation.

The name of Sargon's patrimonial city in the autobiography is called *Azutu*, which seems a dialectic variant of *Agudu* (or "Agade") especially as it is located in this autobiography on "The River of the Sun-temple city of Sipparā," as the Euphrates is poetically called here, and Agudu (or "Agade") is placed by archæologists near that city. The name *Azutu*, moreover, equates fairly well with the Indian name for his capital, namely, *Ayodhya*, which is

[1] This name also reads *Ish-tar*, and is usually translated here as Goddess Ishtar. But see p. 220 on it as a title of King Tar or Dar.

[2] On *Iatu* or *Pu* Land, as Egypt, see next Chapter.

[3] *Dur-ash* (or *-ilu*)*-ki-gal*. This city is usually identified with Dur-Ili supposed to be a name of Dēr, an Elamite city state east of the Tigris; but it was clearly remote from Mesopotamia and presumably in the west, beyond or to the north of Egypt; and, as noted below, I suggest that it may be Tarsus port of Cilicia or Ilos, *i.e.*, Troy.

spelt in modern Hindu as *Ajodhya*, for its namesake in the Ganges Valley, which is also a sacred city of the Indian Sun-worshippers. It would thus appear that Sargon was not the founder of Agudu (or "Agadē") but only its deliverer and rebuilder.

The incident of the babe in the basket is found in the Indian epics attached to a later Aryan king Karna, possibly through a confusion of him with the Kuni or Gani title of Sargon. It relates that the king as a babe was exposed in a basket on the bank of the river (Ganga) by his mother Prithā.[1]

But one of the most important evidences of identity in the Babylonian and Indian tradition is that in the Babylonian version the Fire-priest's name is "*Urura*, The Man of Fire," which thus equates in name and title with *Urva* or *Aurva*, the Fire-priest of the Indian version. And this identity receives further confirmation from another Babylonian record.

Additional Babylonian Confirmation of Indian Record of Tutelage of "Sargon" by the Priest Aurva or Ūrva

In a Babylonian historical text of about 600 B.C., now in the British Museum,[2] is I find another version of the same historical incident of the tutelage of Sargon and his investiture and restoration. In this the priest is named "The lord *Urura*, the sanctuary shepherd," and significantly the prince's name is spelt variously *Gani* and *Gin*, or possibly "*Saggin*"—this latter Babylonian form thus equating with the Old Sumerian list form of *S'agin*, and with the Indian Chronicle form of "Sargon's" name as *Sakuni*. And it gives prominence to his being instructed in religion as "the religious lord."

Here I place the Babylonian version in my revised reading alongside the Indian version for comparison in the accompanying Table. The cuneiform text is taken from Prof. King's transcription;[2] and the authorities for my revised

[1] WVP. 4, 126.

[2] BM. 96152, published by KC. 2, 15 f., wherein the priest's name is translated as "King Urās'mitti," and the king is disguised as "King Bel-Ibni, the gardener."

reading of the critical names are duly attested in the foot-notes.

" Sargon's " Tutelage under Priest Aurva & Recovery of his Throne in Babylonian & Indian Versions

Indian. (WVP. 3, 290 f.).	*Babylonian.* (Cuneif.Tab. BM. 96152).
" AURVA (or ŪRVA), the sage of the hermitage conducted the (widowed) queen to his abode and after some time a very splendid boy was born there.	" The lord URURA,[1] the sanctuary shepherd,[2] sat the king, the lord, the religious lord GANI [3] as the man-gardener (of the oracle).
" AURVA gave him the name SAGARA. The same holy sage *celebrated his investiture* with the cord of his class and instructed him in the Vedas and all sciences, and taught him the use of arms, especially those of Fire.	" This unseated [4] SAG-GIN (or Prince GIN) [5] upon the wood-throne he set. " The crown of his kingship he placed on his head. " The lord URURA (him) in the sovereignty of his great palace (and of) his father (who was) overthrown by weapons, he arranged.
" When the boy had grown up . . . he vowed to recover his patrimonial kingdom and exterminate the Haihayas and Tālajanghas by whom it had been overrun. Accordingly, when he became a man he put nearly the whole Haihayas to death.	" In the priestship he seated him.[6]
" SAGARA after the recovery of his kingdom reigned over the seven-zoned earth with undisputed dominion."	" The lord, the religious lord GANI sat. And as king he was established."

[1] Prof. King notes that the tablet was written by a careless copyist (KC. i. 57). This is evident by the first sign for the priest's name, which in line 1 is written with the *Mu* sign by omitting a wedge, but in line 4, where the name recurs, it is rightly written with the *Uru* sign (B. 49; Br. 955). Its second syllable is *ra* (B. 287).

[2] *Ashirtu re'u*=" sanctuary shepherd " (M. 4606, 8181).

[3] *Ga-ni* (Br. 5412, 5310).

[4] *La-shakanu*=" unseated."

[5] *Sag-Gin* (Br. 3502, 2384). Or the first sign may read by its Babylonian value, " Prince "(*asharidu*, Br. 3509), thus giving meaning, " Prince Gin."

[6] *Ena sa-ra-tu-shu im-divut.* Here *saratu*=" priestship " (cp. MD. 781, 785), and *imdu*=" seat " (MD. 55).

The agreement shown in the Table between the Indian and Babylonian tradition is strikingly conclusive, and affords another instance of the historicity of the Indian records as a source of Sumerian history. The prince's name, it is noteworthy, is spelt variously as *Gina* and *Gin*, and there is no *Shar* or *Sharru* prefix whatsoever, thus proving again that his proper name is *Gina* or *Gin*, and *not* " Shargina " or " Shargin." *Thus, moreover, is shown the equivalency of the " Sagara "* title with his proper name of *Gina* or *Gin*.

The priest's name also equates substantially in both Babylonian and in the Indian records, being *Urura* in the former and *Aurva* or *Ūrva* in the latter. His title of " shepherd " also, it will be noticed, agrees with that same title applied to him in the Babylonian autobiography of " Sargon " already cited, wherein as Fire-priest he is styled " Anakki " or " Akki, The Man of Fire."

As this priest-tutor plays such an important part in the history of " Sargon," and nothing is yet known of him in the Babylonian, it is necessary to give here some further information regarding him and his teaching from the Indian records.

Aurva or Ūrva, Fire-priest & Sun-worshipper, the Tutor of " Sargon," is Urura, " The Man of Fire," of the Babylonian Records

Aurva or Ūrva, disclosed by the Babylonian and Indian records to have been the tutor of " Sargon "-the-Great, like Aristotle as tutor and mentor of Alexander-the-Great, in regard to the achievements of the latter, doubtless contributed in no small degree by his teaching to the greatness, glory and vast world-wide successes achieved by his pupil " Sargon." He looms large in the Indian Epics as one of the foremost ancient Aryan sages and teachers ; and bears therein the title of " the master of them that know." And his pupils and descendants figure in the Vedas as the authors of some of the psalms of the Ancient Aryans. He was a Sun-worshipper, his Fire ritual being merely a symbol of his scientific Sun-cult. He is stated to have been of royal descent, a scion of the Panch or " Phœnician " king Cyavana (No. 21 in the main-line list), who reigned sixteen generations before Sargon's epoch.

ARYAN COMMANDMENTS & ETHICS TRADITIONALLY IMPARTED TO PRINCE "SAGARA" (OR "SARGON") BY THE ARYAN SAGE AURVA.

The traditional instruction in Duty and Ethics imparted by the Aryan sage Aurva to the young Prince Sagara ("Sargon") was considered to be so important as an ethical and religious code that it fills some eleven chapters of the Indian Epics. As it presumably embodies a good deal of the actual teaching of this Aryan sage, though doubtless expanded by later priests, I give here a few extracts to show how thoroughly Aryan and "modern" are the ethics which it teaches, notwithstanding that his epoch was about forty-six centuries ago. His ethical teaching, it will be noticed, is based on his scientific Sun-religion, in which the Lord of the Universe is specially identified with that great luminary, the Light of the World, which is still recognized as the ultimate source of all mundane life. And its Lord is made a beneficent glorious Father-God and the source of the Aryan ethical code, one-and-a-half millenniums or more before Moses.

Thus we are told that Prince Sagara ("Sargon") was taught by the Sun-priest Aurva the following code of Duty,[1] which is seen to agree substantially with the Early Sumerian and Hittite codes and the Ten Commandments of Thor in the Gothic Eddas, and to comprise the whole of the ethical portions of the "Commandments" which were latterly borrowed by the Hebrews in their Mosaic code (which substituted for the Aryan Sun-God the Semitic jealous God and added the sacred Semitic day, the Sabbath or Saturday) :—

"The Sun-Lord [2] is most pleased with him who does good to others: who never utters calumny or untruth; who never covets another's wife, or another's wealth; who bears ill-will to none; who neither beats nor slays any living thing; who is ever diligent in the service of God; who is ever desirous of the welfare of all creatures, of his children

[1] WVP. 3, 85.

[2] *Keshava* or "The handsome-haired," a poetic title of the Sun-god in allusion to the halo of rays. The divine horse of Indra's car is also called "The hairy."

and of his own soul; whose heart derives no pleasure from the passions of lust and hatred. The man who conforms to these duties is he who best worships the Sun-Lord."

On the duties of a ruler or king imparted to the prince, it is noteworthy that the ruler is called by the name of *Kshatra, i.e. Khattiyo* in the older Indian vernacular and derived as we have seen from the Sumerian *Khat* or *Khad* "rule" and *Khatti* "rulers," and embodied in Udu's title of *Khatti-sig* or "Governor of the Khatti." The prominence given by this Sun-priest on the duty of kings to bestow alms on priests is significant, as the Sun-Church was the established religion of the State amongst the Early Aryans. And this injunction explains the lavishness with which the Sumerian kings, including "Sargon," endowed the Sun-temples and their priests. The advice to kings is:

"The ruler should cheerfully give presents to the priests, perform the sacrifices and study the scriptures. His especial sources of maintenance are arms, and the protection of the earth. The guardianship of the earth is his especial province. By intimidating the bad and cherishing the good, the monarch maintains discipline and secures whatever region he desires."[1]

Significantly, this instruction in Sun-worship now explains "Sargon's" devotion to the Sun; and the fact that he claims as his personal lord or "god" "The Lord Sagg or Sagaga or Sakh, *i.e.* the deified first Aryan king, otherwise entitled Ikshwāku, from whom he traced his lineal descent, as cited in the record in the heading of this chapter. In his inscriptions "Sargon" repeatedly invokes the Sun-god along with Sagg, and no others;[2] and similarly does his son Manis-Tusu, who dedicated a fine votive stone-mace to the queen of the Sun-god at the Sun-temple of Sippara.[2]

On the art of War, we are told that the instruction given to the prince by this Fire-priest included the use of "The Fiery Weapon," a kind of invincible firearm by which

[1] WVP. 3, 87 f.

[2] Cp. PHT. iv. 176, 182, 183, 184, 185, 188, 191; and see p. 215 of present work. In one only of these numerous inscriptions does Sargon invoke also the wife of Lord Sagg or Sakh. *Ib.* 178.

Sagara is reputed to have vanquished his enemies and recovered his patrimonial kingdom. It was possibly a kind of " Greek fire," and fire-missiles are referred to in the Gothic Eddas. The use of a fire-weapon by " Sargon " seems to be actually referred to in one of the cuneiform tablets on his war with the usurper Zaggisi, see below.

" Sargon's " Recovery of his Patrimonial Kingdom in Indian Chronicles Confirmed by contemporary & other Sumerian & Babylonian Records

Striking confirmation of the authenticity of the Indian Chronicle account of " Sargon's " recovery of his patrimonial kingdom, as well as of his father's name, birth and upbringing, is found in Sumerian and Babylonian records.

Sargon's Ultimatum to the Usurper King Zaggisi & disclosing his Father's Name in Agreement with Indian Lists

In a Sumerian historical text found at Erech or Uruk, the capital of the usurper King Zaggisi, the modern Warka, and published by Prof. Scheil,[1] is a graphic and realistic account of how the young prince " Sargon," before attacking the usurper Zaggisi, sent a messenger to the latter, presumably to effect a settlement without resource to arms, and it narrates the indignities to which his messenger was subjected.

The opening and concluding part of the text are wanting and some lines are defaced ; but it appears that at the time that this messenger was despatched, " Sargon " had regained possession of his father's capital of Kish city and its temple, had secured the favour of its patron deity Sagg, had made a canal and reservoir and had made ready his army. In this latter connection it is especially noticeable that " his oven " is referred to, which seems related to the invincible " Fiery Weapon " of the Indian records.

The following translation of this important historical text is made from the French translation by Prof. Scheil, with a revision of some of the personal names from the cuneiform text. The text opened apparently with a detailed account of

[1] RA. xiii. 177 f.

the preparations for battle which Sargon had made at Kish, the remaining portion continues thus :—

" His port . . . .
His oven . . . .
His canal, the waters of joy . . . .
His fields, altogether cultivated by servants . . . .
In the temple at Kish, like a city of hurricane, the revenue [rushed in].[1]
Regarding its king, who the weapon-emblem of the Lord Sagaga,
In the temple at Kish, like the face of the Sun had (?) set up,
For changing the cycle of sovereignty, from prolonging the ruin of his palace.
God Sakh, by his august orders firmly decided.
At his post was Sharrūm-KĪN ;[2] his city was the city of . .
His father was BARGIN-IBUZ-UM ;[3] his mother . . . .
Sharrūm-KĪN (? grew up) amidst the cattle . . . .
When he was deposited in the world . . . .

He (was sent ?) a wife of King ZAGGISI,
In concubinage he reduced her.
To King Zaggisi (he despatched) a messenger,
Towards the sublime house, Eanna,[4] (he directed) his steps
King Zaggisi, his heart not wishing to listen, to the messenger made no reply.
Till he would reply the messenger remained before the prince :
Meanwhile that he pushed his plaints, he rested in the dust.
King Zaggisi (at length) replied to the messenger :

[1] This within brackets is my suggested restoration.

[2] The prefix here of *Sharru-um* we have seen means " king " and " master."

[3] This critical name was read by Prof. Scheil, without any key to the form of the name, as *La-i-pu-um* (*loc. cit.*, 177). But by our Indian keys it is seen to read *Bar-du-i-buz-um* or *Par-du-i-buz-um*, corresponding to Indian *B'aradvaja* and to the *Buru-u-buz* of his own Indus Valley seal. The first sign is certainly not *La*, as the initial horizontal wedge is crossed by a vertical wedge, making the usual sign *Bar* or *Par* sign (Br. 1722) ; and this is followed by the *du* sign (Br. 9577, B. 417, pl. 108, Gudea period ; and on *Buz*, Br. 7503).

[4] *Eanna* or " Temple of Goddess Aana " is the chief temple at Erech.

O messenger! King KĪN [1] has never bent the neck!
King KĪN (refuses) to submit to King (Zaggisi) . . . . .
King KĪN (said) to King Zaggisi:
Why . . . ."

[Here fragment ends.]

This recovery of *his father's name* in this Babylonian document is of immense historical importance, as it is in agreement with the Indian Chronicle form of his father's name as *B'aradwaja*, and with the form *Buru-u-buz* used by himself in his Indus seal, and in general agreement with the form of that name in the two Old Sumerian King-Lists in the Isin Chronicle (see Table, p. 140). It moreover *confirms the identity of the Indian form of his name as* SHA-KUNI *or* KUNI *with Sharru*-KĪN *or " Sargon."* This equation in his father's name is thus seen :—

Erech Tablet.		Old Sumerian Lists.		Indus Seal.		Indian Lists.
BARDUIBUZ-*um*	=	BARAGIN-*mu*	=	BURUUBUZ	=	B'ARADWAJA.
PARDUIBUZ-*um*		BARAGIN		BARGIN		PRACIN-wat.
		PURUGIN		PURUGIN		

The " weapon-emblem of Lord Sagg (or Sagaga) " is significant, as in one of Sargon's inscriptions, celebrating his victory over Erech or Uruk, he claims to have vanquished his enemies and smote that city " by the battle-mace of Sagaga." [2]

The accounts of " Sargon's " conquests in his own inscriptions or in the certified early copies of them at Nippur Sun-temple are also in general agreement with the conquests of King Sagara in the Indian Epics.

SARGON'S CONQUEST OF ZAGGISI OF ERECH & RECOVERY OF HIS FATHER'S EMPIRE & WORLD-CONQUESTS

Sargon's own accounts of his victory over the usurper King Zaggisi—who we have seen was the chief of the Haihaya tribe of the Indian version—are contained in early certified copies of the collected originals which he set up at the great Sun-temple at Nippur. · And significantly *these*

[1] This reads *Sharra*-KĪN, wherein *Sharru*, as we have seen, is Semitic for " King."

[2] PHT. iv. 180.

inscriptions of Sargon are in the Sumerian language, although it is universally asserted by Assyriologists, to suit their theory that Sargon was a Semite, that he never wrote in Sumerian but in the Semitic or so-called Akkadian language, a statement also unsupported by the few original inscriptions of his own which exist. For the information of his Semitic subjects most of these inscriptions in question exist in bilingual Sumerian and Akkadian or Semitic versions.

Sargon's own account of his victories in his own words on the tablets unearthed at the Nippur temple reads in translation[1]:—

"King Gin, king of Agudu city . . . king of Kish, priest of the Lord of Heaven, king of the Land, the great priest-king of Lord Sakh, the City of Urug (Erech) he smote and its wall he destroyed. With the people of Uruk he battled and routed them. With King Zaggisi, king of Urug he battled and he captured him and in fetters led him through the Gate of Lord Sakh [in Nippur Sun-temple]. Eninmar he smote and its wall he destroyed, and its (entire) territory from Lagash to the sea he smote. His weapons he washed in the sea. With the man of Umma he battled and routed him and smote his city and destroyed its wall. Unto King Gin, king of the Land (or Earth) Lord Sakh gave no foe, from the Upper Sea [Mediterranean] unto the lower Sea [Persian Gulf and Indian Ocean] Lord Sakh . . . subjected the lands to him . . . King Gin, king of Agudu restored Kish (people) to their old place. Their city he gave (back) to them as a dwelling-place. Who shall destroy this inscription may the Sun-god tear out his foundations and destroy his seed."

Here it is noteworthy that Sargon whilst destroying the cities of his foes and transferring his own capital to Agudu, preserved Kish, the cherished old imperial capital of his father and his ancestors and handed it over to its old inhabitants. It is also to be noted that he invokes solely the Sun-god.

[1] *Ib.*, 173 f. I have revised the reading of the god-names according to their real values as already described, *e.g.*, *En Lil* is read "Lord *Sakh*," and so on. And *Shar-um Gin* or "Master Lord Gin" is read "King Gin."

SARGON'S CONQUEST & ANNEXATION OF PERSIA

Sargon has never been supposed hitherto to have conquered or ruled in Persia, beyond his "smiting of Elam," the small hilly province on the South-east border of Persia, to the east of Lower Mesopotamia (see map). But I find that the country called *Barahsi* or *Parahsi*, repeatedly referred to in Sargon's inscriptions as being conquered and reconquered by him as well as by his descendants, is really all unsuspectedly the country of Persia and the source of the latter name.

"Barahsi" or "Parahsi" is supposed by Assyriologists, with their usual minimizing of Sargon's empire, to have been an insignificant district which they thrust within the borders of Mesopotamia to the *west* of Susa, the capital of the Elam province.[1] But as has been remarked, Barahsi or Parashi is usually mentioned in the Sargonic and other inscriptions along with Elam, which, lies to the *east* of Mesopotamia; and it is enumerated after Elam, which indicates that it lay beyond and to the east of Elam. And at times the king of Barahsi was the leading political power in Elam;[2] and Sargon's son Uru-Mush states in an inscription that he "tore out the foundations of Barahsi from the nations of Elam"[3] shows their interrelationship and locations to the *east* of Mesopotamia.

Barahsi or Parahsi now transpires to be the original of the ancient Persis province of the Greeks, with its old capital at Anshan or Persepolis, the central province of Persia to the east of Elam (see map) and the source of our modern names of "Persia" and "Parsī." And it is another instance of the remarkable persistence of old territorial names.

This identity is strikingly confirmed by our Indian Chronicles. These state that King Sagara destroyed not only "nearly the whole of the Haihayas," *i.e.* the tribe of Zaggisi, but also "the Pāradas and *Pahlavas*" (see p. 203). Now *Pahlav* was the ancient Iranic or Persian name for this central portion of Persia. It included Ispahān, Raī, Hamadān, Nikāvand and Adarbaijān, and is supposed also to have comprised Media;[4] and that name still survives in terms

[1] *Camb. Anc. Hist.*, I, 408.
[2] Cp. PHT. iv. 236.
[3] *Ib.*, 233.
[4] M. Haug, ed. West, *Parsī Religion*, 79.

Pahlavi or Pehlvi applied to the Aryan dialect of the Zoroastrian Persians. And *Pārada* now appears to be a dialectic form of *Parthia*, the great eastern province of Persia south-east of the Caspian and Teheran.

Sargon's inscription of his conquest of Barahsi or Parahsi records [1] :—

"King Gin,[2] king of Kish, smiter of Elam and Barashi [here follows curses of the Sun-god and Sakh and also the wife of the latter, "The Lady," on those who would destroy the inscription, followed by missing lines and then an enumeration of the chief prisoners he took and the booty, the name of the king being lost] Dagu brother of the king of Barahsi [here follows the names of other high officials, including the high priest and judge of Barahsi]." And there exist fragmentary duplicates of this inscription.

Significantly, on this record were sculptured portraits of the train of captives and their tribute or spoil, just as Darius from the same Persepolitan provinces over two thousand years later imitated Sargon in sculpturing in his famous fresco at Behistun a similar scene in celebrating his own conquests.[3] So also a finely sculptured inscribed monument of Sargon's, found at Susa in Elam, pictures a battle-scene and rows of captives being brought before the king and his suite—the king's name being inscribed "King Kin." On the reverse, vultures are figured feeding on the slain, and the king (or a god) clubbing the enemies enmeshed in his net, somewhat as in Bidashnadi's well known Victory "stele of the Vultures" in Uruash's Dynasty.

SARGON'S CONQUEST (OR RECONQUEST) OF THE INDUS VALLEY COLONY OF EDIN OR "GARDEN OF EDIN" FROM HIS OWN RECORDS, CONFIRMING MY DECIPHERMENT OF INDUS VALLEY SEALS

Similarly, until I published the discovery of Sargon's official seals in my decipherments of the Indus Valley seals,[4] no one had ever suspected that "Sargon" had reached India or held the rich Indus Valley within his empire—

[1] PHT. iv. 185 f.
[2] *Sharru*-GIN in text, which is a Semitic copy.
[3] See L. King, *Inscripts. of Darius at Behistun.*
[4] WISD. 64-68.

that great Elysium province of Edin of the Sumerian empire, which we have found King Madgal added to the sea-empire of his father, King Uruash, the Khād or "Phœnician" (see Chap. VI).

Now I give here further concrete documentary confirmation of Sargon's conquest and annexation of the Indus Valley from a copy of his own Chronicles, and alongside it place the version preserved in the Assyrio-Babylonian Omen-literature. In the latter it is referred to as a conquest, but in the Chronicle it is called the quelling of a revolt, which is in keeping with the Indian Chronicle record that it was the reconquest of part of his patrimonial empire.

Hitherto, I find that the name of the Edin colony in the Indus Valley in these Sargonic records has been disguised by all previous translators under its Semitic titles of "Subartu" and "Sirihum"; and besides this it has been so grossly misplaced as to be conjecturally located in north-western Mesopotamia![1] Though under its latter title Poebel, while not recognizing its equivalency with "Subartu," has placed it somewhat nearer the truth as lying immediately to the east of Anshan on the Oman Straits of the Persian Gulf. But we now find that it is very much farther to the east, and across the Arabian Sea, and is the Indus Valley itself.

The name in Sargon's own and other records hitherto read "Subartu"—which is merely a Semitic term—reads I find by its Sumerian signs unequivocally *Su*-EDIN or "The Good EDIN Land."[2] While its title, as used by Sargon's sons and descendants and other later Sumerian kings, and hitherto read conjecturally "*Shiri-hum*," reads directly by its Sumerian signs *Shu*-EDIN-*hum*, or "The Garden of EDIN, the fruitful."[3]

Now I have already proved conclusively that the regular name for the great Sumerian colony and city-state on the Indus, with its capital at Mohenjo Daro, which King Madgal established, and from which, as I have shown from his

[1] *Camb. Anc. Hist.*, I., 452 f.

[2] KC. 2, 36. And cp. Br. 198, 162, 4521; MD. 746.

[3] On *Shirihum*, see PHT. iv. 205. On *Shu*=garden, Br. 10509, 10539; and on *Edin* as in previous note.

victory seals, he derived his title of Lord of Edin or Etin,[1] was *Edin* or *Etin.*[2]

"Sargon's" own record of his conquest of Edin as preserved in his Chronicles in their Babylonian copy and in the Omen-literature extract which I place alongside for comparison, states :—

"*Sargon's*" *Chronicle.* (KC. 2, 7.)	*In Omens.* (KC. 2, 36-37.) (5½ revised reading.)
"Afterwards he (King *Gin*)[3] the land of The Good EDIN City attacked. They submitted to his arms. And King *Gin* settled that revolt, and defeated them. He achieved their overthrow and their wide spreading host he destroyed. And he brought their possessions into Agadu."	"King *Ginna*[3] . . . the land of The Good EDIN City in its might he attacked. They submitted to his arms. And King *Ginna* settled their habitations and he smote them grievously and defeated them and their great army . . . his . . . and his mighty host he brought into Agudu."

This fresh and independent documentary confirmation of my decipherment of Sargon's seals amongst those recently unearthed in the Indus Valley is of immense historical importance. Similarly so is this evidence for the name of that city-state as *Edin* or *Etin*, in confirming those readings. It also confirms my identifications of the "*Saki* Land" mentioned in those seals and elsewhere in Sumerian literature with the "*Shaka* Land" (or "Land of the Scyths or Sacæ") title for the Indus Valley in the Indian Chronicles,[4] which was conquered by King Sagara with punishment of its people, by altering the style of wearing their hair, in his reconquest of that portion of his patrimonial empire. Now a mass of contemporary inscriptional proof of Sargon's rule in the Indus Valley is forthcoming from my discovery of no less than six official seals of Sargon in the second batch of seals from that colony, as detailed on page 226 and following pages.

We now come to the records of Sargon's other world-wide conquests.

[1] WISP. 35 f., and see Fig. 19, p. 109.
[2] *Ib.*, 7, with map, 29 f., 75 f., 81 f., 96 f.; and WSAD. 69.
[3] Note here the sign is for "king," and not spelt *shar-ru*.
[4] WSAD. 34, 53, 63 f., 103 f., 108.

Sargon's Conquests in the Western Old World to the Tin-mines (? of Britain) beyond the Western Sea or Mediterranean

We have seen that "Sargon" in his inscriptions at Nippur claims that: "Unto King Gin, king of the Land (or Earth), Lord Sakh gave no foe from the Upper Sea [Mediterranean] unto the Lower Sea [Persian Gulf and Indian Ocean], Lord Sakh . . . subjected the lands to him." And the Omen version of his Chronicles states: "King Gin who marched against the Land of the West, and conquered the Land of the West, his hand subdued the Four Quarters of the World."[1]

Further details of his conquests in the West are given in others of his inscriptions, and in his Chronicles in their Babylonian copy and in the Assyrio-Babylonian extracts in the Omen-literature. Thus the Chronicles state the particular year in which he achieved these conquests, in almost literal agreement with the Omen version, and make the complete conquest to have occurred in the eleventh year of his reign, while the Omens place it in his third year. This is supposed to imply that his first expedition was in his third year and the full conquest in his eleventh.

This Chronicle copy reads:[2] "King *Gin*, king of Agudu City, through the Weapon[3] of Lord Sakhar Tar[4] (or ? Lady Ish-Tar) was exalted. And he possessed no foe or rival. His glory over the world he poured out. The Sea in the East [? West][5] he crossed. And in the eleventh year the Land of the West (or Sunset) in full his hand subdued. He united them under one rule. He set up his images in the West. Their booty he brought over as arranged."

The name of the deity with the invincible "Weapon," to whom "Sargon" piously ascribes his victories, is of much religious historical significance. That name is written in his

[1] KC. 2, 27.

[2] Text in KC. 2, 3 f. The reading is as revised by me.

[3] *Bal*, Br. 278-9.

[4] Br. 5081. *Sakhar Tar* is, I think, the correct reading, in which *Sakhar* corresponds to the Eddic title *Skiri* (or "The Scourer") of Thor as "The Baptizer"—baptism being the initiatory ritual in the Sun-cult of Thor, see WPOB. 273 and my new translation of The Eddas.

[5] The Omen version says "The Sea of the West he crossed." KC. 2, 31.

own monuments as Zagg or Zagaga or Sakh; but in these late Babylonian copies of his Chronicle it is written by signs which read variously *Sakhar-Tar*[1] or "Ish-tar"—the same name and by the same signs which designate his patron deity in his autobiography as we have seen. Hitherto that name has been translated as "The Mother-goddess Ishtar," and it was doubtless so read by the late Babylonian scribes who made this copy, as by that time this goddess had become a favourite object of worship by the late Babylonians and Chaldees and in one of her modes she was an armed goddess of war.

But the name "Ishtar" for this goddess is of late origin. It does not appear until many centuries after Sargon's period; and on the other hand Sargon in his own inscriptions ascribes his successes to Lord Sakh or Sagg or Sagaga and to the "weapon" of the latter as we have seen.[2] And his only mention of a goddess occurs in his invocation of Ninni or "The Lady," that is the wife of Lord Sakh, whom he once invokes in his curse along with her husband. Besides this, there is no reference to goddess-worship in the religious instruction traditionally imparted to him by his tutor the Sun-priest Aurva. It thus seems probable, I think, that in the original text the name was *Sakh-Dar*, *i.e.*, the deified first King *Sakh* or *Dar* or Tar (*i.e.*, Thor), to whom with his weapon Sargon so repeatedly ascribes his victories.

The name for this weapon and its pictorial sign are of significance. Its sign pictures what is regarded as a thunderbolt with an arrow-head;[3] and it appears to be the same weapon which is carried by the Sumerian Hercules, the top of which is sometimes figured as a Cross.[4] It also seems to be the same emblem, somewhat resembling the crescentic Turkish spear-standard, which is found on some of the old Sumerian temples at Ur.

[1] See note 3, p. 220.

[2] In addition to the references given on this weapon of Sagg, in one of the Nippur copies of his inscriptions, he says: "Uruk (Erech) and fifty governors he vanquished with the battle-mace of Sagaga" PHT. iv. 180.

[3] B. 2, p. 6. It has the name *Bal*, and is defined as "spindle" or "axe." Br. 278-9.

[4] See figs. in WISD. 136.

Resuming the conquests of Sargon in the West, some particulars are given regarding the Mediterranean basin, in one of his edicts on the boundaries of his empire.[1] This refers amongst other things to his "conquest of the land of the Muru (Amorites)" and mentions his suzerainty over "*the Tin-land country which lies beyond the Upper* Sea [Mediterranean]." This obviously refers to Sargon's sovereignty over the tin-mines of Cornwall,[2] and I have adduced evidence for the introduction of the Bronze Age into Britain by Amorites before his epoch or about 2800 B.C. And it mentions that "*the produce of the mines* is taken, and the produce of the fields to King Gin has been brought." And Egypt or *Mishir* is mentioned as being within his frontiers. Sargon's conquest of Egypt as now discovered is detailed in the next chapter.

Sargon's Conquest of Asia Minor, and Syria-Phœnicia, including Hittite & Amorite Land & Ionia

Sargon's conquests of the "Upper" or "Western" Land of Syria-Phœnicia, which barred his way from Mesopotamia to the Western Sea or Mediterranean, are referred to in some detail in his inscriptions. One of these, recounting presumably one expedition, states :—

"And he (Lord Sakh) gave unto him (King Gin) the Upper Land, Mari City, Iarmuti City and Dara (?)-la (or Ib- or Ibbi- la), as far as the Cedar Forest and the Silver Mountains. Unto the master-king Gin, the king, the Lord Sakh did not give an adversary." [3]

Most of these places can be identified on the maps with more or less certainty.

Mari City is usually supposed to be a city-state on the Upper Euphrates, "perhaps in the vicinity of Karkemis (Carchemish)," [4] that is in the so-called Amorite Land of North Syria. It was already a powerful city-state which was attacked by the son of King Madgal, "Pasenadi," twenty generations before Sargon's epoch. It was probably, I think, the great and formidable Hittite city-state of Marash, about eighty miles north-west of Carchemish, on

[1] Text in KTA. 1920. No. 92.
[2] See WPOB. 413 f.
[3] PHT. iv. 177 f.
[4] *Ib.*, 223

the northern flank of the Amanus range on the border of Eastern Cilicia[1]—the later Hittites often adding an *sh* to their city names.

This seems confirmed by the statement that these places were " as far as the Cedar Forest and the Silver Mountains. This Cedar Forest has been identified through the directions and descriptions of King Gudia with the Amanus range of the Eastern Taurus, which stretches from Marash down to near Antioch on the Orontes. And the Silver Mountains are identified with the Eastern Taurus mountains to the north, which are rich in silver-mines which were worked in antiquity.[2]

Iarmuti City is known also from the official Amarna letters of the Egyptian archives of Pharaoh Akenaten, the predecessor of Tutankhamen, of about 1400 B.C. It is therein called " *Iarimuta* Land " by the governor of the seaport of Gubla (or Byblos) in North Phœnicia and described by him as being in communication by sea with that port, and so rich in grain that it could supply the Phœnician cities. It has accordingly been located to the north of Phœnicia, " somewhere along the Syrian or possibly the Cilician coast." [3] It was, I venture to suggest, the famous, rich North Phœnician seaport city and fertile city-state of *Arwad* (" Arad ") opposite Cyprus, which was called by the later Hittites *Iaruwattash* in their cuneiform tablets,[4] the letters *t* and *d* being freely interchangeable, and also *w* and *m* in Sumerian and Hittite.

The third city-state or country named reads variously Dara-(?) la, Urash-la or Ib-la. It is supposed to stand further off towards the north or west in the Taurus range, being mentioned last. It is described by King Gudia as a mountainous district in the north, with a city called Uruursu, whence he procured rare mountain woods. And it is associated by Sargon's grandson Naram-Ba with an adjoining country called Armanum (? Armenia).

This proves that Sargon had conquered the states throughout the great mountainous barrier standing between Mesopotamia and the Mediterranean north of the Syrian desert,

[1] See WPOB. 39, 172, with map. [2] PHT. iv. 226.
[3] *Ib.*, 225. [4] *Index of Hittite Names*, Mayer & Garstang, 24.

SHET-LAND
KATA-NESS
(Caith-ness)
CATUV
Qass
Neyton
Aberdeen
Ballymote
SCOTIA
SCOT-LAND
BRITAIN
Aran
Scene
Bantry B.
St. George's Ch.
CATTI
Cassi
CATTI-euchlani
Kassi-terides
Penz-ance
KENTS
Velo-Casse
Bato Casse
Vidu-Casse
Vannes
Veneti
Morbihan
BRITTANY
Paris
Pictavia
Vendee
KELTICA OR GAUL
Vienne
CED-EYRA
Vanesia
CATALONIA
IBERIA
GADES or AGADIR
Frith of the GADIS or GOTHS
CEUTA
MAURITANIA
Muluya R.
Rusicada
UTICA
KOTH-ON
Port of Carthage
AGADIR
(or GUTTA?)
GÆT-ULI
LIBYA
Philænon Aræ
KYR-ENE
Casæ
Gozo
Sea of the KHATS
Cossyra
Syracuse
CATINA
Tyrrh-ene
Cossa
Latium
GÆTA
BRUTII
Venice
VINDELICIA
Vienna
Danube
VANII REG.
Vandalici Mts.
CHATTI
CATTI
CAT-LAUNI
GOTHA
Rhine
Elbe R.
Oder R.
Sleswick
Texel
JUT-LAND
GAUTAR
CATTI
NORWAY
GOTHS
SWEDEN
SIT-ONES
GOTH-LAND
GOTH-ones
VENEDI
PARTHINI
KYTH-ERA
20
10
0
10
20
Meridian of 0 Greenwich

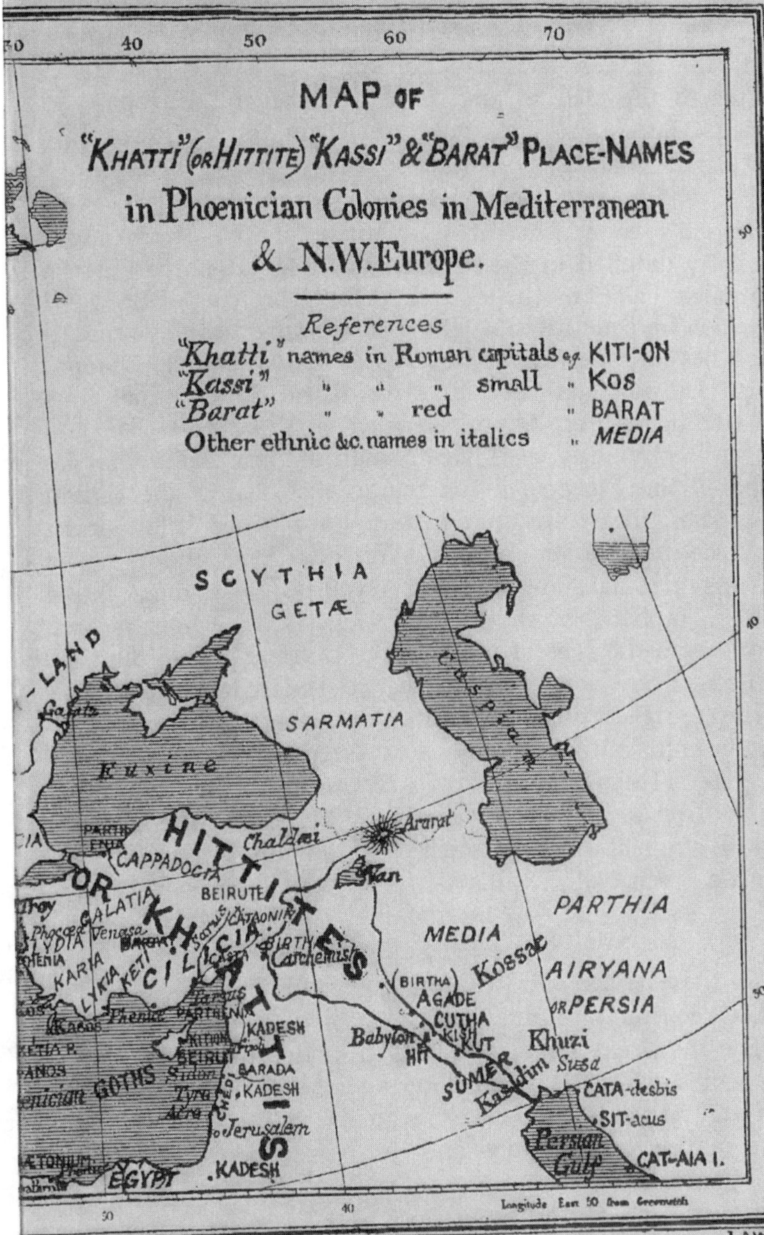
MAP OF
"KHATTI" (OR HITTITE) "KASSI" & "BARAT" PLACE-NAMES
in Phoenician Colonies in Mediterranean
& N.W. Europe.
References
"Khatti" names in Roman capitals e.g. KITI-ON
"Kassi" " " " small " Kos
"Barat" " " red " BARAT
Other ethnic &c. names in italics " MEDIA
SCYTHIA
GETÆ
SARMATIA
Euxine
HITTITES
OR KHATTI
CAPPADOCIA
Chaldæi
Ararat
Van
BEIRUTE
CATAONIA
GALATIA
Troy
Phocæa
Venasa
LYDIA
KARIA
LYKIA
KETI
CILICIA
Tarsus
PARTHENIA
Carchemish
Phenice
Kasos
KADESH
KITION
BEIRUT
Sidon
Tyre
Acre
BARADA
KADESH
Jerusalem
KADESH
GOTHS
EGYPT
MEDIA
Kossæ
PARTHIA
AIRYANA
OR PERSIA
BIRTHA
AGADE
CUTHA
KISH
KUT
Babylon
HIT
Khuzi
Susa
SUMER
Kasdim
CATA-desbis
SIT-acus
Persian Gulf
CAT-AIA I.
30
40
50
60
70
Longitude East 50 from Greenwich
L.A.Vidal.

including the Amanus and adjoining northern districts of the Taurus up to Cappadocia and Cilicia of Asia Minor; and thus gained complete control of the Amorite trade-routes to the Mediterranean, Asia Minor and Europe, and added to his empire Syria and Phœnicia on the Mediterranean.

Sargon's Conquest of Ionia

Sargon's conquests in Asia Minor of the Hittites are specially detailed in the account of his great north-western campaign, called by the later Hittites "The King of Battle"[1] in which he penetrated with his conquering army the mountains beyond the Cilician Taurus as far as Bursha-khanda, which has not yet been exactly identified but which was situated in southern Cappadocia.

It was obviously in this campaign in Asia Minor that he defeated the *Yavans*, or Ionians, as recorded in the Indian Chronicles, thus presuming that he reached the Ionian province and archipelago of Western Asia Minor. The Yavans or Ionians are the same Aryan people as the "*Javan* sons of Japhet" of the Hebrew Genesis, by whom we are told "were the isles of the Gentiles divided"—*i.e.* the isles in the Mediterranean, and especially in the Ionian archipelago.

The great fortified city of *Durash* specially cited by Sargon in his autobiography as captured by him, was, I have suggested, Tarsus, the famous Amorite and Phœnician city-port of Cilicia, and the "Tarshish of Ships" of the Old and New Testaments[2]—"Tarshish" being made by the Hebrew scribe a "son" of Javan.

Sargon's "World Monarchy"

All these world-wide conquests, in the regaining of his father's lost empire and in its extension, were achieved by Sargon-the-Great as a young man under or about thirty years of age, and thus recalling again the parallel between him and Alexander-the-Great, whose vast eastern conquests were in the same regions and also extended to the Indus Valley.

[1] Amarna tablets, translated by E. F. Weidner, *Boghaz Koi Studien*, 1922, 6 Heft, 57 f.; and a later English translation by Albright.

[2] WPOB. 41, 58 f., 68, 346, 395.

The severity of Sargon's revenge on his foes is more than paralleled by that of the later "world-emperors" Alexander and Cæsar, not to mention Napoleon Bonaparte, who wiped out whole cities, with their inhabitants, men, women and children, when it suited their policy, without any expression of horror at their cruelty. The complacent, unsqueamish butcheries committed by Cæsar are commented on by Trollope.

Thus all the foregoing records of world-conquest by "Sargon" or King Gina in his own records, contemporary or in Babylonian and Hittite copies, confirm fully the accounts of his conquests as the Emperor Sagara or Sha-Kuni in the Indian Chronicles. This again strikingly attests the remarkable authenticity and historicity of the Indian Chronicle as an independent source of Sumerian history; and it also confirms the identity of the Sumerians with the Early Aryans. And it is now seen to have been through the "world-monarchy" of Sargon and his Aryan predecessors that the Aryan or Sumerian civilization and laws were mainly spread over the world, and thus accounting for the essential unity in the civilizations of the Ancient World.

Sargon's Imperial Court

The pomp and magnificence of "Sargon's" court is referred to in some of his inscriptions and in his chronicles. Thus we learn:—

"The sons of his palace for five stages [1] around he settled. And over the hosts of the world he reigned supreme." . . . [2] And the man of . . . , and the man of . . . stand (in attendance (before the Master-king Gin, king of the Land (Earth). . . . 5400 men eat daily food before him." [3]

Sargon's Additional Signet-Seals Discovered in Indus Valley & their Decipherment

Striking positive evidence for Sargon's rule in the old Sumerian colony of Edin in the Indus Valley was demonstrated in my *Indo-Sumerian Seals Deciphered* in 1925, where I found and deciphered two seals of that great Sumerian emperor amongst the first batch of seals unearthed there.

[1] *Kasbu.* [2] KC. 2, 5. [3] KC. 2, 175, 178.

One of these was his own official signet, presumably entrusted to his governor or viceroy there for sealing local state documents; and in it he bears the title of "*Sagara* of Agdu,"[1] in which his title is in literal agreement with his imperial solar title in the Indian records. The other seal read "Tax, the minister of the Great *Gana* (*Sa-Gana*) the *Gut* of Agdu."[2]

Now, in the second batch of seals unearthed at the same site, namely, at the capital of the old Edin colony at Mohenjo Daro, I find no fewer than six additional seals of Sargon (see Plate X) including amongst them the most exquisite of all the seals hitherto known of the Sumerian period, and picturing as its chief device the Indian humped Bull, which is a masterpiece of high naturalistic art and technical graver's skill that could not be surpassed at the present day; and eminently it is worthy of the greatest of all the old emperors of the World, see Plate X, Nos. 1 and 2 for the photographs of this seal and of its impression.

In these new seals it will be seen that "Sargon" calls himself respectively, *Sag, Sharu Gin, Shar Gin, Sharum Gin, Gin Bur* and *Gan Bur-Piru*. In three of them he adds the title of *Gut* (or "Goth"), and in one he calls himself "The Great *Khāti*" (or *Khatti* or "Hitt-ite").

The spelling of the same name occasionally by different pictographic signs of the same or nearly similar values in the case of Sargon's and of other Sumerian personal names is noteworthy. The reason seems to have been to introduce other meanings, heroic or poetic, into the names, analogous to the Chinese practice by poets of spelling emperors' names by hieroglyphs different from those usually employed for spelling the name so as to yield poetic or complimentary meanings. Thus Sargon's *Gin* name by its sign here has the meaning of "The Ruler," and his title *Sharu* by this sign here written means "The Universal One," instead of "King."

As the fully detailed decipherment of these new Indus Valley seals is given in Appendix VII with duly attested proofs for the reading of each sign, it is only necessary here to record the literal reading of the inscriptions on these Indus seals of Sargon. Their inscriptions, as usual in all these Indo-Sumerian seals, as well as in the similar Early

[1] WISD. 68 f. [2] *Ib.* 63 f.

PLATE X.

INDUS VALLEY SEALS OF SARGON AND HIS FATHER AS "PHARAOHS," c. 2760-2720 B.C.

(Photographs after Sir J. Marshall.) For decipherments and translations, see pp. 189 f., 225 f., 551 f.

MAP IV

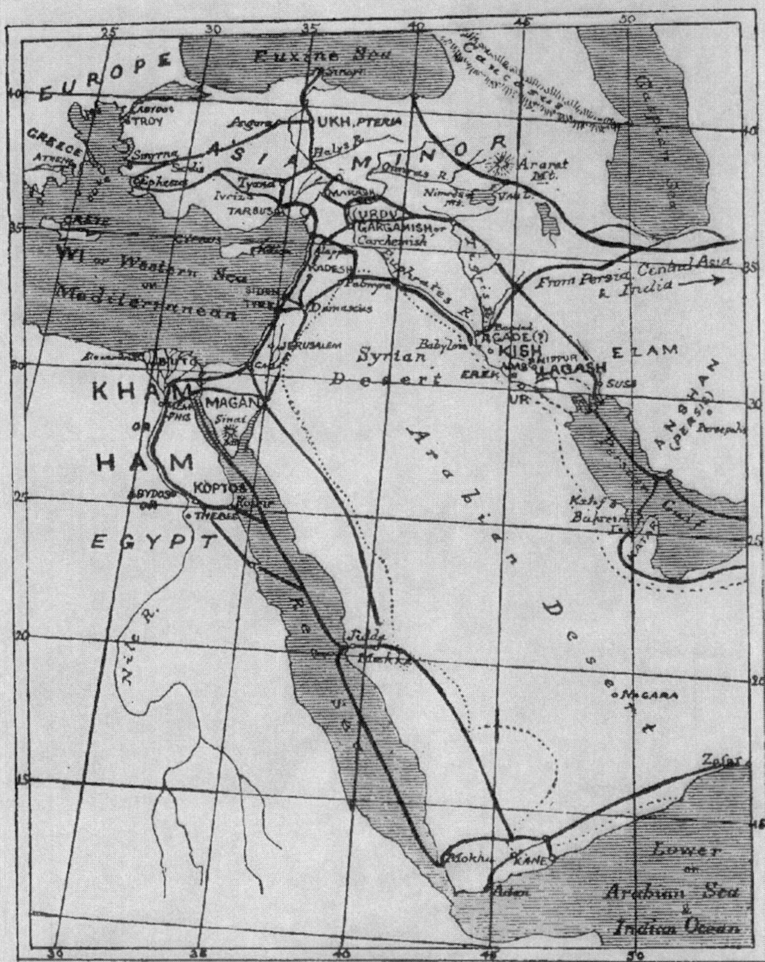

OLD LAND TRADE ROUTES FROM RED SEA, ARABIA, MESOPOTAMIA, INDIA, ASIA MINOR AND SYRIA TO EGYPT

Sumerian seals from Mesopotamia, are graven so as to give the writing in their sealings or seal-impressions in *the reverse or retrograde direction* from left to right. In the following literal translations, the writing is given in the usual Sumerian or Aryan direction for reading from right to left. For convenience of reference I cite these seals in the order in which they are numbered in Plate X.

His beautiful Bull signet (Plate X, Nos. 1 and 2, for seal and its impression) admirably portrays as its central figure the sacred Indian Bull, the Brahmin Bull of modern India, adorned with a wreath or garland as in Indo-Aryan festivals at the present day. But this Bull is here used as the pictograph of his title *Gut*, and the prominence given to it indicates the importance which the king attached to that title. The inscription reads :—

" SAG, The Seer, The lofty *Kad*, the tablet (seal) of the One Lord, The GUT (Goth)."

This title *Sag* is spelt by the identical sign which Sargon uses on his seal previously deciphered by me,[1] in which its fuller form of *Sagara* is given, that is in literal agreement with his solar title as preserved in the Indian chronicles, as we have seen. His title of " Seer " or " Diviner " is in keeping with the foregoing records of his initiation into the priesthood as a priest-king. *Kad* is a Phœnician title which we shall see is used repeatedly by members of his dynasty ; and the prominence given to his *Gut* title here is noteworthy and significant, and in No. 6 he calls himself *Khati*, *i.e.*, " Hittite."

Of his other seals, No. 5 inscription reads :—

" SHARU-GIN of *Uri* (or *Akkadu*) Land."

No. 6 reads :—

" SHAR-GIN, The Great *Khāti* of . . . Land."

No. 7. reads :—

" SHAR-UM-GIN, The *Gut* of *Agdu* Land."

Here the Sumerian form with the syllable *um* is significant as it is in agreement with the early Mesopotamian tablets as we have seen.

[1] *Ib.* 69 f.

No. 8 reads :—

"GAN, The Ruler of *Khamaesshi* (Land)."

On the great historical significance of the name of this land as a name for Egypt, see later on.

No. 9 reads :—

"GAN, The PARU (or PIRU or BARU or 'Pharaoh'), The Gut of Agdu Land." The title here of *Paru* or *Baru* is, we shall find, the equivalent of "Pharaoh"; whilst its variant spelling of *Piru* appears to be the Sumerian source of his Indian *Vīra* title in *Pra-Vīra*, see Table opposite p. 140, No. 37, col. 6.

Altogether, these six newly deciphered seals of Sargon from the Indus Valley colony of Edin, along with the two previously deciphered by me, now fully confirm and solidly establish by concrete contemporary inscriptional evidence as a historical fact that Sargon ruled imperially over the Indus colony, and for a long term of years, as indicated by the number of official seals there, notwithstanding that Assyriologists have never hitherto even suspected that Sargon made any conquests there or that his empire extended to that region.

SARGON'S LAST DAYS AMID REVOLTS

The mighty "Sargon's" glorious reign of fifty-five years as a world-monarch ended in his old age in revolutions and widespread disasters. And we shall find from the Indian Chronicles that his eldest son Manis-Tusu was a leader in the revolt against his father. The unhappy fate which ultimately befell "Sargon" or King Gin is referred to in the later Babylonian Chronicles and in the Omen-literature. Thus we learn :—

"Afterwards in his (King Gin's) old age all the lands revolted against his rule; and they besieged him in Agadu. And King Gin went forth to battle and defeated them: he accomplished their overthrow and their wide spreading hosts he destroyed. . . . The soil from the trenches of Kāshra [Babylon] City he removed and the boundaries of Agadu he made like those of Kāshra City. But because of the evil which he had committed the great Lord the god Marud[1] [of Babylon] was angry, and he destroyed his people by famine. From the Rising of the Sun (East) unto the Setting of the Sun (West) they opposed him and gave (him) no rest."[2]

Here now, before leaving the mighty Aryan or Sumerian emperor, "Sargon"-the-Great, who we have found was by descent an Aryan Phœnician, it is necessary to chronicle the other great discovery which I have made regarding him by our Indian keys, namely that he was all unsuspectedly the greatest of the "Predynastic" Pharaohs of Ancient Egypt, who introduced there the so-called "Egyptian" Civilization, which is now disclosed to be transplanted Sumerian or Aryan Civilization; and that his son Manis-the-Warrior or Manis-Tusu, was Menes, the founder of "The First Dynasty" of Egypt. This requires a chapter to itself.

[1] Or literally "Son of the Sun," latterly called *Mar-duk*, whom the Babylonians adopted as their chief god instead of Sakh or Induru or Bel, his deified father.

[2] KC. 2, 6 f

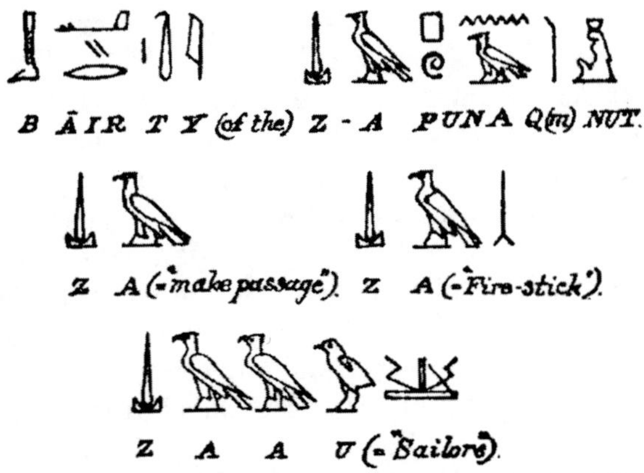

FIG. 22B.—Egyptian hieroglyphs for tutelary goddess Bairthy (or Britannia) of Phœnician sailors. For her Egyptian representation see Fig. 9, p. 22.
(*Punaq* here seems=Panag or Fankhu, the Egyptian for "Phœnician." See details in WPOB. 60 f.)

XIV

Sargon with his Father and Grandfather discovered as "Predynastic" Pharaohs of Egypt & his son Manis-Tusu as "Menes" the Founder of the First Dynasty of Egypt & at a Date no earlier than about 2704 B.C.

Disclosing the Unknown Ancestry of Menes, THE ARYAN ORIGIN OF EGYPTIAN CIVILIZATION AND HIEROGLYPHIC WRITING AND SARGON'S TOMB IN EGYPT.

> *It was within these narrow limits (from the Delta to about Luxor) that Egyptian Civilization struck root and ripened as in a closed vessel. What were the People by whom it was developed, the Country whence they came, the Race to which they belonged is to-day unknown.*—MASPERO, "Dawn of Civilization," 1922, 45.

WE now make the further revolutionary discoveries through the Indian Chronicles, confirmed by the contemporary Mesopotamian, Indus Valley and Egyptian inscriptions, that Sargon was the chief of the historical "Predynastic" kings of Egypt, and that his eldest son Manis-the-Warrior or *Manis-Tusu* is identical with Menes or "Menes-the-Warrior" or *Aha-Manj*, the traditional founder of the First Dynasty of Egypt, and whose ancestry and antecedents have hitherto been wholly unknown; and that Sargon's Father and Grandfather were Predynastic Pharaohs in Egypt before him.

The far-reaching effect of these discoveries upon all ancient history and chronology and on the origin and inter-relations of the early civilizations hitherto conjectured as Egyptian is obvious. It supplies for the first time a synchronism between Ancient Egypt and Mesopotamia, by which a relatively fixed and real date is obtained for Menes, the most widely disputed of all dates in ancient history, and yet a date on which so many theories of civilization are based. And most important of all it discloses the Aryan origin of Egyptian Civilization, as already announced in my previous works when demonstrating the Sumerian origin of the Egyptian language and hieroglyphic writing.

It is impossible in the limited scope of the present book to deal in adequate detail with this fundamental historical discovery, but the main proofs necessary for our theme are here given, all duly attested.

Sargon as a Predynastic Pharaoh with Inscriptions & Tomb at Abydos

Although "Sargon" is admitted by a leading Assyriologist to have held Egypt and to have included Egypt within his empire by its name of "Mizir"[1] and by its Semitic title of "Dilmun,"[2] none of the text-book writers on Babylonian or Egyptian History refer to the subject at all, presumably because it militates against their theory of the independent origin of Egyptian Civilization.

But we now find Sargon's own inscription, as the "oldest" of the inscriptions of Predynastic Pharaohs that have been found at the royal tombs at Abydos, and attesting that his own tomb was there along with that of his queen. And it now appears that Sargon, with his vast world-empire, had selected for his mausoleum for himself, his queen and his dynasty that relatively cool semi-temperate part of his realm in Egypt on the Mediterranean, presumably because it was a more natural resting-place for him and his Nordic race than the torrid sun-baked mud plains of Mesopotamia. And we shall find that both Sargon-the-Great and his son Menes and their dynasty call themselves *Gut* or "Goth" in their Indus Valley seals, as well as *Bar* or *Par* or "Pharaoh."

This discovery of Sargon as a Predynastic Pharaoh was made through the Indian Chronicle account of "Sargon's" son under his title there of *Manasyu*, identifying him with Manis-Tusu and Menes.

[1] Sayce in *Ancient Egypt*, 1924, 2-5.

[2] See refs. later.

SARGON'S SON MANIS-TUSU DISCOVERED AS IDENTICAL WITH MANASYU OF INDIAN LISTS & MENES OF EGYPT

The identity of Menes, the founder of the First Dynasty of Egypt with Manis-Tusu or "Manis-the-Warrior," the great Mesopotamian emperor and son of Sargon of Agudu, first suggested itself to me over twenty years ago, when I observed by my unified tables of the Indian King-Lists that *Manasyu* came out in the table as the son and successor of "Sargon" as Sha-Kuni, or Kuni, the great world-emperor Sagara, and that he also bore the solar title therein of *Asa Manja* or "Manja the Shooter" (see App. I, Nos. 37 and 38).[1]

Menes' identity with this Manasyu or Aha Manjas (or Manj) then became a certainty when I revised the Sanskrit text of the Indian Epic Chronicle record of him.

MENES OR MANIS-TUSU AS MANASYU THE "PHARAOH OF GOPTA" (EGYPT) IN THE INDIAN EPICS

The name of this Aryan king under the form of *Manasyu* is found in the lunar Puru version of the Indo-Aryan King-Lists, and corresponds to the solar form of his name as Asa Manjas or Asa Manja in the unified main-line lists in which he is No. 38 (see App. I)—the solar lists being the most complete and in undisturbed chronological order. And we have seen that Sargon in this Puru version is called by the title of Pra-Vīra or "Foremost hero," in which *Vīra* corresponds to his Sumerian title of *Pir.*

One of the Indian Epic records of this King Manasyu and his ancestry states according to my revised reading as follows:[2]

"PURU had by his wife Paushti three sons PRA-VIRA,

[1] The displacement of this dynasty of "Sargon" in the Puru lunar version of the Indian king-lists by later Indian scribes has already been described. It occurred evidently through these scribes mistaking Puru I (No. 4 in main line) for Puru II, the Puru or Buru title of Sargon's father, the *Puru Gin* of the old Sumerian list (No. 36 in main line). And the reality of this displacement was fully confirmed by the fact that when this misplaced dynasty of Sargon was taken out from its misplaced position in the Puru list, the remaining kings occupied their proper position in the unique list from No. 5 onwards in agreement with the solar and the other lunar lists (see App. I, col. 4).

[2] The Sanskrit text of this critical record in the Mahā Bharata epic is given in App. VIII.

Ishwara and Raudr-āshwa, all of whom were mighty charioteers.[1] Amongst them Pra-Vīra had by his wife ACCHURA Seni a son named MANASYU of the line of the PRABHŪ [' Pharaoh '], the royal eye of GOPTA [Kopt or Egypt] and of the four ends of the earth. Manasyu by Su-Vira's daughter begat three sons Shakta, Samhana and Vagmā, all heroes and mighty charioteer warriors."

Here we have fortunately preserved to us in the Indian epic the concentrated tradition of the Aryan King Manasyu as " Pharaoh of Gopta " or Egypt, all in a nutshell. His genealogy is fully authenticated back to his grandfather Puru II, Puru-Gin of the Isin lists (see Table, opp. p. 140) and Buru or Puru of his Indus Valley seal, as the father of Sargon-the-Great.

Manasyu's father Pra-Vīra we have already identified as Sargon, this Vīra title corresponding to his *Pir* title in the Old Sumerian key-list; whilst the *Pra* in series with the longer form Prabhū, now appears to be the equivalent of the Egyptian *Parăā* or " Pharaoh."[2]

His mother's name of *Acchura Seni* also confirms Manasyu's identity with Manis-Tusu. Her Indian name substantially equates with the Mesopotamian name for Sargon's queen of " Lady *Ash-nar*," also read *Ash-lal*; and *l* and *r* are freely interchangeable dialectically. And we shall find below that Sargon in his own Egyptian inscription calls his queen " The Lady *Ash*."

His designation as " of the line of the *Prabhū* " clearly defines him as " of the line of the Pharaohs." *Prabhū*, the Sanskrit word, here means " ruler, master, lord,"[3] and it is in series with his further prefixed title of *Pra*, and derived from the Sumerian *Bar* or *Baru*, " lord "[4]—the form Prabhū adopted by the Indian scribes was presumably to make this " Pharaoh " title intelligible to Indian readers. And the fact that he is described as " of the line of the

[1] Sargon in his records describes, as we have seen, that he rode in " a brazen chariot."

[2] See WASD. 34 and cp. BD. 238—the Egyptian name had its first syllable latterly spelt with the Sumerian house-sign *Bar* or *Pur*, see WASB., so as to mean " The Great House "; and in Sumerian *Bar*, *Bara*=" great house or palace or temple " (WSAD. 29).

[3] MWD. 684.

[4] WSAD. 34.

Prabhū" is obviously to denote that his father (Sargon) before him was also a *Pra* or *Paraa* or Pharaoh. And we have found that Sargon in one of his Indus seals calls himself "Pharaoh," and in another (No. 8) "The Ruler of Egypt (or Khamaesshi) Land."

The title "Royal Eye" for Manasyu is a strikingly Egyptian metaphor and in series with the name *Asar* (Greek Osiris) for the traditional deified ancestor of Menes, which name is significantly written in Egyptian and Sumerian by the same pictograph of an Eye over a Throne,[1] another instance of the Sumerian origin of a fundamental Egyptian word with the same meaning, word-form and hieroglyph writing. And Menes, in one of his inscriptions in Egypt, actually uses this Eye-Throne Sumerian hieroglyph for his title, see Fig. 35, p. 280.

The title "Eye of the Four ends of the Earth" for Manasyu is, we shall find, the equivalent of Manis-Tusu's Mesopotamian imperial title and of his son Naram Enzu's or Naram Ba's title of "King of the Four Quarters of the World."[2]

The place-name *Gopta*[3] is of great historical importance. It equates with the Ancient Egyptian *Gebt* or *Gabt* name for Koptos;[4] and it survives in the modern "Copt" title for native Egyptians as opposed to immigrant Arabs; and it is clearly cognate with *Kopt-os* of the Greeks, the name of the oldest immemorial trade-city in Upper Egypt on the Nile, to the east of Abydos (see Map I). It was, presumably, the first capital of Menes in Upper Egypt. This name Gopta or Copt is probably, I suggest, the real source of the modern name "Egypt," the "Aiguptos" of the Greeks.

In his name "Manasyu," as it occurs in this Indian text, it is significant that the affix *yu* means in Sanskrit "uniter"[5] so the name would thus be "*Manas*-the-Uniter"; and Menes is designated by Egyptian tradition as "The *Uniter*

[1] WASD. p. 20, and representation, pl. II.

[2] RB. 7, and PHT. iv. 213.

[3] Now recognized as a territorial designation for the first time, it previously having been translated as a mere grammatical expression.

[4] BD. 1044.

[5] MWD. 853.

of the two crowns of Upper and Lower Egypt." Under his other Indian name as *Asa-Manja,* or "*Manja* the Shooter," is described in the Indian Chronicles, his quarrel with, and disinheritance by, his father, Sagara (Sargon), which, we shall find later, appears to relate to his declaration of independence in Egypt during the lifetime of his father in Mesopotamia ; and thus explaining why Sargon's younger son succeeded his father on the Mesopotamian throne and not Manis-Tusu, his eldest son.

Identity of Menes with the Aryan Emperor Manasyu & Manis-Tusu, son of Sargon, confirmed.

It was this startling and revolutionary discovery by me, about a quarter of a century ago, that Menes, the founder of the First Dynasty of Egypt, was clearly identical with the Aryan Emperor Manasyu of Gopta, or Asa-Manja or Asa-Manjas, and with Manis-Tusu, the son of Sargon, disclosed by the Indian Chronicles and King-Lists, that chiefly forced me to take up seriously the gigantic task of mastering the Sumerian language and its linear and cuneiform script, in order to revise the spelling of the names at first hand, after observing the totally different forms of the names which different Assyriologists "restored" from the same Sumerian writing in the same texts. All the more so was I prompted to take up this Egyptian side of the research, as the marvellous civilization of Ancient Egypt had captivated me ever since I had spent some weeks at the Boulaq Museum in Cairo in the eighties, and had acquired even then an amateurish acquaintance with the Egyptian hieroglyphics.

On gaining a working knowledge of all three scripts, Sanskritic, Sumerian with cuneiform, and Egyptian, the detailed examinations and comparisons of the critical names in the several texts with the associated histories of the kings thus made possible, fully confirmed the identities of the latter as is now shown here in detail in the following pages.

The Name "Menes," Manj or Aha-Manj compared with the Sumerian Manis-Tusu & its Indian forms.

One of the earliest critically-important historical results of this trilingual comparison of the Sumerian, Indian and Egyptian proper names was that which emerged from my comparison of the names for Menes (as the Greeks called him, and the *Manj* or *Aha-Manj* of his own inscriptions) with its Sumerian and Indian forms. This disclosed identity in all three. And as this trilingual identity is of critical importance not only for the identity of Menes with Manis-Tusu, but also for the rest of Menes' Dynasty as well, it is desirable here to examine it in detail.

Identity of the name "Menes," Manj or Aha-Manj in Egyptian, Indian & Sumerian.

It is necessary to premise in my comparison of the Egyptian language and writing with other cognate Aryan languages and writing—for I have demonstrated that the Ancient Egyptian language is radically Aryan in its roots and writing,[1] although it adopted latterly a Semitic idiom in using these Aryan roots, as the subjects of Menes, like those of Sargon in Mesopotamia were mostly Semitic-speaking people—that Ancient Egyptian writing, like its Aryan cognates Sanskrit, Pali, Hindi, etc., and Phœnician alphabetic writing, does not usually express the short vowel *a* in its writing. The hitherto unknown reason for this, as I have demonstrated in my *Aryan Origin of the Alphabet*, is that the short vowel *a* is inherent as an affix in each consonantal letter.

Thus "Menes," as the Greeks called him, spells his name (as also do later Egyptians) by the "Egyptian" hieroglyphs read as M-N and also spells it M-N-J. Egyptologists recognized that in order to sound the words written by this consonantal way of spelling, it was necessary to introduce a vowel after each initial and medial consonant. But unaware of the reason for this consonantal spelling with its absence of short vowels, they agreed on the expedient of arbitrarily introducing the vowel *e* after each initial and

[1] WSAD. *passim*.

medial consonantal sign in rendering the words into "Roman" or European alphabetic writing.

But, as I have proved in my *Aryan Origin of the Alphabet*, the unexpressed vowel in Ancient Egyptian was not *e*, but was the *a* inherent in each consonant as in the other Aryan languages which used this consonantal form of writing. Thus the Egyptian name for "Menes," written M-N and M-N-J does not usually read *Men* or *Menj*, as "restored" by Egyptologists, but reads properly *Man* or *Manaj* or *Manj*; just as in the Indian Sanskrit his name is written M-N-S-Y-U and A-S-M-N-J, which are universally transcribed into Roman characters by all Indianists as *Manasyu* and *Asa-Manja*.

The fuller Egyptian form of Menes' name as *Manj*, strikingly confirms the literal identity of the Egyptian with the Sanskrit *Manja* (or Asa-Manja), the son of the Emperor Sagara, that is Sargon; and it equates also phonetically with the *Manis* name of Sargon's son in Sumerian—the affix *Tusu* meaning, as seen below, "The Warrior." This fuller Egyptian form of Menes' name is usually disguised by many English Egyptologists as *Mena*. But the alphabetic value of the last letter is rightly rendered by the Berlin school as *J*,[1] which is now seen to be its proper value by our trilingual comparison; and this is confirmed by the pictorial form of this Egyptian hieroglyph which pictures a flowering reed, which I observed was the same sign, form, sound, and meaning as the Sumerian pictograph of the flowering reed word-sign with the phonetic value *Gi*[2]—thus affording another of the many instances I have demonstrated of the derivation of the Egyptian hieroglyphs from the Sumerian pictographs, with the same pictographs, form, phonetic value and meaning.

We thus get the trilingual equation of Menes' name as follows:

Egyptian.		Sumerian.		Sanskrit.
Man or *Manj*	=	*Manis* or *Manisi*	=	*Manasyu* and *Manja*.

Similarly is it with the title of *Aha* or *Akha* which "Menes" uses sometimes along with his proper personal name of *Manj* or abbreviated into *Man*, and giving him a

[1] GH. xi. [2] Br. 2385.

form of name with title which is usually spelt by English Egyptologists as *Aha Men* or *Aha Mena*; but which should now be properly spelt *Aha* (or *Akha*) *Manj*, though, as we shall find, Menes himself sometimes spells his name on his Indo-Sumerian seal as *Men*, see Plate XI, Nos. 2, 3 and 10.

Here again our trilingual comparison confirms the identity of this title *Aha* or *Akha* in all three languages, Egyptian, Sumerian and Indian, in meaning and generally in word-form. This title *Aha* or *Akha* means in Egyptian "The Warrior," and is derived, as I have shown, from the Sumerian root *Aha* or *Akha* "Fight, strike down," a Sumerian root which runs in the same word-form and meaning throughout the whole family of Aryan language including the English.[1] And the Egyptian hieroglyph for this sign, which is a picture of two arms holding a shield and a battle-mace, is significantly derived as I have shown from the similar Sumerian sign for this pictograph *Aha or Akha*, again showing the derivation of the Egyptian hieroglyphs from the Sumerian with the same pictograph signs, word-form and meaning.[2] Thus it is demonstrated that the Sumerian title of Sargon's son, namely, *Manis-Tusu* or "Manis-the-Warrior," is the equivalent of the Egyptian *Aha-Manj* or *Akha-Manj*, for *Tusu* in Sumerian also means, as I have shown, "War or Fight" and is the Sumerian origin of our English word "Tussle."[3]

So also, the Indian form of Menes' title as *Asa-Manja* means "*Manja*-the-Shooter"—*As* meaning in Sanskrit "Shoot at, cast, throw,"[4] thus showing that the Indian scribes had translated the Sumerian title *Tusu* into Sanskrit to render it intelligible to Indian readers, just as Menes himself had translated it by *Aha* to render it more intelligible to Egyptians to whom *Tusu* was presumably unknown.[5]

We thus find that besides Menes' identity of name in all three languages—Egyptian, Sumerian and Indian—his title also of "Warrior or Fighter" also is identical thus:

Egyptian.		Sumerian.		Indian.
Manj-the-Warrior	=	*Manis*-the-Warrior	=	*Manja*-the-Shooter.
(*Aha-Manj*)	=	(*Manis-Tussa*)	=	*Asa-Manja*.

[1] WSAD. 9. [2] WSAD. pl. I. [3] WSAD. 9-10. [4] MWD. 117. [5] Cp. WSAD. 10.

Thus no proof of identity could be more complete in regard to "Menes," the founder of the First Dynasty of Egypt, being the son of "Sargon"-the-Great or King Gin, to which world-monarch as a predynastic Pharaoh of Egypt we now return. And we shall find that Menes calls himself "the son of Gina or Sha-Gina" in his Indus Valley and Egyptian records.

"SARGON," FATHER OF MENES, DISCOVERED AS THE CHIEF "PREDYNASTIC" PHARAOH IN EGYPT

Having thus established the identity of the Aryan Emperor Manas-yu or "*Manas*-the-Uniter" or Asa-Manja or "*Manja*-the-Shooter," the son of the Aryan Emperor Sha-Kuni or Kuni (or "Sargon"), with Manis-Tusu or "Manis-the-Warrior," the son of King Gin or "Sargon," and with Menes or *Manj* or *Aha-Manj* or *Manj*-the-Warrior, the founder of the First Egyptian Dynasty and "The Uniter" of Upper and Lower Egypt, we now follow up the Indian epic record that he was "of the line of the *Prabhū* (or Pharaoh)."

We have seen that the world-monarch "Sargon," the father of Menes, held Egypt within his empire; and that he bears in the Old Sumerian King-List the title of *Pir*, *Bir* or *Bur*, which seems to be the equivalent of his father's Sumerian title in the same lists of *Bur* or *Buru*, the latter also occurring on one of his Indus Valley seals. And this title appears to be a variant spelling of Sargon's father's title spelt *Bara* in the older Sumerian King-List, and of his *Pra* title in the Indian Lists; which we have seen was obviously the equivalent of the Egyptian *Parā* or "Pharaoh." And this Indian *Pra* form was expanded by the Indian scribes into *Prabhū*, "ruler or master" in Sanskrit, presumably to render it intelligible to Indian readers.

This implies that both Menes' father "Sargon" and the father of the latter also were Pharaohs, and thus Menes or Manasyu was "of the line of the Prabhū (or Pharaoh)." And as the Pharaohs or kings of Egypt before Menes are styled by Egyptologists "Predynastic," Sargon and his father as kings of Egypt are according to this nomenclature "Predynastic" Pharaohs.

THE "PREDYNASTIC" PHARAOHS OF EGYPT

The kings or "Pharaohs" of Egypt before Menes are termed by Egyptologists "Predynastic." This is because the late Egyptian priest Manetho, who compiled in the 3rd century B.C. a list of the Pharaohs for Ptolemy II Philadelphus, for the great library of Alexandria (of which work only fragments are now found in the works of later classic writers), heads his long list of the Pharaohs with Menes, whom he calls the founder of the First Dynasty in Egypt. And similarly Sety I (whose beautiful alabaster sarcophagus is now a chief treasure in the Soane Museum in London), the father of Rameses-the-Great, also begins his list of Egyptian kings with Menes, who was the traditional uniter of the crowns of Upper and Lower Egypt into one kingship and nation.

But Manetho prefixes to Menes a list of ten kings, who it was said reigned before Menes at Thinis near Abydos for a period of 350 years before Menes, and who may be nine pre-Sargonic Sumerian suzerains with Sargon as the tenth. And before these again he prefixes a long list of gods and demigods as kings with fabulous ages, just as did his more or less contemporary Babylonian priest Berosos in his list also compiled for the Seleucid Greek king of Babylon, and somewhat like the Isin priests prefixing fabulous chronology to the historical kings of Mesopotamia. The early list of Egyptian kings, also on the Palermo stele of the Fifth Dynasty, enumerates ten kings before Menes, the names of whom are mostly illegible. But no inscribed remains of any of these ten legendary pre-Menes kings are said to have been found.

The only inscribed objects with personal names recovered at Abydos and other old Egyptian sites which are considered by Egyptologists to be "Predynastic," give the names of eight kings or "pharaohs" who are believed to be Predynastic from the archaic form of the writing and the relatively early culture form of the objects inscribed, coupled with the absence of their names in the First Dynasty list. And these eight historical "Predynastic" kings have been arranged by Egyptologists in serial order according to their supposed relative archæological ages.[1] But as the last

[1] PHE. 1, 6,

two are written in a later style and classed as belonging to the period of " Narmer " who is within the First Dynasty, this leaves only six " Predynastic " kings of whom inscribed remains have been found.

Now, the very first of these historical Predynastic Pharaohs, and heading the list, proves by our new Sumerian and Indian keys to be none other than the father of Menes, " Sargon " himself! And the other two who are placed by Egyptologists immediately after him are disclosed to be his father and grandfather, who preceded him as predynastic Pharaohs.

Sargon's Father & Grandfather as the Predynastic Pharaohs hitherto called " Ro " & " Khetm "

The three earliest of the Predynastic Pharaohs who have left inscriptions are those whose names have hitherto been read *Ka-Ap*, *Ro* and *Khetm*. They are now disclosed to be respectively in reality Sargon himself with his father and grandfather; but chronologically they are in the reverse order to what they have been placed by Egyptologists on archæological grounds—another instance of the unreliability of archæological dating.

Inscriptions of King " Ro "

The inscriptions of King " Ro " were found in his great tomb at Abydos, roughly scratched on large votive funereal jars of pottery which were placed alongside large alabaster

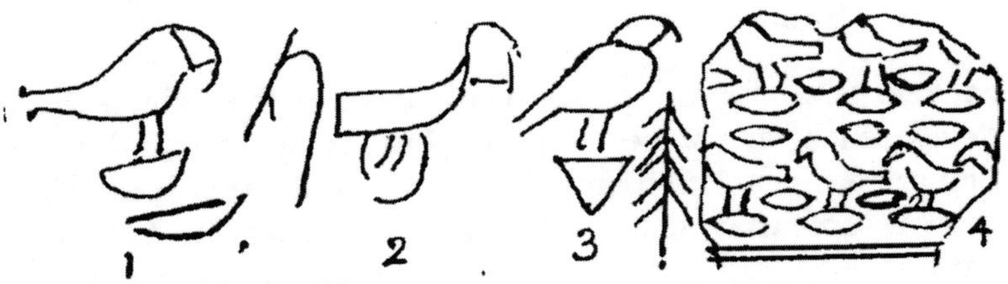

1, 2, 3. On Pottery. 4. On Sealing.
Fig. 23.—King " Ro's " Name from his Tomb at Abydos.

jars,[1] and another was impressed on a clay sealing by a cylinder seal of Mesopotamian style and engraved in finer fashion.[2] They are shown in the accompanying Figure (No. 23).

[1] PRT. I. xliv. 2-9. [2] PRT. II. xiii. 96, and PHE. 1, 5.

Decipherment of the Real Name of Predynastic Pharaoh "Ro," identifying Him with Sargon's Father

For decipherment, I here place the Egyptian writing of this king's name alongside the standard Sumerian writing of the Sargonic period in Mesopotamia in the conventional style of pictographs used for lithic engraving there. The first two signs form his shorter name as written in most of the instances—the other two following signs occur on several of the inscriptions giving his name in its fuller form, and the first of these signs occurs also as an additional sign on the sealing. It is seen that the Egyptian writing is not in the

Egypt.

Sumer Mesop.

Reads: PA,PAK,BAK,HU[1] U BURU[2] GIN[3]

Transl. PĀU or PĀŬ, BĀKU, PĀU-GIN or PA-BURU-GIN.

Fig. 24.—Name of Predynastic Pharaoh "Ro," deciphered as PĀU or BĀKU or PA-BURU-GIN.

[1] B. 831; Br. 2047-8. [2] B. 365; Br. 8632, 8645.
[3] B. 92; Br. 2384.

conventional Egyptian style of hieroglyphs, which was developed after Menes' epoch, but it is essentially in Sumerian linear pictographic script, with the hawk-sign drawn somewhat more naturalistically than in the conventional diagrammatic form generally used in Mesopotamia; and that the signs have their Sumerian phonetic values, which accounts for the name not having been hitherto deciphered or read.[1] On the jars, the writing is in the reversed or retrograde direction; but in the sealing it is in the usual orthographic Sumerian or Aryan direction from

[1] The "Ro" value assigned to it by Egyptologists was obtained from the later Egyptian value of *R* borne by the second sign.

the left towards the right hand. For our decipherment the signs are given in the usual direction for reading, namely from left to right.

It is thus seen that this king's name as written on his tomb in Egypt and on his sealing equates with the form of his name as the 36th king on the main-line lists in the Indian Chronicles and in the old Sumerian prefixed lists in the Isin Chronicle and on his Indus Valley seals, as is displayed in the following equations:

Egypt.		Old Sumerian Lists.		Indus Valley Seals.		Indian Lists.
Pāu or Pāû	=		=	Bu or Buz	=	Bāhu
or Bākû	=		=		=	Bāhuka
or Pāu-Gin	=	Bara-Gin	=	Bara Gin	=	Pra-Cin-wat
or Pa Buru-Gin	=	Buru-Gina	=	Buru or Puru	=	Puru (II)

It is also seen that whilst the later Indian scribes have preserved substantially the same spelling of the name as in the Egyptian inscriptions they have Sanskritized them slightly in order to extract a meaning from them. Thus they have made *Bāu* or *Bāku* into *Bāhu* and *Bāhuka*, both of which latter names mean in Sanskrit "The arm" or "mighty." And *Pāu-Gin* and *Pa-buru-Gin* they have Sanskritized into *Pra-cin-wat* or "The collector or gatherer."

The Predynastic King "Khetm's" Real Name in Egyptian & Sumerian, identifying Him with Sargon's Grandfather

Similarly, the name of the Predynastic Pharaoh[1] hitherto read "Khetm" or "Khatm" is now disclosed to be written in Sumerian hieroglyph and with the Sumerian phonetic value of that sign. That sign pictures a Sumerian cylinder-seal (*Tukh* or *Dukh*) in its realistic form with its attached loop of string, as contrasted with its diagrammatic form in Mesopotamian Sumerian for rapid writing with straight lines, on wet clay-tablets, as seen in the annexed figure, where the Sumerian form of this sign is placed beneath the Egyptian for comparison.

[1] It is on a clay sealing. Petrie, *Naqada and Ballas*, lxxx. 1, and PHE. 1, 5.

It is thus seen that this predynastic Pharaoh's name, hitherto read "Khetm,"[2] reads in Sumerian *Tukh, Tukhu, Dukh* or *Tekhi*, which equates with the name of the 35th king

Egyptian.

Sumerian Mesop.

Reads: TUKH, DUKHU or TEKHI.[1]

FIG. 25.—King "Khetm's"[2] Name deciphered as *TUKH, DUKHU* or *TEKHI.*

[1] B. 157. Br. 3921, spelt *Di-* (or *Ti*)*-ukh* (or *-ukhu* or *-akh*) giving the form *D*(*i*)*ukhu* or *T*(*i*)*ukhu* or *T*(*i*)*akh* or *Dikh*, cp. Br. 8289-90. On *Tekhi*, Br. 3922.

on the main-line list of the Indian Chronicles, who is made therein the father of the king above-named and the grandfather of Sagara or Sargon, and it also equates with the name for this king in the old Sumerian King-Lists. Thus:

Egypt.		Old Sumer Lists.		Indian Lists.
Tukhu or Tekhi	=	Tuke	=	Vri-*Taka* or Dhri-*Taka*.

The Indian prefixes *Vri* and *Dhri* were obviously added for descriptive purposes by the early Indian scribes who converted the Sumerian syllabic pictographic writing into the Indian alphabetic writing. For *Vri* in Sanskrit = "to cover, check, conceal," that is the sense of "a seal," which this word literally means in Sumerian. And *Dhri* has the analogous meaning of "keep down, restrain, preserve" (which are also secondary meanings of this Sumerian "seal" word. Indeed the latter Sanskrit word is obviously derived from this same Sumerian "seal" word, which has also the value *Dih*,[3] and we have seen that Sanskrit frequently intruded

[2] "Khetm" or "Khatm" is the later Egyptian descriptive title for this seal sign, as "the cut or engraved," and is derived from the Egyptian *Khat* "cut or engrave" (BD. 569); which Egyptian word is seen to be obviously derived from the Sumerian *Kut* "cut" (Br. 356), which I have shown to be the parent of our English word "Cut," and of its equivalents in the Aryan family of languages, Sanskrit *Chid*, etc.

[3] Br. 3921.

an *r* Cockney-wise into the old Early Aryan or Sumerian roots.

And incidentally this Sumerian " seal " word, which has also meaning " written tablet," is, as I have shown under its *Dikh, Tikh* and *Dukh* values, the parent of our English words " Tick-et, Tok-en, Dock-et, Docu-ment," etc., and the corresponding words of this form and meaning which run throughout the Aryan family of languages [1]—another instance of the Sumerian origin of the Aryan languages.

" Sargon's " Inscriptions as Predynastic Pharaoh GIN or SHA-GIN in Egypt
(*the so-called King " Ka-ap "*)

That this startling discovery of " Sargon's " inscriptions in Egypt was not made before, is now seen to be owing, partly to the narrow outlook of Egyptologists, with their theory that Civilization and the Egyptian hieroglyphs

Fig. 26.—" Sargon's " Sumerian Inscription as Pharaoh at Abydos. (On a jar, after Sir F. Petrie, PHE. I, 5.)

Fig. 27.—Sumerian Inscription of " Sargon's " queen, " The Lady Ash," at Abydos. (On a jar, after Sir F. Petrie, PHE. I, 5.)

originated in the Nile Valley, and partly to the fact that these predynastic inscriptions are written in the Early Sumerian script and language, and not in the later derived conventional form of the Egyptian hieroglyphs with which alone Egyptologists are familiar. As a result these Sargonic inscriptions have hitherto remained undeciphered and unread.

These highly critical inscriptions of this king, now disclosed

[1] WSAD. 55 f.

to be the great emperor "Sargon" (see Figs. 26 and 27) as a Predynastic Pharaoh of Egypt, were discovered by Prof. (now Sir) Flinders Petrie in one of the oldest tombs at Abydos in Upper Egypt. In this tomb the queen of this king was buried, and also it seems himself.

In summarizing the discovery and contents of this tomb Prof. Petrie says:[1] "The tomb of this king is a brick-lined pit about twenty feet long and half as wide. It had been entirely plundered anciently; but many cylinder jars of pottery remained in the sand, bearing inscriptions [Fig. 26] which gave the name of 'Horus Ka,' with the personal name of 'King Ap.' Besides these there are other similar inscriptions [Fig. 27] of 'Ha, wife of the Horus Ka.' In the same tomb was an impression of a small seal of Ka. From these remains we see that the system of inscribing the royal property, *of sealing on clay with a cylinder seal and the free use of writing*, were already in course of development, leading on to the civilization which followed."

"Sargon's" Sumerian Inscriptions at Abydos

When I first saw these inscriptions about twenty years ago, in the light of my Indian keys to Menes' Mesopotamian origin and with some acquaintance with Egyptian hieroglyphs and Sumerian writing, I observed that the writing generally resembled the Early Sumerian script and differed considerably from the conventional Egyptian hieroglyphs and contained some signs which were absent in the latter.

On scrutinizing the inscriptions in detail some years later, I found that the writing was radically of the old cursive Sumerian type (such as I later found written regularly on the Indo-Sumerian seals of the Sargonic and later period); and that it was obviously intended to be read with the Sumerian phonetic values of the signs, that is syllabically. Moreover, it was clear that both inscriptions were to be read in the retrograde direction, as the Sun-Hawk sign in both faced to the right, a feature which indicates the direction for reading to the left through the beak or nose of bird or animal in archaic Hittite and in Egyptian inscriptions, and also as we now find on the Indo-Sumerian sealings.

[1] WSAD. I, 4-5.

PLATE XA.

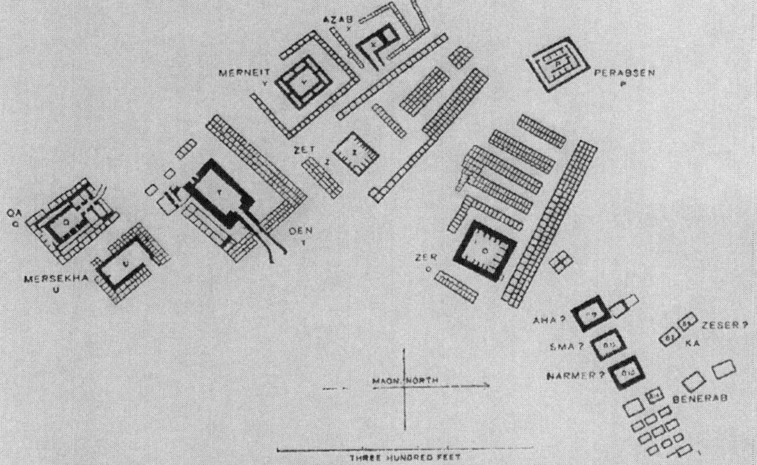

GENERAL PLAN OF TOMBS OF PREDYNASTIC AND FIRST DYNASTY PHARAOHS AT ABYDOS.

(After Sir F. Petrie, PRT., II, Pl. LVIII.)

Note the tomb of Sargon-the-Great as King "Ka" to the right of that of Menes' (Aha); and the tombs of Menes' descendants on the South and North become more and more extensive and developed. See Pl. XVIA for details of Pharaoh Dudu's tomb; and Pl. XVIIIA for details of King Shudur Kib's or Qa's tomb.

On reading the signs with their Sumerian syllabic values, I found that the King's personal name read GIN-UKUS, or GIN-UKUSSI,[1] (see decipherment table, Fig. 28.) This strikingly confirmed his identity with King Gin or "Sargon"; for the usual title of "Sargon" in the Indian Epics is *Kuni* (or *Shakuni*) *Aikshvaka, i.e.* "Kuni descendant of Ikshvāku" —the latter being as we have seen the solar title of the first Aryan king and the equivalent, as we have found, of his Sumerian title in the Kish Chronicle of *Ukusi*. And "Sargon" as Kuni or Shakuni in the Indian Epics is repeatedly called by this proud title of "Descendant of Ikshvāku," and also in the extract cited in the heading of Chapter XIII., p. 196.

The Shield for the Solar Title of the Pharaohs on "Sargon's" Tomb Inscription at Abydos and its Sumerian Meaning.

At the outset it is noteworthy that the king's *Solar title* is enclosed within a sign consisting of an upright panelled frame with three vertical bars in its top register (compared with two in the queen's inscription) and surmounted by the Sun-Hawk, while his solar title occupies its lower register. The Solar title of Pharaoh is called by Egyptologists "the Horus name" from "Horus" or *Haru*, the title of the Sun and of the Sun-Hawk, which is presumably derived from the Sumerian *Hu* or *Ha* name for the Hawk.[2] And this "Horus" title is given the first place of all the plural titles used by subsequent Pharaohs, each of whom claimed to be "Son of the Sun." It is significant that already Sargon had adopted this heraldic shield-like enclosing device for framing his solar title; and it was evidently the model copied by the latter Pharaohs for this purpose, with the alteration that the vertical bars were relegated to the lower register, thus giving more prominence to the Solar title. The vertical bars have suggested to some Egyptologists that this design, which they call *serekh*, represented a banner with fringes, because in the later forms the bottom bars have sometimes free ends; but their early position as erect bars above is against this view. Much more probable, it

[1] Br. 11184 gives the complement *-si* to the *Kus* value.

[2] Br. 2053.

seems to me, is the suggestion that the figure represented the hieroglyph of a temple; for this seems confirmed by the fact that the sign resembles the upper portion of the Sumerian pictograph of the temple-sign, which has the value of *Bar* or *Bara*,[1] which designated him as the *Paăar* or "*Pharaoh* in Egyptian inscriptions of the First Dynasty, as we shall see, and also in the Indus seals. And in its developed forms in the stele of the fourth king of the First Dynasty it is figured realistically as a temple or palace (see Fig. 50 p. 325).

This temple or palace sign, or the upper portion of that sign, is placed within the square sign, which in Sumerian has the value of *Rin*, and meaning primarily "Ring," and secondarily "enclosure, dwelling-place"; and it has the Semitic value of *Saru*,[2] which is thus presumably the source of the later Egyptian name *serekh*; I have accordingly translated it as "of the House of the Pharaoh."

Decipherment of Sargon's Inscription at Abydos

In the decipherment of this Sumerian inscription of "Sargon," in order to enable the reader to follow it, I have in the accompanying Decipherment Table in Fig. 28, arranged in the first line the signs in their usual orthographic Sumerian order for reading from left to right; and in the second line are placed for comparison the corresponding forms of these signs in the standard Early Sumerian script of Mesopotamia, in which it will be noticed the signs are given a slightly more cursive and somewhat abbreviated form for rapid writing; in the third line are placed the Sumerian phonetic values of each sign in roman type, each duly attested for the standard Sumerian lexicons; and in the fourth line is the literal translation all duly attested for each word by the references in the preceding line. The language is Sumerian.

Here it is seen that "Sargon" uses, or is given, for his personal name at Abydos in Egypt precisely the same personal name *Gin* which he uses with the variant *Gani* in his inscriptions in Mesopotamia, and which is used for him in most of the Babylonian inscriptions. And his title

[1] Br. 6871-2; WSAD. 29.

[2] B. 443; M. 7683.

of "The *Ukus* or *Ukussi*," we have seen designates him as a descendant of the first Sumerian king Ukusi of the Sun-Hawk City, or the first Aryan king under his solar title of Ikshwāku of the Indian Epics and Vedas, in keeping with the references to him in the Indian Epics as an *Aikshwaka* or "descendant of King Ikshwāku."

The *Sha*[1] prefix to his solar title is in series with his name and title spelt *Sha-Gin* in the Old Sumerian King-Lists (see Table facing p. 140) and in series with his fuller Indian

Transl.: The Shepherd of the (Sun-)Hawk, of the House of the Pharaoh, KAD (the lofty) GIN, the Ukus (or Ukussi).

FIG. 28.—Sargon's Tomb Inscription as the Solar KAD, GIN, or SHA-GIN, the UKUSSI at Abydos deciphered.

1 *Sha*, "The brilliant." B. 93; Br. 2552.
2 B. 83; Br. 2045, 2047, and see *Bak*, *Pak*, in WSAD. 25. *Rin* 443. Br. 10167.
3 B. 301; Br. 6872.
4 B. 311; *Kad* or *Shu*, Br. 7063-5.
5 B. 283; Br. 6506.
6 B. 273; Br. 6020.
7 B. 508; Br. 11184, *Kus*, with complement *-si*.

form of name as *Sha-Kuni*. The sign for his solar title "KAD" is the pictogram of an uplifted hand with the fingers erect. In its conventionalized Egyptian hieroglyph form this sign is pictured by two uplifted hands conjoined and is given the phonetic value of *Ka*, whence Egyptologists have called the solar title of this king "King *Ka*." This *Ka* value in Egypt is obviously derived from the

1 This *Sha* sign means "protect," "protector," also "shepherd," and "shining," Br. 2560, 2572, 2577. It is clearly not the reed sign *Gi*, with the meaning of "king," from which it differs by its curve below.

Sumerian value of this sign as *Kad* or *Kat*,[1] wherein the final *d*, as is often the case, has dropped out; and affords another illustration of the derivation of the Egyptian hieroglyphs from the Sumerian in pictographic form and phonetic sound. This title *Kad* is used by Sargon also in his beautiful Bull signet (Pl. X, No. 1) from the Indus Valley. And *Kad* as we have seen was a not infrequent title used by the Phœnicians, and we have seen that Sargon was an Aryan Phœnician.

The simplicity in the titles of the great world-monarch "Sargon," without any reference to his empire on this funereal votive vase is noteworthy. Possibly his temporal titles were recorded on his main epitaph (as in those of his descendant Pharaohs as we shall see) which has been lost. Here it should be noted that, this inscription was presumably written by his son Menes, who we shall find revolted against his father and was in revolt against him at the time of the latter's death, and thus lost the immediate succession in Mesopotamia. In such circumstances, if Sargon's body were really buried in this tomb, which was the tomb of his queen (the mother of Menes), who obviously died before him, his body must have been embalmed for its transport from Mesopotamia to Abydos to repose beside that of his queen. For although Prof. Elliot Smith says that mumification does not appear to have been practised in Egypt before the Second Dynasty,[2] we have seen that the body of the second king of the First Aryan or Sumerian Dynasty six and a half centuries before Sargon was traditionally reported in the Indian records to have been embalmed and remained preserved "as if it were immortal."

We now turn to the inscription of the Queen of "Sargon" found in the same tomb.

Sargon's Queen's Tomb Inscription at Abydos Deciphered.

The inscription on Sargon's Queen's tomb vase (Fig. 27) is likewise written in the reversed direction or towards the left, and in the Sumerian language. When arranged for

[1] Br. 7063.

[2] Rept. Brit. Ass. 1912, 612.

decipherment in the usual Sumerian order of reading from left to right it reads as follows :—

Predynastic.

Mesopot. Sumerian.

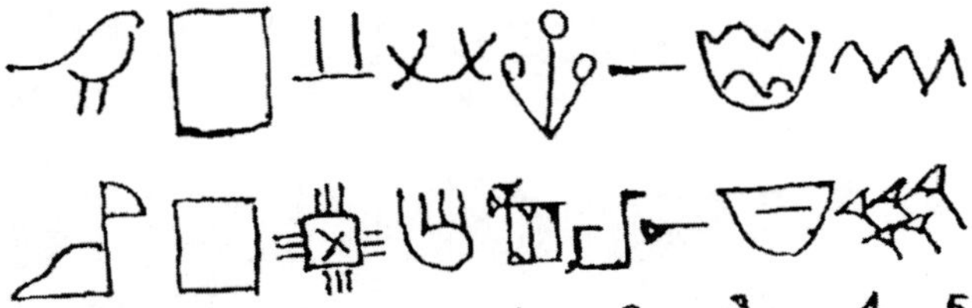

Reads : PA - RIN - BARA KAD[1] MA[2]-ASH[3] NIN[4]-I[5]

Transl. : (Of) The (Sun-)Hawk House of the Pharaoh KAD, my Lady ASH

FIG. 29.—Sargon's Queen, the Lady Ash (*Ash-Nini*), Tomb inscription at Abydos deciphered.

[1] As in previous Fig. [2] B. 137 ; Br. 3682.
[3] B. 1 ; Br. 2 ; WSAD. 19. [4] B. 532 ; Br. 11949. [5] B. 533.

The name of Sargon's Queen here as "The Lady *Ash*" is of immense critical importance. In later Babylonian records the name of Sargon's Queen is given as *Ash-nar*(-tum) or *Ash-lul*(-tum)—*tum* meaning "the exalted," and *l* and *r* are freely interchanged dialectically. And in the Indian Epics her name as the mother of Manasyu, *i.e.*, Menes, is given as *Acchura*(*-Seni*) (see p. 233). Thus both Babylonian and Indian substantially agree with the Abydos inscription, and confirm her identity as the Queen of "Sargon" or King Gin.

The third sign, that immediately following the "Horus" *Kad* title, is the ship-sign or the pictograph of a Nile boat, as distinguished from the high-prowed ship-sign in Mesopotamian Sumerian. It has the literal meaning of "my" or "me," and is, as I have shown, obviously the Sumerian origin of these English words. This gives the reading, "Of the (Sun-)Hawk House of the Pharaoh Kad, my Lady Ash," and shows that Sargon's Queen died within his lifetime and was here buried by him.

KING GIN'S OR "SARGON'S" SEALING AT ABYDOS AND ITS DECIPHERMENT

I find another of King Gin's or "Sargon's" inscriptions amongst the sealings unearthed at the Abydos tombs by

Sir F. Petrie, included by the latter in "Sealings of King Ka and Narmer,"[1] and here reproduced in Fig. 30.

FIG. 30.—Sealing of King GIN or "Sargon" at Abydos. (Photo after Petrie.)

It will be noticed that this royal sealing (for a jar or other article of the royal property) consists of a tenfold repetition of two alternating signs, namely a circle with matted line interior and a branched twig or reed; and from exigencies of space for the circles two of the reeds belonging to the lower row of circles are squeezed into the top row of signs. Now, these signs are the well-known Sumerian

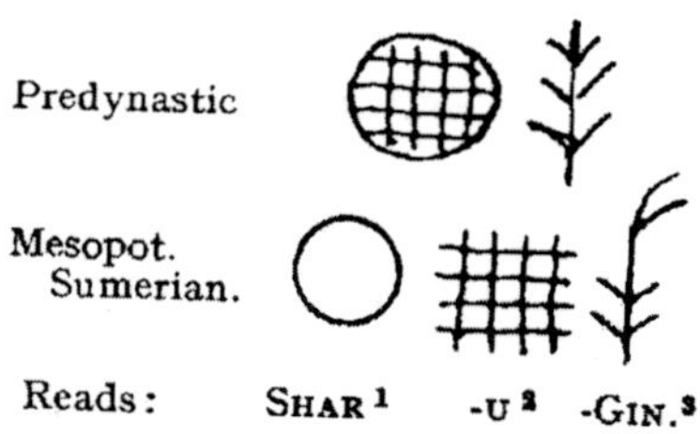

FIG. 31.—King Gin's or "Sargon's" Sealing from Abydos deciphered. Here it is seen that King Gin calls himself *Sharu-Gin*, suggesting that this seal was for use in Mesopotamia.

[1] B. 353; Br. 8208. [2] B. 273; Br. 6020. [3] B. 92, as before.

syllabic signs for *Shar*, *U* and *Gin* as seen in the above decipherment table, which also shows that the sealing reads *in the retrograde direction*, from right to left.

Thus these three inscriptions from the tomb of the Predynastic Pharaoh, Gin, Sha-Gin or Sharu-Gin at Abydos, the tomb of himself and his Queen, with his solar title of *Kad*—and we have seen that "Sargon" was a famous

[1] PRT. II., pl. XII, 95.

Sun-worshipper—now identify him clearly with the mighty world-monarch "Sargon" or King Gin of Mesopotamia, whose empire included Egypt, and with the father of King Manasyu or Asa-Manja "the Prabhu of Gopta" and son of Sha-Kuni and Queen Acchura(-Seni) of the Indian Epics, who was, we have found, identical with Manis-Tusu or "Manis-the-Warrior" of Mesopotamia, and with Manj or Aha-Manj or "Manj - the - Warrior" or the Egyptian "Menes."

Sargon's Annexation or Reconquest of Egypt, & Route & Date

Some light also is thrown on the date and route of Sargon's annexation of Egypt by the references in his chronicles and in the extracts preserved in the Babylonian and Assyrian Omen-literature, and in his traditional autobiography. While the former gives the specific year of his reign for his first expedition of conquest to the Mediterranean as his third year of reign and his culminating conquest of "all the lands of that Western Sea of the Setting Sun" in his eleventh year, his autobiography says: "To the Western Sea-coast thrice did I advance," and it adds, "*Iatu* (or Itu)-Land-Mouth submitted," wherein the word now read as *Iatu* (or *Itu*) has hitherto been read by its Semitic synonym of "Dilmun." [1] And that Sargon regarded this *Iatu*-Land-Mouth (also defined as Pu-Land,[2] a Semitic title for Lower Egypt,[3] presumably from *Pu*, the old name for the early sacred city of Buto in the Delta [4] and the centre of the aboriginal predynastic Serpent cult) as one of his greatest conquests in the West, seems evidenced by its being given the first place of the only two places, both in the West, actually named as conquered by him in his autobiography.

Now it is significant that the old and usual Egyptian

[1] This territorial name has hitherto been conjecturally read *Ni-tuk(-ki)*, with the Semitic synonym Dilmun (Br. 5372). But the standard Sumerian bilingual glossaries give for the first sign the chief value of *I* or *Ia* (Br. 5305; M. 3664-5), and *Iau* is the name of this sign. And the definition of this land name is prefixed by "*Pu*-Land," and it bears the suffix *ka* or "Mouth" (Br. 5372). It thus obviously designated *Iatu* Land as "The Land of the Mouth of the Iatu River or Nile."

[2] Br. 5372; M. 7799. [3] MD. 789. [4] BD. 981 a.

hieroglyphic name for the River Nile is *Iatur*,[1] a name also applied to the Land of Egypt.[2]

This "*Iatu* Land-Mouth," therefore, one of the greatest of Sargon's new conquests in the West, made by him in his eleventh year of reign, appears to designate "The Mouth-Land of the Iatur or Nile," that is Lower Egypt. And this identity is confirmed in the next chapter. This conquest, or reconquest, as it now appears from the new evidence, of Egypt by Sargon, *via* the Mediterranean, from the north is also in agreement with Sargon's records, which make his conquests of "The Lands of the Western Sea (or Mediterranean)" begin from the Muru or Amorite Land in Northern Syria. His penetration to Upper Egypt would doubtless follow from his possession of Lower Egypt with his "predynastic" capital there, presumably at Pu or Buto.

Sargon on the Nile *re* his Birth Legend

Sargon's later Babylonian title of *Ni-lu-ba-ni*, which occurs in the Isin literature of about 2000 B.C., may thus, I think, possibly refer to his having been "born on the *Nile*"—*Nilu* in Assyrian meaning "Flood or high-tide water"[3] and *bani*="beget."[4] So, after all, the legendary story of his being sent adrift in a basket of rushes by his mother on "The River" may thus have occurred on the banks of the Nile, where his father and grandfather before him were the Predynastic Pharaohs. And the Hebrews in borrowing this legend for their Moses, would appear to have helped themselves to the local floating legend of the Aryan Pharaoh Sargon surviving on the Nile. There seems no doubt that this absenteeship of these Mesopotamian emperors in Egypt must have contributed to the usurpation of the Mesopotamian throne by Zaggisi, who dethroned Sargon's father there.

[1] MDC. 6; and see BD. 97 b; and cp. later *Itru*, BD. 99 b.

[2] Lower Egypt was called *Itur*-meh, and Upper Egypt was *Itur*-res, cp. BD. 97 b.

[3] MD. 678.

[4] *Ib.*, 173.

Summary of Discoveries regarding Sargon as Predynastic Pharaoh of Egypt

Thus we find through the keys supplied by the Indian King-Lists and Chronicles, that the "earliest known" of the Predynastic kings of Egypt of whom any contemporary inscriptional evidence has been found, the so-called "King Ka," is the great Sumerian or Aryan emperor King Gin of Agudu, the so-called "Sargon"; that his father and grandfather there before him were the so-called Predynastic Kings "Ro" and "Khetm"; that his son, the emperor Manis-Tusu or "Manis-the-Warrior" of Mesopotamia is identical with Asa-Manja or "Manja-the-Shooter" and Manasyu "the Prabhu of Gopta," son of the world-emperor Kuni or Sha-Kuni of the Indian Epics and Chronicles, and identical with the Pharaoh Manj or Aha-Manj or "Manj-the-Warrior" or "Menes" the founder of the First Dynasty in Egypt; that Sargon and his Queen, the Lady Ash, were buried at Abydos as attested by his three tomb inscriptions there; that by these discoveries is found the first synchronism between Egypt and Mesopotamia by which is now fixed with comparative certainty the date of Menes, hitherto the most disputed of all fundamental dates in Ancient History, at a no earlier period than about 2704 B.C.; and that the Civilization of Egypt was of Sumerian or Aryan Origin.

The further identity of Sargon's son Manis-Tusu with "Menes," the founder of the First Dynasty of Egypt, now requires a special chapter.

Fig. 31a.—Bird-men as Tasia-Michael or St Michael in Ancient Britain monuments. From Inchbrayock and Kirriemuir (SSS. I 43).

XV

Menes, Founder of First Dynasty of Egypt as Manis-Tusu, Son of Sargon, his Unknown Antecedents & Seizure of Egypt from his Father (?), *c.* 2704 B.C.

Disclosing his Governorship of Persia and of Indus Colony with Signet Seals, his Sunworship, apparent Sea-route of his Conquest of Upper Egypt, Identification with King Minos *of Crete, and his* tragic Death in the West.

> "All that we know of the first of the Pharaohs—Menes—beyond the fact of his existence is practically nil."
> —Maspero, *MDC.* 1922, 233.

> "Menes appears to be a 'conflate' personage of legend."—*Cambridge Anc. Hist.*, 1924, i. 267.

Hitherto Menes, the traditional founder of the First Dynasty of Egypt, although regularly cited in the native Egyptian king-lists from the old chronology of Sety I downwards to Manetho as the founder of the First Dynasty in Egypt, has been so shadowy and so little known, that notwithstanding the discovery of his "tomb," with several inscriptions, by Sir Flinders Petrie in the royal cemeteries at Abydos in 1900, he is still regarded by the latest historical text-books as "a conflate personage of legend." And beyond the finding of his name in a few contemporary inscriptions, and the inference that he must have arrived in Upper Egypt by way of the Red Sea with a fully-fledged civilization, nothing whatever is known to Egyptologists of his origin, personality, portrait, ancestry and race.

Menes discovered as Sumerian or Aryan Emperor Manis-Tusu, Son of "Sargon"-the-Great of Mesopotamia, with his Lost Antecedents, History & Ancestry

In the previous chapter we have discovered that Menes, the Pharaoh, is a truly historical personage, and identical with the famous Mesopotamian emperor Manis-Tusu or

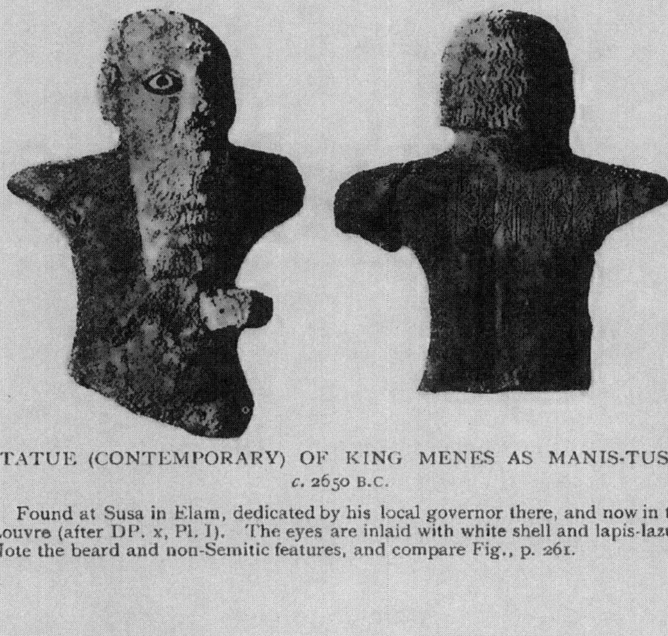

STATUE (CONTEMPORARY) OF KING MENES AS MANIS-TUSU, *c.* 2650 B.C.

Found at Susa in Elam, dedicated by his local governor there, and now in the Louvre (after DP. x, Pl. I). The eyes are inlaid with white shell and lapis-lazuli. Note the beard and non-Semitic features, and compare Fig., p. 261.

" Manis-the-Warrior (see his portrait in Pl. XB and Fig. 32) the son of the Sumerian world-emperor " Sargon "-the-Great, and identical with Manasyu, " the Prabhu of Gopta," or Asa-Manja, the son of the world-emperor Kuni or Sha-Kuni (*i.e.* " Sargon ") of the Indian Chronicles, and that his lost ancestry and genealogy are now recovered, and much of his lost history and antecedents as well through these identifications. And it is seen that he was of the Aryan or Sumerian race and entered Egypt like his father Sargon equipped with the fully-fledged Sumerian or Aryan Civilization, which formed the basis and fabric of Egyptian Civilization.

Genealogy of Menes & his Descendants

The genealogy of Menes' father Sargon was given in the previous chapter, continuously back to the first king of the First Sumerian or Aryan Dynasty on the Dawn of Civilization, disclosing Menes also to be of the Sumerian or Aryan race.

His genealogy, according to the Old Sumerian King-Lists compared with the Kish Chronicle and the Indian lists, is shown in the table facing p. 140. Here I tabulate for convenience of reference his genealogy as Manis-Tusu in Mesopotamia, according to the Babylonian record in the Kish Chronicle, and we shall see in next chapter that the descendants of Manis-Tusu are identical with those of Menes in the First Dynasty of Egypt.

King KIN (*Sharru*-KIN or " Sargon "),
r. 55 yrs. in Agadu.

MANIŚI-TIŚŚU,[1] eldest son, r. 15 yrs. in Kish after brother Uri-Mush.	URI-MUSH, younger son, r. 15 (9?)[2] in Kish before k. Maniśi-Tiśśu.
NARĀM Lord ENZU (" Narām Sin ") son, r. 56 yrs. in Agadu.	
Shar-GANI-ERI, son, r. 24(?) yrs. in Agadu. [Anarchy]. (For continuation of Dynasty, see p. 61).	

[1] This is the dialectic variant spelling of this king's name by the Babylonian scribe of the Kish Chronicle.

[2] Fifteen years is given in Legrain's fragment, *loc. cit.*, No. 1, 7; and nine years in WB. 444.

Menes' or Manis-Tusu's Revolt against his Father "Sargon" *re* his Seizure of Egypt (?)

It will be noticed that although Manis-Tusu (spelt phonetically in this Kish Chronicle "Manisi-*Tissu*,") was the eldest son of King Kīn or "Sargon," he did not immediately succeed his father on the Mesopotamian throne; but the succession passed to his younger brother Mush or Uru-Mush, who reigned as emperor of Mesopotamia for 15 (or 9 ?) years, and claimed in his inscriptions to be King of the Upper Sea (Mediterranean) and of the Lower Sea (Persian Gulf and Indian Ocean)"[1] just as his father Sargon did, though that claim could be only partial as regards the Mediterranean. And Manis-Tusu did not gain the Mesopotamian throne until his brother's death in "a palace revolution," the real character of which is disclosed by the Indus seals as his dethronement by his brother Menes.

Of his brother Uru-Mush's rule in the Indus Valley colony of the Lower Sea, I have discovered evidence in one of his official seals in the second batch of seals unearthed there. This proves that he, like his father Sargon and his grandfather, held the rich Indus Colony as an appanage of the Sumerian empire. In this seal he calls himself "The One Lord," that is emperor. This seal (see Plate XVIII, No. 8) inscription I read as follows as detailed in Appendix IX:—

Reads: *Umun-ash lu-gal-uru uri-mush.*
Translation: The One Lord, The great hero, Uri-Mush.

The reason for Manis-Tusu's non-succession in Mesopotamia immediately on the death of his father Sargon, and not until the death of his younger brother Mush, we now find in the Indian Chronicle record regarding him. This, which is cited in detail below, states that he was disinherited by his father, owing to his having revolted against him. And this revolt now appears to have been his seizure of Egypt from his father, and his declaration of independence there as "Menes" King of Upper and Lower Egypt.

The Indian account of the revolt of the young prince Menes or Manis-Tusu against his father "Sargon" is thus

[1] PHT. 4, 200 f.

related in the solar version of the Indian Epic Chronicles, under his title of Asa-Manja, the eldest son of the world-monarch Sagara (*i.e.* "Sargon"). This record is in the somewhat expanded sacerdotal form it has been given by the later Brahman priests; it states[1]:—

"Asa-Manja—son of Sagara by his queen Keshinī[2]—the prince through whom the dynasty continued, was from his boyhood of very wayward[3] conduct. His father hoped that as he grew up to manhood he would reform; but finding that he continued addicted to the same habit Sagara abandoned him. The sixty thousand fed troops (?)[4] of Sargon followed the example of their 'brother' Asa-Manja. The path of virtue and piety was obscured in the world by the 'sons' of Sagara." [Here the narrative goes on to relate in diffuse Brahmanist fashion, that King Sagara, in order to remedy this disaster, commenced preparations for the victorious sacrifice for a world-monarch's conquests, presumably in anticipation of his recovery of the lost provinces. But this sacrifice did not materialize until his grandson's day. It was obstructed by "the world-monarch's" horse—a late Brahmanist sacrifice—being stolen. And for its recovery other loyal "sons" of Sagara had to dig in a chasm in the earth, where the "sons dug downwards each for a league," and were thereafter killed. The world-monarch's horse was eventually recovered only by Sargon's grandson in the person of *Ansu*-mat (*i.e.* Narām *Enzu*) the son of Manis-Tusu (or Menes) whom his grandfather Sagara adopted. And the chasm which Sagara's "sons" had dug was called "The Ocean" (Sagara).]

This is obviously a somewhat allegorical account of the successful revolt by prince Manis-Tusu (Manis-the-Warrior or Menes), against his father, and his retention of Egypt against the expeditions sent by his father; so that the complete "world-monarchship," including Egypt, was not

[1] WVP. 3, 298 f.

[2] Here Menes' mother, who in the lunar version is called Acchura Seni, is descriptively styled "The Fine Haired" (Keshinī), and is called "a daughter of King Vidarbha."

[3] *Apavritta*="gone out of the way, deport, turn away." MWD. 52.

[4] *Sagaraira padhvasta.* This is translated "Sagara's sons," by Wilson. WVP. 3, 298.

recovered until the accession of Sargon's grandson Narām Euzu, the son of Manis-Tusu, who we shall find succeeded his father, Menes, as second king of the First Dynasty in Egypt as "Narmar," and combined with it the imperial throne of Mesopotamia.

The digging operations referred to were, I venture to suggest, a memory of canals connected with the Mediterranean dug by Sargon's expeditionary force in the Suez Canal region in their attack on Menes' position in Upper Egypt, as the Sumerians were great experts in digging canals. And we have seen that Sargon, in his record of his attack on King Zaggisi, speaks of his canals for military purposes. At that early period the Gulf of Suez, arm of the Red Sea, probably extended up to the Bitter Lakes, and Lake Timsah to the site of the modern Ismailia, that is only about six miles from the Bala Lake, which is continuous with Lake Menzaleh, an old arm of the Mediterranean and presumably then the open sea of the Mediterranean, as geologists find that the the Red Sea extended to the Mediterranean in this line in former times. Thus the cutting of a relatively short canal might have connected it with the Mediterranean sufficiently for the galleys of these days. For Lower Egypt was presumably not originally under Menes; but had to be conquered by him later on, and probably continued to be held by Sargon's governors for a time.

What seems to be historical confirmation of Manis-Tusu's quarrel with his father, Sargon, is found in a record which states Manis-Tusu, King of Anshan (*i.e.* Persia), was deported as an enemy by King "Shar-Gani (?)-Sharri"[1]—for Shar-Gani or Sargon is often confounded with his great-grandson of the former name. And Sargon's son, Manis-Tusu, we shall find was King of Anshan as well as governor of the Indus Valley to its east in the reign of his father, Sargon, as attested by his own seals recently unearthed in the latter region, as deciphered below and numerous contemporary statues of him have been unearthed in Elam in S.W. Persia of which he was for a time governor and latterly emperor.

[1] Cp. KHS. 244.

MENES' PORTRAIT AS MANIS-TUSU OR "MANIS-THE-WARRIOR"

Amongst the many particulars now recovered of Menes and his personality, through his identification with Manis-Tusu, are his portraits as found on several of his statues that have been unearthed in Mesopotamia and Elam, from which latter province is the one shown in Pl. XB and Fig. 32. From the inscription engraved upon it, it was

FIG. 32.—Statue of King Manis-Tusu (or Menes) in alabaster from Susa in Elam and now in the Louvre. (After AIC. 1907, 398.)

erected by an official in the service of King Manis-Tusu during the latter's suzerainty over Elam.

This fine artistic statue in alabaster is sculptured in the round, and shows the king bearded and like his Sumerian or Aryan ancestor King Madgal (Fig. 19, p. 109), who was also governor and latterly King of Elam, which was a colony of the Sumerian Empire along with the Indus Valley Colony, as we have seen, in his day—the shaven face was obviously adopted for sacerdotal purposes under the *ex-officio* priest-kingship. And it is noticeable that his upper lip is shaven, a Sumerian and Ancient Hittite custom (see Plate III) which distinguishes those from the Semites who wore a moustache as well as beard.

The staring effect of the eyes is owing to the eyeballs having been made of white limestone inset into the eye-sockets of the alabaster image, and to the inlaid iris and pupil being lost. The iris was probably of inlaid lapis lazuli stone, as is found in other similarly inlaid eyes, to represent the blue eyes of the Nordic or Aryan race.

Menes as Manis-Tusu in Mesopotamia, Elam, Persia & Indus Valley

The reign of Menes in Mesopotamia as well as in Egypt is implied by the record in the Indian Epics that Manasyu was "the royal Eye of Gopta *and of the four ends of the Earth*," as already cited; though in none of his Mesopotamian inscriptions yet found does he call himself like his father and like his son a "world-monarch."

The actually existing contemporary records of Manis-Tusu in Mesopotamia, Elam, and Persia date only from the period in which he gained the Emperorship as "King of Kish" there, in succession to his younger brother Mūsh or Uri-Mūsh. And Manis-Tusu, as "King of Kish," was amongst the earliest recovered names of a king bearing that imperial Mesopotamian title, and as a Sun-worshipper. But in the Indus Valley I have discovered his seals there as crown prince governor of that colony before his attainment of kingship as detailed below, and see Plates X and XI.

Most of his original inscriptions in Mesopotamia are characteristically carved on the extremely hard mineral called diorite, a stone not found in Mesopotamia and brought there by sea, as we shall find, from the north of the Red Sea *via* the Arabian Sea and Persian Gulf. Others are inscribed on votive vases and on a stone-mace-head, on a cruciform monument, and on the famous Black Obelisk, while others are certified copies in the old Sun-temple at Nippur.

The most historically important of these inscriptions is that of which many multiple copies, more or less fragmentary, exist in which he records as "King of Kish" his vast campaign of reconquests of revolted colonies to the east of Mesopotamia, in Persia, the Indus Valley and across the Indian Ocean or Arabian Sea, through the Red Sea to the Sinai Peninsula on the borders of Egypt, as now definitely established for the first time in these pages. This campaign occurred after he became King of Kish, that is after his gaining the imperial throne of Mesopotamia on the death of his younger brother; and we shall find that it was a reconquest of revolted colonies of his father's, Sargon's, empire. Before examining this record of his vast reconquests with the important geographical information they contain of the extent of his empire, it is necessary here to refer to my discovery of his official seals in the Indus Valley.

Official Seals of Menes or Manis-Tusu discovered in the Indus Valley disclosing him as Crown Prince Governor there, as Son of "Sargon" with title of "Pharaoh"

Startling concrete confirmation of all the foregoing identifications of Menes, Egyptian, Babylonian, and Indian, now emerges, fortunately for History, in my *discovery of no less than nine official seals of Menes in the Indus Colony in the second batch of seals unearthed there, and in several of these he already bears the title of "Bara" or "Pharaoh" and "Aha Men."*

In my pioneer decipherment of the first batch of the Indus Valley seals, I supplied for the first time the key to the signs of these seals in that linear variety of Sumerian writing hitherto undeciphered. With those keys to the script, I experienced little difficulty in deciphering the freshly-found seals.

The previous Indus Valley seals disclosed that it was a custom of the Mesopotamian emperors to send the crown prince for a time as governor of that rich and favourite crown colony on the Indus.[1] The new seals, which included others of Sargon and other Mesopotamian emperors, show that Sargon also followed this practice.

1 WISD. 35 f., 55 f.

The Title of "Under-King Companion" or Viceroy in the Indus Colony Seals

Striking confirmation of my observation, in my *Indo-Sumerian Seals Deciphered*, that it was the custom for the Sumerian emperors of Mesopotamia to send their eldest son as Viceroy to the Indus Colony of Edin is now found in the second batch of seals unearthed there, and now deciphered for the first time.

Whilst the names on many of these fresh seals are those of the crown princes of Mesopotamia of Sargon's dynasty who latterly became emperors, the title which these bear in many of their seals is not "king" or "emperor," but "Under-King Companion," in the form of *Shag-man*, *Shab-man*, or *Sha-man*.

The first element in this title, namely, *Shag*, *Shab* or *Sha*, is very interesting. Its pictograph (see initial sign in Plate XI, Nos. 1, 3 and 7) represents and means "Heart"; and its secondary meaning is "interior, midst, within," and also "below, lower, under";[1] and it is, in the latter sense, the usual sign employed to designate the Persian Gulf and Indian Ocean as "The Lower Sea." Hence the meaning of the full title might be "King-Companion of the Persian Gulf and Indian Ocean." The second syllable *Man* literally means "Two, Second, or Companion," and also "King";[2] and it is significant that it is formed by two short straight strokes like those in the first batch of Indus seals which I deciphered, and not written by its usual crescent form as in ordinary Mesopotamian writing. This title of *Shag-man* thus means literally "The Under-King Companion," which is the equivalent of our modern "Viceroy."

Most of the crown princes of Sargon's or Menes' dynasty in their Indus seals carry this title on some of their seals, thus indicating those seals as belonging to the period of their governorship or viceroyship of the Edin colony. Whilst others of their seals bear the title of "Lord Companion," in which the sign for this "Lord" has the sense of "Emperor," and thus implies a more advanced rank, presumably corresponding to "Co-Regent." And others of their seals in

[1] Br. 7988 f. [2] Br. 9952 f.

INDUS VALLEY SEALS OF PHARAOH MENES AND HIS SON NARMAR OR NARAM.

(Photographs after Sir J. Marshall.) For decipherments and translations, see pp. 265 f., 555 f.

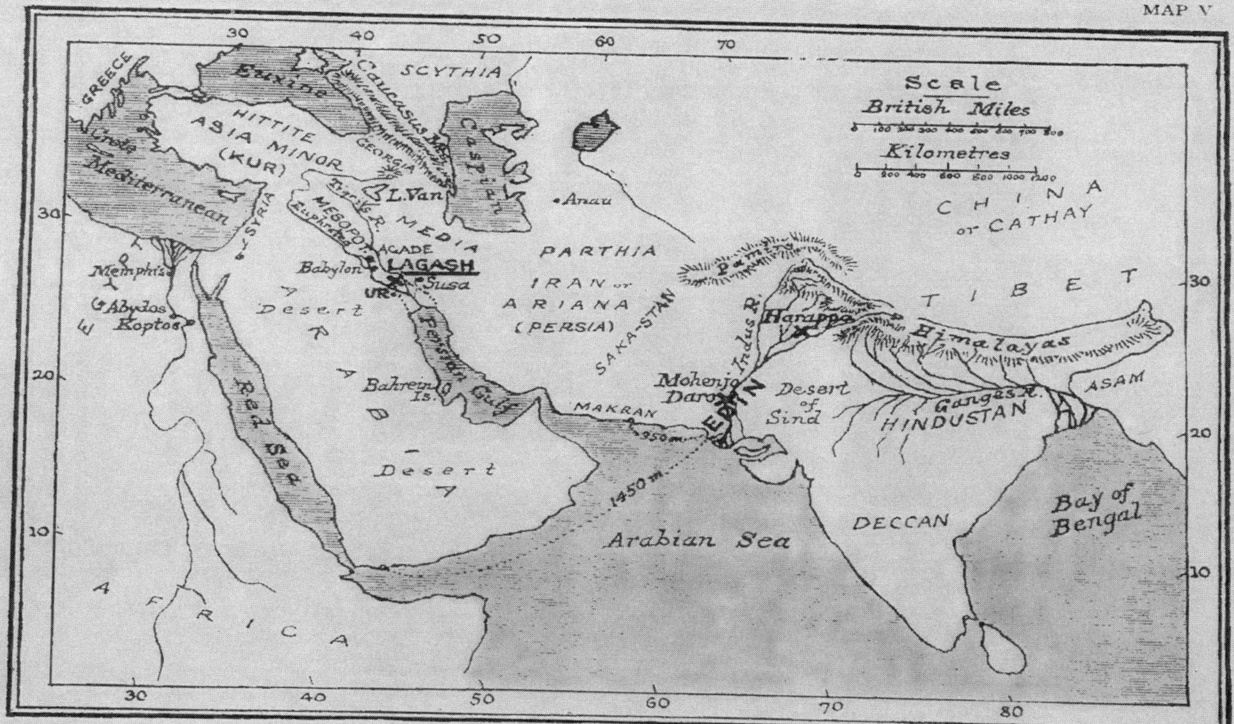

RELATION OF INDUS VALLEY COLONY TO MESOPOTAMIA AND EGYPT

L.A.W del.

which they are called "The One Lord," belong to their period of emperorship.

Menes' Indus Valley Seals Deciphered

The nine seals of Menes or Manis thus discovered in the Indus Valley are figured in Plate X, No. 10, and Plate XI, Nos. 1–8.

In these new Indus seals here deciphered, Menes or Manis calls himself by his names and titles variously spelt as *Men*, *Ash-Mānshu*, *Aha* or *Akha* and *Aha* (or *Akha*) *Men*. And while styling himself *Bara* or "Pharaoh" and son of *Shar-Gin* or *Sara-Gin* (*i.e.* "Sargon"), he also significantly spells the latter name as *Shagāni* or *Shakunu*, thus using substantially the dialectic form of the Indian epics *Shakuni*, a form which is also used in Menes' ebony label at Abydos as we shall see. *Aha* we have seen has in the Sumerian the meaning of "Warrior," just as *Tussu* has, and thus confirms the identification of Menes or Aha Men with Manis Tussu of Mesopotamia. And his title of *Gut* or "Goth," like that of his father Sargon, in his Indus seals is noteworthy.

These Indus seals of Manis, Menes or Aha Men, the detailed decipherment of which is given in Appendix IX, are here enumerated in the order in which they are figured in Plates X and XI, for convenience of reference.

Plate X, No. 10 Seal (Fig. 86).

Reads : *Umun-man a-ha mar sha-ga-ni bara gu-edin-ash.*

Transl. : Lord Companion Aha, the son of Shagani, The Pharaoh at Edin Land.

Plate XI, No. 1 Seal (Fig. 87).

Reads : *Shag-man ma-anshu bara gu-edin* (or *ag-du*)*-ash.*

Transl. : Under-King Companion Mānshu, The Pharaoh at Edin (or Agdu) Land.

No. 2 Seal (Fig. 88).

Reads : *Umun-man a-ha-men . . . gu- . . .*

Transl. : Lord Companion Aha-Men . . . at . . .

No. 3 Seal.

Reads: *Shag-man a-ha-(?)men gut gu-ag-du-ash.*
Transl.: Under-King Companion Aha-(?) Men, The *Gut* (or "Goth") at Agdu Land.

No. 4 Seal.

Reads: *Umun-ash a-ha mar gut gin gu-ag-du-ash.*
Transl.: The One Lord Aha, son of the *Gut* Gin, at Agdu Land.

No. 5 Seal.

Reads: *Umun-man a-ha-(?)man mar(?)azu (ma)-esh-tar Gin.*
Transl.: Lord Companion Aha-(?)Man, son of the Priest-Seer Esh-tar Gin. (On "Seer" table cp. p. 227).

No. 6 Seal.

Reads: *A-ha sig uku mush.*
Transl.: Aha, The Overthrower of King Mush.

No. 7.

Reads: *Shag-man Aha ma-(es)-gan-mush.*
Transl.: Under-King-Companion Aha of Mā-(es)gan and Mush (-sir) [Egypt].

No. 8.

Reads: *A-ha men-a gu uri-du-ash.*
Transl.: Aha Mena at Uriki Land.

The place-name on the smaller seals does not always clearly differentiate the name Edin from the very similar pictograph of Agdu, or "Agudu."

Evidence of Indus Seals on Identity of Menes & Manis-Tusu & his Governorship of Indus Colony

This critically important historical series of official Indus seals of Manis-Tusu, the son of Sargon-the-Great, whilst disclosing his hitherto unknown governorship of the Indus Colony of his father's vast empire, as crown prince, and also as emperor and with the title of Pharaoh in his own seals, confirms absolutely his identity with Pharaoh Men, or Aha Men, the first king and founder of the First Dynasty of Egypt. These seals also confirm his identity with the Aryan world-emperor Manasyu or Asa-Manja, the son of the world-emperor Shakuni of the Indian Lists; and disclose original Sumerian variants in the spelling of "Sargon's" name in series with the phonetic forms of spelling current in the Indian Lists and in Egypt. And the free use of the title *Bara*, *Para* or "Pharaoh" on these seals evidences the free intercommunication of the Indus Valley with Egypt in his reign.

MENES' OR MANIS-TUSU'S CONQUESTS IN PERSIA, INDUS VALLEY, ARABIAN SEA-LANDS & *via* RED SEA TO SINAI PENINSULA

From the vast extent of his victorious conquests, as recorded in his own records, we can now see how Manis-Tusu or Menes earned his title of "Menes-the-Warrior."

There are several instances of Manis-Tusu having crossed the Persian Gulf or Indian Ocean to the Arabian coast with a victorious army;[1] but his greatest expedition there was his reconquest of the lost provinces stretching along the Arabian coast and Red Sea to Sinai.

The fullest text of this inscription is preserved in a series of certified copies set up in the old Sun-temple at Nippur, which are found to be in literal agreement with the texts of his campaign records on his original monuments, as far as the existing fragments of the latter go. One of his original diorite inscribed monuments with the critical paragraph about his defeat of the thirty-two kings actually exists. The fullest text reads as follows[2]:—

"Manish Tusu, King of Kish City, when Anshan [Persia] and Shu-Edin-hum ["The Garden of Edin, the Fruitful" =Indus Valley] he had smitten, the Lower Sea [Persian Gulf and Arabian Sea] in ships he (crossed). Thirty-two kings of cities on the other side of the sea had rallied to battle and he defeated them, and their cities he smote, (and) their lords he cast down, and the whole country . . . as far as the Silver Mines he destroyed. The mountains beyond the sea, their (diorite) stones he broke and his statue he fashioned, and to Lord Sakh he dedicated it. The Sun-

[1] PHT. iv. 238.

[2] Text and translation in PHT. iv. 205 f. His transliteration of *Shirihum*, I have already proved in Chapter X, reads *Shu-Edin-hum*, or "Garden of Edin, the Fruitful."

god and Zagaga. . . . Who shall destroy this inscription, may Lord Sakh and the Sun-god tear out his foundations and destroy his seed."

This critical record by Manis-Tusu of his crossing the Arabian Sea in ships with his great armies after his reconquest of the Indus Valley and his conquest on the Arabian side of thirty-two confederate kings, and his advance to a country of Silver Mines, the name of which is lost, and to "the mountain *beyond the sea*" of the diorite rocks, which we shall find is Magan, in the Sinai Peninsula at the head of the Red Sea, which was afterwards regularly reached by ship from Mesopotamia, is all of immense historical importance with reference to the Red Sea route by which Menes reached Upper Egypt with his metal-armed warriors and Sumerian civilization.

We observe that this expedition took place after Manis-Tusu, who repeatedly calls himself in other inscriptions "The Smiter of Elam," had conquered (or reconquered) Anshan (that is as admitted by the best authorities, Persis, the old central province of Persia) immediately to the east of Elam, and after he had conquered (or reconquered) The Garden of Edin Sumerian colony in the Indus Valley. See Maps I and III.

This great conquest of the thirty-two confederate kings on the Arabian coast-land was esteemed by Manis-Tusu so important an achievement that he records it in identical words in the monuments he set up in the chief cities and temples all over Mesopotamia. The expedition, we are informed on his Cruciform Monument—symbolic of the Sun-Cross of which he was a worshipper—took place "when all the lands . . . revolted against me." It was thus a *reconquest* of the lands within his father's empire.

For the Arabian and Red Sea portion of the campaign, he probably marched his victorious army, after recovering the Indus Valley colony, westwards from the Indus Valley along the coast of Baluchistan and Mekran to the narrow Straits of Oman or Ormuz, just as Alexander-the-Great, over two millenniums later, in returning from his inglorious adventure in India from the Indus to Persepolis, marched his troops along the shore with his fleet under Nearchus in the offing, past the Straits of Oman to Persis or Anshan, or Persepolis with its beautiful palaces which he destroyed.

His point of crossing the Lower or Arabian Sea was probably effected at the Straits of Oman, where on the peninsula the first pitched battle with the confederate kings was likely to be fought, and with his fleet he could attack them in the rear, in a battle which, judging from the great number of kings engaged, must have been one of the greatest in the old world.

The number of the hostile confederate kings and their cities which he "smote," thirty-two, implies the conquest of a vast stretch of the Arabian coast, which is so sparsely peopled and the towns are almost entirely located on the coast and at great distances apart. The statement that he reached the diorite mountains "beyond the sea," *i.e.*, beyond the Red Sea arm of the Lower Sea or Arabian Sea absolutely identifies the limit reached by his expedition with Magan which we shall find was at the base of the Sinai Peninsula in the neighbourhood of Suez. It is thus indicated that he voyaged from the Indus Valley and Persia through the Arabian Sea and the Red Sea to Sinai on the borders of Lower Egypt to the east of Suez.

Magan, the Land reconquered by Manis-Tusu, a Name for the Sinai Peninsula

Magan,[1] the famous sea-port of the mountainous country whence the Sumerians obtained by sea their diorite blocks for statues, is located by Assyriologists in the Sinai Peninsula at the head of the Red Sea.[2] And we shall find by the inscription of Pharaoh Narmar, now deciphered for the first time in next chapter, that it was on the borders of Lower Egypt. It was so very distant from Mesopotamia by sea that King Gudia, about four centuries after Manis-Tusu, records that the voyage took *a whole year* to and from Magan to bring back diorite blocks and precious woods and stones to the sea-port of Lagash in Mesopotamia, by way of the Persian Gulf.[3] And we shall find that it is repeatedly referred

[1] The name by its Sumerian signs means "Receptacle of Ships," implying that its chief town or city had a harbour.

[2] MD. 538.

[3] On products of Magan, Br. 3692 f.; and MD. 886, 537 f.

to along with Egypt in the Indus seals of the descendants of Manis or Menes, cited below.

Manis-Tusu & Egypt in Mesopotamian Literature *re* "Khamasi" Land & "Kham" or "Ham"

In none of the existing inscriptions of Manis-Tusu in Mesopotamia, nor in those of his dynasty, nor in those of the later Sumerian king Gudia, is there any reference to Egypt by its usual Babylonian name of *Misri* or *Musri*,[1] the equivalent of its modern Egyptian and Arabic name of *Misr*. Nor does it appear to be mentioned by them as *Pu*, nor does Manis-Tusu mention *Iatu* ("Dilmun") Land in his existing inscriptions in Babylonia. It is possible that his omission to mention Egypt by name, if it be not the missing name in all the copies of his victory inscriptions, may have been owing to his having for so long held the Land of the Nile outside of, and independently of, the Mesopotamian empire as his personal possession, that he wished his favourite land to continue so; or that it probably remained faithful to him when all the other lands revolted. But we have seen that Sargon in one of his Indus seals (No. 8) called himself "The Ruler of *Khamaesshi* Land, which we shall find was a title of Egypt, and several of his descendants in their Indus seals mention Egypt as their land, as seen below.

What now seems to be a Babylonian reference to Manis-Tusu in Egypt we find in the Old Sumerian King-List wrongly prefixed by the Isin priests to the Kish Chronicle, in which we have an old version of Sargon's Dynasty as Kings of Kish (see Table facing p. 140 and App. III). In this the succession is recorded as here shown on the left, and on the right are placed their usual titles for identification :—

1. Ganni-*Pur* (or *Pir*), the horizon-quartering = King *Ganni, Kīn*, or "Sargon."
2. Mu, in whose r. Kish was smitten by weapons = *Mush or Uru-Mush*, s. of 1.
3. Ha-(?)Manīsh or "*Danīsh*" of *Khama-si* Land = *Aha Manj* or *Manis-Tusu*, s. of 1.
4. Nerra-*En* or Enugge = *Narām Enzu*, s. of 3.

[1] Its name as *Misri* and *Misir* occurs in the Amarna Letters of about 1400 B.C.

In this Old Sumerian King-List, the Isin scribe writes the name of the third king, that is the King of *Khama-si* Land who succeeded Sargon's son Mu (whose reign was ended by "Kish was smitten by weapons" just as we know that Sargon's son Mush's reign ended by his being killed at Kish in a revolution, and the overthrow of Mush is disclosed by the Indus seal to have been by Menes Aha) as "Ha-Da-ni-ish." But this second sign *Da* very closely resembles the ship-sign *Ma;* and as this king in question occupies the identical position of Manis-Tusu or Manish-Tusu in all the other lists of the same dynasty, it is certain that he was Manish-Tusu, and that the Isin scribe mistook *Ma* for *Da;* and that the real name on the Old Sumerian List which he copied was *Manish.* The corruption of this entry is also evident from the prefixed title written *Ha* by the scribe, instead of *Aha,* which we have seen is the synonym of Tusu or "Warrior," and the prefixed *Aha* title used by Menes in both his Egyptian and Indus inscriptions. And we have seen that this scribe wrote King *Mu* for "King *Mush,*" presumably through carelessness.

This Old Sumerian List records that after "Kish was smitten by weapons," at the end of the reign of King Mu(sh), "the kingship passed to *Khama-si* or *Hama-si* City-Land," where King Ha-Danish, properly *Aha-Manish,* reigned.

This Land[1] of *Khama-si* or *Hama-si* is clearly not the *Khmazi* City-Land of Udu's Bowl, which I have shown was an ancient title of Carchemish or Kar-Khamish or "Fort-Khamish," and which never was a capital of the Sumerian or Babylonian kings of Mesopotamia.

On the other hand, it appears to be the Land of *Kham* or *Ham,* the oldest traditional name for Egypt, and a usual name for that land and its people in the Hebrew Old Testament, where the Phœnicians are called "Sons of Ham"; and Sargon and his son Menes we have seen were direct descendants of the First Phœnician Dynasty. The Greeks called Egypt sometimes *Khemia* or *Khīmia.*[2]

Now this *Khama-si* Land is obviously the *Khama-esshi* Land, of which Sargon claims to be "The Ruler" in the

[1] *Ki*="Land." Br. 9636.

[2] Plutarch, *De Iside et Osiride,* 33.

aforesaid Indus seal; and we shall find that the latter land is repeatedly mentioned in the Indus seals of the later members of Sargon's dynasty, and is several times used alternately with Egypt or *Mush-sir* and *Pu* (or Buto).

In the name *Khama-si*, the affix *si* is defined in the bilingual glossaries as (*a*) dialectic for *shar*, great, luxuriant, fat [1]—suggestive of "the flesh-pots of Egypt," and also (*b*) as "bile," perhaps in series with the later traditional Egyptian explanation of the old name of Egypt as *Kami*(*-t*) or *Kam* [2] meaning "dark-coloured or black" in allusion to the darkish colour of its soil, and it is spelt with the Crocodile hieroglyph *Kam*.[3]

Moreover, the country to the west of Mesopotamia across the Arabian desert, *i.e.*, in the direction of Egypt, is called by the later Sumerians and Babylonians *Kimash*, a land from which couriers came overland with merchandise, including sesame oil, to the capital of Dungi at Lagash, and from the mountains of which Gudea obtained copper. It seems to be a later phonetic spelling of this name for Egypt. The country of Kimash is placed by Assyriologists "to the west of Babylonia," [4] and there is no inhabited country west of Babylonia until Sinai and Egypt.

Altogether the identity of *Khamasi* and *Khamaesshi* and *Kimash* Land with Egypt seems now clear.

Menes *re* Manis-Tusu as Sun-worshipper

Menes was essentially a Sun-worshipper, as evidenced by his inscriptions in Egypt. Manis-Tusu likewise was significantly an ardent Sun-worshipper, like his father Sargon, who we have seen regularly invoked the Sun-god and called himself in his Egyptian inscription an "Ukussi" or descendant of Ukusi of the city of the Sun-Hawk, the first Sumerian king.

One of Manis-Tusu's best-known monuments is his massive Cruciform Monument dedicated to the Sun-god at the Sun-temple of Sippar, and its form symbolizes the Sun-Cross.

[1] Br. 4198. [2] BD. 1044-5. Also spelt *Qam*, 770-1.

[3] BD. 787 b. It is also significant that the Crocodile is called in Egyptian *Khams* or *Khems*, BD. 485 b.

[4] PB. 11. There it is stated S.W., but Prof. Pinches informs me "it should be in all probability west."

Its twelve sides are inscribed with long texts recording his conquest of Anshan (Persia), "when all the lands . . . . revolted against me," and in which his gifts to the Sun-god and his temple are detailed, including choice Date fruits—a simple fruit-offering which recalls that of his famous ancestor "Cain," the son of King Ukusi or "Adam," who incurred the wrath of the Semitic god for not offering the sanguinary Chaldean sacrifices, as did his "brother" Abel. In his inscriptions also in the Sun-temple at Nippur Manis invokes the Sun-god along with King Sakh, Zagg or Zagaga, who we have seen was his deified ancestor Ukusi of the city of the Sun-Hawk. And on the back of the great ebony label in Menes' tomb is painted with red pigment a Sun-Cross like a pedestalled Red Cross of St George.

As an Aryan Sun-worshipper, Menes or Manis appears to be the king called in the Indian Vedic psalms *Manasa* or *Mayin* (*i.e.*, Menes or Men) who invoked the Sun and the Sun-Hawk, and significantly for "boons abiding in the Sea." He is associated with *Yayati* and *Evāvada*, apparently his descendants, who may represent *Ata* or *Zetata* and *Ousaphaidos*, the third to fifth kings of the First Dynasty of Egypt in Manetho's list (see p. 298). And it is noteworthy that Manasa bears the title of *Khattiyo*, that is, as we have seen, a title for "ruler," and which as *Kat* or *Kad* is borne by Sargon and the 1st Dynasty Pharaohs in their tomb inscriptions (see later). This Vedic hymn, which was evidently composed in the fierce heat of a torrid clime, such as Egypt is in the hot season, from its appeal for a "heat-sheltered house," joyously says[1] :—

> "O Sun! sage One, free as the unwedded hero, in love of battle moving o'er the foes. . . .
> Self-excellent, grant us a sheltering home, a house that wards off fierce heat!
> Thy Name sung forth by bards soars up to Thee, the loftiest One, with this swift-moving (Fire-offering's) flight.
> One (by thy Name) wins the boon his heart is set on: He who bestirs himself (by thy Name) shall bring the thing to pass.

[1] RV. 5, 44, 7-10. Translation based upon Griffith's.

The chief best (boon) abideth in the Sea, nor does (thy) long libation ever fail (to win it).
The heart of him who praiseth (Thee) trembles not in fear, when his hymn is sung by the pure (in heart).
This (singer) is he with thoughts of the *Khattiyo*[1] MANASA, of YAYATI and *Sadhri* and EVAVADA:
This priest Avatsāra's sweet songs strive to win for us the mightiest strength known.
The (Sun-) Hawk, girth-stretching, is the full source of (the prayed-for boons) as by the libations of the all-bestowing MAYIN and YAYATI.
Sadā-Prina the holy, Tarya, Sruta-vit and Bahu-Vrikta joined with you have slain their foes."

This identity in his Sun-worship, Egyptian, Mesopotamian, and Indo-Aryan, forges, therefore, another link in the chain of the personal identity of Menes with the Sumerian or Aryan emperor Manis-the-Warrior of Mesopotamia.

MANIS-TUSU OR MENES AS A FREE CONSTITUTIONAL RULER & LAW-GIVER

One of the most interesting and important of the monuments left by King Manis-Tusu is his famous "Black Obelisk," so-called from its black diorite stone. It was discovered by M. de Morgan in 1897 in the French excavations at Susa, the capital of the Elam province of the Sumerians in south-west Persia, where it had been carried off as booty, presumably from Kish, in a raid by a revolted king of Elam of later date, who has endorsed it accordingly and it is now treasured in the Louvre Museum.

Its record[2] is a striking illustration of the very advanced free constitutional government which King Manis-Tusu administered; and discloses him as a most enlightened ruler and respecter of the free institutions and rights of private citizens, and quite on a par with our most "modern" times, although about forty-six centuries ago. The text occupies sixty-nine closely-written columns, and records the purchase of several large estates in the neighbourhood of

[1] This old Indian Pali name here, is Sanskritized as usual in the modern Vedic MSS. into *Kshatra*.

[2] STS. 1, 1 f.; and for Summary, KHS. 206 f.

Kish City, his capital, which he required for his official buildings and settlements for his officials and for the estate of his son, wherein, instead of confiscating the necessary land and buildings already occupied, he purchased it legally at its full market-value, by shekels of money, with in addition lavish gifts and payments for the goodwill of the tradesmen and others who were dispossessed, *just as if he were a mere private citizen himself.* The precise area of each estate, as accurately measured, with their defined boundaries, is given, and its value then reckoned in standard measures of grain and afterwards converted into its equivalent in silver: one *bur* of land being reckoned as worth sixty *gur* measures of grain, and one *mana* of silver.[1] An addition of one-tenth the purchase price was paid to the owner or joint-owners of each estate, who also received from the king presents of cattle, garments, vessels, etc., varying in value according to the rank of each recipient and his share in the property. And all the names of the sellers, with their addresses, as well as their receipts with the names and addresses of the witnesses, are all duly recorded. And the names and duties are detailed of the forty-nine government overseers entrusted with the administration and cultivation of the lands thus purchased by King Manis-Tusu or Menes.

Route of Manis-Tusu, Asa Manja or Menes in his Seizure of Upper Egypt, c. 2703 b.c.

We have seen from the Indian Chronicles that King Manis-Tusu as the crown-prince Asa-Manja revolted from his father Sargon, in his early manhood; and this tradition, along with the historical evidence we have gained regarding him, appears to provide material for reconstructing the outline of the lost chapter on his mode of seizing Upper Egypt and the route by which he effected it.

As crown prince of the Sumerian empire, Manis, as we have found, was governor of the Indus Valley colony of that empire.[2] As such, he would have control of the local Sumerian army of occupation in the Indus Valley and of the great merchant-fleet plying between there and the

[1] *Mana* in Sanskrit in Vedas is "golden," MKI. 2, 128.

[2] WISD. 35 f., 55 f.

port of Lagash (for the type of ship in this, Menes' period, see illustrations on the ivory labels from Menes' tomb (Fig. 35, p. 283)). This fleet [1] also presumably voyaged to Magan and Egypt *via* the Arabian coast-ports and the Red Sea, as is implied not only in his father Sargon's title of "King of all the Lands of the Lower Sea," but also by Manis-Tusu's own record that the thirty-two kings of this coast-land up to Magan or Sinai had "revolted," thus implying that they had been under the suzerainty of the Sumerian empire; and Menes, as well as his father, use of the title "Pharaoh" on their Indus seals.

The Indian Chronicles record that 60,000 of "the fed sons" of the emperor Sagara (Sargon) followed the crown-prince in his revolt, which is evidently a memory of the great number of Sargon's military and naval forces which flocked to the standard of their young master, Menes, in his great adventure in a more temperate and attractive clime. With such resources, it would be comparatively easy for Manis or Menes, proceeding *via* the Red Sea, to carve out and hold a kingdom in Upper Egypt, and ultimately over-power the local governors of Sargon in Lower Egypt, which was so very remote by the land route from Mesopotamia, while Sargon was deprived of his Lower Sea fleet. For it was clearly by the Red Sea route that Manis-the-Warrior, the Aryan King Manasyu, with his metal-using warriors, arrived in Egypt to become "The *Prabhu* (or Pharaoh), the Royal Eye of Gopta," as Menes, the founder of the First Dynasty in Egypt.

Egyptologists are generally agreed that Menes must have entered Upper Egypt by the Red Sea, somewhere to the east of Koptos and Abydos, at which latter place is his "tomb" with his inscriptions. And at Koptos exist the oldest known statues of a god in Egypt, indicating the Red Sea route of their erectors. "The oldest statues of gods (in Egypt) are three gigantic limestone figures of Min at

[1] There is no record of the number of ships or size of ships used by Menes. The form of the ships is seen in the hieroglyphs of his ebony-label tomb inscription. In the Third Dynasty King Snefru sent a fleet of forty ships to a Syrian port for cedar wood, and the length of one of these was no less than 170 feet. Baikie, p. 146.

Koptos; these bear designs of Red Sea shells and swordfish. . . . His worship continued down to the Roman period."[1] This god "Min" would now appear to be either the deified Menes himself or more probably *Min* or *Man*, the twin Sun-gods of the Sumerians, Aryans and Phœnicians.[2]

Koptos was an ancient trade-mart town of immemorial antiquity, to which converged the old caravan routes from the Red Sea, Sudan and Lower Egypt. And its Red Sea seaport was Kosseir (see map), which thus seems to have been the probable port of debarkation of Menes and his Sumerian invading army.

The "Predynastic" kings of Egypt, prior to Menes, are said by Egyptologists to have been all confined to Lower Egypt;[3] though we have found that Sargon's father, as well as himself and his grandfather, as predynastic kings had their tombs at Abydos in Upper Egypt—a more fitting and congenial resting-place for Aryans or Nordics than the Delta. Thus Menes would probably meet with comparatively little resistance in establishing himself at Koptos, whence he proceeded to annex the more populous and richer Delta, *i.e.*, Lower Egypt; and it is as "The uniter of the two crowns of Upper and Lower Egypt" that he comes down to us in Egyptian history. And his name *Manasyu* in the Indian records means "Manas-the-uniter."

Menes' Establishment of Sumerian or Aryan Civilization in Egypt

Menes, the first independent king of United Egypt, is the traditional introducer and establisher of Civilization in Ancient Egypt; though we have seen that his father, Sargon, and his grandfather and great-grandfather were also predynastic Pharaohs, and thus possessed the same civilization. What Menes appears to have done was to vastly increase the elements of sporadic Sumerian civilization introduced by his father and other predynastic kings, and to have established it firmly for the first time.

Significantly, the Civilization that he brought with him

[1] PHE. 1, 3.

[2] WPOB. 242 f.; and WISD. 51, 89. *Manu* in Indian legend was son of the Sun-god.

[3] PHE. 1, 4.

and established in Egypt is now seen to be of the same general kind as the Sumerian of the Sargonic period in Mesopotamia and in the Indus Valley. His culture, with its metal industries, irrigation by canals for agriculture, pottery [1] and art, alabaster bowls, cylinder seals for sealing on clay, votive ceremonial stone mace-heads, form of tombs, Sun-worship and writing in Sumerian script and in the Sumerian language soon becoming modified by the introduction of aboriginal Semitic idioms and by a local neo-archaism in forming the Sumerian pictographs resulting in the standard stereotyped " Egyptian " hieroglyphs, yet retaining the same phonetic sounds and meanings—all betrays unequivocally its Sumerian or Aryan origin.

The Aryan race also of Menes and his dynasty and dynastic ruling people is evidenced by their physical type on their monuments and in their skeletons unearthed from their tombs. This reveals them to be of the Aryan type, tall, long-headed, with relatively broad brows and large brains, straight bridge to the nose and of a very vigorous type of face.

Date of Menes' Invasion of Egypt, about 2704 B.C.

The approximate date for Menes' invasion of Egypt, as evidenced by the newly-found synchronism with the Sargonic epoch in Mesopotamia, and detailed in the Chapter on Chronology, is about 2704 B.C. This indicates from the chronology of Sargon's dynasty preserved in the Kish Chronicle that Manis' or Menes' occupation of the throne in Upper Egypt took place about the twentieth year of the reign of Sargon, when Prince Manis was about twenty-one years of age ; and that he continued to hold Egypt as an independent king, outside the Mesopotamian empire, during the remaining thirty-five years of his father Sargon's reign in Mesopotamia, and continued to do so during the fifteen years of the reign of his younger brother Mush in Mesopotamia, whereafter he himself gained the imperial crown of the latter on the death of his younger brother, the emperor Mush, in a " revolution," which is now seen to have been the result of Manis-Tusu's seizure of the Mesopotamian crown.

[1] Pottery of a " Syrian " type is found in the First Dynasty.

Menes' Inscriptions in Egypt in Sumerian Language & in Sumerian Writing

Further striking evidence of the identity of Menes with the Sumerian emperor Manis-the-Warrior of Mesopotamia emerged in the facts, that, as now disclosed, the inscriptions of Menes at Abydos are in Sumerian writing of the Sargonic period and in the Sumerian language; and similarly so are the inscriptions of the rest of his First Egyptian Dynasty, all of which have hitherto remained undeciphered except for the royal names, most of which also have not been correctly read.

In Egypt several inscriptions of Menes have been found by Sir F. Petrie at Menes' "tomb" at Abydos, engraved on ebony and ivory labels, stone vases, on a gold bar from his treasury, and on clay sealings (reading towards the right), which latter

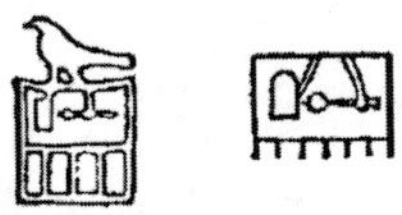

Fig. 33.—Menes' Title of *Aha* (or *Akha*) in Egypt. (After Sir F. Petrie.)

were also found along with an ivory label at Nagada.[1] Most of these inscriptions are merely his solar or "Horus" name of *Aha* (or *Akha*), which is pictured by a pair of hands holding respectively a shield and stone-mace, as seen in Fig. 33. And I have shown that this *Aha* hieroglyph with its phonetic value and meaning of Warrior are derived from the Sumerian.[2] Significantly cup-mark inscriptions are also found there (Pl. XII 4), as in Ancient Britain and Troy.

The largest and longest inscriptions of Menes in Egypt are engraved on the ebony and ivory labels found at Abydos, of which three of the smaller are shown in Plate XII, and the largest in Plate XIII (in duplicate). All of these, with the exception of the smaller ivory label deciphered below, are funereal and now prove to relate to the circumstances of his tragic death as we shall see later on. This small ivory label is of critical historical importance, as in it he uses his title of *Tusu* in Egypt, instead of the usual *Aha*.

[1] PHE. I, 13. [2] WSAD. Pl. I. 9 f.

MENES OR AHA MEN CALLED TUSU MENNA IN ONE OF HIS ABYDOS INSCRIPTIONS

This ivory label of Aha Mena (No. 1, Plate XII) was obtained from the tomb supposed to be that of Narmer[1] (who, we shall find, was Narām, the son of Manis Tusu) the adjoining tomb next but one to that of Aha, which latter had been early rifled and its inscribed objects strewn around near the old surface level, whilst others of Menes' inscribed objects were found in the adjoining tombs of his family.

This small label measuring 2¼ inches in length, and like the other labels pierced by a hole towards its top right

Egyptian

Sumer. Mesop.

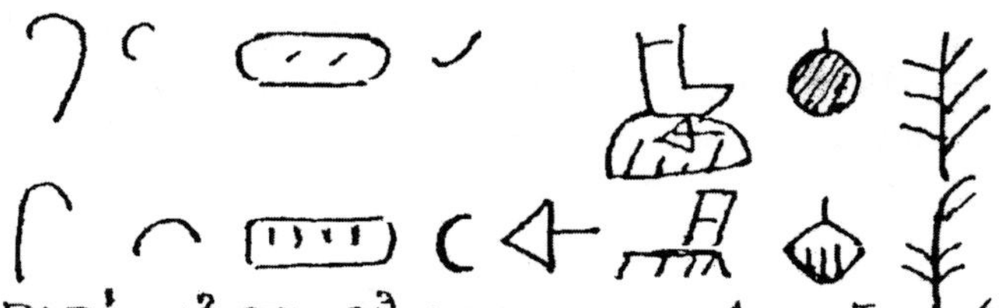

Reads: PAR[1]-U[2] TUS[3]-U-MEN[4]-NA[5]GIN[6]

Transl. The Pharaoh TUSU-MENNA, The Ruler.

FIG. 34.—Menes' Title of TUSU-MENNA in Egypt Deciphered.

1 B. 77; Br. 1722.
2 B. 365, as before.
3 *Tus* or *Tush*. B. 481; Br. 10515="Battle" M. 7999.
4 Br. 10355; PSL. 237. The high seat of Egyptian throne compared with the low in the diagram in Mesop. Sumerian is noteworthy.
5 B. 71; B. 1581.

border, proves to be of unique historical importance, as it preserves in Egypt this king's title of *Tusu*, and substitutes it for *Aha* (or *Akha*), thus *demonstrating the equivalency of "Aha" and "Tusu."* Like all the other First Dynasty inscriptions it is written in the Sumerian script and language. It reads in the retrograde direction, but in the annexed decipherment table I have arranged its signs for convenience from left to right.

Here it is significant that Menes uses in spelling his *Men* name that compound Sumerian sign of an Eye and Throne, which is now disclosed as the obvious Sumero-Egyptian

1 PRT. II, 20 f

a *d* *e-f*

LESSER LABELS FROM MENES' TOMB IN EGYPT.

In ebony and ivory (from photographs by Sir F. Petrie, PRI. II, Pls. III and IIIA). For decipherments and translations of *a*, see p. 280; of *b* and *c*, pp. 290 f. and Pl. XIIIA, facing p. 290. Note in *d* the Revolving Sun Spiral and "Cup-markings," as in prehistoric tomb monuments and "whorls" in Troy and Ancient Britain (see WPOB. 237 f.).

source of his title as Manasyu, in the Indian epics as " The Royal Eye of Gopta (Egypt)."

The other larger inscriptions of Menes in Egypt refer to his tragic death as seen later on and in these he is repeatedly called " the son of the Great Pharaoh Gani (or Sha- Gani)."

His Mesopotamian Emperorship at Kish

On becoming emperor at Kish, in addition to his kingship in Egypt, Manis reigned at Kish for fifteen years, according to the Kish Chronicle, when he was succeeded there by his son Narām Enzu. This would give him a total reign in Egypt of thirty-five years independently, and thereafter conjointly with Mesopotamia of fifteen years, or in all fifty years. But the Egyptian traditional chronology of Manetho, which we shall find is proved by the Kish Chronicle to be grossly exaggerated for the successors in Menes' Dynasty, gives him a reign in Egypt of sixty-two years. Such a long period is only possible on the assumption that he abdicated in Mesopotamia and retired to Egypt to reign for twelve more years there, whilst his son Narām Enzu was reigning contemporarily in Mesopotamia, which is highly improbable.

Menes' or Manis' Death

The Egyptian tradition of Menes' death is that he met with a tragic end. It relates that after reigning for long as an ideal sovereign, architect, warrior, sailor, statesman, promulgator of written laws, and regulator of the worship of the gods, he was killed by a " hippopotamus "[1]—a word *Kheb*, which also significantly, in the light of our decipherment of his tomb inscriptions, means " a wasp."[2]

It has been suggested that Menes was probably identical with a certain king or " Lord " of Magan, called " Mannu-Dannu " or " Mannu-the-mighty," who was " cast down " by the emperor Narām Enzu.[3] And this conjecture of identity has been rejected merely on the assumption that Menes' date was much earlier than that of Narām Enzu; though now it is seen to be also wholly untenable even when, as we have now found, these two emperors Menes and Narām Enzu were contemporary. For apart from Narām

[1] MDC. 235. [2] Cp. BD. 539 a. [3] JEA. 1920, 89, 295; 1921, 80.

being the son of Menes, we find from Narmar's (*i.e.* Narâm's) own Egyptian record in his Slate Palette victory tablet, now deciphered for the first time in the next chapter, that Mannu-Dannu was an aboriginal, uncivilized chief of Magan and not of Egypt. Moreover, the contemporary ebony labels on Menes' "tomb" at Abydos tell us the real story of the circumstances of Menes' death elsewhere.

Tragic Death of Menes disclosed in Inscription on Ebony Labels at his "Tomb" at Abydos

The Ebony Labels found at the "tomb" of Menes at Abydos, which have not previously been deciphered are, I find, written in transitional Sumero-Egyptian hieroglyphs; and contain an account of Menes' tragic death by an accident during a voyage of exploration by sea in the far West. And it is stated that that "tomb" was only the place of "the Label." It was thus merely a cenotaph.

The Great Ebony Labels from Menes' Tomb at Abydos

The largest ebony label (see Plate XIII), which was found in duplicate by Sir F. Petrie in 1901 at the empty tomb of King Mena or Menes at Abydos,[1] is said to show "the earliest known use of hieroglyphs for continuous writing in Egypt."[2] But it has hitherto remained undeciphered and untranslated because its writing, with the exception of a few characters, is not in the stereotyped form of Egyptian hieroglyphs with which Egyptologists are familiar, and which came into use after the period of Menes. And no Assyriologist has hitherto perceived the very transparent resemblance to, and identity with, the Sumerian hieroglyphs in its writing. For convenience of reference I give here my careful transcript of the inscription from the photograph in Plate XIII, where some of the signs require the assistance of a lens to make out their full details.

In view of my discovery that Menes or Aha Manj or "*Manj*-the-Warrior" was identical with the Mesopotamian

[1] PRT. II., pl. III A

[2] PHE. I, 14. But we have seen that his father Sargon's tomb inscriptions are earlier.

emperor "*Manis*-the-Warrior" (Manis-Tusu), the son of Sargon, and thus an Aryan Sumerian who ordinarily wrote in Sumerian characters and language; and that the conventional

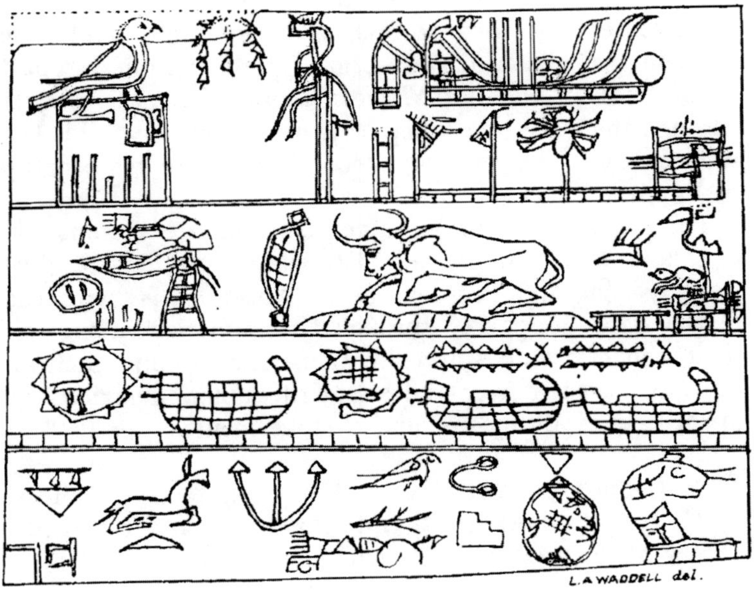

FIG. 35.—Ebony Label Inscription from Menes' "Tomb" at Abydos. (Drawn from Photograph in Plate XIII.)

Egyptian hieroglyphs, with their radical language, were derived from the Sumerian, I several years ago proceeded to re-examine this important sealed label inscription for its decipherment by our new keys.

DECIPHERMENT OF MENES' GREAT EBONY LABEL INSCRIPTION

I then observed that the writing was in Early Sumerian pictographic writing of the same type substantially as in Sargon's inscription at Abydos and in the Early Sumerian and Indo-Sumerian seals, with some of its pictographic signs written more realistically than in the Mesopotamian diagrammatic style, as for example, in the pictographs for "Fly" and "Ship" and "Ox," see Fig. 35, lines 1 to 3.

On deciphering the signs through their Sumerian values,

I found that the record contained a detailed contemporary and official account of Menes' death and its tragic circumstances. It described him as " King Manash or Manshu, the Pharaoh of Egypt, the Land of the Two Crowns," and " the son of The Great Sha-Gana, the Pharaoh," and stated that on his voyage of inspection by ships from Egypt to " The Peak of the Far Western Land," he met his death through the sting of a Wasp or Hornet ; and that this label was merely " The hanging Wood (Label) " of his cenotaph in Egypt.

The full details of my decipherment and literal translation of this extremely important historical inscription are given, sign by sign, and line by line in Appendix X, with each of the signs deciphered through the Sumerian, along with their phonetic values and literal meanings ; and each and all duly attested from the standard Sumerian lexicons, as in the case of all my previous decipherments.

The Record on the Large Ebony Labels in Menes' " Tomb," narrating the Tragic Death of Menes' in an Exploration in the Far West

Thus the full record on the Ebony Label in Menes' " Tomb " at Abydos records in the Sumerian writing and language literally as follows :—

" *The King Manash (or Minash), The Pharaoh of Mushsir (Egypt), the Land of the Two Crowns, the perished dead one in the West, of the (Sun-) Hawk race, Aha Manash (or Minash) of the Lower (or Sunrise or Eastern) and of the Sunset (or Upper or Western) Waters and of their Lands and Oceans, The Ruler, The King of Mushrim (the two Egypts) Lands, son of the Great Sha-Gana (or Sha-Gunu) of the (Sun-) Hawk race, The Pharaoh, the deceased, the Commander-in-Chief of Ships. The Commander-in-Chief of Ships (Minash) made the complete course to the End of the Sunset Land, going in ships. He completed the inspection of the Western Lands. He built (there) a holding (or possession) in Urani Land. At the Lake of the Peak, Fate pierced (him) by a Hornet (or Wasp), The King of the Two Crowns, Mānshu. This bored tablet set up of hanging wood is dedicated (to his memory).*"

PLATE XIII.

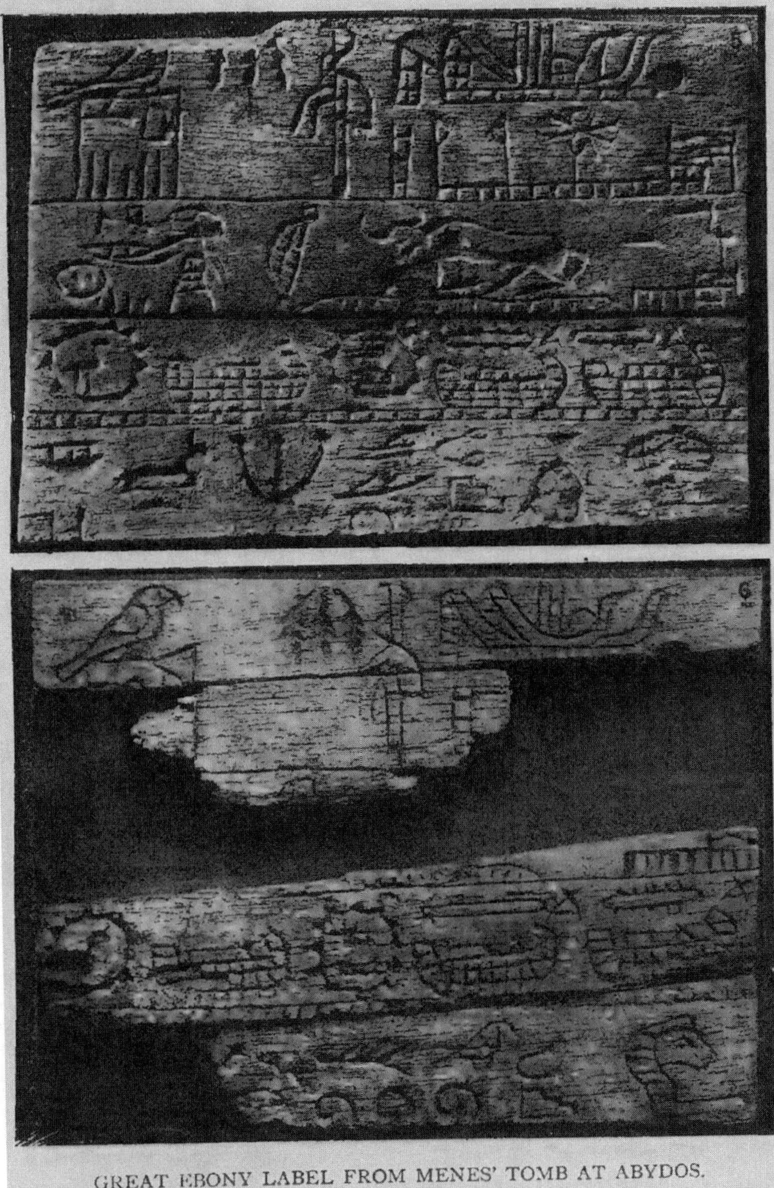

GREAT EBONY LABEL FROM MENES' TOMB AT ABYDOS.

In duplicate (from photographs by Sir F. Petrie, PRI. II. Pl. IIIA). For decipherment and translation, see pp. 283 f. and 559 f.

The pathetic simplicity and dignity of this contemporary record of the tragic ending of the life of this great "world emperor" and early Nordic admiral, whilst on a voyage of exploration and discovery to the furthest west islands in the Atlantic, at the ripe old age of about eighty years, and over four and a half thousand years ago, strikingly reflects the businesslike directness, conciseness, precision, restraint and historical and scientific habits of this adventurous enterprising Early Aryan ruling and seafaring race. Indeed, their record is *so thoroughly modern* that it might well have been composed and written at the present day.

The Fatal Hornet which slew King Menes

This contemporary historical account of the death of King Menes by the sting of a Hornet or Wasp is significantly confirmed all unsuspectedly by the Egyptian tradition of his death.

In Egyptian tradition or legend, Menes is said, after a glorious reign of sixty to sixty-two years in establishing and developing civilization in Egypt, to have been killed by a *Kheb* beast which came forth from the waters of the Nile.[1]

a in Label B. *b* in Label A *c* Sumer pictograph.

Fig. 36.—The Fatal Fly on Menes' Label as a Wasp or Hornet.

This *Kheb* animal in question has hitherto been translated "Hippopotamus." But it does not appear to have been remarked before, in this regard, that *Kheb* in Egyptian also means a "Wasp" (or Hornet),[2] which thus shows that the Egyptian legend actually preserved the true traditional name of the animal which caused Menes' death, though latterly misinterpreted. It is also noteworthy that the beast, according to the Egyptian tradition, came out of the waters of "The Great River" (*Iaur-au*), latterly known as the Nile; and the label records that the death-dealing insect was "at the Lake of the Peak" in Urani Land.

[1] Manetho cited by MDC. 235. [2] BD. 539a.

The identity of the "piercing Fly," which ended the life of the illustrious "world-monarch" King Menes in the Far West, is well preserved in its pictograph on the duplicate label, Plate XIII *B*, when examined under a lens. This clearly portrays it to be a winged insect of the Wasp or Hornet kind; and it has the same general form in the somewhat abraded label *A* (see Plate XIII). These two pictographs are shown in the accompanying Figure (No. 35), alongside of the diagrammatic form of this sign in the old Sumerian writing; and in the Sumerian glossaries this pictograph is defined as "a voracious or wolfish insect of the field." [1]

The Word for "Fate" is a Swallow

The word for Fate on this label is pictured by a Swallow which has the ideographic meaning in Sumerian of "swift" and "Fate" as well as a "Swallow." In Babylonian tradition the swallow was also a bird of Fate or augury. In the Chaldean version of the Deluge, the Chaldean Noah says:—

"I caused to go forth a swallow, the destiny bird . . .
The swallow went and turned about,
A resting-place it did not settle upon and it returned." [2]

"Urani" Land where Menes met his Tragic Death as "Erin" (Ireland)

The later Egyptians in ignorance of the real circumstances and locality of the death of Menes, and interpreting the traditional name of the beast that killed him as an "hippopotamus," naturally placed the scene of his death on the Nile, as that quadruped was and is common in the Nile, and was restricted to Africa in historic times. The later Greek mythmongering bards on the other hand, who were unaware of the identity of King Minos of Crete with Pharaoh Menes or Minash of Egypt and Mesopotamia, yet aware that he met a tragic end whilst on a sea-voyage to the West, made King Minos to be treacherously and miserably murdered in a hot-bath in Sicily whilst he was there in pursuit of his

[1] See footnote to decipherment in App. X.

[2] W. Houghton, *Natural History of Ancients*, 221

fugitive architect, Daedalus. This legend was presumably invented in order to account for the Minoa colony of Egyptians in Sicily, with architecture of the traditional Minos or Menes' type—this Sicilian Minoa, like the other ports of that name in the Mediterranean having been doubtless a port of call established by Minos or Menes.

Now, however, this official authentic and contemporary historical record on the ebony labels in his "tomb" at Abydos, definitely places the locality of Menes' death at "the End of the Land of Sunset," that is to say in the furthest western land in the Atlantic known to the adventurous Egyptian mariners of Menes' day. We have already seen that Sargon, the father of Menes and the predynastic Pharaoh who immediately preceded him in Egypt, records that the Tin Land, which lay *beyond* the Upper or Western Sea or Mediterranean, and thus in the Atlantic beyond the Pillars of Hercules, was tributary to him and sent him the products of its mines.[1] And I have shown that the "cup-mark" gravings on the prehistoric monoliths in the neighbourhood of the Tin and other prehistoric mine-workings in the British Isles are in the ancient Sumerian sacred funereal script of the Sargon period, and we shall find them repeated in the tomb inscriptions of some of the members of Menes' Dynasty in the following chapters. Moreover, I have adduced evidence showing that the Tin Land referred to by Sargon was in Cornwall, which was thus already a recognized part of Sargon's empire before the accession of Menes to that empire. And from its uplands the still further western land of Erin is sometimes visible.

But Menes, the greatest admiral of the Old World, who, as we have seen, had repeatedly made with his fleet the long deep-sea voyage of about three thousand miles from the Persian Gulf and Indus Valley to Egypt by the Arabian and Red Seas, and who, as King Minos was the most famous sea-king in Greek tradition, expressly embarked on his last great voyage of exploration, as we are officially told in this

[1] There were relatively poor ancient tin-workings in South-western Spain to the west of Gades outside the Strait of Gibraltar, but it is doubtful if they were worked in the Sargonic period.

label, in order " to inspect the End of the Sunset Land," in the Far West " going in ships."

This Land of " The End of the Sunset " must have especially attracted a scientific sea-explorer like Menes, who, we are told, " made its complete course," and all the more so, as he was, as we have seen, an ardent Sun-worshipper. For it was the accepted theory of his day, and a theory which continued down through the ages till the comparatively modern time of Copernicus in the fifteenth century A.D., that the Sun moved round the earth ; and that after Sunset in the furtherest western land in the ocean it travelled back to its point of " rising " in the Far East by an underground passage, as the " Night or Resurrecting Sun," as opposed to the " Day or Flying Sun," or " Sun-Hawk." This dual character of the Sun in " going " and " returning " is freely pictured as I have shown in the sacred seals of the Sumerians and Hittites with its respective westing and easting represented by alternating spirals, which as demonstrated in a former work is obviously the unknown source of the decorative " spiral ornament " in the Ægean and elsewhere.[1] And significantly the pictograph for this " End of the Sunset Land " on this Menes label is the Sumerian word-sign for it, representing the Sun entering this supposed dark underground passage, pictured by two curved or wavy lines with the Sun inside (see Fig 59, p. 336). And it was presumably to discover this supposed turning-point of the Sun that Menes made his final great adventure.

This " End of the Sunset Land," which was thus reached by ships, lay clearly beyond the Tin land of Cornwall, which was already a colony of the empire and well known. And the furthest land to the west of the latter is the land of Erin—for at this period the Sumero-Phœnicians had evidently not yet reached the Azores or America, which latter now appears to be " The lost Atlantis " of a later age of Aryan-Phœnician explorers.

The name *Urani*, for this furthest west land reached by Menes or Manj or Mena, thus appears to me to be the original form of the old name " Erin " for Ireland ; and we have seen that the vowels freely interchange in Sumerian and

[1] WPOB. 248 f., 285 f., 308 f.

Early Aryan, and that ancient place-names are surprisingly persistent down to modern times. Moreover, I have demonstrated elsewhere that representations of this "End of the Sunset Land" occur in Ireland, engraved on prehistoric cup-marked stones at New Grange on the Boyne River, near Drogheda, which are essentially replicas of the same pictograms as in the Early Sumerian and Hittite sacred seals.[1]

Remarkable confirmation of the identity of this Urani Land with Erin I found about three years ago in the inscriptions engraved on the boulder stones of the prehistoric rude stone grave at Knock-Many or "The Hill of *Many*," near Clogher on the southern border of County Tyrone. This prehistoric grave tumulus practically crowns the central watershed between the Lough Erne arm of Donegal or Galway Bay of the Atlantic or western side of Erin and Lough Neagh of the River Bann on the North-east, which latter lake was penetrated by Norse galleys within historic times. The inscriptions on the two chief standing boulder stones at Knock-Many, as seen in the remarkably fine large photographs taken by Mr R. Welch in 1896, contain, I observed, inscriptions in Sumerian linear writing which, though largely weathered, were mostly decipherable, and were practically identical in their writing and contents with those of the ebony label from the empty tomb of Mena or Manj or Menes at Abydos. In particular the photograph of *one of the stones*[2] *contains the same monogram of the name "Urani," and is written by the same signs as on the ebony label, but on a larger scale; and the realistic pictograph of the animal which caused the death of Menes in Urani represented it as a Hornet.*

Most unfortunately, however, those venerable engraved stones of this immensely important monument of hoary antiquity were two years ago cleared from their dense incrustation of lichens of thirty years' growth, by coating them with caustic chemicals for some days followed by vigorous scrubbing with brushes and water. Since then, the subsequent photographs now show little or no trace of the majority of the finer inscriptions, and in the larger stone especially a great many defacing additional initials carved

1 WPOB. 249 f. 287, 308 f.

2 Stone D. in drawing by G. Coffey, *New Grange*, 104,

by trippers in the interval. The stone of these boulders is composed of millstone grit, a friable rock consisting of grit concreted with natural cement ; and the action of caustic soda and lime tends to dissolve the cement and set free the grit which with the hard scrubbing tends to remove part of the surface of the stone, and with it the loss of the finer lines of the inscriptions.

But Mr Welch's earlier photographs, which are of great technical excellence, are indisputable facts in themselves. And they preserve many vestiges of the old Sumerian and other inscriptions, the decipherment of which I hope to publish later on.

It thus appears that the Land of Urani in "The Land of the End of the Sunset" in the Far West, to which Menes penetrated in ships and where he met his tragic death through the sting of a Wasp or Hornet was Erin, the furthest West land of Europe (excluding Iceland or Ultima Thule, then doubtless unknown) ; and that his tomb survives on the top of Knock-Many or "The Hill of Many" in County Tyrone, in which the name *Many* seems to preserve the name of that great Aryan "world-emperor" and famous admiral Mena or *Manj* down to the present day. And the so-called "tomb" of Menes at Abydos is disclosed to be not his tomb, but his cenotaph.

Confirmation of Menes' Death in West by Lesser Ebony Labels, and recording his Name as Mani Tussi and Son of Sargon

The three lesser ebony labels from Menes' "Tomb" figured in Plate XII, A to C, fully confirm the larger labels. *Two record that he has "gone in The West," one records that he is "dead," two record that he is "the son of Pharaoh Gani (Sargon)," and one records him under both titles of* Man Aha and MANI-TUSSI,

The detailed decipherments are given in Plate XIIIa.

The record of label B reads literally :—

> "The very great Protector (or Leader) of the (Sun-) Hawk House of the Pharaoh, Aha, Eha Men, the Gone One in The West, the son of Pharaoh Gani (or Guni)."

PLATE XIIIA.

DECIPHERMENT OF MENES' TOMB LESSER LABELS & CUP-MARKS.

(See photographs in Pl. XII, facing p. 280, and Label A decipherment, p. 280.)

B. l. 1.

Egyptian

Sumer Mesop.

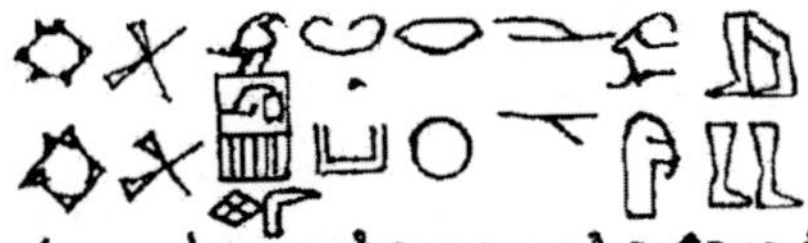

Reads ŚAR-KUR[1] AHA E[2]-BURU KUD[3] GU[4] DU-DU[5]

Transl.: The whole (Earth) Protector, The Hawk-house AHA, The Water-Lord, reported perished

B. l. 2.

Egyptian

S. Mesop.

Reads WI[6]- ES[7] BUR[8] BARU PA-RU[9] GA[10]- NI[11]

Transl.: in The West, The Son of Pharaoh of the Hawk line, GANI,

C. l. 1.

Egyptian

S. Mesop.

Reads MIM[12] MAN[13] PA-BAR[14] WI MA-NI[15]-TUS-SI[16]

Transl.: the dead (king) MAN, The Hawk Pharaoh, in the West, MANI-TUSSI,

C. l. 2.

Egyptian

S. Mesop.

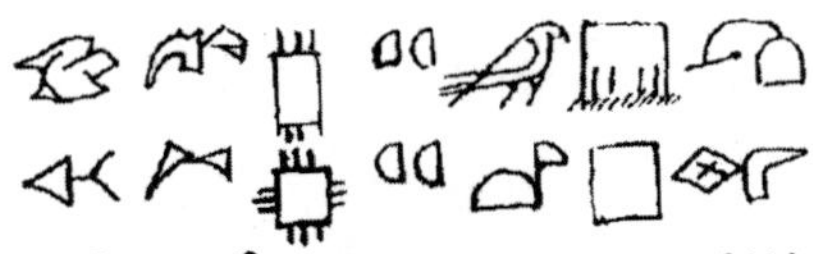

Reads TI[17] - SHU[18] BARA MAN PA - RIN AHA

Transl. TISHU, The Pharaoh MAN of the Hawk race, AHA.

D-F.

Egyptian

S. Mesop.

Reads RA,DAG,ZAL[19] ASH or IMI(N)[20] USSA[21]

Transl.: Revolving Sun (RA). Heaven. The bright Field of Tas (Tasia).

1. B. 59, Br. 1146. The unmarked phonetic values have been given in previous tables. 2. B. 263. 3. B. 12. 4. B. 15, Br. 549, pictures face with protruded tongue = "speak, report." 5. B. 207. 6. B. 380. 7. B. 432. 9. B. 1. 10. B. 275. 11. B. 228. 12. B. 116, M. 1923. 13. B. 431. 14. B. 77. 15. B. 532, Br. 11947. 16. B. 175. 17. B. 76. 18. B. 490. 19. B. 337, M. 5741 f. 20. B. 534, Br. 12196-8, 8371. Also value *Mer*, *Muru*, "Wind or Storm (god)." 21. Br. 11053, 12214, cp. 7527 and WPOB. 243.

The record of label C reads literally :—" The dead (Sun-) Hawk Pharaoh in The West, MANI TUSSI, TISHU the (Sun-)Hawk House Pharaoh AHA."

This gives us again absolute contemporary documentary proof from Egypt itself of the identity of Menes or Aha Men with Manis Tussi, as well as his sonship to Sargon-the-Great.

KING MINOS OF CRETE IDENTICAL WITH MENES OR MANIS-THE-WARRIOR

Disclosing his Son the Bull-Man (Mino-Taur) as Menes' son Narmar or Narām " The Wild Bull Lord "

It also now transpires that the famous legendary hero of Greek myth, King Minos of Crete, is all unsuspectedly the great Sumerian or Aryan emperor Menes or Manis-the-Warrior of Egypt and sea-emperor of the Mediterranean, whose achievements in establishing civilization in Crete and the Ægean were afterwards embroidered with romantic fable by the Greek myth-mongering poets.

It is significant that Sir A. Evans, the brilliant explorer of Cretan antiquities, equates the beginning of his Early Minoan Period I, when Cretan civilization suddenly begins at the end of the New Stone Age, with the beginning of the First Dynasty Period in Egypt; yet no one ever appears to have suggested that Minos and Menes themselves might be personally related or identical. On the contrary, the rich harvest of art treasures unearthed at Crete by Sir A. Evans since 1900 onwards of " Ægean " type with Greek affinities has led him to believe that Cretan or " Minoan " civilization was of independent indigenous origin within Crete itself; and was a chief source of Grecian and European civilization; and that Minos and his civilized Cretans were of the same race as the Late Stone Age aborigines of Crete, amongst whom Minos suddenly appears with his Bronze Age civilization.

The identity of Minos with Menes now becomes apparent, not only from the identity in their personal tradition, and the equation in their names, but also in the essentials of their culture and civilization; and the Sumerian sign for the *Man* element in Menes' name in the Egyptian and Indus inscriptions reads also dialectically *Min.*

In legend, Minos was a son of Zeus, just as Menes or Manis-the-Warrior, like his father Sargon, was a descendant of the human original of Zeus, namely King Zagg, Sakh or Sax. He was like Menes or Manis a votary and priest of Zeus or Zagg. He was a sea-emperor of the Mediterranean and laid Greece, including Athens, under tribute, just as Menes or Manis was sea-emperor of the Mediterranean and its lands; and a seal of the son of Manis has been found in Cyprus;

FIG. 37.—Narmar or Narām or "The Strong Wild Bull," son of Menes or Manis, as Minos' son, "Mino-Taur." (From Slate "Palette" of King Narmar, after Quibell, and compare Plate XVI.)

Note his cognomen of Wild Bull's head in upper register duplicated for symmetry, and at bottom the king personified as Wild Bull destroying citadel of his enemy, the king of Magan. For detailed decipherment see next chapter. Note giraffes' necks forming pigment well.

and the "Minoa" place-names in the Mediterranean from Sicily to the Syrian coast evidently attest former trading stations of the Minoans. Minos was a great sailor, an admiral and builder of ships, just as Manis was. He promulgated wise laws, which he received from Zeus, just as the Sumerians ascribed their laws to King Zagg or Sax, and Manis himself was a famous establisher and observer of constitutional law. His "Labyrinth," the intricate building which he erected and in which his son dwelt, was probably an exaggerated memory of his great palace in Crete, in which his son doubtless dwelt in his voyages of inspection in the Mediterranean; and it is significant that Menes also is credited with the erection of a "Labyrinth" in Egypt.[1] His son was a Wild Bull-Man, so-called "Mino-Taur," just as the son of Menes or Manis was called "The Strong Wild Bull," *Nar-am*—in which *Nar* means in both Sumerian and Egyptian "Strong or Mighty,"[2] and *am* or "Wild Bull" is invariably the sign by which Nar-am wrote his name, *and significantly as we shall see he as "Nar-mar" of* Egypt *represents himself pictorially on his victory Palette as a Wild Bull* (Fig. 37). Minos' death also was tragic in a sea-voyage in the West, just as Menes' was.

The culture, art and civilization of Minos and his period was generally similar to that of Menes or Manis. Both kings were of the Bronze Age. Both used finely wrought stone bowls in diorite or other hard mineral. Both had black hand-burnished ceramic ware and decorated and painted pottery of the same forms. Both used writing on clay tablets with a style, and the Minoan script resembles many of the signs in the linear script of Sargon and Menes and his dynastic successors in Egypt (my decipherments of the relatively few inscriptions found in Crete I hope to publish in a later work). The button-seals of Crete resemble those found in the Sumerian colony of the Indus Valley in the Sargonic period,[3] and also in Mesopotamia, and cylinder seals[4] and clay sealings were used by both. The jointed terra-cotta drain-pipes in Minoan Crete are similar to the Sumerian found at Ur and in the Indus Valley. And the differences which latterly developed in the mannerisms and local style of Cretan artists are no greater than those which latterly arose in Egypt and other colonies of the Sumerians under local inspiration. Funeral rites and cults of Minoan Crete were similar to Egyptians of Delta.

The Double-Axe sign for the god Zeus in Crete also occurs as a sign for the god *Zag* in Sumerian. It is found in the

[1] MDC. 235.

[2] On *Nar*, "strong, mighty," see Br. 7263 f.; MD. 720; and in Egyptian, BD. 378 b, which is another instance of the identity of words in sound and meaning in Sumerian and Egyptian.

[3] WISD. 64 f., 68 f.

[4] EPM. 197.

inscription of Manis-Tusu's grandfather;[1] and it is obviously a fuller form of the diagrammatic axe-sign in Sumerian, which has the phonetic value of *Zag* or *Sag*, and is defined as "axe, sceptre, *two-edged* sword."[2] And significantly this axe-sign is a title in Sumerian of "The Great Lord" (Nar-gal),[3] a martial reflex of the Father-god Zagg, Sakh or Sax, *i.e.* Zeus, who became latterly the "God of War" in Babylonia; and Manis' father Sargon worshipped the weapon of God Zagg as we have seen.

Identity of Minos of Crete with Menes or Manis-the-Warrior

Minos of Crete.	Menes or Manis.
1. Son of god Zeus.	Son or descendant of Zagg or Sax (Zeus).
2. Votary and priest of Zeus.	Votary of god Zagg and ex officio high-priest.
3. Of Bronze Age, replacing Neolithic.	Of Bronze Age, replacing Neolithic.
4. Sea-emperor of Mediterranean.	Sea-emperor of Mediterranean.
5. Sailor and builder of fleets.	Sailor with fleets of ships.
6. Introducer of Civilization.	Introducer of Civilization.
7. Law-giver direct from Zeus.	Law-establisher with code credited to Zagg.
8. Built a Labyrinth.	Built a Labyrinth.
9. His son was a Bull-man (Mino-Taur).	His son was named "The Strong Wild Bull" (*Nar-ām*), and bore title "Men-Narmar" and *Nerāma*.
10. Writing on clay tablets in linear script generally resembling Sumerian and linear Egyptian.	Writing on clay tablets in linear and cuneiform Sumerian script.
11. Used seal-impressions on clay for sealing.	Used seals for clay sealing.
12. Culture and Art generally of Sumerian or Aryan type.	Culture and Art of Sumerian or Aryan type.
13. Funeral rites similar to Egyptian delta.	Funeral rites of delta similar to Cretan.
14. Double-Axe emblem of Zeus.	Double-Axe sign for Zag in Sumerian and Manis' father worshipped the weapon of god Zagg.
15. Physical type of Minoans is Aryan.	Physical type is Aryan.
16. Death tragic on sea-voyage in West.	Death of Menes tragic on sea-voyage in West.

[1] Cp. B. pl. 160, No. (?) 160.

[2] Br. 5573 f.; M. 3925.

[3] M. 10751. Ner-gal from his fatal smiting still later became the God of the Underworld.

The physical type of the Minoans in Crete as seen in the beautiful "Cup-bearer" fresco shows "The profile of the face is pure and almost classic Greek, the physiognomy has certainly no Semitic cast;"[1] and similarly so the ivory carved figures and heads and clay sealings from Knossus are of fine Aryan type;[2] and the Dorians were early located there.

These identities of the legendary King Minos of Crete with the historical King Menes of Egypt or King Manis-the-Warrior, the Sumerian or Aryan sea-emperor of the Mediterranean, are displayed in the preceding table.

Date of Minoan Civilization about 2700 B.C.

We thus obtain a mass of cumulative evidence for the identity of the legendary King Minos of Crete with the historical King Menes of Egypt and the Sumerian or Aryan King Manis, the sea-emperor of the Mediterranean. We also gain for the first time a relatively fixed initial historical date for King Minos of Crete at about 2700 B.C., and thus recover a more solid foundation for the chronological scheme of classification of the strata in Minoan or Cretan civilization, and for the truer appreciation of its racial authorship and affinities.

Altogether, our new evidence identifies Menes, the founder of the First Dynasty of Egypt with King Manis-the-Warrior, the Sumerian emperor of Mesopotamia and son of the world-monarch Sargon, with the Aryan King Manasyu, "The royal Eye of Gopta and of the Four Quarters of the World," and with King Minos of Crete, and discovers the hitherto wholly unknown origin of Menes or Minos, his antecedents, ancestry, race and his tragic death on a sea-voyage in the West; and fixes with relative certainty for the first time his actual date.

As the successors of Menes in his First Dynasty of Egypt are now discovered to be identical with the successors of Manis-the-Warrior in Mesopotamia and in agreement with the Aryan kings in the Indian Lists, this discovery requires a separate chapter.

1 *Monthly Review*, 1900.

2 EPM. 8, and see pl. opp. p. 145, BSK.

XVI

MENES' FIRST DYNASTY OF EGYPT IDENTICAL WITH MANIS-TUSU'S DYNASTY IN MESOPOTAMIA & IN INDIAN LISTS FROM NARMAR ONWARDS

Disclosing NARMAR *as* NARAM-ENZU, *son of Manis-Tusu, with Indus Valley seals giving his genealogy from Sargon, Egyptian Inscriptions as Emperor of Akkad and World-monarch and his conquest of King Mannu-Dan of Magan.*

WE now discover that Menes' Dynasty or The First Dynasty of Egypt is identical in names and chronological order of succession with the dynasty of the Sumerian emperor Manis or Manis-Tusu in Mesopotamia and also with that of the Aryan emperor Manasyu or Asa-Manja in the Indian Lists. These identities thus while confirming the personal identities above demonstrated of King Gin or " Sargon " and his Aryan ancestry and descendants, at the same time establish absolutely the Sumerian or Aryan Origin of Egyptian Civilization.

These identities moreover disclose that Egypt was held as a colony of the Mesopotamian empire from the epoch of Sargon onwards to at least the end of his dynasty ; with the exception of the reign of Menes or Manis himself, in which it was held independently of Mesopotamia as a separate kingdom by Manis or Aha Men personally. Indeed, the Indian King-Lists and Chronicles make it clear that his younger brother Mush did not reign there, as they omit his name altogether from the main-line Aryan kings, and obviously considered him to be a usurper.

MENES' OR MANIS-TUSU'S DYNASTY FROM MESOPOTAMIAN LISTS & MONUMENTS, & IN THE INDIAN-KING-LISTS

The genealogical table of Menes or Manis-Tusu from the Kish Chronicle on p. 61, shows that Manis-Tusu's son and successor in Mesopotamia was Narām, Lord Enzu, the so-called " Narām Sin " of Assyriologists, and that he was the

PLATE XIV.

NARAM-ENZU'S (MINOTAUR'S) STELE OF VICTORY, *c.* 2600 B.C.

Found at Susa, whither it had been carried from Mesopotamia as a raid-trophy, and now in the Louvre (DP. I, Pl. X). The king is represented of heroic size, with horned hat, climbing with his warriors a high mountain rising to the stars and storming a hill fort. His helmet is adorned with horns of a Bull (his homonym). He carries a club or battle-axe and a bow and arrow, and with one arrow he has shot an enemy and tramples on a fallen foe, whilst others plead for mercy. His followers bear standards and weapons. Compare with Narmar's palette of Victory, Pl. XVI, p. 310, with its Bull emblems.

grandson of King Kīn or "Sargon" of Agadu. And the Kish Chronicle goes on to detail the official list of eight kings from Manis to the end of his, or his father's dynasty, including four temporary kings who reigned in all for only three years during a period of revolt or anarchy on the demise of Narām's successor.

MANIS-TUSU'S DYNASTY IN BABYLONIAN & INDIAN LISTS COMPARED

In the annexed Table is displayed the agreement between the official Babylonian Lists (Kish and Isin Chronicles) and the official Indian Lists respectively in regard to the dynasty of Manis-Tusu in Mesopotamia and that of the Aryan emperor Manasyu or Asa-Manja. In column 2 are added the forms of the names of those kings as actually found in their own contemporary monuments in Mesopotamia, which is also confirmed by their names in their Indus seals in Plates XI, etc.

Manis-Tusu's Dynasty in Babylonian and Indian Lists

Babylonian.		Indian Lists.		
Kish Chronicle.	Inscriptions.	Puru.	Solar and Lunar.	No.
(Kīn or Sharru-Kīn).	(Gani or Gin, Shar-Gani).	Pra-Vīra or Puru II.	Kuni, Sha-Kuni or Sagara.	37.
Mūsh (Uru-), s. of 37.	Mush (Uru-).	—	—	
Manis-Tīsshu, s. of 37.	Manis-Tusu (or -Tis's'u).	Manasyu, s. of 37.	Asa-Manja, s. of 37.	38.
Narām-Enzu or Narām-Ba, s. of 38.	Narām-Enzu or Narām-Ba.	Vātā-Yudha, Abha-Yada, or Vāggmin, s. of 38.	Karam-B'a, Ansu-mat or Anjana, s. of 38.	39.
Gani-Eri, Shar-Guni-Eri.	Gani-Eri, Shar-Guni-Eri.	—	Kunti-jit, Rtu-jit or Khat-wanga, s. of 39.	40.
[Anarchy with 4 kings in 3 yrs. of whom 1st was (?) Igigi].	—	—	[Variation in succession] Bhagī-ratha, s. of 40.	
Dudu.	Dudu.	Dhundu, s. of 39 and Bahu-bida	or Soma or Deva-kshatra.	41.
Shudur-Kib [End of Dynasty].	Shudur-Kib.	Subāhu, s. of 41.	Suhotra II, Shruta or Deva-Kshattra, s. of 41 [Break of Dynasty].	42.

It will be observed that the Indian lists agree with the Babylonian absolutely in chronological order of succession, and substantially in the form of the names, the variations in the latter being merely in phonetic spelling and in the use of one or more titles instead of the personal name. And we thus obtain additional evidence of the identity of the Sumerian and Aryan history.

Egyptian King-Lists of Menes' First Dynasty compared with Mesopotamian King-Lists of Manis-Tusu's Dynasty & the Indian Versions

In starting to compare the Egyptian King-Lists of Menes' First Dynasty with the Mesopotamian and Indian lists we are met at the outset by the striking fact that there is practically no agreement amongst Egyptologists nor in the traditional Egyptian King-Lists themselves in regard to the names of the kings of the First Dynasty of Egypt.

Wide Discrepancies amongst Egyptologists & Traditional Egyptian King-Lists in the Names of the Kings of the First Dynasty.

Not only are the readings or restorations of the names of the kings of the First Dynasty by the leading Egyptologists more or less totally different, but these again, excepting the name of Menes himself, are totally different from the traditional names of those kings preserved in the lists of Manetho of the third century B.C. and Sety I of the nineteenth dynasty and others (see cols. 1-5 of the following Table).

This wide difference in the readings or restorations of the names in this dynasty by Egyptologists was obviously owing, I observed, to the names being written in the kings' own inscriptions, not in the later stereotyped Egyptian hieroglyphs, but in the parent Sumerian linear pictographic writing and in the Sumerian language with syllabic values for each sign ; and to the fact that Egyptologists treating the signs as Egyptian hieroglyphs read them mostly with alphabetic value, *i.e.*, using only the initial letter of the each syllabic sign, and where the latter differed markedly from the later Egyptian hieroglyph, different Egyptologists selected arbitrarily the phonetic value of one or other hieroglyph which somewhat resembled it.

Again, as regards the traditional Egyptian list of names of the kings, of Manetho, etc., the almost complete want of equation between these and the monument names was clearly owing, I observed, to the lists having largely used *titles* for the kings instead of their personal names, and thus being in series with the Indian lists which as often as not used different titles, regnal, religious and other, in place of the proper personal names.

Revision of the Readings of the Names of the Kings of the First Egyptian Dynasty on their own contemporary Monuments

On realizing the causes of these serious differences in the existing king-lists of the First Egyptian Dynasty, it thus became necessary, before comparison with the Babylonian and Indian lists was possible, that I should revise the readings of the names of each king in their contemporary inscriptions by my Sumerian and Indian keys. The results of these revised readings are given in the first column of the annexed Comparative Table.

Menes' First Egyptian Dynasty compared with Manis' or Manis-Tusu's Dynasty in the Babylonian and Indian Lists

In the annexed Table are compared Menes' First Egyptian Dynasty of eight kings according to the traditional lists of Manetho and others, with Manis-Tusu's Dynasty in the Babylonian Lists and Manasyu or Asa-Manja's Aryan line in the Indian lists. In column 1 are given the names of the kings on their own Egyptian monuments as revised by me, the detailed proofs for which readings are given in my revised readings and translations of the Egyptian inscriptions of these kings. In columns 2 and 3 are given the names as read respectively by the leading Egyptologists, Sir F. Petrie[1] and Sir W. Budge.[2] In columns 4 and 5 are the traditional forms of the names and titles from the lists of Manetho, Sety I and others. And in columns 6 and 7

[1] PHE. 7. [2] BH. 251.

are the forms in the Babylonian king-lists (Kish and Isin Chronicles) and on the contemporary monuments of King Manis-Tusu's (or Sargon's) Dynasty in Mesopotamia.

Results of Comparison of First Egyptian Dynasty Kings with Babylonian & Indian Lists

From this Table is seen the substantial agreement in the names of the kings of Menes' Dynasty on their Egyptian monuments with those of Manis-Tusu's Dynasty on their Mesopotamian monuments and in the Babylonian and Indian lists. The chronological order of the kings also is essentially identical. It is absolutely identical in all three lists—Egyptian, Babylonian and Indian, as far as and inclusive of the third king, *Shar-Guni* or *Gin-Eri*, the *Kenkenes* of Manetho and *Khent* of Egyptologists and *Kunti-jit* of the Indian lists; and the last king who ended Menes' Dynasty is the same in all three lists: *Kebh* of Egyptian, *Shudur-Kib* of the Babylonian and *Suhotra* of the Indian, who is identical with the king *Shudur Kib* who ended Manis-Tusu's Dynasty in Mesopotamia; and *Shudur Kib* of his Indus seals.

Of the other kings of Manetho's list and the monuments, Nos. 4 to 7, the 5th, namely *Dudu*, bears the same name in all three lists, Egyptian, Indian (where the name is nasalized) and in the Babylonian. In the latter he immediately precedes the last king of the dynasty. The reason for the extra kings in the Egyptian lists is disclosed to be evidently the anarchy in Mesopotamia which followed on the death of the third king, Gani-sharri, as detailed in the Babylonian Chronicles. In the period following this anarchy the Egyptian lists give two kings (Nos. 6 and 7) who were not kings of Mesopotamia, implying either that they were tributary to the emperor Dudu or held Egypt independently of him, until it was recovered by his successor, the last emperor of Manis-Tusu's Dynasty, namely *Kebh* of the Egyptian and Shudur-*Kib* of the Babylonian. Significantly, certain versions of the Indian lists, which latter exhibit considerable variations in the succession of this period, give between them the names of those two Egyptian kings who are absent in the Babylonian lists.

The wide differences also in the traditional Egyptian lists

of Manetho and others from the names as found on the monuments, are now seen to be owing to these Egyptian lists having largely used *titles* instead of the personal names of the kings. Thus the second king of the dynasty, now disclosed as Narmar of the Egyptian monuments or the emperor Narām of Mesopotamia, is styled in the Egyptian lists *Athōthis* or *Teta* (see cols. 4 and 5 of Table). This is now seen obviously to represent Narām's Mesopotamian title of "*Ati*-enshak,"[1] and corresponding to his Indian title of *Vātā-yūdha* and *Abha-yada*. Similarly the third king, whose name in his monuments reads Guni-Sag and "Khent," the Kunti-jit of the Indian and Kenkenēs of Manetho is called *Atta* in the other Egyptian lists. This seems to represent his *Rtu* and *Khat* titles in the Indian lists, the latter word *Khat* becoming in Sumerian dialect *Hat* and *At* through dropping of the initial letters,[2] as is also seen on the Ancient Briton coins of the Catti on p. 8. And similarly with others, though some of Manetho's other differences may be errors of later scribes.

Another and extremely important historical result emerging from our Comparative Table is the conclusive evidence afforded that *the total years' reign for the First Dynasty of Egypt given by Manetho is very greatly exaggerated*; and yet Manetho's chronology is implicitly accepted by Egyptologists. Our identification of Menes with Manis-Tusu enables us to recover the actual length of the reign of this dynasty through the Mesopotamian chronicles. Manetho makes Menes' Dynasty reign for 253 years; but the Babylonian chronicles agree in giving the reign of Manis-Tusu's Dynasty in Mesopotamia from and including Manis himself down to the end of the reign of the last King Shudur-Kib as only 134 years. And we find in the Chapter on Chronology that although Manetho gives Menes a reign in Egypt of 62 years, the utmost that can be allowed for his reign in Egypt prior to his accession in Mesopotamia is 35 years, making, with his 15 years in Mesopotamia, a total of 50 years in all in Egypt. This would give the total reign of Menes and his dynasty in Egypt, including his previous 35 years' rule there as 169 years instead of the 253 of

[1] Cp. PHT. 4, 132. [2] WAOA. 33.

First Egyptian Dynasty of Menes compared \

Egyptian Monuments.			Egyptian Lists.	
Waddell (in Sumerian).	Petrie.	Budge.	Manetho.	Sety I,
. MAN, MANJ, AHA-MANJ, MANASH, MINASH, MANSHU, MANI-TUSSI, TUSU-MENA or AHA-MENA, s. of Puru-GANI.	Nor-mer, MEN.	ÂHA.	MÊNÊS.	MENA.
. NARMAR, NAR-AMA or ABATU.	Aha.	NÂRMER.	Athôthis.	Teta.
. SAG-GINA, GIN-ERI or Shar-GUNI-DILI-PA-RIT.	Zer-Ta.	KHENT.	KENKENÊS.	Attā.
. BAG-GID or BAG-GID-GI-RU.	Zet-Ata.	Tcha.	Uenephês.	Ata.
. DUDU, DUNU, SHU-DUDU, DANA, or BUSAHAP, s. of Gina Sag.	DEN-Setui.	TEN, Semti.	Usaphaidos.	Hesepti.
. BI-DI, Lord MAR.	Azab-Merpaba.	Âtab.	Miebidos.	Mer-ba-p
. SHESHIMMASH, PA or KHAT.	Semerkhat-shemshu.	Hu(?).	Semempsês.	Sem-en-p
. SHUDUR-KIB, KIBBU, KIBI, QIBI, KIA, QA, or XUDARUR, s. of Gana-Sag.	Qa-Sen.	Qa or Sen. (QEBHU(?)).	Biênekhês.	KEBH.
[End of Menes' First Dynasty of Egypt.]				

MANIS-TUSU'S & MANASYU'S IN BABYLONIAN & INDIAN

Indian Lists.		Babylonian.	
Solar.	Lunar.	Lists: K.=Kish, I.=Isin.	Monuments.
Asa-MANJA, s. of Kuni or Sakuni.	MANASYU, s. of Pra-Vira.	MANIS-TISSHU (K.), HA (?)MA-NIS (I.), s. of Sar-Gani.	MANIS-TUSU or Manish Tussu.
Anjana, Ansu-mat, s. of Asa-Manja.	KARAM-B'A, Abha-yada or Vātā-yudha, s. of Manasyu.	NARĀM-BA or -ENZU (K.) NERRA, ENUGGE-ANNA (I.), s. of Manis-Tisshu.	NARĀM-BA or -ENZU.
KUNTĪ-jit, Ritu-jit, or DILĪ-PA, s. of Anjana.	[Break in Dynasty].	Shar-GANI (or GUNI)-Eri (K.), s. of Narām Enzu. [Anarchy with Igigi or Nigigi, Imi Nanum, Iama or Ilulu].	Shar-GANI (or -GUNI)-Eri.
BHAGĪ-ratha, g.s. of Ansu-mat.	—	—	—
DEVANA-kshatra, or Arishta-nemi, s. of Kunti-jit.	DHUNDU, SUDYUMNA, s. of Abha-yada ((?) Madhu).	DUDU (K.) or DUNDU(N).	DUDU or DUNDU(N).
—	Bahu-Bida, s. of Dhundu.		
—	SAMPĀTI, s. of Bahu-bida, or SOMA (or Aham-yati).	—	—
SHRUTA, SUHOTRA (III).	(?) PURU-HOTRA.	SHUDUR-KIB (K.), s. of Dudu.	SHUDUR-KIB.
[Break in Dynasty.]		[End of Manis-Tusu's Dynasty in Mesopotamia.]	

Manetho. That is to say that Manetho has evidently exaggerated the reign of the First Dynasty by 84 years, or one-third more than its approximately actual years. And if, as seems probable, Manetho's other dynastic reigns are equally exaggerated in length as they appear to be when compared with the subsequent contemporary dynasties in Mesopotamia, this reduction along with that for the undoubted overlapping of many of his dynasties will tend to approximate the revised chronologies of Egyptian dynasties to the newly-found date for Menes of about 2704 B.C.

Records of Individual Kings of Menes' Dynasty confirm Identities with Manis-Tusu's Dynasty

The records of the individual kings also of Menes' Dynasty in Egypt fully confirm the identities of the kings with those of Manis-Tusu's Dynasty. Menes himself we have already identified with Manis or Manis-Tusu, so we now take up the other kings of his dynasty, commencing with the second king of that dynasty, Narmar.

Narmar, Second King of Menes' Egyptian Dynasty identical with Narām Enzu or Narām Ba (" Naram Sin ") of Mesopotamia

King Narmar of Egypt is now definitely placed by our new evidence as the second king of the First Dynasty, and as the successor of Menes, of whom we have found him to be the son. He was rightly placed as the second king by Budge; whilst others have conjecturally made him the first king and identical with Menes, or have made him a predynastic king, because they could not find his name in the lists of Manetho and the others which called him only by his titles and not by his personal name (see foregoing Table).

He is found by the comparative king-lists and genealogies, Sumerian and Indian, to be identical with the Mesopotamian emperor Narām Enzu or Narām-Ba (" Narām Sin ") the son of the emperor Manis-Tusu and grandson of " Sargon-the-Great." This identity is now fully confirmed and established by Narmar's own inscriptions in Egypt, not only

NARAM-ENZU (OR NARMAR).

Contemporary portrait on basalt bas-relief, *c.* 2600 B.C.; found near Diarbekr, in Kurdistan, and now in Imperial Ottoman Museum, Constantinople. It records his victories, including Magan, which he ascribes to God Induru or Ia (Jah). He carries a club in right hand and a whip in left, and wears bracelets, and a tall Phrygian hat, as in his Egyptian portrait, see p. 310 and Pl. XVI. His upper lip is unshaved, presumably as he was campaigning in Kurdistan, and his nose is of non-Semitic type.

in his name but also in his records regarding his paternity and Mesopotamian empire and by his portraits resembling those of Narām Enzu in Mesopotamia (see Plates XV and XVI).

NARMAR'S NAME & EGYPTIAN EMBLEMS OF "THE WILD BULL" & "FISH-MONSTER" *re* NARĀM ENZU'S MESOPOTAMIAN TITLES OF "WILD BULL" & "FISH-MONSTER" ("CUTTLE-FISH").

In Egypt King Narmar usually writes his name by the two hieroglyph signs of *Nar* and *Mar*, which have the same pictographic forms, phonetic values and meanings as the corresponding signs in Sumerian, another illustration of the

FIG. 38.—Naram's Name in Egypt as "Narmar" (after Petrie).

Sumerian origin of Egyptian hieroglyphs. But he also spells his name in Egypt as *Nar-ama*, as we shall find, which is identical with the usual spelling of his name in Mesopotamia as *Narām* or *Narāma*; and in his Indian seals.

In Egyptian, the initial *Nār* syllable of his name is written by the pictograph or hieroglyph of a monster fish supposed to be a cuttle-fish; [1] and the second syllable *Mar* is written by the pictograph of a drill or borer,[2] the latter being, as I have shown, derived from the Sumerian *Mar* sign for a drill; [3] and similarly we shall find that the first sign also is of Sumerian origin.

This monster fish or "cuttle-fish" sign has in Egyptian generally the same pictograph form as in Sumerian, with tentacles projecting from its mouth (see Fig. 38 and the top of Figs. 37 and 39). This fish-sign in Sumerian has the usual value of *Pish* or "Fish," [4] and is defined as "mighty fish" and as a title of the Babylonian god of war or death named *Ner* or *Nar*,[5] presuming that the sign also had this

[1] BD. 347 a.
[2] GH. 49.
[3] WSAD. *Mar*, Pl. IV.
[4] WSAD. 80.
[5] MD. 553 and B. 303. Significantly in Egyptian *Narh* is also a god of death, BD. 343.

value *Ner* or *Nar* in Sumerian. It has also the Sumerian value of *Kar*,[1] which obviously explains the Indian variant of this king's name as *Kar*am-B'a instead of *Nar*ām-Ba, by the Indian scribes selecting the former value *Kar* instead of *Nar*, which latter was its value in Egypt.

The second element in his Mesopotamian name of *Narām* or *Narāma*, namely, *Am* or *Ama*, which also occurs in his inscription in Egypt, designates him as "The Wild Bull,"[2] which has also the synonym of "strong lord" or "warrior,"[3] and was a common title of the Father-god and of heroic

FIG. 38A.—Sealing of Narmar (after Petrie).

kings in Sumerian, Babylonian and Indian as well as Egyptian literature; and the Bull was a source of the colossal man-headed Bull-gods of Babylonia. That King Narām actually used this "Wild Bull" element of his name realistically is evidenced by his figuring the Wild Bull on the top of both sides of his Egyptian victory Palette as Narmar (see Plate XV and Figs. 37 and 39), and significantly in the lowermost compartment on the reverse of his Palette *he pictures himself as a Wild Bull* destroying his foes and their citadel. The Bull is also figured beside him on his great stone mace-head. And this title of his, as Wild Bull, we have seen was obviously the source of his being called by the Greek myth-

[1] Br. 6927.

[2] See WSAD. 12 for its occurrence in the leading Aryan languages, including English. Also B. 183; Br. 4545.

[3] Br. 4543-4.

mongering bards "Mino-Taur," or the Bull-man, in his Cretan legend, as the son of King Minos of Crete, who, we have seen, was Menes of Egypt.

The reason why King Narām of Mesopotamia changed his name in Egypt to *Nar-mar*, now apparently transpires in the fact that there is no *Am* or *Ama* word in Egyptian meaning "Bull" or "Wild Bull" or "strong lord." Whereas in Egyptian, *Mar* means "hero,"[1] and it is pictured by the hieroglyph sign of a drill, that is the same sign which in Sumerian with the value *Mar* has the meaning of "pierce, throw down, destroy,"[2] in the same sense as the wild Bull metaphor.

We thus find that the evidence of King Narmar's name and his own victory Palette in Egypt conclusively confirms his identity with the Mesopotamian emperor Narām or Narāma, who was the son of Manis or Manis-Tusu, who was, as we have found, Menes the founder of the First Egyptian Dynasty.

The Semitic title of "Sin" arbitrarily applied by all modern Assyriologists to King Narām, instead of his Sumerian title of *Enzu* or *Ba* in his own Mesopotamian inscriptions is merely an unjustified attempt, as we have seen, to claim him with his father and grandfather Sargon as Semites in order to suit their erroneous theory. But that theory is conclusively disproved by the documents of these Sargonic kings themselves and by the cumulative evidence of the Sumerian and Indian genealogies and records, including the fact that they were Sun-worshippers, a wholly non-Semitic cult. And this false Semitic attribution of Sargon's great Aryan Dynasty has formed one of the chief obstructions to the discovery of the truth in regard to the origin and affinities of the Sumerians and Aryans and the origin of the World's Civilization.

Narām's Inscriptions in Mesopotamia

In Mesopotamia many inscriptions of King Narām have been unearthed on votive vases, plaques, his famous stele of victory statues, seals and stamped bricks, etc.,[3] and in old certified copies of his inscriptions at the Sun-temple of Nippur.

[1] BD. 314 a. [2] Br. 5818-9. [3] TDI. 236 f.

In these inscriptions he claims the title of "King of the Four Quarters of the World," and refers to his booty from "the Land of Magan" and elsewhere. In one of these inscriptions preserved in a copy in the Nippur temple describing his conquests,[1] in which the names of the countries and kings are mostly missing, he ascribes his conquests, like Sargon, to Lord Sakh, and in his curse against those who would destroy his inscription he invokes besides Sagaga, Lord Sakh and the Sun-god, also Lady Inanna, the wife of Sakh, of whom he styles himself "the servant or (?) descendant," also the great god Nar (or Ner) and even the Semitic Moon-god and several others, showing that he had an enlarged pantheon, or that he included as cursers the local tribal gods of the would-be destroyers.

Narām's Conquests in the West, including Magan, Syria & Asia Minor

His conquest of Magan or the Sinai Peninsula, and his defeat of its king Mannu-dannu (supposed to have been possibly Menes of Egypt) have been detailed in the previous chapter.

In the Hittite cuneiform version of his conquests found at the old Hittite capital at Boghaz Koi in Cappadocia in script of about 1400 B.C. or earlier,[2] and which is fragmentary, we find amongst the list of vanquished kings and countries extending from the West Land, and Asia Minor of the Hittites and Syria to Persia, a king of the West Land named *Mana-ila*, who may possibly be identical with this Mannu-dannu. The fragment records:[3] "And I (Narām Enzu) at that time against all the enemy lands made war. Mana-ila king of the Western Land,[4] Bunana-ila, king of Pāgki, Lapana-ila, king of Ulliui, . . . innipa-ila king of . . . , Pāmba king of the Khatti ("Hittite") Land, Khutuni king of Kaniesh, Nur . . . [Dagan king of Burushkhanda], Akwāru-wash king of the Ammuri (Amorites), Tīshenki king of Parashi (Persia) . . . Madakina king of Armani, Iskibbu king of the Cedar Mountains (Amanus), Teshshi . . . , Urlarāg,

[1] PHT. iv. 210 f. [2] FB. 2-3.

[3] This translation is based on Sayce's in AE. 1923, 99, with revision of names from texts.

[4] *Gu-shu-a* in which *Gu*=land (M. 2027), *shu*=Setting of Sun, B. 490.

PLATE XV.

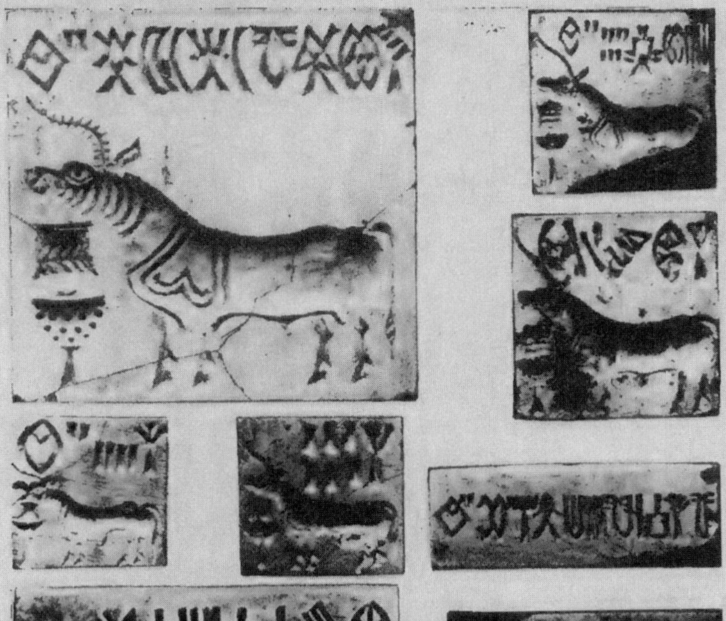

INDUS VALLEY SEALS OF FIRST DYNASTY PHARAOHS FROM NARMAR TO SHUDUR-KIB OR QA, *c.* 2640-2535 B.C.

Including Gan-Eri (Khent), Bugiru (Bhagiratha) and Dudu or Dan. (Photographs after Sir J. Marshall.) For decipherments and translations, see pp. 307 f., 321 f., 327 f., 340 f., 567 f.

king of Larāg, Urbānda king of Nīgki, Ilshunna-īl king of Dur city, Tisbinki king of Kūrshaura. Altogether 17 kings who formed an alliance I overthrew them. I entrusted the troops to a *Khar-i* (*Har-i* or *Uru-i*)." And the second fragment records the tribute received in talents of silver and copper and in lapis-lazuli precious stone which was brought to Agadu.

Naram or Narmer's Seals in Indus Valley.

Amongst the second batch of seals unearthed from the old Indus Valley colonial capital at Edin, I found the following five seals figured in Plates XI and XIV, which presumably belong to Naram, see especially No. 3. The detailed decipherment is given in Apps. IX and XI. Here the literal translation of their inscriptions is given. It is seen that in these seals the name is spelt variously *Nera* and *Marru* and *Mar-Nera*, and also *Ner-Amma*.

1st Seal (Plate XI, 9 and Fig. 103).

"Of the Lower (Eastern) Land, the Gut (Goth or "Warrior") Nera, The Gut at Agdu Land."

Nera is evidently coined so as to give the meaning of Lord of the Deep Waters (*Ner*), the *Narāyana* of the Sanskrit.

2nd Seal (Plate XI, 10–11 and Fig. 102).
The Elephant Seal.

This seal with the Elephant as its chief device reads :—

"Under-King Companion Mar-Nera, The Gut Amma."

Here significantly the Elephant, which is called in Sumerian *Amsi* or "Horned (Toothed) Wild Bull," is clearly introduced for the Bull element in Naram's name. The Elephant is called sometimes in the east "The Great Ox," and our modern name for it is derived from the Greek *Elephas* through the Semitic *aleph* "an ox." This *Nar-amma* name for him is repeated on seal, Fig. 118.

3rd Seal (Plate XV, 1 and Fig. 104).

"Under-King Companion Marru, The Lord, Son of the Gut, the *Ara*, The Lord of the Deep Waters Gin ("Sargon").

It is noteworthy that Naram is called by Nabonidus and late Babylonians "the son" of Sargon.

4TH SEAL (PLATE XV, 2). "Under-King Companion, The heavenly Pharaoh NERA, the Lord at Agdu (or Edin).

5TH SEAL (NOS. 3–4, PLATE XV), THE TIGER SEAL. "Under-King Companion MARRU, the Lord Gut of Tiger Land." This seal as seen at p. 545 apparently belongs to Nar-Mar.

NARAM AS "THE DEMON-KING" NĀRMARA OF THE INDIAN VEDAS

In view of such wholesale intestine wars waged by Narām—for several of these kings were of kindred Sumerian or Aryan stock, such as the Hittites—it seems to me practically certain that he is the King Nārmara referred to in the Indian Vedic Psalms as a "demon" king, who harassed the loyal and orthodox Aryans and was destroyed in consequence by Indra. This Vedic hymn sings :—

> "Thou Indra, who broughtest Nārmara with all his wealth of Ūrjayantī to slay him, so that the demons might be destroyed." [1]

Here his identity with King Narām or Narmar of Egypt seems to be clearly proved by the name of his chief fort called *Ūrjayantī* or "Ūr-the-Victorious." For *Uri* is the Sumerian, that is Aryan name for the Semitic *Akkad* or *Akkadu*,[2] which Assyriologists suppose to be the Semitic name of Agade, the Mesopotamian capital of Narām-Enzu; and we shall see that Narmar in his Egyptian Palette calls himself "king of Uri." And Narām, much more than any other king of his Sargonic dynasty, adopted Semitic idioms into his Mesopotamian inscriptions, and as evidence of his reactionary backsliding we have seen that he had adopted the Semitic Moon-god, the human sacrifices to whom are being revealed by the excavations at Ur.

His inveterately destructive character with the abuse of his royalty is pictured by himself as Narmar in his great Palette and stone mace-head, in which he is gloating over his slain and beheaded victims. And his atrocious destruc-

[1] RV. 2, 13, 8. [2] Br. 7304-5.

tiveness was his leading trait, as we have seen in his Cretan legend as the ravaging Mino-Taur, son of King Minos (or Menes) of Crete.

Narām's Inscriptions as "Narmar" in Egypt

The chief monuments of Narmar in Egypt are his famous great sculptured slate Palette of Victory (Plate XVI and Figs. 37 and 39) and his magnificently carved great stone mace-head, both from Hierakonopolis, and his name on an ebony tablet, several vases and clay sealings by a cylinder-seal, found in his "tomb" at Abydos. But apart from the few short pictographic inscriptions or labels on his great Palette, now read for the first time, and his name-marks, there appear to be no other inscriptions of him yet found in Egypt; whereas his successors in the dynasty have left several more or less longish inscriptions.

Narmar's Palette Inscriptions celebrate his Victory over the King of Magan & confirm his identity with Narām of Mesopotamia

His magnificent victory slate Palette,[1] which is practically his only Egyptian monument containing inscriptions besides his mere name, is disclosed by its written labels, now deciphered for the first time, to celebrate his victory over the King of Magan, and thus strikingly confirms his identity with the Sumerian emperor Narām of Mesopotamia, who repeatedly boasts of his conquest of Magan in his imperial inscriptions in Mesopotamia.

This monument is shaped in the form of the indigenous Egyptian palette of the two-knobbed-head type, with a well or saucer in its centre for grinding cosmetic pigments (here malachite), the use of which for toilet purposes was common in prehistoric Egypt and Mesopotamia, as it still is in the Orient at the present day. The rest of the surface of the Palette on both sides is finely and artistically carved with figures, scenes and a few hieroglyphs.

Its front or face (see Plate XVI, A) is arranged as in Sumerian composite drawings into compartments separated

[1] Discovered by Mr J. E. Quibell at Hierakonpolis or "Hawk City" in 1898; and generally described by Sir F. Petrie in Hierakonpolis, 1900-10.

by horizontal lines. In the first compartment, below the duplicated man-faced Bull emblem of Narmar with his name in a cartouche between the Bull-heads is pictured the king wearing the crown of Lower Egypt in procession. The procession is coming from a fort or building bearing the Sumerian pictograph of *Uru*, meaning "Guard,"[1] and presumably it is his famous fort, which is called in the Indian Vedas "Ūrjayantī, the fort of Nārmara."[2] This procession was supposed by Sir F. Petrie to be "formed by the four

FIG. 39.—Narmar's Slate Palette, Reverse.

chiefs of nomes (or provinces) bearing the standards, the high priest Thet, the king Nar-mer [with hieroglyphs of his name in front of him] and the 'king's servant' behind them. They seem to have come from a building named *deb*. In front of the procession lie the bodies of enemies bound and decapitated. The heads, placed between the legs, are all bearded,"[3] and above them is a hieroglyph description. Below these are two mythological camel-leopard-like animals, with their necks enclosing the pigment basin. And below is the Bull, symbolizing Narām breaking down a fort, scattering the bricks and trampling upon a fleeing foe. The picture inside the fort is supposed to be the hieroglyph for the name of the town.[4]

[1] B. 290, pl. 183; M. 4587. [2] RV. 2, 13, 8. [3] QH. 10.

[4] The picture somewhat resembles the Sumerian pictograph of *Pisan-mat* or *Gur-mat*. B. 272.

A

B

KING NARMAR (MINOTAUR) OR NARAM'S SLATE PALETTE OF VICTORY, *c.* 2630 B.C. 1/2.

Found at Hierakonopolis, and now in Cairo Museum. (After J. E. Quibell and W. F. Petrie.) Both sides are shown, *A*, top with central well, and *B*, reverse. For detailed description and decipherments and translations of the Standard and other inscriptions, see pp. 292 f., 309 f.

The reverse (see Plate XVI, B) with the same Bull emblems and name above, shows the king, with the tall Sumerian and Hittite hat, grasping the forelock of his enemy with the left hand, and with uplifted mace in his right hand preparing to strike his foe, and behind him is his body servant. In front is the Sun-Hawk hooking the captured enemy by the nose; and the six plants are supposed to represent the hieroglyph of 6000, as indicating the number of captives. Behind the captive is the hieroglyph of his name. And in the bottom compartment are two fleeing foes.

Decipherment of Narmar's Palette Inscriptions of his Victory over Magan

These critically important historical inscriptions engraved on the labels and standards of the several personages and scenes pictured in Narmar's Palette, are now discovered to be written significantly in Sumerian script and in the Sumerian language. The Sumerian script employed, though largely of the usual standard linear type of the Sargonic period in Mesopotamia, has certain of the pictographs drawn in full realistic form for pictorial effect, such as the Ship-sign (*Ma*) in the name Ma-gan, and the Lion or Wolf sign on the second standard, instead of by their usual diagrammatic and abbreviated Sumerian forms for rapid writing.

It is also noteworthy that the Sumerian writing is in the reversed direction, as if intended to be read by a Semitic people accustomed to read in the *lunar* or reversed direction from right to left, instead of in the *solar* or Aryan or Sumerian direction towards the right from the left.

In my decipherments I place, as before, in line 1, the form of each sign as written on the Egyptian monument arranged in the order in which it is read when placed from left to right; in line 2 are the corresponding forms in the diagrammatic linear Sumerian writing of Mesopotamia; in line 3 are the phonetic values of the Sumerian signs in roman letters according to the standard Sumerian lexicons; and in line 4 are the severely literal translations into English all fully attested by the references in the foot-notes from the standard Sumerian lexicons.

Most of the inscriptions or labels are found on the front or face of the Palette. The chief inscriptions, apart from the name of Narmar, are those over the enemy dead and on the standards.

Inscription over Enemy Dead Deciphered

This Sumerian inscription is at the upper right-hand corner of the Palette face (see Plate XVI, A), below the man-faced bull on the right-hand side and immediately above the double row of decapitated dead bodies of the enemy. It is in two lines dovetailed; the uppermost line containing the sign of the ship (*Ma*) and the gridiron-like sign (*gan*) touch with their tops the top line bordering the compartment with

Palette.
Egypt.

Sumer
(Mesop.).

Reads: MA[1]- GAN[2] (Hu) BAT[3] -TI[4] -(Hu) WULU[5]-ES.[6]
Transl.: Magan, dead men ("birds").

FIG. 40.—Palette Inscription over Enemy Dead deciphered.

[1] B. 137; Br. 3682. [2] B. 119; Br. 3173.
[3] B. 70; Br. 1475; and see WSAD. 24, for its root in English and other Aryan words, *e.g.*, Bad, Fate, Fatal, etc.
[4] B. 76. [5] B. 289; Br. 6398.
[6] B. 432; Br. 9990 = "three," sign for plural and source of our English plural affix *S*, see WASD. 75.

the scenes; and the second line is slightly lower down and partly within the ship or boat. And these two lines are read as in Ancient Greek, the first line from right to left and the second line from left to right, or in *boustrephedon* or "ploughwise" fashion, in the alternating direction of the furrows of a ploughed field. The two Hawks facing the left, and related to the signs of this second line, appear to be introduced merely to show the direction in which this second line is to be read, namely from left to right; though they at the same time indicate the victory of the king who was professedly of the Sun-Hawk cult. In the Decipherment Table

Fig. 40, the two lines are read as one line; and the silent Hawk sign is placed within brackets.

Thus the inscription actually describes these decapitated and bound enemy dead as "Magan dead and bound men."

HIS STANDARD INSCRIPTIONS

The badges borne aloft on the standards in the procession before King Narmar are now discovered to be his Sumerian

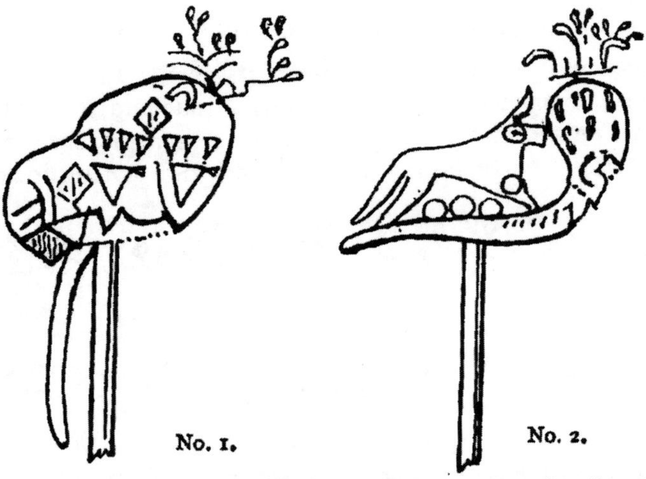

No. 1. No. 2.

FIG. 41.—Narmar's Standards, Nos. 1 and 2. (Enlarged 3 diameters from Plate XV, A).

No. 3. No. 4.

FIG. 42.—Narmar's Standards, Nos. 3 and 4. (Enlarged 3 diameters).

titles as "world-emperor" and sea-monarch. As some of the signs are small and somewhat faint yet distinct in the Plate when examined under a lens, I give here a drawing of the first two for reference; and have numbered them in serial order from the king, that nearest the king being termed No. 1, and so on.

The different shapes of the standard emblems are found to be owing to the groups of the word-signs they contain.

No. 1 Standard Inscription Deciphered

This sausage-like emblem with its tail, which has been variously conjectured to be a liver, a placenta, etc., is now seen to be a dummy effigy of the Sumerian pictograph sign for "King" with the rest of the inscription within inside it.

Palette. Egypt.

Sumer (Mesop.).

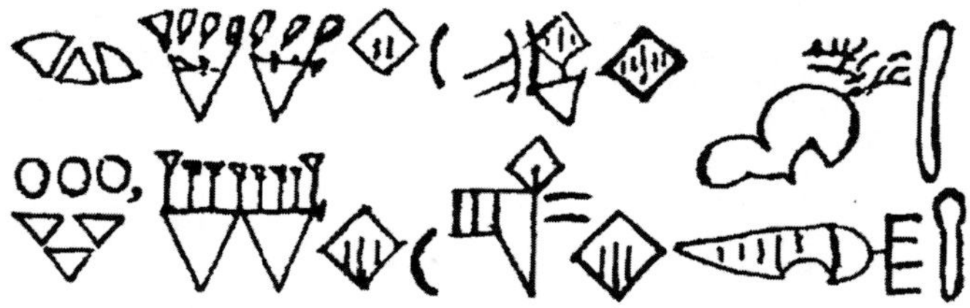

Reads: MAD[1] URI[2] -KI[3] U KISH[4] -TABKI LUGAL[5] -AN.[6]

Transl.: Of the Land of Uri (or Akkad) and Kish City, the One King.

Fig. 43.—Inscription on Narmar's Standard, No. 1 Deciphered.

[1] B. 411; Br. 7386.
[2] B. 316; Br. 7304-8.
[3] B. 217; Br. 9621.
[4] B. 377; Br. 8902.
[5] B. 169; Br. 4259.
[6] B. 1; Br. 17. Literally="The One," see WSAD. 19.

Its outline minus the tail is obviously a shortened form of the Sumerian head-sign with its crown for "king"; whilst the tail is the Sumerian sign for "one," defining him as "The One King," *i.e.* Emperor. The signs which are mostly written within the king-sign I read as above

Here Narmar calls himself "The One King of the Land of Uri," and of Kish City, wherein *Uri* has the Semitic synonym of *Akkad*, which Assyriologists identify with Sargon's and Narām's capital of Agadu. Thus this inscription conclusively identifies Narmar with Narām, the Mesopotamian emperor of Agadu, and grandson of Sargon, who boasts in his Babylonian inscriptions of his conquest of Magan ; and whose title of " The One King " is the equivalent of " Emperor."

No. 2 Standard Inscription Deciphered

In this inscription, the sign for " king " is given more of its usual early form, but it is bent on itself to accommodate and support the Lion-sign for " Western Land," which latter sign is drawn in full form to render its identity evident from afar, instead of merely the Lion's head, as in the diagrammatic Sumerian, and the lion's head with paw,

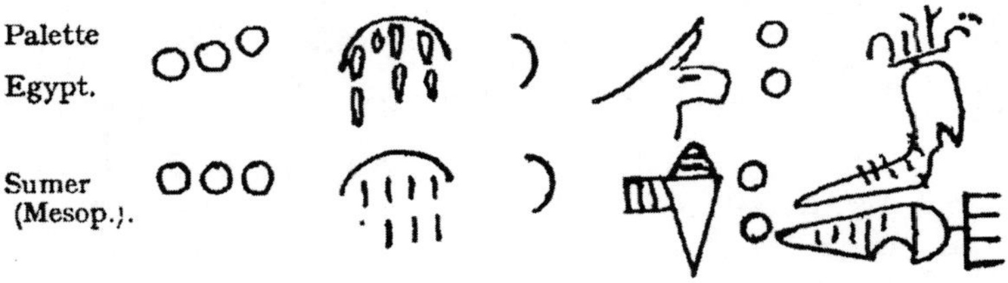

Reads : MAD -WI[1] -U[2] TIANU[3] LUGAL.

Transl. : Of the Western Sunset Land and of Tianu, the King.

Fig. 44.—Inscription on Narmar's Standard, No. 2 Deciphered.

[1] B. 380 ; Br. 8916. [2] B. 365 ; Br. 8770.

[3] For sign see B. 400 and Menes' Ebony Label ; and Br. 9220-23. The two strokes under the Lion duplicate the sign, which ordinarily reads *Pirig*. The glossaries give its possible phonetic values as Ti-a-nu, Ti-id-nu, Amurru, Martu, Axaru, *Akharu*, etc. ; and cp. MD. 30, 1148. It may possibly be related to the Ikarian Sea Land.

as in Menes' ebony label. And the other signs are placed partly within the king-sign as before.

Here Narmar calls himself " King of the Western Sunset Land and of Tianu." This " Total Western Sunset Land " includes the Mediterranean Coast Land, with Egypt and Europe. " Tianu " Land or " Land of the Lions " is variously read by Assyriologists as *Tidnu* or *Tidanu* ;[1] and is considered to be Asia Minor or Amorite Land, that is Syria-Phœnicia ; and one of its definitions in the glossaries is *Amurru* Land, *i.e.*, " Land of the Amorites," including Palestine.

[1] See previous note.

Nos. 3 & 4 Standard Inscriptions Deciphered

These two standards bear the same general emblematic form. This emblem, which replaces the " King " sign of the first two standards, is apparently the effigy of the Sumerian pictographic  sign of the Shepherd's Crook for the title *Bar* or *Par*, " Lord," which Sumerian word-sign we have seen was the source of the Egyptian title of " Pharaoh " ; and it has also in Sumerian the angular form of . And the surmounting Hawk designates him as " Pharaoh of the Sun-Hawk line."

Palette. Egypt.

Sumer (Mesop.).

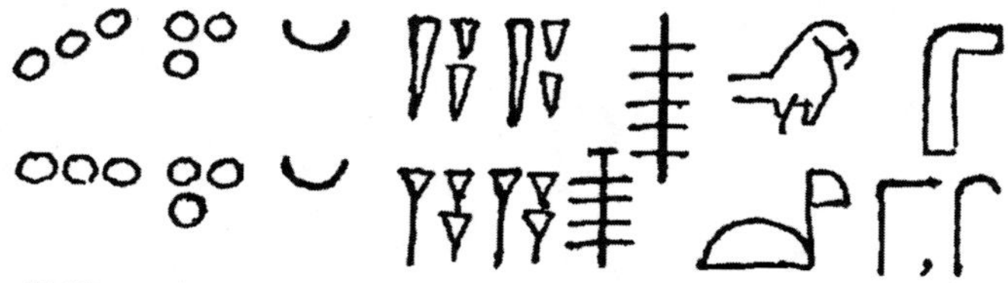

Reads : MAD -MAD -U -A-A[1] NUN[2] - HU[3] -PAR.[4]

Transl. : Of the Lands and Waters, The Great Sea-Lord, the Hawk(-line) Pharaoh.

Fig. 45.—Inscription on Narmar's Standards, Nos. 3 and 4 Deciphered.

[1] As before. [2] B. 94 ; Br. 2622. [3] B. 82 ; Br. 2045.
[4] B. 77 a ; Br. 1722 and 1752 ; and WSAD. 33-34 ; WISD. 31, 40 f.

The two inscriptions differ slightly, the first referring to his Land and Sea empire, and the second to his universal Sea-empire.

Here on standard No. 3 Narmar calls himself " The Great Sea-Lord of The Lands and Waters, the Hawk(-line) Pharaoh," and he uses the same Sumerian sign and title for " Sea-Lord " as we have seen was used by his ancestral Aryan sea-emperors of Uruash's First Phœnician Dynasty for " Sea-Lord," namely, the sign of " the great Fish " or Sea-serpent of the Deep. On his 4th standard he calls himself " The Great Sea Lord of the Lands of The Seven Seas," the earliest occurrence known of the latter title.[1]

Thus, the four Standards of Narmar with their emblems and inscriptions confirm positively the identity of Pharaoh

[1] " The Seven Seas " are not specifically mentioned in the Indian Vedas, but these repeatedly refer to " The Seven Mother Rivers," " The Seven Regions of the Earth," " The Seven Races of Mesi," " The Seven Horses " of the Sun-God's Car, " The Seven Fiends," and " The Seven Days of the Week."

Narmar, "The One King of Akkad Kish, and of the Western Sunset Land and of Amurru and Great Sea-Lord (of the Two Seas), the Hawk (-line) Pharaoh, and conqueror of Magan" with the Mesopotamian emperor Narām, grandson of Sargon, King of Agadu and the Four Quarters of the World and conqueror of Magan, as recorded in his own inscriptions in Mesopotamia.

Inscription over Narmar's Attendant

The Sumerian inscription over the attendant behind the king, carrying what appear to be a pair of sandals and a pot reads: *E, Kha-du* or *Khal-du*,[1] according to whether the top sign is a six-rayed figure or the eight-rayed Sun pictograph; but both compounds mean the same, namely, the "Runner forth."[2]

Name of Magan, Captive Chief on Narmar's Palette as "Manun Dan" as on his Mesopotamian Inscription

The personal name of the captive Magan chief who is pictured on the reverse of the Palette (Plate XVI B) in a kneeling posture, with his forelock grasped by King Narmar with uplifted mace, is enclosed within a rectangular panel. Above this panel is the Sumerian sign for "The Man."[3]

The name written in the panel is presumably that of the vanquished king of Magan, who is called in the copies of Narām's Mesopotamian inscriptions Mannu(?)-Dan." The signs are here so minute that several cannot be deciphered even by a lens. But the name appears to read "Manun-dan."

Narām Enzu's Version of his Conquest of Mannu Dan in his Mesopotamian & Babylonian Records

Having thus discovered and deciphered Narām's own original inscription in Egypt as Narmar, on his victory over the king of Magan, it is necessary for us now to compare it with Narām's own accounts of that victory in his Mesopotamian inscriptions, for it further strikingly confirms the identity of Narām with Narmar.

1 Br. 7873; and WSAD. 68 f.
2 B. 2; Br. 78; and B. 207; Br. 4871.
3 *Wulu*, B. 289.

The emperor Narām Enzu in Mesopotamia considered his conquest of the king of Magan as one of his great victories, for he repeatedly refers to it in his records in Mesopotamia, and it is also recorded in the later Babylonian Chronicle copies of his inscriptions. The Babylonian Chronicle states:

"Narām An-Enzu, the son [1] of King Gin (Sharru-Gin) . . . against Magan City he marched and Mannu-Dānnu (?), the king of Magan City [his hand subdued].[2]

The Omens repeat the same, but using the word "land" instead of "city" and supplying the sentence enclosed above within square brackets. And on the base of a diorite statue of Narām in Elam, the latter claims to have "cast down Manu . . . [(?) Dannu] lord of Magan" on his conquest of that country.[3]

King of Magan defeated by Narmar or Narām was not King Menes of Egypt

It is thus rendered abundantly clear by the testimony of King Narmar or Narām himself on his own Egyptian monument that King Manun-Dan (or Mannu-Dannu) of Magan, conquered by him, was not, as has hitherto been supposed, Menes of Egypt, who we have found was his own father. On the contrary, besides his name and country-name, this king of Magan is pictured by Narmar in this Palette of aboriginal type, with large broad negroid nose, long matted and (?) woolly hair, and like the other oborigines in the scenes, naked except for a loin string.

King Narmar of Egypt identical with King Narām Enzu (or "Sin") of Mesopotamia, son of Manis-Tusu (or Menes) and Grandson of "Sargon"-the-Great.

We have thus established conclusively the identity of King Narmar of Egypt with the Mesopotamian emperor Narām Enzu (or "Sin"), the son of the Mesopotamian emperor Manis-Tusu, who was the son of Sargon-the-Great by a mass of positive contemporary documentary evidence

[1] Here "son" = "descendant."
[2] KC. 2, 38 f.
[3] DP. *Mém.* 6 (1905), 25; STS. 3, 5; TDI, 239.

from their own monuments in Egypt and Mesopotamia, and from the official king-lists of Menes' Dynasty in Egypt and from those of Manis-Tusu's Dynasty in Mesopotamia. The occurrence of his name in some sealings, alternating with *Man,* his father's name, presumes that he was co-regent for a time in his father's old age.

This new evidence also strikingly confirms the previous evidence we have elicited for the *Sumerian or Aryan Origin of Egyptian Civilization.*

The identity of the subsequent kings of Menes' Dynasty in Egypt with those of Manis-Tusu's Dynasty in Mesopotamia is demonstrated in the next chapter.

FIG. 45A.—Seal of Naram's son King Gani II or Gan-Eri, showing Gishsax (the Sumerian original of Hercules) watering his buffaloes c. 2580 B.C. (From the De Clercq collection.) Note the fine naturalistic drawing and the duplication for symmetry.

XVII

Menes' First Dynasty of Egypt identical with Manis-Tusu's Dynasty of Mesopotamia & with Indian Lists from THIRD KING to END of this Dynasty, & their World-Empire, about 2527 B.C.

Disclosing their Egyptian contemporary Inscriptions in Sumerian deciphered for the first time, recording their World-Empire in Mesopotamia, Egypt, etc., and invoking Tasia or Tascio the Sun-archangel for Resurrection as in Sumerian Mesopotamia, Asia Minor, Indus Valley, Troy & Ancient Britain, and their Indus Seals deciphered.

Having established in the previous three chapters the identity of Menes, the first king of the First Dynasty of Egypt and Narmar the second king of that dynasty with the Mesopotamian emperor Manis-the-Warrior or Manis-Tusu and his son and successor Narām Enzu (or " Sin "), we now proceed with the identification of the remaining kings of Menes' First Dynasty of Egypt with those of Manis-Tusu's Dynasty in Mesopotamia.

This general identity of Menes' Egyptian Dynasty with Manis-Tusu's Mesopotamian Dynasty, I have already established by the Comparative Table of the official king-lists of those two dynasties Egyptian and Mesopotamian, confirmed by the official lists of the Early Aryan kings from the Indian Chronicles—the agreement being absolute except in regard to the 6th and 7th Egyptian Kings, who were presumably local kings in Egypt and not emperors in Mesopotamia. From that Table, it is seen that the third king and successor of Narmar in Menes' dynasty in Egypt is the so-called King " Khent " of Egyptologists, the " Kenkenēs of Manetho's list ; but who writes his name on his own Egyptian monuments, as we shall now find, as *Shar Guni-Rit* and *Sag-Gina.*

THIRD KING OF MENES' DYNASTY, SAG-GINA OR SHAR-GUNI-RIT (OR -RI), THE SO-CALLED "KHENT" OR "KENKENĒS" IDENTICAL WITH THIRD KING IN MANIS-TUSU'S DYNASTY IN MESOPOTAMIAN & IN INDIAN LISTS

The identity of the third king of Menes' dynasty in Egypt, the so-called King "Khent," or Kenkenēs of Manetho's list, with the third king of Manis-Tusu's dynasty in Mesopotamia has been demonstrated in the above Table.

In Mesopotamia the name of the son and successor of Narām Enzu is conjecturally read by Assyriologists variously as *Shar-gani-shar-ri*, *Shar-gali-sharri*, *Shar-gani-shar-ali* and *Shar-gani-shar-eri* (or *eru*). As, however, he is seen to be a namesake of his great-grandfather Sargon, whose personal name we have seen as Shar-Gani or Shar-Guni is properly "King *Gani* or *Guni*," the front half of his name therefore reads "King *Gani* or *Guni*." The latter half or the special titular portion of his name is not however spelt in Sumerian *Shar-ri* or *Shar-eri*, but is spelt *Lugal-Ri* (or *Eri*),[1] that is "King *Ri*," and the last sign has also the value *Eridu*.[2] Thus this king's name reads in his Mesopotamian records "King *Gani* (or *Guni*), the king *Ri* (or *Eri* or *Eridu*)."

The Indian lists support this reading of his name, as the solar versions give his name variously as *Kunti*-jit and *Ritu*-jit, that is "*Kunti* or *Ritu* the victorious," wherein *Kunti* equates with the Sumerian *Guni* and *Ritu* with *Ri* of the Sumerian.

INDUS VALLEY SEALS OF KING SHA-GIN II OR GAN-ERI

In the second batch of Indus Valley seals I found the following four seals of this king, shown in Plate XIV, and give their detailed decipherment in Appendix XI. In the first and second he is Under-King Companion in the Indus Valley, presumably under his father Narām. In the others he is emperor. The second seal is especially important in that he calls himself therein by his title of *Dili*, as in his ivory tablet in Egypt and by the Sumerian sign, and also "The King of the Great Khāmaesh Land," that is as we have

[1] B. 39. Br. 889-90.

[2] On *Eridu* value of this sign see HCC. No. 41, p. 39, and Pr. 2645 and 2649.

seen Egypt, thus apparently implying that the Indus Valley was then tributary to Egypt.

The records on these seals read as follows :—

No. 1 Seal (Plate XIV, 4 and Fig. 107)

" Under-King Companion Sha-Gin at Edin (or Agdu) Land."

No. 2 Seal (Plate XIV, 6 and Fig. 109)

" Under-King Companion Gan, The Great Khāmaesh King Dili, The Great Khāmaesh (Egypt) King, The Seal of Gin the Gut."

No. 3 Seal (Plate XIV, 3 and Fig. 106)

" Gan-Eri, The Ruler of the Lands, The Lord Gin."

No. 4 Seal (Plate XIV, 5 and Fig. 108)

" Lord Gin at Edin (or Agdu) Land."

Third King's Name in Egyptian Records

In Egypt, the name of this third king, which has been read variously as " Khent " and Zer-Ta, is found on several

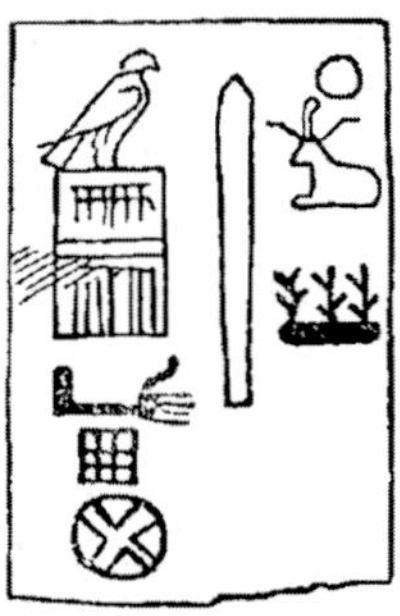

Fig. 46.—Ivory Label of Third King. (After Sir F. Petrie, PRT. ii. Pl. VI.)

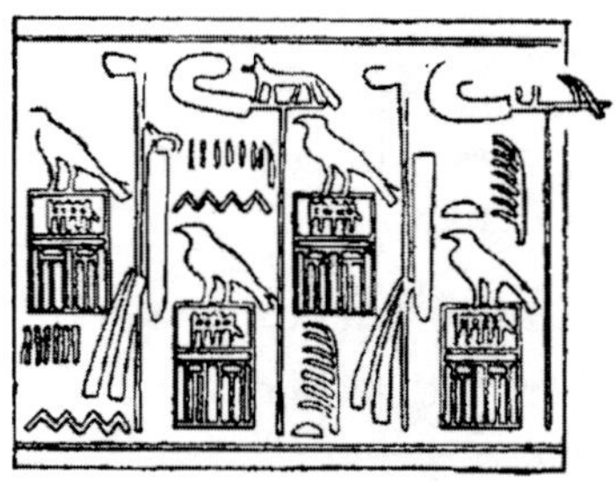

Fig. 47.—Sealing of Third King. (After Sir F. Petrie, PRT. ii. Pl. XV.)

ivory labels and clay sealings impressed by cylinder-seals of Sumerian type from his tomb at Abydos (see Figs. 46 and 47).

The writing on these labels and sealings is seen to be essentially in Sumerian script.

THIRD KING'S NAME ON IVORY LABEL IN EGYPT DECIPHERED & IN AGREEMENT WITH MESOPOTAMIAN & INDIAN FORMS

The inscription on his ivory label (see Fig. 46) is written in reversed direction; and when the signs are arranged to read from left to right they are as follows in Fig. 48, where their equivalent Sumerian signs and values, with translation, are added, as in the other cases.

Here the king calls himself, or is called in his tomb, "King *Guni*, Man of the (Sun-)Hawk (line), *Rit*, the

Egypt Label.

Sumer (Mesop.).

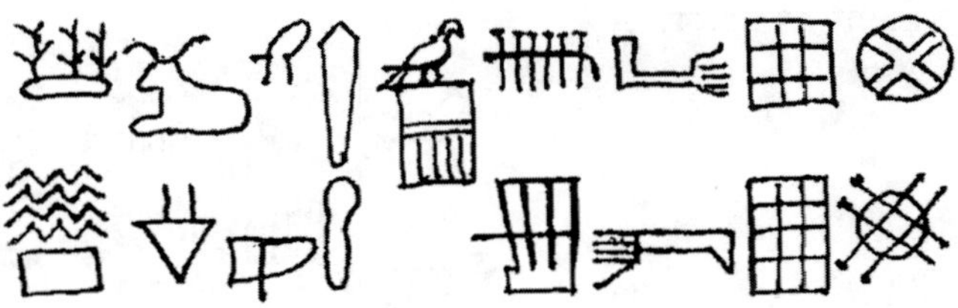

Reads: SHAR[1]-GU[2]-NI[3] DILI[4]-PA[5] RIT[6] A[7] - SAKH[8] GUN.[9]

Transl.: King GUNI, man of the (Sun-)Hawk (House of Pharaoh) RIT, the Lord GUN.

FIG. 48.—Third King's Name on Ivory Label deciphered.

1 B. 170; Br. 4297.
2 B. 275; Br. 6104. On this as cow-sign see WISD. 51 f.
3 B. 228; Br. 5310. This sign is between the horns of the cow. The object represented by this Sumerian sign is supposed to be a Teat.
4 B. 1; Br. 27=" man."
5 B. 83; Br. 2048. Has also *Hu* value.
6 See foot-note on previous page.
7 B. 293; Br. 6542 or *Du* B. 294; Br. 6644.
8 B. 269; Br. 5928.
9 B. 307; Br. 6985.

Pharaoh *Sakh-Gun*." And it is of immense critical significance that his title here as "Man of the Sun-Hawk line," which is spelt in this Egypto-Sumerian text *Dili-pa*, is actually given as his solar title in the Indian king-lists as *Dilī-pa*. This is another striking testimony to the remarkable authenticity of the Indian Chronicles, and shows again that the Indian scribes who transcribed the Sumerian syllabic writing into the Indian alphabetic script were familiar with Sumerian, and also that they evidently differentiated this king from his namesake, his great-grandfather Sargon, by selecting for him this more distinctive part of his title, *Dili-pa*. And the identity is still more striking by the Indian lunar versions giving him the title of "*Ritu* the Conqueror," wherein *Ritu* is in series with his *Rit* title in this Egyptian inscription. This presumes that his Mesopotamian affixed title *Ri* is a shortened form of *Rit*.

Third King's Name on Sealings in Egypt deciphered

In these clay sealings (Fig. 47) the king's personal name is spelt *Gin-ti* instead of *Gani*, in series with his *Kunti* title in the Indian lists and *Khent* in the later Egyptian hieroglyphs. In the annexed figure these signs are arranged for decipherment as before :

Reads : BURU[1] MAR[2] -PA[3] RIT[4] GIN[5]-TI (or NA).[6]

Transl. : Lord (Pharaoh) Son of the (Sun-)Hawk, Rit (or Sag), Gin-ti (or Na).

Fig. 49.—Third King's Name on Sealings deciphered.

[1] B. 365 ; Br. 8632, 8657-9.

[2] B. 392, and cp. form of this sign *mar* in WSAD. Pl. IV ; WPOB. Fig. 36, in present work Fig. 21, p. 149.

[3] B. 83 ; Br. 2048.

[4] As before.

[5] B. 283. As before, in Sargon's Egyptian inscription.

[6] B. 76 ; Br. 1695. This sign seems to be the local Egyptian form of the Sumerian sign *Ti* for a drill, which is defined as "drive away, throw down," and in Egyptian this sign with alphabetic value *T* is considered the picture of a stone-drill cap. GH. 49. But this sign may have been read in Sumerian as *Na*, the Stone-sign.

Here the king calls himself "The *Buru* (Pharaoh), Son of the (Sun-) Hawk, *Rit*, *Ginti*. And significantly in the next compartment of the sealing (see Fig. 47) it will be noticed that he calls himself again *Dilipa Rit* as his solar title, in agreement with his Indian solar titles of *Dilipa* and *Ritu*.

We thus find that the third king of Menes' Dynasty in

Egypt in his Egyptian inscriptions is called by the same name and titles as the third king of Manis-Tusu's Dynasty in Mesopotamia and in the lists of Early Aryan kings in the Indian Chronicles.

Fourth King of Menes' Dynasty Baggid *re* Fourth King of Manis-Tusu's Dynasty and his Name on his Egyptian Monuments

The fourth king in Manis-Tusu's dynasty has his name spelt *Igigi* in the Babylonian lists (see Table, p. 61); but no inscriptions of him have been found in Mesopotamia. He arose and reigned during a brief period of anarchy

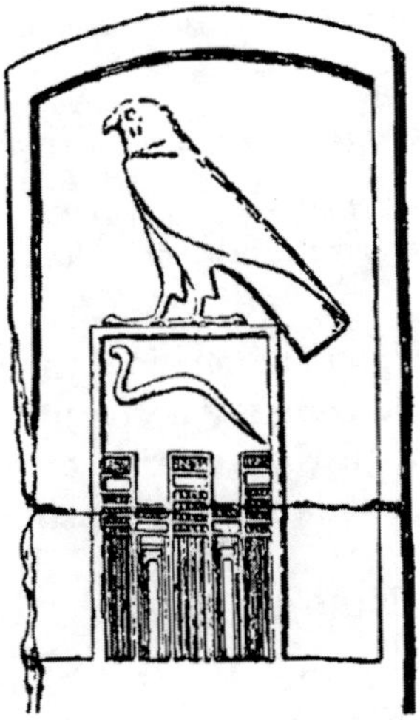

Fig. 50.—Stele of 4th King of Menes' Dynasty. (After Petrie).

Fig. 51.—Seal of 4th King "Zet" in Egypt. (After Sir F. Petrie. PHE. 1, 17.)

or revolution on the death of the third king; and he corresponds to the Indian list king, called Bhagī-ratha or "Bhagī-the-charioteer."

This latter name supplies a key to his name on the Egyptian monuments, see Figs. 50 and 51. In Egypt the fourth king of Menes' Dynasty wrote his solar name by the Sun-hawk and the sign of the Serpent,[1] which last has a phonetic value of *Gid*. Thus with the *Ba* or *Bag* value of

[1] B. 325; Br. 7501 f.

the Hawk-sign followed by *Gid,* we get his name as *Bagid* or *Baggid,* in series with his *Bhagi* name in the Indian Lists, see decipherment table, Fig. 52.

Egypt Seal.

Sumer (Mesop.).

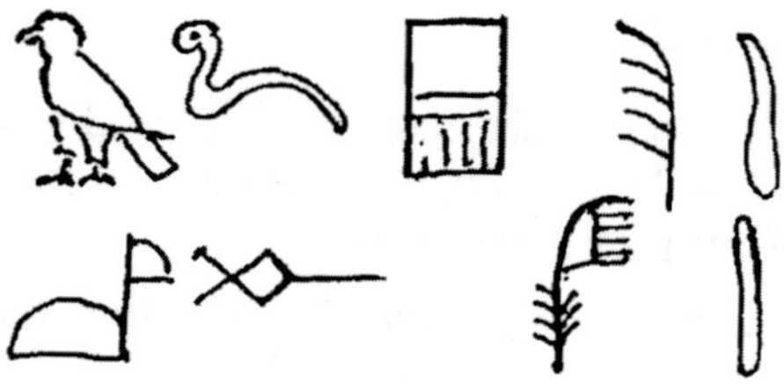

Reads: BAG GID [1] GI [2] - RU.[3]

Transl.: The(Sun-)Hawk (line) Pharaoh GID, GI- T(il).

FIG. 52.—Seal of 4th King of Menes' Dynasty Deciphered.

[1] Br. 7504, and see foot-note 1, p. 325. [2] B. 283; Br. 6307.

[3] This sign on the seal is a long tapered wand with recovered tip, which in later Egyptian has the value of *Ta* or *Ty.* GH. 62. It is now seen to be the Sumerian sign *Tal* or *Til*="stretched out" (M. 9); and thus disclosed as the Sumerian source of our English word "Tall" But its *Ru* value is obviously intended here.

It thus appears that the *Igigi* name for the Fourth Babylonian King of Manis-Tusu's Dynasty is corrupted from his Egyptian solar title of *Gid* with the addition of his name *Gi-ru,* in which the final *d* of first syllable is dropped out.

INDUS VALLEY SEAL OF 4TH KING OF MENES' DYNASTY

I find a seal of his from the Indus colony, see Plate XIV, 7, and deciphered in Fig. 110, p. 574. It reads:—"BAG-ERI of the house of Maru-Ner at Uri-du Land." This seal name thus equates with his Indian name of "Bhagīratha," into which it has been expanded by the Brahmans.

FIFTH KING OF MENES' DYNASTY DUDU OR DUNDU IDENTICAL WITH 5TH CHIEF KING OF MANIS-TUSU'S DYNASTY, DUDU, & WITH DHUNDU OF INDIAN LISTS

The fifth king of Menes' Dynasty, "Den" of Egyptologists, is now demonstrated to be identical with the fifth chief king of Manis-Tusu's Dynasty, *Dudu* or *Dundu* (see Kish Chronicle, p. 61), and the *Dhundu* of the Indian lists.

FIG. 52A.—King Dudu or "Den's" Portrait on a label from Abydos. (After Sir F. Petrie).

INDUS VALLEY SEALS OF KING DUDU OR DAN

In the second batch of Indus Valley seals I found two seals of King Dudu or Dan, figured in Plate XIV, 8 and 9. These are of critical historical importance in giving besides his name *Dudu*, also his synonym of *Dan*, and also his father's name as GANI ERI, who is moreover called GAN-*the-Second*, that is "Sargon-the-Second"; and he appears also to call himself, like Sargon, a descendant of Uku or "Ukushi," the first Sumerian or Aryan king.

The detailed decipherment is relegated to Appendix XI. The records on the seals read as follows :—

NO. 1 SEAL (PLATE XIV, 8, and Fig. 111)

"DUDU DAN, son of GANI (or SHUKUNNI-)ERI. The seal of the Minister Lord at Edin Land."

NO. 2 SEAL (PLATE XIV, 9, and Fig. 112)

"DAN, the son of GAN-the-Second of the House of UKU (Lord) *Neres*, the Great (?) UKUSH, the Gut."

KING DUDU'S NAME & INSCRIPTIONS IN EGYPT

He has left several immensely important historical inscriptions besides his seals and signatures, all of which being written in Sumerian script have not been hitherto read, and are now deciphered and translated here for the first time.

PERSONAL NAME OF 5TH KING AS DUDU OR DUNDU, & DECIPHERMENT OF ITS SIGNS

In Egypt the personal name of the fifth king reads I find in the Sumerian inscriptions of that king as *Dudu* or *Dundu*(*n*), that is just as we have seen it so spelt in his inscriptions in Mesopotamia (see Table p. 298).

In Egypt this personal name is written by duplicating the "Desert" sign or hieroglyph of a three-knobbed mound (see Fig. 53.) The phonetic value of this sign in Egyptian has been unknown, but because it is used as a determinative or pictorial index-sign to words meaning "desert," it has been

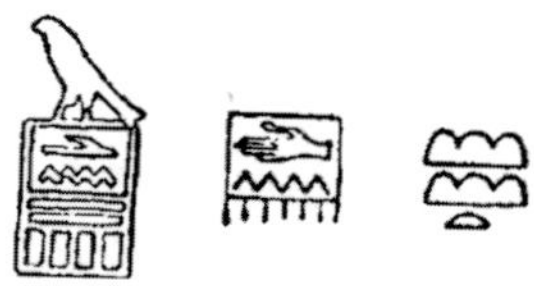

a. *b.* *c.*

FIG. 53.—Personal Name of Dudu, Dan or Dundu in 5th King's Inscriptions in Egypt. (After Sir F. Petrie.)

a. PAT. 1, pl. 5, 11 ; *b. Ib.*, 1, pl. 5, 12 ; *c. Ib.*, 2, pl. 7, 7.

assumed by Egyptologists to have had the phonetic value of the commonest Egyptian word for "desert," namely "*Sem-t*" ; and hence the name of this king has been conjecturally read as "Semty."

But this "desert" hieroglyph, which occurs in the Sumerian inscriptions of this king in Egypt, is now seen to be merely a fuller realistic drawing of the Sumerian pictograph *Du* or *Dun*, meaning "mound, earthwork, hill" (see Fig. 54) ; and it is, as I have shown, the Sumerian origin of our English word *Dune* for "sand-hills," *Downs*, etc., Sanskrit *Dhanu*, "sand-bank," and it runs with this sound and meaning throughout the other Aryan languages.[1] The three knobs in the Egyptian hieroglyph are now seen to be a fuller form of drawing the three strokes inside a circle or triangle, to which the Sumerians in Mesopotamia reduced this picture diagrammatically for speedy writing (see Fig. 54.) And the identity

[1] WSAD. 63.

of the signs is further confirmed by the interior dots within some versions of the Egyptian hieroglyphs (see Fig. 54), which dots are also found in this sign in some Sumerian documents (see Fig. 54)—these dots presumably picturing grains of sand, earth or pebbles on the mound sign.

The Mound-Sign DU or DUN in Egyptian Hieroglyphs deciphered through the Sumerian & identical in Sumerian & Egyptian

The Egyptian phonetic value of this mound sign is discovered through the Sumerian in the following figure, in which the Egyptian forms of the sign are given in the first line, the Sumerian diagrammatic forms in the second line, and the phonetic value of the latter in the third line.

Egypt.

Sumer (Mesop.).

Reads: DU (or DUN).[1] DU (or DUN).[1]

Fig. 54.—The Sumerian Mound sign in Egyptian = DU or DUN as in Sumerian.

[1] B. 417, pls. 108 and 171; Br. 9577. On the *Dun* value for this sign see WSAD. 63, and cp. Br. 4861 and Br. 9577.

This *Du* value for this Mound sign was later preserved also in Egyptian, as the phonetic value of *Du* is occasionally attached to the two-peaked Mound sign; [1] and in some of this king's inscriptions the sign is two-peaked.[2]

It is thus seen that the personal name of the fifth king of Menes' Dynasty in Egypt, written by the duplicated Mound sign, in his inscriptions which are in the Sumerian writing and language, reads *Du-du* or *Dun-du* (*n*). And it is thus in strict literal agreement with his name as the fifth chief king in Manis-Tusu's Dynasty in Mesopotamia.

We now proceed to his solar title or name.

[1] GH. 31. [2] PRT. 2, pl. 7, etc.

Solar Title of 5th King, Dudu, of Menes' Dynasty Deciphered as Dana

The usual solar title of the fifth king of Menes' Dynasty is written as in Fig. 55, by the hieroglyphs of a Hand and the Negation sign; and it is read by Egyptologists as D-N or "Den."

Now both of these hieroglyphs, the Hand and the Negation signs, are derived with their form, sound and meaning from the Sumerian. The Hand sign with its value *Da* I have already demonstrated to be of Sumerian origin.[1] Similarly so is this *Na* or negative hieroglyph, which in Egyptian means "No" or "Not"[2] It is the Sumerian *Na* or *Nu*,[3] which is now disclosed as the source of the English "*No*," "*Not*," and all the negative *N* words in the Aryan family of languages. In Sumerian its sign pictures a line cancelled by a wavy or straight stroke through it (see Fig. 56 line 2); and in Egyptian it is a wavy cancelling line (see Fig. 56 line 1) as in modern conventional cancelling of a written word by a wavy line. These are therefore other striking instances of the derivation of the Egyptian language and writing from the Sumerian.

Thus his solar title as seen in Fig 54, reads *Da-na*[4] or Du-nu,[5] or as one syllable *Dan* or *Dun*. *Dan* in Sumerian as in Egyptian and other Aryan languages means "mighty, powerful";[6] or if its value was *Dun*, it had the same form as his personal name.

Dudu's Title of "Usaphaidos" in Sumero-Egyptian

This fifth king of Menes' Dynasty is called by Manetho "Usaphaid-os," a title which cannot be found on the monuments or explained by Egyptologists, though an

[1] WSAD. 44, Pl. II.

[2] BD. 339 a.

[3] B. 79; Br. 1958. The *Nu* value is inferred from the Akkadian *Nu*=No; but Akkadian words ending in *u* have *a* in Sumerian.

[4] B. 294; *Da*, Br. 6643; on *Du* value, Br. 6644.

[5] See foot-note 3.

[6] WSAD. 49.

inscription has been read as "Den-Setui." This inscription is here given in Fig. 55.

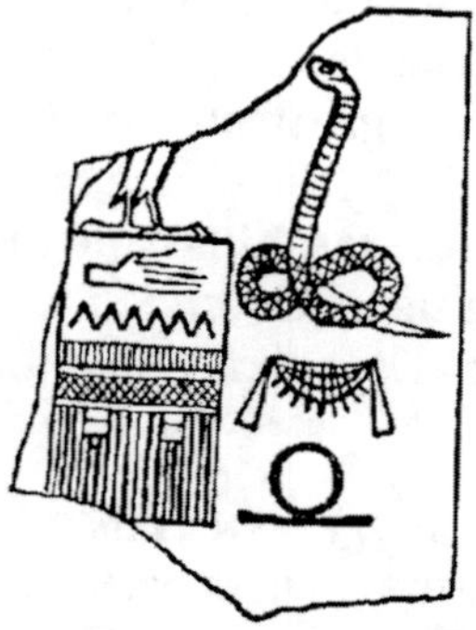

FIG. 55.—Inscription of Dudu or Dundu from Lid of a Seal-box. (After Petrie. PHE. 1, 20; PRT. 1, pl. 7, 12).

This inscription through the Sumerian reads as follows :—

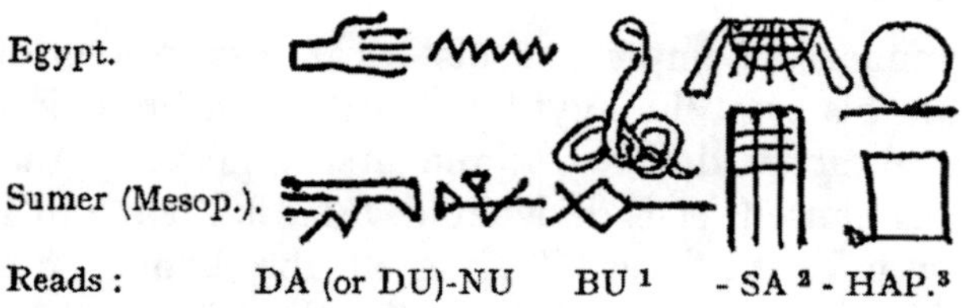

FIG. 56.—Inscription of Dundu with title "Busahap" deciphered.

[1] B. 325. [2] B. 118. A Net.
[3] Br. 10159; B. 443. This square=a circle.

This *Busahap* title in his own inscription in Egypt clearly discloses the Sumerian source of Dudu's Egyptian title of Usaphaid-os of the later scribes. It is moreover incidentally of considerable historical importance, in that it supplies *in all three of its signs* additional evidence to what I have demonstrated in my *Sumer-Aryan Dictionary* of the derivation of the Egyptian hieroglyphs from the Sumerian in form, sound and meaning. The first sign *Bu* figured in Sumerian by a Serpent is seen to be the Sumerian source of the Egyptian value of *Fau* for Serpent and its sign.[1] The second sign *sa*, "a net," and pictured by a net in

[1] Cp. WSAD. 76.

Sumerian is seen to be the Sumerian source of the Egyptian hieroglyph *skha*(*t*) or *sha*(*t*)[1] "a net," and its sign. And the third sign picturing a loop of cord, with the meaning in Egyptian of "loop, circle, ring," and secondarily through its sense of enclosure "great multitude,"[2] is now disclosed as the Sumerian sign *Hap* (the source of the English "Heap") which possesses all these meanings and also that of "Heap"[3] and its Akkadian value of *Shinu*[4] is now discovered to be also the source of its Egyptian name and phonetic value of *Shenu*.

Inscriptions from Egyptian Tomb of King Dudu or Dundu deciphered, Disclosing his World-emperorship in West, Mesopotamia, & East, his Parentage & Invocation of Sun-Archangel Tasia as in Sumerian, Trojan & Indus Valley Seals & in Prehistoric Monuments & Coins of the Ancient Britons

The immensely important historical inscriptions of this king from his tomb in Egypt are written in Sumerian, and are now deciphered here for the first time.[5] In these he designates himself, or is designated, besides "King of Upper and Lower Egypt," also "King of the Lands from the Rising Sun to the Setting Sun in the West" and "King of Kish" and "son of King Gana or Gin-Ri," that is the third king and grandson of Menes or Manis-Tusu; and thus identifying him absolutely with the Mesopotamian emperor Dudu or Dundu. He moreover invokes for his Resurrection the Sun-archangel Tasia, and in the same general formulas as in the Sumerian, Trojan, Indus Valley seals and in the "prehistoric monuments of the 3rd millennium B.C. in Ancient Britain.[6] This discovery of the active prevalence of this Tasia cult (the "Tascio" of the Ancient Briton pre-Roman coins) in Egypt in this Sargonic or Menes' Dynasty in the early part of the third millennium B.C., appears to indicate

[1] BD. 618, 695.
[2] GH. 47.
[3] B. 443.
[4] M. 7695.
[5] The proposed interpretations of some of the signs by Mr Griffiths, PRT. 1, 40 f., were admittedly "tentative" and conjectural.
[6] WPOB. 243 f.; 249 f.; 254 f.; 261 f.; 335 f.; and *passim*; WISD. 37 f.; 79 f.; WSAD. 53.

PLATE XVIA.

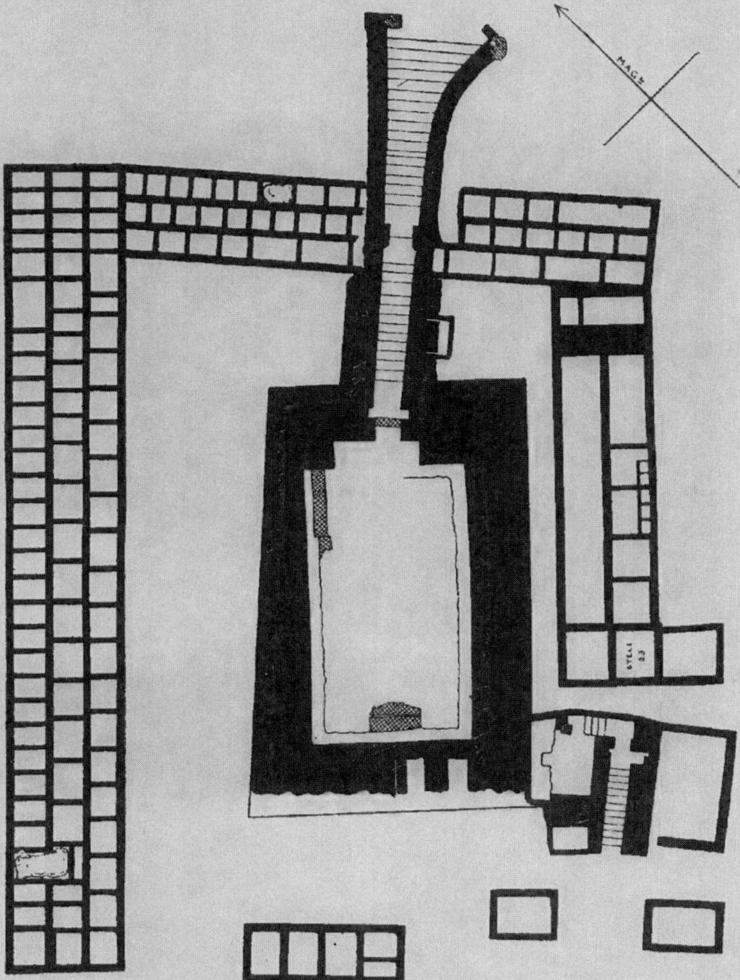

TOMB OF KING DUDU AT ABYDOS.

(After Sir F. Petrie, PRT. II, Pl. LXII.) Note the enormous development of the tomb with surrounding chambers to accommodate the abundant food and other offerings to minister to the supposed comfort of the spirit of the deceased king.

PLATE XVII.

KING DUDU'S ("DEN-SETUI'S") TOMB EBONY LABELS AT ABYDOS, *c.* 2536.

(From photographs by Sir F. Petrie, PRI. I, Pl. XI.) For decipherment and translation, see pp. 333 f.

the route by which that cult reached Ancient Britain about that period (as I have shown that it did), through the seafaring, colonial and mining trade activities of this enterprising Egypto-Sumerian world-empire.

These tomb inscriptions are mostly engraved on ivory and ebony tablets, some of them with portraits of the king. Those selected here for examination and decipherment are the best preserved of the larger of those many fragmentary records (Plate XVII.).

Decipherment of Egyptian Inscriptions of King Dudu or Dundu

The writing in the inscriptions from the tomb of King Dudu or Dundu in Egypt is seen to be unequivocally of Sumerian type in the linear cursive kind, written with pen and ink, and ink inscriptions are found on some of those tomb objects) as found engraved in the earlier Sumerian period in Mesopotamia and in the Indus Valley seals, as opposed to the more angular diagrammatic form in the lapidary and cuneiform style latterly current in Mesopotamia. Some of the signs are already becoming conventionalized into their local Egyptian forms as found in the Egyptian hieroglyphs; and this well illustrates the derivation of the latter from the Sumerian writing.

In this pioneer decipherment of this writing in its transition stage from the Sumerian to the conventionalized Egyptian hieroglyphs and hieratic writing, the readings and translations are made as before through the Sumerian keys of the lapidary script of Mesopotamia. The freely cursive form of the writing in these Egyptian inscriptions, as in the Indus Valley, somewhat modifies the forms of the Sumerian signs occasionally. But although a few signs are thus somewhat doubtful, it is believed that these in no material way alter the sense of the records and their immense historical and religious significance. For convenience of reference I have marked the two chief inscriptions of King Dudu here deciphered as Nos. 1 and 2 on the next and following pages.

King Dudu or Dundu's Tomb Inscription No. 1, Disclosing his World-Empire Titles, Parentage & Prayer to Sun-Angel Tasia for Resurrection

This ebony label inscription (Plate XVII,[1] facing p. 332) is incomplete in its lower edge—the lower fragment in the plate is part of another ebony tablet which was evidently

Egypt.

Sumer (Mesop.).

Reads : BATU [1] LUGAL [2]-DU-DU [3]-GE [4] TUR [5] ENE [6] BARA.

Transl. : Of the dead [1] King Dudu the tomb. The (enthroned) Lord the Pharaoh.

Fig. 57.—Line 1 of column 1, of Dudu's Tomb Ebony Label No. 1 deciphered.

[1] This sign *Batu* or *Bat* (B. 432 ; Br. 9971) is, as I have shown, synonymous with *Bat* " Dead " (Br. 1578 ; WPOB. 243 f. ; WSAD. 24) ; and is the usual sign for " Dead " on Sumerian funereal monuments, with the phonetic variant of *Matu* (WPOB. 255 f. ; WISD. 89 f.). It is also defined as " crushed, beat out " (M. 7543). And it is, as I have shown, the Sumerian source of the English Bad, Fate, Fatal, and their compounds (WSAD. 24).

[2] This sign for " king " in Sumerian is a diagram of the King's bust and crowned head ; without legs.

[3] The prominence given to the legs of the king in the pictograph suggests that they are to be read separately as 2 legs, which have the Sumerian sign value of *Du-du* : especially as this king wrote his name Du-du in Mesopotamia always by the sign of 2 legs with the meaning of run as here pictured. The Leg-sign = *Du* in Sumerian. B. 207 ; Br. 4860.

[4] *Ge* or *Gi* " of " (Br. 7313 ; and cp. WAOA. *Gi* in pl. 1).

[5] This is evidently a pictograph of a tomb (B. 57 and 95), with definitions " dig, dwelling, cave, fold," etc.

[6] Throne sign *Ene* (B 112) with meaning " enthroned " or " lord," 2810, etc.

---

[1] From PRT. 1 pl. XI, 14.

more or less a duplicate of the upper one. This ebony label was found crusted over and varnished with hard resin, which had been poured over it in a melted state, and had to be cleaned off by a needle, "so that it is possible that some points may not have been fully cleaned out."

The writing, which is in two columns, is in cursive Sumerian linear script with syllabic and not alphabetic values, and the

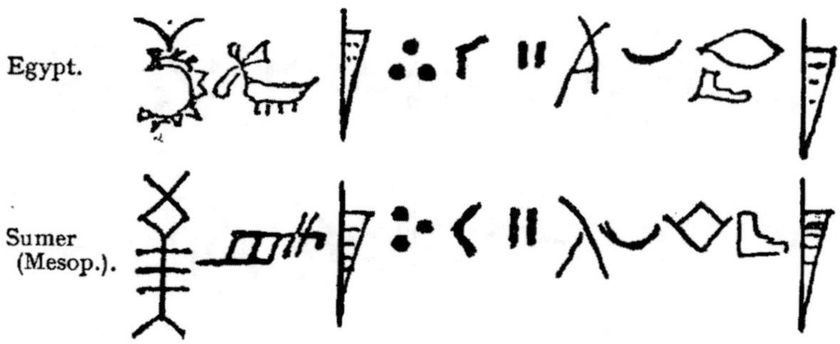

Reads: MUSH [1]-SUR [2]-TAG [3]-MAD [4]-GI-TAB [5] KUD[6]-U [7] E [8] TAG.[9]

Transl.: of Mushsur (Egypt) Land, the Two Lands. The One Judge. And of the Sunrise Land.

Fig. 58.—Line 2 of column 1 of Dudu's Ebony Label No. 1 deciphered.

[1] B. 328; Br. 7637-8.

[2] B. 364 a; M. 6536-7. The cross-bands of the sign are seen in the lower duplicate fragment.

[3] B. 146, M. 2490.

[4] B. 322; Br. 7386.

[5] *Tab* or *Dab*="two" B. 144; M. 2463; and it is source of English "Two, Twain, Double," etc. WSAD. 46.

[6] B. 12; Br. 364.

[7] As before.

[8] *E* or *Khadu* pictured by Sun + Foot or "Sunrise." Br. 7869.

[9] B. 146="Land." M. 2470.

language is Sumerian. The writing is again in the retrograde direction; but for decipherment, the signs are arranged in their usual Sumerian or Aryan direction to read from the left hand towards the right. The first and second lines or registers of column 1 are bracketed together and contain the king's imperial titles. The third and fourth lines are funereal and contain a prayer for the dead king's resurrection. No reference numbers are attached to those Sumerian signs which have previously been duly attested. It is significant that his name *Dudu* is spelt three times in the labels by the same duplicated Foot-sign by which he spells his name in Mesopotamia.

The first line of column 1 is as Fig. 57.

The second line of column 1, which is bracketed in the text with the first line by a curved line on its right border, is a continuation of the first line. It significantly contains amongst his territorial titles the word-sign for "Egypt" in the form of *Mush-sur* or *Mush-sir*, written by the two signs

Reads: EGIR [1]-SHU [2]-USHU [3]-WI [4]-MAD-GI TIL [5] LUGAL DU-DU-U [6] PARA AN.

Transl.: back to the Setting Sun of the West-Land, the complete king, Dudu, and One Lord or Pharaoh.

Fig. 59.—Line 2 continued of Dudu's Ebony Label No. 1 deciphered.

[1] B. 212; 5001.
[2] B. 365; Br. 8675.
[3] B. 403; Br. 9250.
[4] B. 380; Br. 8919 and Pinches, JRAS. 1917, 102 = *Wis* "West."
[5] B. 70; Br. 1500-1.
[6] B. 365.

of the great Serpent (*Mush* or *Sir*) [1] and an Insect (*Mush* or *Sur*).[2] And that land is given also the title of the "Great" or "mighty," as well as "The Two Lands," *i.e.* Upper and Lower Egypt.

The third and fourth lines, which are not bracketed with the above, contain the stereotyped prayer for resurrection from the dead. This significantly is in series with those which I have demonstrated are engraved on the Sumerian

[1] B. 328; Br. 7637-8.

[2] B. 364 a; M. 6536-7. The cross-bands of the sign are seen in the lower duplicate fragment.

burial amulets and tablets of Mesopotamia, the Indus Valley, Troy and the " prehistoric " monuments of Ancient Britain.[1]

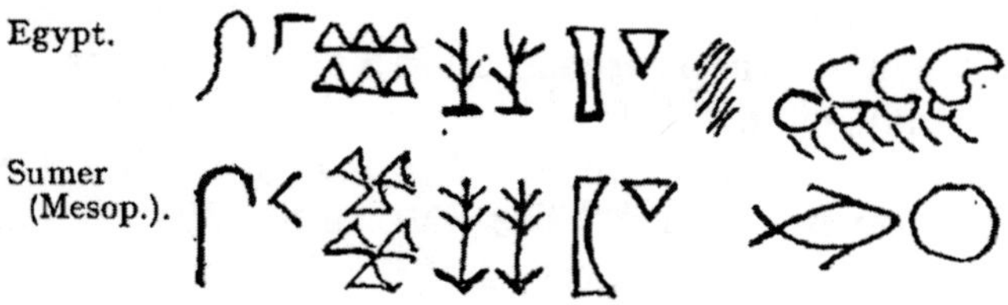

Reads: BAR [1]-U [2] MAD-MAD TAX [3] GIN [4] -SHU-DU [5] . . . . (? SHU)-KHA [6] . . .

Transl.: O (Sun-)Lord of the Lands, TAX (Tasia) The Helper, descend! . . . O (Sun-)Fish. . . .

FIG. 60.—Line 3 of column 1 of Dudu's Ebony Label No. 1 deciphered.

[1] B. 77; Br. 1802, 1752. [2] B. 365; Br. 8659.
[3] B. 182; *Tax* or *Dax*. Br. 4537. On this title for the Sun-archangel Tasia, see WSAD. 53 and WPOB. 258 f.
[4] B. 92. [5] Br. 227.
[6] This appears to be a diagram of the great Sun-Fish or the " Resurrecting " Sun (Shu-Kha) which the Sumerians invoked for resurrection from the dead. WISD. 88 f.

The fourth line is wanting except its last sign.

The second column of this ebony label continues King Dudu's inscription, with his territorial, imperial and solar titles, and his paternity, disclosing him to be the son of the

Reads: PA DA-NU LUGAL KAD [1] (DU)-DU [2] MAR [3]-GI GANA [4] RIT [5] GIN ERI.[6]

Transl.: The (Sun-)Hawk (line) DANU, the King the *Kad* DU-DU son of GANA, RIT, GIN-ERI.

FIG. 61.—Line 1 of column 2 of Dudu's Ebony Label deciphered.

[1] B. 311; Br. 7063. [2] B. 207, pl. 50. [3] B. 392.
[4] B. 160; Br. 4036. [5] B. 270; Br. 5956. [6] B. 39.

---

[1] WPOB. 255 f.

third king of Menes' Dynasty, namely King Gana, Rit or "Khent," that is the *Kunti* or *Ritu* of the Indian lists. The first line reads as Fig. 61.

The prefix here of *Shu* (which is a synonym of *Kad*) to Dudu's name perhaps accounts for his "Sudyumna" name in the Indian lunar lists. The second line continues with a prayer to the Twin Sun-god Min or Man for Resurrection of the King who is called "The Ruler of the Western Lands."

The rest of the lower portion of this label is missing.

Egypt.

Sumer (Mesop.).

Reads: ENE PA-GIN-RA[1] IR[2] SHU[3] -TA[4] -TIANU[5] QUM[6] XAL[7] MIN TIL-TI.

Transl.: Unto the enthroned one of the Hawk-line of Gin hasten! Unto the fallen one of the Western Land, the fallen one hasten, O Min (to) Life!

FIG. 62.—Line 2, column 2, of Dudu's Ebony Label deciphered.

[1] B. 287; Br. 6365. [2] B. 229. [3] B. 490.
[4] B. 158. "Unto, to."
[5] On this title as Tianu, etc., see before. The two strokes which double this Lion-head or *Pirig* sign are seen in front of its head. Compare these doubling strokes with those in Menes' ebony label and in the label from "King Zet's" tomb in PRT. 1, Pl. XI, in which last the doubling two strokes are placed inside the neck of the Lion. On the location of this land as Asia Minor, also the Western Lands generally, including Europe, as the Greater Amorite Land, see before.
[6] B. 193, the Flail sign. [7] B. 2.

SUMMARY OF KING DUDU'S OR DUNDU'S TOMB INSCRIPTIONS

This fragmentary inscription from the tomb of King Dudu or Dundu thus reads as follows:—

"Of the dead King DUDU (this is) the tomb. The (enthroned) Lord the King of MUSHSUR (Egypt) Land, the Two Lands. The One Judge of the Sunrise Land back to the Setting Sun of the West Land, the complete king, DUDU, One Lord. O Sun-Lord of the Lands, TAX, the

Helper, descend! . . . O (Sun-)Fish . . . [resurrect him] . . . The (Sun-)Hawk (line) DANU, the King, the *Kad* DUDU, son of GANA RIT, GIN-ERI. Unto the enthroned one of the Hawk line of Gin, hasten! Unto the fallen one of The Western Land, the fallen one hasten O Min (to) Life!"

SIXTH KING OF MENES' DYNASTY, NOT A MESOPOTAMIAN EMPEROR & ONLY A TEMPORARY KING

The sixth king of Menes' dynasty is seen by our Comparative Table at p. 298 to have not been a Mesopotamian emperor; but was evidently merely a local king and presumably tributary to King Dudu. In keeping with this,

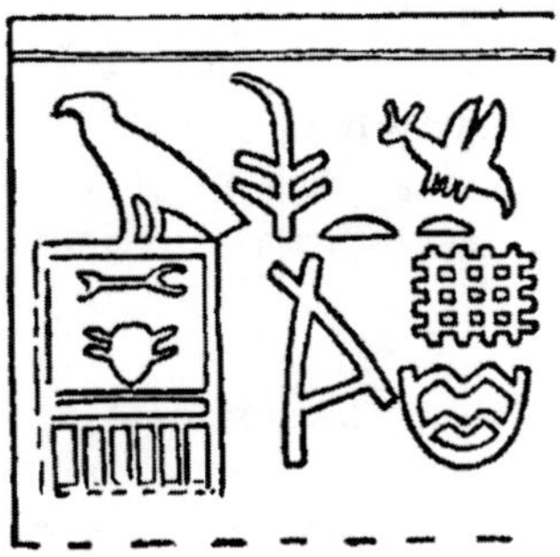

FIG. 63.—Clay sealing of 6th King of 1st Dynasty of Egypt.

seems the statement by Prof. Petrie that "This tomb is the poorest in contents and in remains of all those of the first dynasty." [1]

His name is read by Egyptologists as *Azab Merpaba*—the

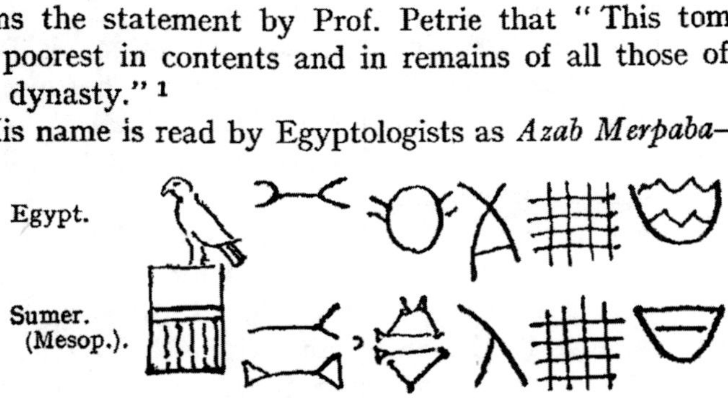

Reads: PA-RIN-BARA [1]-BI [2]-DI [3] KUD -U -MAR. [4]
Transl.: The Hawk-line Pharaoh BIDI, Lord MAR.

FIG. 64.—Name of 6th King of 1st Dynasty of Egypt deciphered.

[1] As before. [2] B. 70; Br. 1477. [3] B. 415. [4] B. 532; Br. 11982

[1] PHE. I, 20.

latter half of which is his title in the Egyptian lists; whilst Manetho calls him *Miebidos*, which is in series with his lunar title in the Indian lists of *Bahu-bida*. His signature on his clay sealings is seen in Fig. 63.

This inscription reads through the Sumerian as in Fig. 64. Here his *Bidi* or *Eshshabi* solar equates with his *Bida* name in the Indian Lists, and explains his *Miebidos* of Manetho; whilst the *Mar* in his personal name seems related to the readings of it as *Mer-paba* by Egyptologists.

Seventh King of Menes' Dynasty, a Temporary or Tributary King & not an Emperor

The seventh king of Menes' dynasty likewise is not shown by the Babylonian lists as an emperor of Mesopotamia, and was probably tributary to King Dudu. His name is variously read with "some uncertainty" by Egyptologists as Shemer-khet Shemsu. He corresponds to *Sampati* in the Indian Lists.

Last King of Menes' Dynasty, SHUDUR KIB or "Qa" identical in Name & Titles with Last King of Manis-Tusu's Dynasty in Mesopotamia & with Indian Lists

The absolute identity of the eighth or last king of Menes' dynasty with the last king and emperor of Manis-Tusu's or Sargon's dynasty in Mesopotamia (see Kish Chronicle, p. 61) *strikingly completes and establishes the identity of the dynasty of Menes with that of Manis-Tusu and the identity of these two personages themselves.*

His name has been read by Egyptologists as *Qa* or *Qa-Sen*, and a seal of his period has been read by them as *Qebhu*, see Comparative Table opposite p. 298. But it is now found by the new keys to the Sumerian script used by the First Egyptian Dynasty that his name reads in one of his Egyptian inscriptions *Shudur Kib*, that is precisely as he spelt his name and by the same Sumerian signs as in his own inscriptions as Sargonic emperor in Mesopotamia. And he is also called curtly, *Kib*, *Kibbu* and *Qa*.

I have, moreover, found several of his official seals in

PLATE XVIII.

INDUS VALLEY SEALS OF PHARAOH SHUDUR-KIB, OR QA, AND HIS SON, AND URI-MUSH.

(From photographs after Sir J. Marshall.) For decipherments and translations, see pp. 341 f., 576 f.

PLATE XVIIIA.

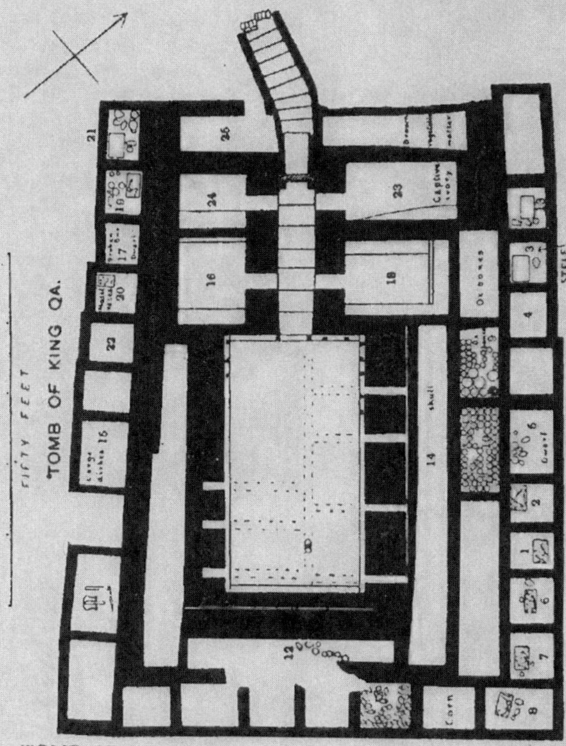

TOMB OF KING SHUDUR-KIB, OR QA, AT ABYDOS.

(After Sir F. Petrie, PRT. II, Pl. LX.)

Note the contents of the various chambers with provisions for the spirit of the dead king.

the Indus Valley collection, attesting his long rule of that Sumerian colony on the Indus.

INDUS VALLEY SEALS OF KING KIB OR QA

In the second batch of the Indus Valley seals, I found no fewer than seven seals of King Kib, the last member of the Sargon-Menes' Dynasty, as shown in Plates XIV and XVIII. They are of especial historical importance in that, while attesting his rule on the Indus and in Egypt, they give his genealogy as well as his title of *Qa*. Their detailed decipherment is displayed in Appendix XI. Their inscribed records read literally as follows :—

NO. 1 (PLATE XIV, 10, and FIG. 113)

" KIB-BU SHUKA, son of the House of AHA at Agdu Land."

NO. 2 (PLATE XVIII, 1, and FIG. 114)

" KIB, the *Pharaoh,* the seal of the Lord at Agdu Land."

NO. 3 (PLATE XVIII, 2, and FIGS. 115 and 116)

" KIB-BU, *devotee of Fire,* KIB the Gut, KIBBU (of line of) SHAR-GIN the Gut (son of) DAN, the son of GIN of the House of NER (?-Mar) at Uriki (Akkad) Land."

NO. 4 (PLATE XVIII, 3-4, and FIGS. 117 and 118)

" For the Life of SUHAHATUR-KIB QA, Turn the Evil from the Gut of the House of Gin! KIB of the House of NER at MAGAN Land."

NO. 5 (PLATE XVIII, 5, and FIG. 119)

" SHUHADUR KIḄ, the Pharaoh (son of) GAN at Agdu Land."

NO. 5A (PLATE XVIII, 5A, and FIG. 119A)

" KIBBU, the Deep-Water Lord, son of Aha-Men."

NO. 6 (PLATE XVIII, 6, and FIG. 120)

" King QA of MA(-ash)-GAN, MUSHSIR (Egypt)."

In addition there is a seal of a son of Kib (Plate XVIII, 10) which reads " The Gut SHU son of Pharaoh KIB."

Name of the King in Egypt, Mesopotamia & Indian Chronicles

Fortunately there are several of this king's Egyptian labels and sealings extant, giving his name and titles in fairly full detail. All are written in Sumerian script and in the Sumerian language; and in one of these *he writes his name with the self-same Sumerian signs as he writes it as Sumerian emperor in his Mesopotamian inscriptions; and in his Indus seals.*

In his Mesopotamian inscriptions he writes his personal name and title as *Shu-dur-Kib*;[1] and similarly it is written in the Kish Chronicle lists (p. 61), where he is called the "son of Dudu." And this name of *Shudur* (or *Shutur*)-Kib, or "*Shudur* or *Shutur* of the Mighty Flood-tides or Oceans,"[2] is seen to equate substantially with the form of his name as *Suhotra*, *Shruta*, or *Xattra* in our Indian Chronicle key-lists.

Similarly in Egypt, he spells his name Shudur Kib by the self-same signs as in his Mesopotamian inscriptions; and also by the phonetic variants of *Shudaru-Kib*, *Shudaru-Quibi* and *Shudur-Gibi*, thus giving the equations:—

Egyptian.		*Indian Lists.*		*Mesop. Monuments & Lists.*
Shudur (or Shutur) Kib	=	Suhotra	=	Shudur (or Shutur)-Kib
Shudaru Kib	=	Shruta		—
Shuduru Quibi	=	Xattra	=	Xudaru Kib
Shudur Gibi.				

And he gives amongst his titles on the objects in his Egyptian tomb, besides that of "King of the Two Lands of Upper and Lower Egypt," also those of "The One Lord of Uruki (*i.e.* Ur or Erech)" and "The King of Tianu (*i.e.* The Western or Amorite Land)." This absolutely fixes his identity with the last Pharaoh of Menes' dynasty and the last ruler of Manis-Tusu's dynasty in the Mesopotamian empire.

[1] See tablets published by Pognon (AOT. b. 69. rev. 1 and 420) and Craig (*Relig. Texts*, I, pl. 57), and TDC. 63; on the attested values of the signs, see Kish Chronicle (p. 61) and below. His name is disguised in *Cambridge Anc. History* (I. 669) and elsewhere as "Gimilduril"—another of the innumerable instances of how students of history are misled by the fantastic conjectures of Assyriologists unpossessed of any keys to the form of the names!

[2] B. 223; MD. 244.

PLATE XIX.

SHUDUR-KIB'S (QA'S) TOMB IVORY LABELS AT ABYDOS.
(From Sir F. Petrie's photographs, PRI. II, Pl. VIII, 2, and I, Pl. XII, 2.)
For decipherments and translations see pp. 343 f.

His solar title in Egypt reads " Kia " or " Qia "—the so-called " King Qa " of Egyptologists.[1]

HIS INSCRIPTIONS ON HIS TOMB IN EGYPT DECIPHERED THROUGH THE SUMERIAN & DISCLOSING HIS WORLD-EMPIRE TITLES

The inscriptions of this king on his tomb, upon votive articles, stone vases, ebony and ivory labels and clay sealings are numerous. The three chief ones are seen in Plate XIX, and they are here deciphered and read through the Sumerian as in the previous cases.

In the first of these, on a weathered ivory label[2] (Plate XIX A) his name is seen on the right-hand column to be written by the same sign as in his Mesopotamian inscriptions, and in his Indus seals. It reads as follows :—

Egypt.

Sumer (Mesop.).

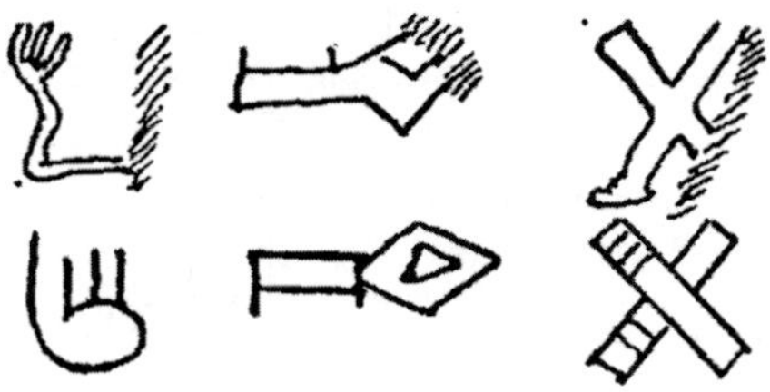

Reads : SHU[1] -DUR[2] -KIB.[3]

FIG. 65.—Name of last King of Menes' Dynasty, Shudur Kib, on Ivory Label A, deciphered.

[1] B. 311 ; Br. 7065. The sign of the Uplifted Hand.
[2] Or *Tur*, B. 122 ; Br. 3331. [3] B. 223 ; Br. 5217.

The other columns on this label are somewhat defaced, but the second contains his title as " King of Tianu (Western or Amorite Land)," which title is repeated on others of his labels.

On another ivory label (Plate XIX, B),[3] broken but with well-preserved inscription as far as it goes, his solar title of *Kia* or *Qia* occurs within the rectangle under the large Sun-Hawk on the left side. Significantly in the last column his name is spelt by other signs of the same phonetic values,

[1] The surname " Sen " given him by Egyptologists is a conjectural alphabetic misreading of the Sumerian signs for Shudur Kib.
[2] PRT. II, Pl. VIII, No. 2. [3] PRT. I, Pl. XII, 2.

to introduce other meanings, and it is recorded that he is "*of the* UKUSH Line"—that is the same as claimed by his dynastic ancestor Sargon-the-Great, namely, descent for *Ukusi*, the first king of the First Sumerian Dynasty of the Kish Chronicle (pp. 59 f.).

This inscription in the last column reads :—

Egypt.

Sumer (Mesop.).

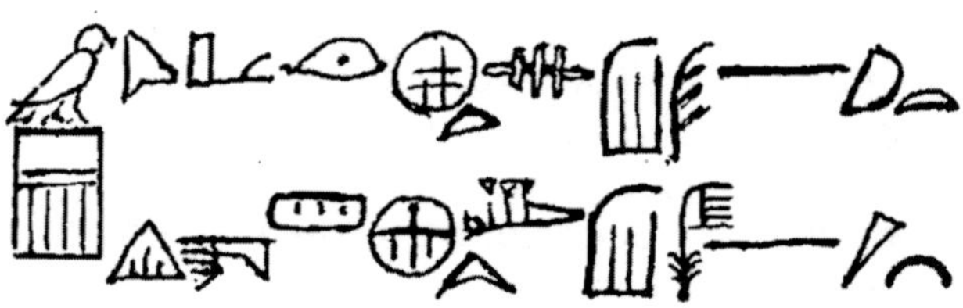

Reads : PA KI-A [1] SHU [2]-DU [3]-U -UR [4] -UKUSH [5] -GI-TIL-GE.

Transl. : The (Sun-)Hawk (line) KIA (or QIA) SHUDUUR, the overthrown one of the UKUSH line.

FIG. 66.—Inscription of Shudur Kib on Label B, cols. 4 and 5, deciphered.

[1] This may be either *Ki* or *Qia* (B. 419) + A.

[2] The Island sign, B. 481.

[3] B. 417.

[4] The spiked Club-sign, B. 529.

[5] B. 495 ; Br. 10882. The Harp-sign.

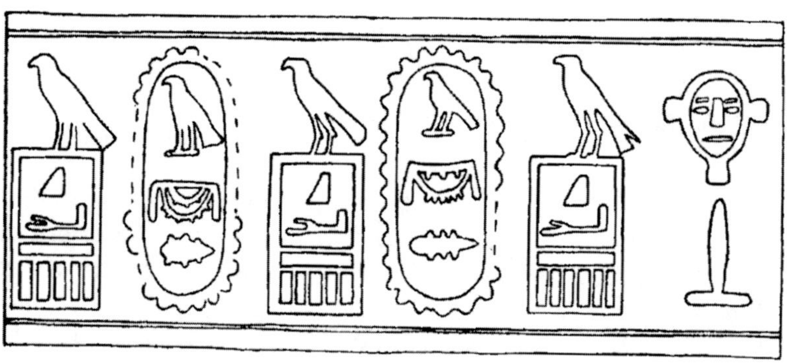

FIG. 67.—Clay Sealing of King Shudur Kib in Egypt (after Sir F. Petrie).

On his Egyptian sealings (Fig. 67) [1] his name and titles are stamped to read in the Sumerian or Aryan, towards the right. His solar title is given first place and it is followed

[1] These are taken for clearness from Mr Griffiths' drawings in PRT. 1, Pl. XXIX.

by his personal name written within an oval cartouche; in the other two it is followed by his title Kib variantly spelt. It is noteworthy that in the first sealing the first syllable of his name is spelt *Xu*, in place of *Shu*, and has the added syllable of *ur;* this coupled with the variations in the spelling of *Kib* in the other sealings suggests that the scribes were Egyptian born and not Mesopotamians.

The decipherment of these sealings through the Sumerian is given in the following Table (Fig. 68). The Net-sign with value of *Dara* used in spelling the second syllable of his name, is seen in its fuller form as the second hieroglyph within the oval cartouche. In other sealings, it is seen that the *Kib* title following his solar name is variantly spelt phonetically *Quibi* and *Quibbi*.

Egypt.

Sumer (Mesop.).

Reads: PA (or XU) KI-A (or QI-A) XU [1]-DARA [2]-UR.[3]
Transl.: The Hawk (line) KIA, XUDARAUR.

FIG. 68.—Name on Sealing A. deciphered.

[1] B. 83; Br. 2045.
[2] The Net-sign, B. 480, is drawn in fuller form in the Egyptian.
[3] The spiked Club-sign, as before.

INSCRIPTIONS OF SHUDUR KIB, LAST KING OF MENES' DYNASTY, IN HIS TOMB IN EGYPT, IDENTIFY HIM WITH SHUDUR KIB, LAST EMPEROR OF MANIS-TUSU'S DYNASTY IN MESOPOTAMIA

We thus find that the inscriptions in his tomb in Egypt identify Shudur Kib, the last king of Menes' dynasty in Egypt, with Shudur Kib, the last emperor of Manis-Tusu's dynasty of Mesopotamia. These inscriptions now deciphered spell his solar name as *Kia* or *Qia*, and his ordinary name as *Shudur Kib*, and describe him as king of Tianu (*i.e.* Western or Amorite Land).

Identity of Menes' Dynasty of Egypt with Manis-Tusu's "World Empire" Dynasty of Mesopotamia

Thus we have demonstrated by actual concrete contemporary documentary evidence the identity of Menes' First Dynasty of Egypt with Manis-Tusu's Dynasty of "World emperors" of Mesopotamia. And at the same time we have demonstrated the identity of the individual kings or emperors of these respective dynasties.

This identity is established not only by the contemporary records of the kings themselves in Egypt and Mesopotamia, and in their official signets and seals in their Indus Colony, but also by the identity in their names and chronological order in both the Babylonian, Egyptian and Indian Chronicle king-lists—the sixth and seventh kings of Menes' Dynasty in the local Egyptian lists proving to be local or tributary kings of the Sumerian empire, as seen also further in the chapter on Chronology.

Menes' Date discovered by newly-found Synchronism between Ancient Egypt & Mesopotamia as no earlier than about 2704 B.C.

This additional concrete contemporary evidence now adduced, by proving that the whole of Pharaoh Menes' dynasty is identical with the whole imperial dynasty of Manis-Tusu, the son of Sargon of Mesopotamia, thus fully establishes for the first time a synchronism between Ancient Egyptian and Babylonian History which definitely fixes by the identification of Menes, the founder of the First Dynasty of Egypt with Manis-Tusu, the son of Sargon, the date of Menes at a period no earlier than about 2704 B.C., and the end of his dynasty at about 2522 B.C., as detailed in the chapter on Chronology.

Aryan Origin of Egyptian Civilization Established

Through this identification of Menes and his dynasty with Manis-Tusu, the son of Sargon, and his dynasty, coupled with our discovery of Sargon-the-Great as the leading Predynastic king of Egypt, with proved Aryan descent continuously back to the first Sumerian or Aryan king of the First Sumerian or Aryan Dynasty, and the fact that both Sargon and his son's dynasty in Egypt wrote their inscriptions there in the Sumerian script and in the Sumerian language, we have demonstrated by unequivocal contemporary inscriptional evidence the Aryan or Sumerian Origin of Egyptian Civilization, as well as the Aryan or Nordic Racial Origin of the Sumerians. And we have seen that the Aryan or Sumerian Civilization was spread abroad more largely over the world, and especially the Western World, including Crete through the "world-empire" and colonial rule of Sargon and his son Menes' dynasty, a dynasty disclosed to be Aryan-Phœnician. At the same time we have also established still further the remarkable historical authenticity of the official Indian Chronicles as an unique and independent source of Sumerian, Babylonian and Ancient Egyptian History.

FIG. 68A.—Tasia or Tax, *Taś-Mikal* of Phœnicians, the deified second Aryan king as Sun-archangel Michael in Egypt, as "Lord of Corn" (Resep). Invoked in First Egyptian Dynasty tomb inscriptions and in prehistoric Briton monuments and figured on pre-Roman Briton coins. (After Renan.)

Note his Goat's head chaplet and his handled Sun-Cross in "Key of Life." For details see WPOB. 353 f.

XVIII

Disruption of Sargon's "World Empire" with Rise of Independent Egypt under its Second Dynasty & Westering of the Chief Centre of Sumerian or Aryan Civilization about 2520 B.C.

Disclosing the Aryan Race of the 2nd Dynasty of Egypt from Indian Lists.

With the end of Sargon's mighty dynasty of World Emperors, with its dual centres East and West, in Mesopotamia and Egypt respectively, about 2522 B.C., we reach one of the most momentous epochs in the History of the Ancient World, especially as regards Europe. For with this disruption began the definite cleavage of Civilization into Western and Eastern branches and types. The centre of the most progressive elements in the Sumerian or Aryan Civilization shifted permanently westwards from Mesopotamia to Egypt on the basin of the cool Mediterranean, which Sargon and his dynasty of Nordics and their clansmen had deliberately selected as their future homeland. And from Egypt the Higher Civilization now spread back to Western Asia Minor and Europe. For this period of transition, however, the Babylonian records do not help us much, as it is one of the darkest periods in Mesopotamian history. Apart from the bare list in the Kish Chronicle of the names and chronology of a short-lived weak dynasty, the "Fifth" Dynasty of that chronicle, which immediately succeeded Sargon's dynasty in Mesopotamia, and of which no monuments have been found, there is no reference whatever to this crisis in Babylonian history with the loss of the Western Section of the empire.

But from what we have elicited regarding Sargon in Egypt, and his son Menes' dynasty, with their tombs in that more favoured western part of their empire, coupled with our existing knowledge of the Second and subsequent early dynasties of the Egyptian empire, and their relationships with Asia Minor, the Levant and Europe, and some references in the Indian Chronicle, we gain considerable light on the happenings at this epoch.

Disintegration of Sargon's "World Empire" on the Fall of his Dynasty in Mesopotamia

It is clear that on the fall of Sargon's dynasty in Mesopotamia, that is the "Fourth" Dynasty of the Kish Chronicle, after a glorious reign for 197 years, as that chronicle records, the vast unwieldly world empire which its founder had built up completely collapsed and broke into pieces, and was never afterwards regained by any Mesopotamian or other king.

Sargon's mighty dynasty had perhaps fulfilled its useful mission in propagating by its world-wide sway the most advanced civilization of that period much more widely over the world than ever had been done before its day. And its far-flung colonies, especially in Egypt and the West, by this time had doubtless become sufficiently developed into separate civilized nations, with experience of ordered government, to undertake their own independence, with ability to defend themselves against the impositions and aggressions of such a remote central government, nominally, if not altogether actually, in distant Mesopotamia, and which no doubt, with its hosts of bureaucratic officials, must have tended to develop an intolerable tyranny. Such movements for independence from the yoke of their parent empire would only be in agreement with those made latterly by the colonies of the Phœnician, Greek and Roman empires in the Mediterranean, Asia Minor and on the European Continent, and with those of certain British colonies, "dependencies" or "dominions" in modern times. The time was evidently ripe for the rise of a crop of new independent, self-governing, civilized nationalities and states within Sargon's old empire.

Amongst the chief independent new states which now emerged are seen to be those of the Guti or Goths in Asia Minor in the old Gothic province whence we have seen a branch of their stock had originally descended as the

" Sumerians " into Mesopotamia, of the Amorites of Syria-Phœnicia and of the Egyptian empire. In Mesopotamia itself we find now only a weak and short-lived dynasty, which within two and a half decades was absorbed by the Guti. But the later Sumerian kings of Mesopotamia although still occasionally carving out small empires, and sometimes assuming the imperial title when dominating the greater part of the city-states within Mesopotamia or Babylonia, with at times the adjoining Elam province of Southern Persia and the Indus Valley colony on the East, never appear to have succeeded in extending their empire to Egypt and the Mediterranean or to Central and Western Asia Minor—though an occasional raid on Sinai and Kimash is mentioned a few centuries later.

Rise of Independent Egypt as the chief Centre of " Sumerian " or Aryan Civilization

The main centre of Sumerian Civilization appears to have been definitely and deliberately shifted from Mesopotamia to Egypt when Sargon and his son Menes, following the practice of their immediate ancestral Pharaohs, and followed by their dynasty, made their mausoleums and those of their families in that more temperate and central portion of their empire on the banks of the Nile, outflowing into the cool basin of the Mediterranean. Egypt was climatically a land much more naturally fitted for the scions of that great ruling branch of the Nordic Race, which from the exigencies of their overlordship had been forced for many centuries to live in exile in tropical Mesopotamia. On the extension of their empire westward to include Egypt and the Mediterranean and Southern Europe, Egypt became a suitable centre for their Western empire. And the fact that Sargon and his dynasty selected that land for their tombs and the residences of their families, presumes that they regarded it as their new adopted home-land.

We have seen how Sargon's son Menes made Egypt his own especial home-land, and the centre for the western half of his " world empire." And the last two kings of his dynasty, Dudu and Shudur Kib, evidently resided largely in Egypt with their families and staff of state officials, as attested by the tombs of their families and officials there, and their lavish monumental remains and the profusion of written documents, especially in the reign of the last king or emperor. And this absence in Egypt from Mesopotamia doubtless contributed to the downfall of the dynasty.

On the revolt of Mesopotamia, on the death of this last king or emperor of Menes' dynasty, Egypt with its body of imperial officials and their families, and doubtless possessing the Western armies and fleets, would automatically become an independent empire and centre for the western half of the old world empire, and all the more so as it was practically secure against attack from Babylonia by the great impassable Arabian desert on its eastern border, which had doubtless tended largely to the disruption of the empire.

The Second Dynasty of Egypt as the First Independent Dynasty of Egypt & as (?) Sargonid

Although Egypt, as we have seen, had been held for a time by Menes independently of his father Sargon, on Menes' accession to the imperial Mesopotamian throne, however, Egypt again became an integral part of the Sargonic empire and practically a colony of the latter. But on the fall of Sargon's dynasty in Mesopotamia, Egypt now obtained complete independence; so that the dynasty which succeeded that of Menes, namely the Second Dynasty of Egypt, was practically the first independent dynasty of Egypt.

Nothing is known to Egyptologists regarding the origin of the Second Dynasty of Egypt, nor of the circumstances which led to the fall of the First Dynasty. And unfortunately the Egyptian lists of the Second Dynasty kings are confused and corrupt, and few of the names and titles of the kings of this dynasty from their own monuments have been equated by Egyptologists with the form of the names on the lists.[1] Hence, I cannot at present give a full comparison of the names with those in the Indian lists, such as I have done with the First Dynasty, until the decipherment of their monumental names is revised in detail.

[1] PHE. 1, 28.

Indian Version of Second Dynasty Kings of Egypt

But here it is noteworthy, that in the Indian list of kings given in the Puru version of the Indian Aryan King-Lists—that is in that version which preserves especially full details of Menes' dynasty as Manasyu of Gopta—we find that *the immediate successors of Manasyu's dynasty are Nine kings, whose names equate to a considerable extent with those of the Nine kings forming the Second Dynasty in the lists of Manetho and the others.* And these nine kings were clearly the *local* successors of Manasyu's dynasty in Egypt and not in Mesopotamia, for they are absent in all the main-line lists of the Early Aryan kings, who, we have found, were kings of Mesopotamia.[1]

In this Indian Puru version of the kings who immediately succeeded Manasyu's dynasty, is given a string of nine names of which the holders are described as the "sons" or descendants of Raudrāshwa, a personage who is therein (MBt. I. 94) called a "brother" of Sargon (or Pra-Vīra, see p. 233); and who is stated to have married "the nymph" Misri-Keshi, whose name *Misri* is suggestive of the old name *Misr* for Egypt.[2] And Sargon's father was, as we have seen, a Predynastic Pharaoh of Egypt. This presumes that Raudrāshwa was an *elder* brother of Sargon and was resident in Egypt. And the fact that he did not succeed his deposed father in the kingship in Mesopotamia could be explained by his having died before the reign of the usurper Zaggisi before Sargon had attained manhood and recovered his father's empire; for Sargon being a posthumous son could not have had a younger brother. In

[1] This list of nine kings is found at the very end of the dislocated Manasyu Dynasty, which we have seen had been transferred by the later Puru scribes *en bloc* back to the fifth place from the first Aryan king, through confusing the later king Puru, the father of Sargon, with Puru I. See App. I, col. 4.

[2] This Raudrāshwa is arbitrarily made by the later Puru scribes, who copied the old lists, to be the "son" of the last king of Manasyu's Dynasty as they were in the habit of gratuitously making, as we have seen, each king the "son" of the preceding king, which we have found by the monuments was often not a fact. Similarly they made, as we have seen, mere titles of the kings into names of different kings or "brothers" of the king whose name preceded.

this view therefore, there were resident in Egypt, contemporary with and during the reign of Sargon's or Menes' dynasty, the descendants of an older brother of Sargon, who overthrew Menes' dynasty and founded the Second Dynasty of Egypt. And apparently confirming this is the fact that the Son of Pharaoh Shudur Kib, whose seal is found in the Indus Valley (see p. 341), did not succeed either to the Egyptian or Mesopotamian throne.

Be this as it may, the fact remains that the names of Raudrāshwa's nine "sons" or descendants present a striking general agreement with those of the nine kings in the lists of the Second Dynasty of Egypt. And their divergences from what is admittedly a confused Egyptian list may be explained or removed when the names of the kings of the Second Dynasty of Egypt on their own monuments are duly revised and deciphered by our new Sumerian and Indian keys.

Second Dynasty of Egyptian Lists compared with Indian

In the following Table, I compare the names or titles of those nine [1] kings of the Indian lists with those of the Egyptian lists for the Second Dynasty.[2] It will be noticed that the names of the first three kings are practically identical in both lists, Egyptian and Indian, except for the initial of the first name, which has *B* in the Egyptian as read by Egyptologists instead of *R* in the Indian, and the third name which has the initial *B* for *Sth.* But in the former name the Indian form with *R* is clearly the correct one; for its initial is the Foot or Leg sign used as the initial of his name in the Egyptian, which has the Sumerian value of *Ra;* whereas it is only in later Egyptian that the Foot or Leg sign has the value of *B*. And similarly the other differences may doubtless be explained on revision of their signs or hieroglyphs. Moreover, as there is no *L* in the later Egyptian hieroglyphs, the old *L* words being spelt therein by an *R* sign, I have accordingly altered the *R* in the Egyptian lists as transliterated by Egyptologists in Nos. 3 and 6 into *L*, when the Indian lists show it to be *L*.

[1] In the Indian texts, whilst their number is stated to be "ten," only nine names are specified. WVP. 4, 128 f.

[2] From PHE. 1, 28.

Second Dynasty of Egyptian Lists Compared with Indian.

Egyptian Lists	*Indian Lists*
1. Razau or " Bezau " or Boētho(s).	Rajeyu, Riceÿu or Ritsyu, " son " of Raudrāshwa.
2. Kakau or Kaiekhos.	Kaksheyu.
3. Banetelen, or Binothlis.	Sthandileyu.
4. Uaznes or Tlas.	Vriteyu or Ghriteyu.
5. Senda or Sethenes.	Jaleyu (or Santateyu).
6. Khailes or Ka. . . .	Sthaleyu (or Jaleyu)
7. Neferkara.	Santateyu.
8. Sesokhris.	Dhaneyu.
9. Kheneres or Hezef.	Vaneyu or (?) Ganeyu.

This comparison establishes a presumption that the Indian list of nine post-Manasyu kings preserves the names or titles of the nine kings of the Second Dynasty of Egypt.

We now take up the Mesopotamian line of kings which immediately succeeded Sargon's dynasty in Mesopotamia. For although these kings, excepting the Guti or Gothic and Kassi Dynasties, are not directly connected with Ancient European History, it is essential to establish their identity with the king-lists of the Indo-Aryans in order to recover the lost Chronology of the Early Aryans and of the World's Civilization.

FIG. 68B.—Captive on Ivory gaming-reed of King Shudur Kib or Kia's period. (After Sir F. Petrie, PHE. i. 25.)

XIX

The "Fifth" or Erech Dynasty of Mesopotamia in the Kish Chronicle, *c.* 2521-2494 B.C.

On the fall of Sargon's mighty dynasty in Mesopotamia, that is the "Fourth" Dynasty of the Kish Chronicle, after a reign at the imperial capital of Agudu [1] for 197 years, that chronicle records: "At Agudu, its rule was changed. Its royalty unto Unug (Erech) was carried off. At Unug, Uru-Nigin became king (and) reigned three years." [1]

It is thus seen that a chief leader in the overthrow of Sargon's dynasty in Mesopotamia was presumably the local Sumerian king of Erech City. He set up a weak, short-lived dynasty in that city, of 5 kings, who ruled only for a total period of 26 years, as the Kish Chronicle records. They left no monuments so far as found, nor are they known to later Babylonian history; and within two and a half decades their dynasty was overthrown by a fresh batch of Gothic invaders, the Guti from the north.

In the Indian lists this king is called Nabhin or Nābhāga, a name which appears to be a Semitized reading of his Sumerian name Nigin [2] and his successor bears therein a name which remarkably equates with his successor in the Sumerian lists, namely *Harish-Candra*, equating with *Urish-Ginar*:—

Sumer.			*Indian Lists*	*No.*
Ur-Nigin [or Nabū-u-ge (?)] [2]	3 years	=	Nabhin or Nābhāga	43
Urish-Ginar	6 ,,	=	Harish-Candra or Ambarisha	44
Tar-da (or Kudda)	6 ,,			
Shu (?)—or Mu (?)—sha-nini	5 ,,			
Uran-uta	6 ,,			

The end of Sargon's dynasty in Mesopotamia thus appears to have been due to a general revolt of the tributary kings

[1] Manish-Tusu appears to have made the older imperial capital of Kish his Mesopotamian capital; though he dates his seals from Agdu.

[2] The compound sign for the word "Nigin" consists of the signs of the Setting Sun, Rising Sun and the sign for *Ge*, and may read separately *Nabū* (Br. 8823); *-u* (Br. 7773); *-ge*; (Br. 592).

of Mesopotamia (such as happened in Sargon's and Manis-Tusu's lifetime), headed by the Erech king, on the death of the last Sargonic emperor Shudur Kib, who presumably died in Egypt. But the withdrawal of the strong guiding and controlling hands of the Sargonic emperor and his staff of experienced Aryan or Sumerian officials, who maintained the international peace, appears to have plunged Mesopotamia into chaotic disintegration, although the local kings who remained were evidently more or less Sumerian. The loss of capable Sumerians in itself must have tended to this disintegration; for the Sumerians in Mesopotamia were always as the ruling race in a relative minority to their Chaldean subjects there, whom they called "the black-headed people." As a result, this period following the fall of Sargon's dynasty is one of the darkest in Mesopotamian history.

The Indian king-lists also reflect the great disruption of this period in Mesopotamia by the totally different lists of kings who are made to be the immediate successors of Sargon's or Shakuni's dynasty in Mesopotamia. No two of these Indian versions, solar and lunar, quite agree in the succession at this period. It is possible that some of them may be using different Sanskrit translations of the Sumerian names or titles; but the chief reason for these discrepancies is manifestly that many different rival and local Aryan kings each laid claim to being the paramount king in Mesopotamia. But the chief solar version of the Indian lists is consistent throughout, carrying on the imperial line through the great period of the Guti occupation continuously down through the other periods to the Kassi Dynasty.

The overthrow of this "Fifth" Dynasty is thus briefly recorded in the Kish Chronicle:—"Five kings reigned for 26 years. At Unug its rule was changed. Its royalty was seized by the troops of Guti Land."

We now come to the historically important Guti or Gothic Invasion of Mesopotamia which ended this "Fifth" Dynasty of the Kish Chronicle, and with which event that chronicle ends, a circumstance from which it is assumed, and with reason, that that chronicle was originally compiled at the date of this Guti Invasion.

XX

The Guti or Gothic "Dynasty" in Mesopotamia, *c.* 2495-2360 B.C., with revised "Golden Age," & including GUDIA & VISHVĀ-MITRA, whose Gothic Aryan Origin is disclosed by Indian Chronicles

Disclosing a Neo-Gothic Rule of Mesopotamia as a Dependency, with Temporary Kings or Viceroys, including "Earls."

"The Troops of Guti Land" who now seized the imperial rule in Mesopotamia, about a quarter of a century after the beginning of the dark period of eclipse following the fall of Sargon's dynasty there, are of immense historical importance. Their national name *Guti* (pronounced *Gooti*) discloses them as "Goths"; and they prove to be obviously descendants of the residual Goths left in Asia Minor, when the "Second" Aryan (or Gothic Dynasty) descended, as we have seen, from Cappadocia into Mesopotamia over eight centuries previously, under King Azag Bakus, as "The Sumerians" of Assyriologists.

This is the first known mention in Ancient History of this famous northern Aryan people, the typical Nordic Race, *by their well-known modern name*; and it is significant to find them as leaders of "Sumerian" civilization. Though, as we have seen, early Sumerian kings from the First Phœnician Dynasty onwards to Sargon's Dynasty called themselves often *Gut* ("*Goot*"). Thus in their Mesopotamian inscriptions some of the kings of that First Phœnician Dynasty use that title,[1] also Sargon's father Urudu Gina,[2] and Gudia and the others of this Guti Dynasty.[3] And in the Indus Valley seals it is freely used by most kings from the second king of that First Phœnician Dynasty onwards and by this Guti Dynasty.

With the advent of this Guti or Gothic Dynasty and their infusion of new blood from the old Gothic or

[1] Cp. RBH. 14, 113, 116-7.

[2] *Ib.*, 48, 51.

[3] *Ib.*, 183, 185, 191, 195.

"Sumerian" or "Hittite" stock into their rule in Mesopotamia, the latter land eventually regained such a measure of prosperity with revival of its civilization that the later Guti period has been called "a Sumerian renaissance" and "a revival of the Sumerian Golden Age."

The Name GUTI, GOTI or "Goth"

The national or tribal name of *Guti*, the name of "The Guti Troops (who) carried off the royalty" of the Mesopotamian empire by their conquest of Erech the imperial capital about 2495 B.C., was recognized as obviously suggesting "Goths" by Prof. Scheil, when he announced in 1911 his discovery of the Guti Dynasty in Mesopotamia, and at the same time remarked that "nothing yet proves that they were the ancestors of the Goths."[1] This mere suggestion, however, that the Goths, a typically Aryan people, were already in existence as a great power at such an early period and actually ruling in Mesopotamia was so destructive of Semitic theories on the alleged lateness of the Aryan race that Assyriologists promptly dropped the Gothic question altogether, and it is now never mentioned in any of the modern text-books.[2] As however their identity is now clear from the new evidence, this first-known mention of this great Northern people and kinsmen of the Britons by their own well-known name, and as advanced "Sumerians" is of immense historical importance.

"Goti," the Goths called themselves in Europe from time immemorial down till about the middle of the Christian era when their nationality was lost or changed.[3] The aspiration of their *Got* name into "Goth" was merely introduced by the Romans into their spelling of that name and was not used by the Goths themselves. And I have shown that *Goti* or "Goth" is a dialectic form of the *Khatti*, *Khadti* or *Kudti* title of the "Hitt-ites," of the *Khad* title used by the Aryan or Sumerian Phœnicians from the time of King Uruash, the *Khattiyo* of the Indo-Aryans and of the *Catti* title of the Ancient Briton kings on their pre-Roman coins, and that the Ancient Britons were Goths.[4]

[1] AIC. 1911, 327. [2] *e.g.*, CAH. 1, *passim*. [3] Cp. VD. 209.
[4] WPOB. 7 f.; 46, 70, 179 f.; 330 f. And on *o* for *u* see before.

This early record of the Goths in Mesopotamia is highly significant in view of our having already elicited in the foregoing chapters that the First Sumerian king of the First Sumerian Dynasty, with his people, who first introduced civilization into Mesopotamia, were Goths.

It is also significant that the first capital of the First Sumerian or Gothic king of the First Sumerian Dynasty, Ukusi or Dar or InDara, the Oku Thor or Dar of the Gothic Eddas, was, we are told, by the Kish Chronicle, at *Ukhu* or Okhu, the Oku of the Gothic Eddas, which seems to be located by the new evidence at Pteria, the modern Boghaz Koi, the immemorial imperial capital of the Khatti or "Hitt-ites" in the heart of Cappadocia in Asia Minor (see map). And it is from Cappadocia, or its border, that these Guti or Goths appear to have descended in their conquest of Mesopotamia.

Guti Land Location

Guti Land, from which these invading Guti "troops" descended into Mesopotamia is generally placed conjecturally by Assyriologists in the highlands of Persia to the east of Babylon; others more correctly locate it in Kurdistan [1] in the Eastern Taurus region, the greater part of which is within the old Hittite area. It is interesting therefore to learn that the latest Assyriologists now admit that "some of the kings (of the Guti) have names which seem to contain Hittite elements"; [2] and that they term this Guti or Gothic Invasion "The Hittite Invasion"; although they stultify themselves by still continuing stubbornly to deny that the Hittites were Aryans, without giving any reasons against the mass of new facts I have adduced for the Aryan racial origin of the Hittites.[3]

This location in the Eastern Taurus is within the ancient Cappadocia, in its south-eastern province of "Cataonia" of the Greco-Roman period, a name obviously preserving the old tribal name of the *Khatti* or *Catti* or Hitt-ites.[4] The

[1] RB. 159. [2] CAH. I, 423.

[3] The sole exception is Prof. Hrozny, the pioneer explorer of the Aryan affinities of the language of the later Hittites in their imperial documents written in cuneiform script from about 2000 B.C. onwards. And his philological results are now being confirmed by Kellogg and others.

[4] WPOB. 45, 65. [5] *Ib.*, 36, 172.

capital of Guti Land is referred to in several Sumerian texts as "Gutium situated in the mountains." It was probably one or other of the old Hittite mountain-cities there, Marash, *Kiššia* or Khurmi to the north of Carchemish. It presumably was not Pteria itself nor Cæsarea, as these were so remote for the effective control of Mesopotamia as a dependency. Yet the name of the second suzerain emperor of this Guti period preserved in the Indian king-lists as *Ayut-āyus*, suggests *Du-ut-a-li* (?)-*ya-as*, who was the Hittite emperor at Boghaz Koi or Pteria about this period.

Reason for the Guti or Gothic Invasion & Annexation of Mesopotamia

The cause of this invasion and annexation of Mesopotamia by the Guti or Goths at this early period may probably have been their resentment of the conquest and ravaging of their country with deportation of Goths as slaves by Sargon's great-grandson (Shar) Gani Eri about seventy years before, although he was distantly of the same kindred. He dated two of his regnal years from wars with Guti or Kuti Land and claimed to have captured its king Shar Lak.[1] Moreover, about this period the contemporary Mesopotamian business documents record that Guti and Amorite captives were sold as slaves in the markets of Lagash, of which city-port that great-grandson of Sargon had declared himself "priest-king." Such outrages on a freedom-loving, courageous, independent people like the Goths, who were distant kinsmen of the Sumerian rulers, must have been intolerable.

Guti or Gothic Imperial Rule in Mesopotamia as a Dependency

Fortunately for history, and especially European history, to which the Goths essentially belong, the Isin king-lists from Nippur, etc., carry on the chronology of the Kish Chronicle from the epoch of the Guti Invasion, with which that chronicle ends, continuously down through the Guti occupation and the succeeding dynasties to the latter end of their own Isin Dynasty, about 2050 B.C. And as this

[1] TD. in AIB, 1896, 359, No. 6.

period was for them so recent, their records seem to be historically authentic, and the monuments of the Guti kings are found to be in agreement with the names in those Isin lists.

According to these supplementary Isin Chronicles "The Guti troops carried off the royalty of Mesopotamia to Guti Land," and it is noted that "The Guti troops had not a king by name"; then it is added "Muruta became king and ruled for three years," and he is succeeded by a long line of 19 more "kings," specified by name, till the end of the Guti "Dynasty," which, it is stated, "reigned for 125 years and 40 days." But as the total regnal years of the kings only amount to 81 years and 40 days in the different copies of these Isin lists, this implies that the initial period in which there "was not a king by name" extended to 44 years; and it presumes that Mesopotamia was held for that period as a Guti Dependency under mere governors of the king of Guti Land, and that later they were given the local rank and title of "Kings" as Viceroys. This is confirmed by the numerous seals of this Guti Dynasty that I have discovered in the Indus Valley collection, in several of which these Guti Kings call themselves "The appointed ruler."

This rule of Mesopotamia by Guti or Gothic governors as a dependency of Guti Land during the period of the Guti occupation is confirmed by the Indo-Aryan king-lists, which show for this period (*i.e.* the total 125 years of that occupation) only six (or seven) imperial kings in the main or imperial line, that is with an average reign in this period of twenty-one to eighteen years, which is about a normal average for a king's reign. And of these imperial kings only two (or doubtfully three) appear in the long list of the Guti "kings" of Mesopotamia in the Isin lists for this period of the Guti occupation, in which the majority of the twenty "kings," reign for only three years or double that period.

It would thus appear that during the initial period of forty-four years in which there was "not a king by name" the Mesopotamian dependency was ruled by mere governors; and that after that period the governors were given the status of temporary local "kings," with a term of office for three years, subject to extension for a second term of office, and subject to the suzerainty of the Guti emperor in Guti

Land, in the Hittite mountains of Asia Minor to the north; and that the two (or three) emperors who held the office of viceroy in Mesopotamia did so while they were crown-princes and before their accession to the imperial throne in Guti Land. And the fact that our Indian king-lists uniquely preserve the names and chronological order of the imperial suzerain kings during the currency of this Guti occupation of Mesopotamia under Guti viceroys—names lost to the compilers of the Isin lists—again illustrates the unique importance of the Indian Chronicles as an independent source of lost Mesopotamian History.

Prominence of "Earls" & of Priest-Kings of the Kusha Line or Dynasty amongst the Guti or Gothic Temporary Kings, including GUDIA, "Ur Bau," "Ur Ningirsu," etc.

One of the most outstanding features of the list of the Guti or Gothic "kings" or viceroys is the title borne by several of them of *Iarla*. The significance of this title has not hitherto been recognized, but it is now seen clearly to be the well-known title of Gothic nobility, namely *Iarl* or *Jarl* or "Earl"; which supplies another striking proof of the identity of the Guti with the Goths or Goti.

Another outstanding feature of these Guti lists, which emerges by their comparison with our Indian key-lists is the prominence amongst these Gothic viceroys of the family of priest-kings of the celebrated Kusha line or dynasty of priest-kings of the Indian Epic chronicles, to whom belong, as I have shown,[1] the famous "Sumerian" priest-king Gudea or Gudia of Lagash, his son "Ur Ningirsu," "Ur Bau" and other priest-kings of this period. It is significant that the first and second of these Guti kings or viceroys were of this Kusha line, the second, namely In-Kishu or "King Kishu," being now shown to be the historical original of King Kusha himself of the Indian Chronicles. And Gudia himself appears as the third of these Guti kings or viceroys, who also bears the title of "Iarla" or "Earl," thus disclosing his Gothic origin. And one of them is a "Duke."

This Kusha line or dynasty, detailed on p. 371, is found

[1] WISD. 55 f.

in the Puru lunar versions of the Indian lists, and this being the line from which a considerable number of the Puru Aryan princes in India claimed descent, they took it out of its proper chronological place, just as they did with Manasyu's or Menes' dynasty, and pitchforked it back to connect directly with an earlier ancestor namesake near to the second king of the First Aryan Dynasty in order obviously to give it vaster antiquity. But its true chronological position is recovered for us by the scrupulously exact Solar version of the King-Lists (App. I, col. I), which has retained throughout the real chronological order from the First Aryan or Sumerian Dynasty down to the Babylonian period, and which discloses the imperial contemporaries of this Kusha line in their due chronological place, namely the solar emperors Su Dāsa II, Kalmāsha-pāda, and others.

Guti King or Viceroy List compared with Indian Lists for this Period

The Indian imperial-line lists as above noted give only the main or imperial line of the suzerain emperors and omit the tributary kings or viceroys. But many of these tributary kings and dynasties are given amongst the collateral tributary dynasties. Amongst these we have the Kusha line of priest-kings, which contain the names of several of the Guti viceroys, including Gudea or Gudia, the Gādhi of the Indian lists, and his son Vishwa-Ratha or Vishwa-Mitra.

In the annexed Table is shown the list of the Guti kings or viceroys, compared with the Indian-list suzerain emperors of this period and the Kusha line of priest-kings of the same period, several of whom are seen to have acted for one or more terms as Guti viceroys in Mesopotamia. In col. I are given the names of the twenty Guti kings (or viceroys) in the long list in the Isin and Nippur Chronicles, with their names as revised by me. In col. 2 are shown their names as spelt in their own monuments or in those of their tributaries, and in their Indus Valley seals, see App. XII. and Plate XX. In col. 3 are the names of the Kusha line or dynasty of the Indian list; and in col. 4 are the names of the imperial suzerain kings of the main-line solar lists, Nos. 46 to 50, of that list (see App. I. col I).

Guti Kings or Viceroys of Mesopotamia compared with Indian Lists.

Isin Lists		Monuments S.=Indus Seal	Indian Lists	
			Kusha Line	Solar Main Line
1. MURUTA	3 yrs.	—	MŪRTAYA s. of 2	Ayut-āyus
2. In KISHU (or GISHU)	6 ,,	KUSHU. *S.*	KUSHA f. of 1	Ritu-parna
3. Irila Tax (or Warla Gaba)	6 ,,	Irla TIŚUĀ or TAX. *S.*	—	Sarva-Kāma
4. Dug-me	6 ,,	(?) Udu-me, priest-k. of Lagash		
5. E-AMA-Mesh	6 ,,	KASHUSHAMAMA ,, AMA. *S.*	KUSHĀMBA, s. of 2	
6. Inima-BAKIES or BAEŚŚES	5 ,,	BAKUS or BASAM ,, or BAK. *S.*	BASU II, s. of 2	
7. Iziaush	6 ,,	AŚIASH. *S.*		
8. Iārla TAX or DAX	15 ,,	TASIA. *S.*	—	Su-DĀSA II
9. Ibate	3 ,,	ABATA. *S.*		
10. Iārla [GASH]	3 ,,	KASHUSHAMAMA ,, (2nd term (?))	(?) KUSHĀMBA (2nd term)	
11. BAGIES(PU)UM	1 ,,	BAKUS and BA-SI-UM, k. of Guti	BASU II, s. of 2 (2nd term (?))	
12. . . . Nikīn (or Nigīn)	3 ,,	NIGIN. *S.*	—	Nighna g.s. of Sarva K.
13. [LA-SI]-RABŪM	2 ,,	LA-SIRAB, k. of Guti		
14. Irarūm	2 ,,	IRIRUMUN. *S.*		
15. Darranūm	1 ,,	DAR. *S.*		
16. Khāblum	2 ,,	KHĀBLAM or KHĀB. *S.*	—	KALMASHA-pāda
17. SURATA-ASH SIN	7 ,,	SARATI GUBI SIN, k. of Guti	—	SRUTA-UPA-GUPTA or (?) SHINI, s. of Satyarathī
18. Iārla GU[1] (-ash) -DA (or Ga-[ash]-da)	7 ,,	GUDIA, p.-k. of Lagash. KUD-(*ash*)-DIA. *S.*	GĀDHI, s. of 5	
19. . . . [EN-RIDI-PIZIR] . . .	7 ,,	*En-Ridi* (or ERRIDI) PIZIR, k. of Guti ·RUDDU and PĪSHĀ. *S.*	VISHWĀ RATHA, s. of 18 and contemp. of TRISHANKU	VASVA-NANTA
20. [TIRI]-GAN	40 (days)	TIRIGAN, k. of Guti		

[1] *Gu*, as we have seen, is the Sumerian name for this sign (Br. 6103), and is therefore its major phonetic value.

It is thus seen from this Table that most of the leading "kings" or viceroys of the Guti period came from the Kusha "Dynasty" of Aryan priest-kings; and that two at least of them held the office of viceroy for more than one term, namely kings Nos. 3 and 6; and that in the intervals and later they were local priest-kings at the Sumerian seaport of Lagash. Nos. 18 and 19 are the famous priest-king Gudia and his son and successor, whose seals as *Gutu* or "Goths" are now discovered amongst the Indus Valley seals in Plate XX. and deciphered in App. XII.

Sumerian, Aryan & Gothic Character of the Names of the Guti Kings & Priest-Kings

The personal names of these Guti kings or viceroys generally attest their Sumerian, Aryan or Gothic origin.

Thus *Muruta,* the name of the first king, is a dialectic variant of the Sumerian *Muru* title for the Morites or Amorites, the great sea-going branch of the Early Sumerians, and a title for them already in Uruash's Dynasty when they first founded the Edin colony in the Indus Valley.[1] It was used as a personal name by those Indo-Aryan kings as *Marutta* or *Maruta;* and by the Kassi king of Babylonia *Maruttash,* and as *Marati* for a personal name in the Kassi period;[2] and it is found as a personal name on the prehistoric monuments of Ancient Britain.[3]

Tax, the name of the third and eighth, is *Thiasa* of the Eddas, the *Tkz, Dzs* title for the same personage on Greco-Phœnician coins, and the *Tascio* on the pre-Roman coins of the Ancient Britons.[4] It was also a name used by ruling chieftains in Brittany and Ancient Britain.[5] *Bakies* and *Bagies* are dialectic for *Bakus* (Bacchus). And *Enridi,* the penultimate king, who calls himself "King of the Guti and of the Four Regions,"[6] bears a distinctively Gothic name; for *Einride* is a dialectic form of the name of King Thor or Indara in the Gothic Eddas. Whilst his full Sumerian name *En-Ridi Pizir* or "Lord Ridi Pizir" is seen to equate with his Indian title as *Vishwā Ratha*, and his Indus seals *Pishā Ruddu.*

1 WPOB. 257 f.; WISD. 9 f.; 50 f. 2 CPN. 201. 3 WPOB. 260 f.

4 WPOB 212 f.; 261, 284 f.; 339 f.; 354 f.; 389 f.; with figures.

5 B. Poste, *Anc. British Coins,* 201.

6 PHT. iv., 134. On *di* syllable. Br. 4859.

SEALS OF GUTI OR GOTHIC KINGS FROM INDUS VALLEY

Amongst the second batch of seals unearthed from the Sumerian colonial capital on the Indus, I find no fewer than 19 seals of this dynasty representing 13 out of its 20 kings. These are shown in Pl. XX. and are deciphered in detail in App. XII. Here are cited the inscriptions on these seals, with references to their numbers in the Plate and their figures in the Appendix. It will be noticed that the Isin scribes spell the names often according to their own phonetics, and I have adopted the Isin form of the name for reference.

KISHU (No. 1 in Pl. and Fig. 123). His seal reads: "KŪSHU, The *Gutum* at Agdu Land." The prefix *In*=" King."

Earl TAX or DAX (No. 2, Fig. 124). His seal reads: "The *Irla*, King-Companion TIS'UĀ, The Great Minister of the *Gut* at Agdu Land."

AMA (Nos. 3-4, Figs. 125-6). The prefix *E* and affix *mesh* respectively =" The Great" and "Lord." His 1st seal reads: "AMA, The *Gutu*, The appointed ruler, at Agdu Land." His 2nd seal reads: "AMA, The *Gut*, The One appointed ruler at Agdu Land."

BAKIES (No. 5, Fig. 127). The prefix *Inim*=" Encanter-priest." His seal reads: "Under-King-Companion BAK, The *Gutum* at Agdu Land."

IZIAUSH (No. 6, Fig. 128). His seal reads: "ASIASH (or AIGIASH), The *Gutum*, The ruler *Gut* at Agdu Land."

Earl TAX or DAX (Nos. 7-8, Fig. 129). His first seal reads: "TASIA, The Lord *Gut*; and the second: "The *Ara* TASIA, The ruler."

IBATE (No. 9, Fig. 130). His seal reads: "ABATA, The *Gutum* at Agdu Land."

BAGIES(PU)UM, see above BAKIES.

NIGIN (No. 10, Fig. 131). His seal reads: "Under-King-Companion NIGIN, The *Gut* at . . . Land."

IRARUM (No. 11, Fig. 132). His seal reads: "IRIRUMUN, The *Gutum* at Agdu Land."

DARRANŪM (Nos. 12-13, Figs. 133-4). His first seal reads: "DAR, The *Gutum* at Agdu Land." His second reads: "Under-King-Companion of The Great *Gutums*, TAR (or DAR), The Lord *Gut* at Agdu Land."

KHĀBLUM (Nos. 14-15, Figs. 135-6). His first seal reads: "KHĀBLAM, The *Gutu*, The appointed Ruler." His second reads: "The *Duke Gut*, KHĀB, The Gut at Agdu Land."

Earl GU(-*ash*)-DA [GUDIA or "GUDEA"], (No. 16, Fig. 137). His seal reads: KUD(-*ash*)-DIA, The *Gutum*, The *Gut*."

EN RIDI PIZIR, Nos. 17-20, Figs. 138-140). His first seal reads: "The Overlord-Companion RUDDU, The *Gut*." His second (*Rhinoceros*) seal reads: "PISHA, The *Gutu*, The Lord, The son of the Shepherd of Edin Land." His third (*Tree and Deer-antelope*) seal reads: "The Overlord PISHĀ, The Shepherd of the Lord NIMIRRUD, The King of Kings, The Lord of Plants."

PLATE XX.

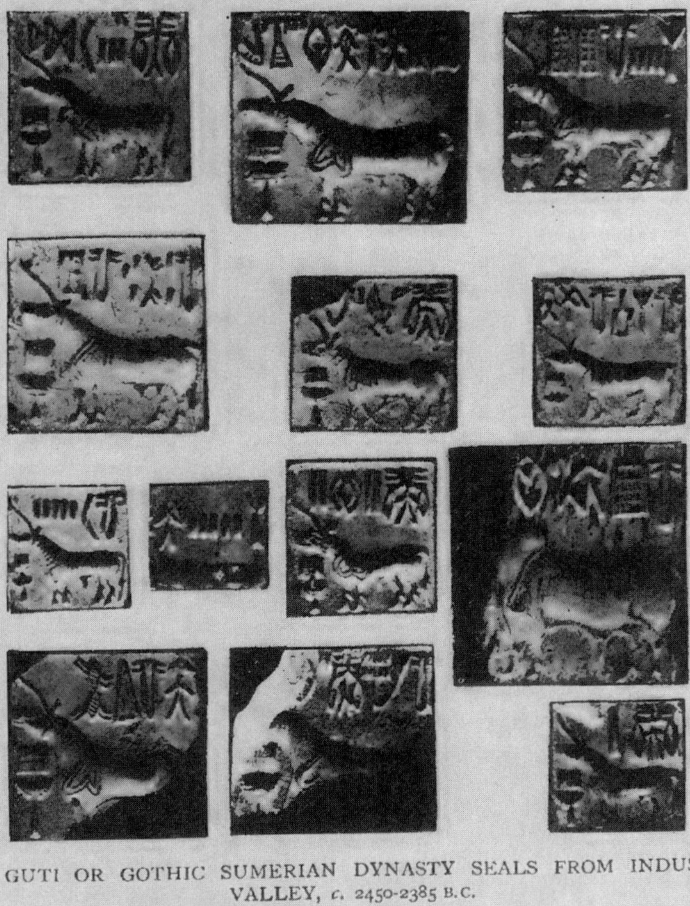

GUTI OR GOTHIC SUMERIAN DYNASTY SEALS FROM INDUS VALLEY, *c.* 2450-2385 B.C.

From King Kushu to Darru (from photographs after Sir J. Marshall). For decipherments and translations, see pp. 366, 582 f. And for continuation, see Pl XXA.

Guti or Gothic Monuments in Mesopotamia

With such short terms of imperial office we would not expect to find in Mesopotamia many records of these kings, especially as so many sites remain unexplored.

Yet there are, apart from the seals and the lavish monuments and records of Gudia and Bakus, seven of these "emperors" who have left records on excavated documents, either of their own or their officials acknowledging their suzerainty. And these records with their sculpturing are engraved in as fine a style of art as the average in the Sargonic period. From these records it appears that the kings were suzerains over the Mesopotamian empire and administered the various provinces and city-states by local kings and priest-kings as governors, just as did the Sumerian emperors of Kish, and Sargon and his dynasty before them.

These local kings and priest-kings were presumably all Goths as permanent officials in the provinces. Thus the local king of Umma under King Basium, bore the name of "King Annatum," a name in series with that of local Sumerian kings under the Sumerian Dynasty of the emperor Uruash, and by its final *um* element it is in series with many of the names of these Gothic kings themselves. This local Gothic king of Umma records the prosperity of Umma, "which he made rich with liberalities for thirty-five years." And as we shall see the famous priest-kings of the old Sumerian seaport city of Lagash on the Persian Gulf, and who are admitted by Assyriologists to be *typical* "Sumerians," namely the celebrated Bakus (or "Ur-Bau") and the still more celebrated Gudia (or "Gudea"), are now disclosed as Guti or Goths of this Guti period which re-established "the Golden Age" in Mesopotamia.

A more detailed account of this Gothic rule of Mesopotamia, apart from the mass of literature left by Gudia, is found in the lengthy record of King En Ridi-Pizir, "King of the Four Regions," extending to about 500 lines of one or two words each, found at the old imperial Sun-temple at Nippur. He dedicated his statue there to the great Sumerian and Gothic Father-god, "The Lord, the enthroned Sakh," just as the Sumerians, Uruash, Sargon, &c., did to that same Aryan and Gothic Father-god. His record appears to have been a praiseworthy pious attempt to collect copies of old inscriptions on the statues in that ancient imperial Sumerian shrine, which were perishing, in order to preserve them from oblivion; and he himself is the famed Vishvā-Mitra, traditional author of the 3rd book of the Vedas.

And we find that the almost unexampled prosperity of the seaport city of Lagash during this dynasty, and the free communications of that city throughout Mesopotamia from north to south, and with Syria and the Taurus Mountains and Cappadocia beyond, and with the Persian Gulf and Indian Ocean, were obviously owing to the universal peace enjoyed under the *pax Gothici*.

Language used by the Guti or Goths

The language used by these Gothic emperors themselves in the few records of this period which have been recovered, although in fairly standard Sumerian contains, like that of Sargon's dynasty, occasional Semitic or so-called Akkad words or idioms, as the documents were intended to be read by the Semitic Chaldees. Yet strange to say, Assyriologists do not conclude on that account, as they did with Sargon, that the Goths were Semites! The language, however, of the Gothic governors of their chief sea-province of Lagash, namely the priest-kings "Ur Bau" and Gudia, whose voluminous records have been unearthed, is always in pure standard Sumerian and in a more developed form than before. Indeed this was to be expected, as the Goths came from the old home-land of the Sumerians in Asia Minor, and were themselves descendants of the old Sumerian stock there, as we shall see.

Gothic Administration of Justice & the Guti Law Codes

The Gothic administration of justice and laws is described by their governor in Lagash, the Gothic priest-king Gudia in his records. The old law-codes of order and justice of King

PLATE XXA.

GUTI OR GOTHIC SUMERIAN DYNASTY SEALS FROM INDUS VALLEY, *c.* 2385-2360 B.C.

From King Khab (Khablum) to Pisha Ruddu or Vishva Ratha, or Vishva Mitra. (From photographs after Sir J. Marshall.) For decipherments and translations, see pp. 366, 588 f.

KING GUDIA, GOTHIC PRIEST-KING OF LAGASH,

c. 2370, B.C.

Diorite statue, one of ten others, found at Telloh, now in the Louvre (after De Sarzec, *Déc.*, Pl. 12, 1). Note his straight non-Semitic nose, quilted Phrygian hat, with brim turned up to give a somewhat turbaned appearance, embroidered robe, inscription graved on front of inner robe, and feet bare when seated on throne in the tropical climate of Lower Mesopotamia. And compare standing statuette in Pl. XXII.

Uruash and his dynasty (see Chapter VI) and of Nimrod or Cain, the founder of the city were, he tells us, again administered. As a result he says: "The maid was the equal of her mistress, and master and slave consorted together as friends; the powerful and the humble man lay down side by side; and in place of evil speech only propitious words were heard. The rich man did not wrong the orphan, nor did the strong man oppress the widow." In the city and the province taxes were levied, but the temple of the patron saint of the city (Nimrod), with its glebes, and fields, were exempted from taxation.

Religion of the Guti or Goths about 2500 B.C.

In religion these Early Goths appear to have preserved generally the higher and purer tenets of the Early Sumerians, in their adherence to the worship of the Sun of Heaven, the one God of the Universe, and latterly represented in human form as their Father-God on the model of their ancestral first king and father of the Sun-cult, The Lord Sakh or In-Dara, that is Thor Andvara or Sig, of the later Goths.

In this regard, it seems from the record of the local priest-king of Erech, who eventually overthrew this Guti Dynasty, and from the late "lamentation" rituals of the Semitic Chaldees of the Mother-goddess cult in the Seleucid era, that the Guti or Goths on their advent into Mesopotamia destroyed several shrines of that aboriginal Chaldee Mother-goddess, whose debasing cult, with its sanguinary human and animal demonistic sacrifices of the Moon-cult and Hell, was abhorrent to Sun-worshippers, with their idea of a beneficent Father-god of Light in Heaven. And this was just as the first Sumerian king Sakh, Dar or Adar himself had likewise previously done on finding that this Mother-son cult opposed the chief obstacle to his establishment of the higher civilization, so that he was forced to destroy those shrines on his advent into Mesopotamia, as celebrated in the Sumerian psalms.

Yet characteristically, Assyriologists generally with their Semitic prejudices and their championship of the degraded Semitic Chaldean Mother-son cult, and shutting their eyes to the admitted fact that "the golden age" of the Sumerians was re-established in Mesopotamia during this Guti period, have seized upon this early destruction of the shrines of the aboriginal Mother-goddess by the Guti or Goths to denounce the latter as " barbarians from the north," " cruel nomads of Gutium of ominous import for the civilization of Sumar and Akkad," " the blight of the occupation of Gutium," and so on ! [1] And they grossly mislead historians, by repeatedly calling the entire period of this Guti Dynasty one of " devastation by the hordes of Gutium . . . in which business records and works of art almost wholly disappear," [2] entirely forgetting that this period admittedly covers their " great renaissance " in Sumerian art and literature with teeming business records of the Guti governors Bakus and Gudea at Lagash ; and which advanced and phenomenal prosperity was only made possible through the imperial peace kept by the rule of these Goths.

The Kusha Line in the Guti or Gothic " Dynasty "

The Kusha line of " Sumerian " or Aryan kings which gave the leading kings to the Guti Dynasty requires some notice here. We have already seen how this Kusha line was arbitrarily displaced chronologically by the later Puru Brahmans in order to give it a pretended antiquity, obviously because the Puru clan, which formed a leading clan latterly in India, claimed descent from it, and because from it branched off through the female line the Ur Dynasty, in which was born the great champion of the Brahman caste, Parasu Rām, whom I have already identified with Purash Enzu or " Bur Sin I " of the Dynasty of Ur (see Fig. 70).

Genealogy of Kusha Line of the Guti in the Indian Lists disclosing the Origin of the Dynasty of Ur

The following genealogical Table of the Kusha Dynasty of the Guti is compiled from the Indian Chronicles.[3] It shows graphically the ancestry and interrelations of most of the leading kings of the Guti Dynasty, as well as the origin of the Ur Dynasty—now so well known from the recent excavations there—through its founder having married the daughter of the famous Guti priest-king Gudia, or Gudea, the princess Satyawati.

[1] So CAH. 1, 421 f. [2] CAH. 1, 424. [3] WVP. 4, 14 f.

In the Table I have placed within square brackets in italic capitals the Sumerian originals of the personal names, with the restorations by Assyriologists within curved brackets, for comparison with the names as preserved in the Indian Chronicles.

Genealogy of Kusha Dynasty of the Guti with Origin of Ur Dynasty.

(From Indian Chronicles).

(d.=daughter; m.=married; p.=priest; s.=son)

Jahnu, s. of Suhotra
|
Sunutu, Suhotra, Sumanta, Pūru
|
Ajaka
|
Balāk-ashwa
|
KUSHA
[*KISHU* or *KŪSHU*]
|
- KUSHĀMBA, s., or Kushāshwa or Pauru-kutsi [=*KASHU SHAMAMA* or (?) *AMA*] ("*Puzur-mama*")
  |
  GĀDHI, s. [=*GUDIA* or *GUDEA*]
  |
  - VISHWĀ-MITRA (II), s. p. [=*URUASH NIMIRRUD*] or *PĪSHA-RUDDU* ("*Ur Ningirsu*")
    |
    Shunah-shepa or Deva-rāta, s., Mādhu-chandas, s., Jaya-krita, s., Ashtaka, s., and others
  - Satya-wati, d. m. ŪRU-RICĪKA, p. [=*URUASH-ZIKUM*] ("*Ur Engur*" or "*Ur-Nāmmu*") Founder of Ur Dynasty
    |
    Jama-DAGNI, s., p. m. Renuka =*DUNGI* or *DUKGIN*
    |
    - PARASHU-Rām, s., [=*PURASH-ENZU*] ("*Bur-Sin I*")
    - Rumanwat, s.,
    - Vasu (III), s.,
    - SUSHENA [=*SHUASH-SIN*] ("*Gimil Sin*")
- Kushanābha, s.,
- MŪRTAYA, s.,
- BASU (II), s. or Ama-Basa II [=*BAKIES, BAKUS, BASAM, BASIUM*] ("*Ur Bau*")

The line on the lower right-hand side, branching off with the princess Satyawati, daughter of King Gudia or Gudea, forms the Dynasty of Ur, which followed the Guti Dynasty after an interval of seven years.

Guti Kings & Priest-Kings of the Kusha Line

Here space permits only of a brief reference to the leading Guti kings and priest-kings of this Kusha line in the light of our new information in order to show their identity with the kings of the Early Eastern Aryans.

Of King Kusha himself, who we have seen is called King *Kishu*[1] in the Isin lists, besides his Indus Valley seal no monuments have yet been found; but most of the others have left numerous monuments and records.

Kashushamama, Gothic Priest-King of Lagash or Kushamba of Indian Lists

The name of this priest-king of Lagash, who has left his name on record near the beginning of the Guti period reads, I find, *Kashshamama* or *Ka-shu-sha-ma-ma*;[2] and thus equates with *Kushāmba*, the name of the eldest son of King Kusha in the Indian lists. The suffix *mama* in Sumerian means " The Appointed ";[3] so that his name reads " Kashsha the appointed," as a temporary king; and he bears " the appointed " title on his Indus seals, see p. 366.

He calls himself in his inscriptions " priest-king of Lagash." He is considered by Assyriologists to be a pure Sumerian, and to have preceded " Ur Bau," who is now disclosed by our genealogical Table to have been his younger brother. This Indian Epic genealogy also discloses him as the hitherto unknown father of Gudia. This Sumerian priest-king is thus discovered to be an Aryan and Guti or Goth.

[1] In the earlier Isin lists he is called " King " by the usual Sumerian sign for " King," which has a value of *In*; but in the later Isin list this *In* is written by another slightly different sign, which also has the value of *In*.

[2] This is the direct orthographic phonetic values of the signs as written, which Assyriologists arbitrarily read as " Puzur-mama," giving the first three signs of this Sumerian name the *Semitic* value of " Puzur," which, moreover, is not found in the lexicons as their equivalent. The first sign is the Mouth sign, with the value of *Ka* or *Gu*, and inside it is the *Shu* sign, evidently to give the value of *Kash* or *Gush* for the compound sign.

[3] *Mama* is defined as having meaning of Assyrian *Śakānu*=" appointed," cp. MD. 1028. And in Sanskrit *Ma* means " authority."

URUASH BAKUS OR BASAM ("UR-BAU") GOTHIC PRIEST-KING OF LAGASH, AS BAKIES OR BASIUM, KING OF THE GUTI & BASU II OF INDIAN LISTS

This great Sumerian priest-king and governor of Lagash almost rivalled Gudia in the magnificence of his monuments and temple building and in restoring the glories of the ancient city of the dynasty of King Uruash; and significantly he takes as his forename that of Uruash, to express his devotion to the worship of the 2nd Aryan king, Bakus, Nimrod or St Michael. And in the Indian Epics the title of "Haryashwas" is applied generically to all the later ruling princes descended from the emperor Haryashwa down to the period of the massacre of "the Haryashwas" by the Brahmans under Parashu Rāma ("Bur-Sin") during the later Ur Dynasty, as seen farther on. His name which reads, on his own numerous monuments *Uru-āsh Bā-kus*, or with the dialectic variant of the last syllable *sam* for *kus*, as *Uru-ash Ba-sam*, is disguised by Assyriologists as "Ur Bau."[1]

His unknown ancestry and antecedents are now disclosed. He, as seen from the genealogical Table, was an Aryan prince, the youngest son of King Kusha and youngest brother of the preceding priest-king Kashshamama, a relationship hitherto unknown.

He is now found to have been originally the sixth Gothic king in the Guti king-lists (see p. 364), in which he is styled "The Incanter Bakies" (*Inima Bakies*), *Inima* or "The Incanter" being a recognized title for "high-priest." As king or emperor under this name Bakies he reigned for five years.

We again find him in office as emperor twenty-seven years later as the eleventh Guti king or emperor under the style of *Bagiesum*, or Basium, which is a dialectic Sumerian variant of Bakies or *Bakus*. The latter name we have seen with reference to "King Bakus, Lord of Grain," the second Aryan king of the First Aryan Dynasty, and the historical human original of Bacchus, possessed the Sumerian variant of *Basam*, through its second syllabic sign *Kus* having

1 "*Ur-Bau*" is coined by omitting the second syllable, and selecting for the last syllable its polyphonous value of *u*.

also the value of *sam*, and it was evidently through this latter form that the Indian Epics derived their name for him of *Basu.* "Basium" is thus a dialectic form for the same Sumerian word variously spelt Bakus, Bakies and Basam.

Under the style of Basium he reigned as king for only one year. This gives him a total official life of 5+27+1 or 33 years. And this is in keeping with his long reign at Lagash, as attested by the great number of monuments and votive records that he has left there recording the building of very numerous temples, in one of which was unearthed an inscribed statue of himself, now headless.

His long reign is also attested by the records of his two daughters and sons-in-law, the latter of whom succeeded him in turn as priest-kings of Lagash. No son of his is anywhere mentioned in the numerous inscriptions of his period; and it is significant that his genealogy in the Indian Epics, as seen in the Table, p. 371, also gives him no son, and is thus in agreement with the historical records. His two daughters, the eldest of whom was named "Lady Gandu" (Nin Gandu) were, according to the contemporary Sumerian records, married to two priests, Nammakhni, who thus gained by this espousal succession to the priest-kingship, and Urgur, who followed the latter in that office after the death of the father-in-law.

The fact that he uses on one at least of his monuments the title of "king," that is temporal king, as opposed to the religious title of "priest-king" (*Khat-ti-si* or *Pa-ti-si*), which latter is his usual designation on his monuments, further identifies him as King Bakies and Basium of the Guti king-lists. And the fact that in his records he does not name any suzerain king is evidently because he twice held the emperorship himself and belonged to the imperial family, and so presumably under the apparently commonwealth rule of the Guti did not require to record his subordination on reverting to the rank of priest-kingship in the great seaport city of which he was the metropolitan pope.

In personal appearance, his statue portrays him as a priest of stocky build, standing with clasped hands in adoration, and wearing the customary Sumerian priests' long plaid or shawl draped over the left shoulder, as still with Buddhist priests and still continued with Brahman priests in India. Though the head is wanting, he was doubtless clean-shaven, like the Sumerian priests of this period.

Gudia ("Gudea") Gothic Priest-King & Governor of Lagash in later Guti Period

Gudia or Gudea is the best known of all the Sumerian priest-kings from the profusion of his records, buildings, magnificent sculptures and statues of himself. He is now disclosed to be a Guti or Goth, and his name "Gudia" was possibly related to his racial name. His records are unusually numerous and are inscribed on his statues, statuettes, clay cylinders (two of great length), bricks, nails, vases, mace-heads, a lion, plaques and cylinder-seals forming a great body of contemporary historical material.

Gudia's Gothic Aryan Ancestry

Hitherto nothing has been known of Gudia's ancestry, as nowhere in his own records or in the Babylonian is there any reference to his father or genealogy. Now his missing genealogy is supplied by the official Indian Epic king-lists, in which he is called King Gādhi; and his power and magnificence were so great that he is called in these Indian Epics an incarnation of the god Indra,[1] that is as we have seen the deified first Aryan or Sumerian king to whom his genealogy is traced back. These Indian Chronicles show that he was a prince of the Aryan Kusha Dynasty, son of Kushamba the Guti king and priest-king Kushshamama and nephew of Basu II, the above Guti king and priest-king Uruash Bakus or Basium, whose sons-in-law he succeeded at Lagash. He married his cousin, a daughter of Uruash Bakus.

His Personal Appearance

His personal appearance is well known from his numerous statues of himself, which he placed in the great temples which he built, and of which no fewer than thirteen of unequal merit have been unearthed by the French Expedition in

[1] MBt. xii. 49; PIT. 136.

their exhaustive excavations at Telloh or "The Mound," the modern Arab name for the ancient site of the seaport city of Lagash, Shirburla or Shirlapur.

The magnificent and artistic life-like statue of him in Plate XXII is one of the latest and finest of his portraits yet found; and I am indebted to the courtesy of the editors of the *Revue d'Assyriologie* and La Librairie Ernest Leroux for permission to reproduce it. This represents him as a tall refined, ascetic-looking intellectual man of Aryan type, clean shaven, and garbed in a flowing embroidered fringed robe and turbaned. And significantly so modern is his appearance and attire that with his features he might pass for a Hindu gentleman of the present day in India, and thus affording still another striking illustration of the Aryan Origin of the Sumerians. In most of his other statues he is portrayed as a priest with swathed shawl leaving the right shoulder bare, as imitated by Buddha and Buddhist priests.

THE PROBLEM OF GUDIA'S IMPERIAL RESOURCES UNDER THE GUTI RULE EXPLAINED

The vast resources for his temple building which Gudia enjoyed under the Guti rule have hitherto formed a vexed and unsolved problem to Assyriologists, who stigmatize the Guti as inveterate "devastating barbarians" and "destroyers of Sumerian civilization."

It is admitted by Assyriologists that "Gudea certainly lived under the kings of Gutium,"[1] that Sumerian art and literature reached its zenith under him, that he lived in a period of profound peace and prosperity, with vast wealth and resources, that he had free access throughout Mesopotamia and beyond its frontiers to Syria, the Taurus Mountains, Cappadocia and the Eastern Mediterranean on the north, to Elam and the Persian Gulf and Indian Ocean lands on the east, all of which places he records having personally visited and ransacked for materials to build and adorn his temples. Thus he records having brought from Mount Amanus in the Eastern Taurus range great beams of cedar wood, 50 and 60 cubits long, and cut a road through the forest for their transport down, also urkarinnu and other precious woods

[1] CAH. I, 433.

KING GUDIA, GOTHIC PRIEST-KING, *c.* 2370 B.C.

Alabaster jade-coloured statuette, .41 m. high, from Lagash, and now in the Louvre. Full face and semi-profile (from photographs after V. Scheil in RA., 1925, 41). He wears the same hat as in the seated statue, Pl. XXI; and is garbed in a rich shawl or robe with tasselled fringe, wound around the body, leaving the right shoulder and arm bare, and the end gathered up and thrown over the left arm. The inscription on the back records that it was a votive offering to the temple constructed by him for "The Lady of the Mead, the dear dame of the god, The Increaser of Plants" (a reflex of the deified second Sumerian king Nimurrud or Nimrod or Bacchus, the patron saint of Lagash city-port).

25 cubits long. From Ursu in Mount Ibla he brought zabalu, plane-tree and other beams. From Basalla and Menua in Amorite Land of North Syria he fetched great blocks of stone for his stelæ, and made roads to the quarries there. From Tiunu in Cilicia-Cappadocia he brought marble. From Kimash (Kamisa or Komisene ?) he brought copper for his great votive mace-head, and silver from The Silver Mount in Cappadocia; from Khakha gold dust, from Madga bitumen and plaster for the great temple platform ; from Melukhkha ushū wood, from Mount Barshib blocks of nalua-stone; which he transported in great boats. From the Mountains of Magan (Sinai) and Gubi and Dilmun *via* the Persian Gulf and Indian Ocean he brought precious woods and the diorite blocks for his statues and friezes by ships to the port of Lagash. And he states that for these purposes he travelled from the lower lands to the upper lands and that his patron-saint, " my beloved King Nimirrud (Nimrod), the son of Lord Sakh, opened the ways for me from the Upper Sea (Mediterranean) to the Lower Sea (Persian Gulf and Indian Ocean)." [1]

This unlimited use of such vast imperial resources by Gudia, who never once calls himself " king " (temporal) [2] nor mentions a suzerain, coupled with its occurrence in the Guti period—a period in which the Guti, according to Assyriologists, were throughout "devastating barbarians," " that period of terrible anarchy and oppression of the barbarians from Gutium," in which Sumerian cities " felt the heavy hands of cruel oppressors," [3] and " during their direful rule the business records and works of art almost wholly disappear " [4] [*sic* !]—this has constituted for Assyriologists a perplexing and unsolved problem.

But this vexed problem of Assyriologists in regard to Gudea is now seen to be entirely of their own making and Semitic prejudices. The solution of the problem is seen to be that Gudia was himself a Guti, the grandson and son-in-law of Guti emperors, and as the metropolitan Guti or Gothic pope he had the run of the vast Guti empire, not only in

[1] Texts and translations in TBI. 146 f. ; and cp. KHS. 261 f.

[2] He is called " king " by Babylonians within two centuries of his death ; but he appears to have been the third last temporary king during his lifetime (see Table, p. 364).

[3] CAH. I, 434.

[4] CAH. I, 434.

Mesopotamia, but beyond. With such royal birth and religious status at a time when the high-priest or priest-kings were allowed apparently by the over-pious Guti rulers to usurp such unlimited powers, it is scarcely surprising that Gudia should omit to name his temporal suzerain.

Gudia's Sumerian Renaissance

The renaissance of Sumerian civilization in Mesopotamia, begun by his father and his uncle and father-in-law Uruash Bau, was continued and further developed by Gudia, as evidenced by his higher art and the more developed literary form of his Sumerian language in his numerous records.

His higher art is displayed in his sculptures, seals, engravings, etc. It is well illustrated in the statue of himself in Plate XXII.

His development of literature is seen generally in his compositions, which are mostly dedicatory and elaborate rituals and litanies.

In architecture he made great advances. His temples were built according to architects' scaled plans (see Fig. 69 for one). And one of his famous statues represents himself as an architect seated with a scaled plan of his great temple upon his knees. His temples surpassed in size and magnificence those of his Sumerian predecessors. They were in reality great palaces, with apartments for the crowd of priests and their servants, with treasure-chambers, store-houses, granaries and stables for oxen and for animals destined for sacrifice—a Chaldean rite practised by him.

In religion, while he energetically restored the old temples and built several fresh ones to the same deified ancestral gods, as his uncle and father-in-law Uruash Bakus did before him, he created several new gods out of titles of the old ones and formed quite a large pantheon, and was a visionary and saw visions and developed the rituals and litanies. In addition to his temples he says that he gave to Lagash a replica more or less of the famous " Hall of Statues " at the old imperial Sun-temple of Nippur. This contained life-sized statues of the old emperors, including Sargon and his dynasty, and was adorned with sculptured bas-reliefs of the exploits of these emperors, and all were protected by engraved curses upon those persons who would destroy them.

His most remarkable building was a great tower-temple of seven stages erected for his city-god Nimirrud (*i.e.* as we have seen the deified second Sumerian king "Michael" or "Cain" and the *Nimi* of the Indian lists), the plan of which —the origin of the later fashionable "Ziggurat" temple-towers [1]—was, he says, revealed to him in a dream.

Gudia's Vision or Dream

This famous vision or dream of Gudia, in which his gods (deified ancestors) appeared and held converse with him, is related and repeatedly referred to by him in his records, and it is interesting as showing the visionary character of Gudia. During a period of great drought, with failures of the crops and threatened famine, which was attributed to "the anger of the gods"—as Gudia had become a downright polytheist—a company of four gods appeared unto him in a dream, two gods and two goddesses, and the leader uttering some words, one of the goddesses drew a plan on a tablet of lapis-lazuli stone. Unable to interpret this dream, he prayed without ceasing to Nimirrud, whom significantly he calls "the dear son of Lord Sakh," and to the deified priestess Gatum-Dug, who was the supposed intercessor with "The Oracular Lady Mother" (Ninā). This intercessor appeared to him and directed him to proceed to the temple of that Oracle Lady herself. The latter goddess then appeared to him in her temple and informed him that the god he had seen was Nimirrud himself, accompanied by Gudia's own familiar tutelary Ninizzida and his sisters, and that the word the god had spoken was an order to rebuild his temple on the new plan which the goddess had drawn. This was the plan which Gudia is represented in his statue bearing upon his knees (see Fig. 69), and the plan of the great tower-temple which he thereupon built. And the old statue of the patron city-god Nimirrud was removed into its new shrine with elaborate ritual.

Confirmation of the great drought which led to the build-

[1] Earlier small temple-towers of the pre-Sargonic period are found at Nippur and elsewhere.

ing of this temple seems to be found in the Indian Epics, which refer to " a twelve years' drought " in the time of the priest-king Vishvā-Mitra,[1] the name of the son and successor of Gādhi *i.e.* Gudia.

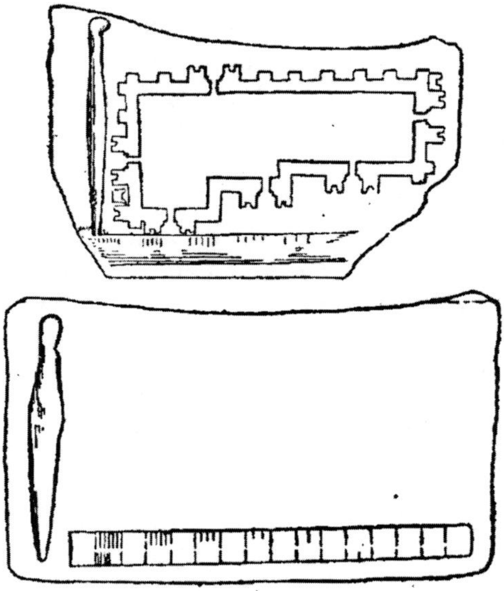

FIG. 69.—Plan of the great Temple engraved on statue of Gudea, showing ground-plan above, and Architect's measured Rule and Stylus below. (After *Déc.*, pl. 15, 1, 2.)

CHARACTER OF GUDIA

Gudia is seen to have been essentially a priest rather than a governor or ruler. He was a mystic and a visionary who saw visions, and developed in a mystical direction the old Sumerian religion into a polytheism.

He evidently believed in his own special inspiration and styled himself " The Good Shepherd," and " The beloved of the Gods "—which latter title was also later adopted by the Indian Buddhist emperor, Asoka, who in many ways resembled Gudia in that he lavished the vast wealth of his empire in covering the land with temples and monasteries and religious monuments and in endowing the priests, to whom he latterly gave up his kingdom and became himself

[1] WVP. 3, 285. Here this Vishva-Mitra is placed much earlier than Gādhi, though he is given the same contemporary Harishchandra as was the son of Gādhi.

a tonsured monk, robed like Gudia and his priests with the right shoulder bare; and is the Constantine of Buddhism.

After a very long reign Gudia died, leaving a son Uruash Nimirrud, who succeeded him, and a daughter who married the founder of the Ur Dynasty (see Table, p. 371).

His Posthumous Canonization

Gudia never himself claims in his inscriptions divine honours, as some of the later kings did. But he was canonized or deified posthumously by the Babylonians within about two centuries of his death and called "The divine Gudia." Perhaps the numerous statues which he made of himself and set up in the temples may have contributed to this deification, although they were apparently intended merely to represent himself as a votary appealing vicariously to his gods. In keeping with his deification by the Babylonians, the Indian Epics call him an incarnation of the god Indra.[1]

King Ridi Pizir, Pisha Ruddu or Uruash Nimirrud, Gothic Priest-King, or Vishwā-Ratha or Vishvā-Mitra of Indian Epics & Vedas

The son and successor of Gudia was En-Ridi (or Erridi) Pizir,[2] that is "King" *Ridi Pizir* of the Guti period, or as he calls himself in his own contemporary inscriptions by his priestly title of Uruash Nimirrud ("Ur-Ningirsu"), as devotee of the patron saint Nimrod of Lagash; and he is now disclosed as the historical original of the famous Early Aryan priest-king of the Indian Epics and Vedas called *Vishwā Ratha* and afterwards priest Vishvā-Mitra.

He is called "king" in one or more of his inscriptions in Mesopotamia; but in most of his contemporary inscriptions he calls himself and is called "Priest-king of Lagash"—the title of his father before him—presumably after he had relinquished or lost his term of office of the temporal kingship. He was the penultimate Guti king—the last king being Tirigan, who was possibly the king "Trisankhu" of the Indian Epics, who was contemporary with and a patron of this priest-king Vishvā-Mitra. In an inscription he states that he re-built part of the temple of his namesake, the patron saint of

[1] WVP. 4, 16. [2] Cp. KHS. 275.

Lagash, and of Enki the canonized son of the latter, and of "Heaven" personified. For further details, see App. XII.

It is inferred that he was deposed from the priest-kingship of Lagash, but retained the charge of the oracle temple there, as one of his name is found over a generation later in the reign of Dungi of Ur as high priest of that oracle temple of Lady Ninā or Nanā and is styled "the beloved high-priest of Ninā." This is in general agreement with the Indian Epics, which state that Gādhi's (*i.e.* Gudia's) son and successor Vishvā-Mitra was deposed by the cow-cult priest Vasishtha and his protégé Kalmasha-pada, *who performed (the Chaldean) human sacrifice;* and as a result the sons of Vishva-Mitra lost their succession.[1] He was one of the most famous Aryan priests, and according to the Brahmanist tradition although of the royal caste he obtained Brahmanhood through his devotions; and he lived to a great age over the reigns of several of the kings, including Jama-Dagni, now seen to be Dungi of the Ur Dynasty.

END OF THE GUTI DYNASTY IN MESOPOTAMIA & ITS LESSONS

After a reign of about 125 years[2] we are told in the Isin lists that under the last king Tirigan (probably Trishanku of Indian Epics[3]) "the troops of Gutum were smitten by the sword. The royalty passed to Unug (Enoch or Erech). At Unug Utu-khe-gal[4] reigned $7\frac{1}{6}$ years and 7 days."

This overthrow of the last king of the Guti, Tiriga or Tirigan, is recorded in an inscription of the victor Utu Khegal, king of Erech, in a manifesto[5] which suggests a Limehouse propaganda declamation of a rival party politician, coming as it does within about three years only after the decease of the Guti Gudia, whose beneficent rule was so

[1] WVP. 4, 22; 3, 306 f.

[2] 125 years 40 days according to Poebel's text; and 124 and 40 days in Legraine's tablet; but the years total only 91.

[3] King Trishanku was a patron of the priest Vishwa-Mitra in the Indian Epics, but later Brahmans seem to have transferred his name, along with the story of Vishwa-Mitra, to the pre-Sargonic king, Satyvrata, giving the latter the appellation of Trishanku (see Table p. 364, No. 20, and cp. WVP. 3, 284 f.).

[4] May also read Ashukha-gal or Anukha-makh.

[5] TD. in RA. IX. 111-120 and X. 99 f.

acclaimed that he was canonized, and even deified a few decades after his death and coming only a few months after the period of his son, "the dear priest," who opposed the practice of Chaldean human sacrifice. In that manifesto this insurrector says that he announced to the people of Erech that the Lord Sakh had sent him to destroy the Guti, "the dragon of the mountains, the enemy of the gods, who had filled Sumer Land with sorrow, had torn husband from wife and parent from child." It goes on to state that the people of Erech thus roused marched forth from the city behind their champion arranged in battle order. King Tirigan sent a message by two of his Guti captains, Ur Ninazu and Nabi En-Shak, without avail. In the conflict Tirigan, deserted by his troops, fled and was captured in the village of Dubruns, and brought to Ashukha-gal, who placed his foot on the neck of the prostrate king. The memory of this defeat of the Guti, which was evidently popular amongst the Chaldeans, lasted down to the Seleuncid era in Babylonia, as there is an Omen entitled "Omen of Tiriqqān the king who perished in the midst of his troops,"[1] which suggests that it was the dead body of the king which was dishonoured by the victor.

The veracity of the charges brought against the Guti Dynasty of Mesopotamia by this usurping king of Erech is countered, as we have seen, by the phenomenal prosperity and peace reaching its climax under the Guti King Gudia a year or two before this epoch, and a material prosperity which we find still continued on into the Ur Dynasty of Gudia's son-in-law, a few years later. And it is significant that this king of Erech who posed as the champion of the people against the alleged oppression by the Gutis, was himself driven from the throne after only seven years' reign by Gudia's son-in-law, and has left no record of anything he achieved beyond his manifesto on this downfall of the Guti. He was evidently the leading chief or king of the *Vriçi* tribe mentioned in the Indian Vedas, the *Vrika* of the Indian Epics, against whom Gudia's son Vishwā-Mitra contended successfully for a time[2] in favour of King Trishanku (? Tirigan) who also abhorred human sacrifice, wherein *Vrici* or *Vrika* or

[1] PT. IV. 135.

[2] MKI. 2, 319; WVP. 3, 284 f.

Wrika now appears to be the Indian equivalent of Uruk, *Uriki* or Erech. And it would seem that a chief objection to the Guti Dynasty was its opposition to the human sacrifice and Moon worship of the aboriginal Chaldees.

The real cause thus of the downfall of the Guti Dynasty in Mesopotamia appears to have been the wasting of their Aryan Guti strength latterly on over-zeal in religion, with excessive building of temples and endowment of hordes of priests, on a scale almost equalling that of the Hermit Kingdom of the Grand Lama in Tibet. Their temporal rule had become subordinated to the priestcraft of their local governors who were ex-officio priest-kings. And to this was added their popular disfavour by opposing the old-established Chaldean Moon-cult, with its human sacrifices. The Ur Dynasty which succeeded seven years later appears to have gained the public favour by its adoption of the Moon-cult, as well as the degraded Chaldean practice of human sacrifice, as revealed by the recent excavations of the tombs at Ur.

Thus the Guti or Gothic Dynasty, which like its fellow-Sumerian dynasties were merely the ruling race over "the black-headed" aboriginal Chaldees and always relatively few in proportion to the Chaldee subjects, after keeping the peace in Mesopotamia for over a century of great prosperity, appears at last to have fallen a victim to their too complacent patronage of their chief priest-king Gudia's excessive temple-building. This endless building and transportation of materials on such a vast and imperial scale was doubtless done largely by forced labour ; and there is repeated reference to the heavy burden of taxation for the support of the army of priests. All these harassing demands, coupled with their opposition to the Moon-cult and human sacrifice, must have placed a plausible excuse in the hands of the leader of the popular Chaldean revolt at Erech.

In the Indus Valley, which I have shown was a Sumerian colony of the Mesopotamian empire, from the First Phœnician Dynasty downwards to at least the Ur Dynasty, further inscriptions and seals of some of these Guti emperors will probably be found amongst the great number of inscribed objects recently unearthed there, but not yet published.

Résumé of Guti or Gothic Dynasty

We have thus found that the *Guti* ruling people of Asia Minor who annexed and ruled Mesopotamia and restored civilization there after the dark period following the fall of Sargon's dynasty were of the same Aryan or Gothic stock as that which originally sent forth from Asia Minor, about eight centuries earlier, the great ruling and civilizing branch into Mesopotamia, which is now called the "Sumerians"; and were the descendants of the residue of that stock left behind in Southern Asia Minor. We have also found that in their relative isolation there they appear to have developed their free institutions in the direction of a commonwealth, with a nobility bearing the title of *Iarla* or "Earl"; and that they had already begun to use as their national title the dialectic form of *Guti*, *i.e.* "Goth," in preference to the other variant forms of Khatti, Kudti, Khad and Hatti, the usual title of the last residue of these people in Asia Minor, the "Hitt-ites."

This Gothic Dynasty restored the glories of the old Sumerian rule in Mesopotamia to such an extent that Assyriologists call its later period "a golden age of the Sumerians." And the activities of this dynasty in the rich Sumerian colony on the Indus are attested by the very numerous official signet seals of its kings now discovered and deciphered above for the first time, see p. 366.

But latterly their kings, through overzeal in their religion, subordinated their temporal government to the priesthood, &c., spent all their energies and the resources of their empire in building and endowing great temples with teeming swarms of priests, who oppressed the people with their exactions, and this, coupled with their opposition to Chaldean human sacrifice, led to the downfall of their dynasty.

We thus have established by a further mass of concrete contemporary historical evidence that the Sumerians, Aryans and Goths were one and the same people—these different titles being synonymous. And again we obtain further striking illustration of the authenticity of the Indian Epic Chronicles and their official king-lists of the Early Aryans, and their unique importance as an independent source of "Sumerian" or Early Aryan or Gothic history.

XXI

Ur Dynasty in Mesopotamia, c. 2350-2200 B.C., with its Unknown Origin discovered by Indian Chronicles

Disclosing its Priestly Origin, Semitization, Orientalist Decadence, Moon-Worship, with Rise of Brahmans to 1st Caste under 3rd King Pur-ash-Sin or Parashu Rama.

The accession of this new Sumerian dynasty at Ur, the so-called "Third Dynasty of Ur" of the Isin lists, under the son-in-law of King Gudia the Guti, who within eight years of the fall of the Guti Dynasty seized the imperial power from the hands of the usurper Utukhegal of Erech, makes the cleavage between the Eastern or Oriental and the Western branches of Civilization much wider and more marked than before.

Its Priestly Origin, Semitization & Orientalist Decadence of the Ur Dynasty, with Rise of Brahmanism to First Caste

This Ur Dynasty, which is at present so much in the public eye through the spectacular and sumptuous finds of massive gold and richly jewelled objects recently unearthed from the tombs there by the Joint Expedition of the British and Philadelphia Museums, under Mr Woolley, was founded by the Sumerian priest Uruash-Zikum, who had married the daughter of King Gudia, the King *Gādhi* of the Indian Chronicles (see genealogical Table, p. 371). He appears to have gained the throne and popularity by embracing whole-heartedly the aboriginal Moon-cult of his Chaldee and Semitic subjects, with its debasing animal sacrifices, including human sacrifices, with the associated immolation of wives at burials, that is the Indian "Sutee"—on the notion that the wives would be of service to their dead lord in the next world, a practice which appears also, as we have seen, to have been adopted at Ur by the reactionary pre-Sargonic dynasty of Duruashi Padda or Drupada.

This lowered position assigned to women, as mere chattels of the husbands, was characteristically Semitic and Chaldean and Eastern (excluding China and Japan); and it was diametrically opposed to the chivalry of the Aryan, Sumerian and Gothic tradition and practice followed by Western Civilization, in which the women have always enjoyed equal social rights with men, subject only to the descent passing in the male line of fatherhood, and with slight political disabilities arising from the father being the "Husband" or "Band or Master of the House."

This Semitizing tendency is also noticeable in the Semitic title for "Moon" as *Sin* attached to the name of the last three members of the dynasty; as well as in the fact that although the official language remained Sumerian, the names of many officials betray their Semitic race, and show that Semites rose to higher positions in the service of their Sumerian rulers than before. And from this period probably dates the considerable number of Semitic roots, which I have shown exist in the Sanskrit language in India,[1] especially as the Indian Brahmans claim to be specially related to and descended from the kings and priests of this dynasty.

The rule also became more priest-ridden even than in Gudia's day; and under the third king, Purash Sin ("Bur Sin I"), the Parashu Rām of the Indian lists, the priests or *Baru* were according to the Indian Chronicles raised as "Brahmans"[2] to be the first hereditary caste in the state, a position which they have continued to possess in the Indian branch down to the present day. And the arrogant adoption by this priestly king-champion of the Brahmans and by his father of the divine title of "The God or Lord-god" in their inscriptions is presumably related to the claim by the Indian Brahmans that their caste is exclusively of divine origin and "twice-born."

Mysticism in religion and polytheism also tended to increase in the Ur Dynasty, with further elaborate develop-

[1] WSAD. *passim.*
[2] On the Sumerian origin of the name *Brahman*, see WISD. 36, 40, 47.

ments in ritual. And Sumerian art, which had progressed more or less down to Gudia's day now becomes conventionalized, stiffened and mechanically repeated with a tendency to decadence.[1] And to crown all, the dynasty made its capital at Ur, the central home of the Semitic Moon-cult, which cult it officially adopted.

Ur Dynasty King-List

The king-list of this dynasty is recorded in the various versions of the Isin and Nippur Chronicles in practically the same words, and at the same time the manner of the accession of the dynasty by the conquest of Erech is thus stated :[2]—

"Unug (Erech) City was smitten by the sword : the royalty passed to Ur City.
At Ur City Uruash Zikum[3] became king and reigned 18 years.
The god Dungi,[4] son of Uruash Zikum reigned 58 (46) years.
The god Purash-Sin,[5] son of the god Dungi, reigned 9 years.
Suash-Sin,[6] son of the god Purash-Sin reigned 9 years.
Ibil, the god (Il) Sin, son of Suash-Sin reigned 26 (14) years.
Five kings reigned 108 years.
Ur City was smitten by weapons ; the royalty passed to Isin City."

Identity of Ur Dynasty with Aryan Dynasty of Ūru in the Indian Chronicles

In the Indian main-line lists, the Ur Dynasty is not recognized as the imperial or suzerain line until after Parashu Rāma's (*i.e.* Bur Sin I) massacre of the rival princely caste, when it comes into the imperial line with the son (?) of the latter as Śatya-ratha and his son Il-Ibila, Nos. 53 and 54 of the main line. But the full list of the Ur Dynasty from its

[1] Ibil's own seal is an exception.
[2] PHT. IV. 94 ; and WB. 19 and text.
[3] WISD. 57.
[4] This may also read *Duk-gin*, WISD. 58.
[5] WISD. 56.
[6] See later.

founder, the brother-in-law of Gudia, is preserved as a collateral dynasty, as we have seen.

The equation of the names of this Ur Dynasty in the Indian lists and in the Sumerian has already been displayed in their genealogical Table on p. 371, with the exception of the last king Ibil, who we shall find is *Il-Ibila* of the Indian main-line lists.

It was seen that this dynasty arose as a branch line of the Guti dynasty at the period of Gudia and entered the imperial line in the solar version with its fourth or its last king Il-Ibila (see App. I., cols. 1 and 4, Nos. 50 f.). The identity of the names of these kings of Ur in both lists, Sumerian and Indian, is displayed in the following Table, in which the current conjectural restorations of their name, when differing from those supplied by our Indian keys to the traditional forms of the names, are placed within square brackets.

EQUATION OF THE UR DYNASTY KINGS WITH THE ARYAN KINGS OF THE INDIAN LISTS

ISIN LISTS		INDIAN LISTS		Serial No. in List
1. Uruash-Zikum [" Ur-Engur "]		Ūru-Ricīka		50
2. Dungi or Duk-gin [Śamu] [1]	s. of 1	Dagni (Jama-)	s. of 1	51
3. Purash-Sin [" Bur-Gin "]	s. of 2	Parashu Rāma	s. of 2	52
4. Suash-Sin [" Gimil Sin "]	s. of 3	Sushena	b. of 3	53
5. *Il* - or Ibil - Sin	s. of 4	Il-Ibila s. of Shatu-rātha [2]		54

[1] See WISD. 58.

[2] This is presumably a translated Sanskrit title of Suash-Sin, and means "The Charioteer of a Hundred."

This striking equation of the names and chronological order and position of the Sumerian kings of the Ur Dynasty with those of the Aryan kings of the same period in the official Indian king-lists establishes the absolute identity of these Sumerian kings with the Early Aryan kings of that period. And it further confirms the remarkable authenticity of the official Indian Chronicles as an independent source of Sumerian and Babylonian History. It moreover further confirms and establishes the identity of the Sumerian people with the Early Aryans.

New Information regarding Ur Dynasty from Indian Chronicles

As the main purpose of this work is to establish the identity of the Sumerian kings with those of the Early Aryans as preserved in the official king-lists of the Early Aryans in the Indian Chronicles in order to establish the identity of the Sumerians with the Early Aryans, it is unnecessary to detail here the achievements of the kings of this Ur Dynasty, which are to be found in the latest text-books and journals on the Sumerians and Babylonians. Here it is only necessary beyond the proofs of their identity with the Early Aryan kings to supply the leading new information regarding them and their origin, which is wholly unknown to Assyriologists, but which is preserved in the Indian Chronicles and Vedas.

Unknown History & Origin of the Founder of the Ur Dynasty, Uruash Zikum, preserved in the Indian Chronicles

The hitherto unknown ancestry and relationships of the founder of this dynasty at Ur are disclosed by the Indian Epic Chronicles.

The founder of this dynasty, Uruash Zikum (hitherto read conjecturally variously " Ur-Gur, Ur-Engur " or " Ur-Namma "), is shown by the Indian records, wherein he is called Ūru or Ricika, to have been an Aryan priest of the Fire-cult, and a descendant of Uru, a priest of the Bhrigu family of Fire-priests, the same who had tutored Sargon. He was rich in horses, which he obtained from " the sea-god

Varuna" (the Indian Neptune),[1] probably implying that he imported Arab steeds by way of the Persian Gulf, and that he was before his seizing the imperial power the local priest of Ur,[2] which city at that period was a seaport on the Persian Gulf.

He is seen by the genealogical Table of the Kusha Dynasty (p. 371) to have married the princess Satya-vati, daughter of Gādhi (*i.e.* Gudia), and was thus brother-in-law to the son of the latter, namely Vishwa-ratha or Nimirrud, the last priest-king of the Guti.

The Indian Epics call Ricika a "priest," and do not usually refer to his being a king or possessing a kingdom, except in two minor references to him as king of Shālva, which kingship was presented to him by King Dyutimant.[3] This may refer to one of his conquests. The country of Shālwa is placed amongst the central countries of the Bharats.[4]

From his own records in Ur we find that he built the great temple to the Moon-god there, that vast staged-tower pile recently unearthed and generally known as "The Ziggurat." He dug a canal and named it after the Moon-god, as a boundary between Ur and Lagash City-state. Yet he claims to have followed the Sumerian law-code ascribed to the Sun-god and says "in accordance with the Laws of the Sun-god he caused peace to prevail." And he restored the old Sun-temple at Nippur.

DUNGI OR ŚAMU-DUNGI IN THE INDIAN EPICS AS JAMA DAGNI IN ASSOCIATION WITH GUTI PRIEST-KING VISHVAMITRA OR URUASH NIMIRRUD (OR "UR-NINGIRSU")

Dungi or Duk-gin, the second king of the Ur Dynasty and son of the founder, succeeded to the imperial throne at Ur after having been priest at Erech during his father's reign. He is now seen to be the famous Aryan priest-king Jama-Dagni, the son of the preceding Ūru Ricika of the Indian Epics, where his name has been obviously corrupted by the

[1] WVP. 4, 16. This reference to the association of the Indian sea-god with horses is interesting as further identifying him with Neptune.

[2] In his inscriptions, which date after his seizure of the temporal emperorship, he does not call himself "priest-king"; but his son was "priest-king," at or very shortly after his father's accession to kingship.

[3] MB. 12, 234; 13, 137.

[4] WVP. 2, 133 f.

later Indian scribes in order to extract a Sanskrit meaning from it as "Fire-priest," as he was a descendant of Uru the Bhrigu or Fire-priest. Yet the prefix *Jama,* I have shown may be a transliteration of the Semitic title of the divine prefix used by Dungi as *Śamu* = "heavenly."[1]

As "Jamadagni"[2] he is frequently mentioned in the Indian Vedic hymns, and is the traditional author of several of these, in which he figures as a priest, and is associated with Vishwā-Mitra, his uncle, there as a friend. This significantly is in keeping with the Sumerian records of Ur, which describes Uruash Nimirrud (*i.e.* Vishwā-Mitra as we have seen) as contemporary with Dungi, and call him "the beloved priest of the Lady (Nina)" at Lagash in Dungi's reign. Dungi was proficient in "the 4 night ritual," in which Vishwā-Mitra was also an adept. His capital is also said in the Indian Epics to have been on the bank of "The River." He enrolled "the Sons of Ur" as a company of archers equipped with the bow, which we have seen was used by King Naram.

Dungi's Development of Ritual & Liturgies in Indian Vedas

His development of liturgies into classic forms for temple service is significant, especially as Jama-Dagni in the Vedas is one of the seven holy singers (Rishi) along with Vishwā-Mitra; and several of the later Vedic singers take his hymns as a type and say in their hymns to Indra and other deities that they are "lauded by Jama-Dagni's song." And Dungi's singers at Ur or Uru are clearly the famous family of sacred singers of the Fire-cult in the Vedas called "Uru dwellers" (*Uru-kshaya*), who are celebrated in the Vedic hymns—

> "The Uru dwellers have kindled thee, O Fire, Oblation bearer, with their hymns,
> Best worshipped among mankind."

[1] See next note.

[2] As this name "Jamadagni" now stands it means in Sanskrit *Jamad,* = "flame or blazing fire" + *agni* = "fire." Probably the old form of the name which the Indian scribes copied was *Shamu-Dungi* or "The Heavenly Dungi," as Dungi calls himself "The Heavenly Lord Dungi," in which "Heaven" or *Ash* has the value of *Shamu* in Semitic Akkadian (WSAD. 19); and *J* and *Sh* are dialectically interchangeable.

Dungi's Hymns to the Moon-god in Sumerian & in the Indian Vedas Compared

Of the liturgies of Dungi and his immediate successors which have been unearthed three are to the Moon-god, and in their general form they resemble the Vedic hymns of Jama-Dagni to the same personage, who is called in the latter *Soma* and *Indu* (possibly his Sumerian titles of *Aśimu* and *Nānndu* or *Enzu*).[1]

Here it is to be noted that the aboriginal Chaldean Moon deity or demon was feminine, and was a form of the Mother "goddess" of Darkness and the underworld of Death. But in the form adopted by these Sumerians of Ur, the Moon which is regarded in its aspect of a luminary is made masculine and cleverly affiliated to the Sun-cult by being made "the first-born son of the Sun-god," personified as the God Sakh. One of the earliest Sumerian references to the Moon deity seems to be that of Naram Enzu (or "Sin"), the grandson of Sargon, in an inscription, in which he invokes the Moon amongst other miscellaneous deities [2] (none of whom have yet been identified with certainty, and who are presumably Semitic) to curse those who would destroy his monument. But as many of these potential destroyers would doubtless be Semites, who always formed the great bulk of the aboriginal and later population of Mesopotamia, he would naturally invoke their own Semitic deities as well as his own, the Sun-god. Yet it is not specified whether the Moon thus referred to at that period was considered male or female.

These Sumerian hymns of Ur to the Moon-god are illustrated in the following extracts. It is noteworthy that in them the god appears to be called a shining Bull, as he is called in the Indian Vedic hymns of Jama-Dagni, with reference to the horned moon; and he is also called a "warrior" in both, in keeping with the Hebrew psalmists

1 The "Nannar" title for the moon-god is merely Semitic. The Sumerian reads *Nānndu* as a synonym for his *Sheshdu* title (*i.e.*, probably his *Shashī* title in Sanskrit), cp. Br. 6453, in which *d* is omitted before the *u*, cp. Br. 10511 and 1068. And the Sanskrit *Indu* seems derived from *Nānndu* by dropping of initial *N* as in *Nindura* for "Indara," with the substitution of *I* for *A* in order to extract a meaning from the names.

2 PHT. IV. 204.

saying "the Sun shall not smite thee by day nor the Moon by night." The hymns sing :—

O holy crescent light of heaven, who is of itself created,
Father Moon, lord of Ur . . .
Lord Moon, first-born son of Lord Sakh . . .
Calf of the crown when for the calves thou carest . . .
Hail thou that in the majesty of a king daily risest, hail!
When over Ur in the sacred boat thou mounted.

The Moon-god, He (Lord Sakh) caused to abide
In Ur, the city which his heart had chosen
The temple like (by ?) a strong bull is glorified.
Of my king may his net (?)
Be upon . . . .
Of the Moon, may his beloved city,
The dwelling-place Ur, with holy decrees a city . . .
Of my king may his chapel . . .
Hail Moon, of the flocks (?) thou art ruler, Lord The One Bull of Light,[1]
First-born son of Lord Sakh, in the land he is ruler.
He that institutes battle as a name I name.[2]

The Indian Vedic hymns of Jama-Dagni to the Moon-god are of a generally similar character, but more fully developed, with special appeals for aid, and they also connote Lord Sakka *i.e.* Sakh (Indara) :

Daybreak sends forth the Sun, the associated sisters [asterisms of night ?] send forth their lord,
The mighty Moon—thou mighty one, their lord !
Pervade, O Clear-going One, all our treasures with repeated light,
God, coming hither from the gods !
Pour on us, O Pure-going One, the rain as service and fair praise for gods :
Pour all to be our nourishment !

[1] *Ash-im-u.*

[2] Langdon, *Sumerian Psalms*, 297, and *Sumerian Liturgies*, 277 f., as revised in CAH. I, 445. For Sin and "Nannar" and Enlil there is substituted "Moon" and "Lord Sakh"; and for his *Ashimu* title its literal translation, "The One Bull of Light."

Thou art a Bull [1] by lustre; we, O Pure-going One faithfully
Call upon thee, the Splendid One!
Do thou rejoicing, nobly armed [with horns] pour on us
heroic strength;
O Indu, come thou hitherward!
Flow onward with thy stream, a Bull inspiriting the
Maruts' Lord (Sakka).
Winning all riches by thy might!

O Indu, visible to all, pour out for us abundant food!
O Moon be thou our prosperer!
Destroyer of our enemies,[2]
Bring us O Indu, hundredfold increase of kine and noble
steeds! [3]

Thus these hymns to the Moon-god in the Sumerian and Indian Vedas further confirm the identity of King Dungi or Śamu Dungi with King Jama-Dagni.

Dungi's Family as disclosed by Indian Chronicles

The Sumerian inscriptions tell us only that his father was Uruash Zikum and that his son and successor was Burash-Sin or Purash-Sin and that he had three other sons and two daughters. The Indian Epics inform us that his mother was the sister of the Guti priest-king Nimirrud, son of Gudia (see genealogical Table, p. 371); and that he married the princess Kāmal Renuka, daughter of Renu or Prasenajit, a prince of the Ikshvāku line, and "had by her the destroyer of the Kshattriya (Khattiyo) race, Parashu-Rāma." [4] The Mahā-Bharata Epic adds that he had four other sons, Rumanwat, *Sushena*, Vasu and Vishvā-Vasu. In the Sumerian inscriptions his other sons were named *Suashen*-Sakh, Nadi and Uruash-Sin, and his daughters were Shat-Sin and Ningmidashu. Here Suashen agrees with his "brother's" name, Sushena, in the Indian Epics; and he was apparently the owner

[1] *Vrisha.*

[2] In the next following Vedic hymn to the Moon, the latter is acclaimed "Thou as Warrior hast ever prevailed." RV.(G.), 9, 66.

[3] RV.(G.), 9, 65, 1 f. The other Jama-Dagni hymns to the Moon-god are of a like character.

[4] WVP. 4, 18.

of the Sumerian seal bearing that name which I previously reported from the Indus Valley.

His Death

Dungi reigned according to his date-lists for 58 years, and this is confirmed by Poebel's Nippur tablets. The Isin list of Weld-Blundell's prism gives his reign as 46 years—the scribe of this record was, however, careless, in that he gives the total number of kings of this Ur Dynasty as " four," while recording in detail the full five.

Nothing is said in the Sumerian or Babylonian records regarding the manner of his death, beyond the statement in the late legendary Babylonian that the god Bel of Babylon avenged himself on him for the sack of his temple and " caused his dogs to eat his corpse." The Mahā-Bharata Indian Epic relates that Jama-Dagni was killed by the sons of Arjuna Kārtavīrya, king of the Haihaya tribe, in revenge for the slaying by Jama-Dagni's son Parashu-Rāma of their father, who had carried off the calf of Jama-Dagni's sacred cow—for the cow as well as the bull was esteemed sacred in the lunar cult of the Mother-Son and adopted by the Brahmans.

Purash-Sin (or " Bur-Sin I "), the Parashu-Rām of Indian Epics & Establisher of Brahmans as First Caste

Dungi was succeeded by his son Purash-Sin, hitherto called " Bur-Sin I," who reigned 9 years as the third king of the Ur Dynasty. He is of especial interest as he is disclosed by the new evidence to be the historical original of the famous warrior-prince *Parashu-Rām* of the Indian Epics, and " The beloved Parashu " of the Indian Brahmans, who is the traditional establisher of the Brahmans as the first hereditary caste in the state, which still persists as the most outstanding feature in Indian society. His name has been assimilated by the Indian Brahmans to *Parashu*, " an axe " in Sanskrit, which word significantly is now disclosed to be derived from the Semitic Chaldee or Akkadian *Parashu*, " to cut or break, as by an axe or hatchet " ;[1] and he is figured in Indian mythology, where he is made a demi-god, carrying this

[1] Cp. MD. 836.

weapon (see Fig. 70), with which Brahmanist tradition alleges he destroyed all the Sun-cult enemies of the Brahmans; and even slew his own mother who followed that cult.

FIG. 70.—Parashu-Rām as Purash-Sin I exterminating the Kings who opposed the Brahmans. (After an eighteenth-century Indian picture in Moor's *Hindoo Pantheon*.)

PURASH-SIN CLAIMS THE DIVINE TITLE

In his own inscriptions and in those of his officials Purash-Sin claims the divine title from the date of his accession. This is in keeping with the Indian Epic tradition that he was an incarnation of the later Brahmanist eponymous abstract god " Brahmā the Creator " or " The Moon on the Waters " (Nārāyana or " The God who moves on the Waters," as defined in Sanskrit), apparently the Semitic origin of the Hebrew belief in Genesis and obviously a form of the Moon-god, who is called in the Indian Vishnu Purāna Epic " The monarch of the Brahmans," and is made the son of the Sun-god—in agreement with the Ur Dynasty title of the Moon as " the first-born son of God Sakh," *i.e.*, the solar father Lord. And Purash-Sin calls the Moon " my god," as personal god.

He evidently believed in himself, as he styles himself " The righteous god of the Land." And he records that he placed an image of himself, which he called " God Parashu-

Sin, the beloved of Ur," in a chapel at Ur. And he was latterly regarded as a minor deity in the court of the Moon-god at Ur. His devotion to the Moon-cult is also evidenced by his aftername of Sin or " The Moon," a name which was now thus rendered in place of the early Sumerian " Enzu."

This deification of these Ur kings by themselves in their own lifetime, instituted by his father and continued by his descendants, was obviously due, I think, largely to their having retained the knowledge that the oldest god Sakh, Ia (Jah) or Indara, the basis of the idea of the Father-God in all the later and modern religious systems, was originally a man, and their own ancestral human king, although they abandoned the old Sumerian belief in the Sun as the One God of the Universe.

His Short Reign as King

His warrior aspect is seen in his immediately continuing and at more frequent intervals the raiding expeditions of his father against the tribes on his eastern or Persian frontier, and especially against Elam, which we have seen was a province of Mesopotamia from the period of Uruash I. In his first and second years he raided Urbillum ; in his third year Shashru and Shurudkhum, in his fifth and seventh year Shashru and Khukhnuri or Huhunuri, and in the latter year he destroyed Bibrabium and Jabrum (or Nebrabelak and Nieshru), with their lands, and Khukhnuri or Huhunuri. These destructive expeditions were probably those which the later Brahmanist legend calls his " extermination of the royal caste," especially the Haihaya ((? Huhu-nuri) tribe of the Sumerian inscriptions) tribal princes, who slew his father. He was suzerain of Susa in Elam, as attested by documents found there dated in his reign. And he used his father's later title of " King of the Four Regions (of the Earth)."

Purash-Sin as Priest-King

The son and grandson of a line of priests, who are regarded as especially pure Brahmans by the Indian Brahmans, he even more than his father united in his own person the chief high-priestships. Already high-priest of the Mother-goddess Anna at Erech, he was invested as high-priest of the Moon-god at Ur in his fourth year and of the Mother-goddess Innini in the next year, and of the god Enki of Urudu in his eighth year, and of the Moon-god temple at Karzida, which now included a shrine of the Moon-god, the next and his last year. He built a great storehouse for the temples at Nippur in his third year and added to the temple buildings of the Moon-god at Ur and of Enki at Urudu, and rebuilt part of the temple of the Mother-goddess at Erech.

The establishment of the Brahmans or priests as the first hereditary caste in the state is credited by the Indian Brahmans to this Parashu Rām as we have seen. As our new historical evidence of Mesopotamia throws a flood of light upon the little-known origin of the Brahmans and the circumstances of their rise to the first caste amongst the Indo-Aryans, I hope to present this information in a subsequent work, as it is beyond the scope of the present one.

Suash-Sin the Sushena of Indian Epics, 4th King of Ur Dynasty

The successor of Purash-Sin was Suash-Sin (hitherto disguised as "Gimil Sin"). He is said to be the son of Purash in the Isin Nippur lists. In the Indian Epics *Sushena* is the brother of Parashu Rām, who is given no son. And Suash-Sin does not appear in his own inscriptions to call himself the son of Purash-Sin.[1] In one of his inscriptions he calls himself "King of the Four Corners of the World."[2]

He appears to have retained possession of the Indus Valley colony, where one of the seals unearthed there gives his name as *Shushena*, as I have shown, and styles him "Prince of Edin,"[3] the latter name being a title of that colony.

Ibil-Sin, last King of Ur, as Il-Ibila of the Indian Chronicles

The fifth and last king of the Ur Dynasty was Ibil-Sin, the successor of Suash-Sin, and his alleged son, according to the Isin-Nippur lists; though he is not called his son in any of

[1] These Isin-Nippur lists also call "Naram-Sin" the son of Manis-tusu, whereas the Babylonian inscriptions call him the son of Sargon, and thus the brother of Manis-tusu.

[2] RBH. 278.

[3] WISD. 55 f.

the inscriptions. His fine contemporary portrait from his own seal is seen in Plate XXIII.

He is now disclosed as the Aryan king *Il-Ibila, Ilibila* or *Ilivila* of the Indian Epic lists, wherein the prefix *Il* is clearly the Semitic prefix *Il* or " God," which he uses as his title in his inscriptions,[1] and thus giving the Indian form of his name as *Il-Ibila,* which literally equates with the *Il-Ibil* of his own inscriptions.

Besides this literal identity in his name and title in his own inscriptions and in the Indian king-lists, his chronological position is identical. In the Indian king-lists of the Early Aryan Kings he appears in the main-line solar list in the second generation after Parashu Rām's massacre, which is his chronological position also in the Sumerian (see No. 54 in App. I). That main line continued the main line of solar emperors down to this period without recognizing any of the previous kings of this lunar Ur dynasty as emperors. This suggests that a remnant of the solar main-line dynasty probably survived Purash-Sin's massacre in Zabshali in North-eastern Mesopotamia (?), where the daughter of Suash-Sin appears to have married the priest-king ; and that Ibil Sin was probably the nephew of Suash-Sin, and thus obtained entry into the solar-line list.

Ibil Sin's Portrait

The remarkably fine and artistic portrait of King Ibil Sin in Pl. XXIII exists, impressed on a clay sealing over the strings of a parcel of his period which was unearthed by the Pennsylvania University Expedition at Nippur, and is preserved in that University Museum, through the courtesy of the Directors of which I am indebted for the photograph in the Plate, with permission to reproduce it. The cylinder-seal which produced this impression was a masterpiece of the engraver's art, cut with such refinement and perfection, as described in detail by M. Legrain.[2] The whole design, including the minute inscription, is only about 1¼ inches long

[1] RBH. 279.

[2] *The Museum Journal*, Univ. of Pennsylvania, Dec. 1920, 169 f.—from which article these details are summarized. The name of the minister is there read Sag-dingvi Nannar-zu, and the god's name En-lil.

PLATE XXIII.

KING IBIL SIN & HIS PRIME MINISTER, c. 2235 B.C.

On a clay-sealing from Nippur in Museum of Pennsylvanian University (from photograph after M. Legrain).

by 1 inch broad, and it had to be cut in a hard material like onyx, agate or lapis-lazuli, such as were used for making these ancient Babylonian seals. It is magnified in the Plate about four diameters. The Sumerian art displayed attains already nearly a classic Greek simplicity, although at such a vastly earlier period.

The inscription records that the seal was gifted by King Ibil Sin to his prime minister, " the premier (first or chief) An-Nānnatu the wise, priest of the god Sakh." It reads :—

" The god (IL) IBIL SIN
the powerful hero,
King of Ur,
King of the Four Regions
has given it
to the premier An-Nānnatu
(or Nannaru), the wise,
priest of god Lord Sakh,
his servant "

This prime minister on whom this unheard-of honour was conferred of the gift of a seal from the king, and who is figured on the seal standing before the enthroned king with clasped hands, was prime minister during three reigns, and appears to have contributed to the downfall of the dynasty, as we shall see.

The king is portrayed as a youngish man seated in the position which the god occupies in seals before this period. He wears a turban like Gudia of the previous dynasty and like the bearded Moon-god of this period, and is clad in the flounced mantle of Sumerian kings, woven so as to imitate the locks of a sheep's fleece,[1] a design possibly related, I think, to their title of " Shepherd of the people," and he is adorned with a necklace and bracelet. His low throne is covered by three cushions covered with the same material. His face, of intellectual and ascetic type, with slightly curved nose, is clean shaven, unlike the gods hitherto figured, who were bearded, and a lock of hair strays below the turban. A smile lurks on the faces of both the king and his minister, and unto the latter the king gracefully hands a small vase presumably filled with precious ointment. The minister, who occupies the same relative position and standing pose of Gudia adoring his god in his seals, is clean shaven and bare-headed and wears the simple fringed mantle of a servant.

[1] This mantle has been identified by M. L. Heuzey with the classic Greek mantle *Kaunakès*.

The Ur Empire under Ibil Sin

The imperial title of " King of the Four Regions " used by the king is of course a rather empty repetition of the title of the Sargonic " world-emperors," as there is no evidence that this Ur Dynasty exercised any authority over Egypt or the West, though he appears to have had suzerainty over the mines in South Cappadocia, as some of the clay-tablet business documents found there are dated in his reign. He devastated Anshan, that is Persis to the East of Elam. Yet it is remarkable that his daughter was married to the priest-king of Anshan,[1] and it was to that place that he himself was afterwards exiled.

The Prime Minister or Grand Vizier of Ibil Sin a Brahman Priest who usurps the Temporal Power

This prime minister or grand vizier and arch-Brahman-priest of Ibil Sin, An-Nanndu, exercised a vast and predominating and malign influence over the fortunes of the Ur Dynasty in its later period, and clearly contributed to the downfall of that empire. Appointed priest-king and governor of the rich seaport city of Lagash towards the end of Purash-Sin's reign, and thus obviously of the Brahman caste, he early became in Suash-Sin's reign the prime minister, and he continued to hold that office under Ibil Sin. From his own records we are informed that his father was an official named Ur-Dunpae,[2] who in the sixth year of Suash-Sin was a trustee for the custodians of the temple built by his son the prime minister for that deified king of Ur, and he bore the title of " Great Messenger (or Ambassador).[3] Now here on the same lump of clay used to seal the strings of the parcel bearing the impress of Ibil Sin's seal, is another seal impression carrying the name of " Dunpae, banker, son of Erindan," suggesting that the father of the prime minister was a banker by profession, and was still alive in Ibil Sin's reign, and used his son's royal seal to safeguard his own or the state's property in his custody.

Already in the sixth year of Suash-Sin this prime minister

[1] Scheil, *Deleg. in Perse Mém*, V. viii.

[2] Or Shulpae.

[3] Tax-max or Sukal-max.

(and son of a banker) had monopolized in his own hands no fewer than twelve of the chief appointments in the empire, and involving the administration of thirteen separate cities and provinces. This we learn from his own inscription on the gate sockets of the temple he built for the worship of his deified master, in which he gives a list of his appointments. In addition to being chief minister to the emperor this pluralist was priest-king of Lagash, priest-king of god Sakh or Enki at Urudu, governor of Uzar-garshana, governor of Babishue, priest-king of Sabu and of the land of Gutebu, governor of Timat-en-Sakh,[1] priest-king of the city of Suash-Sin, governor of Urbillu, priest-king of Khamasi and of Gankhar, governor of Ikhi, and governor of the Su-people and of the land of Kardaka.[2]

The Wealth & Oriental Luxury in Ibil Sin's Reign

The wealth accumulated in Ibil Sin's reign must have been enormous. The tribute of the vast empire of the Ur Dynasty, which seems to have included the mines of mid-Asia Minor, had been flowing into Ur and Lagash for several generations, along with the booty of the raiding expeditions and the products of imperial trade. The mass of commercial documents of this period evidences a continual interchange of products and goods not only between the cities of Mesopotamia, but *via* Lagash from the Persian Gulf and Indian Ocean, and northwards from Amorite Land, Syria and Cappadocia. Of the numerous Cappadocian cuneiform tablets of this period unearthed at the old mining and trade centres in Cappadocia some are dated in the reign of Ibil Sin, implying that some of the richest regions in Cappadocia were within his empire. And many of the records of this Ur Dynasty refer to the comings and goings of couriers and ambassadors.[3]

The luxury of this period is evidenced by the profusion of massive gold and silver jewellery and artistic utensils. It

1 Possibly designating the Indus Valley colony, which I have shown was apparently called Saka Land in Indo-Sumerian seals. WISD. 34, 35 f.

2 Thureau-Dangin, Rit. 5, 90 f.; AIC. 1902, 91 f.; KHS. 301.

3 T. Pinches, *Babylonian Tablets of Berens Colln.* 13 f.

is also reflected in the extensive use of public and private slaves, who were auctioned in the markets of Lagash, and who were mostly prisoners captured in war and in the raiding expeditions, and who must have been seething for revolt in a decadent and effete empire run by a banker-family of Brahman priests in their own self-interest.

The End of Ibil Sin & of the Ur Dynasty

Such centralization of the chief administrative posts of the empire in the person of the Grand Vizier or prime minister, who was also the arch-priest, suggests that the emperor had become a mere puppet in the hands of his intriguing minister. While humoured as to his pretended divinity, he was probably kept virtually a prisoner in the palace by the Vizier and his courtiers who held the reins of government, just as the last emperor of decadent China was, and somewhat analogous to the old Grand Lamas of Tibet and the later Sultans of Turkey, who were also priest-kings claiming semi-divinity.

The collapse of the empire under such conditions along with the effeminacy of over-luxurious living, was merely a matter of time, with one man attempting the physically impossible task of governing personally such widely sundered provinces, with the inevitable weakening of the authority of the local governors or deputy governors. The gift of this seal to this chief minister may, as has been suggested,[1] have been to remind local governors, viceroys and priest-kings of their submission to the central power in a waning loyalty.

The final disaster which overtook and ended Ibil Sin's reign and dynasty was perhaps not so much the fault of Ibil Sin himself, as of the pernicious fiction of divinity instituted by his predecessors into which he had born, and had presumably been brought up in this tutelage since childhood, as we have seen that he probably succeeded to the throne as a minor.

After a reign of 24 years, unbroken by any recorded commotion or wars beyond a raid on Simurum, and having a son named Nitamu, of whom nothing is known and who

[1] L. Legrain, *Museum Journal, op. cit.*, 171.

did not succeed to the throne, the disaster fell. This is recorded in the Isin-Nippur chronicles in these words :—

> "Ur City was smitten by weapons, the royalty passed to Isin City.
> At Isin City Ishbi Ashura was king. He reigned 33 years.
> The divine Katninikat, son of Ishbi Ashshura, reigned 20 (10) years.
> Idin (or Iti) Ash Dakhu, son of Katninikat, reigned 21 years," and so on (see p. 415).

IBIL SIN IS CARRIED OFF CAPTIVE TO EXILE IN ANSHAN (PERSIA)

We further learn, in confirmation of the record of the accession of this new dynasty at Isin from a later omen-tablet portending disaster that "like Ibil Sin, king of Ur who went in fetters to Anshan, they shall weep and perish." And a contemporary lamentation of Ur of this period found at Nippur mourns :—

> "The sacred dynasty from the temple they (the invaders) exiled.
> The city they demolished, the temple they demolished,
> The ruler of the Land they seized. . . .
> Lord Sakh directed his eyes to a strange land,
> The divine Ibil Sin unto Elam (was taken)."

Anshan, as we have seen, was the Persis province of Persia to the east of Elam and the capital later of Cyrus,[1] and it is significant that Ibil Sin had previously devastated Anshan, yet had his daughter married to the priest-king of Anshan.

So ended pathetically this priest-ridden and once powerful Sumerian dynasty, and with it, according to theories of Assyriologists, the "Sumerian" race, which they arbitrarily allege now became totally extinct ! But that theory is like their title "Sumerian," which they have foisted on this great people never had any foundation in fact. And the next dynasty we shall find as distinctively "Sumerian," that is Aryan, as ever, though largely orientalized.

[1] Cp. PHT. IV. 234.

Thus, also, we find that the Ur Dynasty of the Sumerians is identical with the Aryan Dynasty of the priest-king Ūru of the same period in the official Indian Chronicles in names, relative chronological order, achievements, Moon-worship, and in the assumption of divine titles and in establishing the pre-eminence of the caste of the priests or Brahmans. This still further establishes the identity of the Sumerians with the Early Aryans. The official Indian Chronicles also, by this remarkable agreement and by affording fresh information of fundamental importance regarding the unknown origin and relationships of these kings of this dynasty are further proved to be an authentic independent source of Sumerian and Babylonian History.

FIG. 70A.—Deified 1st Aryan king as In-Dur, showing him bearded with his Goat and Bull emblems, and Gothic horned head-dress of self and votaries. From a Cappadocian seal c. 2500 B.C. (After Delaporte DCO. 1 pl. 125, 1.) $\frac{3}{1}$.

Note his Cross emblem as St George.

XXII

Isin Dynasty (c. 2232-2007 B.C.) disclosed as an Elam-Amorite Annexation of Mesopotamia, with Rise of First Dynasties of Elam & Assyria & in Agreement with Indian Lists of Aryan Kings

Discovering Origin of the Elamite, Amorite and Early Assyrian Kings as Sumerians or Aryans. Recovering the proper forms of the Names and Identities of the Elam and Early Assyrian Kings by the Indian key-lists and the historical original of the man-god RAMA CHANDRA *of the Indian Epic romance.*

WITH this period, following the fall of the Ur Dynasty, which according to Assyriologist notions was the fall of the last of all Sumerian dynasties, with the total extinction of the Sumerian race, we enter on a Sumerian era in Mesopotamia almost as priest-ridden as the last, and one in which the divergence between the Eastern or Oriental type of the Sumerian Civilization and its more progressive and scientific Western type becomes still more marked. This period is characterized by weakening of the imperial rule, with the rise of a crop of rival city-states seeking and gaining more or less their independence, with the continuance of the priestly king's pretensions to divinity by assumption of the god-title, and further Semitization by the priests adopting the Chaldean fables of The Flood and Creation myths, and fabricating silly extravagantly fabulous superhuman ages for their ancestors. This period hitherto has been one of the most confused in Mesopotamian history, especially in regard to the interrelations and identities of the rival local kings in Mesopotamia, Elam, Muru or Amorite Land, Babylon and Assyria. This confusion is now to a great extent cleared up by our Indian keys.

Rise of the "Isin Dynasty" as an Imperial Elamite Suzerainty

The new "dynasty" which overthrew the decadent luxurious and priest-ridden Ur Dynasty, in the person of its last king Il-Ibil, established its imperial capital, according to the Isin and Nippur dynastic chronicles, higher up the country at the more central position of Isin City,[1] on an old channel of the Euphrates, supposed to be about 17 miles south of the old Sun-temple city of Nippur; and after this capital city this dynasty is now named the "Isin" Dynasty. This city is repeatedly referred to in the records of the previous Ur Dynasty as subject to the latter.

Notwithstanding that the contemporary literature and the later traditional Omen literature made it clear that the overthrowers of the Ur Dynasty were invaders from Elam and Anshan (Persia), the mountainous countries to the east of Mesopotamia, and that the ex-king of Ur was deported through Elam to Anshan, it has never been suspected by modern writers on this period that the founder of this "Isin Dynasty" was himself an Elamite or Anzanite. On the contrary, it has hitherto been supposed that this deportation of the ex-king to Anzan implied little more than a successful raid on Ur by a local king of Elam—a country which we have seen was held as a colony of the Mesopotamian Sumerians from at least the period of Uruash's Dynasty, but in which the local governors or kings were constantly asserting their independence. And it has been assumed that this supposed raid on Ur by Elam, by removing the central imperial Sumerian power, left Mesopotamia a helpless prey to the ambitions of the kinglets or governors of the various rival city-states—and that one of the latter eventually "soon freed himself from Elamite interference" and established himself as paramount king at Isin; although the Isin and Nippur Chronicles expressly state that the Ur Dynasty was directly overthrown by the first king of the Isin Dynasty. And to crown all, it is dogmatically asserted that this Isin Dynasty and all the subsequent dynasties in Babylonia (excepting the Kassi Dynasty) were Semitic.

[1] The name read "Isin" also reads *Nisin*.

First King of Isin Dynasty of Mesopotamia as former Sumerian Vassal King of Elam-Anshan

On the other hand, we now find through the Comparative Table of the kings of this period with those of the Aryan kings of this period in the Indian dynastic lists (see Table, p. 415), that this first king of the Isin Dynasty, Ishbi Ashurra, was clearly the local king of Elam-Anshan and of Sumerian stock, and was the same personage who overthrew the Ur Dynasty by his invasion and capture of Ur City.

Elam during the Ur Dynasty was held, as usual, as a colony of the Sumerian empire, under a local governor, with the title of "Priest-king," resident at Susa City. The names of several of those local governors under the Ur Dynasty from the period of King Dungi downwards have been found in inscriptions at Susa; but none of them are specified as having been under Ibil Sin in the records hitherto unearthed,[1] though one of them bears a name somewhat resembling the one in question. These governors of Elam we have seen were sometimes scions of the imperial Sumerian family, and under the Ur Dynasty one of them, the priest-king of the province of Zabshali, had married a daughter of the emperor Shu Sin, and thus was a brother-in-law of Ibil Sin according to the Isin dynastic chronicle, and presumably a Sumerian; and the daughter of Ibil Sin married the governor of Anshan.[2] And Anshan was sometimes held conjointly with Elam by the same local king as we have seen; and "King of Elam and Anshan" is found as a common title of the kings of Elam in the period of this Isin Dynasty.

The Sumerian or Aryan racial character of this king and his dynasty is attested not only by his name and his position in the Indian lists of the Aryan kings, but also by him and his dynasty continuing to write in the Sumerian script and language, worshipping the same Sun and other Sumerian deities under their same Sumerian names, and by the personal names of his dynasty being of Sumerian type.

The significant resemblance also between the geometric designs of Elam pottery and those of the Hittite pottery in Cappadocia—which land we have seen was an earlier

[1] STE. V. viii. f.

[2] *Ib.*, viii.; and I. 80.

homeland of the "Sumerians" before their descent into Mesopotamia—has been remarked. And the Hittite "George's" or so-called "Greek" Cross occurring freely in Hittite and Sumerian seals and especially in the Kassi period in Babylonia,[1] is also met with on the early so-called "proto-Elamite" pottery of Elam. Some little confusion has been introduced by a late Assyrian Omen tablet in which Ishbi is supposed to be called "the man of Mari"—that is a city believed to have been located up the Euphrates about midway between Babylon and Carchemish in "Amorite Land," and from which he is supposed to have been an Amorite, and thus according to Assyriologists' notion a Semite. But even if he be traditionally called "the man of Mari," which is doubtful as we shall see, Amorites, as we have found, were of the same Aryan stock as the Sumerians and, as I have shown, the Amorites, who were originally the leading early sea-going branch of the Sumerians, were already in Haryashwa's Dynasty in the Indus Valley and Persian Gulf.

It now transpires that this Elamite vassal king on successfully overthrowing his kindred suzerain at Ur, he, like the Guti who preceded the Ur Dynasty, annexed Mesopotamia to his own kingdom of Elam-Anshan in Persia; but for administrative purposes he established his local Mesopotamian capital at Isin City, in a more central position in the great plains than Ur.

The Isin Dynasty a Composite of Elamite and Amorite

The Isin Dynasty was not homogeneous, of one family of descendants throughout. It was clearly a composite "dynasty" from the contemporary records. Although the dynasty nominally consists of fifteen kings in the Babylonian lists, the original dynasty ended with the fifth king; for the last date-year of the latter is called "the year in which the Muru (Amorites) drove out Libi Ash-Ugun (the fifth Isin king)." This ending of the Elamite section of this "dynasty" with the fifth king was doubtless contributed

[1] WPOB. 294 f.; for numerous illustrations, and for the unknown origin of the True Cross, in the long pre-Christian era.

to by the apparently non-residential character of their kings, as indicated by their Elam inscriptions referred to below, which circumstance must have weakened their imperial rule in Mesopotamia.

With the sixth king came in the new Muru or Amorite section of the dynasty; and this fact militates against the supposed statement that the founder of the Isin Dynasty was a northern Amorite. The kings from now onwards, at least, were residential, and presumably used Isin as their capital, for their dynasty continues to be called " Isin," and they " repaired the wall of Isin City." But although the first Isin king uses the imperial title, neither he nor his successors in the dynasty appear to have held Larsa or New Erech, nor even at first Ur, both in the Lower Delta. For we find that a son of the fourth Isin king, bearing the significantly Sumerian name of Bidasnadi (" Eannatum "), and a younger brother of the last Elamite Isin king, in dedicating an inscription as high-priest of the Moon-god at Ur, calls his suzerain King Gungun of Ur and Larsa; and this king also claims in his own brick inscription the imperial title of King of Kiengi and Uri (" Sumer and Akkad "); just as his contemporary, the sixth Isin king, does. It thus appears that the Elamite faction after losing Isin and Central and Upper Mesopotamia still retained Larsa on the Delta marshes, with the intervening tract to Elam, and raided more or less successfully the Isin territory.

This new Amorite king proves to be of immense importance for Indian history, as he is disclosed to be the historical original of the famous King Dasha-Ratha, the father of Rāma Chandra of the celebrated Indian romance of the *Rāmāyana*, who is now seen to have succeeded his father on the imperial Mesopotamian throne; and was succeeded there by his son. After this, the kings nine to fifteen have no expressed relationship, either to their predecessors or amongst themselves in the Isin dynastic lists or in their extant inscriptions. And their relatively short reigns presume a period of unrest and change, presaging the end of the dynasty through the rise of rival city-states within Mesopotamia.

Arbitrary Semitizing of Names of the Isin Kings by Assyriologists.

Our revision of the reading of the names of the kings of this and associated dynasties by our official Indian keys to the traditional forms of the names again discloses the wholesale manner in which Assyriologists, possessed of no key whatever to the form of these names, have arbitrarily Semitized their readings of the names of most of the kings of these dynasties, in order to forcibly adapt them to their theory that this and all the other subsequent dynasties, like most of the previous dynasties, were Semitic! Whereas, on the contrary, this Isin Dynasty is now disclosed to be Sumerian or Aryan.

Thus, for instance, the name of the second king has been rendered by them as *Gimil-ili-shu*, wherein *Gimil* is not a Sumerian value at all, but is merely one out of fourteen or more totally different Semitic synonyms for this first syllabic Sumerian sign of his name, *which is the same identical sign which they transliterate as "shu" in the last syllable*, and with any pretension to be consistent and scientific the least they could have done would have been to restore the name as "*Gimil-ili-gimil*,"[1] an improbable name even for a Semite. But the name of this king as preserved in the Indian lists, as the fifty-sixth king in these lists (see App. I) is seen to be *Khaṭ-wānga*, with the variant of *Dilipa*. Now the first syllable of this king's name as written in the Isin lists possesses an ordinary phonetic Sumerian value of *Kat*, which is one out of only three possible phonetic values for this sign, whilst the second element has the alternative Sumerian values of *ili* and *nini*, thus giving the Sumerian reading of this king's name as *Kat-nini-kat* or *Kat-ili-kat*. Thus it is seen that the two variant Indian readings of *Khat-wānga* and *Dilīpa* were obviously founded respectively on the two different Sumerian values of the middle element of the name—one Indian scribe having taken its value as *nini* and produced the name *Khat-wānga*, as transcribed in the modern Indian manuscript copies of the lists; while another Indian scribe having adopted the *ili* value, we find

[1] Cp. Br. 7269.

the name as *Dilîpa*, wherein the *D* is presumably derived from the *t* in the preceding syllable *Kat.* Yet in spite of these mutilations by the later Indian scribes the name in both variant forms still retains the chief elements of the name *Kat, nini* and *ili*, and the name occupies the identical place, No. 56, in the king-lists Sumerian and Indian, and the names immediately before and after it are substantially identical in both lists, Sumerian and Indian.

Again the fifth king's name is restored by them as *Li-bi-it Ishtar*, wherein the last sign of the name in question possesses no such Sumerian value as the Semitic Ishtar at all, but has only the one value of *Ugun;* and its preceding sign has also the value of *Ash.* Now in the Indian lists this king is called *Aja*, and in the Isin dynastic lists his name reads "Libi *Ash-Ugun*," wherein "Libi" is obviously a title meaning "the powerful," thus leaving *Ash-Ugun* as the personal name to equate with *Aja* of the Indian lists, and, as we have seen, the Sumerian *g* has often the soft *j* sound, and as *Aja* is an Indian personal name, the later scribes presumably rendered this name *Aja*.

The Indian lists in this particular dynasty and in the following one which corresponds to the First Babylonian Dynasty, exhibit rather more than the usual discrepancies with the Babylonian lists. But this is explicable and detracts little from their unique value as an independent key to the general form of the names and their strict chronological order of succession. Those differences are obviously due, as we have seen, (*a*) partly to the Indian copies having been made from other documentary copies than the late Isin lists; (*b*) partly to differences in the conversion of the Sumerian syllabic writing into alphabetic writing by the Indian scribes; (*c*) partly to mistakes in letters by the Indian copyists of the uncouth names in the manuscripts down through the ages; (*d*) partly to the kings spelling their own names in different phonetic ways (as seen in the name of the first king of this dynasty, whose name as seen in the annexed Table, is variously spelt *Ishbi* and *Ushpia* rendered as *Vishwa* in the Indian lists); and (*e*) very largely due to the Brahman scribes translating many of the Sumerian names into Indian Sanskrit, and occasionally altering slightly the spelling of the ancient names to resemble Indian Sanskrit names, so as to extract a meaning from the venerable names. Thus the *Dagan* or *Dakhu* element of the names of the third and fourth kings of this dynasty in the Isin lists, and also found in their monuments in Mesopotamia, is rendered in the Indian lists as *Dirgha* and *Raghu,* wherein the *R* in both is clearly introduced by later Brahmans to give it the sense and meaning of these two well-known Sanskrit words, which also are used as personal names in India.

Names of Isin Dynasty Kings compared with Aryan Kings of Indian Lists & Discovering First King as First King of Assyria

The names of the kings of this Isin Dynasty as found in the Isin dynastic chronicle [1] and in their own monuments are compared in the following Table with those of the Aryan kings of the same period preserved in the official Indian dynastic lists. The references attesting my revised readings of the Sumerian names, when these differ from those hitherto "restored," are given in the footnotes from the standard Sumerian lexicons.

As this comparison discovers the hitherto unsuspected fact that the first Sumerian king of the Isin dynasty *Ishbi* Ashirra (or Ashurra), the *Vishva* or *Vishwa*-the-Victorious of the Indian lists, is identical with *Ushpia* the first traditional king of Assyria, whose origin and affinities and date have been alike unknown; and seeing that this first Isin king is also disclosed as the first independent and imperial king of Elam-Anshan, I have added in columns 2 and 3 the Assyrian and Elam-Anzan names for reference. The names in column 2 are from the provisional list of Early Assyrian Kings compiled from references by the later Assyrian kings, and these Elamite names in column 3 are from the provisional lists compiled from the monuments by Prof. Scheil, which it will be seen begins with the third king—the names of their two predecessors not having yet been found on the monuments, so far as I am aware. In the Table the personal names are in capitals and the titles in small type; and in the Indian column (No. 4) the names which do not equate are also in

[1] WB. 444, col. viii. ll. 22 f.

small type, and we shall find that much of these are translations of the Sumerian names into Sanskrit.

ISIN DYNASTY KINGS IN SUMERIAN & INDIAN LISTS *with contemporary* ASSYRIAN *and* ELAMITE *Names*

Isin Dynasty	yrs.	Assyria	Elam-Anzan	Indian Lists	No. in List
1. ISH-BI-Ash-ur-ra or Ashirra [1]	r. 33	USHPIA	[USH-I-A-(?)BI-gal, priest-king of Susa]	VISH-VA (or VISH-BA)-saha	55
2. KAT-NINI (or ILI) -KAT,[2] s. of 1	10			KHAT-VĀNGA or DILĪPA, s. of 1	56
3. Iti[3]-ash-DA-KHU[4] (or -GAN), s. of 2	21		Shu-trūk-ash TAKH[20]-KHU -UN nun-gal [21] ("Nahhunte")	DĪRGHA-bāhu, s. of 2	57
4. Ish-shib[5]-ash-DA-KHU (or GAN), [or "Ialūn" As-har],[6] s. of 3	20		Kutir-ash TAKH-KHU-UN nun-gal ("Nahhunte") s. of 3	RAGHU, s. of 3	58
5. Libi (or Li-ul)-[7] Ash-UGUN,[8] s. of 4	11		(?) Lila-ir-tash (?) s. of 4	AJA, s. of 4.	59
6. DASH-ASH-I-URASH [9] (MURU) [10]	28	(?) DAG [17] SHI-ASH MURU [18] ("Shamshi Adad")		DASHA-RATHA III	60
7. AMAR [11]-SIN or BUR(Ash) - SIN II, s. of 6	21			RĀMA CHANDRA, s. of 6	61
8. LIBI . . . IN-SAKH [(?) or KUSH], [12] s. of 7	5			KUSHA & LAVA, s. of 7	62
9. Uru-ra I-WI [13]-TI (or I-MI-TI)	8	ITITI	(?) "SIMTI" Shilhak	ATITHA or Suhotra	63
10. IN-SAKH-BA-NI	24	(?) IN-SAKH GABA-NI [19] -PI ("Bel-kapkapi")		Nishada	64
11. ZA-AM-BI-IA	3			Nala	65
12. TEN [14] - IR - PI - SHA	4				
13. UR-DU-KU-GA	4				
14. SIN-MA-PISH [15]	11		[(?) Kudur MA-PI-UG, *Adda* of West], s. of Simti	Nabha or Nabhas	66
15. DA-WI-IG [16]-NINI (or ili)-shu	23			Pundarīka Kshema-dhanwan	67 68

The notes to above Table will be found on following page.

The substantial agreement in the form of the names in the great majority of those kings and the absolute agreement in their chronological order in the Sumerian and Indian lists is manifest in the Table. The differences are seen to be chiefly due to the Indian scribes having translated some of the names and titles into Sanskrit to give them a meaning for Indian readers, or having slightly altered their spelling so as to adapt them to somewhat similar names current as personal names in India. Thus the name of the sixth king *Dash-ash-i-urash* is made *Dasha-ratha*, meaning "The Charioteer of the Ten (horses)," which was a favourite heroic and royal Indian name. Several of the names possess the same meaning in Sumerian and Indian, again illustrating the essential identity of the two. Thus the seventh king's after-name of *Sin* or "The Moon" is spelt in the Indian *Chandra*, an expanded dialectic form of Sin and also meaning

---

[1] *Ash*, Br. 419; *Ur*, Br. 956; *Ir*, M. 580.

[2] *Kat*, Br. 7063.

[3] *Iti* is a Sumerian title for *Baru*, priest; Br. 9427-30; and is equivalent to Suhotra of the Sanskrit, which is now seen to be the equivalent of Shutruk, the Elamite title of this king.

[4] Br. 4035.

[5] Br. 10353. An incanter-priest, see before.

[6] This name is given the father of No. 5 on a seal. Scheil, *Rec. de Trav.*, XIX, 48; and RB. 229.

[7] Br. 5123.

[8] M. 6636.

[9] Br. 11253, 10982; and cp. 5307, 10478.

[10] He is called *Ash-Muru* . . . in Poebel's text, No. 2, X, 10; and also as *Muru*, "invader," in year name-list.

[11] Br. 9068.

[12] This sign closely resembles the sign *Kush*, Br. 6018, and may be a mistake by the copyists for that sign, which would thus equate with the Indian.

[13] On *Wi* value for this sign, B. 380, see before.

[14] Br. 7698.

[15] Br. 6928.

[16] Br. 2235.

[17] M. 5741 f. This *Dag* = "day," pictured by the Sun is, as I have shown, the Sumerian source of the Gothic, Anglo-Saxon and German *dag*, day, and source of our English "Day," see WSAD. 47.

[18] Br. 8352.

[19] Br. 2684 and 520.

[20] This initial sign in the Elamite name, hitherto read "Nahhunte" or "Nakh-khunte," is unequivocally *Takh*, B. 278 and Br. 6165, with no such value as Nakh.

[21] These two signs hitherto transliterated as *te*, read *Nun-gal*; cp. Br. 7683. And on this Sumerian title of *Nun-gal*; as "Great Sea-lord," see before.

" The Moon." Moreover this king's front name of *Amar* is obviously the Sumerian source of his Indian name of *Rāma*, by the transposing of letters or metathesis, which is recognized as sometimes occurring for reasons of euphony. As further confirming the identities of this dynasty with the Indian, it is significant that kings Nos. 3, 6 and 7, who are the only ones detailed in the Indian Epics, are described as incarnate gods, or having become " gods," [1] and thus in keeping with the Isin dynastic lists and the monuments of these kings which call them " gods."

Name of Founder of Isin Dynasty in Sumerian & Indian & his title of " Ashurra "

The first king of this dynasty, bearing the name of *Ishbi Ashurra* or *Ashira*, immediately succeeded Il-Ibil-Sin in the Babylonian lists, and thus equates with the Indian-list king *Vishva-Saha*, who immediately succeeded King Ilivila in the Indian lists. And his personal Sumerian name *Ishbi* substantially equates phonetically with his personal Indian name *Vishva*.

His title *Ashurra* here now appears to disclose the source of the later patron and national god-name of *Ashur*, adopted by the Assyrians, and which they applied to their land and nation, and used as a personal name for many of their later kings. And this particular king is given the title " god " in the Isin lists.

The god *Ashur* was a form of the Sun-god and was essentially a monotheistic god ; [2] and he is now disclosed as identical with *Asura* of the Indian mythology. *Asura*, or "The divine," was a title of the father-god Indra in Indian religion ; and it is admitted by Sanskritists to be the equivalent of *Ahura*, the title of the Sun-god in the Zoroastrianism of the Persians ; and *Ashira* is also a title of the Sun in Sanskrit, and the Sumerian word in question also reads *Ashira*. Though later on, with the growth of sectarianism and rival creeds, this name came to be given the opposite meaning of " titanic demon " by the Brahmans,[3] presumably because its monotheistic ideal was repellent to them as intolerably unorthodox

[1] Cp. WVP. 310 f. ; and the *Rāmāyana*.
[2] JRB. 51 f. ; 121 f.
[3] WBT. 82 f.

and pagan. This is analogous to what happened amongst the Persians who latterly stigmatized Indra as "a demon," and as one who opposed their Sun-cult!

Similarly his Indian title of *Saha* is significant also of his identity. This word means in Sanskrit "the mighty, overcoming, victorious"; and it is seen to be the equivalent of his title in the Assyrio-Babylonian Omen-texts of "a king without rivals." This Indian *Saha* also spelt *Sahas* is also important as disclosing its derivation from the Sumerian. Aryan philologists are agreed that this *Saha* "victorious" word is cognate with the Gothic *Sig, Sigis*, Anglo-Saxon *Sige* and German *Sieg* "Victory." All these, along with *Saha* or *Sahas*, are now disclosed to be derived from the Sumerian *Sag, Zag* or *Sig*, "Victory," written by the Axe-sign.[1]

His Identity with Uspia, the First Traditional King of Assyria, hitherto of Unknown Origin & Date

His title of *Ashurra* or *Ashura*, as well as the *Asbar* title of his great-grandson [2] suggests his relationship with Assyria; and his personal name is now seen by the Table to identify him with the first traditional king of Assyria, *Uspia*, who significantly bears a Sumerian and not a Semitic name. This king Uspia has hitherto only been known as a traditional "prehistoric" Assyrian king and according to the records of the later Assyrian kings, the first king of Assyria. His origin, affinities and date have alike been unknown, though it was inferred that he could not have lived long before the rise of the First Dynasty of Babylon, which succeeded that of Isin. Now his identity with the first king of the Isin Dynasty fixes his date and affinities. This identity is confirmed by the other stray "prehistoric" Assyrian king *Ititi* being disclosed by our Table as the 9th Isin king, and identical with King Atithi of the Indian lists. And the other early Assyrian king, the so-called "Shamshi Adad I," but whose name reads *Dagshi-ash Muru*, is seen by our Table to be obviously the 6th Isin king *Dashashi Urash*, who is called in the Isin records a *Muru* or Amorite.

We thus obtain for his name the following equivalent

[1] Br. 5576 f.

[2] He is called on a seal "*Yalūn Ashar.*" Scheil, *Rec. de Trav.*, XIX, 48.

phonetic spellings in the Sumerian, Assyrian and Indian lists respectively :—

Sumerian		Assyrian		Indian
Ishbi (Ashurra)	=	*Uspia* (of Assyria)	=	*Vishva* (-Saha)

which thus establishes his identity.

Sixth Isin King & his Son as DASHARATHA & RĀMA CHANDRA of the Indian Lists & the "Rāmāyana" Romance

The evidence for the identity of the sixth and seventh kings of the Isin Dynasty with the famous Indo-Aryan kings Dasha-ratha and his still more famous son Rāma Chandra of the celebrated Indian romance, the *Rāmāyana*, is positive and conclusive. The identity is fixed by the identity of the chronological position in both lists, Isin and Indian, as well as by the names and their relationships ; and the achievements of these two kings are also of the same general kind in the Indian romance and in the Babylonian records.

King Dasharatha was a Sun-worshipper and the sixtieth descendant in the direct line from the first king of the Solar line Ikshvāku, that is Ukusi of Ukh or Akshak of the Kish Chronicle, as we have seen, and the sixth king from Ilivila. He was the paramount Aryan king at the imperial capital of his time, called in the Indian epics Ayodhyā. His inveterate enemy with whom he warred was Ravana, king of Lanka.

As *Dashashi Uruash*, the sixth king of this Isin Dynasty, he is called a Muru or Amorite, which presumes that he was of the northern Aryan " Sumerian " stock from Upper Syria and the Levant ; and he is said to have captured Isin from the fifth king of that dynasty. He had no dominion over Larsa, the city-state low down in the swampy Delta under a local king Gungunu, who also claimed the imperial title,[1] and which was probably the enemy-state of Lanka of the Indian epics, against which Dasharatha and his son warred, and against whose encroachments they defended themselves. In his own extant inscriptions he claims to be " King of Isin, Kiengi and Uri (" Sumer and Akkad "), Lord of Erech,

[1] His descendant, Rim Sin, was subject to Elam. Cp. STE. V, XI.

benefactor of Nippur (the Sun-temple city), Ur and Eridu." And he reigned for the fairly long period of 28 years.

He was succeeded by his son, *Amar-Sin* or "Amar of the Moon," the so-called "Bur Sin II" of Semites. He is seen to be identical with King Dasharatha's son (by his queen Kausalyā) and successor *Rāma Chandra*, or "Rāma of the Moon," wherein "Rāma" is obviously coined from the Sumerian *Amar* by the Brahmans transposing the letters of a word, *i.e.* by metathesis. This king, who gives himself in his inscriptions and is given in the Isin lists the prefixed title of "god," was and is significantly regarded by the Indians as a man-god, and as the incarnation of his namesake Parashu Rāma, the "Bur Sin I" of Semites, as we have seen; and significantly this king is similarly called by the Semites "Bur Sin II." In his inscriptions at Nippur and elsewhere he bears the same territorial titles as his father, and he states that he repaired the wall of Isin City. He reigned 21 years.

In view of his great traditional importance in India as the most popular of all the "men-gods" or incarnate gods of Indian mythology, I give here one of his own actual inscriptions as the historical king of Isin, etc.[1] He records therein :—

"The god Amar Sin, The Good Shepherd of Nippur,
The Mighty Shepherd of Ur,
The Restorer of the Oracle-Tree of Urdu City,
The Lord who delivers the commands of Erech,
King of Isin, King of Kiengi and Uriki (Akkad),
The glorious . . . husband of the goddess Innanna."

Here it is noteworthy that he bears besides the divine title also the man-god title of "The Good Shepherd," claims to be the husband of the Mother-goddess, and restores the famous "oracle-tree of the well of Urd" of the Semitic-Chaldean Mother-cult, as fully described in the Gothic Eddas.[2]

As Rāma Chandra, the prince of Ayodhya (Agudu), he is the hero of the fascinating Indian romance, the *Rāmāyana*, or "Adventures of Rāma." This relates his heroic adventures

[1] HOB. No. 19, and cp. RB. 231.
[2] See my new literal translation of the Eddas.

and prodigies of valour as an invincible knight-errant slaying dragon pests, his winning the hand of the fair princess Sitā, daughter of King Janak of Videha, in a tournament of knightly wooers, his banishment for fourteen years by his father at the instigation of the latter's intriguing, jealous second wife, his accompaniment by his devoted wife Sitā in his wanderings in exile; the birth of his two sons, his refusal to return on the death of his father till the full term of banishment is over, the capture and ravishment of Sitā by the Lanka king, her eventual recapture by Rāma and killing of that king, on the building of "Rama's Bridge" across the straits, his reconciliation with Sitā, his regaining his father's throne and having afterwards a long and glorious reign.

This romance, however, was composed in India only about the fifth century B.C. by the poet Valmiki, and a considerable part of it is later. It is largely unhistorical and full of anachronisms. It brings in as contemporaries King Janak, who, we have seen, was No. 26 in the main list, about eight centuries previously, also the priest Vishvamitra of the Guti period and Parashu Rāma of the Ur Dynasty. And all the scenes are laid within India, and Lanka is the adjoining island of Ceylon to the south. Besides, the name "Rāma Chandra" seems to have been equated to that of Rim Sin, a later king of Larsa, seven or eight generations later than Rāma Chandra, and not in the main or imperial line of kings, and who was the great enemy of Khammurabi of the First Babylonian Dynasty.

But his chronological position in the lists in strict agreement with the Isin lists, and in his name and father's name and achievements fixes the identity of the historical original of Rāma Chandra with the seventh king of the Isin Dynasty. Having now found how the "Amorite" element came into this dynasty with the sixth king, we resume the examination of the first king of this dynasty.

The First Isin King as the Revolted Priest-King or Governor or Viceroy of Elam & Anshan (Persia)

The fact that the last king of the Ur Dynasty was deported to Anshan through Elam indicates, as we have seen, that the overthrower of the Ur Dynasty who "changed the royalty to Isin City," was himself master of Elam and Anshan.

Elam and Anshan were under the Ur Dynasty vassal provinces down to or near the end of that dynasty, as attested by the contemporary inscriptions found at Susa, the capital of Elam; and these provinces were administered by local governors with the title of "priest-king" (Khattisi). The names of several of these local governors at Susa have been found in their inscriptions there, in which they acknowledge the contemporary kings of Ur to be their suzerains. In these inscriptions King Ibil Sin is not specified by name, but one of these governors of Susa, who is admittedly "a contemporary of the last kings of Ur," bears a name which may be read *Ush-i-a-*(?) *ur-gal*,[1] but in which the penultimate sign is somewhat doubtful. I now venture to suggest that this sign in question is the *bi* sign, which closely resembles this *ur* sign.[2] This would give his name as *Ushiabi-gal*, wherein *gal* is a title meaning "the powerful or warlike," [3] and is therefore the equivalent of the first Isin king's title of *Saha* in the Indian version.

Thus we find that this later Elamite governor's name in the Ur Dynasty fairly equates with that of the first king of the Isin Dynasty and with the Assyrian and Indian forms of his name; and the *U* initial is interesting as equating with the *V* initial in the Indian, *U* and *V* being freely exchangeable down to Roman times. Thus we get the variant equation in the spelling of the name of this first Isin king as:—

Isin Lists		Assyria		Elam		Indian
Ishbi (Ashurra)	=	*Ushpiă*	=	*Ushiabi* (-gal)	=	*Vishva* (-saha)

Be this identity of the name of this particular late Elamite governor as it may, the fact remains unaltered that it was clearly an Elamite-Anshan governor under the Ur Dynasty, who had achieved his independence, who dethroned the last king of that dynasty. And one of the latest records of

[1] Cp. STE. V, IX. On *Ush*, Br. 1488, and *i*, Br. 5307. It has hitherto been read *Beli a(u)ru-gal*.

[2] B. 5; Br. 103. I have not been able to see a photograph of this particular inscription; but the signs *Ur* and *Gur* which it resembles are very similar to this *Bi* sign.

[3] Br. 2254.

Ibil Sin refers to a raid on Elam and Anshan, indicating revolts there towards the end of that king's reign.

Third & Fourth Isin Kings identical with Elamite Emperors of Mesopotamia, the so-called Kings "Nahhunte," but whose proper names are disclosed through the Indian Lists

Our Table shows that the fourth Isin king bears the same personal name as a famous Elam-Anshan king who was at the same time emperor of Mesopotamia, namely Kutir-ash *Takh-khu-un* nun-gal, whose personal name is seen to be phonetically identical with that of the fourth Isin king, Ishshib-ash *Dakhu* or *Dagan*—*D* and *T* being always freely interchangeable and especially in Elam, thus the name of the famous Sumerian emperor, Manis Tusu, who, we have seen, was for a time governor of Elam and later its suzerain, is spelt on the Elam monuments variously as *Manish-Dussu* and *Manish-duzzu*, etc.[1] And this Elam king's affixed title of *Nun-gal* or "Great Sea-lord" was, as we have seen, a favourite title of the Sumerian emperors of the First Phœnician Dynasty in the Persian Gulf. His prefixed title of *Kutir* is presumably the equivalent of the Sumerian *Ishshib*, or "Incanting priest," which we have seen was also a title adopted by the early Sumerian kings, who were also priest-kings. This king's name has hitherto been disguised as "Nahhunte," but the evidence for my revised reading by our Indian keys is fully attested in the Table.

Our knowledge of this Elamitic king's dominion over Mesopotamia is based on an extremely important historical record by the later Assyrian king, Ashur Banipal, engraved on his cylinder. In this he states that when he captured Susa in the year 650 B.C., he restored to the Erech temple in his Babylonian empire the image of the goddess Nanā, which had been carried off from that shrine to Susa by Kutur *Takh-khu-un-di*, 1635 years previously. This incidentally gives us a fixed traditional date for this king of 1635+650, or 2285 B.C.[2] And this date it is seen places him within the period of the Isin Dynasty, and is practically

[1] STE. I, 42; IV, I f.
[2] *Ashurbanipal Cyl.*, G. Smith, 250 f.

identical with the period of the fourth king of the Isin Dynasty as obtained by other calculated dates.

It has hitherto been assumed that this deportation of this image had taken place during an isolated raid on Mesopotamia by a powerful Elamite king of that name during the Isin period. But we now find that this Elamite king was himself the fourth king of the Isin Dynasty. And the fact that he transferred the image of this goddess from Erech to his own native capital at Susa in Elam does not imply a raid on Mesopotamia, but merely the transference of a fetish of good-luck, as these idols were considered, to his homeland, of which Mesopotamia in his time was obviously considered a dependency.

The father of this Elamite king and Mesopotamian emperor, Takhkhūn, is stated in a later Elamite inscription to have been named *Shūtruk Takhkhūn*, in which the personal name significantly is identical with that of his son, who, we have found, was identical with the fourth Isin King Dakhu or Dagan. Similarly is it so in the Isin list, the third king bears the same personal name, Dakhu or Dagan as his son, the fourth king. The identity is further clenched by the prefixed title of the third Isin king, namely Iti or " Priest," for his equivalent title in the Elamite texts of *Shūtrūk* is obviously the cognate of the Sanskrit title of *Suhotra* for "The good priest," and indeed I think the Elamite language, hitherto called " Semitic," will prove to be an early form of Sanskrit.

Thus, as the Isin lists show that the third king was son of the second, who in turn was the son of the first Isin king Ishbi, it follows from the identity of the third and fourth kings with the Elam kings, Tukhkhūn I and II, that these latter were also the direct lineal descendants of Ishbi or Ushpia, the founder of the Isin Dynasty.

Other Early Elamite Kings identical with Isin Kings?

Amongst the other known slightly later Elamite kings of this period who claimed to be emperors of Mesopotamia are two, named respectively " *Simti* Shillak " and Kudur *Mabug*, the latter of whom claimed the title of " Adda (or

'Father') of the West."[1] These two are seen from our Table to correspond presumably to the ninth and fourteenth Isin kings. The name of the ninth, reading *Imiti* as well as *Iwiti*, thus resembles the Elamite "Simti," or name which if it reads properly *Si-Imti* (as I have not been able to test the original spelling of this name), would be literally identical, as *Si* in Sumerian also means "priest-king,"[2] and he bears the title of Suhotra or "priest" in the Indian lists.

The Elamite Mesopotamian emperor, Kudur *Mabug* or *Mapiug*, who was the son of the foregoing "Simti," seems from our Table to be identical with the fourteenth Isin king Sin *Ma-pish*, who ascended the throne thirty-five years after the death of I-miti, and this may possibly be owing to his having been an infant on the death of his father, for the latter reigned only for eight years (see Table).

The Elamite king "*Lila*-vi-tash," the son of Takhkhūn II, seems possibly identical with the son of the Isin king Dakhu or Dagan II, whose title or prename reads *Luil* as well as Libi.

Isin Dynasty as Decadent Eastern Sumerians

With this Isin Dynasty the breach between the Eastern or Oriental and the Western or more progressive Sumerian Civilization—the latter represented by the Egyptian and Asia Minor Civilizations—became wider. The priest-kingship became more prominent than before in the titles of their kings and in the pretensions of the latter to be "gods." All of them took that divine title except the second, but he also is given it in the Indian Epics;[3] and Rāma Chandra as the "man-god" is still the most popular of all the ancient Aryan kings in India, where the incarnation idea is still widely prevalent. The Semitic Moon-cult, with its associated polytheism, became again more prominent under Rāma Chandra, and the acceptance of the Semitic Flood and Creation myths, with their fantastic super-human ages of their patriarchs, led the dreamy Isin priests to fabricate those fabulously superhuman ages for their early kings. And although reigning for 225 years this dynasty

[1] STE. V, XI. [2] Br. 3385. [3] WVP. 3, 312.

has left comparatively few records, and only one or two works of art of minor insignificance.

The agency which effected the overthrow of this dynasty and the relatively exact period of that event, hitherto undetermined, are detailed in the next chapter. Significantly this change of dynasty was effected by a family who were so much more matter-of-fact and materialistic as to make no claim at all to the title of "god."

Unknown Origin & Racial Affinities of the Isin Dynasty discovered by Indian Keys

In short, our new evidence elicited by our Indian keys shows that the Isin Dynasty hitherto of unknown origin began with the overthrow of the Ur Dynasty by the revolted Sumerian governor or local vassal king of Elam-Anshan, who became the first king of the Isin Dynasty of the Mesopotamian empire; and thus he was "a king without rivals" in Mesopotamia and the East. Besides this the traditional Sumerian forms of the names of these early Elamite emperors of Mesopotamia are recovered for the first time. The Amorite Sumerian Aryan king who brought in a new line as sixth Isin king is discovered to be the famous Aryan king Dasharatha, the father of the still more famous king Rāma Chandra, the "man-god," and hero of the great Indian romance, the *Rāmāyana*. The first Isin king, moreover, is discovered to be the first "prehistoric" king of Assyria, whose origin, affinities and date have been alike unknown, but these are now recovered, and the introducer of civilization into Assyria is disclosed to be a Sumerian in race and a non-Semite. The wholesale arbitrary Semitization of the Sumerian names of these kings in order to make them appear to be Semites is exposed by our Indian keys. And so far from the Sumerians having ended and become extinct as a race on the downfall of the Ur Dynasty, as is alleged by Assyriologists, they are found in fact to be as dominant and active almost as ever, though assuming the Oriental type, and they are disclosed as the introducers of Sumerian civilization into Assyria.

But the most important of all the historical results of our detailed comparison of the Isin dynastic lists, with our official Indian king-lists is, that it bridges for the first time the great gap which has separated the First and following Babylon Dynasties, including the Kassi Dynasty, from the Sumerian Ur Dynasty, by supplying us with a continuous line of chronology, which recovers for us the lost dated chronology of the Early Sumerian Period. This now requires a separate chapter.

XXIII

Rise of First Babylon Dynasty of Khammu Rabi as an Aryan Branch Dynasty within Isin Period, discovering by Indian Keys the Missing Chronological Link between that Dynasty and the Isin Sumerian Period and Recovering the True Chronology of the Sumerian Period

Disclosing also the Total Absence of Semitic Dynasties in Mesopotamia till end of Kassi Dynasty about 1200 B.C.

THE unique historical importance of our official Indian Chronicles in unlocking the lost history of the Sumerians now reaches its climax. By bridging over directly the chasm which has hitherto separated the Sumerian Ur-Isin period from the Babylonian, which directly connects with our modern period, those Indian Chronicles now recover for us at last the true chronology of the Sumerian period back to the Rise of Civilization.

The Indian Chronicles of the Aryans bridge the Gulf between the Sumerian & Babylonian Periods

Hitherto the chaos in the chronology of the Early Sumerian period, with the continual arbitrary reshuffling of the supposed dates for that period, has, apart from the credulous acceptance of the prefixed fabulous chronology of the Isin priests, been due mainly to the want of any direct connecting link between the lower Sumerian period of the Ur Dynasty and the Babylonian period, which latter is within the period of relatively definitely ascertained chronology extending down to the period of our modern Christian era.

The attempts hitherto made at finding out such a connecting link have been based upon much confident and rather contradictory guess-work from archæological resemblances or supposed affinities in culture in the lower Sumerian strata of Ur and Isin with the upper Babylonian, coupled with the solitary traditional rough date given by the very late Babylonian king Nabonid for Sargon's grandson "Naram Sin"—a date which is admittedly over a thousand years before his possible date—and a supposed reference to the Isin Dynasty as contemporary with the Babylonian king who was the famous Khammurabi's father, but which has latterly been dismissed as untenable, yet its date is retained in the hitherto current provisional scheme; and a reference to the son of the fourth Isin king as a contemporary of a local king Gungunu of Larsa, whose date is obscurely placed by references to some of his successors as contemporaries of certain Assyrian and Babylonian kings, whose dates also themselves are considerably in doubt. But practically no specific synchronism has hitherto been found so as to form a solid or adequate basis for linking up the Babylonian period with the Sumerian.

Now, through our Indian King-Lists of the Early Aryans we find that the official line of the Aryan or Sumerian kings or emperors extends continuously down from the Ur Dynasty through the Isin Dynasty and across the unbridged gulf hitherto separating the Sumerian from the Babylonian period. We are now led by an unbroken chain of imperial Aryan kings from the Ur and antecedent Sumerian period down through the Isin period into the First and following Dynasties of the Babylonian period, including the well-known Kassi period, leading straight down into the well-known classic period and modern era. We thus for the first time recover, and that through our Indian keys, the lost connecting link necessary for converting the dates of the Sumerian period into the terms of our Christian era.

Total Absence of Semitic Dynasties in Mesopotamia and Babylonia until after the Kassi Dynasty, about 1200 B.C.

One of the most striking historical facts which now emerges from this and all the foregoing chapters is that *all the dynasties of Mesopotamia from the First Sumerian Dynasty at the Dawn of Civilization down through the ages to and inclusive of the Babylonian period with Khammu-Rabi's and the Kassi Dynas-*

ties, were without a single exception Aryan and Non-Semitic —no Semitic dynasty whatever having been found in Mesopotamia down to this late period, and none such is found until the late Assyrian period.

As the Indian King-Lists of the Aryans which now bridge this critical gap between the Sumerian Ur-Isin chronology and the Babylonian disclose the definite overlapping of the Isin Dynasty with the First Babylonian Dynasty, it becomes necessary to examine by our new lights the relationships of these two dynasties.

Overlapping of Isin Dynasty by the First Babylon Dynasty in its pre-Imperial Stages

The term "Babylonian" is applied to those dynasties which made their capital at Babylon, a city which only rose into capital importance during the latter part of the Isin dynastic period. And although Khammu-Rabi is the 6th king of the First Babylonian Dynasty the latter is best known as Khammu-Rabi's Dynasty which became imperial with him.

It has been recognized for some time that the First Babylonian Dynasty must have followed soon after the Isin Dynasty and probably overlapped the end of the latter. This was inferred from the contract tablets of the Isin Dynasty bearing a close resemblance to those of the First Babylonian Dynasty in form, material, writing and terminology. And a son of the fourth Isin king, as above noted, was contemporary with a king of Larsa City, Gungunu, a descendant of whom in the fifth generation was contemporary with the third king of the First Babylonian Dynasty. But no direct connection or relationship between these two dynasties, Isin and Babylonian, has hitherto been traced. It was also supposed that a reference by Khammu-Rabi's father at Babylon to the capture of Isin City in the seventeenth year of his reign implied the end of the Isin Dynasty, which if proved would thus have given us a fixed point of connection between the two dynasties. But as no name of any Isin king was mentioned it was decided that "this capture of Isin had nothing to do with the dynasty of that name, but was an episode in the later struggle between Babylon and Larsa. We have thus no means of deciding what interval, if any, separated the two dynasties (Isin and Babylonian) from one another, and consequently all the earlier dates remain only approximate." [1]

The fact of this overlapping of the Isin Dynasty by the First Babylonian Dynasty, with its exact extent, is now definitely fixed by the annexed Table, in which the Isin and Babylonian dynastic lists are compared with the Indian King-Lists. And it now turns out that, after all, the capture of Isin City by Khammu-Rabi's father in the seventeenth year of his reign was evidently the end of the Isin Dynasty. And the circumstance that that Babylonian king may have been at the same time at war with the rival king of Larsa does not invalidate this conclusion, as Larsa City and State was a perennial enemy of the First Babylonian Dynasty.

In order to appreciate this Table, it is to be remembered that these Indian King-Lists of the main line give, as we have seen, only the *imperial* or paramount kings in their chronological order from the first Aryan king of the First Aryan Dynasty namely Ikshvāku, the Ukusi of Uku of the Kish Chronicle, downwards—the branch or contemporary local or tributary dynasties not being introduced into the main-line list. But when a king of a subordinate Aryan dynasty gained the emperorship, his name then appears immediately in the main-line list. Thus the first Isin king " Vishva-the-Victorious " (or Ishbi Ashurra of the Sumerian) is the 55th main-line king in the Indian lists in linear succession from the first Aryan or Sumerian king (see Table). The 6th king of the Isin Dynasty, Dashashi-urash, who brought in the Muru or Amorite section of that dynasty, is the 6th king from Vishva or the Indian Dasha-ratha, the 60th king in the Indian lists; the 9th Isin king *Iwiti* is the 9th king from Vishva or the Indian *Atithi*, No. 63 in the Indian lists, and the 10th Isin King, *Insakh*-bani is the 10th king from Vishva or *Nishada*, No. 64 in the Indian lists, which have slightly distorted his name. But the next king in the Indian lists, namely *Nala*, No. 65, is *the last king of the Isin Dynasty*, and identical, as we shall find, with the last Isin king, who was overthrown by the First Babylonian Dynasty in the person of the 5th king of that dynasty.

[1] KHS. 64.

Connecting Link discovered between Isin & First Babylonian Dynasties by the Indian dynastic King-Lists

That the last king of the Isin Dynasty, bearing the Semitized name of *Damiq-ilishu* (or *ninnishu*) is identical with King Nala, the 65th king in the Indian lists, is evidenced by the etymological equation of these two names, as well as by the name of the next king in the Indian list, the 66th king. *Nal* in the Sanskrit means "to shine,"[1] and is cognate with *Nu*, "a jewel";[2] and it is obviously derived from the Sumerian root *Na*, "shining, bright, full of light," and also "jewel." Whilst *Damiq-ilishu* is the Chaldean or Akkadian-Semitic *Damiqtu*, "light, clear"[2] + *ilishu*, "the lofty"; and this king claimed the prefixed title of "god." It thus appears that this last Isin king, whose personal name was presumably Nala, and who was greatly Semitized, adopted a Semitic translation of his name to conciliate his Chaldean Semitic subjects.

The identity of this last Isin king with Nala, the 65th of the Indian lists, is confirmed by the fact that the 66th king on that list, *Nabha*, is now found to be the father of King Khammu-Rabi of the First Babylonian Dynasty and the capturer of Isin City in the seventeenth year of his reign, an event which is now seen to have ended the Isin Dynasty in that year.

This king of Babylon by his capture of Isin obtained the nominal emperorship of Mesopotamia; for he appears in the Indian imperial main-line Indian list immediately after Nala; and the six kings who succeed him in the Indian list agree in their names and in their exact chronological order of succession with the last six kings of the First Babylonian Dynasty, as seen in the Table, and by the detailed comparison of their names. His Babylonian name *Anu-ba*-Mubaīt (hitherto Semitized as "Sinmubalit") we shall see is represented by *Nabha*, No. 66 in the Indian list. And his son Khammu-Rabi, or "The Great Lotus," of the Babylonian lists and his own inscriptions we shall find is identical with "The Great Lotus" of the Indian lists, which was translated into

[1] MWD. 530.

[2] MWD. 523.

Sanskrit by the Indian scribes in order to prevent ambiguity, as we shall see, as *Pundarīka* or "The Great Lotus."

In the accompanying Comparative Table the extra number

Overlapping of Isin and 1st Babylonian Dynasties
DISCLOSED BY INDIAN KING-LIST KEYS
(*Years' reign within brackets*)

Isin Dynasty	Babylonian Dynasties	Indian Lists	No. in Indian List
1. ISHBI Ashurra (33)	—	VISHVA-Saha	55
2. Katnini-Kat, s. (10)	—	Khatvanga (or Dilīpa)	56
3. Itiash-Dakhu, s. (21)	—	Dīrgha-bāhu	57
4. Ishshib-ash-Dakhu, s. (20)	—	Raghu	58
5. Libi (or Liul)-ash Ugum, s. (11)	—	Aja	59
6. DASHASHI-URASH Muru (28)	—	DASHA-RATHA	60
	1st Babylon Dynasty		
7. AMAR SIN ("Bur Sin II"), s. (21)	1. Sumuabūm or Suābu (14)	RĀMA-CANDRA	61
8. Libi-Insakh (or (?) Kush) (5)	2. Sumu-la-ash (or -ān) (36)	Lava and Kusha	62
9. (Ash-)urra IWITI (or Imiti) (8)	—	Atithi or Suhotra IV	63
10. Insakh-bani (24)	3. Za-bi-um (14)	—	
11. Zāmbīa (3)	—	Nishada	64
12. Tenirpisha (4)	—	—	
13. Urdukuga (4)	4. A-du (or -bil) Sin (18)	Nala	65
14. Sin Mapish (11)	—		
15. Damiq-nini-shu (or Ilishu) (23)	5. Anuba-Mubaīt (20)	Nabha or Nabbas	66
		—	
—	6. KHĀMMU-RABI or "Great Lotus" (43)	PUNDARĪKA or "Great Lotus"	67
—	7. SĀMSUI UDUNA (38)	KSHEMA-DHANVAN	68
—	8. Abieshwa (28)	Devanīka	69
—	9. Ammi Satana (37)	Ruru or (?)Suto-rasta	70
—	10. Ammi Saraga (21)	Ahi-nagu	71
—	11. Sāmsu Satana (31)	Sudhanvan (or Pari-yatra)	72
	2nd Babylon Dynasty		
—	SAHARKI BAL ("Ishki Bal") (15)	SAHASRA-BALA or Bala, with separate line	73
	3rd Babylon or Kassi Dynasty		
—	XATAL ("Gandash") (16)	STHALA	74
—	Agu-um (22)	Auka	75
—	Bizuiru ("Kashti-liash") (22)	Vajra-nābha	76
—	Ushigu (8)	Shankha	77
—	ABISUTTASH ("Abir-attash")	ABYUTTH-ASHVA or Dhyushitashva	78

of the Isin kings in the Isin column as compared with the Indian-list column is owing to the Isin kings 11 to 14 being omitted in the Indian list. This was presumably because they were pretenders or intruders (as their very short reigns of eleven years for three of them suggests) and not of the royal lineage, which is also suggested by none of them bearing any specified relation to each other or to the previous king.

Thus it is seen that the last Isin king, No. 15 in the Isin list, was contemporary with the 4th and 5th kings of the First Babylonian Dynasty, before the accession of the 5th king of that dynasty to the imperial rank with his conquest of Isin City from the last Isin king in the seventeenth year of his reign.

Etymological Translation of Certain Names of First Babylonian Dynasty Kings by the Indian Scribes

In this section of the Indian King-Lists, though most of the names continue to equate substantially with the Sumerian forms of the names of the kings, making due allowance for the variant phonetic spellings as before detailed, we have in this section of the Indian lists a larger proportion than formerly of the names *translated from the Sumerian into Sanskrit.* This was obviously done in order to render the names more intelligible to later Indians. Although this translation of the names at first sight seems unfortunate for our comparison, it is really the opposite, for it shows that the Early Brahmans who converted the kings' names from the Sumerian syllabic sign writing into alphabetic Sanskrit letters were competent Sumerian scholars, and gave the etymological meaning of the older Sumerian names tending to become obsolete in the Sanskrit vernacular, for the information of Indians. This fact therefore that several of the Sumerian kings' names occur in a translated form in the Indian version, further confirms the authenticity and independence of the Indian King-Lists; and the historical value of the Indian Chronicles and Vedas as independent sources of Sumerian and Early Babylonian History.

KHAMMU RABI'S NAME MEANING "THE GREAT LOTUS," TRANSLATED IN THE INDIAN LISTS AS "PUNDARĪKA" OR "THE GREAT LOTUS"

As the name of King *Khammu Rabi*, who re-established a great renaissance in Mesopotamia on extending the empire, now becomes chronologically critical in this determination of the connecting link between the Isin and Babylon dynasties, it is necessary here to establish its equivalency with the Sanskrit name *Pundarika* or "The Great Lotus" in the Indian King-Lists.

The name *Khammu Rabi*, hitherto supposed to be Semitic, means in Sumerian "The Great Lotus," one of the names of the Lotus in Sumerian being *Khammu* or *Khamu*, as well as in Akkadian,[1] and *Rabi* is dialectic for the Sumerian *Raba* "great."[2] That the name Khammu-Rabi is not Semitic, as hitherto alleged, is also evidenced by the fact that it had to be translated into Semitic for the benefit of his Babylonian and Assyrian Semitic subjects. It was thus rendered *Kimta-rapashti*,[3] meaning in Semitic "Plant" + "great."[4] The references in Sumerian and Assyrio-Babylonian literature and business-documents to the Lotus, one of the most beautiful and graceful of all flowers, and one esteemed especially sacred and a symbol of divinity in Egypt and India (see Fig. 71), and sometimes representing the Sun in Sumerian sacred seals (and in India the Sun-god

[1] This plant *Khammu* of the Sumerian and Akkad-Semitic does not appear to have been identified botanically before ; but its detailed meanings in the bilingual Sumerian-Assyrio-Babylonian glossaries leave no doubt as to its identity. It is variously defined as "The plant of the Deep" (Br. 11840 and cp. MD. 196), the habitat of the Lotus being in deep pools. It is also "The plant of wells, ponds or rivers" (cp. MD. 320) ; also "The Boat plant" (MD. 320), presumably with reference to its leaves and flowers floating unsullied on the waters ; also "The lofty, sovereign or priests' plant" (Br. 10266, MD. 130) ; also "The Pû plant" (Br. 10266), wherein *Pū* appears to designate Egypt, and is written by the same sign. And its sacred character is indicated by its title "The One God priests' rod . . . (*Ash-an-barish* . . . [rest illegible], Br. 11857). It is also called the "*Pūsha* plant," which significantly equates with one of the other Sanskrit names for the Lotus, *Pushkar*. And another Sumerian name for it, *Hamiāg* (Br. 11849), seems probably the source of its Sanskrit epithet of *Ambhaja*. There is a great deal of material still to be worked out regarding this and allied plants in Br. 11825 f. and M. 7784-7817.

[2] Br. 4243. [3] MD. 40. [4] MD. 398.

is called "Lotus-eyed"), seem to refer to it as imported from Egypt,[1] the Land of the Lotus, as it is not indigenous

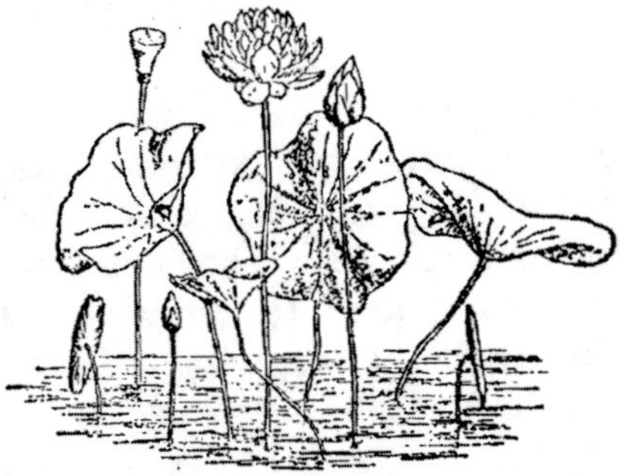

FIG. 71.—The Great Lotus in Nature.

FIG. 71A.—The Great Lotus in Indian Art.

FIG. 71B.—Indian Sun-god on Lotus showing Lotus as Chariot-wheel. (From an eighteenth century drawing in Moor's *Hindoo Pantheon.*)

NOTE.—The Sun-god is figured in Indian sculptures of the seventh century A.D. as shod in Gothic snow-boots, standing within a lotus and holding in each hand an expanded Great Lotus, typifying the Sun.

to Mesopotamia. Indeed it seems now possible that the Sumerian name for Lotus as Khāmala or Khammu may be

[1] See note 1 on p. 435, and p. 437.

KING KHAMMU RABI RECEIVING THE LAW FROM THE SUN-GOD, *c.* 2000 B.C.

Top of diorite stele of this king's Law Code, now in the Louvre (after Scheil, DP. IV, Pl. III). This monument, 8 ft. high, inscribed with 44 cols. of Laws, aggregating 2644 lines, originally set up in the temple of Marduk at Babylon, was found at Susa, whither it had been carried as an Elam raid-trophy. The sculptures in bas-relief on its top, besides portraying the king with straight non-Semitic nose, represent the seated Sun-god (the deified 1st Sumer king) of fine Aryan type, bearded, long-locked and wearing a Phrygian hat, adorned with four horns (set in sockets), as in the portrait of 1st Aryan or Gothic king on the carved ivory handle in Pl. I. In this comparison, see also the line drawings at p. xlvi, which are based on a large number of photographs in different lighting, with the omission of the extra length of beard, which is continued to the waist in the sculpture, although showing an interval in front between the short beard of the profile head.

A Lotus flower, the symbol of the Sun-god and the name of the king (Khammu Rabi), is seen above the god's head near the margin of the tone, and between its two chipped portions.

derived from the Egyptian name of *Khub* for that plant,[1] as the labials *b* and *m* are freely interchangeable, thus Bombay is ordinarily called "Mombay" in India. And significantly a Lotus flower is seen on the top of Khammu Rabi's famous Law-Code stele, above the heads of the Sun-god and of that Aryan Babylonian king Khammu Rabi or "The Great Lotus" (see Pl. XXIV).

This *Khāmmu* or *Khāmu* Sumerian name for the Lotus is obviously a shortened form of its fuller Sumerian name of *Kha-a-ama-la* or *Khāmala*,[2] which significantly discloses the Sumerian source of the ordinary Sanskrit and modern Indian name for the Lotus as *Kamala*—this is again another of the many hundreds of striking illustrations I have demonstrated of the Sumerian source of Sanskrit and Indo-Aryan words.

But as the name of King Khammu Rabi means "The *Great* Lotus," that name is rendered in the Indian King-Lists by the single Sanskrit word for "The Great Lotus," which is the great white and most sacred of all the Lotuses, namely *Pundarīka*,[3] which translated the king's name in one word; and thus therefore dispensed with the use of a separate word for "great," and also the use of *Kamala*, which is now restricted in India to the lesser or rose-coloured Lotus.

Thus, the identity of King Khammu Rabi of the First Babylonian Dynasty with the Aryan king Pundarīka, the 67th king in the Indian main or imperial line of the Early Aryan kings is established, not only by the etymological identity in the two names, but also by the chronological position of this king in the Indian lists. For, the kings immediately succeeding him in that list we find by the Table to be identical in name and chronological order with the kings of the First Babylonian Dynasty which immediately succeeded Khammu Rabi down to the last king of that dynasty. And his son and successor, *Sāmsu Iduna*, of the Babylonian dynastic lists and of his own monuments is seen to be identical with *Kshema Dhanvan*, the son and successor of King Pundarīka and No. 68 in the Indian lists.

[1] BD. 539a. [2] Br. 11859.

[3] The great white Lotus and a symbol of beauty. Perhaps its initial *pu* may be related to the Sumer-Babylonian title of *Pu* for this plant and also for Egypt.

KING KHAMMU RABI AS THE ARYAN KING "PUNDARĪKA" OR "THE GREAT LOTUS" IN INDIAN VEDIC & EPIC LITERATURE

In Vedic literature King Pundarīka is mentioned as the father of Kshema-Dhrtvan, who made a famous sacrifice on the banks of the Sudāman river.[1] This name Kshema-Dhrtvan is a recognized variant of *Kshema-Dhanvan,* who we have seen, was the 68th main-line Aryan king and son of King Pundarīka, and identical with Khammu Rabi's son and successor *Sāmsu-Uduna.* There are references to King Pundarīka in the Mahā-Bharat Epic, and several later Brahman priests bore his name.

With regard to King Khammu Rabi's famous stone-engraved Law-Code, which in the usual Sumerian fashion he represents as having received in person from the hands of the Sun-god (an Aryan priestly fiction borrowed by Moses, when helping himself to some of those Aryan Commandments for the benefit of his race), it is significant that in the theistic Indian, Chinese and Japanese Buddhism of "The Great Revelation or Vehicle," wherein Buddha is deified as the Sun-god, the famous Law-Code of the latter is called "The *Pundarīka* (or Great Lotus) of the Good Law" (Saddharma Pundarīka).

King Khammu Rabi boasts in his inscriptions and letters of his especial worship of the Sun-god, and his unequalled lavish adornment of the Sun-temple at Sipara, and calls himself "the darling of the Sun-God" and "the beloved of Marud (or Tasia) the son of the Sun." And while calling himself "King of Babylon and King of Sumer and Akkad," he also claims the old title of "King of the Four Quarters of the World," and there is evidence that his empire included Muru or Amorite Land of Northern Syria and part at least of the eastern Taurus region in Asia Minor. He adopted for his inscriptions and letters the Semitic dialect of his subjects.

THE FATHER OF KING KHAMMU RABI, AS NABHA OF THE INDIAN LISTS

Of almost equal critical importance with the Aryan identity of Khammu Rabi is that of his father, in the

[1] MKI. 1, 212.

connecting link between the First Babylonian Dynasty and the Isin Dynasty.

The name of Khammu Rabi's father in the dynastic lists of the First Babylonian Dynasty and in his own inscriptions is written by signs which may read *Anu-ba Mu-ba-i-it*, a name which has hitherto been read, leaving out the first sign, as "Sin-mu-ba-li-it." In the Indian lists his name appears as *Nabha*, which seems a corruption by the Indian scribes of his first name Anuba, in order to extract a meaning from it by equating it to a well-known Sanskrit name meaning "sky, heaven, a cloud—especially of the Soma (or mystic Moon-juice)"[1]—*Anuba* in Sumerian meaning literally "the Moon-god," the popular deity of the Chaldees.

The second part of his Babylonian name, *Mubaiit*, appears to be his title, and meaning "The Finisher" (? Finisher of the Isin Dynasty, which would be appropriate), from the Akkadian.[2]

In any case this King Nabha, who is the father of Pundarīka (*i.e.*, Khammu Rabi), and who comes between the last king of the Isin Dynasty and Pundarīka, is clearly identical with Anuba Mubaiit, the so-called "Sinmubalit," the father of Khammu Rabi.

First Babylonian Dynasty in the Indian Chronicles disclosing its Unknown & Aryan Origin

The First Babylonian Dynasty with its first kings of Babylon City, was founded traditionally by Sumu-abūm, Sumu-abu or Su-abu, whose origin has hitherto been unknown, and who with his dynasty have been universally called Semites.

The Indian Chronicles now bring this dynasty into their imperial or main line of Aryan kings with the 5th king of that dynasty, who overthrew, as we have found by the new evidence, the last king of the Isin Dynasty, and thus became the emperor of Mesopotamia, and who with his dynasty is conclusively proved by our new evidence to be of the Aryan or "Sumerian" race.

The founder of this dynasty, whose full name had the

[1] MWD. 527.

[2] Mubatti (-tum)=Batatu ; MD. 509 and 208.

Sumerian and Guti form of Sumu-abūm, was also known during the period of his dynasty and later as *Sumu-abu* and *Su-abu*.[1] Now it is significant that the Indian Chronicles record that the nephew of Rāma Chandra (or " Bur Sin II "), the 7th king of the Isin Dynasty, was named Subāhu. His father Shatrughna, the brother of Rāma Chandra, son of King Dasha-ratha, established himself as king of Mathurā City by slaying the Rākshasa chief there, named Lavana, the son of Madhu,[2] and was succeeded there by his son Subāhu, with whom was his younger brother, Shurasena. And we are informed that Rāma Chandra slew his nephew, Subābu, whilst the latter reigned at Mathurā as king.

It now appears that this king Subāhu of Mathurā, slain by his uncle, Rāma Chandra, was almost certainly Sumu-abu or Su-abu, the first king of Babylon. For our new evidence shows that whilst Sumu-abu or Suabu was a contemporary of Rāma Chandra or " Bur Sin II," he was much younger than the latter, yet died three years before the latter. This interfamily tragedy seems confirmed by the name of the traditional attacker of Suabu in the later Assyrio-Babylonian Chronicle,[3] in which the defaced name reads, I suggest, *Ra-ma*. The defaced first sign of the name has been read *Shu;* but it seems quite as probably the foot-sign, which has a value, *Ra;* and this would give *Ra-ma*, as in the Indian lists. In keeping with this identification with Rama, is his prefixed divine title, such as was borne by Rāma as 7th Isin king, and also his title of " King of Ashur Land (or Assyria)," a title which we have seen was borne by the 1st Isin king, and also presumably by Rāma's father, the 6th Isin Dynasty king (see Table, p. 433). In any case, be this name of this particular attacker of Suabu in this chronicle fragment as it may, our other evidence is nowise affected adversely for the identity of Suabu with King Subāhu of Mathurā, killed by his uncle King Rāma.

The name of King Subāhu's city Mathurā, also appears to represent Babylon. The name " Babylon " is merely a late Semitic translation of the front part of the name of this city, which the Semites latterly rendered *Bab-ili* or " The Gate of God," for the name " Babylon " has no connection

[1] KC. 1. 117. [2] WVP. 3, 316-18. [3] KC. 2, 14.

whatever with "Babel," as "a confusion of tongues," as invented by the Hebrews for their "Tower of Babel" legend.

The real name of the city latterly known as "Babylon" was during the period of the First Babylonian Dynasty, and before that time by Sargon's great-grandson Gani II, in his inscriptions, written by a name which significantly ended in *-ra,* and which according to the Sumerian values of the signs as far as at present known reads *Ka-ash-ra* (or *Ka-an-ra*), with a variant title of *Tin-tir*;[1] both of which names continued to be the sole proper official title for Babylon down to the latest Babylonian period of Nabonid, the last king of "Babylon," and also later in the Persian occupation under Darius.

That Sumu-abu or Su-abu was a junior contemporary of the 7th Isin king Amar Sin (Rāma Chandra or "Bur Sin II") is now definitely proved by our Comparative Table (p. 433), with its exact and positive traditional, regnal and dynastic years. Thus, by our newly-found definite synchronism of the seventeenth year of Khammu Rabi's father's reign with the end of the Isin Dynasty, and by the preservation of the full regnal years for each of the kings in each of these two dynasties, it is a mere matter of arithmetical calculation to find the exact number of years during which Sumu-abu or Suabu lived as a contemporary ruler with the 7th Isin king Amar Sin or "Bur Sin II," or Subāhu with Rāma Chandra.

Our Table, in view of the ascertained end of the Isin Dynasty being in the seventeenth year of Khammu Rabi's father, the 5th king of the First Babylonian Dynasty, shows that the accession of Suabu at Babylon was ninety-nine years before the end of the Isin Dynasty; whilst Amar Sin's (or Rāma Chandra's) accession was 103 years before that epoch. This makes the accession of young Suabu to have occurred in the fourth year of the reign of Amar Sin (or Rāma Chandra), who reigned for twenty-one years. And as Suabu reigned only fourteen years, he died three years before the end of the reign of Amar Sin (or Rāma Chandra). Amar Sin's much greater age on his accession than Suabu

[1] See L. A. Waddell, *Shinar*, 1922.

is evidenced by the fact that his father had reigned twenty-eight years before his own accession, showing that he was a relatively elderly man on his accession; whilst the fact that Suabu's son reigned for thirty-six years presumes that his father, Suabu, had died young; and his death was, as we have seen, three years before the end of Amar Sin's (or Rāma Chandra's) reign. All this agrees with Suabu being identical with Subāhu, the nephew of Amar Sin or Rāma Chandra, the 7th Isin king.

It would thus appear that Sumu-abu or Suabu was identical with Subāhu of the Indian Chronicles, and was the grandson of the 6th Isin king, who brought in the Muru or Amorite element into the Isin Dynasty; that Suabu's father was the younger son of the latter king and conquered Babylon from its local kinglet Lavana, who appears to have been independent of the Isin empire; that Suabu's father was allowed by his imperial father, the 6th Isin king, to retain Babylon as a hereditary city-state; that Suabu succeeded his father in Babylon in the fourth year of the reign of his uncle Amar Sin, the 7th Isin king; that the latter slew his nephew Suabu in the fourteenth year of the latter's reign; and that Amar Sin continued to reign for three years more after that event.

This direct royal solar descent of Sumu-abu or Suabu from the first king of the First Sumerian Dynasty, Ukusi of Ukh of the Kish Chronicle, the Aryan Ikshvāku of the Indian lists, through his grandfather Dasha-ratha, the 6th Isin king, who is repeatedly called "descendant of Ikshvāku" in the Indian Chronicles, would explain why the usurping later kings of the Isin Dynasty (11-14) are omitted in the Indian King-Lists, and why Suabu's line enters the main line of the solar Aryan kings, all traditionally descended from Ukusi, with the 5th king of his dynasty, that is the First Babylonian Dynasty.

Names of First Babylonian Dynasty Kings in the Imperial Line in Agreement with the Indian Lists

We have seen that the First Babylonian Dynasty kings enter the imperial line in the Indian King-Lists of the Aryans with the 5th king, for the reason that it was he who became the first emperor in that dynasty by his conquest of the imperial Isin Dynasty; and that the founder of the First Babylonian Dynasty, Suabu, the Subāhu of the Indian Chronicles, not being an emperor, is only shown as a collateral local king of Mathurā, presumably Babylon, as the grandson of the sixth Isin emperor.

Our Table then shows the comparison of the names Indian and Babylonian of the First Babylonian Dynasty emperors, beginning from that first emperor of that dynasty, namely, its 5th king, onwards through his son, the 6th king, Khammu Rabi, " The Great Lotus " and his son, Sāmsu Iuduna—the Pundarīka or " The Great Lotus," and his son, Kshema Dhanvan of the Indian lists—to the end of that dynasty with the 11th king, Sāmsu Satana, the Sudhanvan of the Indian lists; in which *Sudhanvan* obviously is intended for the Babylonian *Satana*.[1]

The names of the remaining imperial kings of this dynasty, Nos., 8 to 10, now require comparison in the Babylonian and Indian lists. These names it will be noticed do not agree in form in the Babylonian and Indian lists; and thus imply that the Indian forms of the names are either translations of the Babylonian into the later Indian Sanskrit, or are clerical mistakes by Indian scribes in copying the ancient MSS. of these Aryan King-Lists down through them any centuries in India. Let us now take up these three names *seriatim*.

The 8th king's name, *Abieshu'a* or *Abiskat'a* (the meaning of which is quite unknown in Sumerian and Akkadian), is rendered as *Devānīka* in the Indian lists.[2] This seems clearly an Indian clerical error of the copyists, as there is no such word in Sanskrit, unless it be a title of the Fire-god. The 9th king's name, *Ammi-Satana* (or *-Ditana*) is rendered in the Indian lists as Ruru. This latter word in Sanskrit means " a species of Antelope (or Goat-Antelope), a wild animal."[3] Now in Akkadian *Ditana* means " a He-Goat, a leader, and hence a king ";[4] and thus is in essential

[1] This name may also read *Di-ta-na*; but the Indian list shows that it traditionally read *Satana*.

[2] The resemblance of this name to that of the last Isin king Damiq-ninishu is obviously accidental.

[3] MWD. 884.

[4] MD. 971.

agreement with the Sanskrit *Ruru*. The prefixed title *Ammi* appears to be an expanded form of the Sumerian *Am* or *Ama*, "a warrior," which would make the whole name read "The Warrior He-Goat"—the He-Goat being the sacred-defensive animal of the Sun-cult [1] and a title of the first Sumerian king Ukusi. The 10th king's name, *Ammi Sarāga* is rendered in the Indian lists as *Ahi Nagu*. *Ammi* is the "Warrior" prefix as before, and *Sara* means in Sumerian "Serpent" [2] and *ga* = "to go." [3] Now in Sanskrit *Ahi Nāga* means "The Great Serpent of the Deep and the Sky-clouds"; [4] thus disclosing that the Indian name is a translation of the Babylonian name into the later Indian Sanskrit, with a final dialectic *u* for *a*.

End of the First Babylonian Dynasty

The 11th king was the last of this dynasty, which had effected such a glorious renaissance under Khammu-Rabi's strong and extended empire. He is given a reign of thirty-one years in the traditional king-lists, and this is supported by the contemporary business documents which specify thirty of the year-names of his reign. These year-names give us great insight into what this king deemed the chief events of his reign. They are almost entirely of a religious kind, and call the year after the king's dedication of particular images of gods or of himself as a worshipper, to certain temples, showing that he had become hopelessly priest-ridden and spent his strength on endless religious rites.

We also learn from contemporary inscriptions and the later Babylonian Chronicles some of the other events which weakened his rule and led to the downfall of his dynasty. Towards the end of the reign of Khammu-Rabi's son, the 7th king of this dynasty, the latter lost the "Sea-land" province in the lower Delta bordering the Persian Gulf and extending to the Elam hills. Here, one named An-ma-an or Anu-ma-anu, a name hitherto read in Semitic fashion "Iluma-ilu," set himself up as an independen tking and waged war successfully against the seventh king of

[1] WPOB. 250, f.; 330, f.; with many illustrations from Sumerian and Hitto-Phœnician Seals and Ancient Briton monuments. WSID. 20 f.

[2] Cp. Br. 1170. [3] M. 4343.

[4] MWD. 125, 525, 532 and cp. MVM. 70 f.

Babylon; and the son of the latter also failed to conquer or expel him. As a result, he was left in undisputed possession, and founded a powerful dynasty, which held the Sea-land independently of Babylon for eleven generations, until the stronger Kassi Dynasty later conquered and annexed that province to their Babylonian empire.

The name of the founder of this local contemporary "Sea-land" dynasty, namely *An-ma-an* or *Anu-ma-anu*, suggests the name of Rāma Chandra's dauntless ally *Hanuman*, the so-called "monkey-king." And as this Anumānu was a contemporary of Rim Sin II, the last king of Larsa, a city-state which immediately adjoined this Sea-land province, it supports the view that the Indian poets in composing the *Rāmāyana* romance had mixed up the tradition of Rāma Chandra (or "Rāma of the Moon"), the son of King Dasharatha, the sixth Isin king, with that of Rim Sin (or "Rim of the Moon") whose names were practically identical in form.

Along with this weakening of the Babylonian Dynasty by the loss of this Sea-land province on the south, there eventually came in this eleventh and last king's reign a Hittite invasion of Babylonia from Cappadocia on the north. This is recorded in the Babylonian Chronicle of the Kings, which states: "Against Shamash-sa (or *di*)-ta-na the men of the Land of the Khatti (Hittites) [marched] against the Land of Uri ('Akkad')."[1] The rest of this record is wanting, leaving us in the dark as to the results of this Hittite invasion.

A contemporary reference to this Hittite invasion or raid appears to be made in an actually existing original letter of this last king in reply to an urgent appeal from his governor of the city-state of Sipara, on the Euphrates to the north of Babylon. It states: "Concerning what you wrote to me saying: The corn (crop) which is in Sipar fields, it is not right that it be left on the land to the mercy of the enemy troops; let the king our lord command that an order be sent to us to open the Sun-gate, and then this corn can be brought into the town. In reply: as soon as they have finished (cutting) the corn, which is the town crops, open the

[1] KC. 2, 22. Note the late Babylonian scribe has misspelt *Sāmsu* as "Shamash," a word meaning "the Sun-god."

Sun-gate, and when bringing in the corn send the 'judges' (in the gate) to carefully guard the gate." This suggests that the king had limited his opposition to the invading Hittites to merely timorously shutting the gates of his cities, and doubtless had done similarly also at Babylon.

While it is generally inferred that this Hittite invasion ended the First Babylonian Dynasty in the thirty-first year of its last king, it is also assumed that it was merely a raid, and that the victorious Hittites immediately thereafter returned to Cappadocia laden with their booty, and left the defenceless Babylonia a prey to its rival factions and neighbours, amongst whom, after an interval of several generations, the Kassi from "the mountains of Media" proved to be the strongest. The new light shed on this period by our Indian records is given below.

Historical Results of these Discoveries of the Aryan Racial Origin of the First Babylonian Dynasty & its Affinities & Chronological Relations to the Isin Dynasty

Thus we find that all the names of the First Babylonian Dynasty imperial kings, with the single exception of the corrupt No. 8, are in substantial agreement in form or etymological meaning with those in the official Indian lists of the Early Aryan kings.

The critical historical results of these discoveries disclose and establish the Aryan racial origin of the kings of the First Babylonian Dynasty; and the family descent of the latter from the sixth king of the Isin Dynasty; and they discover and establish for the first time a fixed and definite chronological connecting link between the Isin Dynasty and the First Babylonian Dynasty in the fact that the seventeenth year of the reign of the fifth king of the latter dynasty was the date-year for the end of the Isin Dynasty. And through this fixed date we now recover for the first time by dead-reckoning the real dates of the Sumerian kings back to the first king of the First Sumerian or Aryan Dynasty.

Having thus identified the kings of the First Babylonian Dynasty with the Aryan imperial kings of this period in the Indian Chronicles we now come to the kings of the so-called

" Second Babylonian Dynasty " of the period immediately succeeding this.

THE SO-CALLED " SECOND " OR " SEA-LAND " BABYLONIAN DYNASTY

The dynasty commonly called the " Second Babylonian " Dynasty is paradoxically not really a Babylon dynasty at all. That title was formerly applied to the Sea-land dynasty above mentioned, when it was believed from the late traditional Babylonian King-Lists to have followed immediately after the First Dynasty of Babylon, and before it was known to have been merely a local dynasty in the lower Delta, independent of but contemporary with the latter part of the First Babylonian Dynasty and the beginning of the Kassi Dynasty. And this title is still mechanically repeated, although no adequate evidence has been forthcoming to show that any kings of this dynasty occupied the throne of Babylon at all.

In the latest review of the earlier dynasties of Babylon,[1] whilst this Sea-land Dynasty as a whole is properly relegated aside as a contemporary of the latter part of the First Babylonian and the earlier half of the Kassi Dynasties, nevertheless two of its middle kings, the fifth and sixth, whose dates fall after the end of the First Babylonian Dynasty, are arbitrarily picked out and made to be kings of Babylon in the period intervening between the end of the First Dynasty and the advent of the Kassi. These two kings, Shushshi and Gulkishar, are thus selected, it is said, in order to justify the title given to this Sea-land dynasty, by the later Babylonian scribes, who compiled the traditional king-lists, of *Uruku* or " Holy City "—a title which has once been found applied to Babylon. But as against this, it may be pointed out that there were many holy cities in Babylonia, and the analogous title of *Unu*, which dialectically becomes *Uru*, was applied to the different sacred temple-cities of Ur and Larsa as well as Uunuk, Uruk or Erech ; and it may indeed turn out, I venture to suggest, that Uruk (or Erech) was latterly the capital of the Sea-land Dynasty.

[1] T.D. in RA. 1927, 181 f.

Fourth King of "Sea-land" Dynasty rules at Babylon (?) & his Identity in the Indian Lists

Now our Indian key-lists again come to our aid in clearing up the real succession at this dark critical period of later Mesopotamian History. The Indian lists actually give us as the immediate imperial successor of the last king of the First Babylonian Dynasty a solitary king *bearing a name which equates with that of the Sea-land king of that period.* This name intervenes between the last king of the First Babylonian Dynasty (No. 72 in main-line list, see Table) and the first king of the Kassi Dynasty (No. 74 of the main-line list).

This imperial Sea-land dynastic king, however, is neither of the two arbitrarily selected as above—the fifth and sixth kings; but is their predecessor, the fourth king. The Indian-list name for this king (No. 73 in main line), who immediately succeeded the last king of the First Babylonian Dynasty, is *Bala*, with a variant of *Sahasra Bala.*[1] This name is seen to equate well with *Sahar-ki Bal* or *Saxar-ki Bal*, the fourth king of the Sea-land Dynasty, and *a king who was admittedly the contemporary of the last king of the First Babylonian Dynasty.*[1]

The date of this fourth king of the Sea-land Dynasty thus becomes of some critical importance. His date, according to the latest calculations, is estimated at 1820-1806 B.C.,[2] as compared with the date of the last king of the First Babylonian Dynasty at 1836-1806 B.C., thus making him a younger contemporary of this last king, whose date is fixed with relative exactitude at that period, as detailed in the chapter on Chronology. But this date for the fourth Sea-land king is merely based on the theory that the first king of the Sea-land, Anumānu, established himself independent of the seventh Babylonian king no less than *twenty-eight or twenty-nine years before the latter king began to war against him as a usurper*, which is extremely improbable. For this war against Anumānu was continued by the eighth Babylonian king, thus presuming that the former had ascended his throne only a few years before the death of the seventh Babylonian

[1] WVP. 3, 321. [2] RA. 1927, 197.

king in 1923 B.C., which is now a relatively fixed date. Thus it seems to me much more probable that the first king of the Sea-land arose near the last year of the seventh Babylonian king; and in this way making his accession about 1925 B.C., with this date we then would gain for the fourth Sea-land king, who reigned fifteen years, a date of about 1805-1791 B.C.; and this would also allow a considerable margin for reducing the extravagant regnal years of sixty and fifty-six respectively for the first and second Sea-land kings, which the late Babylonian King-Lists assign them.

The identity of this fourth Sea-land king with the imperial king Bala or Sahasra Bala, who in the Indian lists immediately succeeded the last king of the first Babylon Dynasty, is also strikingly confirmed by the fact that under the latter name Sahasra Bala he left a collateral line of descendants, whose names do not appear in the main or imperial line,[1] just as this fourth king is credited with eight successors in the collateral Sea-land dynasty, whose names are not in the main or imperial Babylonian line. Indeed the comparison of these Indian names with the Babylonian, also yields us *absolute proof of the identity of this king through the identity in the name of his successor in the Sea-land Dynasty in the Babylonian and Indian.*

This fifth Sea-land king's name in the Babylonian is *Shūsh-shi*, a title which is significantly pure Sumerian and meaning "Moon + see,"[2] or "Seer or beholder of the Moon." Moreover the signs for this Sumerian word are ordinarily written by the pictographs of the Crescent Moon and of an Eye; and this latter word-sign, *Shi* or *Shī*, is of especial interest for English readers in that it is another of the many thousands of instances I have given in my Sumer-Aryan Dictionary of the Sumerian origin of English and other Aryan words; for this *Shī* word-sign, pictured by an eye and meaning "see," is disclosed as the Sumerian origin of our English word "See."

Now the Indian-list name for this collateral line king

[1] His successors were Chandra-avaloka, Tāra-pida (or -dhisha), Chandra-giri, Bhānu-ratha (or -mitra or -chandra) and Shrutāyus and (?) Bahula WVP. 3, 321.

[2] *Shūsh*="Moon," Br. 8643 and 8740; and *Shi* or *Shī*="see," Br. 9284

corresponding to the fifth Sea-land king, whose name means "Moon + See," or "Seeing the Moon," is translated into the Sanskrit as *Chandra-avaloka*, which also literally means "Moon + See,"[1] and significantly another Sanskrit name for "Moon" besides Chandra is *Shashin*, now disclosed as derived from the Sumerian *Shushi*, while *Chandra* or *Chaud* itself is seen to be a dialectic derivative for the Sumerian *Sin*, "Moon," as "The Shining One"—the Sanskrit, as we have seen, being in the habit of intruding an *r* Cockneywise into the Sumerian words. Doubtless the rest of the names of the successors of Sahasra Bala in the Indian collateral list will be found on scrutiny to equate with those of Saharki Bal in the Babylonian list, but I have not yet found time to compare them, as this one is sufficient for our present identifications.

Thus we find absolute proof in the identity of this fourth Sea-land king as an imperial king with the Indian-list king who immediately succeeded the last king of the First Babylonian Dynasty, not only in his own name, but also in that of his immediate successor in his collateral Sea-land Dynasty.

The Hittite Invasion of Babylonia *re* the End of First Babylonian Dynasty about 1806 B.C.

The Hittite invasion in the reign of the last king of the First Babylonian Dynasty, as above recorded, is generally supposed to have been the immediate cause of the end of that dynasty. And it has further been supposed that the Hittites did not settle at Babylon to rule there, but after ravaging that city and ending the Babylonian Dynasty they returned to their cool capital in Cappadocia with their rich spoils and left torrid Mesopotamia to its fate.

These inferences are now seen to be supported to some extent by the fact now ascertained that the fourth king of the Sea-land immediately succeeded the First Babylonian Dynasty on the imperial throne in Mesopotamia.

But at the same time this succession suggests that if the Hittite invasion were really the cause of the end of the First Babylonian Dynasty, the Hittites themselves were

[1] MWD. 386 and 103.

presumably the allies of Anumānu's Sea-land Dynasty and placed the throne of Babylon at the disposal of the fourth king of that dynasty; for there is no interregnum in the imperial line in the Indian lists, all the various versions agreeing in placing Bala as the immediate successor of the last king of the First Babylonian Dynasty.[1]

And, as we shall now find that the next following king in the Indian imperial line, No. 74 of the Indian list, is the first king of the Kassi Dynasty, it thus transpires that after all there was a "Second Babylonian Dynasty," but that it consisted only of one king, namely, the above Saharki Bal, or Sahasra Bala of the Indian lists. This is most conveniently demonstrated in the next chapter on The Aryan Origin and Affinities of the Kassi Dynasty.

[1] In some of the Indian MSS. the name is written besides *Bala*, also *Dala* and *Nala*, which latter are clearly clerical errors of later Indian copyists, especially as the letters B, D and N may be easily confused if not carefully written.

XXIV

THE KASSI DYNASTY OF BABYLONIA, C. 1790 TO 1175 B.C., DISCLOSED AS AN ARYAN DYNASTY BY THE INDIAN KING-LISTS & THE LAST OF THE "SUMERIAN" OR EARLY ARYAN DYNASTIES IN MESOPOTAMIA

Disclosing their Homeland in Hittite Asia Minor, the Aryan Affinity of their Language and the End of the Aryan Ruling Race in Babylonia.

OUR Indian key-lists of the Early Aryan kings now again bridge over for us another and the last of the great gaps in Babylonian or Mesopotamian History. This is the hitherto unmeasured gap separating the First Babylonian Dynasty from the Kassi Dynasty, the nominal "Third Babylonian" Dynasty. This Kassi Dynasty was founded, as we shall find, by a new clan of vigorous aristocratic Aryan invaders from the southern portion of the old Sumerian or Aryan highland homeland in Hittite Asia Minor, to the north of the Mesopotamian or Babylonian plains.

This new Aryan dynasty brought back many of the purer old Sumerian features into Babylonia, including a return to the Sumerian language or a dialect of it in their official documents. It proves to be one of the most interesting of all the later Mesopotamian dynasties as regards its Aryan and Western affinities, and one which continued to rule Babylonia for the exceptionally long period of nearly six centuries, and contained those powerful emperors, whose actual voluminous letters, written in a dialect allied to the Hittites, to the well-known Pharaoh Aken-aten and his father of about 1400 B.C., have been unearthed, along with letters from the Hittite governors from the archives of the Ancient Egyptian Foreign Office at Tell-el-Amarna in Upper Egypt.

The Name "Kassi" or "Cassi" & their Homeland

The name of this imperial ruling Aryan people of Babylonia, though now generally spelt "Kassi" or "Cassi" by Europeans, was spelt by those people themselves in Babylonia as *Kāshshi*, and in the singular the Babylonians spelt the name *Kashshū*.

They are presumably the *Kāshi* clan of Aryan people of Indian Vedic literature and the Epic Chronicles, who were associated with the Aryan tribes of the Koshala and Chedi,[1] the latter being, as we have seen, a section of the Khad, Kad, or "Panchala" or Aryan Phœnicians. They were also associated in Vedic literature with the people of Videha (which we have seen probably designated the Hittite capital at Boghaz Koi); and were at times opposed to the Syrio-Phœnicians (Kuru-Panchala).[2] The later Indian Brahmans ascribe their title to a city of the name of Kāshi,[3] so-named they say after a King Kasha, and they give a list of Kāshi kings, which may prove to contain titles of kings of the Kassi Dynasty; but the lists appear to be corrupt.

The mountain homeland of the hardy Kassi tribe is usually placed conjecturally on the western border of Media or north-west Persia, overlooking the northern Babylonian plains. The later Assyrian King Sennacherib gave the name *Kashshu* to a people he conquered in the hills above Holwan near the source of the Divala River in the Zab area to the east of Assyria; and earlier Assyrian kings likewise record their conquests over Kashshu people, though the coupling by Nebuchadnezzar I of Kashshu with Amurru or Amorite Land is against an eastern location for the former. The eastern Kashshu were doubtless, as has been suggested, the Kosseans of the hills north of Elam, and the *Kossai* robber tribe of Strabo,[4] who were certainly not Kassi.

1 WVP. 2, 157, 161, 172, 341.

2 MKI. 1, 154.

3 Kāshi City the Brahmans identify with Benares (!)—for as usual they place all the Early Sumerian and Mesopotamian kings within the limits of Gangetic India, and believe that the Aryans originated in Gangetic India.

4 S. 743, 17-18.

THE KASSI AS "HITTITES"

On the other hand, it has been suggested by Prof. Pinches, with, I think, much more probability, that the Kassi "are apparently the *Kashshi*, *Kashi* or *Kasi* of the Tell-el-Amarna tablets, who have been identified with the *Kusāa* or Cappadocians of the late Assyrian texts."[1] In the Amarna letter (No. 58 of Winckler's Collection) the Egyptian governor of the seaport of Gebal (Byblos) in Northern Phœnicia, which the Egyptians had seized from the Hittites, in writing to his master, the Egyptian Pharaoh, complains that the Hittite governor of an adjoining city, also under the Egyptian occupation, sought to recapture all the cities of his Egyptian suzerain "for the king of Mitana and the king of *Kashshi*." In letter No. 86 the sons of that disaffected Hittite governor are called "dogs of the King of *Kashshi* and the King of Mitanni (Mitana) and take the and of the (Egyptian) king for them." And in letter No. 87 the recapture of these cities is spoken of as a fact accomplished by these "dogs of the King of Mitana and of the King of *Kashi*, and of the King of the *Khata* (*i.e.*, Khatti or "Hittites")." In letter No. 181 the land of Kashshi is associated with that of Nahrima (or The Riverine-Land, a title of the strip of land extending from North Syrian coast of the Mediterranean to the Euphrates in the Carchemish region, and forming the so-called Muru or "Amorite" Land) as being accessible from Egypt by ship, as the Egyptian governor of Jerusalem of that day (several centuries before the advent of the Jews into Palestine and their seizure of the old Hittite capital city of Urusalim) wrote to Pharaoh Aken-Aten, reassuringly and reminiscently saying: "As long as there were (Egyptian) ships in the sea, the arm of the mighty (Egyptian) king took the land of Nahrima and the Land of *Kashshi*."

This Hittite, Mitani (confederates of the Hittites) and Nahrima association for Kashshi Land indicates, I venture to suggest, that the Kassi homeland city-state was the Hittite city-state in S.E. Cappadocia bordering Cilicia, within the Nahrima area, called *Kishshia* or *Gashshia* in the Hittite official

[1] Cuneiform Tablet from Yuzgat, 1907, 18.

cuneiform letters of about 2000 B.C. found at the imperial Hittite capital at Boghaz Koi. It was situated on the Upper Euphrates at the great bend above Carchemish and near the head-waters of the Pyramus River of Cilicia.[1] It is a rich agricultural area, and the Kassi were noted agriculturists; and from there the old caravan routes led to Armenia and the steppes beyond, thus placing the Kassi in connection with a rich horse-supply, for which the Kassi in Babylonia were famous.

This location in Hittite Asia Minor in south-east Cappadocia for the Kassi homeland is confirmed by an inscription of a Kassi sailor prince who has left an inscribed monument in the Don Valley of Scotland about 400 B.C., as I have fully described and figured elsewhere.[2] In his bilingual inscription with the Sun-Cross he tells that he erected his great stone monument to the fire-god Bil, and in it he calls himself by all four titles of Phœnician, "Hittite," Barat and *Kazzi* or *Qaz*, and that he came from the city of Kast in Cilicia. This Kast, I have shown, was the old Sun-temple city of Kasta-bala on the upper Pyramus River, near its head-waters on the border of south-east Cappadocia, and is on the border of this old Hittite provincial city-state of Kishshia or Gashshia. We shall also find that the Kassi language has affinities with the Hittite and other Aryan or Indo-European languages.

Early Relations of the Kassi with Babylonia

The first mention of the Kassi tribe is a raid by them on Babylonia in the eighth year of the reign of Khammu-Rabi's son. Later, during the dynasty of the latter, there are incidental references to harvesters of the Kassi tribe being engaged in Babylonia, and also in the reign of the last king of that First Babylonian Dynasty a contract at Babylon for a two years' lease of an uncultivated field to a Kassi for farming. And the Kassi appear to have been essentially an agricultural people like their Early Aryan ancestors who established systematic agriculture. They reformed the land tenure in Babylonia to some extent, erected inscribed boundary-stones in fields, and they figure themselves plough-

1 HI. 28, and map. p. 54.

2 WPOB. 32 f.

ing under the sign of the Sun-Cross on their sacred seals (see Fig. 72).

FIG. 71C.—Kassi or "Cassi" ploughing and sowing under the Sign of the Cross. From a Kassi official seal of 1400 B.C. (After Clay.)

Note the plough is fitted with a drill, which is fed by the right hand of the sower from his bag, and the corn-seed passes down directly into the fresh furrow opened by the plough. The master, as on the Kassi seals generally, is of fine Aryan type, the men are presumably aboriginal Chaldeans.

KASSI INVASION OF BABYLONIA

Although no specific record exists of the conquest of Babylonia by the Kassi, this conquest by force of arms is implied in the fact that they were non-Babylonians and foreigners from the North, though of the same kindred as the Early Sumerian invading ruling race. Moreover, a copy, though a late copy, of an inscription by the first Kassi king, the so-called "Gandash," spelt by the late scribe "Gaddash" (or ? Gaddal), referring to the repair of a temple in Babylon, presumably the great temple of Bel, speaks of the damage done "in the conquest of Babylon," thus implying that the city had been taken by storm. As evidence also of his own paramount rule, he calls himself therein not only "King of Babylon" and "King of Sumer and Akkad," but also "King of the Four Quarters of the World"—this last, however, was clearly an empty boast, as we know that he had not even conquered the Sea-land Kingdom in the Delta, and he certainly had no authority whatsoever over Egypt, though some of his early successors appear to have had access to, if not authority over, Muru or Amorite Land in Upper Syria, and the ninth king claimed to be king also of Gutium Land.

In Babylonia the Kassi were, like the Sumerians and the other previous dynastic people, a ruling caste or aristocracy, relatively few in numbers to their Chaldean subjects "the dark-headed people." And to start with, they long kept aloof from intermarriage with the Chaldeans. They brought back the use of the Sumerian language or a dialect of it, in their official and business documents and inscriptions, which are in a non-Semitic language. They were admittedly a vigorous and practical people and successful administrators; and they introduced a more scientific method of recording time by dating their years by the year of the king's reign. Whilst extending the feudal system by the grant of lands to their feudal barons and encouraging agriculture (see Fig. 65), they improved in certain directions the system of land tenure, which was on the basis of tribal or collective proprietorship by village communities, as in India at the present day. They erected inscribed stone-boundary pillars to demarcate fields and estates. They introduced the horse into Babylonia as the ordinary beast of burden instead of asses and oxen as hitherto; and their riches in horses doubtless contributed, I think, to their capture of Babylon and associated cities. With wide political outlook their kings, like the Hittite and Mitanni kings, made treaties with each other and with Egypt, and they , like the former, cemented their friendship with Egypt by giving their daughters in marriage to the Egyptian Pharaohs over several centuries.

Kassi King-List in Agreement with Indian Lists of Aryan Main-line Solar Kings of this Period

Our Comparative Table on p. 433 discloses that the name of the king immediately following the solitary imperial Sea-land king who gained the Babylonian throne is identical with the name of the first king of the Kassi Dynasty of Babylon, and further that the names of the kings immediately following him are substantially identical in form, and absolutely identical in chronological order in both lists, Babylonian and Indian.

I give here for reference this comparative list of the names of the first five Kassi kings, with those of the corresponding Aryan kings of the Indian lists; and I have added in the second column the names of these Kassi kings as hitherto conjecturally "restored" from the polyphonous Sumerian syllabic signs without any key to the actual traditional forms of these Kassi kings' names.

KASSI KINGS' NAMES AS NOW RESTORED BY THE INDIAN KEY-LISTS

No. in Dynasty.	Names as now read.	Names as hitherto restored.	Names in Indian Lists.	No. in Lists.
1.	XA[1]-TAL[2]	Gan-dash	STHALA or Gaya	74
2.	A-GU-U(M)	A-gu-um	AUKA	75
3.	BI[3]-ZU[4]-I-RU[5]	Kash-til-ia-shi	VAJRA-sābha	76
4.	USH-IGU[6]	Ush-shi	SHANKHA	77
5.	A-BI-SUT[7]-TASH	A-bi-rat-tash	AB'YUTTHIT-ASHVA or DHYUSHIT-ASHVA	78

The substantial identity of the form of the names and the absolute identity in their chronological order in both dynastic lists, Babylonian and Indian, are thus demonstrated.

MISLEADING "RESTORATIONS" OF THE NAMES OF KASSI KINGS HITHERTO

My comparison of the Babylonian and Indian lists of the names of the Kassi Dynasty, it will be noticed, does not at present extend in the Table beyond the fifth king. This is entailed because I have not yet had an opportunity of comparing the spelling of the names of the few kings whose inscriptions have been found with that in the late Babylonian lists of this dynasty. For in regard to this Kassi Dynasty, even more than usual if possible, *the forms of the names as hitherto arbitrarily restored conjecturally from the polyphonous Sumerian syllabic signs without any key whatever to the traditional forms of these kings' names*, gives us as often as not little or no idea of the real forms of these Kassi kings' names, as preserved in our Indian King-Lists.

[1] Br. 4032. [2] Br. 7. [3] Br. 5119. [4] Br. 1489.
[5] Br. 3. [6] Br. 9260. [7] Br. 2293.

My readings of the names of these first five Kassi kings, as heretofore, are all duly attested from the standard Sumerian lexicons in the Table on p. 458, and cannot be gainsaid. And the complete identity here established between the first five kings of the Kassi Dynasty and the five corresponding Aryan kings of that same period in our Indian key-lists, Nos. 74–78, is quite sufficient for establishing the identity of this dynasty and the complete identity of the Early Aryan kings in the Indian Chronicles from the first king of the First Aryan Dynasty at the Rise of Civilization continuously downwards, with the Sumerian kings from the first king of the First Sumerian Dynasty continuously downwards through all the later dynasties in Mesopotamia to and inclusive of this Kassi Dynasty in the middle Babylonia period.

Aryan Affinities of the Kassi Language

The Kassi are disclosed by our Indian Epic Chronicles to be Aryans in race and tradition, personal names, and presumably in language. It has been supposed that the Kassi people, who were so obviously non-Semites, might possibly prove to be Aryan through their affinities with the Mitani (who I have shown were evidently the Early Medes) whose gods bore Vedic names identical with those of the Indo-Aryans ; and especially so as the Kassi called their Sun-god *Shuriăsh*, compared to the Indian Sanskrit *Surya*, and their war-god *Maruttash*, compared to the Sanskrit *Maruta*, for the storm-god invoked by warriors, and their wind-god-title of *Ubriăsh* suggested Boreas, and one of their titles for god, as *Bashkhu* or *Bugash*, compared with the Phrygian name *Bagaios*, "god."[1]

But as regards the Kassi language itself nothing in it distinctively Aryan or Indo-European has hitherto been recognized. The affinity or identity of the Kassi language with one or other of the composite group of different dialects found in the imperial Hittite archives at Boghaz Koi and elsewhere in Cappadocia, has been remarked by Prof. Pinches,[2] but the affinities of these with the Indo-European is still under discussion and controversy. And though the

[1] *Tablet from Yuzgat*, 1907, 15 f. [2] *Op. cit.*, 18.

Kassi in Babylonia wrote their official documents in a dialect of Sumerian, the few known words in their own Kassi dialect have not been recognized as having any Sumerian or Aryan or Indo-European affinities, beyond the four god-names or titles above specified.

Now, a basis for beginning the determination of the linguistic affinity of the Kassi language is found in a short bilingual glossary of Kassi words, in the Kassi language and in the Semitic dialect of Babylonia, which was drawn up by later Semitic Babylonian scribes in order to explain to Semites the meaning of the names of the later Kassi kings who ruled at Babylon.[1] Although the Kassi words thus translated in respect of their meaning are very few in number, they are sufficient to disclose the radical affinity of a considerable proportion of Kassi words with the Aryan or Indo-European and Sumerian.

Our fresh comparison of these Kassi words with the Sumerian and Aryan or Indo-European discovers that where no Aryan or Sumerian affinity whatever could be made out (except the god-names, Nos. 1, 3 and 5 in the accompanying Table), on the contrary a large proportion of these Kassi words is disclosed to be of Aryan and Sumerian affinity, and most of the remaining words will probably be found also to be of Sumerian origin when the spelling of the Sumerian words is revised and their meanings more fully elicited. The reason why these Kassi affinities were not observed before is seen to be for the most part because the previous arbitrary "restorations" of the Kassi words have masked the real form of the latter by selecting in most instances the wrong particular polyphonous value of one or more syllables in their cuneiform syllabic spelling, just as has been done habitually hitherto in "restoring" the Sumerian names.

The results of this comparison of my revised readings are displayed in the annexed Table, wherein any particular polyphonous value which differs from that previously guessed at is duly attested from standard Sumerian authority. For brevity, I have limited the comparison of the Kassi words to the Sumerian, Sanskrit, Gothic and English—the latter

[1] It is published in cuneiform with translations by Prof. Pinches in JRAS. 1917, 101 f.

KASSI WORDS COMPARED WITH SUMERIAN & ARYAN OR INDO-EUROPEAN

Kassi.	Sumer.	Sanskrit.	Gothic.	English.
Shu-ri-ia-ash	Shur [11] (" Sun-god " *Ashur*)	Suriya or Surya	—	The Sun and Sun-god
Pā[1]-ut-ha or	Pa-ut-tu [12]	Vāta or	Vedr, " wind " & "weather "	Wind & Wind-god
Pā-u-ha	Pa, " wind, blow "	Vāyu	Waiau, " to blow "	(and "Weather")
Ma-rat-tash	Maruta [13]	Maruta	—	Storm and War-god (?) *Mars* [28]
Mi-ri-zi-ir	—	Marīcī [25]	—	Mother-goddess
Ba-ash-hu and Bu-ga-ash	Buzur [14]	Bhaga	Bogu (Slav) Bagaios (Phrygian)	God, chief god (?) Bogey, goblin
Tu [2]-gu [3]-ash or Ta[4]-ra[5]-ash	Du-gu [15] Dingir [16]	(?) Triksha[26] Tārā, Taraka	Tuggl Tungl	Star AS. *Tungol*
Du [6]-gi-gi	Du [17]	Dyo Dyaus (" Sky")	—	Heaven
Mi-di-[7]-ia-ash	Mad	Medinī or Mrittika	(?) Mid-gard "The Earth")	Earth (Mud)
Ia-ash [8]-si	Ash [18]	Īsha, " lord "	Asa, " lord "	King, *Æsc* AS
Ia-shu	Eshshe [19]	Ashā	—	Country
Ash-mu [9]	Azu [20]	Oja (" wizard ") [27]	Weis, " wise "	Wise one
Sir	Shu or Shi-ru [21]	Sharavāp	Sarva, " weapons "	Bow (weapon) AS. *Searo*, " weapons "
E-me	Em [22] " go forth " (of Sun, etc.)	Evam "going"	—	Go or come forth, Greek *Iōeimi*
U-zi-urash [10]	Ag, Agga [23]	Āchar, " do " *Aj* (" move ")	—	Act (Latin *Ago*)
Si-im-mash	Simmu [24] reproduce, make	Samja, " bring forth "	(Sama-kun, " kindred ") Sama, "same"	Same, Semblance

[1] Br. 2048. [2] Br. 6644. [3] Br. 519 f. [4] Br. 6645. [5] Br. 514.
[6] Br. 6644. [7] Br. 2550. [8] WSAD. 20. [9] Br. 10911.
[10] Br. 10478. P. translates its meaning as " do." [11] Br. 8212.
[12] Br. 5638 ; and cp. on *Shupū* " Storm." MD. 1000.
[13] Br. 5564 ; M. 3914, 3955. [14] Br. 8747 f. ; 9953 f. [15] Br. 3855.
[16] Br. 420. [17] Br. 8233. [18] WSAD. 22. [19] Br. 9619. [20] WSAD. 22.
[21] Br. 9098-9. [22] Br. 7870. [23] WSAD. 6. [24] Br. 7378.
[25] Solar mother-goddess or *Sakti* of Hindus and Buddhists. WBT. 219, 361
[26] *Triksha*=" Star " in *Apte's English-Sanskrit Dict.*, 410. [27] WSAD. 22.
[28] It seems probable that the war-god Maruta was the source of Mars ; for the former bore the Sumerian synonym of *Maru*, and a Latin synonym of Mars was *Mavors*. The final *s* in Mars' name was probably added to equate it with the Greek suffix *Arēs*. Mars was a son of Jupiter or Zeus, *i.e.*, Zagg or Sakh of the Sumerians and the Saka or Indra of the Indians ; and Maruta and his sons are called in the Vedas, " Sons of Indra." And he is figured in shining armour and riding in a chariot, just as Maruta in the Vedas.

in column four gives the *literal* English meaning of the words in the same line in the other three columns, which, however, does not equate with the English form of the word except in the case of the second and eleventh words, those other words, except one or two, being absent in the Gothic, Anglo-Saxon and other Western Aryan languages, including the English, having become obsolete in Western Aryan speech.

The most striking and historically important effect of this Comparative Table is to confirm in regard to the Kassi language what our Indian keys have disclosed in regard to the Aryan racial origin of the Kassi rulers.

Moreover, this brief bilingual glossary of Kassi words has in its turn proved to be a key which with the Aryan oil has unlocked the shut meaning of several Sumerian words, thus, for example, *Pā-ut-tu,* No. 2 in the Table. This word, the Sumerian meaning of which has been unknown, is disclosed to mean " The Wind or Storm Wind," and to be the Sumerian source of the Sanskrit *Vāta,* " The Wind or Storm Wind,"[1] and the Sumerian source of the Eddic Gothic *Vedr,* " Wind or Storm," and secondarily " Weather," and of the Swedish *Vaider,* Danish *Vaeder,* German *Wetter,* Anglo-Saxon and Old English *Weder,*" Weather," and of our latter English word—P, V, F and W and T, Th, and D being freely interchangeable in Aryan and Sumerian words dialectically, and V and Th being very late letters.[2]

And its Sumerian root *Pa,* " to blow, to storm (of the wind)," represented in the Kassi *Pā-u-ha,* is now disclosed as the Sumerian source of all the " Wind " words in all the family of Aryan language.[3] Thus the Gothic *Wai*-an " to blow (as the wind)," the Sanskrit *Vā,* " to blow or storm (of the wind)," nasalized also into *Pavana,*" the wind," and similarly when nasalized in the European languages, namely the Greek *Femi,* Latin *Vent*-us, Maeso-Gothic *Winds,* Eddic Gothic, Icelandic, Danish, Swedish, and Anglo-Saxon as *Vind* and the English *Wind.*

[1] MWD. 934. [2] WAOA. 28 f.
[3] Skeat *Maeso-Gothic Glossary.*

The Perversion of Kassi & Sumerian Words by the False "Restorations" of Semitists disguise the radically Aryan Affinities

It thus transpires again that the true forms of Kassi as well as of many Sumerian words have hitherto had their radically Aryan affinities disguised and hopelessly masked by the false haphazard, conjectural "restorations" by Semitic scholars. The only hope for real scientific progress in recovering the true forms of Sumerian words, the Aryan origin and affinity of which I have conclusively established in my *Sumer-Aryan Dictionary* and supplemented in the foregoing pages, lies in that work being now undertaken by its own natural representatives and exponents, namely Aryan scientific scholars and philologists equipped with a competent working knowledge of Sumerian and cuneiform script, in order to recognize through the Aryan languages which of the ambiguous polyphonous values in the cosmopolitan imperial Sumerian script is the correct one for the particular word in question.

In my pioneer *Sumer-Aryan Dictionary* I have fully demonstrated by this scientific comparative method, with the aid of our new Aryan keys, the radical identity of the "Sumerian" language with the Aryan or Indo-European family of languages of the Aryan Race in vocabularly, and have indicated the essential identity in elementary grammatical structure. It is there demonstrated in particular that over 70 per cent. of the words now used by us to-day in our English Language, the origin of many of which could not be traced at all, and the rest of them no earlier than supposedly to cognates or direct borrowing from the Greek, Roman or Sanskrit of the fourth to sixth centuries B.C., or to the Gothic, Briton and Anglo-Saxon of the early Christian era, have, on the contrary, their roots and most of their elementary word-forms already growing and blossoming on the parent Aryan tree, the "Sumerian" or Early Aryan, back several thousand years before the furthest hitherto known period.

The Remaining Kings of the Kassi Dynasty

The later Babylonian dynastic lists give twenty-five to thirty-one additional Kassi kings beyond the fifth king in our above Comparative Table. But of these only a few are found in inscriptions, and I have not yet had an opportunity of fully comparing their names with that in the Indian lists. The latter record only fifteen kings in the main or imperial solar line beyond the fifth above identified; and as the third last Kassi king in the Babylonian lists is the eighth from the end of the Indian list it seems probable that several of the kings on the Babylon lists were contemporaries and not successive.

The third last king of the Kassi Dynasty in the Babylonian lists, namely "*Maruta*, the son of *Signa*" (the so-called "Marduk-apal-iddina I" of the Semites) is now disclosed as "*Maruta* son of *Shīghra*" of our Indian King-Lists of the Aryans.[1] With him, several versions of the solar line in the Indian King-Lists close; but other versions extend the list for five or six generations more, when the line of the old pre-Indian solar Aryan kings ceases altogether.

This absolute identity of the third last king of the Kassi Dynasty, Maruta, in both lists Babylonian and Indian, is further confirmed by the names of the Kassi kings following him in both lists. Thus the two kings immediately following him in the late Babylonian lists have their names spelt respectively as *Sa-ga-ga-mu-dil* and *En-mu-shesh*; and obviously correspond to the second and third kings following Maruta in the Indian lists, namely *Sugavi* or *Susandhi* and *Amarsha*, making due allowance for the corruption in the repeated copying of the MSS. by Indian scribes down through the long centuries and the tendency to Sanskritize the general form of many of the old names, and in particular their intrusion of the Sanskrit *r* into the old names. Thus we have the equation for these last Kassi kings as:—

Babylonian Lists.		Indian Lists.
Mar-uta	=	*Maruta.*
Sa-ga-ga-mu-dil[2]	=	*Sugavi* or *Susandhi.*
En-mu-shesh[3]	=	*Amarsha.*

[1] See App. I. [2] Br. 5. [3] Br. 6437.

Altogether, therefore, this identity of the first five Kassi kings in name and order of succession in both lists, Babylonian and Indian, along with the absolute identity in name of the third last king Maruta, and the practical identity in name of his successors in both lists, Babylonian and Indian, is sufficient to establish the identity of the Kassi Dynasty with that of the last of the line of pre-Indian solar kings preserved in the Indian lists.

End of "Sumerian" or Early Aryan Rule & of the Aryan Race in Babylonia, with the Fall of the Kassi Dynasty by the Semites

With the fall of the Kassi Dynasty at the hands of the Semites, the "Sumerian" or Early Aryan Rule ended in Babylonia, and the Aryan racial element there appears to have become soon practically extinct.

The subsequent Babylonian dynasties which followed the Kassi Dynasty, namely the Fourth Babylonian Dynasty under Nebuchadnezzar, and its successors, including the Assyrian are all transparently Semitic, although adopting the later forms of the religion, laws, and writing of their former overlords and civilizers, the Sumerians or Early Aryans.

Foreign Aryan rule again dominated Babylonia for a time with the conquest of the last Semitic king of Babylon, Nabonidus, by Cyrus the Persian, as Babylonia was a strategic half-way house between Persia and the Levant and Egypt. The Persians continued to dominate the country till the Macedonian conquest by Alexander-the-Great, who was credited with the dream of restoring Babylon as the capital of his "world-empire." On his tragic death, it continued to be held by his eastern Seleucid governor and his descendants till the Roman occupation; and on its abandonment by the Romans it reverted to its own Semitic aborigines, with the rapid decline in its civilization. And incursions from their Arab kinsmen from the Desert eventually trampled out the last remaining embers there of the once radiantly glorious and mighty Sumerian or Aryan Civilization.

As to the disappearance of the Aryan or Nordic racial element in Babylonia, the main body of the ruling Aryan race, including the purer and more progressive and adventurous Aryan stock, had evidently, as we have seen, abandoned the sun-baked and unhealthy Mesopotamian plains very many centuries before this epoch for the more inviting temperate, residential colonies in the West, imitating the exodus of Sargon's dynasty to the Nile and Mediterranean, and to their old homeland in the North and to their eastern colonies in Persia and the Indus Valley. And there seems, besides, to have been a profound change meanwhile in the Mesopotamian climate since the advent of the Sumerians in the direction of extreme arid desiccation, as observed by Mr Pumpelly's Expedition in the Steppes and in Persia, to the north-east, which rendered it even more unfitted than before for a Nordic people.

This practically complete disappearance of the Aryan race from Babylonia is analogous to its disappearance from Greece, which formerly in classic times when at its zenith was one of the chief centres of the Aryan race in Europe. This disappearance from Greece of the Aryan racial type, which gave that land undying fame over the world, has been well-traced and analysed by Macdougall and others as due to wholesale emigration and deportation, and the relatively low birth-rate of the Aryans as compared with the lower races, amongst other causes. It has resulted in the present-day population of Greece being, as Ripley shows, almost wholly of the non-Aryan type, namely, the round-headed Slav or "Alpine" race, along with the narrow-browed, long-headed, dark Mediterranean race, two wholly different races from the classic Greeks, who were of the Nordic or Aryan race.

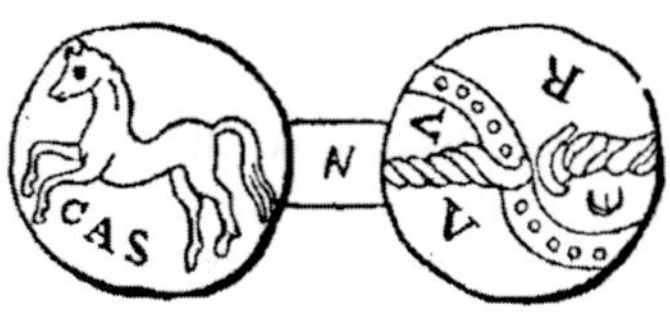

FIG. 71D.—Cassi (Kassi) coin of pre-Roman Ancient Britons, with *Cas* legend and Sun-Horse. (After Poste. For details see WPOB. 48.)

XXV

Summary of the Discoveries on the Originators, Chief Propagators and Developers of the World's Civilization in Personalities, History, Achievements and Race from the Rise of Civilization

Here it is desirable to summarize very briefly the more outstanding of the fundamentally important historical discoveries which have been elicited and established in the foregoing chapters by our new keys, before proceeding to estimate for the first time by our newly-found concrete data the true Chronology of the Ancient World and its Ancient Local Civilizations from the Kassi dynastic period, within modern classic history, continuously back to the epoch of the Rise of Civilization.

In brief, we have found by our new keys in the official Indian Chronicles and King-Lists of the Early Aryans, confirmed and established by the testimony of Sumerian and Babylonian history and a vast mass of contemporary inscriptions and documentary records of the Sumerians and Babylonians and Ancient Egyptians themselves that :

I. The " Sumerian " kings from the first king of the First Sumerian Dynasty at the Rise of Civilization continuously downwards to and including the Kassi Dynasty in the later Babylonian period are identical in name, chronological order and achievements with the Early Aryan kings from the first king of the First Aryan Dynasty at the Rise of Civilization continuously downwards to the classic historical period of modern times.

II. The " Sumerian " ruling people were of the same racial physical type, with the same culture, traditions, religion, writing and language as the Early Aryans, who were of the Aryan, Gothic or Nordic race, and they were identical with the leading stock of the latter. And the Early Sumerian kings sometimes called themselves in their monuments in Mesopotamia and in their Indus Colony *Gut* or *Got;* whilst one of the leading Sumerian dynasties in Mesopotamia called themselves *Guti, Goti* or "Goths."

III. The "Sumerian" stock of this Aryan, Gothic or Nordic race first appears in "Sumerian" history in Cappadocia in Asia Minor, at or near Pteria, the old imperial capital of the Khatti or "Hittites" or "White Syrians"; and here also is located by the traditional epics of the Nordics, the Eddas, the capital of the first traditional Gothic king and the founder of Civilization. These Early Aryans or Nordics, who suddenly appear there with a fully fledged Civilization, were presumably immigrants from the immemorial Gothic Land in South-eastern Europe, from the Danube to the Euxine or Black Sea and the Caucasus up to the Caspian region. And I have found that the owners' marks inscribed on prehistoric pottery in the Danube Valley in the 3rd to 4th milleniums B.C., are written in Sumerian script, as demonstrated in Plates XXIV and XXV and App. XIII.

IV. The first "Sumerian" or Aryan king, a Sun-worshipper, and traditionally pictured in Gothic dress, was the historical original of the legendary culture hero, afterwards canonized or deified, and variously styled by his different titles and personal name Thor, Ar-Thur, Dur, In-Dur, Indra, Sagg, or Sig, Zeus, Prometheus, Bil or Bel, St George of Cappadocia, Odinn, Ad or "Adam," who in the Copper Age built in Asia Minor the first city, used "Sumerian" Writing, established Agriculture, monogamous Marriage, improved Fire-Production, Industrial Life and the first Civilization, properly co-called, about 3378 B.C.—all the alleged vastly earlier dates for Civilization and kings before this epoch being merely imaginary speculations, with no foundation whatsoever in fact. And he captured the famous magic Stone-Bowl fetish of the Semitic Chaldean Serpent-worshippers of "The Garden of Eden" at Carchemish on the Upper Euphrates, who opposed his great uplifting Reformation of Mankind, which famous trophy bowl still exists, with its contemporary historical and genealogical inscription of his great-grandson as "Udu's Bowl," now disclosed as the original "Holy Grail" of the original King Arthur.

V. The Second "Sumerian" or Aryan king, the son and successor of the first, was the historical original of the legendary culture hero, variously styled by his different titles and personal name, Bakus (Bacchus or Dionysos), Nimrod, Ayus, Marduk, St Michael, Tascio (of the Ancient pre-Roman Briton coins and prehistoric Briton inscriptions), Gan or Conn, Sir Gawain or "Cain." Greatly extending agriculture and inventing the plough, he vastly increased the food-supply of the ancient world and made industrial town-life possible, so that he was latterly deified as Bacchus and Tascio by grateful humanity. He descended from Cappadocia into Mesopotamia, in the thirteenth year of his reign in Cappadocia, and established there the first Mesopotamian kingdom and empire over the aboriginal Chaldee "black-headed people," with his chief capitals at Kish and Enoch (Erech), which he built; and his advent there, along with his aristocratic ruling Aryan or Gothic clan, forms "The advent of the Sumerians" of modern writers.

VI. The "Sumerian" stock of these ruling Aryans, already in "The Copper Age" or "The Bronze Age," if not to some extent in "The Iron Age" (as their king at least used a weapon made of meteoric Iron) in their Mesopotamian empire continued rapidly developing Civilization, and became adventurous seamen on the Persian Gulf. The fifteenth king or emperor formed the First (Aryan) Phœnician Dynasty of merchant-princes who established thriving colonies in Elam and the Indus Valley and first spread Civilization there.

VII. The official title of *Gut* or *Got* used by most of these kings and their governors, as also the title used by their governors of *Khatti-Sig* or "Prince or Priest-king of the *Khatti*," indicates their Khatti, "Catti" or "Hitt-ite" or Gothic Nordic race, as rulers.

VIII. The thirty-seventh Sumerian king and emperor, Guni or Sa-Guni or "Sargon"-the-Great, began introducing occasional Semitic words of his Chaldee subjects into official inscriptions, and extended his empire westwards to the Mediterranean and Egypt, where he and his father and grandfather before him were Predynastic Pharaohs as well as emperors at the same time in Mesopotamia, and introduced Civilization (Aryan Civilization) into Egypt, with the Sumerian Langauge and Writing (Sumerian pictograph hieroglyphs), and Sargon's ships reached the Tin-mines "beyond the Western Sea," or Mediterranean, presumably in Cornwall.

IX. His son, Menes, was identical with the emperor Manis Tussu of Mesopotamia and Minos of Crete, and founded the First Dynasty of Egypt about 2704 B.C.—all the alleged earlier dates for Menes and his dynasty are unhistorical, and the culture of his dynasty is in keeping with this newly-found date.

X. The division of Civilization into Western and Eastern began with the separation of Egypt and the Mediterranean from the Mesopotamian empire on the fall of Sargon's dynasty, the Mesopotamian empire tending to adopt more and more Chaldean Oriental traits, whilst the Gothic stock left in Asia Minor and Egypt and Syria-Phœnicia retained generally the "Western" features of Civilization, and so diffused it.

XI. The "Sumerians," so far from having died out and become totally extinct in race, civilization and language with the downfall of the Ur Dynasty about 2233 B.C., as is dogmatically asserted by all Assyriologists, on the contrary, continued to be the sole imperial rulers in Mesopotamia throughout all the subsequent dynasties down to and inclusive of the Kassi Dynasty. The reason why these dynasties do not call themselves "Sumerian" is merely the same as with the other so-called "Sumerian" dynasties, namely, that "Sumerian" as an ethnic title does not exist, and was merely fabricated by modern Assyriologists and thrust upon these Aryan people, who never once used it for themselves. As a fact, these so-called "Sumerians" are found to have continued down to the classic period to be the ruling aristocratic caste in all the known civilized states in the world. And they emerge in the classic European period somewhat mixed with local tribal elements under the different local titles of the various widely-scattered Aryan colonial city-states or nations as: Egyptians, Hittites, Cilicians, Ionians, Trojans, Carians and Phœnicians, Cretans, Dorians, Achaians and Athenians, Thracians, Tuscans and Lâtiums, patrician Romans, Venetians, Goths, Jutes, Swedes, Norse, Danes, Angles, Chatti and Catlauni Germans, Saxons, Royal Scyths, Medes and (Ancient) Persians, Parthians, Indo-Aryans (a modern title, especially appropriate for the Kshattri and Brahman castes), Bretons, Britons, etc. And the "Sumerian" Civilization, Language and Writing are shown to be the basis of the civilization language and writing of those tribes and nationalities, as well as those of their descendants at the present day.

XII. The "Sumerian" Language is demonstrated to be the parent of the whole family of Aryan or Indo-European Languages, ancient and modern, and especially of the English Language.

XIII. The Aryans are disclosed as the originators and chief developers and propagators of the World's Civilization; and Civilization may thus be broadly termed "Aryanization."

XIV. No Semitic dynasty whatever is found to have existed in Mesopotamia (nor so far as known to history elsewhere) down to the end of the Kassi Dynasty.

XV. The new historical evidence also bridges over the hitherto unmeasured great chronological gap which has separated the middle Sumerian period from the Babylonian, and thus now enables us for the first time to recover the real Chronology of the "Sumerian" period with approximately exact dates for the individual kings continuously back to the first king of the First "Sumerian" or Aryan Dynasty at the Rise of Civilization, as detailed in the next chapter.

XXVI

Chronology of the "Sumerian," Aryan or Nordic Kings Recovered from the First Dynasty at the Rise of Civilization.

Disclosing the Dates from Odin Thor, the original King Ar-Thur or St George or King "Adam," c. 3378 B.C., *with Regnal Years down to Classic Period and the Date of Menes as c.* 2704 B.C.

The present-day notoriously chaotic condition of the Chronology of the Early Sumerians and of Early Mesopotamia and of the Ancient Civilizations generally is seen to be owing to the want hitherto of all knowledge of the historical identity of the first Sumerian king and his traditional name and titles and approximate date, and the want of any complete continuous list of the ancient Sumerian kings from the first king down to the Babylonian period connecting with our modern era. And in the absence of these data there has been the confusion introduced by the acceptance of the semi-mythic and legendary prefixed dynasties fabricated by later priests and arbitrarily altered, grossly in the case of the prefixed Isin dynasties, in different ways by different writers, each to suit their own different archæological and other theories and computations.

Total Failure of All Previous Attempts at Estimating the Chronology of the Early Sumerian & Egyptian Periods from Babylonian & Egyptian King-Lists, and by Archæology & Astronomy.

All previous attempts at solving the great outstanding problem of the Chronology of the Early Sumerians, now demonstrated to be the Early Aryans, on which depends the real dates for all the Ancient World Civilizations, have up till now (December 1928) proved abortive.

All the hitherto known legendary and traditional Babylonian chronological lists purporting to give a continuous line of the kings from the first dynasty of the civilized period down to the modern periods, which have been used as a basis for the attempted recovery of dated Ancient History, have been compiled by late Oriental priests, a class admittedly unhistorically minded. They make the earliest kings to be generations of gods and demi-gods and legendary heroes, with fabulously vast superhuman ages and reigns, and in regard to none of these could any remains ever be found. This inveterate defect exists in the lists hitherto used for Mesopotamia, namely those of Berosos and the Isin priests, and in respect of Egypt in Manetho's lists. Added to this is the further defect that dynasties purporting to be successive were in reality sometimes more or less contemporary. And the archæological and palæographic arguments employed by historians to control the vagaries of their texts are in themselves necessarily vaguely relative and incapable of fixing any dates with any approach to historical precision. The astronomical data also for Mesopotamia, while fixing with comparative exactitude the end of the First Babylonian Dynasty still left the latter dynasty separated by gaps at either end of unmeasured width, from the Second and Third Babylonian Dynasties below, and from the Sumerian of Ur-Isin above, and so failed to connect with the Early Sumerian period and recover the earlier Sumerian Chronology.

In illustration of the conflicting chronological inferences which result from the archæological and palæographic arguments—not to mention the discrepancy of 2246 years between the estimates for the date of Menes by the two different schools of present-day Egyptologists, each claiming support by an appeal largely to archæological arguments, and the date of 4000 B.C. for Minos of Crete arrived at also by the same means—numerous instances of their misleading results may be found in regard to Mesopotamian chronology in Radau's *Early Babylonian History* of 1900. Thus on archæological and palæographic grounds Manis-Tusu, before it was known that he was the son of Sargon I, was placed very considerably earlier than the latter.[1] Similarly, to come down

[1] RB. 28.

to present-day beliefs, Udu, now disclosed to be the fourth king, is placed after the thirty-eighth king of the "post-diluvians" in the very latest text-book [1] by these two classes of arguments. Similarly the Sumerian king Medi, No. 20 in our list (whom by the way they call Semitic and Semitize his name into "Me-silim") is placed conjecturally c. 3638 B.C., whilst the first and earlier king of his dynasty (No. 15 in our list) is placed arbitrarily several centuries later at c. 3100 B.C.[2] Such misplacements show how very inexact and misleading these two classes of arguments may prove in estimating chronology.

This confused condition of early Mesopotamian chronology has recently become acutely intensified by the unscientific and credulous acceptance by Assyriologists of the long string of purported dynasties, with absurdly fabulous ages, which the superstitious and ill-informed later Isin priests prefixed to the First Dynasty of the Kish Chronicle, which latter we have demonstrated to be the first of all Sumerian dynasties and the first of all historical dynasties in the Ancient World. As we have already in Chapter VII exposed the fictitious character of all this prefixed Isin chronology, with its prefixed dynasties purporting to extend for geological (241,200 years) ages "before the Flood," and downwards for some 35,000 years after "the Flood," with reigns of individual kings for 43,200 to 1500 years for each king—an average of several centuries for each postdiluvian king, none of whom could be traced,[3] and all of them before the First Dynasty of the Kish Chronicle, it would be a mere waste of our time to refer further to it. And yet it is made the basis of the present-day Early pre-Sargonic Mesopotamian Chronology of Assyriologists!

Failure of Traditional Babylonian "Synchronisms" to solve the Problem of Sumerian Chronology

The Babylonian "Synchronistic Tables," compiled by later Babylonian and Assyrian scribes, relate merely to kings and dynasties subsequent to about 1400 B.C., and do

[1] CAH. 1924, I, 667. [2] *Ib.*, 668.

[3] The fictitious chronology and misplacement of "Mesannipada" has been explained in Chapter VII.

not connect with the Early and Middle Sumerian periods at all.

The chief Babylonian traditional "Synchronism," which has been used in the endeavour to fix a date in the earlier period, is that which relates to Sargon's dynasty. It is an isolated reference given solely by the last king of Babylon, Nabonidus, who reigned 555-538 B.C., and nowhere else. In repairing the Sun-temple at Sippara, this king recorded on a clay cylinder, now preserved in the British Museum,[1] that he found in the foundations the foundation-tablet of "Narām Sin, the son of Shar-Gena," which that founder had deposited there "3200 years previously." Now as Narām Sin was the grandson of Sargon I (the "Shar Gena" of King Nabonidus' Babylonian record) it was hoped that this figure would fix the date of the latter. But Nabonidus does not specify either his own regnal year in which he made the discovery nor the regnal year in which Narām Sin deposited the tablet in his long reign of 56 years, thus leaving an uncertainty of 56 + 18, or 74 years, even supposing that his figure of 3200 years was correct; though it is obviously a mere rough estimate.

Yet, despite these uncertainties it was arbitrarily assumed that the date of Narām Sin was "approximately 3750 B.C." and that of his grandfather Sargon "3800 B.C."; [2] and mainly on the basis of these early dates the beginning of Sumerian history has been set back as far as 5000 B.C. and even 10,000 B.C.

It was then found, however, that such an early date for Sargon at about 3800 B.C., and based on an isolated statement by the last Babylonian king and a Semite, and unsupported by any other reference in either early or late Babylonian texts, was entirely incompatible with all the known archæological facts which had been elicited regarding the short interval of time which separated the well-known Sumerian king Gudia from Sargon's dynasty. The buildings, culture, art and form of writing and shape of the clay tablets of Gudia are so very similar to those of Sargon's dynasty

[1] CIWA. V. pl. 64, 2, 2, ll. 54-65. For a literal translation of this inscription, see RB. 5.

[2] KHS. 1920, 60. Narām Sin was then believed to be the "son" of Sargon.

as to show that the two ages followed each other without any considerable break. The date of Gudia had become relatively fixed at "about 2450 B.C.," not only by his art, business documents, etc., but also by local synchronisms with the equally well-known Ur Dynasty, including Dungi, and the actual buildings of Gudia and Dungi were found to be almost directly on the top of the foundations of Sargon's dynasty, with practically no intervening stratum separating them. It was therefore supposed that Nabonidus had made a mistake of 1000 years in his inscription, and that the date of Sargon was "about 2800 B.C." This date, thus arbitrarily arrived at, is nevertheless that which is now generally adopted as the date of Sargon, and it has been further arbitrarily extended to "circa 2872 B.C." in the latest text-book [1]—a figure which by its semblance of exactitude misleads historians and other readers into believing that Sargon's date has been definitely ascertained, whereas it merely rests, as we have seen, on a chain of more or less doubtful suppositions of the most vague and indefinite kind. Yet it is upon this admittedly concocted and unsolid basis that all the dates of the Sumerian period above and below Sargon's epoch have hitherto been placed.

New Solid Basis for the Chronology of the Sumerians or Early Aryan Period, from First Sumerian Dynasty downwards, Discovered by the Official Indo-Aryan King-Lists

The chief obstacle hitherto encountered in all the attempts at solving the problem of Sumerian Chronology and at placing that chronology on a solid scientific basis, has been the want of any complete chronological list of the Sumerian kings from the First Sumerian Dynasty continuously down to the Babylonian dynastic period which connects with our modern era; and apart from the non-recognition of that First Dynasty, not even the name of the first king of the First Sumerian Dynasty has hitherto been known, through misreading of its polyphonous writing.

This fundamental want is now supplied by our official King-Lists of the Early Aryans which have been uniquely

[1] CAH. I, 669.

preserved in the Indian Epic Chronicles by the eastern branch of the Aryans, and the marvellous authenticity of which has been fully demonstrated in the preceding chapters, which also establish the identity of the Sumerians with the Early Aryans. And these king-lists, it was seen, are not compilations by priests, but are the official copies of the original official records of the old archives scrupulously preserved by the ruling kingly caste and jealously treasured as sacred heirlooms by their royal Indian descendants.

These uniquely complete Indian copies of the king-lists by preserving for us the traditional forms of the names of the Aryan or Sumerian kings in due chronological order, from the first king of the First Sumerian Dynasty continuously downwards to the modern period, and bridging over all the gaps left in the Kish Chronicle and its supplementary Nippur and Isin Chronicles and the late Babylonian dynastic king-lists, enable us for the first time to reconstruct *a complete dated chronology* of the Sumerian period on a solid basis, by means of the regnal years for individual kings and dynasties preserved in the Kish Chronicle and its supplements.

The Indian lists themselves preserve no *dated* chronology whatsoever, as the Indian scribes and Brahmans have always been notoriously lacking in the historical sense, presumably because in their dreamy Oriental fatalism in India the passage of time was of little consequence to them. The unique value of the Indian King-Lists consists in their scrupulous preservation of the complete official lists of the kings' names in their traditional forms, and in the strict chronological order of their succession, by which they record for us the traditional forms of the names of the Sumerian kings, and by bridging the gaps left in the Kish and Babylonian lists complete the chronology of the latter for the first time.

Authenticity of the Dated Chronology of the Kish Chronicle & its Supplements

The authenticity of the years of reign of kings and dynasties preserved in the Kish Chronicle and its Nippur, Isin and Babylonian supplements is evidenced by their recorded years being always found to be strictly in agreement with those recorded in the contemporary monuments of the respective kings, wherever the latter have been found available for testing. The regnal and dynastic years of the Kish Chronicle and its supplements were presumably copied from the original contemporary records, or from the official copies, of each of the dynasties, from the First Dynasty downwards. For the Sumerians are found to have been an essentially scientific people, and had always since their emergence the historical sense highly developed; and they were already familiar with writing very many centuries before the founding of their First Dynasty of Kings. This is evident from the form of the writing in the contemporary inscription of that First Dynasty (Udu's Bowl), in which the pictographs are already reduced to conventionalized diagrams, showing very long practice in their picture-writing, which must have been in vogue for many centuries before the epoch of their First Dynasty. And one of the most striking traits of the Sumerians from their earliest known period is their remarkably developed historical sense, manifested by their free recording of genealogies, and their profuse use of dated and attested business documents, contract tablets, etc.—as they were great traders—and their practice of recording the names of the kings in the foundations and walls of their buildings, and even on the individual bricks; and their ancestor-worship led them to preserve especially the names of their earliest kings of their First Dynasty.

The Sumerian Time-Reckoning by Years

Time-reckoning by years must have been early prevalent amongst the Sumerians, and very long before the foundation of their First Dynasty of Kings. The Sumerians were the most advanced Sun-worshippers and were the first systematic agriculturists, for whom a yearly system of reckoning was indispensable. They are admitted to have evolved the system of the calendar year of 360 days, which was borrowed by the Ancient Egyptians,[1] divided into three seasons of four months each, thus forming twelve calendar months, with the expedient of adjusting it to the solar year by intercalary additions of a month at the end of a specified number

[1] F. Hömmel, ERE. 3, 73.

of years, which the Egyptians modified to an annual addition of five days, thus making the year 365 days.

Full years are employed in the Kish Chronicle for recording the regnal years of the kings and dynasties. And the scientific precision of these Sumerian records is seen in their giving not merely the regnal years for each individual king in each dynasty and his relationship to the preceding king, if any, with the name of his capital city ; but they also give at the end of each dynasty the total number of years for each dynasty. They are in fact models of terse, scientific, historical chronology for the periods they cover (see, for example, Kish Chronicle, pp. 59 f.).

Materials from which the Dated Chronology of the Sumerian Period is Recovered & Reconstructed

The materials from which we are now enabled to recover and reconstruct the *dated* Chronology of the Sumerian Period back to the First Sumerian Dynasty are (*a*) the complete unbroken List of the Sumerian kings from the First Sumerian or Early Aryan Dynasty on the Rise of Civilization continuously down to the modern period which has been recovered by our Indian key-lists ; (*b*) the regnal years for each king and dynasty preserved in the Kish Chronicle and its supplements ; and (*c*) a fixed date in the later or Babylonian period which connects with the anterior and unbroken Sumerian period above and with our modern Christian era below.

From these materials the reconstruction of a complete *dated* Chronology of the Sumerian Period back to the first king of the First Sumerian Dynasty now becomes a mere matter of arithmetical calculation by " dead-reckoning " from the fixed point below.

Fixed Date of First Babylonian Dynasty by Astronomical Computation

This fixed date below from which our reckonings are now made is that of the Foundation of the First Babylonian Dynasty. Previously, this date was approximately estimated variously by complicated calculations from various different sources, from the " Babylonian Dynastic Chronicles," "Babylonian List of Kings," several local synchronisms, the "Synchronous History" of about 1400 B.C. to 800 B.C., and controlled by Ptolemy's Canon from 747 B.C. down to the last Babylonian king Nabonidus, and by the contemporary monumental records of many of the kings of those later dynasties themselves.

Now, however, the date of the Foundation of the First Babylonian Dynasty has lately been definitely fixed by astronomical data and calculations with precision. The astronomical observations which now fortunately fix for us this date are an admirably exact series made at Babylon on the morning and evening disappearances of the planet Venus, recorded by the orders of Ammi-"Zadugga," the tenth king of this dynasty, for the twenty-one years of his reign. Of these observations, the most critical of all for the exact fixation of the date, are those taken in the sixth year of his reign. The original calculations made by Father Kugler, S.J., who was the first to recognize the unique importance of these observations for dating purposes for this king and his dynasty, have now been revised by other astronomical experts, Schoch and others, with better values for the apparent acceleration of the Sun and Moon in relation to the Gregorian calendar. The results of these revised calculations have been published,[1] and show that the date of the Foundation of the First Babylonian Dynasty, which satisfies alike astronomy, the Babylonian seasonal calendar and history, is the year 2105 B.C., with a possible alternative of 2113 B.C., being one eight-year period of Venus;[2] but that the former date is the more probable. In any case, it is stated that the actual date must be either the one or the other, I have therefore adopted in our reckonings the former date, namely the year 2105 B.C., as the fixed date for the Foundation of the First Babylonian Dynasty, though it must be remembered that the actual date may possibly be eight years earlier.

[1] F. T. Dangin, RA. 1927, 181 f.

[2] *Ib.* These dates were calculated by Schoch, who, however, abandoned them, presumably under the influence of the school which tends to further reduce the date of this Babylonian Dynasty. But these dates are shown by Dangin to be the only ones which satisfy the calendar references of history.

Dated Chronology of the Sumerian or Early Aryan Kings, from the First King at Rise of Civilization to the Kassi Dynasty, c. 3378 b.c. to 1200 b.c.

With this fixed date for the Foundation of the First Babylonian Dynasty, along with our recovery of the other two classes of fundamental data above cited, it now becomes merely a matter of arithmetical calculation by "dead-reckoning" backwards to recover all the dates of the Sumerian kings and dynasties back to the first Sumerian or Aryan king on the Rise of Civilization. The results of this reconstructed Chronology are shown in the accompanying Table.

The connecting link between the First Babylonian Dynasty and the imperial Sumerian or Aryan main-line list of imperial kings we have already found was the capture of Isin City by "Sin Mubalīt" (the father of Khammu-Rabi), the fifth king of the First Babylonian Dynasty in the seventeenth year of his reign, and who reigned as emperor three years. From this point the imperial line of kings goes continuously back to the first king of the First Sumerian Dynasty. The omission from our Indian key-lists of the imperial line of the name of Sargon's immediate predecessor, the "usurper" Zaggisi, does not in any way affect the other dates, as in addition to the length of his reign being known, we know also the total regnal years for the preceding dynasty, the Second Dynasty of the Kish Chronicle. The exact duration of the overlapping of the First and Second Dynasties of the Kish Chronicle has already been examined and fixed in Chapter IV.

The omission of the individual regnal years for the 27 kings of the Great Gap of the Kish Chronicle and of its supplementary Isin and Nippur Chronicles, namely kings Nos. 10 to 36 in the main-line list, does not in any way affect the exactitude of the dating of the kings above and below this gap, because the total duration of this gap is definitely specified as 430 years. The Ur Dynasty in the Isin Chronicle gives King Dungi a reign of only 46 years, but his own date-years in his monuments and business documents specify 58 years of reign, which is the figure here adopted.

Dated Chronological List of Sumerian or Early Aryan Kings from Rise of Civilization to Kassi Dynasty, c. 1200 B.C.

(The years of Reign are within brackets)

Date B.C. (approximate).	Sumerian Names in King Lists and Monuments.	Dynasty.	Indian List Names.	No.
3378–3349	Ukusi of Ukhu City or Udu, Uduin, or Udin, Indar, Induru, Dur, Pur Sakh, Sagaga, Zagg, Gaur or Adar (30)	1st Dynasty	Ikshvāku or Indra or Sakko or Purū (-ravas)	1
3348–3337	Azag Ama Basam or Bakus, Tasia Mukhla, Gin, Gan or Kan (12)	—	Āyus, Ama-Basu or Bikukshi-Nimi	2
3336–3273	Azag Bakus or Gan at Unuk, Enoch or Erech City (64)	2nd Dynasty	(As above)	
3272–3248	Naksha, Enuzu, Anenzu, Unnusha, In, Enu (25)	—	Nahusha, Anenas or Janak	3
3247–3242	Udu, Uduk (6)	—	Udā-vasu, Yadu, Yayati, ((?) Puru)	4
3241–3312	Zimugun, Dumuzi (30)	—	Janamejaya or Jina	5
3211–3206	Uziwitar (6)	—	Vishtara or Wishtara	6
3205–3195	Mutin Ugun (11)	—	Matinara	7
3194–3184	Imuashshu or Pishmana (11)	—	Vishamsu or Tamsu	8
3183–3181	Naili (or Nandu) Iaxa Sumaddi or Duag (3)	—	Anila, (?) Ucchaya, Dushyanta or (?) Sun-anta	9
3180– (or 27) Kings.	Baratutu, Bardū, Barti Pirtu	—	Burata, Brihad, Prithu	10
	Gaudumu or Dūdumunu	—	Gautama, Dhundhumara	11
	Dutu-Gindara	—	Dwat, Candra-ashva	12
	Azag, or Ashita-ab	—	Aja-midha or Siteshu	13
	Ishzax or Gishax Gamesh	—	Chaxus, Riksha, Rucaka or Ruk-meshu	14
	Uruash-Khād, Urusag-Khaddu Bara-ma'hasha or Arwasag ((?) 30)	Uruash's Dyn. of " Panch "	Haryashva or Barmyashva	15
	Madgal, A-Madgal Mukh	—	Mudgala or Mogallo	16
	Bi(d)ashnadi, Bi(d)sar, Biugun or Biguaxu	—	Badhryashva, Pasenadi or B'ujyu	17

The Great Gap of 430 years with 26	Enun-nad Enash-nadi		—	Yuvanashwa	18
	Tarsi (Ene- or " divine ") or Dixxi (Di- or " divine ")		—	Dāsa (Divo- or " divine ") or Trasa-Dasyu I	19
	Medi or Meti		—	Mettiyo or Mitrayu	20
	Kiuga, Mūkuda		—	Cyavana or Muckunda	21
	Tarsi, Dix-saax or (?) Shu-Dix		—	Su-Dāsa, Dussaha or Trasa Dasyu II	22
	Tizama		—	Somaka, Sambhuta	23
	[(?) Anda]		—	Jantu	23a
	Rumau or Pashipadda (" Mesanni-padda ")		—	Prishada or Suvarna Roman	24
	Uruduki Raman Duruashi-padda or Rutasa Rāma (" Anni-padda ")		—	Drupada I, Hrashva Roman or Rohida-ashva	25
	(?) Eama . . .		—	Vyoman, Vasumanas	26
	. . . Biama		—	Jīmūta	27
	(?) Paunukha (" ? Meshkalamdug ")		—	Bhanu or Ban-kirti	28
	(Illegible)		—	Satya-brata	29
	"		—	Harish-candra II	30
	"		—	Harita or Rohit-ashwa II	31
	Gungun, Kingubi-Dudu		—	Cuncu or Dhundu	32
	Mama-gal		—	Vijaya	33
	Kalbu- (?) ru		—	B'aruka or Ruruki	34
	Tuke		—	Vri-Taka or Dhri-Taka	35
–2751	Bara-Gina, Puru-gin, Pardui-Bazum or Urudu-Gina, or Uruka-Gina		—	Pra-Cinvat, B'arad-Vaja, Bāhu or Bahuka or Puru II	36
2750–2726	Zaggisi or Saggisi	(25)	" Erech Dyn."	—	36a
2725–2671	Guni, Shar-Guni " Sargon "	(55)	" Sargon's " Dyn.	Kuni Sha-Kuni or Sagara	37
2670–2656	Mūsh (Uru-)	(15 or 9)	—	—	37a
2655–2641	Manis-Tissu (in Mesop.)	(15)	—	Asa-Manja, Manasyu	38
2640–2585	Narām-Anenzu (or " Sin ") or Narām-ba	(56 or 38)	—	Anjana, Ansu-mat or Karamba	39
2584–2561	Shar-Gani Shar-Ri or Dilipa	(24)	—	Kunti-jit Khatwanga Dilīpa	40
2560–2558	Nigigi, Imi, Nanum, Iama (in inter-regnum) four kings	(3)	—	Bhagī-ratha	
2557–2537	Dudu	(21)	—	Dhundu	41

Date B.C. (approximate).	Sumerian Names in King-Lists and Monuments.	Dynasty.	Indian List Names.	No.
2536–2522	Shûdur-kib (15)	—	Suhotra II, Shruta Shrutâyus	42
2521–2519	Uru-Nigin (3)	2ND ERECH DYN.	Nabhin, Nābhāga	43
2518–2513	Urish-Ginar (6)	—	Harish-Candra or (?) Ambarisha	44
2512–2507	Tardu (or Kudda) (6)	—	((?) Rathi *Tara* "g.g. son" of Ambarûshu)	44a
2506–2502	Ba-Sha-nini (or -ama) (5)	—	Sindhu-dhipa, Sanjaya	45
2501–2494	Uru-ash (or -an)-uta (6)	—	—	
2493–2452	Guti occupation without kings (44 or 42)	GUTI DYN.	[KUSHA DYN.] Ayutâyus (or ? Duthaliyās, k. of Khatti)	46
2451–2449	Muruta (3)	—	[Mûrtaya] Ritu-parna	47
2448–2443	In Kishu or Gishu (6)	—	[Kusha]	
2442–2437	Irilla Tax [or Warla Gaba] (6)	—	—	
2436–2431	Dug-me or Ug-me (6)	—	—	
2430–2425	Eamamesh or Kashushamama (6)	—	[Kushâmba] Sarva-Kāma	48
2424–2420	Inima Bakies, Baeśśes, Bakus or Basam (5)	—	[Basu II or (?) Bhaji]	
2419–2414	Iziaush (6)	—	—	
2413–2399	Iārla Tax or Dax (15)	—	Su Dâsa II	49
2398–2396	Ibate (3)	—	—	
2395–2393	Iārla ((?) Gash) or Kashushamama (?) 2nd term) (3)	—	[Kushâmba (2nd term)]	
2392– —	Basium, Basam or Bakus (2nd term)	—	[Basu II or Bhaji (2nd term)]	
2391–2389	. . . Nikîn (or Nigin) (3)	—	—	
2388–2387	[Lasi]-rubûm or La-Sirab (2)	—	((?) Sarva-bhauma)	
2386–2385	Irarum (2)	—	—	
2384– —	Darranûm (1)	—	—	
2383–2382	Khāblum or Khab-Kalamu (2)	—	Kalmâshu-pāda	50
2381–2375	Suratāsh Sin or Sarati Gubi Sin (7)	—	(Sruta, Upa-Gupta)	
2374–2368	Iārla *Gu*(ash)*da* (? Gudia) (7)	—	[Gâdhi]	
2367–2361	[En-Ridi-Pizir] Pisha Ruddu (7)	—	[Vishva-Ratha, s. of Gâdhi]	
2360– —	[Tiri]-gan (40 days)	—	[Trishanku, contemp. of above]	
2360–2353	Ashukhamukh or Utukhe-gal (7½)	3RD ERECH DYN.	Ashmaka	51

2352–2335	Uruash-Zikum	(18)	UR DYN.	[URU BRANCH DYN. Uru-Riūka] **Mūlaka**	52
2334–2277	Dungi or Duk-gin (Shamu-)	(58)	—	[Dagni (Jama-)]	
2276–2268	Purash-Sin (" Bur-Sin ")	(9)	—	[Parashu-Rāma and his massacre] Dasha ratha or (?)	
2267–2259	Suash-Sin (" Gimil Sin ")	(9)	—	[Sushena] Shata-ratha	53
2258–2233	Il-Ibil-Sin	(26)	—	Il-Ibila or Ilivila	54
2232–2200	Ishbi-Ashurra	(33)	ISIN DYN.	Vishva-saha	55
2199–2190	Katnini-Kat (or Shu-lilishu)	(10)	—	Khatvanga or Dilīpa	56
2189–2169	Itiash-Dakhu	(21)	—	Dirgha-bahu	57
2163–2149	Ishshibash-Dakhu	(20)	—	Raghu	58
2148–2138	Libiash Ugun	(11)	—	Aja	59
2137–2110	Dashashi-urash, Muru	(28)	—	Dasha-ratha	60
2109–2089	Amar-Sin (" Bur-Sin II ")	(21)	—	Rāma (-Chandra)	61
2088–2084	Libi (Insakh)	(5)	—	Lava and Kusha	62
2083–2076	(Ash-)urra Iwiti	(8)	—	—	
2075–2052	Insakh-bani	(24)	—	Atithi or Suhotra IV	63
2051– —	Zāmbi (3), Tenirpisha (4), Urdukuga (4), Sin Mapish (11)		—	Nishadha	64
— –2007	Damiq-ilushu	(23)	—	Nala	65
2023–2004	Anuha-Mubalit (" Sin Muballit " (20), of which four as emperor)		1ST BABYLON DYN. as Emperors	Nabha or Nabhas	66
2003–1961	Khammu-Rabi or " Great Lotus "	(43)	—	Pundarīka or " Great Lotus "	67
1960–1923	Sāmsui-Uduna	(38)	—	Kshema-Dhanvan	68
1922–1895	Abieshu'a	(28)	—	Devānīka	69
1894–1858	Ammi-Satana (or -Ditana)	(37)	—	Ruru or (?) Suto-rusta	70
1857–1837	Ammi-Saraga or -Saduga)	(21)	—	Ahi-nagu	71
1836–1806	Sāmsu-Satana	(31)	—	Sudhanvan or Pariyatra	72
1805–1791	Saharki-Bal	(15)	SEA-LAND DYN.	Sahasra Bala or Bala (with separate line)	73
1790–1775	Xatal (" Gandash ")	(16)	KASSI DYN.	Sthala or Gaya	74
1774–1753	Agu-um	(22)	—	Auka or Uktha	75
1752–1745	Bizuiru (" Kashtiliash ")	(8)	—	Vajra-nābha	76
1744–1737	Ushigu	(8)	—	Shankha	77
1736– —	Abisuttash		—	Ab'yutthit-ashva or Dhyushit-ashva	78

Regarding the Babylonian Dynasties we have seen that the Second Babylonian Dynasty contained one king of the contemporary Sea-land Dynasty who held imperial rule, namely, the fourth king of that dynasty, therefore the date for the beginning of the Kassi Dynasty is 1790 B.C. The new date for Menes is more conveniently examined after our Table has been studied.

Here it is to be remembered that as different versions of the Nippur and Isin Chronicle tablets give slight variations in the total length of reign of Narām Sin and some others and of the total reign of the Guti Dynasty, although we have adopted the generally accepted versions in such cases, the results are only exact approximately to within a few years. But in this regard it will be remembered that even so relatively recent an event as the birth of Christ has not yet been definitely fixed, and its estimate ranges from 6 B.C. to 0 A.D. It is also to be noted that the uneven date for the accession to the throne of the Sumerian-Aryan or Gothic king Odin Thor, Ar-Thur, or St George, is necessarily determined by the process of dead-reckoning of regnal years from below upwards.

From the Kassi Dynasty (which I have not detailed in the Table beyond the fifth king for the reasons stated above) the chronological connections downwards are fixed with comparative exactness through their contemporary inscriptions and synchronisms, and the later Babylonian and Assyrian King-Lists and "Synchronous Tables" and the Ptolemaic Code, down to the Persian occupation or so-called 27th Dynasty in 527 B.C., and onwards through Alexander's empire to the Ptolemaic period of 305-50 B.C. and through this to our Christian era.

Date of the First "Sumerian," Aryan or Gothic King Odin Thor, Her Thor or Ar-Thur, St George of Cappadocia, Indara, Sagg or Zax or Pur or Bur, Ia or Jah, Adar or Ada or "Adam," c. 3378 B.C.

By this Table we now gain at last the fixed date for the greatest of all kings and culture heroes, the first traditional civilized king in the Ancient World at the Rise of Civilization, the immortal Aryan, "Sumerian" or Gothic king who first established Civilization and Agriculture and built the first town or city; and he is disclosed as a historical personage, whose inscribed sacred stone-bowl or "holy grail" still exists. His date is seen to be fixed at c. 3378 B.C., with approximate exactitude to within a few years of the actual date.

This unsuspected relatively recent date of 3378 B.C. for the advent of the first civilized king and the first establishment of Civilization, whilst now explaining the surprising "Modernness" of all the Ancient Civilizations from their earliest known period and their essential one-ness in character, at the same time exposes the grossly exaggerated chronology which has been conjecturally thrust upon Civilization, that is Civilization properly so-called, and not the mere primitive culture with which it is so often loosely confounded.

His world-wide immortal fame as the greatest of all culture heroes amongst all civilized peoples, ancient and modern, under either his personal name or one or other of his "Sumerian" titles confirms his identity as the establisher of Civilization. Thus we have seen he was early canonized and latterly deified by grateful mankind. As the greatest man known to the civilized world, he was made the basis of the first conception of God as a king and father, thus making God in the image of Man. And as such, most of the names and titles of God are coined from his human personal name or titles, such as Sagg, Zagg or Zeus, Ia or Jah, Indara or Indra, Asar or Osiris, Bil or Bel, Ilu or Allah, etc. And under his human heroic character we have seen that he is the historical original of King Arthur (thinly disguised and embroidered by Briton-Welsh bards in Christian dress), as St George, the patron saint of England and Cappadocia, as St Andrew, the patron saint of Britons, Scots and Scyths; and his heroic son Gan as Sir Gawain, Nimrod and St Michael. He is also seen to have been the historical original of "Adam," the father of "Cain," in the Hebrew legend of the Garden of Eden, which latter has misrepresented him as "the first created man" and a lowly common ancestor, instead of the first noble man of great creative genius, who first made men of men, the pre-Adamite men; and his glorious tradition of great achievements in effecting

"The Rise of Man" and destroying the degraded Semitic Serpent and Moon-worship with its sanguinary sacrifices, as well as the glorious achievements of his almost equally heroic son Gan, are spitefully mutilated and inverted therein; though it is remarkable how near to the historical fact the Hebrews have preserved his date.

New Date for Menes of Egypt at c. 2704 B.C.–2641 B.C.

The other most critically important date emerging from our Table is the new fixed date for Menes, the founder of the First Dynasty of Egypt. The date of Menes in Egypt, which hitherto has been the most widely disputed of all dates in Ancient History, although one of the most critically important of dates, in that it is the basis for those of the ancient civilizations of the Mediterranean and the West, including Europe, is now recovered for the first time with approximate exactitude by our new historical keys.

Hitherto that date was estimated by accepting the traditional lists of the Egyptian dynasties as given in the surviving mutilated copies of the lists compiled by the late priest Manetho of the Ptolemaic period, which contained the traditional regnal and dynastic years, and purported to be consecutive dynasties. When the lists were compared with other fragmentary ones and with the known reigns of certain kings, the variations were so great that different Egyptologists each made Menes' date widely different, ranging from 5869 B.C. of Champollion to 4400 B.C. or less;[1] and at present the "long-date" school of Egyptologists still places his date "about 5546 B.C." which, with the other dates, give the misleading impression of well-ascertained chronology. On the other hand, the "short date" Egyptologists under Meyer, recognizing the relatively late or developed stage in the culture of Menes and his dynasty, including the use of metals and systematic writing, have dismissed the early chronology of Manetho, and have more or less arbitrarily reduced the date to "about 3300 B.C.," and they support it by astronomical arguments based on some late references to the Sothic cycles—the heliacal

[1] BKI. I, LIV. f.

risings of the Dog-star Sirius or Sothis; although there seems no evidence that the Egyptians ever used the Sothic cycle as an era. But now his real date is fixed at about six centuries still lower than that hypothetical "short date."

Our recovery of the real date of Menes is now made possible by our discovery of the identity of Menes or Manj with the great Mesopotamian emperor Manis Tusu, the son of Sargon, as demonstrated in the previous chapters, through our new Indian keys; and fully confirmed by the actual contemporary inscriptions of Menes himself and his dynasty in their Egyptian records and in their Indus Valley official signets.

The regnal dates of Manis Tusu preserved in the Kish Chronicle and its Isin and Nippur supplements refer only to his emperorship in Mesopotamia, which began, according to those chronicles (see Table, p. 61) fifteen years after the death of his father Sargon, by whom we have found through the Indian Chronicles that he was disinherited for his revolt against his father through his declaration of independence in Egypt; and thus did not immediately succeed the latter on the Mesopotamian throne. In order to ascertain, therefore, the date of Menes' founding of his dynasty in Egypt we have to calculate on the basis of the Egyptian circumstantial tradition that he reigned in Egypt for sixty-two years, and that the last year of his reign as emperor of Mesopotamia was the year of his death. This reckoning yields us from our Table the following date for his founding of the First Dynasty in Egypt thus:

Death of Menes or Manis Tusu	=	2641 B.C.
Reign in Egypt	=	62 years
Date of Founding First Dynasty in Egypt (completed year)	=	2703 B.C.

That is to say, Menes ascended the throne in Egypt in the year 2704 B.C.

And this date of 2704 B.C.–2641 B.C. for Menes is quite in keeping with his culture, which we have seen was that of the Sargonic period, to which he and his dynasty belonged.

This date of 2704 B.C. for the founding of the First Dynasty in Egypt by Menes or Manis Tusu implies that the latter established his independence there in the twenty-second year of the reign of his father Sargon, who commenced to reign in 2725 B.C. (see Table), thus 2725–2703 = twenty-two years. The Indian Epic chronicles emphasize that Prince Asa Manja or Manjas revolted from his father in his early youth. Our figures suggest that the age of Menes when he declared his independence in Egypt against his father was probably about twenty-one, if his father did not marry till he recovered his patrimonial empire. But as we have found that the young Sargon is described as having recovered Kish before he dethroned the Emperor Zaggisi of Erech, he may have been married before the latter event, and thus Menes might be a few years older, say twenty-five years old, when he established his independence in Egypt. This would make Menes, when he died about twenty-one plus sixty-two, or eighty-three years old, or about twenty-five plus sixty-two or eighty-seven years old; and all Egyptian tradition credits Menes with having reached a very old age when he met his tragic death; and the vast works which he performed in the Delta in reclaiming Memphis from the sea imply a very long reign.

It may be objected at first sight by Egyptologists, accustomed to placing the date of Menes so very much earlier, that the new date does not allow sufficient space for the long string of twenty-six dynasties down to the Persian period of 527 B.C. But it is now being recognized that some of these traditional dynasties were not consecutive but more or less contemporary; that the lengths of several dynasties, especially the eleventh, twelfth and the Hyksos dynasties are very vague, and the allowance by Brugsch of an average of thirty years' reign for each king is considerably above a normal average. And as a fact, we have found that the length of reign of the First Dynasty is grossly exaggerated in the lists. The period from the accession of Menes to the last king of this dynasty, Shudur-kib, we have found by the precise and authentic records of Mesopotamia was only 182 years (2703–2522), and with six kings, of whom one reigned less than one year, as opposed to the eight kings with a reign of 253 years, as given in Manetho's lists, that is an excess of dynastic years of no less than seventy-one years for this one dynasty. Such exaggerations are probably inherent in many of the other dynasties; and it may be that some of even the long dynasties may prove to have short individual reigns, like the Guti Dynasty of Mesopotamia, which had twenty kings reigning for only eighty-one years.

In any case, this newly-found date for Menes of 2704 B.C. is obviously the real date, and it is well-established by the mass of new concrete facts and is consistent with the leading facts of contemporary history. And the intervening dynasties between his dynasty and the eighteenth dynasty of c. 1550, with which the more solid dated Egyptian history begins, will doubtless be capable of automatic adjustment within the new limits thus imposed by our discoveries.

Dates of the Intervening Aryan Kings of Imperial Line from First King of First Aryan Dynasty at Rise of Civilization continuously down to the end of the Kassi Dynasty, about 1200 B.C. (1175 B.C.).

All the dates for the individual kings of the imperial or main line of the Sumerians or Early Aryans, from the first king of the First Dynasty continuously down to the end of the Kassi Dynasty, about 1175 B.C., and including the First Dynasty of Egypt, and through Menes for Minos of Crete, follow as a matter of mere calculation by "dead-reckoning" from the official lists of their regnal years as preserved in the Sumerian and Babylonian records.

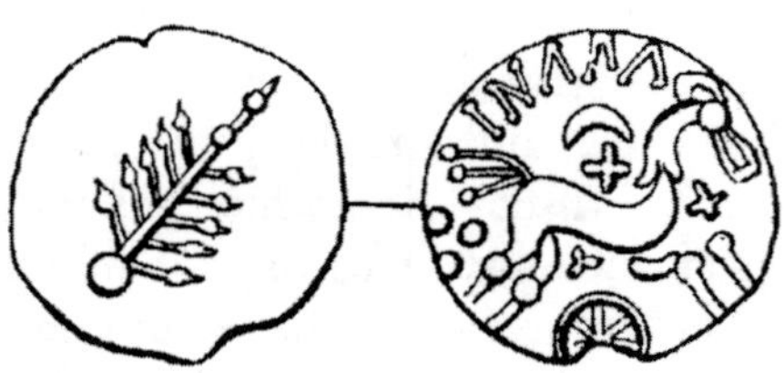

FIG. 71E.—Ancient Briton Catti coin of 2nd cent. B.C. with Sumerian Sun Crosses, Sun-Horse, etc., and legend *INARA*, that is the Gothic Eindri or Andvara or Andrew.
From Evans *Ancient British Coins*, 149.)

XXVII

Historical Effects of the Discoveries

> "*Science is teaching the world that the ultimate court of appeal is Observation and Experiment and* not *Authority.*"—Huxley, *Essays*, 372.

Whilst it is impossible here to discuss adequately the far-reaching historic consequences of the discoveries set forth in the foregoing pages, which are more or less revolutionary of current fundamental theories of established authorities, a few general reflections and references to some of the specially outstanding points seem called for, supplementary to those in the Preface.

Prolific and essentially constructive as these discoveries are, and solving by scientific methods not a few of the long outstanding fundamental vexed questions on human origins, history, chronology, civilization, sociology, eugenics, archæology, ethnology, language, writing, mythology, and religion, the new research at the same time strikingly discloses the difficulties under which History and the Study of Human Origins have laboured, owing to the false theories universally entertained and propagated by scholars.

In consequence of these theories, and of a kind of vested interest in delusion which they have created, the whole field of History and of Antiquarian Research, Eastern and Western, has been overlaid with Prejudice, fixed, dense, and impenetrable; and discoveries which have lain as open secrets upon its surface have had to wait many decades and generations and centuries before they could be realized.

In the main, the errors arose from attributing to mere speculations and generalizations of the intellect a greater finality than they ever can possess. No doubt certain scientific results, those, for example, connected with chemistry and physics, with gravitation and the planetary movements have great fixity and permanence, whilst others in descending series are marked by a steadily lessening durability. Regarded in this light such established theories as those relating to the origin of the Greek, Minoan or Cretan, Semitic and Indian Civilizations, the pre-Roman barbarism of the British, the race, language and culture origins of the Early Dynastic Egyptians and Mesopotamians, and the non-historicity of the Homeric, Vedic, Eddic, Gothic, and Arthurian heroes and demi-gods, and "the antediluvian patriarchs" of the Hebrews, evidently stood low in the scale of probable finality. One or other of them might clearly, at any moment, have been upset by the progress of discovery; and it is difficult to acquit altogether of blame the distinguished scholars and archæologists, who allowed such flimsy constructions to blind and hypnotize them so long to the many indications tending to their overthrow and demanding a complete restudy of the ground which they covered.

It is in no spirit of self-complacent superiority that I am led to make these observations upon fellow-workers, for whom I have a high regard, for assuredly no ingenuous enquirer into human origins has suffered more grievously from deference to established prejudice than I have. It was a too implicit belief in the established opinions of the Sanskritist authorities that the Indian Epic heroes were fabulous which, in my life-long pursuit of Aryan Origins, delayed for about twenty-five years my initial discovery that the names in the Indian Epics and Vedas were identical with the kings' names inscribed on the Sumerian, Babylonian, Hittite and Egyptian monuments. And it was the too ready acceptance by philologists, archæologists and anthropologists, and to some extent by myself of the Assyriologists' and Egyptologists' theory of the Semitic affinities of the Mesopotamian and Egyptian radical vocabularies, culture, mythology, religion and ruling race which interposed a further delay of many years before I realized its misleading character, and was then able to establish conclusively the historicity of the so-called "mythic" Indian, Eddic, Gothic, Roman and Greek heroes, gods, and demi-gods by comparing their names and exploits in detail with my own revised readings at first-hand of the names of the historic ancient Sumerian, "Akkad," Babylonian, Early Egyptian and "Hittite" kings with their exploits on their own monuments.

The inveterate resistance offered by otherwise reputedly scientific savants and by the docile public, led by them, to new basic facts that radically conflict with the prejudices and false theories they have been taught to believe, is well-expressed by Prof. Sayce, when he laments: "It was [is ?] hard to part with the prejudices of early education."[1] And Prof. Elliot Smith, says, with not a little truth: "It is mainly the *errors* in accumulated 'Knowledge' which are diffused, rather than the solid acquisitions of Knowledge, which are accepted with great resistance by most human beings. . . . Most people are able to get on without thinking at all, the views they would entertain being determined by the society in which they lived."[2] In this way the great Gibbon's hard scientific facts shattering the superstitions of the older "historians" met with long and virulent opposition; and even more so did Darwin's revolutionary *Origin of Species* and *Descent of Man*, substituting the Evolutionist for the Creational theory of things, which are only now beginning to be generally accepted; and Jenner's discovery of Vaccination, Lister's discovery of Antiseptics, and the new "Higher Criticism" in Religion, not to mention the epoch-making discoveries of Copernicus and Galileo, evoked long denunciation, and to some of their authors excommunication and to one even death. Similarly, Herodotus, whose history is now found to be true, in most of its details where they can be tested, was stigmatized as "the father of Lies," and Sir Henry Rawlinson's discovery of the Sumerians and their Non-Semitic race, Non-Semitic civilization, language, writing and religion and their authorship of Babylonian Civilization, was received with ridicule and hostility by Semitic scholars and leading Assyriologists, who, nevertheless, stultified eventually, were forced to admit the logic of the new facts, destructive of their false fundamental theories.

In the new and truer historical and traditional perspective now opened up for us, the various Ancient Civilizations,

[1] *Archæology of Cuneiform Inscriptions*, 1908, 68.
[2] Gresham College Lects. on "The Study of Mankind," 11th Jan. 1926.

hitherto generally believed to have been separately invented or created *ab origine* by different races as independent species, each within its own narrow water-tight geographical compartment in Mesopotamia or Babylonia, Egypt, Asia Minor, Syria, Phœnicia and Palestine, Crete, Greece, Persia and India (and ? China) are now seen to be one and the same species, evolved and established by the one highly specialized Aryan Race at a now relatively fixed and dated epoch, and diffused from one common centre into all those ancient centres of Civilization by that race as the ruling imperial caste of the Ancient World who formed a military aristocracy. The Unity in the essentials of the ancient Civilizations and in their lineal descendants the modern Civilizations is now seen to be due, not to the Kantian dogma, as generally accepted, that all men, savage and civilized, think and invent spontaneously alike down to minute details, but to the authors and early propagators of these ancient Civilizations having been members of one and the same highly gifted race, the fair long-headed "Aryan" Race of Huxley. And this race is now disclosed as already forming from about 5000 years ago onwards mighty empires that embraced the greater part of the then known world, and planted the same tree of their Civilization in each of those old centres in those different lands, where its leaves, branches and fruit took on different hues in keeping with the different soils and environments and the local cultivation of the tree by that ruling Aryan race, along with the local talent of the aboriginal race regenerated and inspired by that Civilization.

In short, the new evidence shows that Civilization was essentially racial, and that it was Aryanization; and that even now, when Civilization has become diffused over the divers races in the world, it still appears to flourish most vigorously where the Aryan racial elements are relatively numerous. For although there is no such thing nowadays as a purely Aryan nation—if, indeed, there ever was one, as a "nation" implies a political community of more or less mixed races, though the ruling elements in the early civilized nations were Aryan—and the long prevalence of intermarriage between different racial elements or stocks, fair and dark, within the nations, with commingling of racial blood diluting the pure Aryan strain, Nature, nevertheless, with her remarkable process for securing "the survival of the fittest," refuses to lose the painstaking progress made through long evolution towards a higher type by permitting any chance interference with her machinery or by diluting her products. It has been found that the progeny of a marriage between two races of different physical types and head-forms are not the mere mean or average or mixture between the two parent types, but belong to one or other of the separate parent (or grandparent) types as regards head and brain formation, the different racial head-forms refuse to mix, like oil and water. Thus the intermarriage of a long head and a round head usually results in one or other of the children being long-headed and another round-headed, like one or other of the parents, and not an intermediate type of head. The result is not a mixture, as if we mixed red and white wine, but is often a manifest reversion to the original types. In this way good old types, once fixed by long interbreeding, do not necessarily get lost by intermarriage, but often return with astonishing energy.[1] In this way the subsequent intermarriage of individuals of a relatively pure Aryan physical type, would tend to enhance and fix the predominance of the Aryan blood-strain with all the superior intellectual endowments for Progress which the Aryan type stands for. As a result we have at the present day, especially amongst the Nordic nations of Europe, and amongst the higher castes of the Indians, with whom mixed marriages have long been restricted by caste regulations, a large number of individuals and even communities of relatively pure Aryan type. And in Europe, especially in Nordic Europe, this Aryan type is by no means confined to the "upper" classes, which, indeed, nowadays contain all sorts of different racial types, but is found most numerous perhaps amongst the "middle" classes, and it is also found to a not inconsiderable extent amongst the masses of the people, which would thus seem to explain to some extent perhaps the rise of "self-made" men to the foremost ranks in the van of Progress. But this is a subject for the consideration of the eugenists.

[1] Cp. Prof. F. von Luschan, J.R.A.I. 1911, 239; and WPOB. 369 f.

This Early Aryan Race, which is now seen to have evolved and established Civilization, is demonstrated by our new evidence to be identical in its leading branch with the "Sumerians" of Assyriologists. And so far from the "Sumerians," the earliest civilized historical people of the Ancient World, being an alien race of unknown affinities, and more especially a Non-Aryan race, which along with its marvellously high civilization, art, language, and writing, had died out and become totally extinct about 2250 B.C., and a sort of fossil curiosity in no way related to any modern people in race, civilization, and language, as Assyriologists believe, the very reverse now proves to be the fact. They are now found to be the ancestors and affines of the modern Nordic or Aryan Race of people in Europe and of the purer high-caste Hindu elements in India, and of the classic Greeks and Romans and Ancient Britons, to whom they passed on from hand to hand down the ages the torch of Civilization.

The "Sumerians," who never called themselves by that title, nor were ever so called, as far as is known, except by Assyriologists, are now seen to have no more died out and become extinct than did the Goths in Europe and the Picts in Scotland, when they gave up those "pagan" titles for territorial ones on their conversion to Christianity, or than did their later sea-going branches, the Phœnicians (who seldom ever called themselves so); and Amorites or Morites and their inland kinsmen, the Hittites, when they adopted the national titles of their city-states and colonies. The "Sumerians" are seen to have continued as the ruling race in Mesopotamia, without interruption, down to the end of the Kassi Dynasty there, about 1200 B.C., giving off hives of their officials, priests, industrialists, and merchants with their families as emigrants to their various flourishing colonies east and west, to which they transplanted their Civilization. Then, at last, the relatively small Sumerian residue left in Mesopotamia seems to have soon disappeared thence after the overthrow of the Aryan rulers of the Kassi Dynasty by the native Semitic Babylonians and Assyrians, who adopted the Sumerian or Aryan Civilization of their former over-lords in its decadent form. And just as the Aryan elements disappeared in the population of Greece after the Roman occupation, with decadence of Civilization by racial impoverishment, so eventually the Semite and Arab population left to themselves trampled out the embers of the torch of the once mighty Civilization of Mesopotamia, lit, and kept alight, by the Sumerians or Early Aryans.

The westward trend of the Sumerians or Early Aryans from Mesopotamia appears to have begun about 3000 B.C., under their chief sea-going branch, the adventurous "Phœnicians," as we have seen; but their great westward migration commenced with Sargon and his son Menes' dynasty, also seen to be Aryan Phœnicians, about 2700 B.C., on their annexation and colonization of Egypt, which country they adopted as their new homeland and made their mausoleums there. It was a land much more climatically suited to a Nordic race than the stifling pestiferous plains of Mesopotamia, where their Sumerian ancestors had perforce been located for some six centuries, and where the climate appears to have been steadily deteriorating by undergoing more intensely torrid and desiccatory change.

Egypt, where the Nile debouched into the cool Mediterranean basin, also offered a more strategical centre for dominating the western and more desirable portion of the great Sumerian or Aryan "world empire" along the Mediterranean sea-board. And it appears probable that the ancient classic name for Egypt and Crete of *Aeria* or *Heriē* or "Land of the Arya or Aryan,"[1] dates from this epoch. It seems to have been from this Aryanized Egypt as a centre that a great portion of the Mediterranean basin and beyond the Pillars of Hercules received its early civilization—as Prof. Elliot Smith has brilliantly shown in respect to many elements of culture, though regarding Egypt as the original centre of Civilization itself; and as Sir Arthur Evans has shown to some extent in regard to Cretan or Minoan Civilization; and Sir Flinders Petrie and Mr W. Airy respecting the British units of weights and measures, etc.; and Sir Arthur Keith as to the plan of the megalithic tombs in Sardinia and Britain. An interesting memory of Sargon and his dynasty as "the protectors of the *Northern Countries*" is preserved in the Indian Epic tradition cited

[1] WSAD. 15.

in the heading of Chapter XIII, p. 196. And Sargon and his dynasty, as well as their Sumerian predecessors and successors, freely called themselves *Gut* or "Goths."

In these various colonial Aryan city-states and civilized nationalities thus established along the basin of the Mediterranean and in Europe, these Early Aryans or Egyptian Sumerians and their kinsmen on the North, the Amorites or Morites, Hittites, Phœnicians and Goths, appear to have called themselves mainly after their city-states and colonies, as: Keftui (Cretans), Ionians, Dorians and Trojans, Achaioi (Achaians), Carians, Kitions (Cyprians), Cilicians, etc., just as in modern times the British colonists, largely as it now appears the descendants of those Sumerians, in the new colonial homelands of their adoption do not call themselves Briton or British, but Canadian, Newfoundlander, Australian, New Zealander, etc. And it appears probable, from the evidence I have adduced in my Phœnician Origin of the Britons regarding the activities of the great sea-going branch of the Sumerians, the "Phœnicians" in the Atlantic, coupled with the solar religious symbolism on their monuments and their Cyclopean architecture, that from their bases in Iberia, Morocco or the British Isles, these daring and resourceful Early Aryan mariners may have reached America, where their conquests were afterwards forgotten, and survived only in the tradition of the lost Atlantis (America ?), and in the mighty sculptured ruins of cities in Peru, Mexico, Easter Island, etc., recalling the architecture and religious symbolism of the Phœnicians.[1]

The "Phœnicians," *who have never been found to have called themselves by that title, nor by the name of "Punic," anywhere in the Mediterranean, Levant, Mesopotamia or the East in their many thousands of inscriptions in Phœnicia, Syria-Palestine, Carthage, Gades, Asia Minor, Cyprus, Mesopotamia, etc., nor in any of their many thousands of coins, and who are called Non-Semites by the typical Semites or the Hebrews or Sons of Shem themselves in their Old Testament,* are now disclosed by still fuller proofs than in my previous works to have been the leading sea-going branch of the Sumerians or Early Aryans. The First Phœnician Dynasty

[1] WPOB. 1924, 298, 380.

of these daring Early Aryan pioneer mariners, with their capital on the Persian Gulf, is seen to have founded their great commercial colony overseas in the Indus Valley about 3100 B.C., or *four centuries before the epoch of Menes;* and their emperor of that day used the title of *Khād* or *Khad-du,* presumably in the sense of " Sea-king " or " Ruler of the Waves," and apparently coined it on the form of the old *Khad-ti* or Khatti title of their old kinsmen, the " Hitt-ites." This identity and early location for them is strikingly confirmed by Herodotus, who records for us the tradition that the Phoinīk-es or " Phœnicians " (whom he otherwise calls Tyrians and Sidonians) *came from the Persian Gulf* to the Levantine Mediterranean and founded Tyre about 2750 B.C.; and both he and the other classic Greek as well as Roman writers speak in glowing terms of the great contributions made by the " Phœnicians " or Tyrians and Sidonians to the Civilization of Greece and Rome, apart from the introduction of alphabetic writing by Kadmos, the Tyrian Phœnician. Even Homer, who so frequently refers to these gifted merchant mariners, only once calls them " Phœnician " in his *Iliad* and only seven times in his *Odyssey,* his usual title for them being Sidonians or Tyrians after their chief colonial seaports in the Levant. And significantly the Levantine Mediterranean was called by the Early Egyptians, " The Sea of the Qadi (or Qedi)," obviously after the Khād or Kad title of the " Phœnicians " and the *Cedi* Aryans of the Indian Chronicles; just as the Straits of Gibraltar in the west were called by the Romans " Fretum Gaditanum " or Frith of Gad-es (or House of the *Gads* or ' Phœnicians ')."

The Aryan racial character of the Phœnicians and of Sargon-the-Great and his " Akkads " (the hypothetical " Western Semites " of Assyriologists) is also further established in this work by a mass of direct and confirmatory, contemporary, inscriptional evidence, proving their Aryan and Non-Semitic physique, personalities, language and religion. Their later introduction into their official Aryan language of a considerable number of Chaldean or Semitic words, and the still later practice of the later " Phœnicians " to write largely in the Semitic language and in the reversed direction, which are the only two arguments by which Assyriologists claim them as Semites, are now seen to have been mainly confined to localities in which the great majority of their subjects were Semites speaking a Semitic language. It was analogous to the great Aryan emperor of India, Asoka, in the third century B.C., employing retrograde writing for his edicts in those provinces of his empire which were inhabited mainly by Semites accustomed to reversed writing. And Sargon-the-Great, the so-called "Semite" and "Akkad," but whose Aryan race is now absolutely established, wrote his inscriptions usually if not always, in pure Sumerian, and some of them bilingually, respectively in pure Sumerian and in Semitic Akkadian for the information of his Semitic subjects. And the current Semitized readings of his inscriptions by Assyriologists are now seen to be merely arbitrary forced readings under the spell of their Semitic theories. The retrograde or reversed style of writing generally used by the later Eastern "Phœnicians" was also used by the old Hittites in their hieroglyph writing and by the Early Greeks, yet Assyriologists admit that neither of those two nations were at all Semites. And *the Sumerians habitually used retrograde writing for their sealings*, from the time at least of their First "Phœnician" Dynasty about 3100 B.C., as fully demonstrated in the profusion of illustrations of their seals in these pages and in the Appendices. Besides, I have fully demonstrated in my *Sumer-Aryan Dictionary* the radically Aryan or Sumerian character of the chief cultural psalms and Epics, not a single one of which had hitherto been known, even in the remotest conjectural fashion, and which all three of those languages.

The remarkable Modern-ness of Civilization when it first appears on the stage of the world's history, on the advent of the Sumerians or Early Aryans, over 5000 years ago, is astonishing. It shows how comparatively small has been the really solid advance in general Civilization since then, beyond developments in details, new mechanical inventions and widespread material luxury tending towards a mechanized and "hygienic paradise" of physical comfort in our much boasted present-day "modern" civilization—though in the Higher Civilization, namely Science and Art, profound advance has also taken place. We find at that early period the Early Aryans or Sumerians, from whom we have inherited our Civilization, already a vigorous law-abiding industrial and agricultural people, living in cities, under established government, with free institutions, practising scientific arts and crafts, great sea-traders, familiar with writing, literature, poetry and history, and possessed of a lofty religion of Heaven on the monotheistic lines of the present day. We thus find a Sumerian king, some generations before Menes, recording that " He is the champion of the weak against the strong, in place of servitude he established liberty throughout his kingdom . . . he delivered the children from want, theft, murder and other ills . . . to the widow and the orphan the strong man could do no harm." And he issues or reissues a great number of laws, including many for protecting the people against extortions by officials and priests, which are precisely similar in form to those found in the later law-codes of the Hittites and on the famous stone-graven code of the Sun-worshipping Babylonian emperor Khammu-Rabi (c. 2003-1961 B.C.), now disclosed as an Aryan king, and whose law-code is now generally admitted to be the immediate source from which Moses and the Israelites borrowed the chief ethical and fiscal portions of their law-codes and " The Commandments," and their name for God, along with his imagery in human form, solar symbolism, monotheistic character and attributes as Lord of Hosts, for the exaltation of their own tribal god.

Finely built cities of these Early Sumerians are found in Mesopotamia, Elam, Egypt, Crete and the Indus Valley with comfortable, spacious houses and palaces, public buildings and temples adorned with sculptures, paved courts, staircases, garden ponds, canals and quays, hydraulic and sanitary engineering, with bathrooms fitted with covered drains and water-supply. Their jewellery of gold and silver is often of the most delicate kind, sometimes inlaid with lapis-lazuli or enamelled with colours, indicating that the wearers were of fair complexion ; and faience and coloured glass beads are not uncommon. Their furniture was of elegant artistic form. Their dresses were often richly embroidered, and they played chess with carved " men," and children's toys are numerous.

Their vases of alabaster or other stone or of embossed silver are often masterpieces in design and execution; and their pottery is of highly artistic type and decoration; and their seals are delicately engraved with drawings of men and animals, done with admirable technique and naturalistic art.

Even in Religion there appears to have been little if any real progress since those early Aryan days. As Emerson says: "The Days were ever divine to the First Aryans."[1] The Early Aryans already at the epoch of their first king (c. 3378 B.C.) are found to have evolved a really scientific religion on the idea that Nature's God was a beneficent, vitalizing Force resident in the Sun, which with rare scientific acumen they recognized as the Single Power that rules this world, and that luminary even now, according to modern scientists, also is the ultimate source of all life in this world. And the Sun as The Light of the World was regarded as the emblem of Purity and champion of Right over Wrong and Darkness, and required no living sacrifices, but only praises, with offerings of Fire and the fruits of the earth. This was a tremendous uplifting ethical and moral advance beyond the primitive debasing religious belief of the Semitic-Chaldean aborigines, who had no idea of a god or heaven, but only belief in widespread malignant devouring demons of Darkness and Death, who held mankind in perpetual terror, and demanded cruel sanguinary sacrifices and even human victims. This simple, early Aryan monotheistic idea of the Sun, or the force behind the Sun, as being Nature's God, was evidently too abstract for the multitude, as we find within a few generations that although many still adhered to this simple Sun-worship, others of the Aryan men "created God in the image of Man." They imagined him as the invincible King of Heaven and fashioned him on the model of their own great first human king, the invincible superman who established their Civilization, and they even gave him two of the titles of that earthly king, which latterly have become the usual titles of God in the modern "higher" religions, which are all seen to have been derived along with the monotheistic idea of God from this Early Aryan one. They imagined him in human form as a universal and protecting

[1] *Society and Solitude*, 7, 137.

Father, a lord of righteousness and hearer of prayers, with the Sun or the Sun-Cross, that is the True Cross and the Cross carried by St John the Baptist, as his symbol, and with Baptism as the initiatory rite of entry into that solar religion of purity. Their first human king's son and great battle champion, namely Michael, they also canonized and made him an archangel (the St Michael of the New Testament), intercessor and a resurrector from the dead. And this religion—though degraded latterly in Babylonia by making the One God into a Trinity godhead and introducing Semitic goddesses and godlings to form a polytheistic pantheon—still remained the religion of many of the pure monotheistic Aryans, and especially of the so-called pagan Goths and of the Ancient Britons under their Aryan Catti kings before their conversion to Christianity,[1] Druidism, with its human sacrifices, being merely the religion of the Non-Aryan Moon-worshipping aboriginal "Celts" in Britain.[2] Amongst the Goths especially was this pure traditional Monotheism held so unflinchingly, that on their conversion to Christianity (into which they introduced the True Cross as the symbol)[3] they altogether refused belief in the Trinity and also in the Mother-Son cult of the Romish Church, which resulted in the famous "Arian" controversy and schism in the Christian Church, which again asserted itself at the Reformation.[4] That great Early Aryan advance in Religion has on the whole been maintained, though no doubt the pure monotheism of the Aryan Sumerians has often been degraded by corrupt ecclesiastics, who to maintain their power and privileges have not hesitated to incorporate with it magical rites of savagery and the popular superstitions about devils and Hell.

The true Chronology of the Ancient World back to the Rise of Civilization is now recovered for the first time from concrete official contemporary and other inscriptional evidence and other authentic official traditional historical evidence, by which the Chronology is exactly fixed, or fixed

[1] WPOB. 262 f. [2] *Ib.*, 232 f., 271, 331.

[3] *Ib.*, 290 f., where it is shown with many illustrated proofs that The True Cross was not and never was a Crucifix, but was the old Aryan Sun-Cross emblem of the Sun as "The Light of the World."

[4] *Ib.* 301 f. and ERE. I, 775 f.

to within a few years of the actual dates. This has been made possible by discovering in the complete official King-Lists and Chronicles of the Early Aryans from the first king of the First Aryan Dynasty continuously down in unbroken line to the classic historical period, which have been fortunately preserved by the Eastern or Indian branch of the Aryans, the unique key to the King-Lists of the Sumerians and Babylonians and Early Dynastic Egyptians. This key which has preserved the traditional forms of the names of the kings, hitherto obscure and largely conjectural in their ambiguous polyphonous Sumerian writing, and has disclosed unequivocally the personality and titles of the first of all Sumerian kings, has also bridged over for the first time the great gaps in the Sumerian King-Lists, which gaps have hitherto proved unsurmountable obstacles in all previous attempts at recovering those dates in terms of our modern era. And this key has disclosed and established for the first time synchronisms between Ancient Mesopotamian Chronology and that of Ancient Egypt and Crete. Whilst thus restoring order into the History of the Ancient World from the Rise of Civilization continuously downwards, with a true perspective of the origin, progress and early developments of Civilization, we at the same time recover through the Sumerian dynastic records the exact dates of all the famous Aryan kings and priest-kings celebrated in the Indian Vedic psalms and Epics, not a single one of which had hitherto been known, even in the remotest conjectural fashion, and which had been the despair of all Sanskrit scholars.

As to Language, we have observed how this world-wide expansion of the Early Aryan or Sumerian dominion over the greater part of the known world, along with their official Aryan speech, and especially through their Amorite, Phœnician and Egyptian seafaring branches, went far towards establishing that linguistic Unity, the dangers of which the jealous God of the Israelites had foreseen when he desired to confound the language of the ambitious early inhabitants of the plain of Shinar. And although we know that the top of our tower can never reach to Heaven, we can see how vital to the purely terrestrial culture which we hope to rear, has been that widespread prevalence of the Sumerian or proto-Aryan speech, which this earliest world sea-power established. It would be difficult to exaggerate the extent to which Civilization has advanced by the ancient implicit science of the language spread by these early navigators to the most distant lands. We know how poetic associations become attached and cling to words through long usage, and may surmise that the enormous progress of Science since the revival of letters, and the " word-magic " which characterizes the best poetry of both ancients and moderns, that of Homer and Virgil, of Dante, Shakespeare and Milton, has been due in hitherto unsuspected degree to the long and world-prevalence of the Aryan languages, which resulted from the enterprise of these early sea-going " Sumerians." Even the Gothic Edda or " Norse " poetry, long regarded as of independent growth, is now seen to be a late fruit of the old Aryan heredity, preserving in discernible if fainter form the signs and even the themes of its true parentage and affiliation.

Although the modern Aryan family of languages, as well as its older classic members, the Greek, Latin and Sanskrit for example, are of the inflective type, the most highly developed and complicated stage of languages, yet scientific philologists, by analysing these Aryan languages, find that they betray unmistakable traces of having been evolved from the less developed type called " agglutinative," that is joining together the simple root-words or word-roots to form sentences without inflections to modify their terminations so as to express the relation of number, gender, person, tense, etc. At the present day Turkish, Finnic, Hungarian and Basque in Europe, and Japanese, etc., are still in the agglutinative stage. Moreover, it is found that the later Aryan family of languages possesses many vestiges of the still simpler and most primitive of all types of language, namely the monosyllabic, in stringing the simple word-roots together to form sentences, as in the Chinese.[1] Now it is characteristic that notwithstanding that it has been thus found by scientists that the Aryan language has undergone evolution, like everything else in Nature from a lower to a higher type, from monosyllabic through the agglutinative

[1] A. Hovelacque, *Science of Language*, 32 f.

to the inflective stage, Assyriologists, nevertheless, dogmatically declare that the Sumerian language (which we have demonstrated to be the proto-Aryan language) "*has no affinity with the Aryan,*"[1] *merely because it was still largely agglutinative at the remote period according to them of 7000 years ago or more!* Yet these same Assyriologists admit that the Sumerian language was steadily undergoing structural change down through the later millenniums and centuries in the direction of inflection, and they even devote a chapter in their text-books to "Inflection and Postfixes" in the Sumerian language.[2] Their absolute denial of any Aryan affinity to the Sumerians seems merely to be a lingering vestige of the notorious prejudice of the older Semitic Assyriologists, who even denied Sumerian the status of being really a language at all. They are apparently unaware of the fact that scientific philologists and grammarians find that even the modern English tongue still retains to a considerable degree agglutinative features in its well-known deep-rooted present-day habit of using compound words and phrases, consisting of agglutinated word-roots, and that the English language is by-no-means even now-a-days a purely so-called inflective language. And the still older monosyllabic structure seems still to persist in it in such common sentences as "No work no pay."

The Sumerian or proto-Aryan language still survived in Babylonia in its earlier form as a classic speech amongst the Semitic Babylonians, long after it had developed and became locally diluted by the incorporation of elements from the local Chaldean Semitic dialects and idioms of the Babylonian aborigines, as did the Latin in Britain long after the Roman occupation. In later Babylonia, legal judgments were still written in the old Sumerian language and Sumerian liturgies were chanted in the temples and continued to be so chanted down to the last century before our era, like the dead Sanskrit in modern Brahmanist temples in India, the dead Pali in Buddhist temples and like the dead Latin in modern Romish Churches. The Church and Law were as loath to give up the old "dead" language of their early Sumerian civilizers as

[1] S. Langdon, *Sumerian Grammar,* II.
[2] *Ib.*, 62-90.

they are in modern England to give up Latin in the present "*Anno Domini.*"

The Aryan Race of the originators of Civilization, who we have found by unequivocal historical evidence were the "Sumerians," is confirmed by the radical identity of the "Sumerian" language with the Aryan family of languages, of which it has the most primitive form and is disclosed as the parent, or the proto-Aryan. The developers and propagators of Civilization also in the early and middle periods are seen to have been in most part, if not wholly, of the same Aryan race as the founders. This is in series with the recent conclusions of Profs. M'Dougall and Günther, Sir Arthur Keith and others from their analyses of the race-strain in European history, from the classic Greek period onwards, resulting in their One-race, One-brain theory of Civilization, and accounting for the Unity in the elements of Civilization, and their emphasis on the One-brain theory of individual great men of creative genius as leading factors for the Progress of Civilization.

The simultaneous and almost world-wide efflorescence of science, art and literature, that is in the main elements of the Higher Civilization, between the ninth to the fifth centuries B.C., in such widely separated centres as Greece, Ionia and Phrygia, Tuscany and Latium (including Rome), Persia and the Gangetic Valley of India (and in China), is held by some modern writers to be a strong, and as they think a conclusive, argument against the World's Civilization having been the product of any single race strain or any single race influence. But this efflorescence appears to me on the contrary to support the Aryan Origin of the World's Civilization.

All these different centres specified were already old colonies of the Aryans or "Sumerians"—Ionia, Phrygia-Cappadocia, Persia and the Indus Valley having been so from early times, also Achaian and Doric Greece, where the cyclopean buildings in Mycenæ and Tiryns are dated to about 1400 B.C.; and the prehistoric "whorls" of Troy contain Sumerian writing; whilst Tuscany was traditionally a settlement formed by sea-going Lydians from Ionia shortly after the Fall of Troy (about 1200 B.C.), and Latium tradition ascribes its Civilization to Æneas as a fugitive at the same epoch; and China we have seen presumably owes its early Civilization and hieroglyphic system of writing also to Mesopotamia, and the philosophy and religion of Confucius and Lao-tsze of the sixth and seventh centuries B.C. have much in common with those of the Indo-Aryan of Buddha of the same period and the older Brahmans, whilst early Chinese art, with its Fish-men heroes, is shown by the explorations in the Central Asian halfway-house to have been largely influenced by the Mesopotamian and Indo-Persian and even by Grecian art.

Moreover, the physical type of the people amongst whom this efflorescence of Civilization appears (excepting the Chinese) was of the Aryan type. And all these local outcrops of Civilization that thus appear at the epochs in question were already in more or less fully-fledged form, and that form was Aryan in type, even including to some extent the Chinese.

The reason for this sudden efflorescence of active Civilization at those various old Aryan colonies at this particular period, from the ninth to the fifth centuries B.C., was, I venture to suggest, owing in no inconsiderable degree to fresh immigration waves of refugees from the older centres of Aryan Civilization in the Near East, from Asia Minor, Mesopotamia and Syria-Phœnicia, caused by the pressure of the exterminating wars waged by the ravening Semitic Assyrians with wolfish ferocity against these old Aryan centres. The fall of the Aryan Kassi Dynasty in Babylonia about 1200 B.C. doubtless accounted for some remnants of those last of the old ruling Aryans migrating to Europe on the west and to Indo-Persia on the east; and the Fall of Troy about the same period is traditionally credited with the flight of Æneas, with his men and household goods to Italy. But the brutally destructive wars of the Semitic Assyrians against the old Aryan city-states from Mesopotamia to the borders of Cappadocia, and from Carchemish to Cilicia and Syria-Phœnicia on the Mediterranean must have driven swarms of fugitives westwards to the old colonies along the Mediterranean and eastwards into Indo-Persia, which latter they did do in fact. Such were the wars, especially of the Assyrian king Tiglath Pileser I (1115–1103 B.C.), and of Ashur Nasir Pal II (883–859 B.C.), who brutally boasts of having crucified his enemies wholesale and of having tortured and flayed alive those leaders who opposed him, and deported gangs of the remainder to Assyria as hostages and slaves. Similar and even more barbarous atrocities were perpetrated by his later successor, the notorious Assyrian Sargon II (722–705 B.C.), the same who sent the Jews into captivity, in his exterminating wars in Upper Mesopotamia, Eastern Taurus, Carchemish, Cilicia and Syria-Phœnicia-Palestine, which left very few of the Aryan racial elements remaining in those regions. Many fugitives must have escaped along the Mediterranean, and others north into Central Asia and even to China. A leading consequence of this particular exterminating war was, as I have shown, the great flight or migration of the Hittites or *Khatti* eastwards *via* Persia to the Gangetic Valley in India, where they suddenly appear about 700 B.C. as the *Khattiya* (or Kshattriya) ruling Aryan race, carrying with them their precious ancestral king-lists with a fully-fledged Aryan Civilization of the "Sumerian" type, which still remains in practically the same form at the present day as "Indian Civilization." And the Assyrian occupation of Egypt, which lasted till 650 B.C., led to the opening up of intimate friendly relations between the Egyptian ruling Aryan race (predominantly Aryan) with the Greeks, accompanied, doubtless, by the settlement of many Egyptian fugitives in Greece. With the blending of these accretions of fresh blood from so many of the old Aryan centres of Civilization with that in the later Aryan colonies at the sites above specified, it seems only natural that there should have now been a somewhat sudden efflorescence of more active Civilization and a more active development and progress in it at those various local centres than before that epoch.

The Mixed Race factor which has entered into Civilization, especially since its propagation over the world amongst Non-Aryan races that have been born and bred up in civilized communities, with the increased intelligence resulting therefrom, is undoubted, and it now plays an important part in the present and future Progress of Civilization. The happy blending of the more intellectual elements of the Non-Aryan races with the Aryan or Nordic in developing and modifying Civilization is seen to have resulted in the various local and temperamental phases of Civilization, forming the various ancient and modern Local Civilizations; though other results of the blending of these different mental types have proved to be not quite so happy. Thus, the happy blending of the Aryan Civilization of the fair long-headed Nordic ruling race with the native racial elements in serpent-worshipping Ancient Egypt, the so-called Hamitic or Libyan and Semitic Arab races, resulted in the developed Egyptian phase of Civilization; in Mesopotamia with the Semitic or Chaldean Serpent-, Eagle- and Lion-worshipping race in the later phases of the Mesopotamian and Babylonian Civilizations; in Crete, with the north-east Pelasgian or dark long-headed, narrow-browed Mediterranean race in the Minoan Civilization; in Ionia, Lydia and Greece, with the Northern Pelasgian or Mediterranean race in the Ionian and Hellenic Civilizations; in Italy and Spain, with the Iberian or Western Mediterranean race in the Early Roman and Spanish Civilizations; in Syria-Phœnicia-Cilicia and Cyprus, with the Levantine Pelasgian or Mediterranean and Semitic races with the later Amorite and "Phœnician" Civilizations; in Central and Eastern Asia Minor, with the round-headed "Turanian" or Alpine race in the later Hittite and the Turkish Civilizations; in China and Japan, with the Mongol and Indonesian races in Ancient Chinese and Japanese Civilizations. In Peru and Mexico, with the Indo-American races in the Inca, Aztec and Maya Civilizations; in Persia and Media, with the round-headed Alpines or Turanians and Sassanian Semites in the Median and Persian Civilizations; in India, with the dark long-headed narrow-browed, aborigines, and in the north with Scyths in the Indian Civilization; in Burma and Tibet with the Indonesian, Mongol and Turkic races in the Burmese and Tibetan Civilizations; in Gaul and Germany, with the Mediterranean and round-headed Alpines in the French and German Civilizations; in Scandinavia with Alpines and in Finland, with Scythic Mongols as

Scandinavian and Finnic in the later "Gothic" Civilizations; in the Danube Valley and Russia, with the "Scythic" and round-headed Slav races; and in the British Isles, with the dark long-headed narrow-browed aborigines, the Picts and "British Celts," and with the fair round-headed "beaker-folk," especially on the East Coast, in the British or English, Irish and Scottish Civilizations; and the English-speaking American Civilization is admittedly essentially British, adopted by the mixed trans-Atlantic races.

Race-Intermixture also, through the intermarriage of different race stocks, which has ensued since Civilization became widespread with the formation of Nations out of miscellaneous mixed racial elements, now necessarily plays a very important part in the present and future Progress of Civilization as well as in the factors making for its Decline. For a long time the ruling and civilizing race, essentially an aristocratic military caste, appears to have kept aloof from intermarrying with its subject "lower" races, through "race-pride" or "race-prejudice" or "race-instinct," and allowed only selected individuals with their families as residents within their settlements and towns and with the privileges of citizenship. But in the course of time, when the townships or cities developed into States and Nations, comprising tribes of mixed races, and their Non-Aryan races rose in the scale of Civilization by passing through the mill of Aryanization in laws, customs, habits of life and speech under the community of Nationalities, with equal rights of citizenship and a common patriotism, then more or less intermarriage of the different racial stocks began to take place, and this practice has steadily increased till the present day, when it is now universal throughout the leading Civilizations. As a result, there is nowadays practically no such thing as absolute purity of racial stock, even amongst European nations, each individual being physically a complex of different race stocks, with one or other race-strain usually predominating. Yet, as we have seen, Nature has so arranged that this predominating race-strain can become so intensified under favourable circumstances as to revert almost to a relatively pure racial type, which carries with it, according to biologists, the mental qualities, aptitudes or endowments of that type, which in the case of the Nordic type are Aryan.

The weakening of the Aryan racial element or race-strain in the mixed population of modern Europe at the present day, that is a weakening in that particular racial element which founded and mostly developed Civilization in the Past, is observed by recent biologists and with grave concern as to its influence on the future Progress of the World's Civilization. Although the Aryan racial element always formed a relatively small proportion of the population of the world, and especially of the total population of the Nations which they organized into being, it is a notable fact that anthropologists have found that the fair long-headed, broad-browed people are decreasing in relative proportion to the round heads in the modern period as well as in the middle period, where there has been a steady change from long to short heads all over Europe. Thus, according to the single-race view of the Aryans as the originators and chief early developers of Civilization, the latter would seem to be getting into a less and less favourable position as the centuries proceed. This danger from the relative decrease of the Aryan elements (which is explained by the biologists through the cumulative effect of the relatively less fertility of the higher civilized and intellectual types of humanity as compared with the " lower ") is considered, however, to be to a great extent modified by the superior importance nowadays of accumulated intellectual and moral traditions over race influence in the later history of nations and of mankind. To this saving influence of improved tradition might be added the benefits to the future Progress of science and art likely to flow from the improved Heredity of the mixed races born and bred up in Civilization.

One of the greatest dangers to Civilization at the present day appears to be much more from the very rapid cumulative numerical increase of the prolific " inferior " racial elements than from the racial impoverishment of the higher elements further up the social ladder. Biologists show that it is from these more prolific " lower " racial stocks that the inefficient and unemployable mainly come, and who, being unable to keep pace with the Civilization created by " the Master caste of the world" into which they were born, are desirous of overthrowing it. Perhaps the biologists hardly do justice, however, to "the lower orders of mankind," in denying them the capacity for any wider group-feeling than patriotism. For sometimes these lower people have a feeling of temperamental community with other races which makes them more cosmopolitan in sympathy than other classes; though it is a commonplace that many of them cannot assimilate Civilization through defective natural endowment, as expressed in the Turkish proverb: "Allah never divides anything equally among men."

It must come as a shock to most people who have not seriously studied History nor are aware of the manner in which the Civilization that now enriches their lives was established and developed to find the important and necessary part that War and Conquest have played as extenders and developers of Civilization. This aspect of Civilization is strikingly illustrated in our recovered history in these pages from the Rise of Civilization downwards, through the period of the "world-emperors" Sargon-the-Great and Menes onwards; and it has been the same experience in modern times in the spread of Civilization to Africa, America and all modern colonies. Indeed, it is seen that Civilization itself could never have been established at all except by the conquest of the neighbouring hordes of primitive Stone-Age backward races, who inflamed by their Serpent (Dragon) and Devil-worshipping priests virulently fought against it and wrecked the fields and factories of the pioneers of Civilization, who with their simple, benign Sun-worship, which was an essential part of their Civilization, upset the immemorial savage superstitions of the aborigines and deprived the armies of parasitical Devil-worshipping necromantic priests of their unholy livelihood.

The subjection of those lawless barbarous races was not only necessary to establish Civilization and safeguard it from attack with its systematic agriculture, industries and its reign of Law by just laws, but it was also necessary to secure that internal armed peace essential for its development and progress. And it is significant that a fairly true historical memory of the first epoch-making great war of Civilization by which the first historical "Sumerian" or Aryan king Gaur or St George established Civilization, c. 3378 B.C., with the aid of his gallant son Prince Michael and his men in his first mountain capital in Cappadocia, called Imin or "Heaven," the *Himin* of the Goths, against these Devil-worshipping aborigines, still survives in the Gentile tradition incorporated in the Apocalypse. This is "the War of Heaven against the Devil and his angels," in which the historical Sumerian Prince Michael is seen to be the Archangel of Heaven who cast out "the great Dragon, that old Serpent called the Devil and Satan who deceiveth the whole world," in which the Devil is seen to be merely the totem of the cult of these Serpent-worshipping Chaldees who, with their Devil-priests, were ejected from the neighbourhood of the Aryan city-state.

Conquest by a more advanced race is seen to affect Progress, and more especially a sudden progress in Civilization, as far as its higher elements of Art and Science form essentials of civilized Progress. This effect of such warfare is evidently due to the automatic diffusion of the ready-made developed culture of the more advanced race over the wider area embraced within their extended empire, moulding men to a fixed type, and to the internal peace that results favouring further development and progress in the culture itself within the larger empire and the lands with which they are in contact. Thus we have seen how the Pax Sargonica at Menes led to the sudden rise of the Egyptian and Minoan Civilizations, and similarly the sudden rise of Civilization in the Indus Valley, and in later times the Pax Romana and Pax Britannica effected also sudden extensions of Civilization over widespread backward people with notable Progress as well. The notion of some modern writers that success in war means penury of Art seems to be only half true, and even then requires much qualification and reservations, as indeed was recognized by that great apostle of Art, Ruskin. The great material advantages tending to Progress resulting from a stable empire peace, with flourishing trade by land and sea, that are enjoyed under an enlightened, civilized non-corrupt representative government, are well recognized; and even an enlightened despotism has manifestly had its advantages sometimes in the Past. And Progress in Civilization would doubtless become still more rapid could a Pax Mundi ever be attained amongst the comity of Nations, through the League of Nations or other co-ordinating or controlling force equipped with the necessary organized, practical machinery to settle international disputes by peaceable means and abolish War. For War, on the modern scale, waged between civilized scientific states professing to be Christian, yet harbouring Hate in their hearts, has become the greatest of all menaces to human existence as well as Civilization; and for its riddance the nations must organize themselves for Peace with the same intensity that they have hitherto been and are organizing themselves for War, which destroys the best specimens of the race. As an aftermath of War sometimes upon the material comforts of Civilization, may be mentioned here the sudden and enormous rise in the general standard of living which has followed the Great War, with all its heavy burdens of terrible suffering and disastrous loss. Another contemporary instance of sudden advance in Civilization following War, with its shrinkage of barriers, is seen in the phenomenally rapid Westernizing of the Turkish republic under the hands of the masterful Mustapha Kemal Pasha.

The manner now disclosed in which our supremely gifted Aryan ancestors invented Civilization for us and developed and propagated it along solid progressive lines in the Past with passionate devotion, supplies us with inspiring indications for further solid Progress in the Present and for the Future.

The foregoing are a few of the outstanding results and reflections which have so far followed from comparison of the monumental inscriptions with the literary remains of our Aryan ancestors. Important as the results are in themselves, they are still more so by the promise they afford of the harvest of new knowledge that awaits us when the method of research by the new comparative keys have been more fully exploited.

Attention may here be invited to the Appendices, of which many contain numerous details of the new discoveries which, apart from their historical importance, are of interest to the general educated reader, especially from Appendix V on Nimrod-Cain onwards through those on the Indo-Sumerian Seals, with their profusion of illustrations showing the high naturalistic and pictorial art attained by the Sumerians or

Early Aryan Goths, to Appendix XIII on the Sumerian Writing now discovered as " owner's marks " scratched upon the finished Prehistoric Pottery in the Old Gothic homeland in the Danube Valley and attesting the early presence of the " Sumerians " in Middle Europe.

In conclusion, it may be observed that amongst the modern peoples of Aryan strain and Aryanized nations, the British Nation owes its Aryan racial elements, as I have demonstrated in a previous work, largely to those introduced by the Phœnician sea-going branch of the Early Aryans or " Sumerians " in their early colonization of Ancient Britain and the lands of the Angles, Saxons, Jutes and Norse, with accretions from Ancient Greece, Troy, and to a less extent from Rome. And these passed on from hand to hand a-down the centuries the Torch of Civilization, which never became extinguished. More perhaps than any other people, the English or Britons represent both sides of the Aryan faculty, the organizing, incorporating talent of the Aryan Phœnicians and Romans and the artistic quality of the Greeks, Babylonians and Egyptians, the former of which can alone guarantee the growth of the latter in a world in which Progress is still so largely determined by ability to survive in competition with other races. It is their fuller participation in the " Sumerian " heredity, with its commerce of the seas, also which may give the British an advantage over non-Aryan and non-seafaring people, the Jews for example and the Chinese, in the contest for the future control and development of Civilization. And for this purpose it is necessary to take fuller account of, and draw inspiration from, the manner in which the old Truth-seeking scientific Early Aryans or " Sumerians " achieved and developed for us Civilization which, except for advances in Art, Literature and Science, and especially in the applied Science of mechanical invention and increased luxury, still remains essentially so very much as they left it.

Let us hope that the Future of the modern Aryans and Aryanized Nations be worthy of their glorious ancestral Past.

APPENDICES

I

Indian King-Lists of the Early Aryans, with Solar & Lunar Names & Titles embedded in the "Purānas," or Ancient Epics of the Indo-Aryans

It has been described in Chapter II how I discovered that the ancient King-Lists and Dynasties of the Early Aryans, which are now embedded in the Indian *Purānas* or "Epics of the Ancients" were the official lists of the Early Aryan kings and emperors of Mesopotamia and Asia Minor of the pre-Indian period, before the eastern or Indian branch of the Aryans migrated from their pre-Indian homeland to Gangetic India about the beginning of the seventh century B.C., and were carried off by them to India as their most precious ancestral possession and embedded in these epics where we now find them. It is also there described how I observed that the several so-called "Solar" and "Lunar" Main-lines of these kings and dynasties therein were not as hitherto imagined different lines of different kings, but were the selfsame lines of the selfsame kings under their different Solar and Lunar names and titles as preserved independently by different clans and tribes of the Indo-Aryans; and that these different independent lists of the same kings were collected together and "pooled" as they stood with scrupulous care in their joint and composite epic, the *Purānas*, when the various clans and tribes united to form a new nation in India, the new land of their adoption.

These several versions of the King-Lists of the Main Lines have been critically edited, as to the spelling of their names in the different MSS., with admirable painstaking care by the late Prof. Fitz-Edward Hall in his classic edition of Wilson's *Vishnu Purāna* (WVP.), in which all the variant spellings in the different versions of the *Purānas* (eighteen in number), and in the different MS. copies of these versions, are laboriously collated and compared with meticulous care. That comparative analysis disclosed that certain of the *Purāṅas* were older and more authentic than others, the oldest being the Vāyu, Vishnu and Brahmānda, which although manifestly independent, generally agreed in essentials, whilst many of the others, also obviously independent, occasionally preserved titles for certain kings where personal names were recorded in other versions of the lists.

In order to establish a standard categorical list of the kings of the main or imperial line of the Early Aryans, showing their Solar and Lunar names and titles, in view of our discovery that the Solar and Lunar lines were independent versions of the same line of kings under their Solar and Lunar names and titles, I compiled the annexed Table from the two Solar and the two chief Lunar lines by juxtaposing the lines; and I have numbered the kings from the first king of the first dynasty onwards in their consecutive order for convenience of reference. Of these main-line lists the "Solar" are the most complete.

The first Solar-line list, called also "The *Ayodhya* Line" after that capital city (which represents the Agudu or "Agade" capital of Sargon-the-Great), where it was presumably compiled, is absolutely complete from the first king of the Early Aryans continuously down to the End of the Kassi Dynasty. It is therefore taken as the standard, and forms column 1 of our Table. The second Solar-line list called "The *Videha* or *Mithila* Line" is nearly as complete, being only slightly contracted in a few places. It forms column 2 of our Table.

The Lunar versions, which give the Lunar names and titles of the kings, are less complete, expecially in their later portions. They are called respectively after the eponymous ancestors of the two leading tribes of the Early Aryans, namely, *Yadu*, the fourth king in the main-line Lunar list,[1] and *Puru*, the fifth king in that list; and

[1] Yadu is shown by the Solar lists and by the Old Sumerian King-Lists to be clearly identical with Yati or Yayati, and not a son of the latter as is gratuitously supposed by the later Brahmans.

significantly the latter king is actually called *Pur* in the old Sumerian Erech Dynasty list. Of these two Lunar lines, that of Puru is the more fragmentary and mutilated. As disclosed by comparison alongside the other three lines, it is seen that the later Indian Brahmans have taken great liberties with the Puru line, from the lunar titled priest-kings in which they mostly claim their descent. They have dislocated the succession beyond the fifth king Puru I (see annexed Table col. 4), by substituting there the succession of King Puru II (No. 36 in the main line) for nine generations, thereby thrusting down all the others, including King Bharat, by a corresponding number of places. They have likewise introduced several generations between King Bharat, the tenth king and Haryashwa, the fifteenth king, presumably by rendering mere titles or descriptive epithets as personal names of successive kings. These additions also are exposed by the practical agreement to the contrary in the other three trustworthy line texts. And they have taken the liberty with the dynasty of their great benefactor, Parashu Rāma of the Ur Dynasty, who raised the Brahmans to the first caste, of carrying up his dynasty with that of his mother from the period of No. 52 of the main-line list and attaching it to the second king of the First Dynasty of the main line; but this dislocation is also exposed by the other lists. In the Table I have rectified these displacements by means of the complete and intact Solar version in column 1.

The succession is usually gratuitously expressed in the modern MS. versions of the *Purānas* by the later Indian copyists as "son," even when a new dynasty appears. And similarly titles of the son and successor of a king are sometimes expanded in the modern MS. versions into different individuals, as, for example, in the case of the second king, whose title of *Āyus dhīmat Amā-Vasu* or "Āyus, the upholder Ama-Vasu," is made into three separate brothers Āyus, Dhīmat and Amā-Vasu. And similarly in the Solar version this second king, under his Solar title of Vikukshi-Nimi, has been made, as we have seen, into two brothers, respectively named Vikukshi and Nimi; and this notwithstanding that the text clearly makes them only one personage.[1] And several of the so-called "brothers" are clearly merely different titles of the king himself arbitrarily separated out as "brothers" by the later copyists, as for instance with the titles of Ama and Vasu for the second king, Ayus. It thus appears that the original Indian lists consisted of simple strings of names and titles in their due chronological order of succession, with few, if any, expressed relationships, except when a narrative was introduced; and that the systematic use of "son of" was added by later scribes. I have, therefore, omitted the stereotyped phrase "son of," which follows nearly every name.

The names of a few of the more outstanding kings are printed in capitals, and those which recur in similar or dialectic spellings in more than one column in the same line are printed in italics. The differences in phonetic spelling are discussed in Chapter IV, pp. 65 f. Several of the old Sumerian names and titles have been translated into Indian Sanskrit by the early Indian compilers of the lists presumably for the information of Indians. As *V* is admittedly a very late letter, and is in Sanskrit mostly derived from B, which closely resembles it in written form, I have reconverted that letter into B in several cases, to facilitate comparison with the older name-forms. *W* is sometimes retained for the *V* of Sanskrit when it has attained currency amongst Sanskrit translators. (P) in the Table = Pali, the pre-Sanskritic vernacular of the Indo-Aryans.

[1] Cp. WVP. 3, 259, wherein the sons of the first king are specified as "Vikukshi Nimi and Danda," and they are counted as only *two* persons in the total of the fifty category in the next sentence.

See Table over the page:

Indian Main-line King-Lists

From the

SOLAR Names and Titles.	
Ayodhya (WVP. 3, 259 f.).	Videha or Mithila (WVP. 3, 327 f.).
1. IKSH-VĀKU, Founder of First Dynasty.	IKSH-VĀKU.
2. *Bikukshi* (or Vikukshi)-*Nimi* or Shashada and brother Danda.	*Nimi*.
3. Pur-*Anjaya* or Kakutstha.	*Janaka* or Vaideha or Mithi.
4. Su-*Yodh*ana.	*Udā*-Vasu or Udara Vasu.
5. *Prithu*.	Nandi-Vardhana.
6. *Vishtara*-ashva or *Vish*vag-ashwa.	Suketu.
7. Ārdra, Ayu or Andhra.	Devarata I.
8. Yuvan-ashva I.	—
9. Shāvasta or Shrāvasta.	—
10. BRIHAD-ashva.	BRIHAD-UKTHA.
11. Kuval-ashva or Dhundhu māra.	Mahā-vīrya.
12. *Dridh*-ashva or Candra-ashva.	*Dhriti*-mant.
13. Kapil-āshva ((?) brother).	*Satyā-Dhrita*.
14. Pra-moda (" The joyous ").	Dhrishta-ketu (" The daring leader ").
15. HARY-ASHVA.	HARY-ASHVA.
16. Nikumbha or ? Samhatashva, Akrisha-ashva.	Maru.
17. Prasenajit, Pasenadi (Pali).	*Pratīndha*-ka, *Prasiddha*-ka.
18. Yuvan-āshva II.	*Kīrti*-ratha.
19. Trasa-*Dasyu* I.	—
20. *Māndhā*tri.	Deva-*Mīdha* or Krita.
21. Muc*kunda* (and (?)) Puru-kutsa.	Vibudha, Vishruta.
22. Trasa-*Dasyu* II. or *Dussaha*.	*Dhriti*.
23. *Sam*-bhūta.	Kīrti-rāta.
23a. Anaranya I (slain by Rāvana).	Mahā-Roman.
24. *Prishada*-ashva.	Svarna-Roman.
25. *Hary-ashva* II or *Rohid*-ashva.	*Hrashwa*-Roman.
26. *Vasumanas*.	Janak II, Sīradhvaja.
27. Tridhanvan (or Tridhatva R.V.).	Kusha-dhvaja.
28. Trayyāruna Aiksh-vāku.	*Bhānu*-mat.
29. *Satya* Vrata (or Trishanku).	*Shata*-dyumna.
30. Harish *Candra*.	Shuci (=*Candra*) or Muni.
31. Rohit-ashva or Harita.	—
32. Cuncu or Dhundhu.	—
33. Vijaya (" The Conqueror ") or Sudeva.	—

OF THE EARLY ARYANS

PURĀNA EPICS.

LUNAR Names and Titles.		
Yadu (WVP. 4, 13 f., 61 f.).	Puru (WVP. 4, 13 f., 127 f.).	
PURŪ-ravas or Aila, Founder of First Dynasty.	PURŪ-ravas or Aila.	1.
Āyus, Amā-Vasu.	*Āyus, Ayu, Amā-Vasu.*	2.
Nahusha, Anenas.	*Nahusha, Anenas.*	3.
Yati, Yayati or (?) *Yadu.*	*Yati, Yayati.*	4.
Jina, Anjika or (?) Kroshtu.	*Puru* I (here misplaced Manasyu's dyn. No. 36–42).	5.
Vrijinī-vat.	Riceyu or *Janam*ejaya or Riteyu	6.
Swāhi or Ahi.	Matināra.	7.
Vishāmsu, Rusheka or (?) Citra-rātha.	Tamsu or Dushyanta, Dushmanta	8.
Shasha-bindu.	Anilā.	9.
PRITHU-YASHAS or PĀRTHA.	B'ARATA or UCATHYA.	10.
Tamas or *Gotama* or (?) Antara (here great variety).	*Gotama,* Aushija or Suhotra I (here great variety).	11.
Ushanas or Ushat.	Shara-*Dvat.*	12.
Shiteshu, Marutta, Kambala-barhis.	*Shatā*-nanda, Sushanti or (?) Aja-mīdha.	13.
Ruk-Meshu or *Rucaka.*	Cakshu or *Riksha.*	14.
PARĀ-vrit (or " The Restorer ") and five Sons.	HARY-ASHVA or B'army-āshva and five sons (founds Panch-ala dynasty).	15.
Jyā-*Magha* married Shaibya.	Mudgala or *Mogalla* (P.).	16.
Bidar-bha.	Badhry-ashva.	17.
Kratha-Bhīma.	Brahmishtha.	18.
Kaishika or Kaushika.	Divo-*Dāsa* or " Divine Dāsa."	19.
Cidi, founder of Cedi dynasty.	*Mitrayu* or *Mettiyo* (P.).	20.
Kunti (s. of Kratha).	Cyavana I.	21.
Dhrishta.	Su-*Dāsa* I.	22.
Nirvriti.	*Soma*ka.	23.
—	Jantu.	23a.
Vidū-ratha.	Prishata.	24.
Dashārha, destroyer of copper-faced foes.	Drupada I, famous Panch-ala king.	25.
Vyoman.	Dhristha Dyumnsa, with sister Draupadi.	26.
Jīmūta.	Dhrista Ketu.	27.
Ban-kirti or *Van*-kirti.	—	28.
—	—	29.
—	—	30.
—	—	31.
—	—	32.
Bhīma-ratha.	—	33.

INDIAN MAIN-LINE KING-LISTS

FROM THE

SOLAR Names and Titles.	
Ayodhya (WVP. 3, 259 f.).	Videha or Mithila (WVP. 3, 327 f.).
34. *B'aruka*, Kuruka, or Ruruku.	—
35. Wri-Taka, Dhri-Taka.	Urja-vaha, " son " or descendant of Shuci.
36. Bāhu or Bāhuka, vanquished by Haihayas.	B'aradvāja.
36a. —	((?) Satyadhvaja).
37. SAGARA, s. of 36, born posthumously.	SHA-KUNI or KUNI, s. of 36.
38. Asa-MANJA.	—
39. *Anshu*-mat.	Anjana.
40. Dilī-pa.	Kunti-jit or Rtu-jit.
41. Bhagī-ratha.	Arishtā-nemi.
42. *Suhotra* II or *Shruta*.	*Shrutāyus*, Satāyus.
43 Nabhin, Nābhaya.	—
44. Ambarīsha.	Su-Pārshva.
45. *Sindhu*-dvipa.	*Sanj'aya*.
45a. (Rathī-Tara, great-grandson of Ambarisha).	Kshemāri.
46. Ayutāyus.	Anenas.
47. Ritu-parna (friend of Nala).	Mīna-ratha.
48. Sarva-kāma (or (?)-bhumi).	Satya-ratha.
49. Su-Dāsa II or Mitra-saha.	Upa-Guru.
50. Kal-masha-pada, contemp. of VISHVĀ-RATHA.	Sruta or (?) Upa-Gupta.
51. Ashmaka.	Vasva-nanta or (?) Svāgata or Shashwata.
52. Mūlaka or Nārīkayaca, with PARASHU'S massacre.	Suvarcas or (?) Sudhanvan.
53. Sata-ratha or Dasha-ratha II.	Shruta or (?) Subhasa.
54. IL-IBILA (or Ilivila).	Sushruta.
55. Vishva-saha I.	Jaya.
56. Khatvānga or Dilīpa II.	Vijaya.

OF THE EARLY ARYANS

PURĀNA EPICS—*Continued*

LUNAR Names and Titles.			
Yadu (WVP. 4, 13 f., 61 f.).	Puru (WVP. 4, 13 f., 127 f.).		
Ratha-*Bara*.	—		34.
Nara-ratha or Nava-ratha.	—		35.
Dasha-ratha I or Dridha-ratha.	Pra-Cin-wat (or Puru II) (and dynasty displaced as No. 5 in text).		36.
—	—		36a.
SHA-KUNI or KUNI, s. of 36.	Pra-Vīra or "The Foremost Hero," s. of 36.		37.
—	MANASYU.		38.
Karam-b'a.	Abha-yada, Vāta-yudha or (?) Shakta, Samhanana (here great variety).		39.
—	((?) Shakta).		40.
Deva-Rāta.	Dhundu, Su-Dhanvan or Shambhu.		41.
Deva-*Kshattra*.	Bahu-Gava.	(Kusha Dyn.) [Suhotra, s. of Kāncana, displaced in WVP. 4, 14.	42.
Devana (here great variety).	Sampāti or Samyāti.	Jahnu.	43.
—			44.
Madhu.	Aham-yāti or Bahu-vadin.	*Sunaha* or Sujanta.	45.
Puru-vasha.	Raudr-āshva and ten "sons" by Misra-Keshi.	Ajaka.	45a.
Purud-vant.	[Riceyu or Rīksha, followed by Samvarana and "after a thousand years" by *Kuru*, and this last dynasty ending with *Vicītra-Virya*, the father of Dhrita-rashtra, the 1st King of Gangetic India.]	Balak-ashva.	46.
Jantu or Amshu.		Kusha.	47.
Satvant (with great variety).		Kushāmba and br. Basu II.	48.
Satvata, and sons Anamitra, Nighna, etc., sons.		Gādhi.	49.
Bhajamāna, Andhaka, etc.		VISHVĀ-RATHA, Vishvā-Mitra, and contemp. Uru-Ricika.	50.
Kukura.		Suneyu. Jama-Dagni.	51.
Vrishni.		PARASHU-Rāma, Sushena.	52.
Kapota-roman or (?) Deva-Midhasha.		(End).	
Vilo-man.			
Nala or (?) Shūra.			
Abhī-jit.			

Indian Main-line King-Lists From the Purāna

SOLAR Names and Titles.	
Ayodhya (WVP. 3, 259 f.).	Videha or Mithila (WVP. 3, 327 f.).
57. Dirgha-bāhu. 58. Raghu (or (?) Prithu-shravas). 59. Aja. 60. DASHA-RATHA III. 61. RĀMA-CANDRA 62. Kusha and Lava. 63. Atithi or Suhotra. 64. Nishadha. 65. Nala. 66. Nabha or Nabhas. 67. Pundarīka or " Great Lotus." 68. Kshema-Dhanvan. 69. Devānīka. 70. Ruru or (?) Suto-rusta. 71. Ahi-nagu. 72. Sudhanvan or Pāriyatra. 73. Bala or Sahasrabala, with separate line. 74. Sthala or Shala or Gaya. 75. Auka or Uktha. 76. Vajra-nābha. 77. Shankha. 78. Ab'yutthit-ashva or Dhyushit-ashva. 79. Vishva-saha II. 80. Hiranya-nabha [?Bur-naburiashe] 81. Pushya. 82. Dhruva-sandhi or Artha-siddhi. 83. Su-darshana. 84. Agni-varna. 85. Shīghra. 86. Maruta. 87. Prasushruta. 88. Sugavi or Susandhi. 89. Amarsha. 90. Mahaswat or Sahaswat. (End.)	Rita. Shunaya. Vītahavya. Dhriti. Bahul-ashva. Kriti or Kritak-Shana. (End.)

OF THE EARLY ARYANS

EPICS—*Continued.*

LUNAR Names and Titles.	
Yadu (WVP. 4, 13 f., 61 f.).	Puru (WVP. 4, 13 f., 127 f.).
Punarvasu. Āhuka. Devaka and Ugrasena and Dhriti. Kansa. Vasudeva, s. of Shūra. (RĀMA-) KRISHNA. Sāmba. (End.)	

II

Kish Chronicle Text

(See Plate IV & p. 59 for Translation, with Names revised by Indian Key-Lists).

Obverse

[1st Dynasty at Ukhu, Uxu or Akshak.]

Line

1. *Ukhu*[1]*-ki-a Uku-si*[2] *lugal-am*, 30 *mu-in-ag.*
2. *Azag*[3]*-da-Ama* (*or Baa'kus* or *Bau'sam*)[4], 12 *mu-in-ag.*
3. *Tan-tan*[5], 6 *mu-in-ag.*
4. *Nak*[6]*-śa-an-sir*[7], 20 *mu-in-ag.*
5. *I-śu-il*, 7 *mu-in-ag.*
6. *Śu-an-en-zu ban I-śu-il-ge*[8], *mu in-ag.*
7. 6 *lugal-e-ne mu-bi*, 99 *in-ag-eś.*
8. *Ukhu-ki-a bal-bi ba-kur nam-lugal-bi. Kiś-ki-śa ba-tum.*

[2nd Dynasty at Kish.]

9. *Kiś-ki-a Azag aś Ba-kus* (or *Ba-sam*) *śal-lu ul-tin-na suxus Kiś-ki mu-un-gi-na*[8].
10. *lugal-am*, 60+4(0) [9] *mu-in-ag.*
11. *Nak*[6]*-śa-an-enu-zu ban Azag aś Ba-kus-ge*, 25 *mu-in-ag.*
12. *Uru*[10] *aś-Sa-ga-ga ban Nak-śa-en-zu-ge*, 6 *mu-in-ag.*
13. *Zi-*(or *Gin-*) *mu-gun*, 30 *mu-in-ag.*
14. *U-zi-wi-tar ban Zi-mu-gun-ge*, 6 *mu-in-ag.*

[1] *Ukhu* (or *Okhu*), Br. 8125; on *Akh*, Br. 8124 and 8290=" Eagle," see WSAD. 9, and B. 346 and 355; cognate with *Bak*, " Hawk," WSAD. 25), and the obvious source of that English word as well as " Eagle." On its *Akshak* value, see p. 71.

[2] *Si* or *Zi* or *Zig*. On *S* for *Z*, see Br. 11720.

[3] *Azag*, Br. 9887; B. 428, is clearly the sign here.

[4] The signs *Lu-lu*=*Ama*, M. 8172 (where duplicate has same Assyrian value as single *Lu*). On *Baa'kus*, Br. 10727. On *kus*=*sam*, cp. Br. 6018, 5025 and 6019.

[5] *Tan-tan*, Br. 11252.

[6] The sign is *Nak*, *Nag*, " drink " or " beverage," Br. 868; B. 37.

[7] *Aś-sir* or *An-sir*=" Lord+serpent."

[8] On the masculine character of *Azag*, Lord *Bakus*, see text. *Śal* in text=" to pour out, libate " (M. 8378 and MD. 1082)+*lu*=" man."

[9] In text 60+40 is obviously a mistake of scribe for 60+4, and repeated by later copyists.

[10] *Uru*=" devotee," M. 8642, 8648, 8684; MD. 384.

Line

15. *Ugun-Mu-tin,* 11 *mu-in-ag.*
16. *I-mu-aś-u,* 11 *mu-in-ag.*
17. *Na-ili*[1]*-ia-kha,* 3 *mu-in-ag.*
18. 8[2] *lugal-e-ne mu-bi,* 586 *in-ag-eś.*
19. *Kiś-ki bal-bi ba-kur nam-lugal-bi Unug-ki-śu ba-tum.*

[3rd Dynasty at Unug or Erech.]

20. *Unug-ki-ga lugal Zag-gi-si lugal-am,* 25 *mu-in-ag.*
21. 1 *lugal mu-bi,* 25 *in-ag.*
22. *Unug-ki-ga bal-bi ba-kur* [*nam-lugal*] *bi A-gu-du*[3] *ki-śu ba-tum.*

[4th Dynasty at Agudu (or Agade).][4]

23. *A-gu-du-ki-a Śar-ru-Ki-in* . . . [*ni-lu-ba-ni*] . . . *nu-iś-sar.*
24. *ga-śu-du* . . . *uru aś-Zag-ga-ga.*
25. *lugal A-gu-du-ki* . . . . *du-a.*
26. [*lugal-am,* 55 *mu*]*-in-ag.*

[*a, b. Uru-Mu-uś ban Śar-ru-Ki-in mu* 9 (15), *ni-ag.*

[*c. d. Ma-ni-is-Ti-is-śu śeś-gal Uru-Mu-śu-uś.*

[*e, f. ban Śar-ru-Ki-in mu* 15 (7), *ni-ag.*

[*g-i. Na-ra-am an-En-zu ban Ma-ni-is-Ti-is-śu mu* 56 (38), *ni-ag.*

Reverse

Line

1. *Śar-Ga-*[*ni*[5]*- lugal*[6]*- Ri,* 24 *mu-in-ag*].
2. *a-ba-am* [*lugal, a-bu-am-nu-gal*].

[1] *Ili,* Br. 5308.

[2] 8 is got by merely totalling the names of the kings who only reigned for 156 years—*plus* is thus obviously omitted in giving the total reign of this dynasty as 586 years. For the names of the 27 kings of Kish of this dynasty reigning for 430 years, see App. I, Table Nos. 10-36; and Table opp. p. 140.

[3] See note to translation.

[4] The restorations within square brackets are from the fragmentary Isin lists from Nippur in Univ. of Pennsylvania, edited by Poebel (PT. 1914) and Legrain (LHF. 1922), and from the Weld-Blundell 444-prism version edited by Langdon, with readings revised by new keys.

[5] This *ni* sign has also a value of *li.*

[6] This name is usually transcribed as *Shar-gani sharri* or *Shar gali-sharri,* notwithstanding that the fourth sign is *Lugal* or "King" (Br. 4266) and has no *Shar* value in Sumerian. For evidence of the real form of his name see his Egyptian inscriptions in text, Indian list names and Indus Valley seals in Appendix XI.

Line

3. *I*[1] *-gi-gi lugal, I-mi lugal.*
4. *Na-nu-um lugal, I-ama lugal.*
5. *gar-bi,* 3 *mu-in-ag.*
6. *Du-du,* 21 *mu-in-ag.*
7. *Śu-dur-kib bandù-du-ge,* 15 *mu-in-ag.*
8. 12 (? 11) *lugal-e-ne mu-bi* 197 *in-ag-eś.*
9. *A-gu-du-ki bal-bi, ba-kur.*
10. *nam-lugal-bi Unug-ki-śu ba-tum.*

[5th Dynasty at Unug (Erech).]

11. *Unug-ki-ga Uru-Nigin lugal-mu,* 3 *mu-in-ag.*
12. *Ur-is-ginar-ban Ur-Nigin-ge,* 6 *mu-in-ag.*
13. *Kud*[2] *-da,* 6 *mu-in-ag.*
14. *Nak-śa-li-li,*[3] 5 *mu-in-ag.*
15. *Ur-aś-utu,* 6 *mu-in-ag.*
16. 5 *lugal-e-ene mu-bi in ag-eś.*
17. *Unug-ki-ga bal-bi ba-kur.*
18. *nam-lugal-bi ugnim Gu-ti-um ki- śu ba-tum.*

. . . .

Itu in[4]*-na ud* 30 *kam.*

III

Early Sumerian King-Lists prefixed to 1st Dynasty of Kish Chronicle in Isin Chronicle as "Antediluvian" & "Early Postdiluvian" Dynasties in Prism WB. 444

With revised Reading of Names by Indian and Nordic Eddic Keys. (*And see Table opposite p.* 140.)

The discovery that these uniquely important historical King-Lists prefixed to the First Dynasty of the Kish Chronicle in the Isin Chronicle were genuine old official Early Sumerian versions of the King-Lists from the First Sumerian Dynasty, which the credulous Isin priests had erroneously believed

[1] *I* also reads *Ni*, but see text and Appendix XI.

[2] Or *Tar-*, thus giving Tar-da.

[3] Or Nak-śa-ni-ni. On *Nak* see f.n. 6, p. 528.

[4] On *In* as the name of this month (the *Simanu* of Assyrians), cp. Br. 11197 and 6287.

were earlier dynasties than the First Kish Chronicle Dynasty, and had added to them fabulous ages, has been detailed in Chapters VII–XII.

Our comparative analysis of those ancient dynastic lists, by the light of our Indian and Nordic Eddic Keys, disclosed that they were three separate ancient versions of the Sumerian King-Lists, each beginning from the same first king as the first king of the First Sumerian Dynasty in the Kish Chronicle, but much earlier compilations than the latter. The dates on which these three early versions were compiled, as estimated by the date of the last king in each list, were, we found, about 3180 B.C., for the first or so-called "Antediluvian" List, which ended with King Barat; for the second so-called "Early Postdiluvian," ending with Sargon-the-Great, about 2700 B.C.; and for the third, which ends with Sargon's grandson, Naram-Enzu, a date of about 2600 B.C. It is thus seen that the traditional antiquity of these ancient lists had not been forgotten, as we find them strung together by the Isin priests in their due order of antiquity; though in ignorance of the identity of the kings, through some of them bearing other titles, solar or lunar, the Isin priests imagined that they were all totally different lines of kings. This was similar to the present-day Indian Brahmans, and following them the European Sanskrit scholars, who believe that the solar and lunar lines of the Early Aryans are totally different lines of kings and dynasties.

In this Appendix is given my revised readings of the proper names in these old lists in the light of our Indian and Eddic Keys. All these readings, when they differ from those arbitrarily selected from the polyphonous values of the Sumerian signs by previous decipherers without any key to the traditional forms of the names, are duly attested from the standard Sumerian lexicons, and therefore cannot be gainsaid. As the translation is literal, the fabulous ages are necessarily given, but these in nowise detract from the authenticity of the names and their chronological succession. It will be noticed that the record is formed on the same general model as the Kish Chronicle recording the capital city, King's name, regnal years, and the total regnal years for each dynasty. *For List of these kings see Table opp. p.* 140.

'ANTEDILUVIAN" DYNASTY from Isin Dynastic Prism WB. 444

Revised Decipherment and Translation.

Col. 1.
Lines

1–2. Kingship from Heaven was made arise: At Urdu[1] City kingship was.

3–4. At Urdu City UDU-IN[2] the king reigned 28,800 years.

5–6. A-AMA (or A-KU)[3] of the Jar reigned 36,000 years. Two kings.

7–8. 64,800 years they reigned. Urdu City was overthrown:

9–10. the royalty to the walled Kishib[4]-nagar City passed.

11–12. At the walled Kishib-nagar City ENU (or IN)[5] Priest-King,[6] lord of men[7] reigned 43,200 years.

13–14. The king,[8] the great priest-king, the lord reigned 28,800 years.

15–16. The lord DUMU-ZI (or -GIN), the shepherd,[9] reigned 36,000 years. Three kings,

17–18. they reigned 108,000 years. Walled Kishib-nagar City was overthrown,

19–20. the kingship passed to Larāk City. At Larāk City SIBA-ZI the lord

21–22. reigned 28,800 years. One king,

23–24. he reigned 288,000 years. Larāk City was overthrown:

[1] Eri-du, Br. 2645; wherein ERI is dialectic for *Ur*, see Br. 289-90, and before.

[2] Br. 10672, 9261. The *a* preceding *Udu-in* is ablative suffix of the preceding word *Ki*, "City," forming *Ki-a* "in or at the City" as in opening line of Kish Chronicle (see p. 528). On *Udu* sign see Br. 10723.

[3] The second sign is transcribed so as to somewhat resemble B. 124, which has values *Ku* and *Lal;* but the sign is clearly the Wild Ox sign *Ama*, B. 183; Br. 4545, as is also seen in the duplicate text, WB. 62, see App. IV. The following sign *Gar*=" Jar," Br. 12184, and refers to the magic stone-bowl of which he was the co-capturer.

[4] *Bad*=" Wall," Br. 4386. *Kishib*, M. 2601, 2614. Is evidently a corruption for Kish City.

[5] Br. 2806-8.

[6] *Me-en* or *Shib-en*, priest (or enchanter) + king, Br. 10368 f., 2816.

[7] *Lu-ash-na*=" lord of men." *Ash*=" Lord," Br. 419, 428; WSAD. 20, and *Ash-na* literally=" heavenly lord" (cp. Br. 448 f.). It is obviously the source of the Sanskrit *Īshāna*, " Lord, ruler, master," MWD. 171.

[8] In, En=" King," Br. 2816.

[9] *Siba*=shepherd, Br. 5688.

Col. 1.
Lines

25–26. the kingship passed to "Sippar". At "Sippar" City the king-priest UMUSH,[1] the lord,

27–28. was king, he reigned 21,000 years. One king,

29–30. he reigned 21,000 years. "Sippar" was overthrown:

31–32. the kingship was established at Sumadru City.[2] At Sumadru City BAR-DU-DU (or BARA-TUTU)[3]

33–34. was king and reigned 18,600 years. One king,

35–36. he reigned 18,600 years. Five cities,

37–38. Eight kings, they reigned 241,200 years.

39. The Deluge came up.

"Early Postdiluvian" Dynasty at Kish from Isin Dynastic Prism WB. 444.

Revised Decipherment and Translation.

40–41. After the Deluge had come, Kingship from Heaven was made arise.

42–43. At Kish City kingship was. At Kish City GA-UR (or GA-URU.[4]

44–45. became king. He reigned 1200 years.

46–47. MUKH-LA,[5] lord TASIA[6] companion, lord A(?)-ZAG[7] reigned 960 years.

Col. 2.
Lines

1–2. . . . . (abraded and illegible).

3–4. . . . . (do.).

5–6. MA-(or BA-) . . . . , PI–ASH-(?)EN-ZU[8] . . . .

[1] Br. 10517.

[2] Su-mad-ru. In the variant WB. 62, the last sign is written *di*, giving the form *Sumaddi*, which corresponds to the old capital city name *Sumati* of the Pali texts.

[3] *Bara-du-du* or *Bara-tu-tu*. The first sign is *Bar*, *Bara* (B. 301, Br. 6871-2).

[4] This *Ur* sign has also *Uru* value.

[5] The first sign is *Mukh*, B. 366; M. 9166; and not *Gul*, B. 381, which is distinctly different.

[6] Tasia, see before and Br. 10038, 11253 and 12190.

[7] *Zag*, B. 270; Br. 5962. The prefixed *A* is somewhat defaced.

[8] These are same signs that have been read *Bu-Sin*, with substitution of *Pi* value (Br. 7506) for *Bu*, and Sumerian *Enzu* as written for Semitic -in, and the intervening *Ash* sign which is present in text.

Col. 2.
Lines

7–8. GU-NI PI-(or BU-)URUDU [1] reigned 950 years.

9–10. GU-UDU-MU-MU [2] reigned 840 years. DU-TU-GIN-DARA [3]

11–12. reigned 900 years. AZAG(?) [4] reigned 600 years.

13–14. AZAG(?)-BA [5] reigned 840 years. AR-WA-SAG, [6] son of priest (*Mash*) RU-ZAX [7]

15–16. reigned 720 years. E-TA-NA, the shepherd ((?)GAL) [8] who to Heaven

17–18. ascended, who made the foreign lands faithful,

19–20. became king and reigned 1500 years. BA-(or BI-) GU(B)-'U, [9]

21–22. son of Etana, reigned 400 years.

23–24. EN-ISHIB, [10] sea-lord, reigned 660 years. ME-DE, [11] of Kish, son of Enishib,

25–26. sea-lord, reigned 900 years. Priest GA-AG (or MUG) [12] sea-lord, s. of Enishab,

27–28. sea-lord, reigned 1200 years. DIX-SA-AX, [13] s. of Priest Gaag (or Mug),

29–30. reigned 140 years. TIZ-KAR, son of Dixsaax,

31–32. reigned 306 years. RU-MA [14] - U, reigned 900 years.

33–34. RU-TA-SA RA-UM, [15] reigned 1200 years.

[1] *Gu*, Br. 6103 ; SS. 244. *Pi* or *Bu*, Br. 7501-6. *Urudu*, M. 2600.

[2] *Gu*, Br. 504 or *Du*, Br. 506. *Udu*, Br. 10673.

[3] *Du*, Br. 506. *Tu*, Br. 6107. *Dara*, Br. 10475.

[4] The second mutilated sign here is clearly the Axe-sign and gives *Azag*, Br. 6591.

[5] The same two signs with addition of *ba*.

[6] Second sign is B. 339, with value *Wa*. JAOS. 31–43. *Sag*, B. 270 ; Br. 5962.

[7] *Ru*, Br. 5245. *Zax* or *Sax*, Br. 5928.

[8] The Isin scribes have treated *Gal* grammatically as "who," but in old text that word probably represented the name of A-Mad-*Gal*.

[9] *Gub*, Br. 1103. *'U* or *'I*, B. 354 ; Br. 8285.

[10] As before, may be title of "King-priest."

[11] Second sign has value *de*, Br. 4568.

[12] This sign is not B. 497 but Br. 1905, *Gak* or *Gaag*. It seems, however, from Indian lists to have been sometimes confused with B. 497, with the value *Mug*.

[13] *Dix*, Br. 3923.

[14] First sign is clearly not *Il* but *Ru*, B. 181 ; Br. 4524 ; and 2nd sign is *Ma*.

[15] First sign as in last ; and second last sign is *Ra*, Br. 4856.

Col. 2.
Lines

35–36. The king-priest BARA-GIN-MA,[1] who the land of Elam

37–38. with weapons subdued, became king. He reigned 900 years.

39–40. SHA-GIN (or -KIN, or -GUR),[2] s. of king-priest Bara -Gin-ma.

41–42. reigned 625 years. Twenty-three kings.

43–44. They reigned 24,510 years, 3 months, 3 days and half-a-day.

44–46. Kish City was smitten by weapons. The kingship passed to Bid-(or In-)na-na.

"Early Postdiluvian" Dynasties at Inanna, Enoch (Erech), &c. from Isin Dynastic Prism WB. 444.

Revised Decipherment and Translation.

Col. 2.
Line

47. At Inanna (or Biddingirna),[3]

Col. 3.
Lines

1–2. [SAG[4]-GI]-AG-GU-[SHE, the swift,[5] son] of Udu[6] as lord,

3–4. became king. He reigned 325 years. Saggi Aggushe, the swift,

5–6. penetrated to the sea and went up into the mountains.

7–8. King-priest GAN (GUN or KAN),[7] s. of Sagki Aggushe, the king of Unug (Enoch) City, who built Unug City:

9–10. MU-UKU,[8] the begetter of Plants,[9] became king.

[1] The last sign is evidently *Ma*, B. 230.

[2] *Sha*, Br. 2774. *Gin* or *Kin*, cp. phonetic sign Br. 6105 with 10748-49. On *Gur*, Br. 6105.

[3] *In*, Br. 6237; or *Bid*, "abode," Br. 6235; WSAD. 37. *An*=*dingir*, Br. 418-20.

[4] *Sag* or *Zag*, Br. 5962.

[5] *Ag*, Br. 4735; *Gu* or *Ga* as before; *Ir*=swift, Br. 5381.

[6] *Ash Udu*=" The Sun-god."

[7] *Gan*, *Gun* or *Kan*, B. 119; Br. 3173. *In-men*, "King-priest" as before.

[8] *Mu*, Br. 1225; *Uku*, Br. 5912.

[9] *Du*, "plant," Br. 5270; *A* "beget," Br. 11330.

Col. 3.
Lines

11–12. He reigned 420 years. Lord IN, shepherd of the vessel,

13–14. reigned 1200 years. Lord DUMU-ZI (or -GIN), prince PUR (or PURU),[1]

15–16. whose city was *Kha-me* (or Ha-me or Hā-ā) City, reigned 100 years.

17–18. Lord IZ-ZAX GA-MESH,[2] whose father was ZAX, the mighty,[3]

19–20. the king of Kub -(or Zir-) abba. He reigned 126 years.

21–22. URU-ASH,[4] great sea-lord,[5] son of Izzax Gamesh,

23–24. reigned 30 years. MUKH of the sea-lands,[6]

25–26. son of Uruash, great sea-lord, reigned 15 years.

27–28. The protector BA-USSA, the swift,[7] reigned 9 years.

29–30. ENNUNAD, the lord, reigned 8 years.

31–32. DIX-XI, the divine (Di) reigned 36 years. ME-DE[8] the lord,

33–34. reigned 6 years. King KI-AGA, reigned 36 years.

35–36. Twelve kings, they reigned 2310 years.

37–38. Unug (Enoch or Erech) City was smitten by weapons. The kingship passed to Ur City.

39–40. At Ur City PA-ASH-I-PAD-DA,[9]

41–42. reigned 80 years. URUDU-KI RAM-AN,[10] of Uru City,

43–44. son of Pāshi-padda, became king.

45. He ruled 36 years.

Col. 4.
Lines

1–2. [E-AMA[11] reigned 25 years. BI-AMA[11] reigned 36 years.

[1] *Pur, Puru*, B. 306; Br. 6971.

[2] *Iz*, Br. 5968; *Zax*, Br. 4577; *Ga-mesh*="Lord of Oxen."

[3] *Zax*, Br. 5928; *la*, "mighty," M. 7588.

[4] Note his simple name of *Uruash*=Indian Haryashva.

[5] On *Nun-gal*="great sea-lord," see text.

[6] *Mukh*, B. 366; M. 9166. *Unu*="land," Br. 5915; *ma*="ship," Br. 3683.

[7] *Ba* (or *Bi*), Br. 102-3. *Ussa*, Br. 10051-3, 12214.

[8] *De*, Br. 4568.

[9] *Pa*, B. 270; Br. 5954. *Ash*, Br. 419. *i*, Br. 5307.

[10] *Urudu*, M. 2600; *Ram*, Br. 4737; *an*, Br. 418.

[11] On *Lu-lu* *Ama*, see before.

Col. 4.
Lines

3–4. [Four kings. They reigned 177 years.

5–6. [Ur City was smitten by weapons. The kingship to " Awan " City.

7–8. [passed. At " Awan " City.

9–10. [. . . . . . . became king. He reigned . . . . . . years.

11–12. [. . . . . . . reigned . . . . years.]

13–14. BA-RU[1] . . . . reigned 36 years.

15–16. Three kings. They reigned 356 years.

17–18. " Awan " City by weapons was smitten. The kingship

19–20. passed to Kish City. At Kish City . . . .

21–22. became king. He reigned 201+ years.

23–24. DU-DU-? GUN[2] reigned . . . . years. MA-MA-GAL . . . .

25–26. reigned 360 years. KA(?)-ALBU . . . . (or INIM-AL-BU . . . . . .),[3]

27–28. son of Ma-gal-gal[4] reigned 195 years.

29–30. TUK-E[5] reigned 360 years. BURU-(or PURU-)GIN[6] sea-lord[7] reigned 180 years.

31–32. The horizon-quartering[8] GAN-NI PUR[9] reigned 290 years.

33–34. King MU reigned 360 years. Eight kings:

35–36. They reigned 3195 years. Kish City was smitten by weapons.

37–38. The kingship passed to Kha-ma-si[10] City.

[1] *Ru*, Br. 9132. [2] *Du*, Br. 6644. *Gun*, Br. 6985.

[3] *Inim* or *Ka*, Br. 508.

[4] Prism has here *Ma-gal-gal* and not *Ma-ma-gal* as above.

[5] *Tuk*, Br. 10513.

[6] This compound sign is clearly, as seen by the Indian key-lists in Table opp. p. 140, the *Bur*, *Pur* or *Puru* sign, B. 234; Br. 5480; with the *Gin* sign enclosed. The full value *Buru* or *Puru* is got from the *Uru* value of its phonetic, Br. 5480, 11245.

[7] On *Nun-na* as " Sea-lord," see text.

[8] *Ibi*, " Quarter of horizon," Br. 18477 and PSL. 184.

[9] This sign somewhat abraded is seen by Indian key-lists to be obviously *Gan*, *Kan*, B. 119; Br. 3173; *Gunu*, M. 2011; *Pur*, B. 234.

[10] The affix *Si* is defined as *Ma-la* . . . M. 2776, which was probably *Malakhu*, " boat man," and cognate with Phœnician *Malah*, " god of sailors," cp. MD. 546; and Ma-kan or " Field of boats " was a title of Egypt as we have seen in the text.

Col. 4.
Lines

39–40. At Kha-ma-si (City) KHA-(?)MA-NI-IS[1] ruled 360 years.

41–42. 1 king: he reigned 360 years.

43–44. Khamasi City by weapons was smitten, the kingship passed to Unug (Erech) City.

45–46. At Erech EN-UG-GE-AN-NA[2] became king. He ruled 1 *sos* (60 years).

47–48. The kingship was for 2 *sos* (120 years) (?) For 420 years they reigned.

IV

Second Version of "Antediluvian" Kings from WB. 62, with Names revised.

This somewhat later Babylonian version contains the full list of the ten "Antediluvian" kings, and significantly they are in full agreement with and in the identical order of the first ten kings in the Indian Official Lists (compare Table opposite p. 140). Their fabulous reigns, which are generally double even the fantastic ages in the Isin version, and ranging for the individual kings from 72,000 to 21,600 years are omitted in this translation.

Line

1. . . . . -KI UDU-IN[3] . . . .

2. . . . . AMA of the Jar[4] . . . . . . Kha-me[5] City.

3. At . . . . . . City UN-NU-SHA[6] the commander of commanders[7] . . . .

4. . . . . [UDU ?]-UK ?-KU ?[8] . . . . City.

5. . . . . [DUMU]-ZI, the shepherd . . . .

[1] In the transcript this second sign is written an abbreviated *da*, but it resembles the *Ma* or boat-sign. See discussion on p. 271.

[2] On *Ge* value for this sign, cp. M. 3336.

[3] Written by same signs as in Isin version (see p. 532 l. 3).

[4] Same as in Isin version (see p. 532).

[5] The second sign also reads *A*, *Bur* or *Dur*.

[6] *Sha*, B. 310; Br. 7047.

[7] *Kin-Kin*, B. 483.

[8] Uk ?-ku ? is as read by previous decipherer. On *Udu*, see f.n. 5, p. 540.

Line

6. . . . . EN, lord of men, ... the walled Kishib-nagar City.
7. . . . . SHIBA-ZI, lord . . . . Larāk City.
8. King-priest, The Jar (*Dur*)[1] lord, [PISH-MA-MA] . . . .
9. SU-MAD-DI[2], son[3] of Pish-ma-ma.[4]
10. The established BAR-RAD-DU[5], son of Sumaddi . . . . 2 kings of Sumaddi City.

V

THE NAME "NIMROD" FOR THE SECOND ARYAN KING GAN OR "CAIN" IN SUMERIAN & INDIAN CHRONICLES

The usual early Sumerian name for the second Aryan king, the son and successor of the first king, and the first great extender of his father's Aryan empire and its civilization—with the extension into Mesopotamia and his building of the city of Enoch there—was, as we have seen from the contemporary and other early inscriptions, his own personal names variously spelt *Gin*, *Gun*, *Gan* or *Kan*, along with the titles of *Azag* (presumably a patronym as "Son of Zag or Sag") and *Bakus* ("Bacchus") as the extender of agriculture.

Besides this personal name and those two titles we found that in the old Sumerian King-Lists, prefixed by the Isin priests to the Kish Chronicle he is given besides this Gan name and Azag title the titles of Lord *Mukhla* or *Mūku* and *Tasia;* and we found in Chapter I that he was called Lord *Miklu,* now seen to be a dialectic form of the former title, which we have seen was the source of the modern title of "St Michael." *Muku,* it is to be noted, was also a title of

[1] On *Dur* for "divining jar," see WSAD. 64. His personal name is given in next line.

[2] *Su,* Br. 162; *mad,* 7386; *di,* B. 415; Br. 9518.

[3] B. 161.

[4] *Pish,* B. 303; Br. 6928; and WSAD. 80; *Ma,* B. 190; Br. 4290.

[5] *Bar,* Br. 7768; *Rad*—the sign here written has ordinary value of *Sud;* but on *Sud=Rad,* cp. Br. 2293-4. Significantly this sign is written by the *Rad* sign in the Assyrian version of this list published by Dr Weidner.

his deified form as Marduk, the son of Bel[1] his deified father, the first king, which further identifies him with his human prototype Azag by his title of Muku being written as "Azag of the Garden," and defined as "related to a Skin(-ful) of strong Wine,"[2] thus identifying him again with Bakus or Bacchus. And all of these titles are preserved for him in the Nordic Eddas as Gun or Kon, Aegis, Bauge and *Miok*, and all except the first and last in the Indian Epics, as we have seen.

About two and a half centuries after his death, when we find him canonized or semi-deified as the patron saint of the great Sumerian seaport city of Lagash on the Persian Gulf, he bears the title of *Nimirrud*, and he is styled "The first-born son of Lord (or God) Sakh, the King of the Lands and "The Hero of King Sakh"—the old spelling of Sagg for the first king having been thus altered to *Sakh*, in order presumably to give his name on his deification the mythological meaning of "Lord of the Wind or Storm," as we have seen in the text of this work.

This title, *Nimirrud*, which is presumably coined from *Nimi-in* or "Forty-fold"[3] in which the affix *in* = "a plant,"[4] has hitherto been conjecturally restored by Assyriologists from the polyphonous Sumerian signs, without any key whatsoever to its traditional form, as "Nin-gir-su." But our Indian King-Lists give this second king the traditional solar title of *Nimi*, as we have seen, with the associated title of *Bikukshi*, which is the Indian spelling of his Bakus or Bakush or "Bacchus" title. With this Indian key, we find that his name in Sumerian really reads *Ni-mir-rud*,[5] and significantly the affix *rud* means "increase,"[6] just as in

[1] Br. 4379, 4291, 9888.

[2] Shi-kur su al-lit.

[3] Br. 10030.

[4] Br. 4227-8.

[5] *Ni*, Br. 10982; *mir*, Br. 301, Sb. III, 31, B. 10; *rud*, cp. Br. 164, where phonetic does not read *Tuk*, but *ru-du*, Br. 506, and *ru-udu*, cp. second sign in 3860, which is wrongly read *ku* instead of *du*. see Br. 10511, where *tu* is read instead of the *du* value of that sign, Br. 1068. This incidentally discloses that all the *Uk* and *Uku* values of sign B. 150, Br. 3860 and M. 2549 f., must be altered to *Ud* and *Udu*, which is also in keeping with their meanings of "Sun," day, light, etc., as written by the Sun signs. This value of *Rud* for this sign is also in agreement with its Semitic value of *ruddu*, Br. 168, which has the same meaning of "increase."

[6] See previous note.

several of his other titles, from being the extender of agriculture, he is gratefully called "The Increaser of Plants."[1] And as showing that the affix *rud* was merely an expletive, we find the name sometimes written in Sumerian as "Rud Ni-mir" or "The Increaser Nimi or Nimir," and thus confirming the Indian Chronicle form of his title *Nimi* as the shorter style for Nimirrud.

Positive evidence for the real form of his name as *Ni-mir-rud* is given in the beautiful Indus Valley seal, Fig. 140 in Appendix XII, in which the first two syllables of his name are spelt by different syllabic signs, but with the same phonetic values.

Interesting confirmation of this "Nimi" form of his title is found in the variant title coined for him by King Gudia on his votive offering to him of the Serpent-Dragon stone-bowl, see Fig. 15, p. 31 (in commemoration, as we now see, of the capture by Nimirrud of the original fetish bowl), and it is used also by him in other temple inscriptions and hymns, in which Gudia makes him a reflex of "Nimirrud," as *Ni-mish-zi-da* (or *-ta*)—a name hitherto conjecturally read "Nin-gish-zi-da." This new form of spelling his name gives it the meaning of "Lord of the Tree of Life," a suitable title for the idealized Bakus or Bacchus, whom he was.[2]

All this now identifies him clearly with the historical original of "Nimrod" of the Hebrew Genesis, where the name is written "Nimrud," whose human original has never hitherto been found. In that Hebrew narrative we are told[3] that "Nimrod" was the son of "Cush," which is evidently a corruption of Nimirrud's father's solar title of Ukusi or Agushe. We are also told that "he began to be a mighty one (literally "giant" in the Hebrew)[4] in the earth. He was a mighty hunter before the Lord, wherefore it is said, even as Nimrod the mighty hunter before the Lord. And the beginning of his kingdom was Babel and Erech (Erek in Hebrew) and Accad and Calneh in the land of Shinar."

This "mighty" hunting reputation of this second Aryan king or emperor, as Nimi (or Nimrod), is also preserved

[1] WSAD. 7, 22, 26.
[2] *Ni*, "lord"; *mish*, "tree"; and *zid*, "life"; Br. 2322.
[3] Gen. x. 8-9.
[4] EB. 3410.

in the Indian Epics, which also refer to it as hunting "for the Lord." These Indian traditional accounts, however, although occurring in the solar versions, have been expanded by the later moon-worshipping Indian Brahmans, who had latterly captured the Epics, with silly fabulous additions founded on transparently false etymologies of the names, in order to make out that the first Aryan king, Iksh-Vāku, although solar, was addicted to moon-worship, with its demonist animal sacrifices, a cult which we have seen he had especially revolted against. In the Indian Epic account of this hunting exploit, as edited by these lunar Indian Brahmans, we read: "Upon one of the sacred festal days, the eighth day after the full moon, Iksh-Vāku (being desirous of performing ancestral obsequies[1]) ordered Bikukshi (-Nimi) to bring him flesh suitable for the offering. *The prince accordingly went into the forest and killed many deer* and other wild animals (for the celebration). Being weary with the chase and being hungered, he ate a hare, after which (being refreshed) he carried the rest of the game to his father. The family priest of the house of Iksh-Vāku was summoned to consecrate the food, but he declared that it was impure, in consequence of Bikukshi's having eaten a hare from amongst it (making it thus, as it were, the residue of his meal). Bikukshi was in consequence abandoned by his offended father; and the epithet *Shashāda*(hare-eater) was affixed to him by the priest. On the death of Iksh-Vāku, the dominion of the earth descended to Shashāda (that is Bikukshi)." [2]

Another Brahmanist version of King Nimi's sacrifice and the curse imposed on him by the moon-worshippers relates that because he, Nimi, did not employ the lunar priest for his oblation, he was cursed by the latter, with the result according to the Brahmans of instant death.[3] And it is added: "The corpse of Nimi was preserved from decay by being *embalmed with fragrant oils and resins, and it remained as entire as if it were immortal.*" [4] This incidentally shows that the Hindus were acquainted with the tradition of

[1] Significantly the first king who is made to perform this celebration for the manes of his ancestors is stated to be Purū-Ravas (WVP. 3, 168), that is the lunar title of Ikshvāku himself, and thus connecting these two in Indian Epic literature.

[2] WVP. 3, 260 f. [3] WVP. 3, 327. [4] *Ib.*, 328.

embalming dead bodies. Now comes the even more absurd climax. As the lunar Brahmans had gratified their imagination by killing off the obnoxious sun-worshipper Nimi, for not employing and feeing their lunar priests, they have to invent the following miracle in order to account for the fact that his son was the third king. Thus they say: "As Nimi left no succession, the priests, apprehensive of the consesequences of the earth being without a ruler, agitated the body of the prince and produced from it a prince who was called Janaka, from being 'born without a progenitor' (Janaka), and Mithi, from being 'produced by agitation' Mathana)." On the Sumerian original of this son's name here rendered "Janak," see previous Tables. Despite these childish expansions of the hostile Brahmans by these false etymologies, it is clear that ancient tradition recorded that Nimi was "a mighty hunter," and that it was remembered in relation to sacrifices "before the Lord"; and that he, as a worshipper of the Sun and Heaven, was cursed by the Moon-worshipping and animal-sacrificing priests of the aboriginal cult of Darkness and Death.

In Babylonian tradition also, the hunting fame of this second Aryan or Sumerian king is reflected in the four hunting dogs which were attached to the suite of the god Marduk or Marud of Babylon, and of which sculptured effigies were offered in his temple there. And we have seen that Marduk was this deified second king Nimirrud under a much later title as "The Son of the Sun." The name Nimrud also still clings to the great tower of Birs Nimrud to the southwest of Babylon, which was popularly believed to be the "Tower of Babel." Nimrud is also the name of the great Assyrian city with sumptuous palaces on the Tigris to the south of Mosul (Nineveh). And the great Nimrud Mountain on the western shore of Lake Van in Armenia, to the east of Cappadocia, and draining, on its western side, into a tributary of the Upper Euphrates or Omiras (the Vimur of the Eddas) carries this king's name far to the north.

In the Nordic Eddas this second king as Miok (Muku, Mukhla or "Michael") is the owner of a famous hunting falcon, and as Kon he is a keen hunter and lover of hounds.

Altogether, it is thus seen that Nimrod is now identified

with the historical second Aryan or Sumerian king or emperor, the son of King Adar, Ad or Adamu or "Adam" on the one hand; and he is identified on the other hand with that son, whose personal name was Kan or "Cain." It will be observed that in the Indian version Bikukshi Nimi (that is Kan) was made by the hostile lunar Brahmans to have his offering rejected like "Cain," according to the hostile Semitic story: "Unto Cain and his offering he (the Hebrew Lord) had no respect." And like Cain, he is made to have been "abandoned," and to have an obnoxious label (or "mark") attached to him. Yet like Cain also, so far from suffering by the lunar curse, he, on the contrary, flourished and succeeded to "the dominion of the earth," and "began to be a mighty one in the earth," and he built, according to the Hebrew tradition the (first ?) city in Mesopotamia of Enoch (or "Erech," and so named after his son, whose Sumerian name we have seen was *Unuk* or *Eno*).

The City of Enoch, we have seen, is admitted by all the leading Biblical experts to be identical with the City Unug or Unuk and latterly Uruk of the Sumerians, and identical with the "Erech" of the later Hebrew Old Testament texts. And traditionally it was built according to the Babylonian King-Lists of the Sumerians by this second Sumerian king, and according to the two Hebrew traditions by Cain, and also by Nimrud. Moreover, in the later Babylonian legend in "The Creation Tablets," its building, as we have seen, is ascribed to Marduk, son of Bel the Lord, who has been demonstrated in these pages to be this deified second Sumerian or Aryan king. In this regard it is noteworthy that "Erech," which is spelt in the Hebrew (which does not express short vowels) as *E-R-K*, that is *Erek* or *Erak*, and is at the site of the modern Arabic village of *Warka*, appears to me to be the source of the modern territorial name for Mesopotamia, namely *Irak* or *Iraq*.

The further identity of this second Sumerian or Aryan king Kan or Nimirrud or "Nimrod" with "Cain" is confirmed by his traditional relationship with "Abel," as preserved in the Nordic Eddas. In these epics *Epli* (that is "Abel") of "the Garden of Iotun," with the "Tree of Knowledge" at the Well of Urd, is neither the son of Ad,

Adar or Thor nor the brother of Miok or Gunn; but on the contrary the arch-enemy and assailant of both, and the champion of the moon- and serpent-worshippers of the Geld (or "Chaldees") sorcerers of Ginnung Land (the Kinengi name of the Sumerians for Mesopotamia), and who in his attack with his followers upon Thor and his son was killed in a duel by the latter when crown-prince, as is related in circumstantial detail in the Nordic Eddas.

VI

New Seals of Sumerian Emperors and Governors from Indus Valley deciphered; *Disclosing Seals of* A-MADGAL and TARSI *of First Phœnician Dynasty c.* 3080-3050 B.C. *and* Keys to their Curvilinear Sumerian Script.

The immense number of official signets of Sumerian emperors, priest-kings and governors that have been unearthed during recent years at the capital of the rich Indus Valley colony of the Sumerians at Mohenjo Daro presumes, as I previously suggested,[1] that the excavations have exhumed the actual graves of some of these kings and those of their governors to whom these official seals had been entrusted, and who had them buried beside their bodies as relics.

The Curvilinear Sumerian Script of I. V. Seals and its Decipherment.

The Sumerian character of the writing on the seals unearthed by the Indian Archaeological Survey, under Sir J. Marshall at Mohenjo Daro and Harappa, I at once recognized entirely independently on first seeing the photographs of the first batch of these seals published in the *Illustrated London News* of September 20th 1924, pp. 528 f. For I had been for the previous eighteen years devoted to the study of Sumerian writing and had significantly *four months previously* in my book on "The Phœnician Origin of the Britons" demonstrated that Indian Civilization with its Writing was of Sumerian origin. Later, I observed that several Assyriologists in subsequent numbers of the same journal remarked

[1] WISD. xii. f.

on the resemblance of some of the signs to the linear Sumerian script of Mesopotamia; but none of them could decipher a single one of the inscriptions nor have they been able yet to do so, either for that first batch or the many hundreds more seals in the subsequent batches up till the present date, December 31st 1928.

This total inability of Assyriologists to decipher these Indus Valley inscriptions, which I termed "Indo-Sumerian" though latterly the same script has been found on seals unearthed in the lowest Sumerian strata at Kish in Mesopotamia, is obviously owing, as I pointed out in 1925 in my *Indo-Sumerian Seals Deciphered*, to this script being written mostly, not in the angular lithic and cuneiform style of Sumerian inscriptions in Mesopotamia, to which alone Assyriologists have hitherto been accustomed, but in the pen-and-ink curvilinear style of the earlier pictographic Sumerian, for writing on parchment or bark or wooden tablets. This form of writing preserves in many cases a fuller objective and naturalistic pictograph of the sign than in the angular Mesopotamian script, in which through the exigency of writing on moist clay tablets, in a climate where parchments soon perished, by dabbing with a flat straight-edged style, the signs became reduced into angular diagrams, often giving little or no indication of the original object pictured by the sign.

Yet, Assyriologists with their inveterate Semitic prejudices, whilst universally admitting that Mesopotamian Sumerian writing must have been originally full pictures of the objects expressed by its signs, nevertheless in their narrow outlook, strange to say, refuse to recognise as "Sumerian" any sign which differs in the slightest degree from the cramped diagrammatic form of the later Sumerian writing in Mesopotamia.

In my decipherment tables, both in my former work and in the following appendices, I exhibit each of the Indus Valley seal inscriptions with its corresponding signs in the angular diagrammatic Mesopotamian Sumerian alongside and sign-by-sign, so that the unprejudiced reader may perceive for himself the absolute identity of the signs, Indo-Sumerian and Mesopotamian Sumerian.

The proof of the correctness of my decipherments is that each of the very large number of these Indus seals of the second batch, 63 in all, thus treated, yields in every case good Sumerian language with good sense and the names and titles of well-known historical Sumerian kings and emperors and their capitals of the early Sumerian period. And besides this, the art and culture of the objects and buildings and graves at the sites where these seals were unearthed are in type distinctively Sumerian.

In these decipherment tables I have numbered the seals as in the Plates, and as before, have given in the 3rd line the phonetic Sumerian value of each sign duly attested from the standard bilingual lexicons, wherever the sign has not been attested in previous pages; and the literal translation in the 4th line. These seals, like the majority of Sumerian seals, are engraved in the orthographic direction from left to right as in Aryan writing; but their impressions read in the reversed or retrograde direction as in Phœnician writing. This is evident by comparing Nos. 1 and 2 and 4 and 5 of Plate IX, which represent respectively the seal and its impression. On the governors' titles of "King Companion" and "Under King-Companion," see p. 264.

INDUS SEALS OF A-MADGAL OR A-KUR DECIPHERED.

Nos. 1 & 2, Pl. IX. Seal of A-Madgal or A-Kur, at Edin.

This seal of the founder of the Indus colony calls him by his alternative title of A-Kur (the affix *gal* meaning "The Great," as we have seen), but also gives his title of "The Shepherd," as in the official plaques of his father (see p. 167); and his title of "Minister" is written by the self-same sign as in his victory-seal (Fig. 19, p. 109).

Indus Seal.

Sumer (Mesop.).

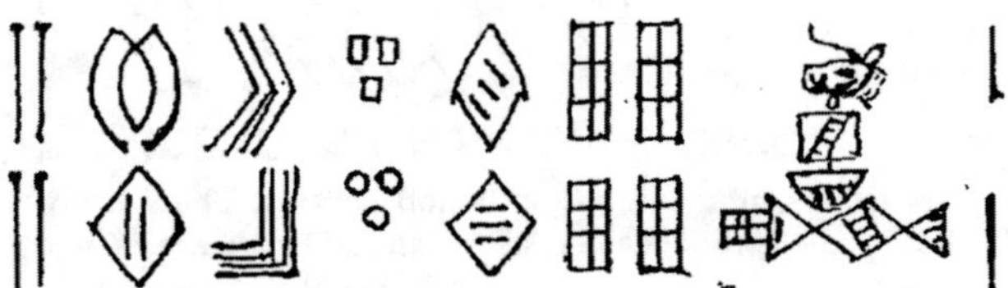

Reads: A-KUR[1] TAX[2]-MAD-KI UDU-UDU[3] EDIN[4]-ASH

Transl.: A-KUR, The Minister, Shepherd of Shepherds of Edin Land.

FIG. 72.—Seal of A-KUR, The Minister, The Shepherd of Shepherds of the Land at Edin deciphered.

[1] B. 429; Br. 9924.
[2] B. 278; Br. 6165.
[3] B. 482; Br. 10673.
[4] B. 181; Br. 4526 f.

No. 3. Seal of Madgal as Viceroy

In this seal, which repeats his title of "The Shepherd of

Shepherds" and uses his viceregal title of "Under King-Companion (or Interior King-Companion)," instead of "Minister," he also calls himself "The First Son" (*i.e.*, crown-prince), and the word for "son" here becomes afterwards his title as *Marru* in others of his seals, and in the Indian King-lists—*Mar* meaning "Son" in Sumerian.

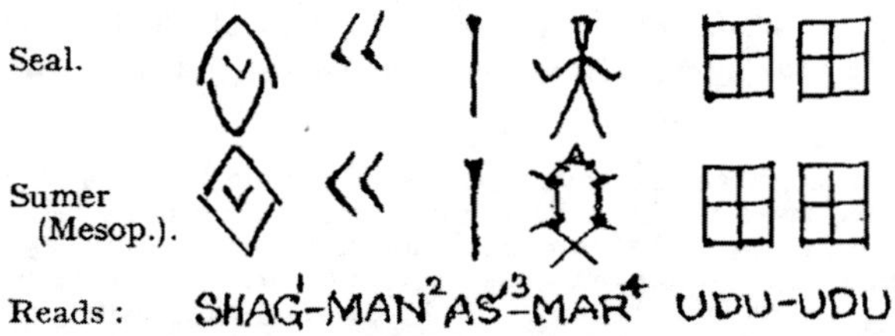

Transl.: Under King-Companion, First Son (*Mar*), Shepherd of Shepherds.
FIG. 73.—Seal of Madgal as Viceroy, First Son and Shepherd deciphered.

[1] B. 340; Br. 7987. [2] B. 431; Br. 9945. [3] B. 1; Br. 13. This sign has also value when written erect of *Makkas*. Br. 10063.

[4] B. 392; M. 6821. This linear sign sometimes closely resembles the *Gin* sign, B. 501, but the latter has a larger head, as seen later.

Tiger Seal, Nos. 4 and 5, of Magdal or Marru, the Viceroy Gut of Tiger Land

This fine artistic seal, with the Tiger as its chief device, reads as follows:—

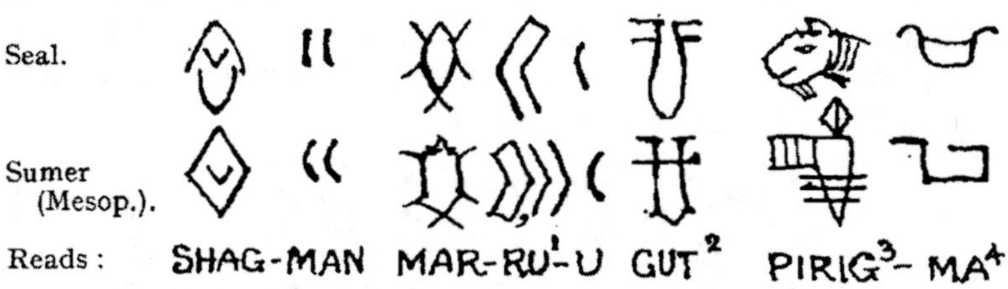

Transl.: Under King-Companion MARRU, The *Gutu* of Tiger Land.
FIG. 74.—Seal of Madgal as MARRU, The Viceroy *Gutu* of Tiger-Land deciphered.

[1] B. 69; Br. 1421. [2] *Gut* as before.

[3] B. 400; Br. 9188, with the meaning of "leopard or panther," MD. 688. The same sign with value of *Ug* or *Tianu* = "Lion."

There seems a possibility, as seen later, that this seal may belong to Menes' son Narmar or Narām, as he also was called "Marru", and he has an Elephant seal in same style. For the Sumerian sign for *Gut* of an Ox-head differs only from that for *Am* or "Wild Bull" by the addition in the latter of two (or three) wedges inserted on its face.

Now in the Ox-head sign in that Elephant seal, there seems besides the large dot (representing a wedge) on the forehead of the Ox-sign, to be two other smaller dots below it, which would make the sign the Wild Bull sign with the value *Am*—the same sign by which Narām wrote his name in his Mesopotamian inscriptions. But if these two smaller dots are disregarded, the sign reads *Gut-u;* and is thus in keeping with A-Madgal's title of *Gut* as he is called in his father's plaque (p. 114).

The name "Tiger Land" reads in Sumerian *Pirig-ma*, wherein *Pirig* appears to be the Sumerian source of the late Sanskrit name *Vyāghra* for "Tiger," and *Vrika* "wolf"; but *Pirig* has also in Sumerian the alternative values of *Ner*, *Gir* and *Ug*, of which *Ner* is a title of Naram.

His use of the name "Tiger Land" for the Indus colony presumes the existence of the Tiger at that period in the Lower Indus Valley or at Harappa, the upper city of the Edin colony near the Himalayas (see Map, p. 116), where tigers are still found at the present day. But according to the best modern authority the tiger nowadays is only found "in a few places in Upper Sind and the Western Punjab—it is wanting in Lower Sind."[1] In this regard an old topographical Indian tradition places a "tiger-faced people" (Vyāghra-mukha) "in the eastern division of India."[2]

No. 6. Seal of Madgal as Marru, King-Companion, The Gut

In this large seal, of which only the upper left-hand fragment was found, he bears the still higher title of "King-Companion," which seems the equivalent of "Co-regent." The inscription reads :—

Seal.

Sumer (Mesop.).

Reads : LUGAL MAN MAR-RU GUT....GU

Transl. : King-Companion MARRU, The *Gut* of the Land of . . . .

FIG. 75.—Seal of Madgal as MARRU, The Gut, deciphered.

1 Cp. WPOB. 239.

1 W. T. Blanford, *Mammalia of India*, 60. 2 IA. xiv. (1893), 5.

No. 7. Seal of Madgal as Gal-the-Great, The Gut of Edin

In this seal Madgal is styled " Gal-the-Great " and also The *Gut* of Edin.

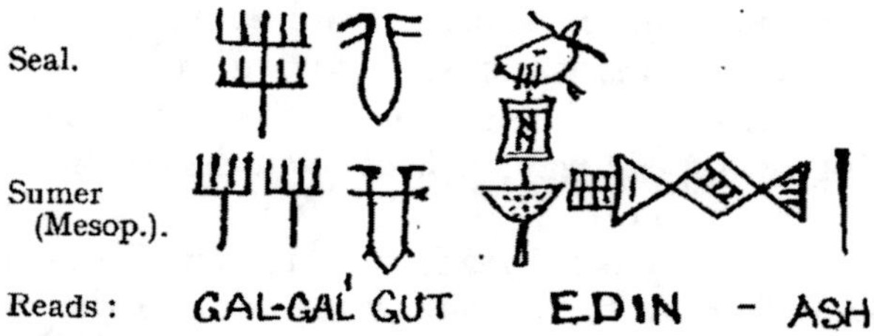

Trans : GAL-the-Great at Edin.

FIG. 76.—Seal of Madgal as GAL-the-Great, The Gut at Edin deciphered.

This seal affords striking proof, by the three strokes through the jaw of the ox, of my identification of the pictographic Sumerian sign B. 275, *Ga* or *Gu* (the 1st element in the Edin monogram), with a Buffalo ox.

No. 8. Seal of Tarzi or Tarsi as King-Companion, The Lord Gut at Uridu

This seal of Tarzi or Tarsi, the grandson of King Madgal (see p. 104), describes him as " Under King-Companion and The Gut at Edin." And his name is written by the self-same signs as in his own records found at Lagash city-port in Mesopotamia. It reads :—

Transl. : Under King-Companion TARZI, the Lord Gut at URIDU.

FIG. 77.—Seal of TARSI, Under King-Companion, The Lord Gut, at URIDU deciphered.

[1] B. 12 ; Br. 359. [2] B. 91 ; Br. 2301. [3] B. 316 ; Br. 7304.
[4] B. 417. The sign is clearly not *Ki*, but *Du* with its projecting lines.

On the site of Uridu see text.

VII

New Sumerial Seals of SARGON & his Father King BUR-GIN (PURU II) from Indus Valley deciphered

The great nest of imperial Sumerian seals in the second batch unearthed by the Indian Archæological Survey Department, under Sir J. Marshall, at Mohenjo Daro, which I have shown was the capital of the Edin colony of the Sumerian emperors of Mesopotamia, was, I found, especially rich in the seals of Sargon and his son Menes and their dynasty, and contained besides these also seals of Sargon's father, the Emperor Bur-Gin or Puru II, as shown in Plate X. Of Sargon himself I discovered no fewer than six new seals, as enumerated at p. 227, in addition to the two formerly deciphered by me.

In detailing the decipherment of Sargon's new seals and those of his father, I here follow for convenience of reference the order in which they are figured in Plate X, the last seal in which No. 10 is one of Menes Aha as "The son of Shagani," *i.e.*, of "Sargon."

The Great Bull Signet of Sargon, Nos. 1–2

This exquisitely beautiful seal, with the Indian humped bull as its chief device, and which is figured as No. 1 in Plate X, and its impression showing the reversed direction in No. 2, reads as follows :—

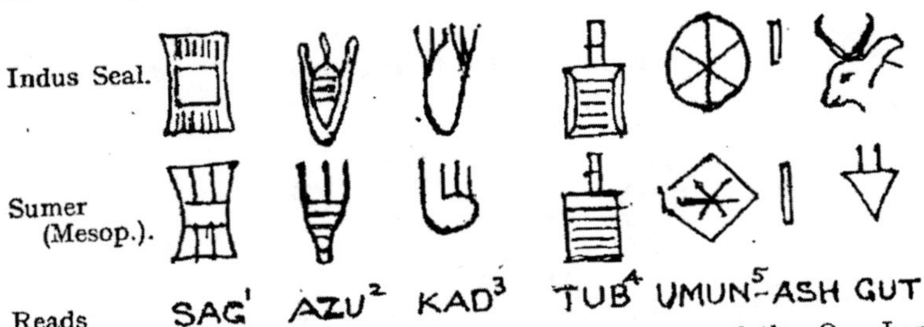

Transl. : Sag, the Seer, the lofty *Kad*, the tablet of the One Lord The *Gut*.

Fig. 78.—Seal of Sargon as Sag (-(?) ara), The *Kad*, The *Gut* deciphered.

[1] B. 291 ; Br. 6461.
[2] B. 188 ; Br. 4666.
[3] B. 311 ; M. 5059.
[4] B. 157 ; Br. 3935.

Here the title *Sag* appears to be short for *Sagara*, his title in the Indus seal previously deciphered by me, and the solar title as frequently used for him in the Indian Epics. And his title of "Seer" is repeated in the Indus seal of his son Aha-Men, No. 6, App. IX.

No. 3. Seal of Sargon's Father as Puru-ar Gana of Egypt and Magan

This Seal No. 3, Pl. X, reads :—

Seal.

Sumer (Mesop.).

Reads : PURU[1]-AR[2] GAN[3]-A MUSH-SIR MA-GAN

Transl. : PURU the Ar, GANA of *Mushir* (Egypt) and *Magan*.

FIG. 79.—Seal of Sargon's Father as PURWAR or PUAR or BUAR-GANA of Egypt and Magan deciphered.

[1] B. 325 ; Br. 7502 ; and cp. 6971 and 11255. As we have seen, it possesses also the polyphonous values of Bu and Buz and PI.
[2] The plough sign Ar. B. 261 ; Br. 5776.
[3] This Indus form of the sign is diagrammatic, so as to resemble the Sun sign somewhat.

The name in this and in the next seal are in series with those in the archaic prefixed Isin Lists, as seen in the Table opposite p. 140, No. 36, cols. 1 and 2.

No. 4. Seal of Sargon's Father as Puru (or Bu) Par-Gin of Uridu Land

This seal reads :—

Seal.

Sumer (Mesop.).

Reads : UMUN PURU PAR GIN URI-DU[1]

Transl. : Lord of Lords PURU PAR-GIN of *Uridu* (or *Uriki*) Land.

FIG. 80.—Seal of Sargon's Father as PURU Par-Gin of *Uridu* or *Uriki* Land deciphered.

[1] As in previous seal, and the other signs as in former seals.

No. 5. *Seal of Sargon as Sharru Gin*

This seal reads :—

Seal.

Sumer (Mesop.).

Reads : SHARU[1] - GIN GU- URI[2]-KI-ASH

Transl. : SHARRU-GIN of *Uriki* Land.

FIG. 81.—Seal of SHARRU-GIN of *Uriki* Land deciphered.

[1] B. 364A ; Br. 6630. [2] B. 316 (as before).

Here *Uriki* Land is the usual Sumerian name for the Semitic *Akkadu* and Amurru as we have already repeatedly seen in the foregoing pages with detailed proofs. *Uri-ki* is sometimes read arbitrarily by Assyrologists as " Ur City."

No. 6. *Seal of Sargon as Shar-Gin, The Great Khāti*

This seal reads :—

Seal.

Sumer (Mesop.).

Reads : SHAR[1] GIN GAL-KHA-A-TI[2] GU-...

Transl. : SHAR-GIN, The Great *Khāti* of . . . . Land.

FIG. 82.—Seal of SHAR-GIN, The Great *Khāti* of . . . Land deciphered.

The great importance of the use here by Sargon of the title *Khāti* or " Hittite " has been remarked in the text, see p. 226.

[1] B. 353 ; Br. 8221. [2] Br. 7685.

No. 7. Seal of Sharum-Gin, The Gut of Agdu Land

This seal reads :—

Seal.

Sumer (Mesop.).

Reads : SHAR-UM-GIN GUT GU-AG-DU-ASH

Transl. : SHARUM-GIN, The *Gut* of *Agdu* Land.

FIG. 83.—Seal of SHARUM-GIN, The *Gut* of Agdu Land deciphered.

[1] B. 353 ; Br. 8221.

No. 8. Seal of Gan, The Puru (or Pharaoh) of Khamaesshi at Agdu Land

This seal reads :—

Seal.

Sumer (Mesop.).

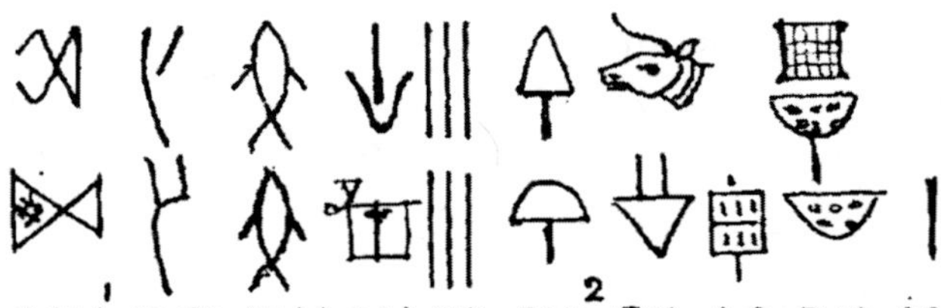

Reads : GAN[1]-PUR KHA-MA-ES-SHI[2] GU-AG-DU-ASH

Transl. : GAN, The Pharaoh of *Khamaesshi* at *Agdu* Land.

FIG. 84.—Seal of GAN, The Pharaoh of *Khamaesshi* Land deciphered.

[1] B. 160 ; Br. 4036. [2] As before.

No. 9. Seal of Gan, Bur the Piru or Baru (Pharaoh), The Gut of Uri-du Land

This seal reads :—

Seal.

Sumer (Mesop.).

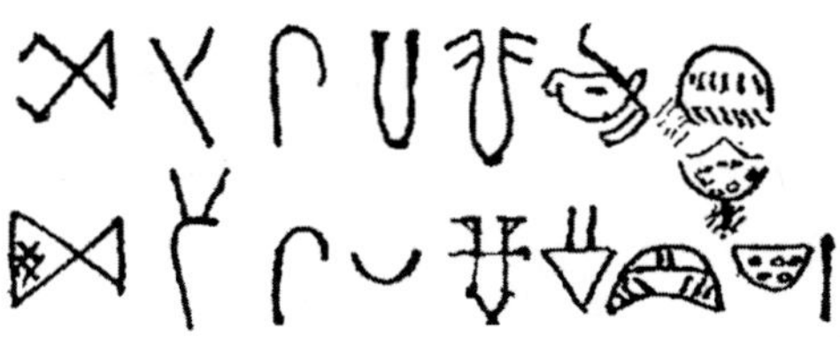

Reads : GAN-PUR PAR-U GUT GU-URI-DU-AŚ

Transl. : GAN, PUR, The *Pharaoh*, The *Gut* of Uridu Land.

FIG. 85.—Seal of GAN, PUR, The *Pharaoh*, The Gut of Uridu Land deciphered. (See p. 228 for these titles.)

Seal No. 10 in Plate X is that of Aha as King-Companion and the son of *Sagani*, and is included in the Menes series of Indus Seals deciphered in Appendix IX.

VIII

Sanskrit Text of the Mahā-Bhārata Version of Manasyu's or Menes' Genealogy

The stanzas of the Sanskrit text of the *Mahā-Bhārata* on Manasyu's genealogy, of which I have given a literal transliteration on pp. 232–3, occur in the text of the great Calcutta edition of that Epic, published in 1834, Vol. I, section 94, slokas 3695 to 3697.

This genealogy of King Puru's dynasty purports to have been recited by the Brahman priest and Vedic teacher Vaishampāyana to the Puru-line king Janamejaya (III), immediately after the Great Bhārata War, that is, as we have seen, about 650 B.C.

I here transliterate the Sanskrit writing of these three slokas into roman letters :—

" Pravīreshvara-raudrāshvastrayah-puttrā mahārathāh |
pūroh paushtyāmajāyanta pravīro vamsha krittatah |
Manasyura bhavatta smācchuraseni-sutah prabhuh |
prithvyāsh-catur-antāyā goptā rājīvalocanah |
Shaktah samhanaanovāgmī sauvīrītanayāstrayah |
manasyorabhavan puttrāh sūrāh sarve mahārattāh | ."

IX

MENES' Sumerian Seals from the Indus Valley Deciphered

The nine seals of Menes or Manis, which I discovered amongst the second batch of seals unearthed at Mohenjo Daro in the Indus Valley by the Indian Archæological Survey Department, under Sir J. Marshall, are figured in Plates X, No. 10, and XI, Nos. 1 to 8 ; and enumerated at pp. 265–266.

In these Menes, as the ruler of the Edin colony, calls himself Men, Mānshu, Aha (or Akha), Aha (or Akha)-Men, and Aha-Mena. In three he bears the title of "Under King-Companion," in three the higher title of "Lord-Companion," and in one the imperial title of "The One Lord." In two he is styled "The *Gut* (or 'Goth')"; in one he is "Aha the Overthrower of King Mush" (that is his younger brother in Mesopotamia); in one he is "Under King-Companion in Magan and Mush (-(?) sir), or Egypt; and in three his sonship of Shagani or Gin (that is "Sargon") is recorded.

It is also noteworthy that in the seals of this dynasty we now find for the first time the use of the "Ligature" in Sumerian or Aryan writing, that is the use of signs written by attached strokes to other signs when forming compound words. This especially occurs with the use of the possessive *ge* stroke for "of."

Seal of Aha, son of Shagani, The Pharaoh at Edin Land

This seal, No. 10 in Plate X, reads :—

Indus Seal.

Sumer (Mesop.).

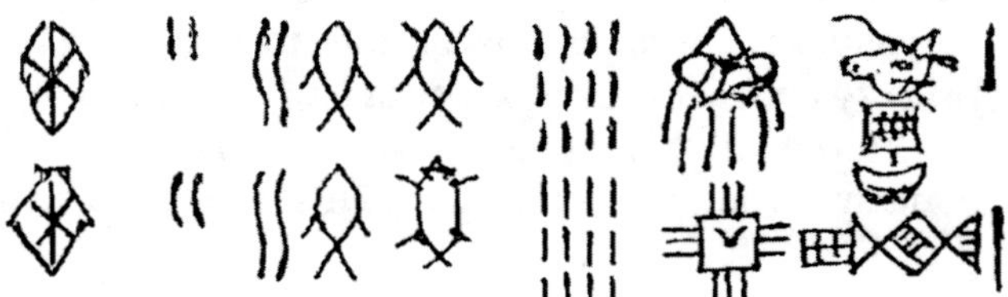

Reads : UMUN-MAN A-HA MAR SHA-GA-NI[1] BARA[2] GU-EDIN-AŠ

Transl. : Lord-Companion AHA, the son of SHAGANI, The *Pharaoh* in Edin Land.

FIG. 86.—Seal of AHA, son of SHAGANI, The *Pharaoh*, deciphered.

[1] B. 532; *Shakanu* or *Shakunu*, Br. 6821, 12182-5. On *Sha-ga-ni*, Br. 11952, 11942, 11947.
[2] B. 301; Br. 6880.

This seal indicates that Aha Menes was joint king with his father Sargon at the Edin colony; but whether this was before or after his revolt is not evident.

No. 1. *Seal* (*Pl. IX*) *of Menes as Mānshu, The Pharaoh, at Edin Land*

This seal reads :—

Reads : SHAG-MAN MA – ANSHU[1] BARA GU-AG-DU-AS

Transl. : Under King-Companion Mānshu, The *Pharaoh* at Edin (or Agdu) Land.

Fig. 87.—Seal of Mānshu, The *Pharaoh* at Edin, deciphered.

[1] On Horse-sign *Anshu*, B. 211 ; Br. 4981, defined as "Mountain ass."

No. 2. *Seal of Aha-Men*

This seal reads :—

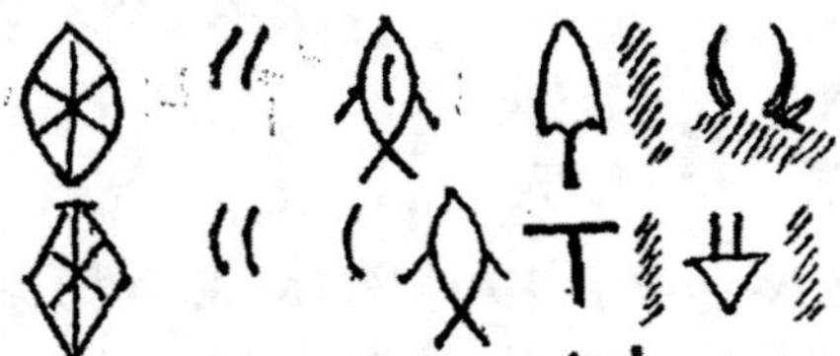

Reads : UMUN-MAN A-HA-MEN[1]... GU.......

Transl. : Lord-Companion Aha Men . . . . at . . . .

Fig. 88.—Seal of Aha Men deciphered.

[1] B. 478 ; Br. 10355.

No. 3. *Seal of Aha-*(?)*Men the Gut*

This seal reads :—

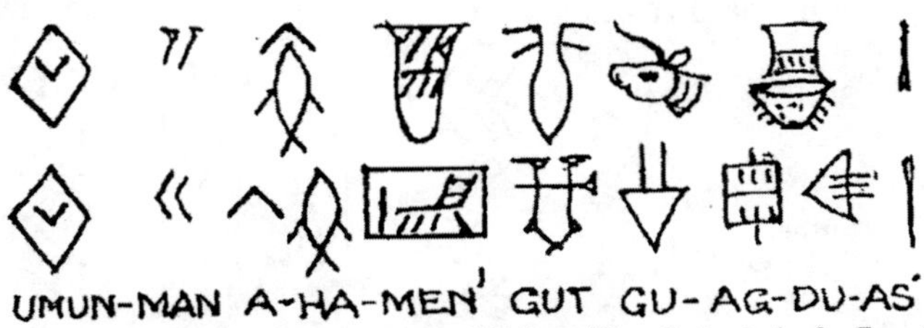

Reads : UMUN-MAN A-HA-MEN[1] GUT GU-AG-DU-AS

Transl. : Under King-Companion Aha-(?)Men, The *Gut*, at Agdu Land.

Fig. 89.—Seal of Aha-(?)Men, The Gut, deciphered.

[1] B. 240 ; Br. 5510.

No. 4. *Seal of Aha The One Lord, Son of The Gut Gin*

This seal reads :—

Transl. : The One Lord Aha, son of The Gut, Gin at Agdu Land.

Fig. 90.—Seal of The One Lord Aha, son of The Gut Gin, deciphered.

No. 5. *Seal of Aha-*(?)*Man, son of Seer Gin*

This seal reads :—

Transl. : Lord-Companion Aha-(?)Man,[1] son of the Seer [2] Esh-tar Gin.

Fig. 91.—Seal of Aha-(?)Man, son of Seer Gin, deciphered.

[1] These four strokes may read *Man-Man* as before ; or the whole sign, with its enclosing tabulature, may read, " Of the house of *Sha,*" *i.e., Sha-Gani* (see above, Fig. 86).

[2] This sign, although its interior is not cross-lined, is clearly the same sign as in Sargon's seal as " The Seer " (Fig. 78).

No. 6. *Seal of Aha as Overthrower of King Mush*

This seal reads :—

Transl. : Aha, The Overthrower of King Mush.

Fig. 92.—Seal of Aha as Overthrower of King Mush deciphered.

[1] B. 175 ; Br. 4420. [2] B. 150 ; Br. 3862.

No. 7. Seal of Aha of Magan and Mush(-sir)

This seal reads :—

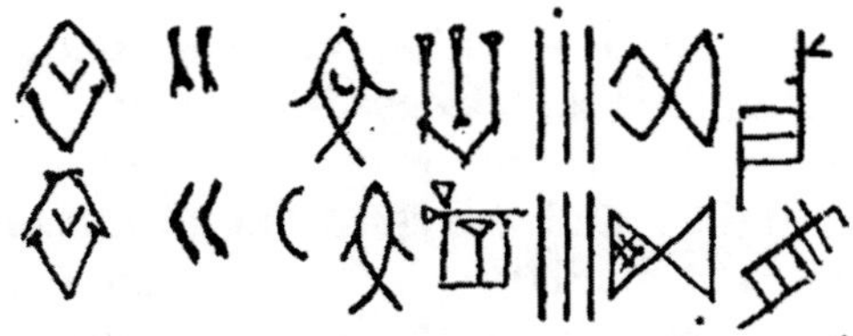

Seal.

Sumer (Mesop.).

Reads : SHAG-MAN A-HA MA -ES-GAN-MUŚ

Transl. : Under King-Companion AHA of MA(esh)-GAN (and) MUSH(-sir).

FIG. 93.—Seal of AHA of *Ma-gan* and *Mush(-sir)* deciphered.

No. 8. Seal of Aha Mena at Uri-ki (Akkadu) Land

This seal reads :—

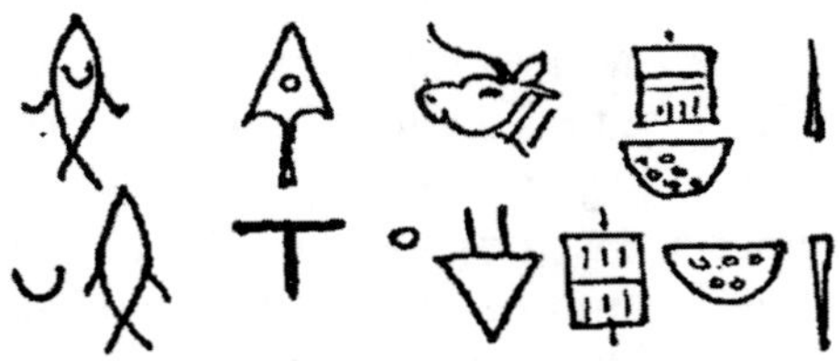

Seal.

Sumer (Mesop.).

Reads : A-HA-MEN-A GU-AG-DU-AŚ

Transl. : AHA MENA at Uriki (Akkadu) Land.

FIG. 94.—Seal of AHA MENA at *Uriki* (*Akkadu*) Land deciphered.

X

GREAT EBONY LABEL WITH SUMERIAN INSCRIPTION FROM MENES' "TOMB" AT ABYDOS DECIPHERED

THIS large ebony label figured in Plate XII (in duplicate), which was found in the "tomb" of Menes at Abydos by Sir F. Petrie, as described on pp. 282 f., is of astounding historical importance through its inscription.

In the following pioneer decipherment of this inscription, reference should be made to my careful drawing of the signs in Fig. 35 on p. 283.

The inscription is in four lines, each separated, as is usual in Sumerian writing, by horizontal bars into separate compartments or registers. The direction in which the writing is to be read is indicated by the direction in which faces of the animal signs in the pictographs are turned, the reading being through the face of the animals. Thus the first line is seen to read in the retrograde direction, from right to left; the second line in the reverse direction to that, namely from left to right; and the third line in the same direction as the first; and similarly so the last line. Therefore the inscription is written in "The Ox-plough-furrow" or boustrophedon fashion, as in the ancient Hittite and Early Greek inscriptions. The pictographs are artistically grouped and composed for pictorial effect.

The first hieroglyph of the first line, beginning at the pierced hole for the string of the label (see Fig. 35), has been supposed by Egyptologists to picture "two ships." This may be so, but it also resembles a conventional form of the plumed-crown head-sign for "king" in Sumerian, as shown in the annexed decipherment table (Fig. 95.) All the other hieroglyphs readily equated with those of the Early Sumerian writing of the Predynastic and First Dynasty Pharaohs, and those of the Indo-Sumerian seals and the standard Sumerian diagrammatic lithic script of Mesopotamia, as seen in the tables below, though several of the signs are drawn in more realistic and naturalistic fashion. And all yielded directly good sense in the Sumerian language when read syllabically.

The language is Sumerian or Early Aryan. Only one Semitic idiom occurs, in the Semitic plural form of *Mushrim* for "The Two Egypts (Upper and Lower)"—the Chaldean and Hebrew *Mizraim*—as the subject aborigines of Egypt were Semites, and presumably at that time called their land Mushrim. The Sumerians, as we have seen, called it *Mushsir*, and the Akkads *Mushri* and *Mushur*; and that land is still called by the Arabs *Misr*.

First Line of Menes' Great Ebony Label

Let us now take up the lines seriatim for decipherment as in my previous Tables, and place the signs in the usual Sumerian or Aryan direction for reading from left to right. Full references are given for the authentication and literal translation of all new signs; but where signs have been identified in previous Tables their references are here mostly omitted.

The first line reads:—

Label.

Sumer (Mesop.).

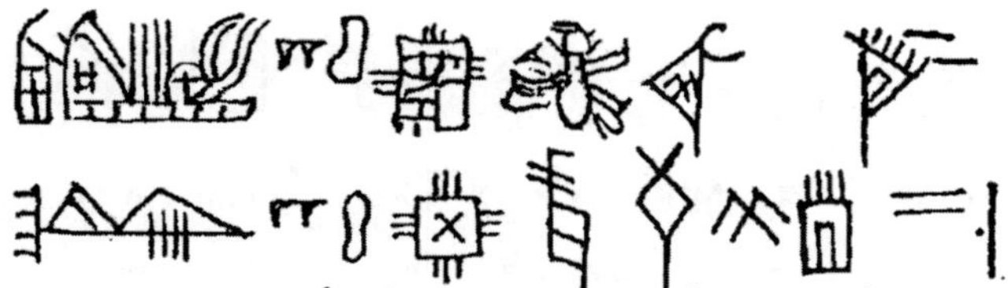

Reads: LUGAL MIN-AŠ[1] BARA MUŠ-SIR-MAD-[2]AGA-[3]TAB-GE

Transl.: "King MIN-ASH (or MAN-ASH) (or Manash of Ships), the Pharaoh of *Mushsir* (Egypt), the Land of the Two Crowns.

FIG. 95.—Line 1 of Menes' Tomb-Label deciphered.

[1] On *Man* value, Br. 9945; and on *Min*. 9946. The first sign may possibly read *Ma-ma* or "Ships."

[2] B. 325; Br. 7507.

[3] B. 304; Br. 6949.

The king's name here spelt *Manash* or *Minash* has been obviously inserted in small signs within the king sign, after the latter was written. Its *Minash* phonetic value is in series with his *Minos* title amongst the Cretans and Greeks. The Fly sign here, drawn naturalistically, with the phonetic value of *Mush* and forming the first syllable of Mush-sir or "Egypt," has hitherto been supposed by Egyptologists to be "the shield and arrows of the goddess Neith," a late goddess, although the sign is seen to be decidedly different from the Neith emblem.

The Sumerian name *Mush* for this winged insect, which is here represented like a winged Scarab beetle, seems to me possibly the source of the later Egyptian name *Mukhrr*[1] for the scarab beetle, the sacred flying beetle of the Egyptians. And this suggests that this ancient name of *Mush-sir* for Egypt, in which the affix *Sir* is pictured by a Serpent (disclosing the source of our modern word "Serpent"); a sacred totem animal of the pre-Sumerian Semitic aborigines in both Egypt and Mesopotamia, probably designated Egypt as "The Land of the Scarab and the Serpent."

[1] BD. 295A.

The continuation of the First Line of the Label reads :—

Label.

Sumer (Mesop.).

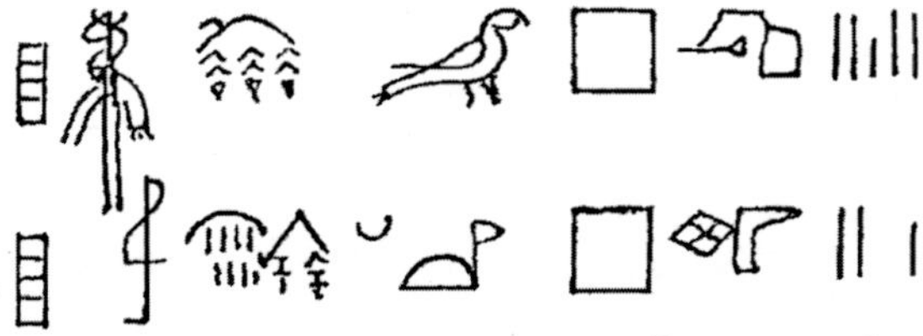

Reads : KU[1] MIM[2] WI[3] - SU XU(BAK)[4] GIR[5] AHA[6] MIN[7]-AS[8]

Transl. : " the perished dead one in the West, of the (Sun-) Hawk race, AHA-MIN-ASH."

FIG. 96.—Line 1 of Menes' Label continued, decipherment.

[1] *Ku* " perished," B. 481 ; Br. 10526 f.

[2] *Mim*=die, M. 1923, pictures a pole surmounted by the skin of an animal, B. 116.

[3] *Wi*=" West " as before. The *shu* affix is seen on full sign in the duplicate label, 4–8, as before. The pair of long strokes with a shorter medial one inside the square seem probably to be the name *Man* or *Min* duplicated with the intermedial stroke *ash*, thus giving the name *Minash* or *Manash*. Otherwise it is a diagrammatic form of *Bara* or " Pharaoh " as before. 4–8 as before.

Second Line of Menes' Great Ebony Label

The second line of this label I read as follows :—

Label.

Sumer (Mesop.).

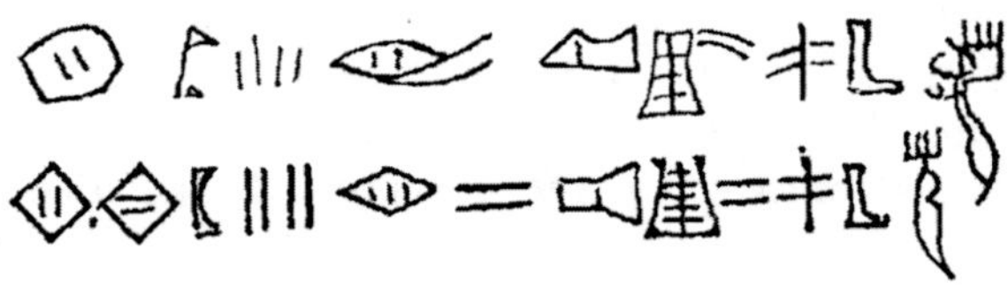

Reads : SAB[1] SU[2] A-A[3] KI[4]-TAB[5] AB[6]-ZU[7]-TAB[8] KHAD[9]-DU[10] LUSA[11]

Transl. : " of the Lower (Sunset or Eastern) and Sunset (Upper or Western) Waters and their Lands and Oceans, the Ruler the King.

FIG. 97.—Line 2 of Menes' Label deciphered in first part.

[1–11] As before. The king sign reads *Lu-sa* as well as Lu-gal (see previously)

This imperial title of " King of the Lower or Sunrise Ocean (*i.e.*, the Persian Gulf, Indian Ocean or Arabian Sea with Red Sea) and of the Upper or Sunset or Western Ocean (*i.e.*, the Mediterranean) and of their Lands," was the regular world-empire title used by Sargon and most of his dynasty on their own monuments in Mesopotamia, and *it is here written by the same Sumerian signs.*

The Sumerian pictographic signs for this imperial title are artistically grouped together to form a whole design, which has suggested to Egyptologists, who were unable to decipher them, "a man making an offering, with two signs above, possibly *uâau*, 'alone.' Behind him is a bull running over wavy ground into a net stretched between two poles. . . . At the end is a crane or stork standing on a shrine. The third line shows three boats in a canal or river passing between places. In the fourth line is a continuous line of hieroglyphs the first of such that is known. . . . On the backs of these tablets are painted signs; a spindle and a *men* sign, with two kinds of gaming pieces."[1] And Prof. Griffith conjectured that the hieroglyphs in the last line read "who takes the throne of Horus."[2]

Proceeding with the decipherment of the rest of this second line, we find it reads as follows:—

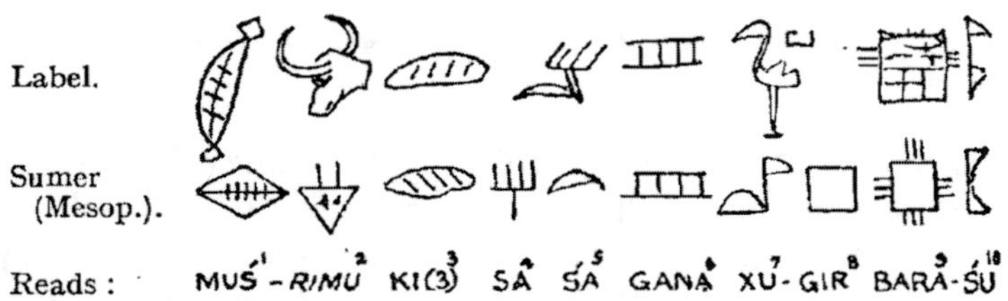

Transl.: of MUSHRIM Lands, son of Great SHA-GANA (or SHA-GUNU) of the (Sun-) Hawk race, the Pharaoh, the (pre-)deceased.

FIG. 98.—Line 2 of Menes' Label continued decipherment, recording his sonship of SHAGANA or "Sargon."

1, 3-10 As before.
2 *Rimu* is the Semitic Akkadian for *Am* or Wild Bull.

Here Menes in this Egyptian label is called "The son of the Great Sha-Gana," that is "Sargon." And significantly the second syllable of his father's name is spelt here by the identical Sumerian hieroglyph as in some of the First Egyptian Dynasty inscriptions and in one of his Indus

1 PRT, ii. 21. 2 *Ib.*, 51.

seals.[1] The form *Sha-Gunu* is seen to be in series with the common Indian Epic form of his name as *Sha-Kuni*.

Third Line of Menes' Great Ebony Label

The third line reads :—

Reads : MÀ[1]-EŠ[2] KAD[3] NIR[4] U[5]-URU[6] RÀ[7]-DU[8] MA-EŠ[9] XU[10]-RÀ[11]-DU[12]

Transl. : The Commander-in-Chief of Ships. The Commander-in-Chief of Ships, the complete course made to the End of the Sunset Land, going in ships. He completed the inspection of,

FIG. 99.—Line 3 of Menes' Label deciphered.

1–3, 4, 7 As before.

5 *Du*=command of a ship, B. 180 ; M. 3014. The sign resembles somewhat *Nir*, " Lord," B. 282.

6 The S sign here is not *Uru* as figured but *Ushu* " The end of the Sunset " (B. 403) as in Fig. 59, p. 336.

8 *Du* or *Shar*=great, complete, Br. 8231.

9–12 Signs as before—the word thus formed *Xura-du*=" inspect, behold," Br. 8526.

The realistic ship-pictographs in this line give us the earliest Sumerian or Egyptian drawings of a multiple-decked ship or galley with cabins and high prow for deep-sea voyaging at this early period. These pictures may be compared with the earlier single-decked masted deep-sea ship carved on the reverse of the ivory dagger handle in Plate V (the upper ship). It was doubtless with this multiple-decked class of ship that Menes invaded Upper Egypt by way of the Red Sea. It is noteworthy, however, that the mast appears to have been omitted, presumably for want of space ; for in the inscriptions of Manis Tusu himself in Mesopotamia, the diagrammatic Sumerian ship-sign has a mast with a yard near its top, as seen in second line of Fig. 99. Significantly, the ships on the label present a general resemblance to the old Phœnician triremes of the ancient navies of the Mediterranean, which were propelled

[1] WISD. 64 f.

by oars in three tiers, with cabin at the stern, and which were the regular warships of the Phœnicians and Greeks until about 360 B.C., and which though carrying a mast and sail are usually drawn without them, as they were only used occasionally. The 30 (or 31) strokes on the double bar line below the ships may possibly represent the number of the vessels of Menes' fleet which took part in his voyage to the Far West ; or they may be reduplications of the sign for "land," as in lines 1 and 2.

It is also noteworthy that Menes bears here the title of "Commander-in-Chief of Ships," by a name spelt *Kad-du*, which is in series with, and apparently coined on the model of, the Khād or *Khaddu* title borne, as we have seen, by his remote ancestor the Sumerian sea-emperor Uruash, the founder of the First Phœnician Dynasty, some four centuries earlier, and which is the earliest known naval power in history. This title is evidently synonymous with the "Sea-lord" (*Nunna*) title which was borne by Uruash and his descendants. And as King Minos in Greek and Cretan tradition, he was a great admiral, with "swift ships," who sailed the seas to extend and defend his dominions.

Fourth Line of Menes' Great Ebony Label

In the fourth and last line of the label is given the very important territorial name of the land in the Far Western Ocean where Menes' "built a holding" and died. The name is artistically formed into a monogram. I have provisionally deciphered this monogram with the aid of a lens as reading "*U-ra-ni-i* Land" as detailed below, and I venture to believe that it will prove correct. It is unfortunately omitted in the rougher duplicate label (Plate XII B) presumably from being too complex ; but a space was left for it, and its associated wedge-sign of "built" is duly graved therein, and gives with its hieroglyph context the same reading, minus the place-name, as in the more complete label.

This fourth line I read :—

Label.

Sumer (Mesop.).

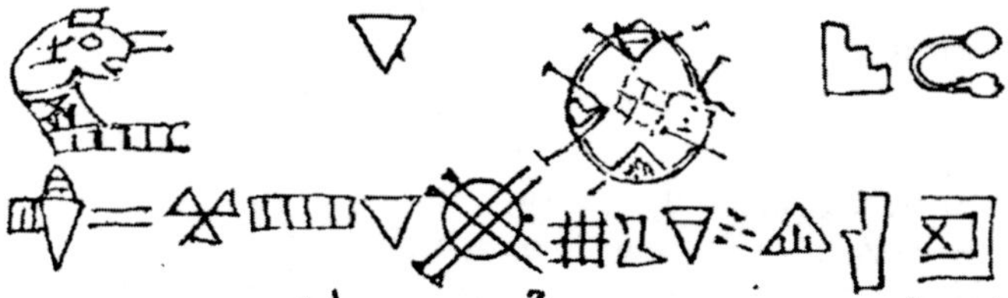

Reads : TIANU-MAD-SÚ[1]-DU GUN[2] U-RA-NI-I-KI UR[3]-E[4]

Transl. : of the Western Lands. He built a holding (or possession) at URANI Land. At the Lake of the Peak.

FIG. 100.—Line 4 of Menes' Label deciphered.

[1] B. 481 ; Br. 10509.
[2] B. 307 ; Br. 6985.
[3] B. 205 ; M. 3311.
[4] B. 61 and 263 ; Br. 1182, 5841.

The term for " The Western Lands " is here written by the usual Sumerian sign of the head of a lion, doubled by two strokes, but the sign is drawn more realistically. This term designated the Western Lands as " The Lands of Lions," that is the old shaggy alpine lion of Phrygia and the Taurus of Asia Minor, as figured in the Frontispiece, and the African lion of the Libyan and Mauretanian or Moroccan border of the Mediterranean. This same sign we have seen used in the same sense in the Egyptian inscriptions of Menes' descendants in his dynasty. The sign has also the phonetic value of *Pirig*, and is defined as " a people," which thus appears to give us the Sumerian source of the name " Phrygian." And its Akkad value of *Labu* or " Lion " probably gives us the source of the name " Libya." It was commonly used in later Mesopotamian inscriptions for Amurru or Amorite Land, including Tyana (? *Tiana*) in Southern Cappadocia, an old Hittite capital, which was latterly a prefecture of the Greeks and Romans, and thus implying that " The Western Land " of the Sumerians commenced at Hittite Asia Minor and Syria-Phœnicia, and included the Mediterranean lands west of Egypt. This totemistic title of " The Land of the Lions " would seem to be analogous to that for Egypt as " The Land of the Scarab Beetle and the Serpent " (*Mush-sir*).

The continuation of the last line of the label reads as follows :—

Label.

Sumer (Mesop.).

Reads : NAM[1] XAL[2] MUŠ LUGAL MA-ANŠU-ŠU[3] GAR[4] LAL[5]-IŠ[6]-DU[7]

Transl. : Fate pierced (him) by a Wasp (or Hornet), The King of the Two Crowns MĀNSHU. This bored tablet set up of hanging wood is dedicated (to his memory).

FIG. 101.—Line 4 of Menes' Great Ebony Label completed decipherment.

1 *Nam*, " Fate," pictured by a swallow, B. 85 ; Br. 2103.

2 *Xal*, " pierce," B. 2 ; Br. 78.

3 " Tablet writing," also " bored," B. 365, 8673, 8688.

4 " Set up, or place," B. 532 ; Br. 11978.

5 " Hang," Br. 10081.

6 " Wood," B. 258 ; Br. 5697.

7 " *Ru* " present, dedicate, B. 1 ; Br. 24. This sign which I have accidentally omitted in my tracing in Fig. 35, will be seen quite distinct on the last sign in the photograph in Pl. XIII A.

On the identification of the locality of this " Uranī Land " in the Far Western Ocean, where Menes' met his tragic death, see text, p. 286 f.

XI

FIRST EGYPTIAN DYNASTY PHARAOHS' SUMERIAN SEALS FROM THE INDUS VALLEY DECIPHERED—COMPRISING KINGS NARAM OR NARMAR, GANERI (KHENT OR KUNTI), BUGIRU (BHAGIRATHA), DUDU OR DAN (DHUNDU), AND SHUDUR KIB OR KING KIBBU OR QA (OR SUHOTRA)

THE seals of the other Pharaohs of the First Dynasty of Egypt, the descendants and successors of Menes, which I discovered amongst the second batch of Sumerian seals unearthed at the old capital of the Edin colony in the Indus Valley, are shown in Plates XI, XIV, XVIII and XIX, and are enumerated in the text thereat. Here I give my pioneer decipherments of their inscriptions on the same model as the others.

These seals whilst concretely evidencing that the First Dynasty Pharaohs, subsequent to Menes, continued to hold the Indus Valley as a colony of their Egyptian empire along with Mesopotamia, are also of the immense further historical importance in that they give in many instances the genealogies of the Pharaohs back to King Gin or "Sargon;" and to his son Aha Menes—the seals of the last two kings Dudu or Dan and Shudur Kib or Qa being especially rich in genealogical details. And significantly King Gin or "Sargon" is again given his title of UKUS, or descendant of the first King of the First Dynasty of the Kish Chronicle, which he uses in his own inscription in Egypt (p. 249), and which is his *Aikshvaki* title in the Indian Chronicles.

PHARAOH NARMAR OR NARAM'S SEALS FROM THE INDUS VALLEY.

We have seen how the son and successor of the Emperor Manis or Menes, namely *Narām Enzu* in his own Mesopotamian inscriptions, wrote his name with the Sumerian pictograph of "The Wild Bull," and used that pictograph freely in his inscriptions in Egypt, where he adopted the form of name of *Nar-mar*.

In his Indus Valley seals we now find that he also calls himself NERĀM, in which *AM* is written by the same Sumerian sign as used by him in his Mesopotamian inscriptions as *Naram*. This title for him, as Nerām, is also repeated on seal, Fig. 118, as *Neramma*. He used therein usually the name of *Ner* and *Maru* and *Mar Nera*. And like his father Menes and his grandfather "Sargon," he as well as his descendants freely call themselves *Gut* or "Goth." This title of *Ner* or *Nera* is written by a Sumerian sign which designates him as "Lord of the Deep Waters." And we have seen that traditionally as "The Wild Bull" or Minotaur son of Minos he ruthlessly dominated Crete and the adjoining isles of the Mediterranean.

In three out of his four seals he bears the viceregal title of "Under King-Companion," with the addition, as in most of the other Indus seals, of the words "at Agdu Land"—

that is *Agudu*, or "Agade" in Mesopotamia. In one, however, he is called without any subordinate title "The Gut of The Lower Land," that is the land of the Lower Sea or Indian Ocean. Significantly, in two of these he calls himself "The *son* of the great Lord Gin" (*i.e.*, "Sargon"), and not as the grandson of the latter. This is in keeping with the later Babylonian tradition, as we have seen, which calls Naram Enzu the "son" and not the grandson of King Gin or "Sargon."

No. 1. *Elephant Seal of Narmar as Mar-Nerām*

This seal, with its chief device as the Elephant or "Great Bull," is figured in Plate XI, Nos. 9 and 10, for seal and its impression respectively. The Elephant was an appropriate symbol for this king, whose name was "Wild Bull," as it is generally styled in the East "The Great Wild Bull," and this is also its name in Sumerian as *Am-si*; [1] and our modern word "Elephant" is supposed to be derived from the Semitic *Aleph*, "an ox." But besides the Elephant he is also called *Ama* or *Am* in this seal by the Wild Bull sign.

The name here if reading "Land of Ships" is of historical interest as identifying Edin presumably with the ancient "Potala" of Indian tradition, the site of which had become lost. Pot-ala, or "Abode of Boats (*Pot*)," was supposed by some to have been possibly on the Indus, and "Patala" was the name given by the Greek historians of Alexander to the last port in the Delta of the Indus, whence the Macedonian on leaving the Indus Valley sailed westwards to the Persian Gulf and Mesopotamia.

As the Tiger seal, which we have seen in Fig. 74 bears the name of *Marru* and is of the same general form as this seal, seems to have two dots within its Ox-head sign besides the large top one, and thus may also read *Am*, it thus seems possible that it also may be a seal of Narmar or Naram, and not that of his earlier namesake, Maru or Madgal.

[1] Cp. MD. 826; and in Tibetan, as translated from the Sanskrit, WBT. 390.

This seal reads :—

Indus Seal.

Sumer (Mesop.).

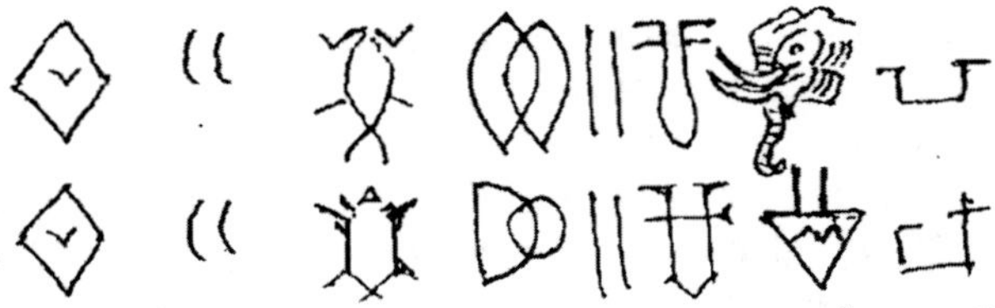

Reads : SHAG- MAN MAR - NER[1] A GUT AM[2]- MA[3]

Transl. : Under King-Companion MAR-NERĀM-MA the Gut, or Nera the Gut Amma.

FIG. 102.—Seal of NARMAR as MAR-NERĀM MA deciphered.

[1] On this sign and its meaning of " Lord of the Deep Waters " (Anunaki), see before. On the *Am* value of this *Gut* sign when it bears two dots, see under seal Fig. 74.

[2] The usual Sumerian word for " elephant " is *Am-si*, and in Akkadian *Pilu* or *Piru*, MD. 826. The sign is here obviously used for " Ox " as a territorial word for " Land " (M. 4038).

[3] *Ma*=" ship," as before.

The name here of Narām as Governor in the form of *Mar-Nera-am* is significant of his identity. The naturalistic drawing of the Asiatic elephant on this seal at this early period is of much zoological interest, as remarked in the text ; and see p. 307.

No. 2. Seal of Narmar as Ama-Nera

This seal, No. 11 in Plate XI, reads as follows :—

Seal.

Sumer (Mesop.).

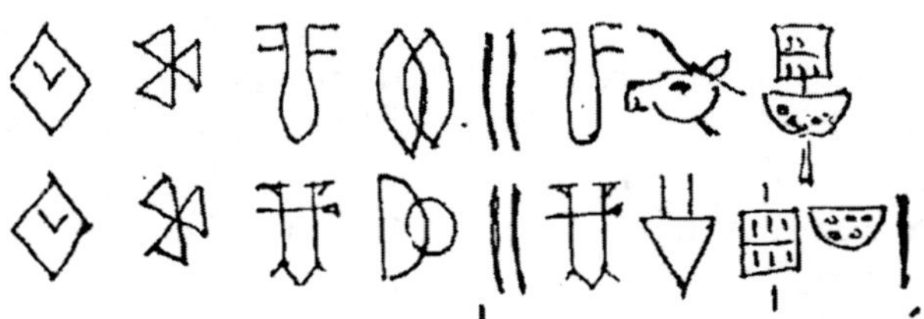

Reads : SHAG-MAD GUT NER[1]A GUT GU-AG-DU-AS

Transl. : Of the Lower (Eastern) Land, the *Gut* NERA, The Gut at Agdu Land.

FIG. 103.—Seal of Narmar as AMA NERA deciphered.

[1] On this *Ner* name, see before. Here the first Ox-head sign contains three small dots inside, thus giving it the value of *Ama*.

No. 3. Seal of Narmar as Marru, son of the Lofty Gut Gin

This seal, No. 1 in Plate XIV, reads :—

Seal.

Sumer (Mesop.).

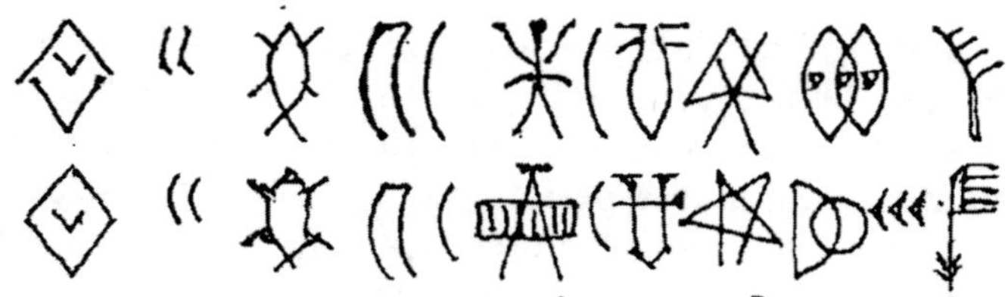

Reads : SHAG-MAN MAR-RU-U TUM[1]-U GUT ARA[2] NER-ES GIN

Transl. : Under King-Companion MARRU, the Lord, Son of the *Gut*, the *Ara* of The Lords of Deep Waters GIN.

FIG. 104.—Seal of Nuder, King-Companion MARRU, Son of ARA, The Gut of the Deep Waters.

[1] A Fly, B. 390 ; Br. 6058. It is significant that the Fly sign *Tum* is used to spell out the Sumerian word Son (*Tumu*), so as to leave no ambiguity as to this designation here.

[2] This is the Plough sign, which as *Ara* has the meaning of "Lofty," the source of *Ara* or " Aryan."

Here Narmar is called "Son" of the Gut Gin or "Sargon" ; and the *Ara* title of the latter appears to designate him as " The Aryan," and is in series with his Indus Valley seal as *Sag-ara*.

Here *Ara* is evidently a shortened form of his father's name as *Arwa-Sag*, the Haryashwa of the Indian lists.

No. 4. Seal of Narmar as Nerau.

This seal, No. 2 of Plate XIV, reads :—

Seal.

Sumer (Mesop.).

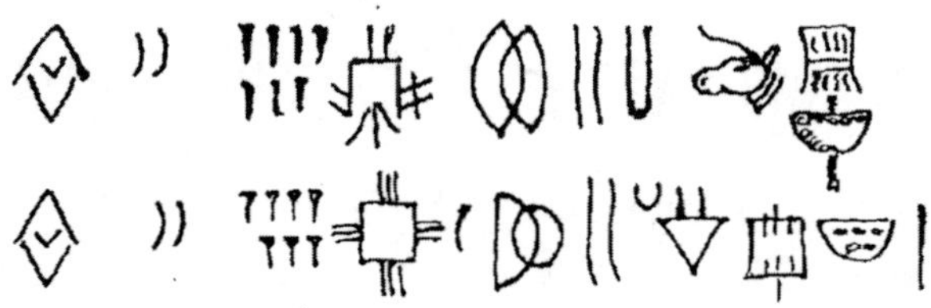

Reads : SHA-MAN IMIN[1]-BARA-GE NER-A-U GU-AG-DU-ASH

Transl. : Under King-Companion of The Heavenly Pharaoh, NERAU at Agdu Land.

FIG. 105.—Seal of Narmar as NERAU deciphered.

[1] Br. 12200. On this *Imin* or this *Himin* or " Heaven " of the Goths, see before.

PHARAOH, SHA-GIN II, GAN-ERI, OR "KHENT'S" SEALS FROM INDUS VALLEY

The Indus Valley seals of this Pharaoh, the third of Menes' Dynasty, and the great-grandson of his namesake, the Great Gin, Gan or Shar-Gin or "Sargon," are four in number and are especially interesting as disclosing along with his Egyptian tomb-inscriptions the proper form of his name as written in his Mesopotamian inscriptions as Sumerian emperor, which is now shown to read *Gani-Eri*, and not "Gali-sharri" or "Shar-Gali-sharri," as hitherto read by Assyriologists. And we have seen that in one of the contemporary Egyptian inscriptions he is actually styled "Sha-Gani II." He is the "Kent" of Egyptologists and the *Kunti* of the Indian lists. His title also in the first of these Indus seals now deciphered, namely "Lord Gin of Serpent (*Bu*)-Land," is interesting as a designation of The Land of Egypt; and it probably implies that his capital was at Buto in the Lower Delta.

These seals are shown in Plate XIV, Nos. 3–6. The first seal reads as follows :—

No. 1. *Seal of Gan-Eri of Serpent Land* (*Bu*) *and Agdu*

Transl. : GAN-ERI of Serpent (*Bu*) Land, The Lord GIN at *Agdu* Land.

FIG. 106.—Seal of GAN-ERI of Serpent Land, Lord GIN of *Agdu* Land deciphered.

[1] B. 229; Br. 5377. Pictures a Sling. In the more realistic Indus pictogram the strings of the sling, which are absent in the Mesopotamian diagram, are shown.

No. 2. Seal as Sha-Gin

This seal, No. 4, Plate XIV, reads :—

Seal.

Sumer (Mesop.).

Reads : ŚAMAN-ŚAGIN-AGDU

Transl. : Under King-Companion SHA-GIN at *Agdu* Land.

FIG. 107.—Seal of King SHA-GIN deciphered.

No. 3. Seal as Lord Gin

This seal, No. 5, Plate XIV, reads :—

Seal.

Sumer (Mesop.).

Reads : AŚ-GIN AG-DU

Transl. : Lord GIN at *Agdu* Land.

FIG. 108.—Seal of Lord GIN at *Agdu* Land deciphered.

[1] B. 534 ; Br. 12196, and cp. 428 f.

No. 4. Seal as King Gan, Gin or Dili, the Gut King of Khāmaesh (Land)

This seal, No. 6, Plate XIV, reads :—

Seal.

Sumer (Mesop.).

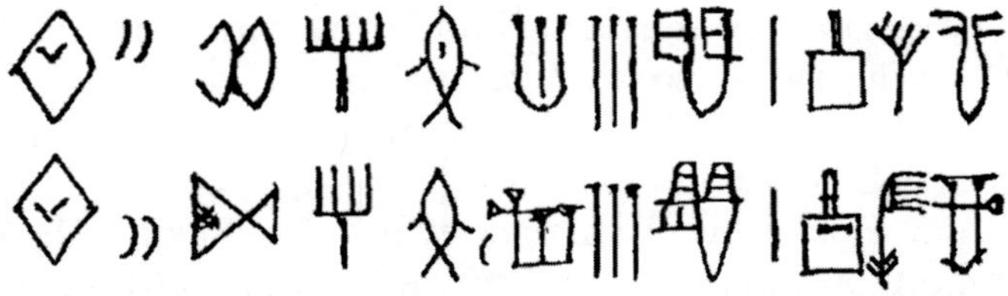

Reads : ŚAG-MAN GAN GAL-KHA-A-MA-EŚ UK-DILI TUB GIN GUT

Transl. : Under King-Companion GAN, the Great *Khāmaesh* King DILI, the tablet of GIN the *Gut*.

FIG. 109.—Seal of King GAN, GIN or DILI, King of *Khāmaesh* deciphered.

[1] B. 150 ; Br. 3862. [2] B. 1 ; Br. 27.

The title of *Dili* borne by him here is significant, as it is found on his ivory label in Egypt, and is his title in the Indian King-lists of *Dili-pa.*

Pharaoh Bugiru or Bageri's (or Bhagiratha's) Seal from Indus Valley

One seal of the fourth Pharaoh of Menes' Dynasty I found in the Indus Valley second collection. It is somewhat roughly carved, and forms No. 7 in Plate XIV. It reads as follows:—

Seal.

Sumer (Mesop.).

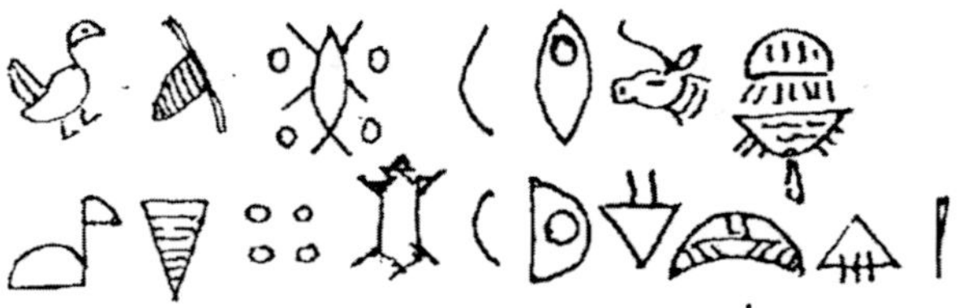

Reads : BAG-ERI GAR-MAR-U NER GU-URI-DU-ASH

Transl. : Bageri of the House of Maru-Ner, The *Gut* of *Uridu* (Akkadu).

Fig. 110.—Seal of Bageri, the *Gut* at *Uridu* deciphered.

This seal is very important historically as disclosing the short reign of this Pharaoh, the 4th of Menes' dynasty, and his identity with Bugiru, the 4th Egyptian King of that dynasty and with Bhagiratha of the Indian King-lists. He is seen to be obviously the first of the four temporary kings who ruled in Mesopotamia only for a total period of three years in the interregnum following the death of King Gani-Eri and the accession of the son of the latter, King Dudu. In the Kish Chronicle (p. 61) and in the Isin lists, those scribes write his name as "Ni-gi-gi" or "I-gi-gi," of which name no inscription has ever been found. It now seems probable that in their corrupted reading they mistook the sign *Bu* for the somewhat similar *Ni* sign; and it is evident that he held the Indus Valley as well as Mesopotamia and Egypt.

It is noteworthy also that he claims descent from Maru-Ner, that is Narmar, and not from Gan-Eri or Sha-Gin the Second.

PHARAOH DUDU, DAN OR "DEN'S" SEALS FROM INDUS VALLEY

Two fine large seals of this Pharaoh, the 5th of Menes' Dynasty, and the son of the Emperor Gani-Eri, I find in the second Indus Valley collection. They are shown in Plate XIV, Nos. 8 and 9. He also bears in his Mesopotamian inscriptions the same title of Dudu, as well as in the Kish Chronicle, (p. 61).

No. 1. Seal of Dudu or Dan as Son of Gani-Eri

This very large seal (No. 8 in Plate) reads :—

Seal.

Sumer (Mesop.).

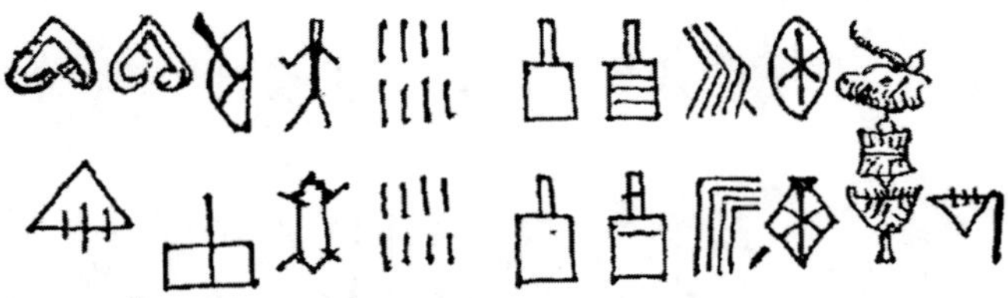

Reads : DU-DU[1] DAN[2] MAR GANI[3]-ERI[4] TUB TAX-GE-U GUAG-DU

Transl. : DUDU DAN, Son of GANI-ERI, the tablet of the Minister, The Lord at *Agdu* Land.

FIG. 111.—Seal of DUDU DAN, Son of GANI-ERI, The Lord Minister at Agdu deciphered.

1 This is clearly a conventional form of the Sumerian "Mound" sign *Du* duplicated.

2 B. 279.

3 These eight strokes have the Akkadian value of *Shakanu* or *Shukunu*, Br. 11978, 12185. These values are obtained by giving different polyphonous values of the four stroke-sign as *Sha*+ga+ni (cp. Br. 11942 f.). Thus the double four strokes give us *Ga-ni*.

4 B. 39 ; Br. 889.

Here the spelling of the second element in this king's father's name is by the same sign as the father himself uses in his own inscriptions in Mesopotamia. And he gives the equivalent title of *Dan*.

No. 2. Seal of Dudu or Dan, son of Gan-the-Second and of the House of Aha and Gin the Ukus

This second seal (No. 9 in Plate) is of immense historical importance as giving his genealogy back to Gin-the-Great or

"Sargon," who is significantly called herewith "The UKUS," that is a descendant of the first Sumerian king of the First Sumerian Dynasty and the King *Ukusi* of the Kish Chronicle and King Ikshvaku of the Indian lists, as we have seen. And Sargon calls himself, or is called in his Egyptian tomb inscription, *Ukus* or *Ukussi* (p. 249), thus strikingly confirming the accuracy of my decipherments. We have also seen that "Sargon" in the Indian Chronicles is repeatedly called "a descendant of the first Aryan solar king Ikshvaku." And it is noteworthy that in this seal Dudu or Dan calls himself literally "The Son of GAN-*the-Second.*"

This seal reads :—

Seal.

Sumer (Mesop.).

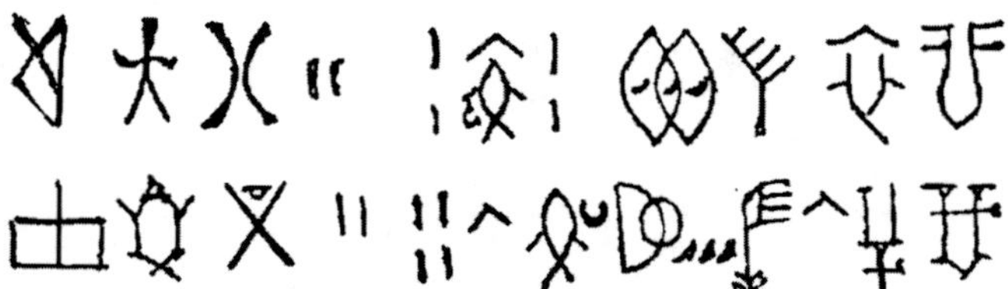

Reads : DAN MAR GAN-TAB GAR A-HA U NER-ES GIN-U-KUS GUT

Transl. : DAN, the son of GAN-*the-Second* of the House of AHA and the Lord of Deep Waters, GIN-*the*-UKUS, The *Gut*.

FIG. 112.—Seal of DAN, son of GAN-*the-Second* of the House of AHA and the Lord of Deep Waters GIN-*the*-UKUS, The Gut, deciphered.

[1] B. 251. The only known specimen of this sign recorded is the late Assyrian one figured in this second line ; but it essentially agrees with this ancient Indus Valley form. On the *Kus* value for this sign instead of *Kush*, cp. Br. 5615 and 5024.

PHARAOH SHUDUR KIB, KIBBU OR QA'S SEALS FROM INDUS VALLEY

I found no fewer than six signets of Shudur Kib,[1] the last of the Pharaohs of Menes' Dynasty, in the second batch of the Indus Valley seals from Mohenjo Daro or Edin. They, like those of his father Dudu or Dan, are rich in genealogical details, and they show that this Pharaoh ruled the Indus Valley colony of the Sumerian empire as well as Mesopotamia, where some of his records have been found.

[1] See TDC. 63, where, however, the transcription of the name is hopelessly misread and Semitized.

In seal No. 1, the *Shuha* title for King Kibbu is seen to approach his title in the Indian lists as *Suhotra*, which latter title is fully given in his Indus seal No. 4, p. 579 as *Shuha-hatura.*

No. 1. Seal of Shudur Kib as Kibbu Shuha

This seal, No. 10 in Plate XIV, reads :—

Transl. : KIBBU SHUHA, son of the House of AHA at *Agdu* Land.

FIG. 113.—Seal of KIBBU SHUHA of House of AHA deciphered.

In his Indus seal No. 2, he significantly bears in the Indus Valley the title of " Pharaoh."

No. 2. Seal of Shudur Kib as The Pharaoh at Agdu

This large seal, No. 1 in Plate XVIII, reads :—

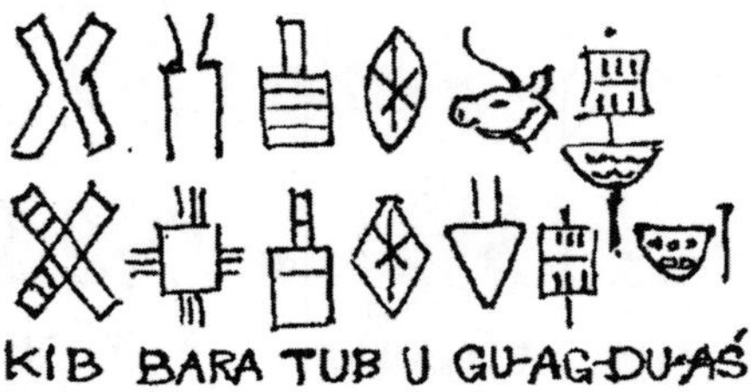

Transl. : KIB, The Pharaoh, the Seal of the Lord at *Agdu* Land.

FIG. 114.—Seal of KIB, The Pharaoh deciphered.

The title of " Lord " in this seal is written by the sign of " Overlord " or " Emperor."

The Fire-worship of this king, which was an aspect of his Sun-cult is devoutly expressed in his seal No. 3. And significantly he calls himself therein " the Son of Shar Gin II and Dan, the former being the great-grandson of Sar-Gin I or Sargon the Great.

No. 3. Seal of Shudur Kib as Kib the Gut, Kibbu, son of Dan and Shar-Gin and of House of Ner(-Mar ?)

This seal, No. 2 in Plate XVIII, reads in its first line :—

Transl. : KIBBU, devotee of Fire, KIB the *Gut*, KIBBU of SHAR-GIN *Gut*.

FIG. 115.—Seal of SHUDUR KIB as KIBBU, son of DAN (the son of) SHAR-GIN the *Gut*—1st line deciphered.

[1] B. 516. The pictograph of a Dog and Dog's head respectively, with sense of " devoted," M. 8684 f.

[2] B. 347 ; Br. 8141, 8147. *Pir* = " Fire," and Sumerian source of that English word.

The second line of this seal reads :—

Transl. : End of DAN the son, of the House of NER (-MAR ?) at *Uridu* (Akkadu) Land.

FIG. 116.—Seal of SHUDUR KIB or KIBBU, son of DAN, 2nd line deciphered.

This seal inscription thus literally reads : " KIBBU, devotee of Fire, KIB the Gut, KIBBU of SHAR-GIN *Gut* and DAN the son, of the House of NER(-MAR ?) at *Uridu* (Akkadu)."

This king's title in his seal No. 4 equates with his *Suhotra* title in the Indian king-lists.

No. 4. Seal of Shudur Kib as Shuhahatura Kibbu, Kib the Gut, of House of Sha-Gin and Neramma

This large seal, Nos. 3-4 in Plate XVIII, is important in containing the name of his ancestors as Shagin (II) and *Neramma,* that is Naram Enzu, reads in its first line :—

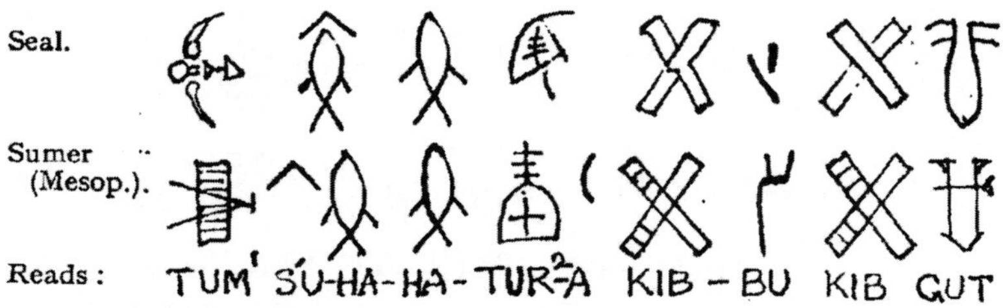

Transl.: For the life of SHUHAHATURA KIBBU, KIB the *Gut.*

FIG. 117.—Seal of SHUHAHATURA KIBBU, KIB the Gut, 1st line deciphered.

[1] B. 390. Fly sign = "Life," M. 6816.

[2] B. 95; B. 2665; MD. 181, pictures a Tomb.

The second line, in Fig. 118 is of great historical importance in giving his genealogy back to Nerāmma or Narām or Narmar.

The second line of this seal reads :—

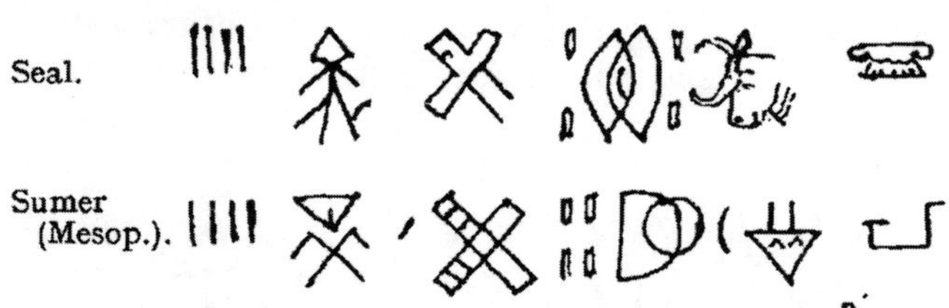

Transl.: of (the House of) SHA-GIN, KIB of the House of NERAMMA.

FIG. 118.—Seal of SHUHAHATURA KIB, 2nd line deciphered.

[1] Br. 11952. [2] *Gu* = "Land," M. 4038.

The inscription on this large seal thus reads: "For the Life of SHUHAHATURA KIBBU, KIB the *Gut* of (the House of) SHA-GIN, KIB of the House of NERAMMA. Compare with this *Neramma,* the form of that name in seal Fig. 102.

His next seal, No. 5, appears to designate him as the Pharaoh of Magan, in which, however, the *Ma* syllable is not expressed. As *Gan* means "Garden," it may thus read "The Garden," which was, as we have seen, a designation of the Edin colony on the Indus.

No. 5. Seal of Shuhudur Kib, Pharaoh of (Ma-)Gan at Agdu

This seal, No. 5, Plate XVIII, reads:—

Seal.

Sumer (Mesop.).

Reads :

Transl.: SHUHUDUR KIB, Pharaoh of (Ma-?) GAN at *Agdu*.

FIG. 119.—Seal of SHUHUDUR KIB Pharaoh deciphered.

[1] B. 160; Br. 4035.

[2] On *Dur* value, cp. Br. 8631 and 11319.

In his next seal he bears the title of Sea-emperor (if this *Ner* be not intended for *Ner-a* a contraction, as we have seen, for Narām or Narmar). And he records his descent from Aha Men or Menes.

No. 5A. Seal of King Kib as KIBBU *Lord of the Deep and Son of* AHA MEN

This seal, No. 5A in Plate, reads:—

Seal.

Sumer (Mesop.).

Reads :

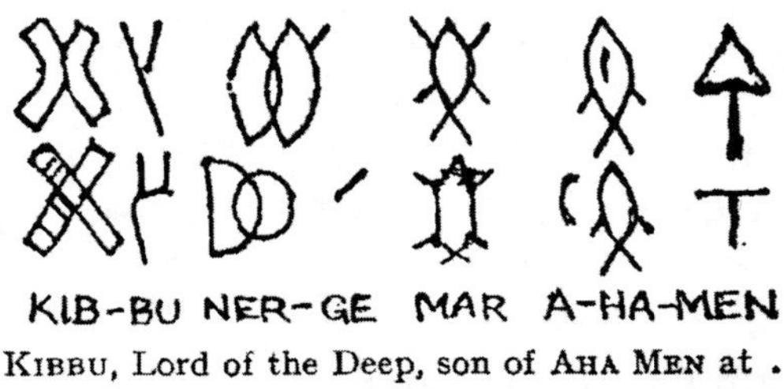

Transl.: KIBBU, Lord of the Deep, son of AHA MEN at . . . Land.

FIG. 119A.—Seal of KIBBU, Lord of the Deep and son of AHA MEN deciphered.

Here the description as "Son" of Aha Men means as not infrequently "descendant."

No. 6. Seal of Shudur Kib as King Qa

This small seal, No. 6 in Plate XVIII, which is noteworthy as being engraved to give an impression which reads in the non-reversed direction, reads :—

Seal.

Sumer (Mesop.).

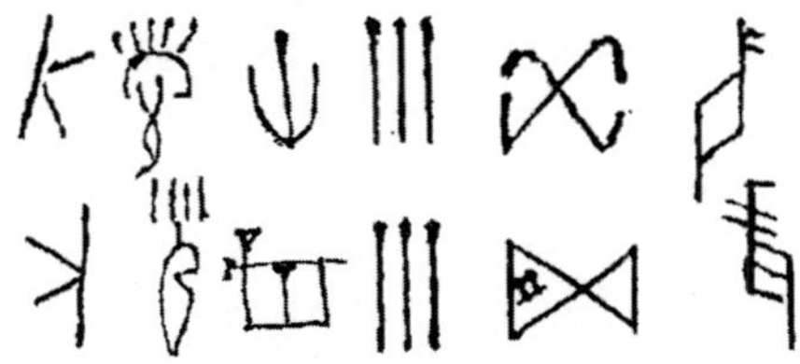

Reads : QA LUGAL MA-ES-GAN-MUSH

Transl. : QA, King, of MA(-*esh*)-GAN, MUSH(-sir).

FIG. 120.—Seal of Shudur Kib as King Qa of Magan and (?) Egypt deciphered.

[1] B. 63.

The final *Mush* in this seal is presumably short for Mush-sir or "Egypt."

SEAL OF SHUDUR KIB'S SON GUT-SHU

This small seal of a son of Shudur Kib, named Gut-Shu, No. 7 in Plate XVIII, reads :—

Seal.

Sumer (Mesop.).

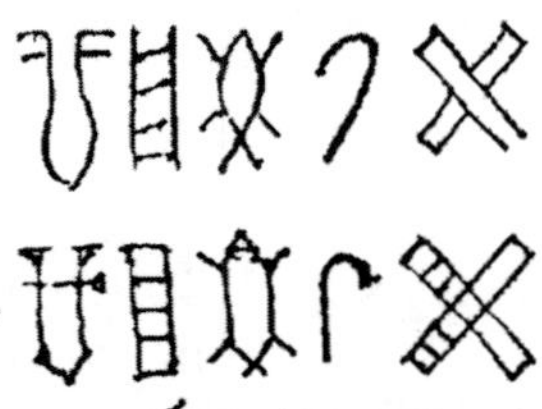

Reads : GUT-ŠU MAR PAR KIB

Transl. : GUT-SHU, son of Pharaoh KIB.

FIG. 121.—Seal of GUT-SHU, son of Pharaoh KIB deciphered.

Nothing is otherwise known of this son of Pharaoh Kib. He did not succeed his father, who ended The First Dynasty of Menes in Egypt and the Dynasty of Sargon-the-Great in Mesopotamia. But he is now seen to have been in the Indus Valley colony, though without any official title.

SEAL OF KING URIMUSH, YOUNGER SON OF SARGON-THE-GREAT

Here it is convenient to give the seal of King Urimush, the younger son of Sargon-the-Great, who succeeded the latter for nine years on the Mesopotamian throne (see Kish Chronicle, p. 61), who has left several inscriptions as emperor at Agudu, and who was massacred and succeeded by Manis-Tusu or Menes in Mesopotamia, as fully recorded in our text.

This seal, which I found in the second Indus Valley collection, is No. 8 in Plate XVIII. It reads :—

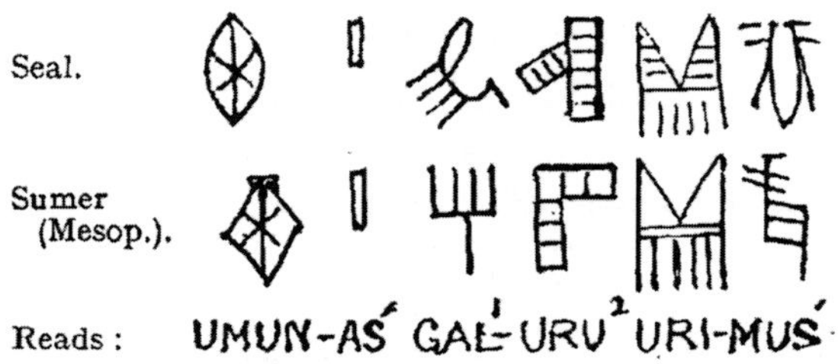

Transl. : The One Over-Lord, the Great Hero URI-MUSH.

FIG. 122.—Seal of King URI-MUSH deciphered.

[1] This sign might also read *Pesh*, " The Monster Fish," B. 303, a title of Lord of Deep Waters, *Anunaki*, MD. 553.

[2] B. 516.

[3] B. 316 ; M. 5311 f.

Here it is seen that King Uri-Mush uses the imperial title ; and in his Mesopotamian inscriptions he also calls himself emperor, as we have seen.

XII

GUTI OR GOTHIC DYNASTY SUMERIAN SEALS FROM THE INDUS VALLEY DECIPHERED—*comprising Kings Kūshu (Kusha), Earl Tishua, Ama, Bak (Bakus), Aigiash, Tasia (Tax or Su-Dās), Abata, Nigin, Irirumun, Dar, Khablam, Gudia and Ruddu or Pisha Nimirrud (Vishwa-Ratha or Uru-Nimirrud or " Ningirsu ")*

THE Indus Valley seals I find are especially rich in the official signets of the kings of the Guti or Gothic Dynasty, showing their activities in that Sumerian colony. Amongst those hitherto wholly undeciphered seals of this dynasty (a dynasty which effected in Mesopotamia " a great Sumerian renaissance "), I find no fewer than nineteen seals, belonging to fourteen out of the total twenty kings of that dynasty (see list, p. 364), as figured in Plate XX and here deciphered in detail.

The Guti seals are of immense historical importance in establishing the Aryan and Sumerian origin of the Guti Dynasty; and of the Guti ancestry and race of Gudia and his famous son, the priest-king Uru Nimirrud (" Ur Ningirsu "), whose origin and ancestry were wholly unknown. They also confirm absolutely by contemporary alternative spelling my reading of that important name *Nimirrud* (a title of St Michael), the patron Saint of the Early Sumerians, and the canonized second king of the First Sumerian Dynasty, the " Nimrod " of later Chaldean and Oriental tradition, in addition to the evidence already detailed in Appendix III.

It is noteworthy that the racial and official title of the Guti kings is frequently spelt on their seals *Gutum*, that is the same form of title that is applied to them in the Isin Chronicles. These seals are here deciphered in the order in which they are numbered in Plate XX; and reference should be made to the list of the Guti kings at p. 364.

Seal of King KŪSHU or Kusha, the Founder of the main line of "The Guti Dynasty."

It has already been disclosed in the text how King Kushu was the founder of the main line of the Guti Dynasty Kings, and his unknown ancestry is there detailed as King Kusha of the Indian lists and chronicles.

His seal, No. 1 in the Plate, reads :—

Seal.

Sumer (Mesop.).

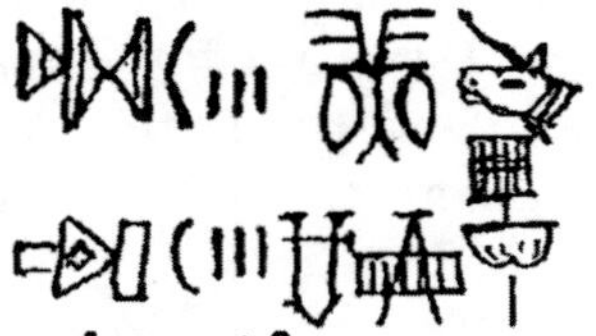

Reads : KU[1]-U-UŠU[2] GU-TUM AGDU

Transl. : Kūshu the *Gutum* at Agdu Land.

Fig. 123.—Seal of King Kūshu the *Gutum* deciphered.

[1] B. 124; SSb. 128.

[2] Br. 9976. In the Isin list his name is spelt *In-Ki-shu*, with the prefix of *Inim* or priest-encanter.

The vowels *u* and *a* are interchangeable in Sumerian; thus *Kūshu* = *Kusha* of the Indian lists.

SEAL OF 3RD GUTI KING, EARL TAX OR TISHUA OR SU-DĀSA II

The 3rd Guti King's name is spelt in the Isin lists as "Iarla Tax or Dax"—*Tax* being, as we have seen, one of the variant spellings of *Tasia*. In his own seal here deciphered he spells his name *Irla* (or *Erila*) *Tishua*, wherein *Irla* or *Erila* = "Earl" as described at p. 362, and he calls himself "Earl Companion or King." His seal, No. 2 in the Plate, reads:—

Seal.

Sumer (Mesop.).

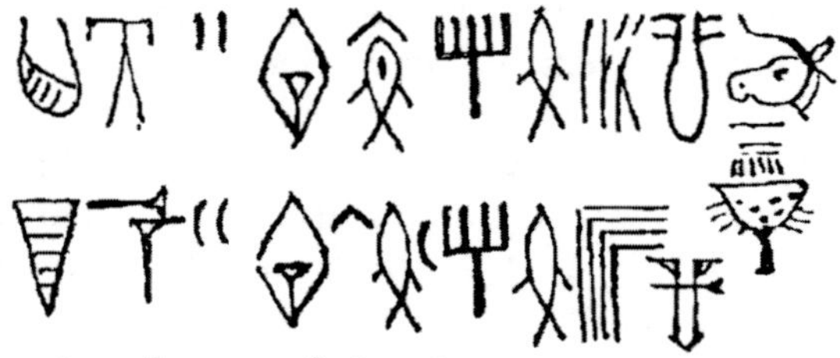

Reads: IR[1]-LA[2]-MAN TI[3]-SU-A[4] GAL-A TAX GUT AGDU

Transl.: The *Earl King-Companion* TISHUA the Great Minister of the Guts at Agdu Land.

FIG. 124.—Seal of *Earl* TISHUA (or TAX) the Great Minister of the Guti deciphered.

[1] *Ir*, or *Eri*, the Sling sign as before. [2] Balance sign, B. 440; Br. 10082.
[3] B. 323; Br. 7685. [4] Br. 11816.

This Guti king we have seen held apparently a second term of office as the 8th Guti king of the essentially identical name Iarla Tax or Dax, and the Tasia of his seals, and he latterly became as crown-prince the paramount Guti emperor of the main-line emperors, Su-Dāsa II of the Indian lists.

SEALS OF 5TH GUTI KING AMA

The 5th king is called in the Isin lists *E-Ama-mesh* or "The Great *Ama* the *Appointed*;[1] and significantly in both his Indus seals he bears the name and title of "Ama the

[1] Br. 5977.

Gutu, *the Appointed Ruler.*" He was evidently, as we have seen, *Ama*-vasu, the youngest son of King Kusha in the Indian lists, the Kusha line furnishing the leading Kings of this Guti or Gothic dynasty; see pp. 364 and 370 f. His first seal, No. 3 in Plate, reads:—

Seal.

Sumer (Mesop.).

Transl.: AMA the *Gutu, the Appointed Ruler* at *Agdu* Land.

FIG. 125.—Seal of AMA, the *Gutu*, Appointed Ruler at Agdu Land deciphered.

[1] B. 482, as before. The seal sign has two more cross-bars than in the Mesopotamian, but there is no other Sumerian sign of a bisected oblong, and its identity is confirmed by the next seal.
[2] Br. 11978, "appointed."
[3] Br. 2400, "Command, rule" = literally "a General" (*Gin*).

His second seal, No. 4 in Plate, reads similarly:—

Seal.

Sumer (Mesop.).

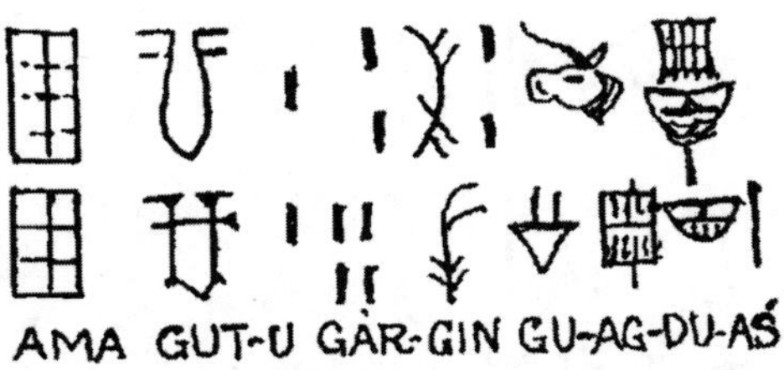

Transl.: AMA the *Gutu, the Appointed Ruler*, at Agdu Land.

FIG. 126.—Seal of AMA the *Gutu* deciphered.

SEAL OF 6TH KING BAK OR BAKIES OR BAEŚŚEŚ

This king, styled BAK *Gutum*, bears in his Indus seal the title of "Under King-Companion." He is clearly the Guti king *Bakies* of the Isin lists, with the title of *Inim* or Priest-encanter, who immediately succeeded the above king; and the Bakus or Basam or Basium who acted as king 27 years later for a period of one year. His seal, No. 4 in Plate, reads :—

Seal.

Sumer (Mesop.).

Reads : SAG-MAN BAK GU-TUM AGDU

Transl. : Under King-Companion BAK the *Gutum* at Agdu Land.

FIG. 127.—Seal of BAK the *Gutum* deciphered.

The immediate successor of the foregoing Gothic king, called Iziash or Igiash in the Isin lists has also left his seal in the Indus Valley colony.

SEAL OF 7TH GUTI KING AIGIASH OR IZIAUSH

This seal, No. 6 in Plate, reads :—

Seal.

Sumer (Mesop.).

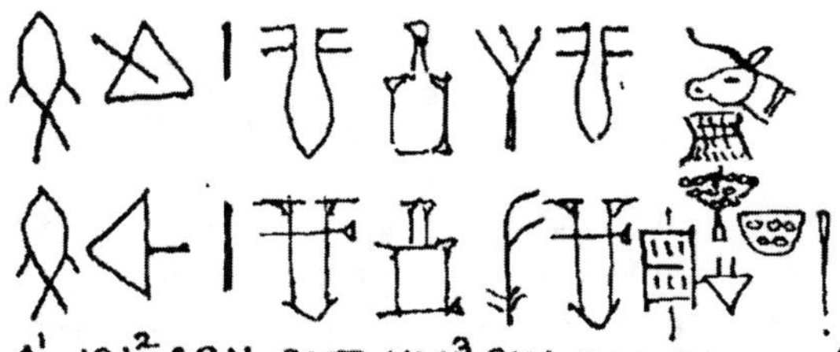

Reads : A[1]-IGI[2]-ASH GUT-UM[3] GIN-GUT AGDU-AŚ

Transl. : AIGIASH *Gutum*, The Ruler Gut at Agdu Land.

FIG. 128.—Seal of AIGIASH *Gutum* Ruler deciphered.

[1] Br. 11816. [2] B. 406 ; Br. 9259 also may read *Shi*.

SEAL OF 8TH KING TASIA THE GUT

This Tasia Gut, who bears in one of his two seals the prefix of *Ara*, is obviously the King Iarla (or "Earl") *Tax* or *Dax* who was next in succession to the above king, who reigned only 6 years. He thus is identical with King

Su-Dās II of the Indian Epics. His first seal, No. 5 in Plate, reads as in Fig. 127 :—

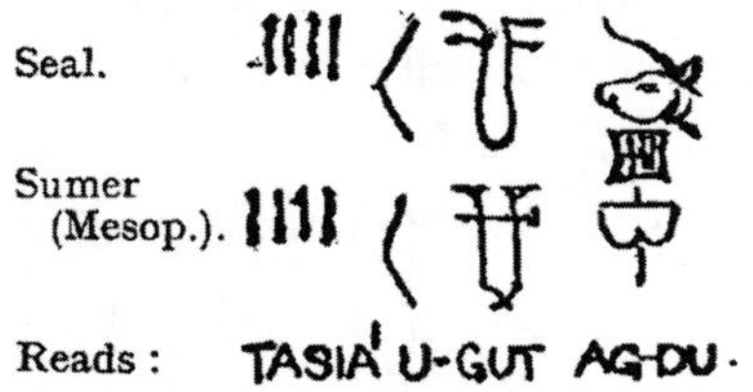

Transl. : TASIA, the Lord *Gut* at Agdu Land.

FIG. 129.—Seal of TASIA *Gut* deciphered.

[1] See previous notes on their phonetic value.

His second seal, No. 6 in Plate, reads *Ara Tasia Gin* or "The Arya or 'Aryan' Tasia, the fully appointed Commander or General."

SEAL OF 9TH KING ABATA THE GUTUM

This king is clearly the Guti king "Ibate" of the Isin Chronicles, who immediately succeeded the above Tax or Tasia. His seal, No. 7 in Plate, reads :—

Transl. : ABATA the *Gutum* at Agdu Land.

FIG. 130.—Seal of ABATA deciphered.

SEAL OF 12TH KING NIGIN OR "NIGHNA."

The 12th Guti king in the Isin lists is called *Ni-ki-in* or *Nikīn* (on the *Ni* value of 1st sign, see Br. 4574). In this Indus seal he spells his name *Nigin*. This identifies him with Prince Nighna of the Indian lists, who was grandson of the 48th main-line Emperor Sarva Kama (WVP. 3, 305), the father of the 8th Guti king, Su-Dāsa II or Iarla Dax, which is in keeping with this chronological position for him, as the 12th temporary Guti king (see Table, p. 364).

The seal of this king, No. 10 in Plate, reads :—

Seal.

Sumer (Mesop.).

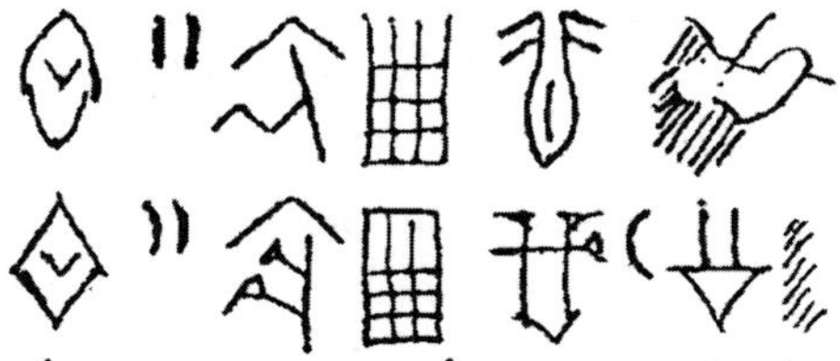

Reads : SAG-MAN NIGIN[1] GUT-U GU-.........

Transl. : Under King-Companion NIGIN *Gutu* at . . . Land.

FIG. 131.—Seal of King NIGIN *Gutu* deciphered.

[1] B. 404. These two signs of the Sun and a House read together as *Nigin*, with the meaning of " Sunrise," M. 6991.

SEAL OF 14TH KING IRIRUMUN

The seal of this king, No. 1 in Plate XXI, and Irarūm of the Isin lists, reads :—

Seal.

Sumer (Mesop.).

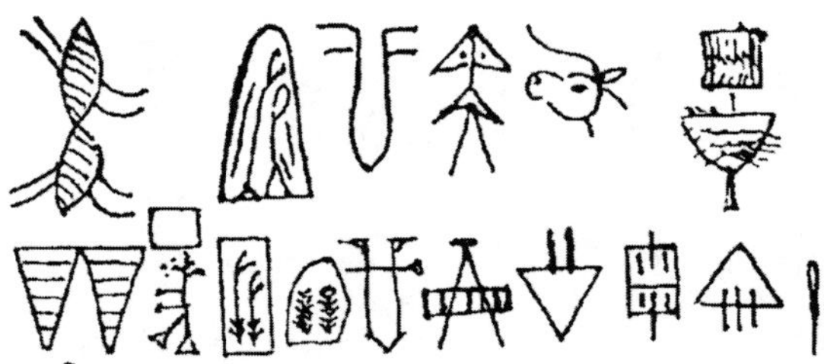

Reads : IR-IR[1]-UMUN[2] GUT-TUM GU-AG-DU-ASH

Transl. : IRIRUMUN *Gutum*, The ruler of the Guti at Agdu Land.

FIG. 132.—Seal of IRIRUMUN *Gutum* deciphered.

[1] B. 229 ; Br. 5378. This is the Sling sign doubled, and in the seal the fuller realistic form of the sling is drawn with its strings, as compared with its diagrammatic form in Mesop. Sumerian of the mere pocket with strokes representing the stones.

[2] B. 66 ; Br. 1371. The sign represents a pair of reeds within an enclosure. No early specimen of this sign has been hitherto noticed, and the later Babylonian form writes it separately as two reeds outside a square, see line 2 of Fig. 132. But the sign (No. 613 in B.) which I figure below it to the right is evidently a form of this sign.

SEALS OF 15TH KING DAR OR DARRANUM

The 15th Guti king, whose name is spelt in the Isin lists "Darranūm," is represented in the Indus seals by two signets, in one of which he spells his name *Dar* and in the other *Darru*. The first of these seals, No. 2 in Plate XXI, reads :—

Reads : DAR GU-TUM GU-AG-DU

Transl. : DAR *Gutum* at Agdu Land.

FIG. 133.—Seal of DAR *Gutum* deciphered.

His second seal, No. 3 in Plate XXI, reads :—

Reads : SÁG-MAN GU-TUM GAL DAR-RU[1] GUT AGDU

Transl. : Under King-Companion of *the Very Great Gutums*, DARRU the *Gut* at Agdu Land.

FIG. 134.—Seal of King-Companion DARRU *of the very Great Gutums* deciphered.

[1] B. 1; Br. 3. This sign *Ru* forms a ligatured tail to the *Dar* sign.

SEAL OF 16TH KING THE "DUKE" KHĀBLUM OR KHAB

The name of the 16th king in the Isin lists is spelt "Khāblum." In his two Indus seals he spells his name

Khāblam and *Khāb*, and in one styles himself "Duke." The first seal, No. 4 in Plate XXI, reads :—

Seal.

Sumer (Mesop.).

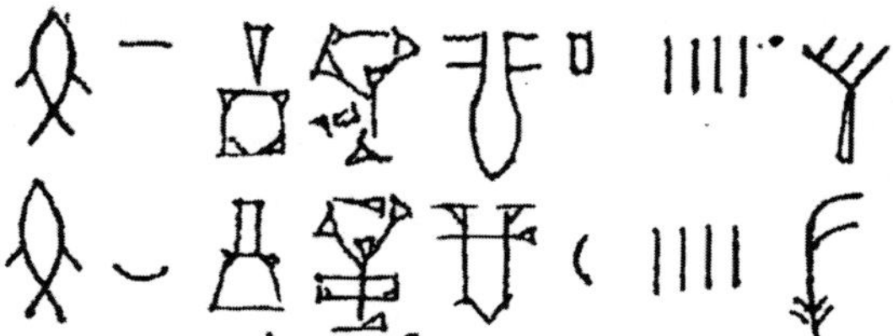

Reads : KHA-A-AB[1]-LAM[2] GUT-U GAR-GIN

Transl. : KHĀBLAM *Gutu*, The Appointed Ruler.

FIG. 135.—Seal of KHĀBLAM *Gutu*, The Appointed Ruler deciphered.

[1] B. 147 ; Br. 3813. [2] B. 500 ; Br. 11106.

His second seal, No. 5 in Plate XXI, reads :—

Seal.

Sumer (Mesop.).

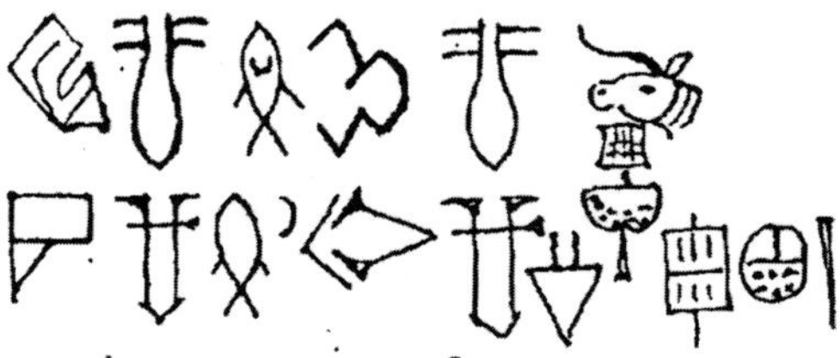

Reads : DUK[1]-GUT KHA-A-AB[2] GUT GU-AG-DU-AS..

Transl. : The *Duke* of the Gutis, KHAB, the *Gut* at Agdu Land.

FIG. 136.—Seal of *Duke* of Guts, KHAB deciphered.

[1] B. 515 ; Br. 9868-9="Lord." Its phonetic value is *Dūk*, and not *Dun*, as given in Br. 9864, cp. spelling *Du*+*uk* or *uku*, Br. 5912. It appears to have pictured a kind of leader's hat, cp. M. 7495. And as the designation of a "lord" it appears to be with its associated Gothic "Earl" title the literal equivalent of our "Duke."

[2] The Cow sign, B. 373 ; Br. 8870. The horns are pictured more realistically in the seal sign than in the Mesopotamian diagram.

SEAL OF KUDIA, GUDIA, OR "GUDEA," THE 18TH GUTI KING

This critically important seal, identifying the famous Sumerian priest-king Gudia or "Gudea," is found in the Indus Valley amongst those others of the Aryan ancestors of the priest-king Gadhi of the Indian records, who, I have proved from quite other different sources, was identical with "Gudea" of the later Sumerian period in Mesopotamia.

And along with it are found three seals of his famous son and successor. This seal, No. 6 in Plate XXI, reads :—

Seal.

Sumer (Mesop.).

Reads : KU[1]-(AS)DI[2]-A[3] GU-TUM . GUT

Transl. : KU-(*ash*) DI GUDIBIR (or GUDIA) the *Gutum*, the *Gut*.

FIG. 137.—Seal of KUDI GUDIBIR (or GUDIA) the *Gut* deciphered.

¹ B. 124 as in seal Fig. 123.

² B. 297 ; Br. 67151, with value of Di, pictures a Furnace with issuing flames. Significantly this is the same sign habitually used by " Gudea " in Mesopotamia for the 2nd syllable of his name.

³ B. 68 and 577. On *Gudibir*, cp. Br. 1445.

The first syllabic sign by which his name is written on this seal is given by Assyriologists the phonetic value of *Ku*, but *K* and *G* are always freely interchangeable ; and the initial sign by which Gudia wrote his name in his Mesopotamian records has similarly the values of both *Ka* and *Gu*. The introduction of the syllable *Ash* before the syllable *Di* was to claim the divine meaning for that word-sign, as with the prefix *ash* or " Lord " it means " The god *Induru* or *Ia* of Smiths." But as usual in later Sumerian of this and the following Ur period the divine prefix *ash* is not sounded in personal names. His seal-name thus reads *Kudi* or *Gudi Gudibir*, this last being a late solar title for Marduk as *Tak*, *i.e.*, Tascio, cp. Br. 1404-5.

SEALS OF THE PRIEST-KING URU NIMIRRUD (" UR-NINGIRSU ") AS PĪSHA RUDDU OR VISHWĀ-RATHA OR VISHWA-MITRA OF INDIAN LISTS, THE 19TH GUTI KING

Three seals of this famous Sumerian and Indian Vedic priest-king, and son of " Gudia " I find in the collection of Indus Valley seals from the old Sumerian colonial capital, as shown in Plate XXI, Nos. 7 to 10, in the photographs of each seal along with the impression of the last. In the Indian records we have seen that he was called Vishwā-Ratha, and that latterly he is said to have adopted the religious title of Vishwā-Mitra, with the meaning of " Friend of all." Now in his first seal he calls himself *Ruddu* or *Rudtu*, which is disclosed as the Sumerian source of his *Ratha* name in the later Sanskrit traditions.

The seals are also of much historical importance in confirming absolutely his identity with the son of the Sumerian King Gudia, under the former's title of *Uru Nimirrud*,[1] thus confirming my reading of that name; and on the other hand they confirm his identity with the second last king, Lord *Ridi Pizir* (= *Vishwā-Ratha*) of the Guti Dynasty, which dynasty we have found was mainly of the Kusha line. And his employment of the Rhinoceros on one of the seals as the pictograph for *Edin* is characteristic.

It is significant that in his Vedic hymns as Vishwā-Mitra, he calls himself " the son of *Kushika*," that is " son of a descendant of *Kushi* "; and in the Indian Chronicles his father King Gadhi is the son of Kushika and is called a *Kaushika*, that is " a descendant of Kusha," [2] who, we have seen, is identical with the second king of the Guti Dynasty. This Guti ancestry for this celebrated Aryan and Sumerian priest-king is now strikingly confirmed by the concrete contemporary proofs in his own Indus seals, as *Pisha*—P, V and W being phonetically interchangeable.

Seal of URU-NIMIRRUD (" *Ur-Ningirsu* ") *or* PISHA *or* VISHWA-RATHA *as* KING RUDDU *the* GUTI

It is now seen that King Uru-Nimirrud or " Devotee of Nimirrud " had besides the personal name of Pīsha also the title of Ruddu spelt by the same sign as the last syllable in his fuller religious title, and it is the obvious source of his *Ridi* or *En-Ridi* title in Babylonian records. His title of " Overlord " King-Companion is in agreement with the later

[1] In my WISD., p. 59, No. 4, Col. 1 should read Vishwā-Mitra instead of his sister Satya-wati, who married No. 5 in that Table; and in No. 6 " 4 and " should be deleted.

[2] WVP. 4, 16.

title of King En-Ridi as "King of the Guti and of the Four Regions."

This seal, No. 7 in Plate XXI, reads :—

Transl. : The Overlord King-Companion RUDDU, the Gut.

FIG. 138.—Seal of King RUDDU the Gut deciphered.

[1] B. 7. The value of this sign as *Rud* has already been fully attested under the name Nimirrud, of which it forms the last syllable ; cp. its spelling in Br. 164 as *Ru+-du ;* Br. 506 ; and similarly its spelling by alternative signs as *Ru+udu,* Br. 3860, where the spelling should be *udu* (cp. Br. 1068) and not *Uku.*

King PĪSHA'S *Rhinoceros Seal as Priest-king at Edin*

His seal with the Rhinoceros as its chief emblem is seen in No. 8 in Plate XXI. Its inscription reads as follows :—

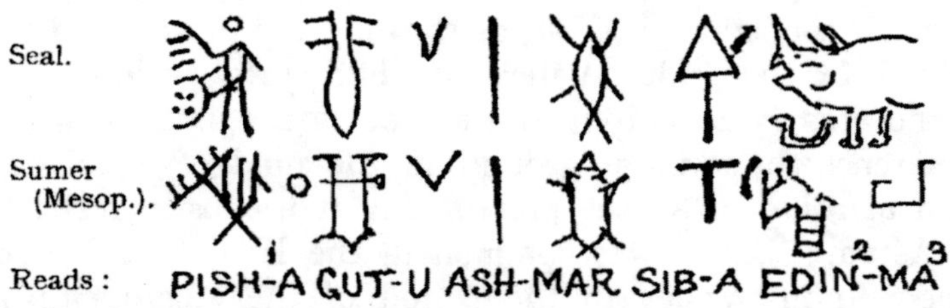

Transl. : PĪSHA the *Gutu,* the One (or Eldest) son, the Shepherd at *Edin* (or Rhinoceros) Land.

FIG. 139.—Seal of PĪSHA the *Gutu* at *Edin* Land deciphered.

[1] B. 303 ; Br. 6928 and WSAD. 80.

[2] B. 531 ; Br. 11936 f., and cp. related Pig sign, B. 52, here figured as clearly a horned Rhinoceros.

[3] This sign seems to be a conventionalized ship-sign *ma* which, as we have seen, means also "land," for *Ma* is the shortened form of *Mad,* "land."

The Rhinoceros on this seal as the name for Edin is interesting. That animal is called in Sumerian *Pish,* which is homophonous with this priest-king's name of *Pīsha* in both of his latter seals, but which is written by a different pictograph from that of the Rhinoceros. The latter pictograph was thus presumably used on this seal for word-play. But the Rhinoceros name in Chaldean or Semitic also meant "Edin." The Sumerian word *Pish* for Rhinoceros with the pictogram shown in Fig. 139, is also defined as "Wild Pig," the Rhinoceros being of pig-like form; and this word *Pish* or "Pig," with its Sumerian variant *S'ah*, "a Sow," I have shown in my *Sumer-Aryan Dictionary* is obviously the Sumerian source of our English words "Pig" and "Sow." In Chaldean or Semitic Akkadian and Assyrian the name for the Rhinoceros is *Humsiru* or *Humsiri*,[1] which is defined as "a four-footed animal related to the *Anunnaki*,[2] that is "The Lords of Deep Water"; and *Hamu* is "an animal living in or near the water";[3] and the Rhinoceros frequents marshy swamps.

Now we have seen that the Semitic name for Edin was *Shirihum* or *Sirihum* (p. 218), in which *Siri* or *Siru* = Edin.[4] Thus by the transposing word-play of metathesis *Siri-hum* or EDIN, presumably became *Hum-siri* or "Rhinoceros" in this seal phraseology.

This fine naturalistic portrait of the great Indian Rhinoceros by the Gothic King Pīsha's artist about 2365 B.C. is of much zoological interest, as showing the presence of that animal in the Indus Valley at that early period. This Rhinoceros is a denizen of the giant grass jungles, with a preference for swampy ground, in the mud of which it is fond of rolling. At the present day it is mostly restricted to Assam; but it was common in the Punjab and in the Upper Indus Valley in the period of the Mogul emperor Baber (1505-1530 A.D.), as far north as Peshawar. Despite its huge bulk and strength it is, as a rule, a quiet and inoffensive animal.[5]

The Fig-tree Seal of PĪSHA, *the Priest-king* URU NIMIRRUD, *defining* NIMIRRUD *as* "THE LORD OF PLANTS."

This remarkably picturesque seal (Plate XXI, Nos. 9-10), in which the sacred Indian Fig-tree, the *Pipal* (*Ficus*

[1] Br. 11936 and MD. 323.
[2] MD. 323.
[3] *Ib.*, 320.
[4] Cp. MD. 888 f.
[5] W. Blanford, *Mammalia of Brit. India*, 1891, 473.

religiosa) is the device in its upper part, with its fruit disposed around the margin, supplies definite proof of the proper spelling of the religious title of the priest-king *Uru Nimirrud* which means " Devotee of Lord Nimirrud." The name of that latter saint we have elicited was *Nimirrud* (not " Ningirsu ") ; and we demonstrated his identity with the Gothic saint, St Michael, the canonized second Aryan king, and Bakus or Bacchus, as " The Lord of Plants,"[1] the Nimi or Bikukshi of the Indian King-lists.

The composite pictographs on this seal are analysed in the following decipherment figure No. 140 ; and it will be noticed that the first sign, " The Overlord," is written in the same ornamental character as that sign has in his *Ruddu* seal. Fig. 138, p. 593, showing its cuneiform wedge-lines.

Transl. : The Overlord Pīsha, The Shepherd of Lord Nimirrud, The King of Kings, *The Lord of Plants*.

Fig. 140.—Seal of Pīsha, the Shepherd of Nimirrud, the Lord of Plants, deciphered.

[1] B. 387 ; Br. 9011. *Ir*, the Sling sign as before.

[2] *Rud*, Sign B. 7. On the value *Rud*, revise the spelling in Br. 164, *Rug* for *Rud* in both detailed spellings, which read *Ru-ud* or *Rudu*. Cp. constituent signs in Br. 506 and 1068, wherein sign B. 481 reads *du*. Cp. Br. 10511, 3860 and 1068. And the great Bull sign for the Sun now reads *Udu* or *Ud*, a usual name for the Sun by other signs (as well as *Uku* or *Ug*).

[3] *Dara*, the Deer sign, B. 113=" king," M. 1867.

[4] *Ezu*, B. 327 ; Br. 7591, 7609, and M. 5575, where it is defined as the name of many kinds of Plants ; and " Lord *Ezu* " is defined as " Grain and Blossom Son, the Lord . . . *Ezu* " ; and as " Grain *Ama-a*, Lord *Buześ*," thus giving King Azag's titles of *Amā* and *Bakuś* under variant dialectic spellings.

The critical importance of this seal is that it gives the spelling of the name of *Nimirrud* by different signs for its

[1] See pp. 144 f., App. III, and WSAD. 7, 22, 26.

first two syllabic signs from those ordinarily used in spelling it in Mesopotamia, in order presumably to bring out more clearly the attributes of that divinity as "The Lofty One (*Nim*)," "The Swift Bringer (*Ir*)," and "The Increaser (*Rud*)."

I was led to discover the decipherment of the name *Nimirrud* in the complicated monogram in which the priest-king Pīsha has here enshrined it, by observing that the latter personage, whose ordinary title in Mesopotamian records was "Devotee of Nimirrud," had written on this seal in ordinary Mesopotamian writing his name and title of Shepherd or "priest" as "The overlord Pīsha the Shepherd of," and then the ordinary Mesopotamian-Sumerian writing stopped, and the rest was in realistic pictographs, where one expected to find the name Nimirrud. Amongst these naturalistic pictographs an outstanding one between the duplicated Deer head was clearly the Sling sign, fully pictured, with its bag of stones and the edges of the mouth of the bag at the top, with the two strings attached to it, each ending in a ring or holder. The Sling sign has in Sumerian the phonetic value of *Ir*, which is a syllable of the name *Nim-ir-rud*. I then observed that in the fan-like strokes below this Sling sign and immediately above the *Ash* or "Lord" sign, attached to the left side of the top of the oblong bar or *ish* sign in the middle of the lowest line of writing, was the pictograph of a Fly, which has the Sumerian phonetic value of *Nim*; and alongside it was the *rud* sign, written by the identical Sumerian sign in which the last syllable of this priest-king's name is habitually written in Mesopotamia (see Fig. 132). Here, then, were found the full Sumerian syllabic signs for the name Nim-ir-rud, and all were written in their due sequence on the seal from left to right.

The rest of the decipherment was then easy. The next following sign, the Deer sign duplicated, has in the Sumerian the meaning of "king," and duplicated it means "the king of kings." And the uppermost signs were clearly "The Lord of Plants," as are shown in the Decipherment Table, Fig. 140 and its foot-note.

Thus this seal inscription reads in the Sumerian writing and language, in its literal translation: "The Overlord

PĪSHA, The Shepherd of Lord NIMIRRUD, The King of Kings, The Lord of Plants." And this designation is in literal agreement with this priest-king's ordinary title in Mesopotamian records as "The devotee of the Lord Nimirrud (*Uruash-Nimirrud* or Bacchus)." This religious priestly practice of designating himself by the title of his patron saint or divinity is seen to be in series with that of the fourth Aryan or Sumerian king, the priest-king Udu of The Bowl, who is designated in the Kish and Isin Chronicles, not by his own personal name, but as "The devotee of Lord Sagg (*Uru-Sagaga*)," the latter being his great-grandfather, the first Aryan or Sumerian king, whom he had himself apparently deified, and to whom he dedicated The Sacred Stone Bowl or "Holy Grail." The 6th Gothic King Bak or Bakies also calls himself usually in his Mesopotamian inscriptions "The devotee of Lord Bakus" (*Uru-ash-Bakus*), and many other Sumerian priest-kings call themselves "The Devotee" of a particular saint or deity.

KING PĪSHA AS "VISHWĀ-MITRA" IN THE INDUS VALLEY IN THE VEDIC HYMNS

Interesting confirmatory evidence of the presence of this Guti or Gothic priest-king Pīsha as Vishwā-Mitra in the Indus Valley, in the old capital of which his seals were unearthed, is preserved in the ancient Vedic Hymns, of which collection he is the traditional author of the 3rd book containing 68 hymns, though it is probable that several of them were composed by the class of priests, his descendants and followers, who bore his name as their patronymic. Of the hymns in this 3rd book no less than 25 are addressed to Indra and 24 to the Fire-god, either alone or in association with Indra, and the rest are to friendly deified spirits, including the tutelary goddess *Bharati* (Britannia), styled "The Lady of the Waters," Indra's son (that is Nimirrud), under his title of *Pushan* (or The Meal-god) and *Tvashtar* perhaps a variant of *Tasia*, and with generally similar functions), and the Maruts, or canonized warriors and seafaring early Morites or Amorites. And significantly the sacrificial offerings are simply fire, wine and fruits; this

Gothic priest-king having, as we have seen, abhorred sanguinary sacrifice, and lost his throne, through opposing the human sacrifice of the Chaldees.

In one of these hymns he, as Vishwā-Mitra (or "The Friend of All," as his name has been rendered by the later Brahmans), is the leader and priest of an expedition of the Bharats "from afar" into the Upper Indus Valley, at the junction of the Bias and Sutlej affluents of the Indus to the east of Harappa, and south-west of Umballa (see Map, p. 116); and they were obviously coming from the West or South-West. Here he and his party are held up by the flooded rivers. "The Friend of All" then prays to the twin spirits of the rivers as "friends" to abate their waters for his crossing; and thereupon the waters fell, permitting the passage of his party and their waggons. As this hymn has considerable poetic beauty, besides locating definitely his position in the Upper Indus Valley and giving him his title as "Son of *Kushika*," that is "son of a descendant of Kusha," who we have found was the 2nd king of the Guti or Gothic Dynasty, I cite here its main stanzas. This Gothic priest-king sings, addressing the Rivers:[1]—

"Impelled by Indra whom ye pray to urge you on, ye move as 'twere on chariots to the ocean.
Flowing together, swelling with your billows, O lucid Streams, each of you seeks the other.
I have attained the more maternal River, we have approached Vipās, the broad, the blest.
Licking, as 'twere their calf, the Mother pair flow onward to their common home together.
Linger a little at my friendly bidding! Rest Holy Ones a moment in your journey!
With hymn sublime soliciting your favour Kushika's son hath called unto the Rivers.
List quickly, Sisters, to the bard who cometh to you from afar with car and waggon!
Bow lowly down, be easy for traverse! Stay Rivers with your floods below our axles!

[1] RV. 3, 33, from Griffith's translation.

(*The United Twain Rivers reply* :)

" ' Yea, we will listen to thy words, O singer, With wain and car from afar thou comest :
Low, like a nursing mother, will I bend me, and yield me as a maiden to her lover.'

(*Friend of All*)

" Soon as the Bharatas have fared across thee, our warrior band urged on and sped by Indra,
Then let your streams flow on in rapid motion! I crave your favour who deserve our worship!

(*Envoi*)

" The warrior host, the Bharats fared across: the singer won the favour of the Rivers.
Now swell with your billows, hasting, pouring riches! Fill full your channels and roll swiftly on!"

The presence, therefore, of King Pīsha's or Vishwa's three fine official signets in the old capital of the Sumerian colony in the Indus Valley is thus accounted for in ancient literary Indo-Aryan tradition.

XIII

Sumerian Writing as " Owners' Marks " on Prehistoric Pottery (Töpferwaare, Scherben) in the Danube (Donau) Valley of Middle Europe

In the foregoing pages the Sumerians are proved to be the Early Aryans or the primitive Goths, and of that race which is now generally called " The Nordic " or North European, who as the most advanced people of their time entered Asia Minor about 3380 B.C. from the North or West, and established there the first great state, and built there the first city, with Civilization, in the dictionary meaning of that word.

The immemorial homeland of the Goths is the mighty fertile and richly metalliferous Danube Valley, with its long corridor interpenetrating the Rhine Valley, and forming with the latter and the associated parallel valleys of the

Elbe, Oder and Vistula, branching off from its northern plateau watershed, a great branched overland corridor for trade, intercommunication and migration, connecting the Euxine or Black Sea and the Ukrain and Dacia northwestwards with the North Sea, and the amber trading Baltic Sea, Cattegat and Jutland or Northern Goth Land and Scandinavia.

This Danube Valley basin in the old Gothic homeland is of especial importance in the history of European Civilization, in that in its great salt-mine area in the Trias formation, with its salt springs—which produced from immemorial times a chief European supply of salt which was for man and beast an essential of life—there stands Hallstatt, near Salzburg, rich also in iron and other metallic veins with many prehistoric mines. For Hallstatt is now regarded as one of the earliest centres of the early Iron Age industry, which reproduced its earlier weapons and tools generally of the same shape used by the later Neolithic and Bronze Age people of the Early Aryan region in Europe and the Caucasus and Caspian areas ; and amber was found there.

Now, in this Danube (Donau) region, Professor M. Vassits of Belgrade, in his excavations in the prehistoric strata of the early agricultural settlement at Vinca, near ancient copper and cinnabar mines, about 15 kilometres below Belgrade, and at Tordos in the tributary Maros Valley in Transylvania with their ancient gold and copper mines, has unearthed a large collection of prehistoric pottery (Töpferwaare) and clay figurines of types and decoration recognized by him and others as similar to those found at Early Troy, Asia Minor and Crete ; and as regards the pottery, as similar to some found in Predynastic Egypt.[1] But what has not been remarked is that this prehistoric Danubian pottery, with figurines and anthropomorphic lids is similar to some of that found on Early Sumerian sites in Mesopotamia, and latterly in the Indus Valley at the Early Sumerian sites there. And the skeletal remains of the early Danubian people are of the long-headed or dolichocephalic type and presumably Aryan—though the shorter statured long-headed men who lived there in pit-dwellings were probably

[1] *Præhistorische Zeitschrift*, Berlin, 1910, 23 f.

of the Mediterranean race and subject to their civilized Aryan overlords.

Most important of all, for our recovery of exact historical and chronological data for this prehistoric period, is the fact that many of the potsherds (Scherben) were found to bear "pictographic" markings, some of which were recognized as resembling the markings or writing on the "spindle"-whorl (querl) from Early Troy,[1] which "whorls" I have shown to be amulets and their markings as Early Sumerian writing.[2]

These markings, which are engraved or scratched upon the finished Danubian pottery, are extra to the normal decorative ornament on the ware. They are obviously the owners' or proprietors' markings or writing; and are thus analogous to the "owners' marks" inscribed or scratched upon the pottery and potsherds of the Predynastic and First Dynasty periods in Ancient Egypt, as observed by Sir Flinders Petrie.[3] And nearly all those owners' marks on Early Egyptian pottery I have demonstrated to be Sumerian pictographic writing, and presumably bearing the phonetic values of the latter, as the same pictographic signs actually do in the contemporary Predynastic and First Dynasty Sumerian inscriptions in Egypt; and they are obviously the personal names or initial syllables of the personal names of the owners of the pottery, written in Sumerian or Early Aryan script.

The similarity or identity of these prehistoric Danubian markings with the Sumerian writing is displayed in the annexed Comparative Table. In this Table the Danubian markings from Professor Vassits' photographs are shown (in the order figured by him) in col. 1; their equivalents in the standard Early Sumerian linear writing of Mesopotamia[4] in col. 2; the Egyptian equivalents from the owners' marks on Predynastic and First Dynasty pottery[5]

[1] *Loc. cit.*, *Tafel* 16, pp. 31 f.

[2] *Phœnician Origin of the Britons*, London, 1924, 238 f.

[3] From W. F. Petrie, *The Royal Tombs of the Earliest Dynasties*, I, 1901, plates xliii. f. and *Formation of the Alphabet*, 1912, plates i. f.

[4] From G. A. Barton, *Origin and Development of Babylonian Writing*, Leipzig, 1913.

[5] See foot-note 4, p. 4.

OWNERS' MARKINGS ON PREHISTORIC DANUBIAN POTTERY COMPARED WITH SUMERIAN, EGYPTIAN & TROJAN WRITING WITH THEIR PHONETIC VALUES

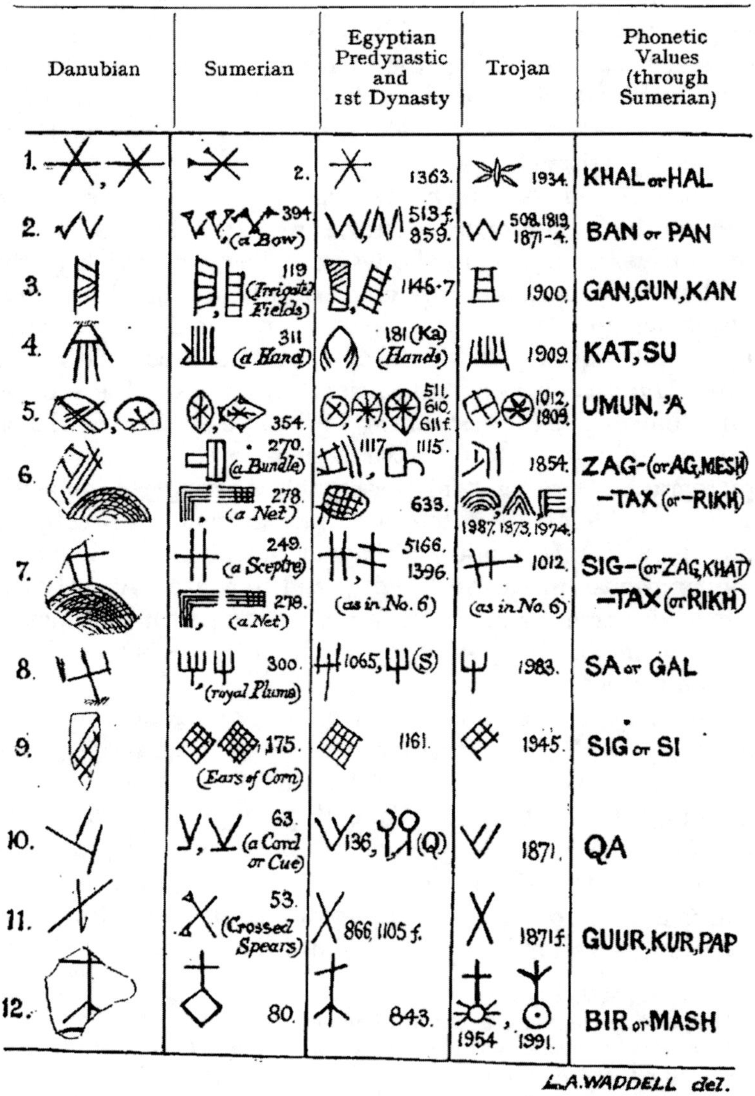

PLATE XXV.

TABLE OF DANUBIAN POTTERY MARKS—*continued*

Danubian	Sumerian	Egyptian Predynastic and 1st Dynasty	Trojan	Phonetic Values (through Sumerian)
13.	298.	1305, 1366.	1939, 1857.	ASH
14.	481.	1185; 1150.	1953	DUK, DUR, KHUN
15.	(as in No. 14) (as in No. 6)	(as in No. 14) (as in No. 6)	(as in No. 14) (as in No. 6)	DUR- (or DUK- -TAX (or RIKH)
16.	70. (as in No. 15)	606, 124, 494 (as in No. 15)	1843, 1984. (as in No. 15)	ETIL- (or TIL, BIL-) -TAX (or RIKH)
17.	532 (a Jar) (as in No. 15)	714, 717. (as in No. 15)	1972f. (as in No. 15)	GAR- -TAX (or RIKH)
18.	12. (a Tree-branch) (as in No. 15)	1434f. 805, 783. (as in No. 15)	1878, 1973. (as in No. 15)	DAR- (TAR KUD-) -TAX (or RIKH)
19.	443. (a Circle or Ring)	610f. 517, 513.	1972	GIR, KIR or KUR
20.	81. (Tree growing by Water) (as in No. 15)	595f. (as in No. 15)	1984. (as in No. 15)	ZI- (or ṢI-) -TAX (or RIKH)
21.	373.	1156 f.	1945.	U or KUS
22.	77. (Wood Cross sceptre)	1109, 1926f.	1871, 1926.	BAR, MASH
23.	365. (Setting Sun)	346f. 348f.	1918, 1860	U, BURU, UMUN
24.	490.	1013, 1270-1.	1265.	SHU
25.	94.	114f. 1371f.	1995.	NUN or SIL
26.	(In Uruash's inscription of 3100 B.C.)	94.	1849f.	

L. A. WADDELL *del*

n col. 3; the Trojan equivalents from whorls[1] in col. 4; and their phonetic values as recovered through the Sumerian are given in col. 5. The authorities for all these comparative signs are duly attested by the reference numbers attached to each sign in each of the columns. Thus the numbers in col. 2 indicate the corresponding Sumerian script signs of Mesopotamia in the standard lexicon; those in col. 3 the Egyptian owners' marks in Petrie's work; those in col. 4 the Trojan whorl markings from Schliemann's work; and the phonetic values in col. 5 will be found in the works cited under the numbers in col. 2. Here it will be noted that the same pictographic sign often possesses several different values in the polyphonous imperial Sumerian language—the same sign bearing often different word-forms in different dialects of the great Sumerian empire, though those words usually possess the same meaning in those different dialects.

From this comparison, the substantial identity in the forms of the Danubian signs with the Sumerian, primitive Egyptian and Trojan writing is evident. The Danubian signs, like those of the primitive Egyptian and Trojan, are seen to be written at a period when the Sumerian pictographic writing had become through rapid writing and long usage converted into mere conventionalized diagrams which had largely lost their detailed naturalistic and objective pictographic features. Though, as seen in Nos. 5, 6, 8, 16, 17, 18 and 20, the writing still retained, to some extent, the early curved form which in the Mesopotamian Sumerian writing became altered into angular lines, from the exigencies of writing by impression with a flat style on moist clay-tablets. And the realistic pictographs of the Net in Nos. 6, etc. are noteworthy.

These palæographic features fix *the Date* of this Danubian writing at between *about* 3300 and 2700 B.C.

The *Personal Names* of the owners of this Danubian pottery, as seen from the phonetic values of the signs in Sumerian, are more or less common personal Sumerian names or titles, or the initial syllables of personal names in the Sumerian; as well as in the names of the Early Aryan kings and heroes preserved in the Indian epics. This con-

[1] From H. Schliemann, *Ilios*, London, 1880.

firms the inference that they were the personal names of the owners of the pottery in question. Many of these names, such as Sig, Dar or Tar, Dur, Duk, Tus, Tax, Khun, Guur and Etil, I have shown in my latest work to be the Sumerian originals of Gothic personal names in The Eddas and in later Gothic and Nordic history. And the title of *Tax* or *Rikh*, meaning "The Supervisor or Ambassador," borne by the owners in Nos. 6, 8, 16, 17, 18 and 20, is an official title borne by the colonial governors in the Sumerian empire,[1] and suggests that those Danubian sites in question were colonies of, or tributary to, a central civilized power which used the Sumerian writing and language. Whilst No. 8 bears the title of "Prince or Great Ruler" (*Sa* or *Gal*).

Appeal to Archæologists & Historians in Middle, South-Eastern & Northern Europe for an Active Search for further Markings on Prehistoric Pottery

In view of the enormous historical importance of these discoveries in opening up a new and promising source of exact scientific contemporary information on the Racial Affinities and Chronology of the Early Civilizers of Middle Europe in times hitherto regarded as Prehistoric, it is confidently hoped that all archæologists and historians resident in the Danube Valley and its associated valleys will now take up without delay an active search for further specimens of Sumerian Writing on the Prehistoric Pottery and Potsherds in these regions. Search should also be made of all prehistoric pottery from the other valleys of the Euxine or Black Sea in South-Eastern Russia, and in the associated valleys of the Danube corridor in Northern Europe, the Rhine and Neckar, Elbe, Oder and Vistula and in Scandinavia, not to mention Switzerland, Italy, France, Spain and the British Isles.

All specimens of prehistoric pottery and potsherds in local museums and private collections should, therefore, be

[1] See my *Indo-Sumerian Seals Deciphered*, 35 f., and compare Brünnow, *List of Classified Ideographs*, Leyden, 1889, 6162-4, and Muss-Arnolt, *Assyrian Dictionary*, Berlin, 1905, 756.

carefully scrutinized for such Owners' Marks; and photographs be taken of all markings found.

Points to be Noted regarding the Marked Pottery

The following points should be noted regarding all further specimens of Marked Prehistoric Pottery which may be found in addition to their photographs :—

1. Finder or Excavator of the Marked Pottery or Potsherd (Scherben), and Date of Find.
2. Find-Place (Fundort), with direction and distance in kilometres from the nearest well-known town.
3. Depth of stratum in metres in which found.
4. Colour and texture of the ware, polished, decorated or not.
5. Any stone or metal tools or weapons or bone relics in same stratum.
6. Any ancient mine-workings in neighbourhood, and if so, what mineral; and any ancient Stone Circles or Megaliths.
7. Location and name of Museum where specimen is now deposited, and museum number, if any.
8. Observer's Name and Address.

Decipherment and Publication of Results of New Finds

I shall be glad to receive and to undertake the task of decipherment of all photographs of further specimens of such marked prehistoric pottery which may be sent to me at the address below; and I shall promptly communicate the results to the sender. And in the event of publication the names of the observers or discoverers of the markings will be duly acknowledged therein.

Dr. L. A. Waddell,
55 Campbell Street,
Greenock,
Scotland.

THE MASS OF NEW BASIC HISTORY ON THE UNKNOWN ORIGIN OF THE WORLD'S CIVILIZATION AND ITS AUTHORS AND THEIR RACE NOW RECOVERED

This great mass of new basic History on the unknown Origin of the World's Civilization and its Authors and their Race, now recovered in the foregoing Appendixes, as well as in the text of this work, affords striking testimony to the richness of the wide fields of new History opened up by our new method of scientific historical research, by comparing the ancient monumental inscriptions of the Sumerians with the literary remains of our Aryan ancestors.

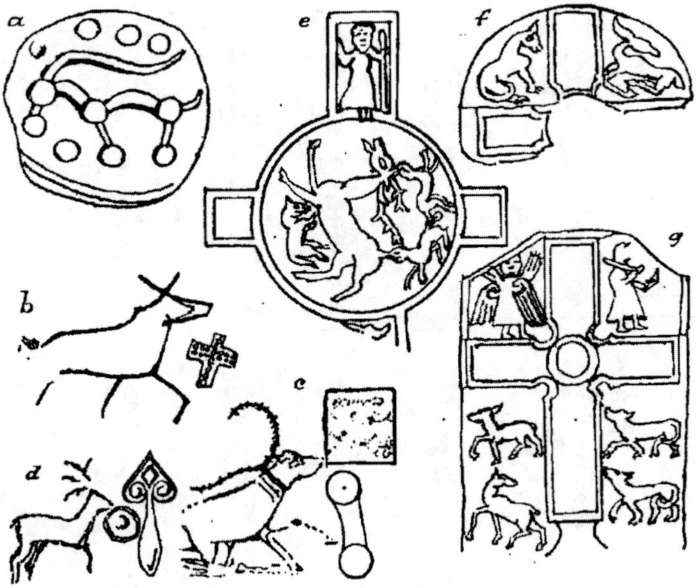

FIG. 141.—Ancient Briton pre-Christian monuments and pre-Roman coins showing Goats and Deer as " Goths " protected by the Sun Cross and In-Dara or Thor and his Archangel Tasia-Michael against the Lion and Wolf demonist totems of the Chaldees (or " Kelts ").

For detailed descriptions see WPOB. 335 f. And compare with Sumerian and Hitto-Phœnician examples on p. 607 ; and Egyptian on pp. 30, 347.

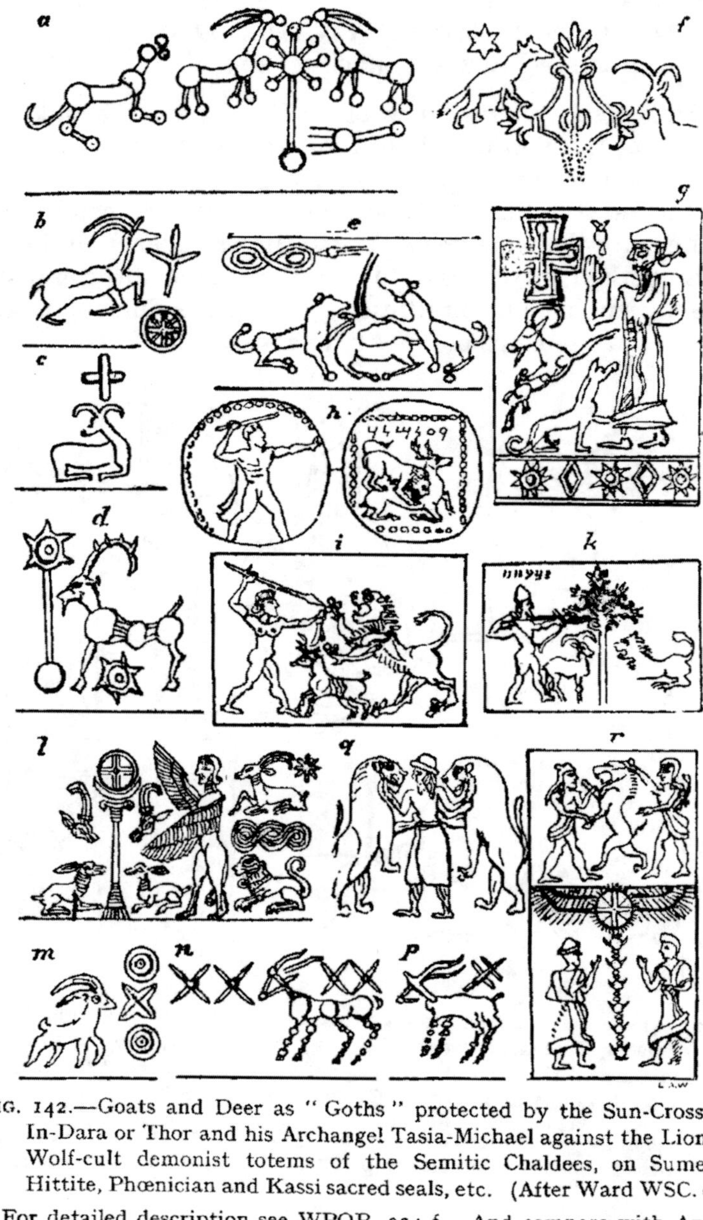

FIG. 142.—Goats and Deer as "Goths" protected by the Sun-Cross and In-Dara or Thor and his Archangel Tasia-Michael against the Lion and Wolf-cult demonist totems of the Semitic Chaldees, on Sumerian, Hittite, Phœnician and Kassi sacred seals, etc. (After Ward WSC. etc.).

For detailed description see WPOB. 334 f. And compare with Ancient Briton representations of same (pp. 195, 607), and with Egyptian (pp. 30, 347).

INDEX

Abbreviations: A.=Aryan; C.=Civilization; E.=Egyptian; I.L.=Indian King-Lists; I.V.=Indus Valley; M.=Mesopotamian; S.=Sumerian; c.=city; dyn.=dynasty; f.=father; k.=king; l.=land; n.=name; s.=son; t.=title.